"The economics of energy resources and their markets is one of the most active areas of research today. We have been in need of a text that can match the demands of an important and rapidly changing field. There is no doubt Schwarz has given us that text! He has produced a *unique* text that brings readers inside and up to date on this rapidly changing field. His book is comprehensive in its coverage of all energy resources. Readers will appreciate how he is able in each chapter to integrate the institutional, scientific, and economic dimensions unique to each energy resource. Rather than separate chapters on economics, geology, and regulations he brings them together and demonstrates how each contributes to understanding the special allocation questions posed for each type of energy resource. The book closes by considering how decisions on which energy resources society should use must confront the broader questions of environmental protection and sustainability. The book's design, with integrated treatment of each individual energy resource, allows instructors to use it as a full text or select components for specialized courses."
V. Kerry Smith, Emeritus Regents Professor and Emeritus University Professor of Economics, Arizona State University, USA

"Schwarz's work is an adroit combination of explanations of energy markets and the environmental issues that arise from such markets. The text ably combines traditional market structure issues with the impact of new and potential energy technology in a way that will open students' to the challenges and opportunities in today's energy issues."
Andrew N. Kleit, Professor of Energy and Environmental Economics, The Pennsylvania State University, USA

"Energy markets and policies are moving targets; economics is an important way to maintain one's ability to understand and assess what we see and what may come next. Applying his extensive research and teaching experience in energy economics, Prof. Schwarz provides here a comprehensive and accessible introduction to the field. He covers the background and evolution of traditional sources and upcoming fuels, the basic economics of competitive markets, resource management and market failures, as well as policy concerns relating to the environment and sustainability. Teachers and students with a wide range of interests will find much gain from this book."
Tim Brennan, Professor of Public Policy, University of Maryland Baltimore County, and Senior Fellow, Resources for the Future, USA

"Schwarz's book, *Energy Economics*, integrates microeconomic theory and applications into the technical, regulatory and policy complexities of alternative energy uses, substitutes, sources, technologies, and prices. He carefully keeps front and center consideration of the multiple energy-related environmental damages, national security concerns, reliability issues, and potential for technological change. The students this text is designed to serve will find it is easy to understand, as it is written by a scholar with a lifetime of widely-respected research on energy economics and a firm grasp on key principles. This book is a valuable, up-to-date survey that will provide a comprehensive framework for those engaged in energy economics research, and those who want to understand this complex and important field."
Darwin C. Hall, Professor Emeritus of Economics, California State University Long Beach, USA

"I am happy to strongly endorse the publication of Peter Schwarz's book *Energy Economics*. I actually wish I had such an introduction to the field of er

energy policy in Germany and in the U.S. From my perspective, the specific value of this book lies in the application of many things we know from Economics to the very dynamic field of energy. This application makes the book unique and important. I particularly like the straightforward way of describing and explaining economic terms. In this regard, the highlighted keywords throughout the book help to quickly look up specific terms. I can very well imagine that students of Economics and other Social Sciences will find the book helpful to get an orientation in the field of energy economics. For professionals, the book can be a guide on how to maneuver through the complex world of energy policy, economics, and technology. Finally, it is very welcome that the book is not only titled "energy economics" and then continues by addressing electricity economics only but actually addresses all aspects of energy, i.e. also oil, shale gas, transportation, heating, sustainability, climate, security, etc."

Dr. Steffen Jenner, Policy Fellow, Das Progressive Zentrum, Germany

"This book is a comprehensive treatment of the energy markets as they relate to economic efficiency, government regulation and environmental policy. The book extensively uses the tools of economic analysis to establish a framework for evaluating past, present and future energy market operations and government policies, but at a level that is useful for economist and non-economist readers alike. Although the pivotal point for serious analysis of energy was the oil crisis of the 1970s, there are many current and near future energy issues that receive a thorough treatment in this book, such as market-based instruments for renewable resources (including financial instruments), energy sustainability and security, and other environmental concerns. This book is must read for anyone seriously interested in the evolving energy public policy debate."

Herb Thompson, Former President at Thompson Consulting and Associate Professor at J. Warren McClure School of Information and Telecommunication Systems, Ohio University, USA, now retired

"Peter Schwarz's new book, *Energy Economics*, is a must read. College students, activists of all stripes, the informed layman and government policy makers can profit from all or parts of his comprehensive treatment of this all important subject."

Christopher Garbacz, Ph.D., Formerly Professor of Economics, Director, Economics, Mississippi Public Utilities Staff, USA

"I can't wait to read *Energy Economics* with my students! The book begins with an accessible discussion of market efficiency and market failures. This sets the stage for discussions of the history, science, and economics of different energy resources: oil, natural gas, coal, nuclear, renewables, and next-generation alternatives with specific attention to electricity. The book closes with chapters focusing on policies related to the environment, national security, and sustainability. Along the way students are introduced to a host of topics in industrial organization, environmental, and natural resource economics through well-motivated examples from energy policy. A great way to learn about both energy and economics!"

Stephen Holland, Professor, University of North Carolina, Greensboro Department of Economics, USA

Energy Economics

With interest in topics such as climate change, energy security, and alternative energy sources being at an all-time high, the effects of today's decisions now rest on the shoulders of future generations. There are no easy answers to our energy issues, so costs and benefits must be considered when evaluating all energy alternatives; alongside that, prices must be right and need to reflect the full social costs to society of a given source of energy.

Energy Economics outlines the fundamental issues and possible solutions to the challenges of energy production and use, and presents a framework for energy decisions based upon sound economic analysis. It considers market forces and policy goals, including economic prosperity, environmental protection, and other considerations that affect societal well-being. This book focuses on both energy choices and the impact of these choices on market performance, environmental conditions, and sustainability. The initial section covers the fundamental economic concepts for analyzing energy markets. Following this, a detailed analysis of established energy sources, specifically fossil fuels and nuclear energy, leads into consideration of energy alternatives such as renewable energy and next-generation alternatives. Electricity production and regulatory trends are covered in depth. The final section considers policy, environmental considerations, sustainability, and energy security. The concluding chapter is a comprehensive vision for our energy future.

Drawing on current energy headlines, perspectives familiar from the popular press, and views outside economics, this text sharpens students' ability to understand, evaluate, and critique policy using appropriate economic analysis. The text builds a foundation that culminates in a view of a comprehensive energy policy that improves upon the vacillations of past decades.

Peter M. Schwarz is a Professor of Economics and Associate, Energy Production and Infrastructure Center (EPIC) at UNC Charlotte, USA. He has published numerous articles on energy, environment, and electricity pricing that have appeared in such journals as the *American Economic Review*, the *RAND Journal of Economics*, and the *Energy Journal*. He has travelled internationally to present his work in these areas, including Israel, Germany, and China (five times).

Routledge Textbooks in Environmental and Agricultural Economics

For a full list of titles in this series, please visit www.routledge.com/Routledge-Textbooks-in-Environmental-and-Agricultural-Economics/book-series/TEAE

Energy Economics

Peter M. Schwarz

LONDON AND NEW YORK

First published 2018
by Routledge
2 Park Square, Milton Park, Abingdon, Oxon OX14 4RN

and by Routledge
711 Third Avenue, New York, NY 10017

Routledge is an imprint of the Taylor & Francis Group, an informa business

© 2018 Peter M. Schwarz

The right of Peter M. Schwarz to be identified as author of this work has been asserted by him in accordance with sections 77 and 78 of the Copyright, Designs and Patents Act 1988.

British Library Cataloguing in Publication Data
A catalogue record for this book is available from the British Library

Library of Congress Cataloging in Publication Data
A catalog record for this book has been requested

ISBN: 978-0-415-67677-9 (hbk)
ISBN: 978-0-415-67678-6 (pbk)
ISBN: 978-1-315-11406-4 (ebk)

Typeset in Bembo
by RefineCatch Limited, Bungay, Suffolk

Visit the companion website: www.routledge.com/cw/schwarz

Contents

Figures

Tables

Preface

Economics in general, and energy economics in particular, is one of those subjects where everyone thinks she is an authority, whether or not she has any training. Academics outside of economics and much popular opinion fear we will run out of oil. Hollywood produces movies and documentaries showing the dark side of nuclear energy and hydraulic fracturing (fracking) for oil and natural gas. Climate change scientists and environmentalists urge us to end the age of fossil fuels, especially coal and its carbon emissions.

There are myriad suggestions from noneconomists to use cleaner energy, or better yet, less energy. The environmentalist's mantra is reduce, reuse, recycle, in order of preference. Energy efficiency and conservation reduce energy use. Waste-to-energy could reduce waste while providing energy. Hydrogen vehicles would use the most common element instead of petroleum and would emit nothing but water.

Reprocessing nuclear fuel would recycle uranium and reduce radioactive wastes. Cogeneration, also known as combined heat and power (CHP), recaptures waste heat for a second energy use. Coal ash has reuses in road asphalt and gypsum board for houses. Carbon capture and storage (CCS) not only prevents carbon dioxide emissions that are widely believed to be warming the planet, but has the potential for reuse to enhance oil and natural gas recovery.

There is one key ingredient missing from these energy proposals and the countless others that appear daily in the press, and that is economic considerations. We can abandon fossil fuels and nuclear energy, but at what cost? Oil is the largest primary fuel source in the United States, and accounts for almost all of our transportation fuel. We can use hybrid or electric vehicles to reduce or eliminate our use of oil. However, without subsidies, auto manufacturers in 2016 lost money on each electric car they produced. The vehicles require expensive infrastructure to provide recharging stations so that owners will not suffer from range anxiety from a car that cannot go beyond 200 miles without a charge. The vehicles also use electricity; unless it is produced using renewable fuels, we risk merely transferring the pollution from the vehicle to the power plant. Hydrogen vehicles emit nothing but water, but obtaining hydrogen from water is itself a high-cost, energy-intensive process that only avoids carbon emissions if the electrolysis uses renewable fuels. The vehicles require large tanks to contain the gas, if you can find a station to fill the tank.

Society often makes its energy decisions in this freewheeling fashion, resetting its objectives with each election cycle, often devoid of economic analysis. I wrote this book in the hope that economics will be a central part of energy decision-making.

Economic thinking can sharpen the evaluation of the benefits and costs to the individual and to society of each energy source, whether used for transportation, for electricity generation, or as industrial feedstocks for plastics and petrochemicals. In the absence of economic considerations, we run the risk of phasing out fossil fuels and nuclear energy prematurely and accelerating the adoption of renewables that are imperfect substitutes. In the absence of affordable battery storage, wind and solar energy can only provide electricity when the wind blows or when the sun shines. There is a saying that comparing conventional fuels to renewables is like comparing a new car and an old car. The new car runs when you want, while the old car runs when it wants.

There are many energy issues in this book where economics will provide a new vantage point. Key energy and economic concepts are in *italics*, typically followed immediately by a definition or explanation of the term. Should we ban Edison's incandescent bulb, the first commercial use of electricity, in favor of CFLs or LEDs? Will OPEC be successful in withholding supplies in order to raise the price of oil? Should we subsidize solar and wind energy in order to reduce carbon emissions, and phase out nuclear energy given its risks? Germany offers an example of both of those policies that can provide lessons.

We need a well-educated citizenry if we are to make the best use of our scarce energy resources; to contribute to decisions about whether the age of oil is over; old King Coal is dead; nuclear energy is coming or going; and fracking is a blessing or a curse. Should we subsidize wind and solar? How should we evaluate the many alternatives that seemingly come along daily: a new method of carbon capture and storage that turns the gas into a rock; a breakthrough in nuclear fusion research that makes it achievable at lower temperatures; using wave, tidal, and ocean currents as sources of energy; next-generation biofuels that use algae to create fuel; and almost unimaginable technologies such as wind towers suspended in the air, and other technologies we have not yet imagined.

There is another saying that those who do not know the past are doomed to repeat it. We have experienced energy crises: gasoline shortages and wars to protect oil supplies; nuclear energy disasters and no agreement on a permanent waste repository; natural gas fires and fears of water pollution and even earthquakes from its extraction; and deaths from coal mining and the smog that comes from burning coal. We can learn from examining past energy events to illuminate our future. Economics provides guidance for improving the use of fossil fuels and nuclear energy, or if phasing them out is a better option. It can evaluate the extent to which growth in renewable fuels should be left to the market, or if government can better achieve our societal goals in the use of energy.

There is more material in this book than most instructors will be able to cover in a semester. Instructors can likely cover Chapters 1 through 9, covering energy economics foundational tools in Chapters 1 through 4, and then the major fuel alternatives—oil, natural gas, coal, nuclear, and renewable fuels—in Chapters 5 through 9. They can choose from the remaining chapters based on their interests to cap off their courses.

For instructors with an interest in electricity, they will find Chapters 12 and 13 on traditional electricity and electricity restructuring. They may choose to cover these chapters before covering all the separate energy sources, with the organizational principle that each of the primary energy sources has a secondary use to provide heat and steam to generate electricity.

Instructors and their students with a strong interest in alternatives to fossil fuel generation can include Chapter 10 on next-generation alternatives and Chapter 11 on energy efficiency and conservation. They may also want to cover the policy chapter on sustainability.

Instructors and students with interdisciplinary or policy interests can include all three policy chapters on environment, sustainability, and energy security. The text ends with a chapter that sketches a comprehensive energy policy that can serve as a suitable capstone for all courses.

Finally, instructors who want to get to the energy topics quickly and have time for additional topics in energy alternatives, electricity, or policy can forgo as little or as much as necessary of the first four chapters. This option is also suitable in classes where students have a strong economics background and can use the first four chapters as a reference.

Peter M. Schwarz
UNC Charlotte Professor of Economics and Associate,
Energy Policy and Infrastructure Center (EPIC).

Acknowledgments

I wish to acknowledge the many people who have helped to make this book a reality at many stages of its development. In its initial stages, Michael Herron, Adedolapo Akinde, Chinedu Ifionu, Joseph Cochran, and Brent Johnson took independent study courses that helped to launch the project. Groups of students in an energy economics topics course and in a Senior Seminar on the same topic tested out the materials and offered comments and corrections. Dr. Andy Kleit, who I have had the pleasure of knowing for many years and who teaches an energy economics course, was a silent voice in my head, with his periodic emails asking, "Is it done yet? We're not getting any younger!"

Gwendolyn Gill, Brian Jones, and Melissa Duscha read drafts of chapters and made many suggestions that have improved the book. Joseph Cochran has read chapter drafts since the book's inception to its near-completion and has provided many useful suggestions.

Hualiu Yang provided steadfast help in the final stages of the project, reading and critiquing drafts and keeping track of the manuscript components. He and Brian Jones have also tried their hand at suggesting homework questions and potential test questions. I congratulate Hualiu, Brian, Joseph, and Melissa, for earning their Ph.D.s even while giving their all to assist in this project. Dr. Carol Swartz, a faculty colleague, offered her unparalleled skills at editing, including text and graphs. I cannot thank her enough for her generous contributions as well as her cheerful words of encouragement.

I acknowledge McKinsey & Company for granting permission to reproduce their illustration that appears as Figure 11.1 in the text.

The editorial staff at Routledge have been encouraging and patient every step of the way. I am particularly grateful to Robert Langham who initiated the project and Elanor Best who has seen it through to the finish line. I also acknowledge Andy Humphries, Senior Editor for Economics, who I met at an international conference on energy and environmental economics and look forward to meeting again.

I thank my wife Jennifer for her belief in this project, her support and tolerance for the demands of writing, and most of all for her love. I also thank my children, their spouses, and their children—my grandchildren were born during the writing of this text—for their love and support. Son Jordan, daughter-in-law Kristina, and granddaughter Julianne; daughter Meredith, son-in-law Zack, and granddaughter Caroline, thanks for sharing me with this project and encouraging me to get it done sooner rather than later.

Abbreviations

AC	Alternating current
ACEEE	American Council for an Energy-Efficient Economy
AE	Alternative energy
AEC	U.S. Atomic Energy Commission
ANWR	Alaskan National Wildlife Refuge
ATC	Average total cost
AVC	Average variable cost
BBL	Billions of barrels
Btu	British thermal unit
CAA	Clean Air Act
CAC	Command and control
CBA	Cost–benefit analysis
CBL	Customer baseline load
CWA	Clean Water Act
CCS	Carbon capture and storage
CEGB	Central Electricity Generating Board
CFD	Contract for difference
CFL	Compact fluorescent light
CNG	Compressed natural gas
CSP	Concentrated solar power
CV	Contingent valuation
CWIP	Construction-work-in-progress
DC	Direct current
DG	Distributed generation
DOE	U.S. Department of Energy
DR	Demand reduction
DSOs	Distribution system operators
DWL	Deadweight loss
EE	Energy efficiency
EIA	U.S. Energy Information Administration
EMP	Electromagnetic pulses
EOS	Economies of scale
EPA	U.S. Environmental Protection Agency
EPRI	U.S. Electric Power Research Institute
ERCOT	Electric Reliability Council of Texas

EU–ETS	European Union Environmental Trading Scheme
FERC	Federal Energy Regulatory Commission
FGD	Flue gas desulfurization
FIT	Feed-in tariff
FPC	Federal Power Commission
FV	Future value
GDP	Gross domestic product
GHG	Greenhouse gas
HC	Hydrocarbon
HVAC	Heating, ventilation and air conditioning
IB	Incentive-based
ICE	Intercontinental Exchange
IEA	International Energy Agency
IOU	Investor-owned utility
IPCC	Intergovernmental Panel on Climate Change
IPE	International Petroleum Exchange
IPP	Independent power producer
ISO	Independent system operator
ITER	International Thermonuclear Experimental Reactor
kWh	Kilowatt hour
LCOE	Levelized cost of electricity
LDC	Local distribution company
LED	Light-emitting diode
LEED	U.S. Leadership in Energy and Environmental Design
LMP	Locational marginal pricing
LNG	Liquid natural gas
LPG	Liquefied petroleum gas
LRAC	Long-run average cost
LRATC	Long-run average total cost
MAC	Marginal abatement cost
MB	Marginal benefit
MC	Marginal cost
MEC	Marginal external cost
MFC	Marginal factor cost
MMBtu	Million British thermal units
MNB	Marginal net benefit
MOX	Mixed-oxide fuel
MP	Marginal product
MPC	Marginal private cost
MRP	Marginal revenue product
MRTS	Marginal rate of technical substitution
MSC	Marginal social cost
MUC	Marginal user cost
MWh	Megawatt hour
NASA	National Aeronautics and Space Administration
NG	Natural gas
NGC	National Grid Company

NGL	Natural gas liquid
NIMBY	Not in my backyard
NOx	Nitrous oxide
NRC	Nuclear Regulatory Commission
NSPS	New Source Performance Standards
NYMEX	New York Mercantile Exchange
O&M	Operations and maintenance
OCC	Overnight construction cost
OTC	Over-the-counter
OPEC	Organization of Petroleum Exporting Countries
PM	Particulate matter
PS	Producer surplus
PUC	Public utility commission
PURPA	Public Utilities Regulatory Policy Act
PV	Present value
R&D	Research and development
RECs	Renewable energy credits
REP	Retail energy provider
ROM	Run-of-mine coal
RoR	Rate-of-return
RPS	Renewable portfolio standard
RPT	Rate of product transformation
RTO	Regional transmission organization
SMCRA	Surface Mining Control and Reclamation Act
SMR	Small modular reactor
SPR	Security petroleum reserve
SWA	Social welfare analysis
TMI	Three Mile Island
TVA	Tennessee Valley Authority
VoLL	Value of lost load
WTI	West Texas Intermediate
WTP	Willingness-to-pay

Part I

Fundamentals of energy economics

Chapter 1

Introduction

> "Those who do not know history are doomed to repeat it."
>
> Variously attributed to Edmund Burke and George Santayana

> "Those who do not know economics are doomed to repeat past energy crises."
>
> The author of this text

Why energy economics?

In 1973, the Organization of Petroleum Exporting Countries (OPEC) nationalized oil resources, expelled U.S. oil producers, and withheld oil supplies. As a result, the price of oil and gasoline increased by 50% within months. Almost overnight, the field of energy economics emerged. Economists began to apply supply and demand to energy concerns of national security and everyday well-being. Energy policy became an important issue as the United States set a goal of energy independence.

Energy economics uses the tools of economics to analyze the supply and demand of energy.[1] There are many basic principles involved such as the law of demand, consumer preferences, elasticity of demand, substitutes in consumption, economies of scale, elasticity of supply, market structures (perfect competition, monopoly, and oligopoly), inefficient outcomes due to market as well as government failures, substitutes in production, the impact of technology changes on costs, and the markets for inputs including energy, labor, and capital. In addition, there are some ideas that are unique to the energy markets such as the problem of allocating a nonrenewable resource between present and future periods. External costs and benefits play a big role in energy markets and in energy policy. Comparisons of marginal costs and marginal benefits are important for understanding policy options and for choosing among possible policies to meet a given objective.

This chapter introduces many of the themes and concepts that will be the focus of later chapters. We begin with an overview of the crude oil markets since 1970. After that, we consider the scope of energy economics, some applications, and economic principles of particular value to understanding energy markets. The chapter ends with an overview of the remainder of the book.

Oil market performance from the 1970s to the present

While energy has always been a scarce resource, the dramatic events of the 1970s captured the attention of citizens, government officials, and scholars. Few commodities experience the kind of price rise that oil saw in the early 1970s.

In the United States, the government attempted to moderate the price increase by controlling energy prices at the gas pump. They imposed price controls which led to shortages and gas rationing. Initially, the government limited how many gallons car owners could buy at one time. This scheme led to long lines, as drivers bought gas more often than if they had filled the tank.[2] The government then restricted sales on a given day based on whether the last digit of the car's license plate was odd or even. Entrepreneurs seized upon the shortage to earn profits. Some gas station owners required drivers to buy a car wash along with gas, with the price of the car wash inflated to capture the buyer's willingness to pay more for gas than the legal limit.

The U.S. economy suffered through years of stagflation, simultaneous inflation and unemployment. The government took additional measures to conserve energy, as mundane as requiring businesses (and universities) to use only half their lights and asking people to wear sweaters. In the late 1970s, buyers turned to natural gas to avoid the high cost of oil. However, there were also price controls on natural gas that had been in place prior to the 1970s. The controls led to shortages of natural gas, and natural gas fell out of favor as it was viewed as unreliable to meet the winter demand for heating fuel.[3]

In 1979, oil supply declined further as Iran took action against the United States for providing a haven for the deposed Shah of Iran. Gas prices soared to new highs.

By the 1980s, consumers and businesses reduced energy use in response to a decade of high prices. OPEC had less power over price and energy prices declined throughout the 1980s and the 1990s. Consumers cheered. However, energy economics languished as there was less reason to search for energy alternatives or to seek energy independence. Gas prices remained low until September 11, 2001, when terrorists attacked the New York City World Trade Center and the Pentagon. The United States restricted imports from countries that were seen as sympathetic to the terrorists, initiating a new price spike. After a period of ups and downs, prices reached an all-time high in the summer of 2008. However, energy prices once again collapsed, this time in the aftermath of a global recession that was the deepest since the Great Depression. By the end of 2010, prices began to rise. Pundits cited inexorably rising demand in China and India and predicted higher prices for years to come. Yet by early 2016, oil prices were at the lowest level since 2003. In the latter part of 2016, OPEC took actions to restrict oil supplies. While prices partially recovered, the new normal no longer asserts that oil will inevitably return to its lofty peaks.

The U.S. Energy Information Administration (EIA) is a division of the U.S. Department of Energy (DOE) that provides a wealth of energy data. Those statistics will be the primary source of data in this text. Figure 1.1, based on EIA data, provides prices for oil, in $/barrel, inflation-adjusted with 2013 as the base year from 1970 through 2016, identifying key events driving price swings. Where is the price as you read these words? Would you want to speculate on the price of oil one year from now? If you can be right a little more than half the time, you could be a millionaire.[4]

The content of energy economics

Energy economics, as well as the related fields of environmental and natural resource economics, have established places in the news, in academia, and in government policy. Energy receives special attention because it is an essential input to everything we produce and consume. Environmental economics considers *externalities*—uncounted

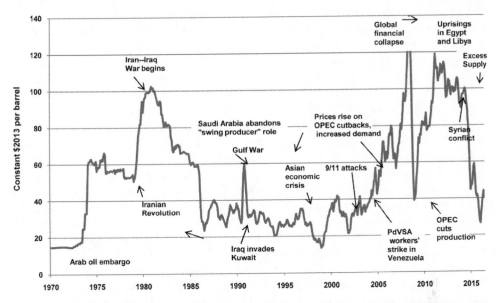

Figure 1.1 Key events in recent crude oil price history. Adapted from *Fact #859 February 9, 2015 Excess Supply is the Most Recent Event to Affect Crude Oil Prices,* by DOE, n.d. Retrieved August 22, 2016 from https://energy.gov/eere/vehicles/fact–859–february–9–2015-excess-supply-most-recent-event-affect-crude-oil-prices.

and unintentional spillover effects on other parties from the actions of producers or consumers—such as air and water pollution; these effects are ubiquitous with energy use. Natural resource economics considers how today's use of renewable and non-renewable resources affects future availability; oil in particular raises concerns about whether today's use will leave enough for future generations.

Economists often take a different view of energy issues than the media, the average citizen, or government officials. People often base their energy views on the latest soundbite, endorsing *renewable fuels*—replenishing sources of energy such as wind, solar, and biofuels—as well as energy efficiency and conservation, without weighing cost or reliability. They champion nuclear energy without addressing a way to permanently store nuclear waste. Others lambast wind and solar for their cost, effect on views, and large land requirements without carefully evaluating the alternative, be it nuclear energy or the burning of *fossil fuels*—sources of energy such as oil, coal, or natural gas composed of hydrocarbons formed from the decay of plants and animals—that emit carbon most scientists believe contributes to human-caused climate change.

Energy economics provides tools for positive and normative analysis. *Positive analysis* examines what is while *normative analysis* evaluates what should be. Positive analysis evaluates the determinants of energy use, while normative analysis addresses the optimal use of energy. The motivation for separate consideration of energy, as opposed to a topic within environmental and natural resource courses, is to apply economics to energy questions to evaluate the merits of market outcomes and government policies in directing the use of energy resources. Economists first evaluate positive market outcomes, focusing on how markets determine gasoline price and quantity. They then evaluate the normative issue of whether markets produce the best outcome for society. Where markets do not produce the best outcome, there is a potential role for government. However, economics acknowledges that the government has its own objectives which will not necessarily improve the outcome.

Consider U.S. policies that mandate use of corn-based ethanol to reduce gasoline use in automobiles. Economics first examines market use of gasoline, and asks if there is a better outcome for society than the market outcome. We have already mentioned one such possibility, the desire to reduce carbon emissions. There is a potential role for government to reduce these emissions. Most economists favor *incentive-based policies* (IB) that work through markets to achieve society's goals. Cap-and-trade is an incentive-based policy where carbon emitters must purchase carbon permits. Economists argue against *command-and-control* (CAC)—policies that prescribe technology or mandate standards to achieve a goal—such as the ethanol requirement. If the goal is to reduce gasoline use to lessen carbon emissions, IB policies encourage a variety of approaches to achieve the goal, whereas CAC mandates one approach with no assurance that it is the least-cost approach.

Economics is commonly defined as the choices we make in a world of scarce resources. Price has the central role in consumer and producer choices. One key ingredient in improving energy use is to get the prices right. If society is using a scarce resource such as air quality for which there is no price, we have suggested one mechanism, a cap-and-trade system, as a way of improving upon the unfettered market outcome.

To consider another application, the American Council for an Energy-Efficient Economy (ACEEE) is a nonprofit organization that promotes energy efficiency as a goal. An economic perspective leads to an insight that may surprise you: from a normative perspective, energy efficiency is not always desirable. If energy is cheap, it makes sense to use more of it, assuming the price includes all costs of its use. When gasoline prices are low, it may be economically efficient to enjoy a larger car with greater comfort vs. a small, fuel-efficient car. However, if the larger car emits more carbon, the market alone will not lead to the socially optimal choice. As we have seen, we would need to price carbon if we seek to reduce emissions, which would increase the cost of driving a large car and lead to the socially optimal choice of car size.

Private cost is the direct cost to the market participants, such as buyers and sellers. The full cost is the social cost. *Social cost*, the cost to society, includes both private costs and externalities. External costs such as pollution and climate change are pervasive in energy markets. If we are to get the prices right, they must reflect social costs including externalities. Markets will overuse and underprice goods such as gasoline in the absence of a price for externalities such as air pollution or carbon emissions that contribute to climate change.

While most externalities, such as pollution, are negative, there can be positive externalities, in which case the social cost is less than the private cost. Mass transit often receives government funding to reduce the use of private vehicles and unpriced pollution.[5] Hybrid and electric vehicles have received subsidies with the justification that they pollute less than conventional vehicles.

Subsidies in the absence of external benefits lead to getting the prices wrong. There is little justification for an oil-depletion allowance that accelerates drilling for fossil fuels. However, we should not jump to the conclusion that there is a justification for subsidizing the production of ethanol. It received cash subsidies even though the production of this fuel is itself an energy-intensive process and so may not result in less pollution than conventional fuels. In addition, the CAC requirement that gasoline include a minimum percentage of ethanol is an implicit subsidy, increasing demand and, consequently, price of ethanol. To add to the inefficiency, the United States only allows corn-based ethanol, and bans imports of sugar-based ethanol, which is cheaper to produce. Still another source of inefficiency is that the subsidy for corn-based ethanol pushes up the price of corn-based foods, not only food where corn is a basic ingredient, but almost all foods given the prevalence of corn syrup and corn oil in processed foods.[6]

Are subsidies to wind and solar producers justified? Certainly, they are cleaner than fossil fuels as a source of electricity production and have a zero fuel cost. However, the construction costs of solar and wind facilities are high, and their availability is at nature's whim. When the sun goes behind a cloud, electricity operators must quickly ramp up an alternative, such as natural gas. We must carefully examine whether these sources have a lower social cost than fossil fuels as well as carbon-free hydroelectric power, nuclear energy, or energy efficiency and conservation.

While competition ordinarily produces an efficient outcome, it can fail to do so in the presence of external costs such as pollution and climate change. Where external costs go unpriced, there is a missing market. Society is using valuable resources without paying for them. Where possible, one remedy may be to create a market where none currently exists, such as the European carbon trading market that determines the price of carbon dioxide emissions.

Some critics of the economic perspective define an economist as "someone who knows the price of everything and the value of nothing."[7] And indeed, energy has impacts on society that may challenge our ability to assign a price. Consider death from exposure to nuclear radioactivity, the loss of species due to the mining and burning of coal, supporting dictators to ensure oil supplies, leaving future generations worse off due to the depletion of energy resources, degrading the environment, and doing irreversible damage to ecosystems.[8] We can try to monetize these resources. But we may well have to develop alternative decision-making approaches when we are not satisfied with our ability to get the prices right.

Our approach in this text is to start with the market approach and the unfettered competitive price system. However, for energy economics, the competitive market is only a starting point. While competition achieves the lowest price, it may not be the lowest social cost once we allow for external costs, including damage to the environment. So the second step is to account for effects that fall outside the market exchange, and internalize those external costs into market transactions. If we cannot find a way to translate external effects into measurable costs, then we must take a third step and investigate alternative approaches that fall outside traditional economics. We have to investigate other frameworks, such as *sustainability*—making decisions today in a way that does not compromise the ability of future generations to be as well off as we are— that reject economic orthodoxy.

Energy is indispensable to modern life

Energy is essential at each moment of our lives, including now when I am writing this introductory chapter on my computer. A loss of electric power can lead to deaths of people who depend upon medical equipment for their survival, individuals unable to heat or cool their homes during extreme weather, or even drivers entering a busy intersection when traffic signals cease to operate.

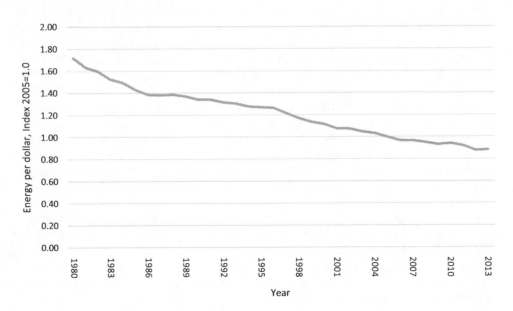

Figure 1.2 Energy intensity from 1980 through 2013. Adapted from *U.S. Energy Intensity Projected to Continue its Steady Decline through 2040*, by EIA, 2013. Retrieved Aug. 18, 2015 from http://www.eia.gov/todayinenergy/detail.cfm?id=10191.

Energy intensity

Energy intensity (EI), the ratio of energy spending to output, accounted for approximately 8% of output in 1970 before the first Middle East oil embargo in 1973. EI rose to 14% by the early 1980s, and then fell as low as 6% in the late 1990s as OPEC's pricing power waned. Figure 1.2 shows EI (energy per dollar of output) from 1980 through 2013 as an index, with 2005 as a base with the index = 1.0. While energy is essential to our lives, the declining trend shows that it is possible to use less energy per unit of output (U.S. gross domestic product).

Why has EI decreased dramatically since the 1970s? One driver is the law of demand. As energy prices increase, market participants increase *energy efficiency*, output per dollar spent on energy. A second reason is that at higher energy prices, firms substitute lower-cost inputs such as labor for more expensive energy. A third reason is that the composition of output in the economy shifts towards industries with lower energy intensities. Finally, there has been an ongoing shift towards less energy-intensive service industries and away from manufacturing.

Transportation

Most forms of transportation require fuel, with the automobile the major focus because of its use of oil.[9] The car is the dominant form of transportation in the United States, and the number of cars has been increasing faster than the population. It provides unparalleled freedom to its owner as a mode of transit. While China relied upon bicycles even into the 1990s, that country is now the fastest-growing market for cars.

European countries make greater use of trains, justified because of their greater population density. Boats play niche roles, such as on rivers and canals and traveling to and from island nations. Air travel is the quickest form of long-distance travel. Walking and bicycles are fuel-free modes of transportation.[10] Without the use of fuel for transportation, we would live in a much less global society.

There are a number of concerns associated with the use of oil for transportation, of which we have already discussed air pollution and carbon emissions. Oil also raises *national security* concerns, requiring additional defense spending and military actions to secure supplies. Finally, oil price spikes have caused economic downturns as well as inflation.

Mass transit can transport more people per unit of fuel. However, buses and trains do not offer as much individual freedom as they run at fixed intervals and on predefined routes. Trains in particular run on a fixed rail and cannot easily adapt if there are shifts in demand.

To what extent can automobiles reduce their use of oil? We can drive less, adopt car sharing, or save fuel with autonomous self-driving vehicles. We can transition to hybrid fuel vehicles that use a combination of gasoline and electricity or switch to all-electric vehicles. Next-generation vehicles may run on hydrogen. We can support mass transit and may one day travel by hyperloop that would transport people at 600 miles per hour through a type of pneumatic tube. We can walk, ride bicycles, with or without a motor, and use conventional and motorized skateboards.

How will these decisions evolve? The key is getting the price of oil right. The right price is not necessarily a high price to discourage use and stretch our oil supplies. It is the price that equals social cost, including all externalities. We are willing to pay for gasoline vehicles because of the utility we get from being able to drive where we want, when we want, and with whom we want.

U.S. drivers have demonstrated repeatedly that they crave large vehicles such as SUVs and full-size trucks. Drivers in Japan prefer small cars. Economists do not pass judgment about what gives people utility. We advocate getting the price right and then letting individuals make their own utility-maximizing decision. If a car buyer chooses a stretch limousine, the choice is socially optimal as long as the price includes all relevant externalities. Some car owners want a car that has all the comforts of a house, while other drivers seek basic transportation and get maximum utility from a car that sips rather than guzzles gas.

Electricity

Consumers aspire to ever-more electronic devices. TV screens are omnipresent, showing up in every room, restaurant, and bar. Computers have evolved from mainframes to desktops, laptops, and tablets. Phones have morphed from landlines to cells and now to miniature computers.

Consumers may have little interest in the technology needed to create the power to run and recharge all these devices, but they want electricity when they flip the switch. In developed countries, we put a premium on reliability, having sufficient electricity available at all times. In India and other developing countries, electricity may not be available at all times, with frequent outages lasting hours or days. When California restructured its electricity industry in the year 2000, the state dealt with repeated blackouts and brownouts before abandoning the failed attempt.

While consumers may not care how electricity is generated, they do care about its price. If price were all that mattered to society as a whole, we would generate electricity at the lowest private cost. However, burning fossil fuels such as coal, oil, and natural gas results in unwanted emissions such as sulfur, nitrous oxides, and carbon, so we want to choose the sources of electricity generation that minimize social cost.

Nuclear energy does not emit carbon or other fossil fuel emissions. Around the year 2000, there was hope for a nuclear renaissance with a wave of new plant construction and carbon-free power. However, nuclear energy has other challenges. The use of nuclear fuel for electricity generation creates radioactive waste. As of yet, no country has a solution for how to store spent fuels or nuclear waste on a permanent basis. In addition, nuclear fuels such as uranium and plutonium can make nuclear weapons if they fall into the wrong hands. Then there are immense safety concerns. The industry may operate safely 99.8% of the time, but the world has trembled when there were accidents at Three Mile Island in the United States, Chernobyl in the former Soviet Union, and most recently, at the Fukushima-Daiichi plants in Japan. The last event put an end to talk of a nuclear renaissance.

In 2010, the International Energy Association (IEA), composed of 29 member countries mostly in the European Union (EU), proclaimed a possible golden age for natural gas. The advent of *hydraulic fracturing* (*fracking*), a technology that uses horizontal and vertical drilling to extract previously inaccessible natural gas (and oil) from shale rock formations, dramatically increased the supply of natural gas as well as oil. However, there are ongoing concerns of water contamination, the need for large supplies of water, damage to land, suffering to nearby residents from noise and air pollution from drilling, and even earthquakes.

There is a strong desire to shift towards greater use of renewable fuels to generate electricity. Wind has the largest market share of renewables, while solar is the fastest growing. However, with greater familiarity come objections. There have been protests against the effect of wind towers on viewscapes, as well as its effects on the well-being of birds and bats. While there are fewer objections to the effect of solar panels, there must be proper disposal of the silicon used to make the panels. Both wind and solar have large land requirements. Finally, wind and solar differ fundamentally from fossil fuels and nuclear energy as they are dependent on nature and not on the electric grid operator. They are intermittent sources of energy, only available when nature dictates until there is wider availability of battery storage that will allow these natural sources to be available when they are needed and not just when they are produced.

Solar and wind are forms of *distributed generation*—electricity produced near the customer rather than by a centralized electric utility—presenting challenges to the electric utility to coordinate its supply with the centralized electric grid. The electricity grid itself is largely unchanged since it was first built in the 1880s.

Looking towards the future, there will be next-generation technologies and even more distant technologies we cannot yet imagine. Next-generation technologies include smaller-scale modular nuclear plants as well as new and safer technologies for large plants and new fuels for both small- and large-scale plants. There will also be smaller-scale hydroelectric plants, as well as greater use of waves, tides, and ocean currents. Automobiles will run on a variety of fuels that will compete with gasoline, including electricity, natural gas, and possibly hydrogen. We will be able to make greater use of coal as well as other fossil fuels if we can develop affordable carbon capture and storage (CCS) to prevent carbon emissions from escaping to the atmosphere.

The market system rewards entrepreneurs who can improve existing technology or invent new methods. For example, it is feasible to convert algae and biowaste into energy, but not yet economical. Electric utilities are replacing the original grid with a *smart grid*, that will provide the electric utility and its customers with real-time information on the type of technology and associated costs as well facilitate two-way transmission of electricity, so that customers as well as the utility can sell as well as buy power. The smart grid will also enhance the ability of utilities to supply power to each other.

Recall that economists do not favor mandates to increase energy efficiency or conservation to reduce the demand for electricity. Electronic devices increase the demand for electricity, but they also improve the lives of people. The key, as always, is that the price needs to equal social cost. If prices are high, people will economize on their use of TV screens, or TV screen manufacturers will work towards equipment that uses less energy. At low electricity prices, we will enjoy ever more electronic devices.

Buildings

There is a tendency to overlook one of the largest energy users, the built environment. According to the Pew Center on Global Climate Change (2011), buildings account for approximately 40% of overall U.S. energy use.

In recent years, there is more attention to reducing energy use in new construction, as well as retrofitting existing construction. The U.S. Leadership in Energy and Environmental Design (LEED) program created standards aimed at constructing buildings that will use less energy and have a smaller impact on the environment. The LEED system is a points-based approach based on construction and use. It differs from an economic approach which would compare the added benefits and costs of greener construction.

The U.S. Environmental Protection Agency (EPA) promulgates its rules without a legal obligation to compare benefits and costs. It can require electric utilities to reduce emissions based on additional benefits, even if on balance, they are less than the additional costs. The EPA ENERGY STAR is a voluntary program that encourages the use of energy-efficient technologies in existing buildings as well as in purchases by consumers. Voluntary programs overcome the objection that they force adoption of new technologies even if costs exceed benefits. However, the ENERGY STAR program may still encourage utilities and consumers to use energy-efficient appliances whether or not the benefits exceed the costs. They may tout an energy-efficient dishwasher that saves $10 a year in energy costs while adding $100 to the manufacturing cost. The typical dishwasher lasts ten years, not long enough to make the purchase worthwhile.

Key energy issues

Are we running out?

The appropriate energy policy depends upon whether or not we must plan for a day when we will run out of fossil fuels, particularly oil. Those who are concerned we will run out of oil, likely within decades, emphasize physical supply and absolute scarcity. They are likely to cite the *Hubbert curve*. Shell Oil geophysicist M. King Hubbert predicted that U.S. oil production would follow a bell-shaped curve, with its peak in the early 1970s and declining thereafter. U.S. oil production did decline until fracking released massive new supplies. By 2014, U.S. production matched its early 1970s peak. *Peak oil* adherents predict that the increase in supply is only temporary, and that we must plan for the inevitable decline.

Economists challenge the peak oil perspective. To economists, it is relative scarcity, as reflected by price, that is relevant, not absolute scarcity, measured by physical quantity. They point out that estimates of proven reserves have risen dramatically over the last several decades. From an economic perspective, the flaw in these physical models is that they do not include price. If resources are diminishing, we can expect price to increase over time. The higher price will motivate the use of previously uneconomic reserves and technologies, the search for new technologies, and the search for alternative resources. George Mitchell, credited as the developer of modern fracking, took enormous risks to achieve his vision of tapping previously uneconomical oil and gas reserves.

There is a famous bet between economist Julian Simon and biologist Paul Ehrlich. In 1980, Simon invited Ehrlich to choose five nonrenewable resources. If the resources cost more in 1990, Ehrlich won, and Simon would pay Ehrlich the difference between the value in 1980 and 1990. If prices decreased, Ehrlich paid Simon. Ehrlich's view was that the price of nonrenewables would rise as the supply was depleted. Simon predicted that the price would fall, as a higher price would bring about technological advances that would allow the use of less accessible resources and the increased use of alternatives. By 1990, all five of the resources had decreased in price and Simon won the bet.

Simon offered a rematch, but Ehrlich declined. Still, say those who side with Ehrlich, the long-term trend will be up. Would you accept the bet that the price of a barrel of oil will be lower ten years from now than it is today? Is the new oil production only a delay in the inevitable decline predicted by Hubbert? Your willingness to bet real money will indicate your conviction, or lack thereof, that technology and the availability of substitutes will continue to advance at a rate sufficient to head off the depletion of oil and other fossil fuels.

The *Hotelling model* provides further foundation for the view that the price system will insure a sufficient supply of nonrenewable resources, including oil and other fossil fuels. Harold Hotelling developed a model of *dynamic efficiency*, the economically efficient allocation of scarce resources over time. In the model, a producer in a competitive economy decides how to allocate nonrenewable resources such as oil over time. If she extracts most of the oil in the present, today's price will be low and the future price will be high. Hence, producers will not put all of their oil on the market today. Instead, they will keep some of the oil in the ground for sale in the future. The larger the amount they set aside, the lower the future price will be, giving an incentive to not keep all of the oil for the future. Price will increase over time, with some resources remaining for the future. In fact, *Hotelling's rule* states that oil and other nonrenewable resources will give a return equal to the real (inflation-adjusted) rate of interest, the same return as other investments.

Those who are unwilling to count on technology look for the government to take an active role to increase conservation and leave more for the future. Whereas the Hotelling model implies that the market can allocate oil and other nonrenewable resources efficiently over time, those who disagree see a host of potential *market failures,* where markets do not produce a socially efficient outcome. Consumers may be myopic (near-sighted), overemphasizing short-term benefits. Another concern is that interest rates may not reflect full social costs. If private interest rates exceed social interest rates, the private rate will give too strong an incentive to use resources today, so there is no assurance that future generations will have sufficient resources. Opponents of the market solution may object that the market outcome does not achieve sustainability, as there is no assurance that the future will be as well off as the present. Even if there are sufficient energy resources, the outcome could fall short of sustainability by damaging ecosystems.

One famous environmental mantra is "Reduce, reuse, and recycle." Environmentalists view reducing as the most desirable, since it is the only one of the three that actually leaves more of the resource for the future. However, we have already seen that even energy efficiency and conservation need not be economically efficient. They can also have unintended consequences.

As long ago as the 1850s, the famous economist William Stanley Jevons put forward the *Jevons paradox*, whereby increased energy efficiency could actually increase energy use! Jevons was writing in England during the Industrial Revolution. Higher energy efficiency would accelerate the use of industrial machinery and potentially lead to higher, not lower, energy use. While the Jevons paradox is an extreme case where energy efficiency actually increases energy use, there is likely to be a *rebound effect*.

The Club of Rome is a global think tank born during the oil crises of the 1970s that warned that we will run out of resources. Donella Meadows and coauthors at the Massachusetts Institute of Technology (1972) presented *Limits to Growth* that predicted the inevitable collapse of nonrenewable resource supplies. Economists contested their predictions, pointing to the absence of price. As their predictions failed to materialize at the forecasted dates, Meadows and her team predicted in *Beyond the Limits* (1992) the collapse of environment and ecosystems, even if the resources themselves did not collapse. *Limits to Growth: The 30-Year Update* (2004) predicts that even if we do not suffer a resource collapse or ecological calamity, world population will exceed the earth's carrying capacity within decades.

Economists challenge that prediction as well. They cite the failed perspective of Thomas Malthus, who predicted in the early 1800s that humankind would be limited in its growth. He predicted that population growth would outstrip food supply, with population growing exponentially (1, 2, 4, 8, etc.) while food supply grew at a slower arithmetic rate (1, 2, 3, 4, etc.). Initially food supply would be more than sufficient for a small population, spurring rapid population growth. However, population would outstrip food supply before long, leading to mass starvation. Only when there had been a sufficient die-off would there again be enough food. This cycle would repeat itself over time, with periods of starvation followed by deaths and new births.

What was missing in the Malthus perspective? By now, you should recognize that his model omitted price. As population increases and with it the demand for food, price increases, motivating the search for better ways to produce food. Economists refer to the *Limits* adherents as neo-Malthusians.

Effects on the planet

Those who hold to the views of Hubbert, Ehrlich, and Meadows see markets as the root of environmental problems. Economists see markets as the basis for solving environmental problems. The problem is too few markets, not too many. Where there is no price for carbon emissions, there is no reason to reduce carbon.

Climate change is largely inseparable from energy use. The focus is generally on CO_2 since it has the longest-lived effect in the atmosphere, and it is produced in the largest quantity.

Electricity generation using hydrocarbons releases emissions that differ somewhat by the fuel source. Burning coal to generate electricity emits sulfur, nitrous oxides (NOx), particulate matter (PM), and mercury (Hg). Coal also emits the most carbon per unit of electricity. NOx (nitrous oxides) and VOCs (volatile organic compounds) combine with heat and sunlight to form ground-level ozone, also known as smog. Sulfur dioxide (SO_2), associated with acid rain in the 1980s, has even more costly health effects. Particulate matter (PM), essentially soot-like particles, can cause lung problems such as asthma.

Natural gas releases carbon at a lower level than coal. However, natural gas is essentially methane, which when emitted into the atmosphere, is also a greenhouse gas. Methane is of growing concern. It has a shorter atmospheric life, but a global-warming potential (GWP) many times that of carbon dioxide. Methane can leak during the natural gas production process. Sometimes producers will intentionally flare (burn) natural gas when it is not worth bringing to market. Noneconomists clamor for a ban on flaring. Economists clamor for a price on methane.

We reviewed hopes for nuclear energy as a carbon-free fuel. We saw an end to talk about its renaissance with the Japanese Fukushima-Daiichi nuclear plant disaster. Germany and other countries have vowed to phase out nuclear energy, while other countries, even Japan, see them as essential if we are to reduce carbon emissions and meet our demand for energy.

These severe challenges for existing fuels hasten the search for alternatives. The current emphasis is on renewable energy, primarily wind and solar, but also biofuels, geothermal energy, and hydrogen. Hydroelectric was one of the earliest methods to generate electricity, but the best sites have now been taken. Water is technically a renewable source, but energy competes with other uses of water including drinking water, recreation, and irrigation. With climate change, drought is more likely, further threatening hydro supplies.

Renewables are not a panacea. As already noted, wind and solar affect views and require land. Offshore wind must withstand ocean conditions, which drives its cost higher than land-based wind. Materials used to make solar panels, such as silica, create waste. Biofuels made from food crops such as corn-based ethanol can drive up the price of food. And net energy from ethanol and other current generation biofuels may be small, as the process of converting food into fuel is energy-intensive.

Economic approach

We now consider some of the economic tools and theories that are particularly useful in understanding energy markets.

Efficiency and inefficiency

Economic efficiency means getting the most from our scarce resources. In this text, efficiency is closely aligned with *cost–benefit analysis* (CBA). The goal is to maximize net benefits, the difference between benefits and costs. At the margin, a change is economically efficient as long as marginal benefit (MB) is at least as great as marginal cost (MC). At the economically efficient point, MB equals MC.

When exchanges take place in a market, we have a measure of the benefits and costs. If the underlying market is competitive, we may be able to use that measure as an accurate value. But many of the evaluations that we must consider in energy economics are not revealed in the marketplace, such as the willingness to pay more for carbon-free sources of energy.

Where there is inefficiency, there is room for a deal. Someone who would gain from a rearrangement of resources could potentially compensate someone who currently owns the resource. One source of inefficiency is when a government regulation uses the CAC approach. At its extreme, the government not only dictates what a company must do, such as cut SO_2 emissions from the use of coal by 50%, but how to do it, requiring a specific technology, a "scrubber" to catch the sulfur emissions. The inefficiency is that the company might have a lower-cost solution, such as burning a lower-sulfur coal or switching to natural gas. One company located close to low-sulfur coal supplies might choose that remedy, while a company far from low-sulfur coal might convert its plants to natural gas.

Incentive-based approaches can achieve socially efficient outcomes. The main IB approaches are emissions taxes and trading. A tax on carbon emissions increases its price and causes a firm to reduce use of carbon-emitting inputs. With carbon trading, a firm that emits carbon must own a permit. Taxes work through price, while permits work through quantity. Under simplifying assumptions, the two achieve equivalent outcomes that minimize the cost of reducing emissions.

Market failure and government failure

Energy markets may not produce socially efficient outcomes, especially given the ubiquity of externalities. The government may be able to improve upon these outcomes.[11]

Government failure can also occur. The *public choice* perspective views government as pursuing its self-interest, not necessarily society's interest. In particular, government may seek votes and money, which can produce policies other than those that maximize society's best interests.

In addition, some imperfections are not worth correcting. We contribute to climate change by exhaling CO_2 with each breath. However, there is little we could do to control our emissions, even if the government imposed a CO_2 breathing tax. And even if we could respond, the *transactions costs*—costs of monitoring and enforcement—would be prohibitive.

As previously cited, few economists think corn-based ethanol is an efficient source of energy. Yet U.S. oil policy mandates a percentage of ethanol in each gallon of gasoline and bans imports of sugar-based ethanol. Public choice economists would explain these policies as aiming to win farm votes. While Mexicans protested higher food costs, they do not vote in the United States and so have relatively little influence.

A roadmap

Part I of the text introduces energy fundamentals. Chapter 1 provided an overview of energy economics. The chapter introduced the some of the major topics and tools in energy economics.

Chapter 2 focuses on economic efficiency, maximum social welfare, and sustainability. The emphasis is on how energy markets work, potential market failures such as externalities, and consideration of government intervention to achieve society's goals. External costs include pollution, climate change, and the costs of national security to obtain oil from unfriendly regimes. Social welfare includes all external costs as well as considerations of *equity*, the distribution of costs and benefits. Sustainability requires us to use resources today in a way that does not diminish future opportunities. Economic efficiency, social welfare, and sustainability may coincide or they may conflict.

Chapter 3 addresses supply, demand, and static efficiency. *Static efficiency* is appropriate when today's use of resources has a negligible effect on the availability of resources in the future. Under certain conditions such as the absence of externalities, perfect competition achieves static efficiency. The chapter then provides a way to measure the social welfare loss from energy market failures such as restrictions on supply by OPEC or externalities from burning fossil fuels. Finally, we will consider why *public goods*—goods that are nonrival in use and from which no one can be excluded—cause problems for the market. We connect this market failure to the challenge of reaching an effective global climate change agreement.

Chapter 4 introduces dynamic efficiency. Dynamic efficiency considers efficient allocation over time, where today's resource use leaves less for the future. The Hotelling model is the foundation for using oil and other nonrenewable resources efficiently. In a dynamic market, prices change over time. Forward, futures, and options markets help manage risk. These markets are particularly active for oil, which displays high price volatility over time.

Part II of the text examines nonrenewable fuels, beginning with oil in Chapter 5. Oil is a global market, with oil supplies throughout the world seeking the most profitable market. We examine the application of dynamic efficiency to the production of oil. The Hotelling model predicts that oil producers will efficiently allocate resources between now and the future. In contrast, we consider the perspective of physical scientists who predict the exhaustion of oil supplies. Finally, we consider financial instruments used by buyers, sellers, and speculators to deal with oil price uncertainty.

In Chapter 6, we examine the natural gas market, from its start as a regulated public utility to its deregulation. Hydraulic fracturing offers great hope for natural gas to account for a greater portion of energy supplies, as well as concerns ranging from water use and contamination to earthquakes. Natural gas is a regional market because of high transportation costs, but is becoming more global with an increase in importing and exporting. There is rapid growth in the *liquefied natural gas* (LNG) market—converting natural gas to a liquid—leading to greater convergence in global natural gas prices. Japan is the major buyer of LNG, purchased from many countries. We examine whether Japan can get a lower than competitive price through the power of *monopsony*—a single buyer of an input. Natural gas price can be highly volatile, so there is a growing use of financial instruments even extending to the LNG market.

Chapter 7 addresses coal. Coal has characteristics that fit a competitive market, although the largest firms may have exerted market power as suggested by high prices on occasion that do not seem attributable to a sudden increase in costs. We also examine the relevance of the *monopsony* model for the labor market for coal. Labor markets had characteristics of a *company town*, where one employer dominates hiring. While many countries have large reserves, coal faces ever-rising challenges to its use. In addition to a multitude of negative externalities—pollution from emissions, coalmine safety, degradation of the landscape, and coal ash spills—the major impediment to its future is its contribution to climate change. We review existing coal technologies, as well as proposals for cleaner technology such as carbon capture and storage (CCS) that may be necessary for coal's survival. We look at likely further developments in CCS in Chapter 10 on next-generation alternatives.

Chapter 8 evaluates nuclear energy, the largest source of carbon-free energy. The primary environmental issue is radioactive waste. As of yet, no country has established a permanent depository for spent fuel or nuclear wastes. Reprocessing spent fuel is one way to reduce waste, and we consider this option. Costs of new plants threaten the technology's future. Safety regulations contribute to the expense of building and operating plants, and construction can easily take a decade. In addition, nuclear energy has a history of substantial cost overruns, with each plant built to order depending on local conditions.

Part III of the text examines alternatives to conventional fuels, with Chapter 9 focusing on renewable fuels, Chapter 10 on next-generation alternatives and Chapter 11 on energy efficiency and conservation.

Renewable energy offers the potential for less environmental damage, especially lower carbon emissions. Their costs have fallen rapidly with greater use. Wind and solar energy have grown rapidly, although some of the growth has been driven by subsidies. Renewable energy also increases energy security since it reduces dependence on imports from countries with unfriendly political regimes. With greater use of wind, there is growing opposition to siting. Wind, solar, and biomass require large amounts of land. Also, sources may fluctuate with weather conditions and be far from the electric grid, so that they can augment but not replace fossil fuels and nuclear energy. Batteries to allow energy storage will allow renewable energy to better meet demand.

Chapter 10 introduces next-generation alternatives including battery storage. Next-generation alternatives are feasible but not yet commercially viable. The private sector may underinvest in *research and development* (R&D) of energy alternatives, which has public goods characteristics. Developers may be unable to prevent other companies from copying successful innovations. Hence, government may have a role in subsidizing and protecting R&D. Government support may be directed to a particular technology more for political gain than society's gain, which is why economists argue for the use of IB solutions and against allowing government to "pick winners." The nuclear industry may lobby for support of small modular reactors or nuclear fusion, while coal and possibly natural gas will seek dollars for CCS.

Chapter 11 uses economic tools to offer some surprising findings, akin to the Jevons paradox introduced in this chapter that suggests caution in adopting energy efficiency to reduce energy use. Economists caution that the energy rebound effect can lessen savings from energy efficiency. We also consider the possibility of the energy efficiency gap, a market failure specific to energy efficiency where consumers forgo energy efficiency improvements despite apparent substantial cost savings. Most fundamentally, we distinguish between energy efficiency and economic efficiency. As this introductory chapter has suggested, we must compare the costs and benefits of energy efficiency just as for any other good or service.

Part IV of the text contains two chapters on electricity. Chapter 12 addresses traditional electricity regulation and Chapter 13 focuses on electric industry deregulation, more accurately called restructuring. Electricity regulation began in the 1930s on the basis that production exemplified a natural monopoly. Under regulation, the Public Utility Commission (PUC) uses average cost to determine a normal rate of return comparable to what is earned by firms in competitive industries. Economists have long proposed marginal-cost-based rates rather than average cost pricing. With greater interconnections among utility networks, and smart grids that will allow utilities and their customers to better monitor use, the gains from prices based on real-time marginal costs will increase.

Deregulation came to a number of industries in the 1970s and 1980s, including natural gas. Advocates of the gains from markets and the limitations of regulation pushed for electricity deregulation. Increasingly, electricity generation can be done on a smaller scale, opening the door to competitive generation. There is also the potential for competition at the retail stage, with marketers offering to shop around for the utility with the lowest price or the greenest source of energy. In the 1990s, the UK privatized and restructured its electricity industry. California, motivated by having some of the highest electric prices in the country under regulation, was an early adopter in the United States. California's model for deregulation contained incompatible elements such as deregulating the wholesale price while capping retail rates, which led to its abandonment. Other restructured electricity markets have been more successful. Texas has deregulated its market, and PJM, an expanding network of states that began with Pennsylvania, New Jersey, and Maryland, is a leader in operating a competitive whole-sale electricity market. One concern of deregulation has been dramatic price volatility, at times making electricity the most volatile commodity. As a result, it is necessary to have accompanying financial markets to manage price risk.

Part V closes the book with energy policy. Chapters 14 through 16 take up environ-ment, security, sustainability, and Chapter 17 is a capstone chapter laying out a compre-hensive energy policy as an alternative to existing policy that is largely unplanned.

Chapter 14 gathers issues that connect energy and environment by contrasting CAC with IB approaches. The discussion shows the inefficiency from government standards to protect the environment, and the efficiency gains from using market-based approaches. We relate the Pigou (1932) tax approach and the trading approach inspired by Coase (1960). In turn, the two leading approaches to IB regulation are emissions taxes and cap-and-trade markets. The chapter applies CAC and IB approaches to sulfur, NOx, and carbon emissions.

Chapter 15 addresses sustainability. Sustainability requires that we use today's resources in a way that does not leave the future worse off. The term is becoming ubiquitous in every aspect of the economy, from statements of business objectives to university curricula. Energy sustainability is a prominent focus. We apply the economic approach to sustainability, best characterized by Robert Solow's definition that we use resources today in a way that does not compromise the *capacity* of the future to be at least as well off. We contrast the economic perspective with the perspective outside the economics discipline that invokes ethics as well as the Porter hypothesis that businesses benefit from sustainability. Economists doubt that businesses "leave $20 bills lying on the sidewalk," and focus on the costs should society incorporate sustainability as a goal. We consider policies aimed at energy sustainability, such as LEED standards.

Chapter 16 delineates energy security issues. The United States sought energy inde-pendence to lessen its reliance on unfriendly suppliers. Such reliance can conflict with domestic interests. In addition, there are military costs to maintaining access to oil supplies. There are also concerns about terrorism aimed at LNG terminals, nuclear plants, and electricity grids.

The final chapter offers a comprehensive energy policy. While there is wide agreement among economists that we "need to get the prices right," there is a danger doing so in a piecemeal fashion. Considering the parts without the whole will result in inefficient substitution from one source to another, and inefficiency as businesses make decisions only to find that they would have done things differently if all the policy pieces were determined together. In this final chapter, we lay out a holistic energy picture. By incorporating the full social costs of energy, we will be able to make maximum use of the power of the market for determining our energy future. At the same time, we will illuminate areas where we may want government to assist in order to make the best use of energy resources.

Welcome to the study of energy economics. By taking this journey you will join those citizens who will help us to make the best use of scarce resources in meeting our future energy needs, as you challenge prescriptions that fail to take into account economic considerations.

Notes

1 We take a predominantly microeconomic approach in this text. Macroeconomics is also relevant to topics such as the relation between energy prices and business cycles. Energy price spikes contributed to U.S. recessions since 1973, as well as to inflation.
2 Fear of shortages can result in panic buying, increasing the average amount people hold in their car's tank and so contributing to perceived shortages.
3 It would take until the 1980s for the government to lift price controls on natural gas, and for consumers to regain confidence in the fuel.
4 If this text helps you make a profit, all I ask is 10%. If the text does not help, you do not owe me anything (a joke!).
5 Mass transit may also reduce congestion and the need for parking.
6 In 2007, Mexicans protested a huge increase in the price of tortillas that resulted from a surge in the demand for corn to produce ethanol.
7 The definition comes from Oscar Wilde's definition of a cynic (Wilde, 1892).
8 The EPA does put a value on statistical life, also known as the value of mortality risk. It is an estimate of what people are willing to pay to lessen the chance of death, such as paying more for a house farther away from a contaminated site, or taking a job with a lower risk of a fatal accident, and not the value of a particular human life. Even so, studies show we place a higher value on dying from nuclear radiation than from a fatal ski accident.
9 The National Academy of Sciences (2016) reports that cars, light trucks, and motorcycles make up 60% of total energy use. Transportation of goods, including transportation of energy, also uses fuel.
10 E- and H-bikes are available for those who want an assist from electricity or hydrogen to power their ride.
11 The government may also intervene when a market outcome is seen as inequitable. Public utilities commissions may require electric utilities to impose a fee on the majority of ratepayers to subsidize low-income consumers. In this text, I will refer to inefficiency, but not inequity, as a market failure. Economists have no special qualification for dictating what is equitable.

References

Coase, R. (1960). The problem of social costs. *Journal of Law and Economics*, *3*, 1–44.
Meadows, D., Meadows, D., Randers, J., & Behrens, W. (1972). *The limits to growth*. New York: Signet Books.

Meadows, D., Randers, J., & Meadows, D. (1992). *Beyond the limits.* White River Junction, Vermont: Chelsea Green Publishing.

Meadows, D., Randers, J., & Meadows, D. (2004). *Limits to growth: The 30-year update.* White River Junction, Vermont: Chelsea Green Publishing.

National Academy of Sciences. (2016). *What you need to know about energy: transportation.* Retrieved August 23, 2016, from http://needtoknow.nas.edu/energy/energy-use/transportation/

Pew Center on Global Climate Change. (2011). *Building overview.* Retrieved July 26, 2011 from http://www.pewclimate.org/technology/overview/buildings

Pigou, A. (1932). *The Economics of Welfare,* 4th edn. London: Macmillan.

U.S. Department of Energy. (n.d.). *Fact #859 February 9, 2015 Excess Supply is the Most Recent Event to Affect Crude Oil Prices.* Retrieved August 22, 2016 from https://energy.gov/eere/vehicles/fact-859-february-9-2015-excess-supply-most-recent-event-affect-crude-oil-prices

U.S. Energy Information Administration. (2013). *U.S. energy intensity projected to continue its steady decline through 2040.* Retrieved Aug. 18, 2015 from http://www.eia.gov/todayinenergy/detail.cfm?id=10191

Wilde, O. (1892). *Lady Windermere's Fan.* New York: Quill Pen Classics.

Chapter 2

Energy, markets, and society

"I have not failed. I have just found 10,000 ways that won't work."

Thomas Edison

"With hydraulic fracturing, finding oil and gas has gone from a 1 in 100 chance to a 90 in 100 chance."

The author of this text

Introduction

Economics focuses on making the best use of scarce resources, the concept of *economic efficiency*. The theory applies to energy resources as it does to any other scarce resource. Societies have a wide range of objectives and we want to attain each objective in a way that uses energy efficiently. Economic efficiency can be thought of as maximizing the size of the pie, where the pie encompasses the well-being of consumers and producers.

We can make the distinction sharper by distinguishing between private and social efficiency. *Private efficiency* involves only the parties participating in the market exchange. *Social efficiency* also includes those who were not directly involved in the exchange. In this text, economic efficiency is synonymous with social efficiency. Under certain conditions, the privately efficient outcome will also be socially efficient, and we will want to clearly establish the conditions where that happy outcome holds. When it does, the market produces the socially efficient outcome without any government intervention.

In energy markets, private and social interests often diverge. If I sell you my used Hummer automobile that gets 10 miles per gallon, you and I both gain from the exchange. If we account for the carbon emissions from driving the Hummer, society might be better off with the Hummer in a landfill.[1]

Society may object to market outcomes for reasons other than inefficiency. We may object on *equity* grounds. Markets distribute income, and some people object to outcomes that increase inequality. On efficiency grounds, some propose a tax on fuels based on their unwanted emissions. However, such a tax takes a larger percentage of income from the poor than from the wealthy.[2] Another source of inequity is when production in one location results in pollution in another. North Carolina sued the Tennessee Valley Authority because emissions from Tennessee coal-burning power plants blew into North Carolina. Another possible inequity is that impoverished areas often experience higher levels of pollution, the issue of *environmental justice*.

Social welfare is a broad measure that encompasses social efficiency and equity. If efficiency is the size of the pie, equity refers to how we slice the pie. A *social welfare function* encompasses both efficiency and equity. For any objective, there can be many efficient points, some of which favor the poor and some the rich. Of these efficient points, the Bliss Point is the one that achieves the highest level of social welfare. The social welfare function is a theoretical ideal, but difficult to operationalize.[3]

A practical alternative to the social welfare function is cost–benefit analysis (CBA). The explicit purpose of CBA is to identify socially efficient uses of resources; implicitly, it embeds an equity judgment that a dollar is a dollar, no matter who receives it.[4] In essence, CBA typically ignores who receives the dollars.[5]

One other criterion for decision-making is sustainability. *Sustainability* requires that we use today's resources in a way that does not compromise the ability of future generations to be at least as well off as we are. Sustainability incorporates an intergenerational equity perspective. It constrains today's generation to resource uses that leave future generations at least as well off. The most widely referenced definition is that of the Bruntland Commission: *sustainable development* meets the needs of the present without compromising the ability of future generations to meet their own needs.[6]

Sustainability is a challenging idea for economists because it is ambiguous. How much weight should we give today relative to society in 10 years? 50 years? 1,000 years? Further understanding the meaning of "Future generations to meet their own needs" creates issues about assumptions of technological change and resource substitutability.

Let us sharpen the distinction about what we mean by future generations meeting their needs. Those who adhere to the Bruntland definition are referring to specific resources, such as oil or ecological services. In contrast, economist Robert Solow (1991) defined sustainability as using resources today in a way that allows future generations to have the *capacity* to be as well off as we are. The difference between the two is the degree to which we can substitute one resource for another. *Strong sustainability* does not allow substitution. Economists allow substitution to a greater degree, referred to as *weak sustainability*.

While economic efficiency and maximum social welfare may achieve sustainability, the objectives can conflict. Economic efficiency may favor the use of fossil fuels over renewable fuels based on cost considerations, while social welfare may consider both cost and who pays. Sustainability might reject continued use of fossil fuels if it leaves future generations with a smaller supply.

Efficiency and sustainability as goals have different underlying ethical assumptions. Ethics guide human actions to distinguish good and bad. Economics embeds the ethical viewpoint that we should maximize our well-being or *utility*, implicitly accepting the philosophy of utilitarianism developed in the eighteenth and nineteenth centuries. The corresponding social welfare function indicates we should choose the action that produces the greatest good for society, depending on the weights we assign to individual well-being. In utilitarianism it is consequences that matter, not the morality of the actions leading to the consequences.

Under the utilitarian ethic, sustainability has no special meaning. If society today views itself as better off leaving future generations with at least as much productive capacity as we have today, then sustainability is a candidate for the best choice. If on balance we judge ourselves better off using resources today in a way that leaves the planet less habitable for future generations, then utilitarianism does not lead to a sustainable outcome.

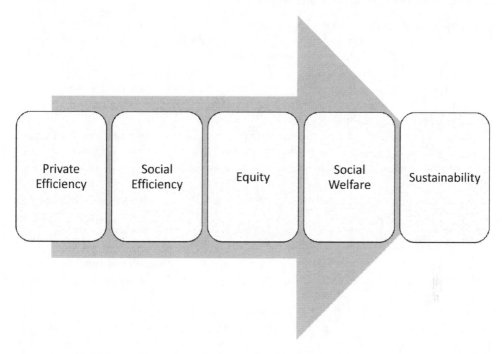

Figure 2.1 Criteria for decision-making.

Sustainability has a different ethical underpinning. From perspectives such as to consider the seventh generation, or the Boy Scout dictum to "Leave no trace," the ethics of sustainability include the action, not just the consequence.[7] Furthermore, economics uses an anthropocentric perspective, where we only consider how our decisions affect human beings. Sustainability may use a broader biocentric perspective, where we consider all living things, whether or not they directly benefit us as human beings.[8] To the extent that today's decision damages ecosystems needed for life support, it may be that our traditional concept of efficiency is too narrow and tends to emphasize short-term benefits at the expense of long-term costs. Sustainability advocates might challenge the use of hydraulic fracturing (fracking) to release more oil and natural gas for many reasons, including the use of large quantities of water, damage to ground-water, and increased risk of earthquakes. Economists also consider these factors, but only within an efficiency framework. Strong sustainability advocates would call a halt to activities that make the future worse off regardless of the trade-off between short- and long-term gains.

Figure 2.1 provides a snapshot of the normative criteria that guide what is best for society. Throughout this text, we first consider private efficiency for the parties directly affected and then whether it coincides with social efficiency for all members of society. We bring in social welfare to incorporate income distribution. We consider sustainability if we want to restrict outcomes to those that leave future generations at least as well off as the present generation.

What is different about energy?

There is broad dissatisfaction with leaving energy questions to the market, not always derived from sound economic reasoning. Concerns include running out of oil, energy security considerations, and environmental damage, especially climate change. In order to consider whether we share these concerns, we first determine the outcome of unfettered markets and their ability to achieve efficiency—private and social—and maximum social welfare. We can also consider sustainability, bearing in mind that the measure goes beyond traditional economic analysis.

Market failure results when markets produce an economically inefficient outcome. Some definitions include inequitable outcomes. However, in this text, we typically restrict the failures to inefficiencies. Energy markets are often missing one or more of the necessary conditions that assure economic efficiency, such as an absence of externalities. When there is market failure, we consider whether government can improve the outcome. At the same time, we need to bear in mind that there can be *government failure*, where the government has an objective other than economic efficiency.

Consider the following policies concerning coal use, nuclear energy, and renewables. Sometimes countries choose their policies using criteria other than economic considerations. Energy economics offers tools to make the best use of scarce energy resources to achieve maximum well-being.

Policies on coal range from rapid expansion to abandoning its use. China was building new coal plants at a feverish pace to supply the electricity needed to fuel its economic growth. The United States has virtually no new coal-fired electricity plants on the drawing board, and electric utilities are shutting down many existing coal plants before their planned retirement date. Coal reserves are plentiful in both countries, yet the use of coal differs. Until recently, China chose coal for its low cost, with less attention to the effect of coal emissions on its air quality or towards global climate change. U.S. policy gives greater attention to climate change, despite having enough coal reserves to last another 200 years.

Nuclear energy also provides electricity generation and does not emit carbon. Yet since the late 1970s, the United States had a virtual moratorium on the construction of nuclear plants after an accident at Pennsylvania's Three Mile Island facility. As the twenty-first century began and climate concerns grew, some observers predicted a nuclear renaissance. However, those prospects faded when, in 2011, Japan was hit by an earthquake and tsunami that devastated the Fukushima-Daiichi nuclear plant. Germany called a halt to its nuclear plans, while the United States took a go-slow approach. China upgraded its nuclear technology and planned to press ahead with new nuclear construction.

Even before Fukushima, nuclear plant construction proved to be far more expensive than projected, and there is still no long-term solution for storing nuclear wastes. Yet, the sudden rejection of nuclear energy in Germany after Fukushima was due more to a change in the political winds than to a change in its cost. Despite climate concerns, many who oppose fossil fuels also oppose nuclear energy, but do not necessarily base their position on careful consideration of costs and benefits.

Proponents of renewable fuels may base their case on finding continued use of carbon-based and nuclear fuels unacceptable, rather than making a case that the alternatives have a lower social cost. The costs of wind and solar have dropped dramatically, and some argue that by forcing more use of these technologies today, we will hasten the improvements that will bring down costs further and faster. However, renewables have their own imperfections.

Wind impacts views, as well as the flight path of birds and bats. Solar requires large amounts of land, and the mining and waste of silica that goes into solar panels. More fundamentally, wind and solar are intermittent sources that are only available when the sun shines or when the wind blows, which does not necessarily coincide with when we need the power. Demand may be highest late on a hot summer day, just when the sun is setting. Wind may blow more at night, when electricity demand is low. Solar and wind await developments in battery technology so that energy can be available even when the sun or wind is not. Alternatively, it may be possible to link wind and solar facilities so that renewable energy is available at more times.

Two of the most widely used programs to accelerate the use of renewables are feed-in tariffs (FITs) and renewable portfolio standards (RPSs). FITs are a price-based mechanism, while RPSs are quantity-based. Feed-in tariffs require utilities to buy renewables at a price above conventional alternatives. While it accelerates the use of renewables, the downside is that it also drives up the cost of generating electricity. Germany and Denmark are among those countries using FITs.

The United States has chosen the RPS. It requires electric utilities to generate a given percentage of electricity using alternative fuels, including renewables and in some cases energy efficiency. The United States has not instituted RPS as a nationwide standard. Instead, it has left it up to the states to decide whether or not to implement a renewables standard. A majority of U.S. states have implemented RPS policies, with each state tailoring its approach to its local conditions. California specifies that over 20% of the fuel used to generate electricity must come from renewables by 2020. North Carolina has a lower target of 12%, but recognizes hog and swine wastes as potential sources of fuel despite their high cost. It also counts energy efficiency and wood chips. Most economists would prefer that we simply price carbon, rather than FITs and RPSs that pursue carbon reductions in ways that do not minimize costs.

Efficiency

In 1776, Adam Smith wrote *The Wealth of Nations*. In the book, Smith explained the ability of markets to produce the best outcome for society. Individuals seeking their own self-interest will end up achieving society's best interest, as if guided by an *invisible hand*. Moreover, they will better accomplish society's interest by pursuing their own self-interest than if they had set out instead to achieve society's best interests.

Over the years, economists have identified a number of conditions necessary to assure this result. The most prominent conditions include: (perfect) competition, (perfect) information, absence of externalities, absence of public goods characteristics, and macroeconomic stability. These conditions are necessary to ensure that markets will achieve efficient use of resources from a societal perspective.

Market failure

In this section, we focus on three sources of market failure that are prominent in energy markets: monopoly, externalities, and public goods characteristics. We also introduce economies of scale. We give briefer treatment to imperfect information, macroeconomic market failure—inflation and unemployment—and second-best considerations, where inefficiency in one market can change the most efficient policy in a related market. In the next chapter, we will present formal models to show the social welfare loss due to market failures from monopoly, externalities, and public goods characteristics.

Finally, we revisit equity and sustainability. While these topics are not efficiency concerns, some would include them as market failures that merit attention in designing energy policy.

Monopoly

Market power exists when individual firms can influence the market price. At the *monopoly* extreme, there is only one producer in the market, and that producer determines the industry price. There must also be barriers that prevent new firms from entering the industry.[9] These conditions allow the monopolist to earn a positive economic profit.

Economists prefer competition to monopoly because the loss to consumers from higher prices exceeds the profit gain to the monopolist, so that on balance society is worse off. Implicit in this statement is the equity criterion that a dollar to consumers is worth the same as a dollar to producers. The objection to the Organization of Petroleum Exporting Countries (OPEC) is not that they earn more profit than they did in the years before their formation, but rather that the world as a whole would be better off if energy were produced competitively. This loss in social welfare is a *deadweight loss*, the loss to society from forgoing output with larger benefits than costs.

Unlike monopoly, economic profits in a perfectly competitive industry tend towards zero, as firms enter the industry when other firms are earning profits and exit the industry when firms are losing money. This long-run tendency of surviving firms to earn zero economic profits leads the survivors to produce at the lowest possible long-run average cost (LRAC). In a competitive market, long-run price equals minimum LRAC. In addition, at the output level that minimizes average cost, marginal cost equals average cost. Competitive markets are efficient because price equals marginal cost, and in the long run, price (P), marginal cost (MC), and minimum average cost are all equal.

The condition that price equals minimum LRAC indicates efficient resource use, insofar as there is no other combination of labor and capital that could produce a given level of output at a lower cost. In addition, P = MC is the *hallmark of efficiency*. *Marginal cost*, the addition to total cost from producing an additional unit of output, can also be thought of as *opportunity cost*, the value of resources in terms of the best forgone alternative. When price equals marginal cost, there is an incentive to produce the efficient output. Monopolists charge a price above marginal cost. OPEC tries to coordinate its decisions to mimic monopoly to share monopoly, so it too charges P > MC, and while OPEC gains, there is a social welfare loss to society as a whole.

Economies of scale

There is a situation where monopoly is potentially more efficient than competition. This is the case of *natural monopoly*, where the lowest-cost method of production is to have a single firm in the industry. *Economies of scale* exist as long as LRAC is declining in the relevant range of demand. To minimize LRAC, we only want one firm.

In electricity production, for example, we only want one set of electricity transmission and distribution lines. While *electricity generation*—the production of electricity using conventional and alternative fuels—was also characterized as a natural monopoly for many years, small-scale generation can now be cost-effective.

Externalities

Externalities, also known as third-party or spillover effects, occur when two parties make a decision that affects others, but the two parties do not internalize those third-party effects into their decision. Consider a steel firm choosing between coal and natural gas to heat a furnace to melt steel ore. In an unfettered market, the producer chooses the fuel that minimizes the cost of heating, but not the cost to society for unpriced resources such as air. We cannot assume that energy users or producers will voluntarily take into account emissions that reduce air quality or contribute to climate change.[10]

Gasland is a documentary about hydraulic fracturing that shows potentially alarming externalities. Among other effects, it depicts flames coming out of kitchen water faucets, purported consequences of chemicals used in the fracking process. Left unregulated, the producers disregard these spillover effects.[11]

You may argue that consumers would be willing to pay more for cleaner energy than for fracked fuels. However, even if some consumers would pay a premium for cleaner energy, we will still stop short of the socially efficient outcome. Some consumers will buy dirtier fracked fuel, while benefiting from less pollution if others are willing to pay more for cleaner alternatives. The benefits of cleaner fuel go to everyone, and no one can be excluded from them. Clean air has the characteristics of a pure public good—nonrival and nonexcludable—which brings us to the next source of market failure.

Public goods

Public goods are an extreme case of *positive externalities*, where the provision of a good has external benefits. In the case of a global public good such as less global warming, everyone benefits.[12]

A pure public good has two characteristics. It is nonrival and nonexcludable.[13] Nonrival means that my use of the good in no way diminishes the amount available to you. Nonexcludable means no one can be prevented from using the good. In contrast, pure private goods are both rival and excludable.

Viewing pure public and private goods as opposites in a taxonomy of goods, there are goods that are rival but nonexcludable (referred to as "the commons"), and nonrival but excludable (impure or quasi-public goods, also called club goods).

Figure 2.2 classifies goods according to these two characteristics.

Markets will not provide nonrival goods efficiently, whether or not they are nonexcludable. Markets usually sell goods to individuals who in turn do not share with society in general. But where benefits are nonrival, the good should be freely available to all.[14] Where the good is also nonexcludable, markets will not only fail but fail miserably, as *free riders* will recognize that they can obtain the benefits of the good without paying. Where the good is excludable, it is technically feasible to sell the good in private markets, but it is generally not efficient to do so from a societal perspective.

	Rival	Nonrival
Excludable	Pure private goods	Club goods
Nonexcludable	The commons	Pure public good

Figure 2.2 Range of goods between public and private.

Public goods characteristics are at the core of why it is so difficult to achieve a climate change agreement. All countries benefit from greenhouse gas (GHG) reductions, and no country can be excluded from those benefits. Hence, each participant has the incentive to free ride by advocating for a reduction in GHGs, while finding a way to avoid participating. For example, China argued during initial rounds of climate-change talks that the United States polluted when we were an industrializing nation and they should be given the same opportunity until they achieve development.

The efficient amount of research and development (R&D) into *nuclear fusion*—the process by which atoms fuse together and release energy, as on the sun's surface—is where the sum of the marginal benefits equals marginal cost. Suppose a company invents cold fusion technology, a way to produce nuclear fusion without the need to achieve the sun's temperature. Efficiency calls for a zero usage fee, to allow everyone to benefit. However, if no one can be excluded, the developer will have difficulty profiting from the discovery. Patents protect the developer by awarding monopoly rights for a period of time, but they inefficiently exclude other companies from using the new knowledge. In this case, there will be some R&D, but less than the efficient amount.

Other potential market failures

We complete the taxonomy of market failures by reviewing other potential challenges to market outcomes. Further sources of inefficiency include imperfect information, second-best considerations, and macroeconomic instability. Other challenges to market outcomes are due to inequitable income distribution or unsustainable outcomes.

There can be market failures in energy markets due to *imperfect information*. Consumers may be unaware of the connection between energy use and climate change. Or they may have little knowledge of energy prices, as seems to be the case in studies that show that consumers know the average price, but not the marginal price, of electricity. Average price includes fixed costs, which are irrelevant to efficient short-run decisions, whereas marginal price indicates the opportunity cost of using electricity. Where there is *asymmetric information*, one party has superior information. Manufacturers of compact fluorescent bulbs know the bulbs contain mercury and should be handled carefully. If you knew of that hazard, you might be less likely to purchase their product.

Competition achieves efficiency when the starting point is that all other markets are efficient. In a *second-best* world, our starting point is that there is an existing market failure in one or more other markets. If two markets are interrelated and it is not possible to correct the failure in the imperfect market, it may be beneficial to intervene in the perfect market. If the use of fossil fuels is contributing to global warming but carbon emissions go unpriced, there may be a justification to subsidize cleaner alternative fuels. Ordinarily, efficiency requires price to equal marginal cost. However, in the world of the second best where one market, such as fossil fuels, has a distortion, it may actually be more efficient to introduce a distortion in a second market for renewable fuels or energy-efficient appliances rather than to price them at marginal cost.

A macroeconomic market failure occurs when there is market instability due to inflation or unemployment. These failures cause inefficiency insofar as the economy performs below its potential GDP. High fuel costs have triggered recessions beginning with the 1973 Middle East oil embargo. In the 2008 Great Recession, there were subsidies for green infrastructure projects as a way to create jobs. The justification for such subsidies depends on their opportunity cost. How many jobs are created per dollar spent? Would the overall gain in jobs be greater if the money were invested into R&D for traditional fuels? Or would society be still better off if the dollars were spent on mass transit, more roads, cleaner air, or nonenergy expenditure such as investment in public education (especially at the university where you are studying)?

Equity can be considered a market failure of a different type than market ineffi-ciency. Taiwan has become a depository for old car batteries which can leak dangerous battery acids.[15] Some would argue it is morally wrong to place developing countries in a position where they have to decide between profits and health. Advocates of environ-mental justice maintain that it is wrong for poor people, whether in lower-class neigh-borhoods in the United States or in developing countries, to suffer a disproportionate amount of environmental hazards. This exposure may be voluntary as in the case of Taiwan, or involuntary, as in the case of Chester, Pennsylvania, an impoverished town that became an unwitting depository for toxic wastes.[16]

Sustainability might be categorized as a market failure to the extent that markets may not adequately protect future generations. There is even an economic efficiency argument made by Brock and Xepapadeas (2003) that we discuss later in the chapter that insofar as evolution is an efficient process that takes millions of years, economic efficiency evaluations are likely to undervalue such long-term changes. There could also be an equity argument that it is unfair for us to improve our well-being at the expense of the future, who are not here to represent their interests. Given the import-ance of this topic in public discourse, we return to it later in the chapter and in Chapter 15 as well.

Social welfare

There are an infinite number of ways to allocate our scarce resources. The United States stockpiles oil in a strategic petroleum reserve (SPR), for use only in the event of adverse developments in the oil market. Is the SPR a sensible policy to smooth oil price fluctuations? If it is, has the United States stockpiled the right amount of oil, or is it too large or too small? If there is another oil embargo, should we ration gasoline, or leave it to the market even if it means that the price could double overnight with the poor impacted disproportionately? Social welfare analysis (SWA) provides a framework for choosing the best outcome based on efficiency and equity considerations.

Pareto and Hicks–Kaldor efficiency

Efficiency provides a menu of all the outcomes that make the best use of societal resources. *Pareto improvements* restrict us to those outcomes that make at least one person better off, without making anyone else worse off. When we have reached the point where it is impossible to make someone better off without making someone else worse off, we have reached a *Pareto efficient* point.

The Pareto criterion has the advantage that we do not need to make interpersonal comparisons, as there are no losers. It gives us a measure of absolute efficiency. Something is either efficient or it is not. However, from a policy standpoint, Pareto efficiency is a very restrictive standard, as there may be few changes where there are only winners and no losers. A change that makes 1,000 people better off by $1 million each at the expense of making one person worse off by $1 would not meet the Pareto criterion.

Hicks–Kaldor efficiency is a relative efficiency measure. An outcome is Hicks–Kaldor efficient if the winners could compensate the losers for accepting a change, even if compensation does not take place. In that sense, it is a "potential Pareto improvement." If compensation does take place, it would then be a Pareto improvement.

On balance, countries that are not major oil producers likely benefit when gasoline prices fall. Consumers have more money to spend, and the economy benefits. Producers that use energy as an input also benefit. Losers include companies and workers in the oil and gasoline industry. Also, we all lose insofar as emissions increase. Lower gas prices may meet the Hicks–Kaldor definition of efficiency, but not the Pareto definition.

Efficiency vs. equity

Efficiency and equity can be conflicting goals. It may be efficient to allow the market to allocate oil, even if it means high prices during a time of tight supplies. The higher cost may fall disproportionately on lower-income households who use a larger proportion of their budget on gasoline purchases than do the wealthy. Alternatively, if we allow the poor to purchase gas at a below-market price, they will increase their purchases, resulting in still tighter supplies. If price does not cover opportunity cost, producers will lose money and production will decrease still further.[17]

Cost–benefit analysis

Maximum social welfare in **cost–benefit analysis** (CBA) sums up *consumer surplus* (CS), the difference between willingness to pay and the price, and *producer surplus* (PS), the difference between price and marginal or opportunity cost. If a decision only involves consumers and producers, then CBA says to choose the decision that results in the maximum sum of consumer and producer surplus.

In the absence of market failures, we will find in Chapter 3 that a competitive market maximizes the sum of CS + PS. If there are market failures, such as external effects or public goods characteristics, then some form of government intervention may be able to achieve a better outcome as measured by CBA.

CBA is an art as well as a skill, as in many cases, we cannot turn to markets to establish the value to society of an external effect or a public good. We may have missing markets, such as is currently the case in countries that do not have restrictions on carbon emissions. Cost–benefit analysis requires as good a proxy as possible to the competitive market price. Where markets do not exist or where markets exist but are inefficient, the best we can do is to ascertain a *shadow price*, a proxy for price. We might consider the price from the European carbon market to arrive at a shadow price. However, that price would likely need adjustments to be a good proxy. Initially, the European Union (EU) issued a large number of licenses, possibly to get industry support for the carbon market, resulting in a low price for carbon emissions. Another potential problem for determining a good proxy for price is thin trading, indicating a low volume of exchanges. In such a market, buyers or sellers might have market power, so that the outcome deviates from the competitive price.

Box 2.1 How not to choose a route for the Alaskan pipeline

Cicchetti and Freeman (1973) compare two routes for the Alaskan pipeline—the Trans-Alaska Pipeline (TAP) and the Mackenzie Valley Pipeline (MVP)—that were alternatives for transporting oil from the Prudhoe Bay of Alaska to the lower 48 states. The authors show that TAP, the chosen route, was inferior to MVP on both efficiency and equity criteria. The cost of transporting oil was higher using TAP and there was greater environmental damage going through an ecologically sensitive region of permafrost. The alternative route comes out better from an equity perspective as well, producing more gains for lower-income groups. Yet TAP was chosen. Ultimately, Cicchetti and Freeman suggest that the choice of route was determined by (a) the greater profitability to oil companies from exporting oil to Japan from the chosen route at a greater profit than selling the oil domestically, and (b) the corresponding incentive for oil companies to lobby the government to choose the more profitable route.

Sustainability

The term "sustainability" is open to many dimensions and interpretations, making it a difficult criterion to apply rigorously. There are economic, environmental, and social dimensions, also referred to as the triple-bottom line. Sustainability proposes that we expand the notion of capital beyond physical capital (plant and equipment) and human capital (education) to encompass natural capital (natural resource accumulation and depletion) and social capital (relationships among individuals that foster production). We have defined economic sustainability according to Solow's (1991) definition that emphasizes leaving the future the *capacity* to be as well off as we are and allows for resource substitution. Economic sustainability asks that we use our economic resources today in a way that would allow future generations to continue at this level or higher indefinitely. Environmental sustainability directs our attention to aspects of production provided by nature, such as ecological systems. Environmental sustainability argues for leaving ecological systems intact to support life in the future. Social sustainability refers to the availability of human resources for future generations: intergenerational equity, cultural characteristics that promote quality of life, and human rights, including property rights, that empower all members of the society to achieve their potential.

Energy sustainability requires that we use energy today in a way that does not compromise the ability of future generations to be at least as well off. Strong sustainability requires that we leave future generations at least as much of a *specific resource*. It assumes that there are no substitutes for a particular resource. Weak sustainability requires that we provide at least as much *productive capacity*.

If we use oil today, we can meet the definition of weak sustainability if we leave the future productive capacity equal to what we have today, even if we leave them fewer oil reserves. The equivalence need not be oil or even alternative fuels. In fact, we could achieve weak sustainability by simply investing the proceeds from using oil today in a way that increases future production capability by at least as much. Norway invests surplus funds from its sale of North Sea oil into a pension fund for future citizens. In the United States, Texas invests its oil funds into its state university system, weakly sustainable if it creates sufficient human capital to offset the loss of natural capital. The better educated citizenry are more likely to find new extraction methods, new resources, or new forms of energy conservation, all of which could allow future generations to be at least as well off as the current generation. The Alaska Permanent Fund aims to put aside a percentage of oil revenues in a permanent fund, where the interest is used to pay an annual dividend in perpetuity.[18]

Sustainability may conflict with efficiency and social welfare

If economic efficiency and maximization of social welfare also ensured sustainability, then there really would be no need to consider sustainability separately. But the three need not coincide. Consider taking an action to lessen climate change. Suppose spending $1,000 today to sequester carbon in the ocean will prevent the planet from getting hotter, while failure to take the action will result in a temperature increase of 0.1 degrees 50 years from now. Let us suppose that society values preventing the temperature increase at $3,000. It would seem that if we can spend $1,000 today to prevent damage worth $3,000 50 years from today, we should take this action. Yet we cannot draw this conclusion.

We must consider opportunity cost. What are the other options for spending $1,000 today? Could it be used to improve public education? Could it be invested into R&D of renewable fuels? Could it be invested at 3% a year for each of the next 50 years, worth $4,384 in year 50?[19]

Brock and Xepapadeas (2003) suggest that sustainability may actually compensate for a bias in the way economists apply efficiency. Evolution is a very slow process, and yet few would argue we would want to use resources in a way that would compromise evolution. The search for economic efficiency rarely considers a time horizon longer than one or two generations, whereas evolutionary change requires millions of years. Thus changes in ecosystems or species characteristics typically fall outside efficiency calculations. It could be viewed as a type of market failure, an extreme case of what A. C. Pigou (1932) called "defective telescopic faculty," whereby we prefer present pleasures to future ones. Explicitly considering sustainability may correct that shortsightedness.

On the other hand, considerations of sustainability may overcorrect. In place of efficiency, ecologists and other advocates of strong sustainability call for a *precautionary principle*.[20] According to this principle, an action should not be taken if there is a measurable possibility that it might do harm. Economists find this principle of little use. There is always uncertainty, but we would not want to preclude all action. The precautionary principle offers no guidance as to which actions are permissible, and which are not.

Equity for future generations

Sustainability expresses an equity perspective. The future is not here to represent itself, and so we have a responsibility to protect unborn generations. It is a view of equity that is reminiscent of *A Theory of Justice*, a classic philosophical treatise by John Rawls (1971).

Rawls asks us to operate behind a "veil of ignorance" in determining fairness. Before we are born, we do not know if we will be rich or poor. If that were the case, what would be fair? Rawls posits that we are only as well off as the least well-off person, so the only way we can become better off is to help the worst off. The sustainability ethic indicates that we are worse off if future generations cannot achieve what we can do today. We will only become better off if we use resources in a way that allows the future to be at least as well off as we are today.

Summary

The public tends to be wary of markets when it comes to energy. They may object to the magnitude of profits earned by oil companies and that these companies willingly sacrifice the environment in order to earn more profit. Some concerns may be justified, others are not. In order to make such judgments, we need a systematic way of linking our goals, our actions, and our outcomes.

Economic efficiency is foremost in economic analysis. Efficiency is making the most of our scarce resources, in essence maximizing the size of the pie. Private efficiency only takes into account the costs and benefits of the direct participants. Social efficiency incorporates the effects on any affected party, as if we were one large family. When comparing fossil fuels to renewables, fossil fuels have long had lower private costs than wind or solar. Social costs of fossil fuels would also account for pollutants including carbon emissions that have global effects beyond those of the fossil fuel buyer or seller. The social efficiency case for nuclear energy or renewables is that they do not emit carbon. However, the comparison also needs to recognize that nuclear energy produces radioactive wastes and that wind and solar are intermittent, impact views, and require large amounts of land.

There is also public concern about equity, or how we divide the pie. Most of the time, there is an equity–efficiency trade-off, so that to achieve greater equality, we may weaken efficiency incentives. Higher energy prices affect the poor disproportionately. Assisting the poor by subsidizing the price of electricity could lead to higher than efficient electricity use, as well as weakening the incentive to earn income and losing eligibility for the subsidy.

Social welfare analysis aggregates individual well-being into a measure of societal well-being that includes efficiency and equity. A common equity assumption is to treat a dollar as a dollar, regardless of the recipient. This assumption is implicit in cost–benefit analysis. Sometimes, CBA will show that one project dominates on both efficiency and equity criteria. The study of the route chosen for the Alaskan pipeline shows that government failure can result in choosing an outcome that is inferior in both efficiency and equity.

Sustainability rules out an outcome that leaves the future worse off than today's generation. Economists emphasize efficiency. To the extent that they consider sustainability, they are more willing to accept weak than strong sustainability. Weak sustainability accepts depletion of today's oil in return for investing a portion of the proceeds in ways that benefit the future, such as more R&D into energy alternatives or depositing the money in an interest-earning bank account for the use of future generations. As with equity, economists have no special qualification for determining what is fair, whether within the current generation or between current and future ones. If society accepts certain fairness guidelines, economists maintain that we should achieve these goals in a way that minimizes the trade-off with efficiency.

Pareto improvements are exchanges where there are gains to one or more individuals, without any losers. We have reached Pareto efficiency when it is no longer possible to make someone better off without making someone else worse off. While Pareto efficiency avoids controversial judgments about interpersonal utility, it is conservative, preventing most changes because we cannot permit even a single loser. Most changes create both winners and losers. Hicks–Kaldor efficiency allows changes where the winners could compensate the losers, although compensation need not take place. Lower energy prices tend to increase Hicks–Kaldor efficiency, but would not pass the Pareto criteria. On balance, there are net benefits, but oil companies, their workers, and nearby businesses will be among the losers. CBA has a similar underlying equity judgment, except we are dealing with dollars, rather than a more abstract notion of well-being such as utility. A Rawlsian would in fact only permit changes that help the least well-off person, a social welfare function that emphasizes equity over efficiency.

The starting point for efficiency is to fully understand how markets work, and how they can produce an efficient outcome, as if moved by an invisible hand. However, market failure leads to inefficient outcomes. Causes of market failure include non-competitive markets, economies of scale, externalities, public goods characteristics, imperfect information, second-best considerations, and macroeconomic problems of inflation and unemployment. Some would add equity considerations such as environmental injustice and unsustainable outcomes such as depleting oil. Examples of market failure in energy markets are ubiquitous, including OPEC's noncompetitive pricing, missing markets for carbon emissions, failed attempts at climate change agreements, and electric utility economies of scale. In a second-best world where one market is inefficient, it may not be efficient to strive for competition in related markets. If fossil fuels escape carbon pricing, it may be efficient to subsidize alternative fuels. Lastly, energy has macroeconomic effects. High energy prices can create inflation and unemployment.

Economics can help evaluate how best to achieve society's goals with regard to the use of our scarce energy resources. Society ultimately gets to set the priorities assisted by CBA, although we may have to rely upon shadow prices rather than actual ones in the absence of real markets, such as for carbon emissions in countries that do not price greenhouse gases. The alternative to imperfect markets is often imperfect government, which may pursue money and votes rather than economic efficiency.

Once we approximate society's priorities, economics focuses on achieving these objectives in an economically efficient manner to leave as many resources as possible to tackle other concerns, such as investing in energy R&D, reducing emissions, or providing more money for the education institution of your choice.

Notes

1 More often, the Hummer may end up in a developing country and not in a landfill. In the U.S. Cash-for-Clunkers program, where the government provided subsidies for drivers who traded in their low-mileage vehicles for higher-mileage ones, a critical factor was what the car dealerships did with the low-mileage vehicles. If they simply sold them to low-income consumers in developing countries, then the program did relatively little to help reduce carbon emissions. When it comes to climate change, social efficiency encompasses all countries. The effect of carbon emissions on climate change is the same no matter where they are emitted.

2 JP Morgan (2015) reported that while high-income consumers spent more in absolute terms on gas, the relative percentage expense was 1.5% for high income vs. 5.6% for low income.

3 Social welfare functions and the Bliss Point are hard to operationalize because they require cardinal measures of well-being; that is, they assume we can measure well-being on a numerical scale. Economics rejected that approach in favor of an ordinal scale that allows us to say that consumers prefer A to B, but does not say by how much. While we can say that lower gas prices increase your well-being, we cannot say that it makes you twice as well off. Nor can we make interpersonal comparisons, such as whether you or I gain more well-being from lower gas prices.

4 CBA may appear to have an innocuous equity assumption, but in fact it is anti-egalitarian. A gain of $1.01 to a millionaire at the expense of a loss of $1 to a pauper would be a net benefit. Yet most would agree that the rich person gains less additional well-being from the million and first dollar than the poor person loses from forgoing a dollar that was needed to purchase necessities. Before you reject the use of CBA because of this judgment, be aware that it is less flawed than maximizing GDP, the most widely used measure of society's well-being. The GDP measurement also assumes a dollar is a dollar, since it does not consider who gets the dollars. Furthermore, it fails to account in a systematic way for a host of issues, including resource depletion and external costs such as carbon emissions.

5 It is possible to incorporate other equity judgments in CBA. We can give a greater weight to dollars received by the poor. But then the question becomes how much greater: 2 : 1, 3 : 1, 4 : 1? You can assume the ratio is 1 : 1 unless stated otherwise, because of the difficulty of justifying other weightings.

6 The definition can be found at the International Institute of Sustainable Development (n.d.).

7 A consequentialist might favor white lies such as complimenting someone's new car even if you think it is hideous, because the gain in happiness to the new owner outweighs any cost to the one telling the lie. Deontology is a rules-based approach to ethics; a deontologist would not tell a white lie as lying is always wrong. Under value ethics, it is permissible to tell a white lie if the underlying motive is benevolent, namely not to hurt the feelings of the new car owner.

8 Some will argue for sustainability on moral grounds. One moral argument is that future generations are not here to defend their rights, so we should not usurp their rights by leaving them with fewer resources than we have today. Others would extend rights to all living things, so that trees for example have standing in the criteria for what has the right to future resources. While economic arguments are anthropocentric, other disciplines such as deep ecology may view all living things as having equal rights, in the realm of a biocentric view.

9 In this text, a barrier to entry is a cost deterrent to potential entrants that was not faced by firms already in the industry. Tesla, the developer of a luxury electric car, desires to sell its cars through the internet rather than through the traditional means of selling cars through distributors. North Carolina is among the U.S. states that has so far not allowed Tesla to sell its cars without a distributor. If Tesla cannot find a distributor, then Tesla may be unable to sell cars in North Carolina. Other texts define a barrier to entry as any cost that makes entry more difficult. There are high capital costs to starting a new car company. But as long as existing companies also faced these costs, this text does not consider high capital costs a barrier to entry. New firms are not at a disadvantage as compared to established firms.

10 We are concerned about real (nonpecuniary), not money (pecuniary) externalities. When a new firm enters a competitive industry, it reduces price which helps consumers but hurts firms already in the industry. There is no inefficiency, just an income distribution effect. Producers suffer a money externality, not a real externality. In this text, the term "externality" refers to a real externality.

11 *Gasland* was nominated for the 2011 Academy Award for best documentary and was followed by *Gasland II*. The oil and gas industries disputed the claims. If flames do come out of faucets, they may be caused by chemicals in the water that predate fracking.

12 More precisely, almost everyone benefits. Cold countries such as Canada and Russia may have positive net benefits from global warming, such as reduced heating bills and increased agricultural output. And while the average global temperature is rising, some locations will actually experience cooling. If the jet stream shifts, Great Britain may be plunged into a much colder climate. However, for the time being, warmer temperatures are allowing England to grow wine grapes. France is still growing grapes, but if it continues to warm, their wine industry could be hurt.

13 The nonrival property is sometimes referred to as nonexclusive. We avoid this terminology, as the similarity of the words "exclusive" and "excludable" can lead to unnecessary confusion.

14 Be careful to distinguish between the marginal cost of production vs. use. There is a marginal cost of production, and consumers must be willing to pay that cost if the good is worth producing in the first place. Typically, governments charge a tax to pay for public goods. However, once the good has been produced and there are no marginal costs associated with its use, the price for use should be zero.

15 See Williams and Chang (2008), especially p. 49, for a discussion of Taiwan's willingness to accept old car batteries to provide revenues to accelerate the country's development.

16 To read more about the Chester, PA, case, go to Kearns (1998), who reviews a U.S. Supreme Court ruling dismissing the case. Banzhaf (2009) cautions against focusing on environmental justice. Lower income means less ability to pay, including for environment. The poor may elect to live in places with lower rents and more pollution. If we then single out these locations for cleanup, we are taking an inefficient action. We may even drive up rents, and drive out the poor in a way analogous to gentrification.

17 Price controls could actually hurt the poor. Producers will have an incentive to evade the controls, as gas stations did during the price controls of the 1970s. They required gas purchasers to also obtain an overpriced car wash. In the end, the wealthy were the most likely to be willing to buy gas and a car wash.

18 The fund is proving unsustainable. With lower oil prices, it has had to cut the dividend, so that fewer generations could get smaller dividends than today's citizens, and it is possible that Alaska will dip into the principle to try to maintain today's payment at the expense of the future.

19 Nor do we know the preferences of future generations. In the absence of that knowledge, it is reasonable to assume they will have the same preferences as the present generation.

20 Ecological economics is distinct from environmental economics by incorporating ecological principles such as strong sustainability. It emphasizes the unique role of ecosystems and the inability to find substitutes for them. The International Society for Ecological Economics (ISEE) was established in 1989 and publishes *Ecological Economics*.

References

Banzhaf, S. (2009, May 25). The political economy of environmental justice [Web log post]. Retrieved August 29, 2016 from http://www.rff.org/blog/2009/political-economy-environmental-justice

Brock, W. A., & Xepapadeas, A. (2003). Valuing biodiversity from an economic perspective: A unified economic, ecological, and genetic approach. *American Economic Review, 93*(5), 1597–1614.

Cicchetti, C., & Freeman, A. M. (1973). The Trans-Alaska pipeline: An economic analysis of alternatives. In A. C. Enthoven & A. M. Freeman III (Eds), *Pollution, resources and the environment*. New York: W.W. Norton and Co.

Kearns, R. (1998). *Chester lawsuit declared moot by U.S. Supreme Court: Environmental justice still doable through courts despite recent Supreme Court decision*. Retrieved August 29, 2016 from http://www.ejnet.org/chester/moot.html

International Institute of Sustainable Development. (n.d.). *What is Sustainable Development?* Retrieved July 26, 2013 from, http://www.iisd.org/sd/

Morgan, JP. (2015). How falling gas prices fuel the consumer; Evidence from 25 million people. JP Morgan Chase & Co. Institute. Retrieved August 28, 2016 from https://www.jpmorganchase.com/corporate/institute/document/jpmc-institute-gas-report.pdf

Pigou, A. C. (1932). *The economics of welfare*. London: Macmillan and Company.

Rawls, J. (1971). *A theory of justice*. Cambridge, MA: Belknap Press.

Smith, A. (1776). *An inquiry into the nature and causes of the wealth of nations*. Dublin: NPN.

Solow, R. (1991). *Sustainability: An economist's perspective*. J. Seward Johnson Lecture to the Marine Policy Center. Woods Hole, MA: Oceanographic Institution.

Williams, J., & Chang, C. (2008). *Taiwan's environmental struggle: Towards a green silicon island*. Oxford, UK and New York, NY: Routledge.

Chapter 3

Static efficiency

Applying supply and demand to energy markets

"The reports of my death have been greatly exaggerated."

Mark Twain

"The reports of the death of the Sports Utility Vehicle have been greatly exaggerated."
The author of this text

Introduction

This chapter focuses on static efficiency in energy markets, using the familiar tools of supply and demand. Static efficiency is the appropriate measure of efficiency when time considerations do not play a significant role. In static decision-making, today's decision can be made independently of future decisions. Chapter 4 will focus on dynamic efficiency, appropriate when it is necessary to incorporate temporal considerations in order to make efficient use of resources. In order to consider sustainability, it is necessary to weigh future generations in today's decision, so we delay further consideration of sustainability until Chapter 4.

In this chapter, we revisit the core concepts introduced in Chapter 2, such as efficiency and social welfare. This time, however, we develop the concepts using the supply and demand model and its application to competitive and monopoly markets.

The decision to use a static model is ultimately a judgment call to ignore future periods of time. Consider the decision by a firm of how much natural gas to extract today. In the United States, where recoverable natural gas supplies have increased dramatically with the use of hydraulic fracturing, there is about a 100-year supply of natural gas, and it is likely to be acceptable to simplify the problem to a one-period problem focusing on today.[1]

In countries that have more limited supplies or are unwilling to use hydraulic fracturing, there may be only a 30-year horizon before those countries would deplete reserves based on their current usage rates. It is then more important to incorporate fixed supply considerations, both from the perspective of a firm wanting to maximize profits, and from the standpoint of a society wanting to use its resources efficiently.

Economists make use of *Occam's razor* to choose the simpler explanation if both explanations are equally good. Albert Einstein is often credited with saying, "Make things as simple as possible, but not more so." Unless it is clear that it is necessary to incorporate a time dimension, the usual practice is to focus on static analysis.

After a review of supply and demand as they apply to energy markets, we develop the efficiency benchmark of perfect competition, and the underlying conditions necessary for perfect competition to produce an outcome that is economically efficient and maximizes social welfare. We then revisit market failures such as monopoly, externalities, and public goods that can result in outcomes that neither maximize efficiency nor social welfare. Our emphasis in this chapter is to develop formal tools such as graphs and mathematics to allow a more precise understanding of the virtues and vices of energy market outcomes. The basics of supply and demand are in Appendix 3A. Appendix 3B uses calculus for the same static analysis presented in this chapter.

Supply and demand

Demand

Applying Occam's razor, we choose linear demand for its simplicity, as long as it gives accurate enough predictions for the purpose at hand.[2] Equation (3.1) provides a linear demand curve for gasoline:

$$Q_G = a_1 + b_1 P_G \tag{3.1}$$

where Q_G and P_G represent the quantity and price of gasoline, and the terms a_1 and b_1 correspond to intercept and slope. We expect b_1 to be negative because the *law of demand*: as price increases, quantity decreases, *ceteris paribus* (abbreviated to c.p. and meaning that we are holding other things constant that affect demand).

When we include variables other than price that affect demand, such as income and the prices of other goods, we have a linear demand function as in equation (3.2):

$$Q_G = a_1 + b_1 P_G + b_2 Y + b_3 P_S + b_4 P_C \tag{3.2}$$

where Y is income, P_S is the price of a substitute for gas and P_C is the price of a complement for gasoline.[3]

We expect b_2 to be positive as a consumer with more *income* will buy more gasoline, the case of a *normal* good. As the price of a *substitute* for gasoline, such as an electric vehicle, decreases, the demand for gasoline will decrease, so we expect b_3 to be a positive number. We expect b_4 to be negative; if the price of cars decrease, a *complement* with gas, consumers will buy more cars and use more gas, so the price of cars and the quantity of gasoline move in opposite directions.

Box 3.1 You can't argue with tastes

We will typically exclude tastes as a variable that affects demand. The problem with attributing a change in demand to a change in tastes is that it relegates the explanation to one of psychology and not economics. George Stigler and Gary Becker (1977), two economists who both went on to win Nobel prizes in Economics (Stigler in 1982 and Becker in 1992), argued that changes in prices often explain what had previously been classified as a change in tastes.

Consider changes in the size of cars consumers purchase. Sports utility vehicles (SUVs) first gained popularity in the early 1980s. Did Americans suddenly gain a taste for these large vehicles, lose their taste in later decades, and regain it in recent years? Or is there an alternative explanation based on economic factors?

Before 1973, when gas prices were low, American automobile producers earned big profits on fully loaded full-size American cars (back then, producers charged extra for cruise control, electronic controls to open and close windows, stereo radios, and the like). When gas prices skyrocketed, foreign car manufacturers, especially the Japanese, had a first-mover advantage in the U.S. market as they had already developed small cars suited to conditions in their domestic market. U.S. manufacturers came late to the small-car market with their lower profit margins.

In 1975, the U.S. Congress enacted Corporate Average Fuel Economy (CAFÉ) standards that required automobile fleets to meet a minimum miles per gallon standard. The legal requirement applied to cars, but not trucks. In the early 1980s, U.S. car manufacturers began to produce SUVs. The big three U.S. automakers—Ford, GM, and Chrysler—convinced the government to classify these novel vehicles as trucks. As gas prices fell dramatically in the 1980s and 1990s, consumers bought SUVs in ever larger numbers.

Consumers bought SUVs as a substitute for large cars that U.S. producers phased out because they could not meet CAFÉ requirements. When gas prices—a complement to driving—fell, U.S. consumers returned to large vehicles, and U.S. producers were happy to supply the high-profit margin SUVs.

Many observers thought SUVs would never diminish in popularity. However, as gas prices soared to record levels in the summer of 2008, many consumers downsized and these same observers predicted the demise of the SUV. But to paraphrase Mark Twain, news of their death was greatly exaggerated. As gas prices went into freefall in the second half of 2014, SUVs and full-sized truck sales led the way, with auto manufacturers having to provide steep discounts in order to sell sedans, even luxury cars such as Lexus.

Figure 3.1 shows the changing U.S. demand for SUVs between 1980 and 1990.

The initial demand is D_0. A decrease in gas prices increases demand to D_1. The gas prices shown are representative, and are not adjusted for inflation. The quantities are in line with actual sales that increased from 2.5 to 5 million in that decade. At any given price for an SUV such as $20,000 (again, we would have to adjust for inflation to compare 1980 and 1990 prices), consumers are now buying more SUVs when gas prices are low than they did at higher gas prices.

Consumers allocate their income to maximize their well-being, or utility. Equivalently, they want to maximize *consumer surplus*, the difference between maximum willingness to pay and what they actually pay. Figure 3.2 shows a hypothetical demand for SUVs, and consumer surplus if the selling price is $15,000. The demand curve shows marginal benefit and the corresponding maximum willingness to pay. Actual expenditure is the price multiplied by the number of cars purchased.

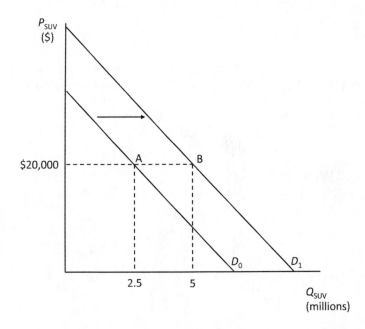

Figure 3.1 Change in the U.S. demand for SUVs between 1980 and 1990.

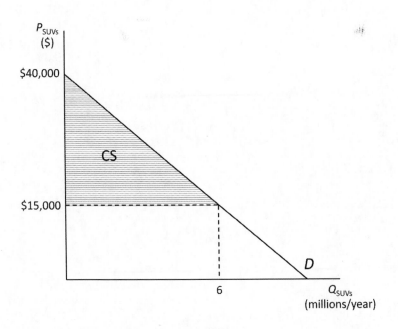

Figure 3.2 Consumer surplus from SUVs.

For linear demand, consumer surplus is a triangle, and the formula is

$$CS = \frac{1}{2}(\Delta Q) \times (\Delta P) \qquad (3.3)$$

where ΔQ is the difference between the change in the quantity demanded between two prices, in this case simply the quantity $Q = 6$, since the quantity at the origin is zero, and ΔP is the change in the price, in this case the difference between the maximum price at the vertical axis and the price corresponding to $Q = 6$.[4]

Example 3.1

Referring to Figure 3.2, consumers purchase 6 million SUVs per year at a price of $15,000. Find the change in consumer surplus if price increases to $20,000.

Solution

Assuming demand is linear, we can write the equation as

$$P = a + bQ$$

where a is the Y-axis intercept and b is the slope.

To solve for slope, find any two points on the demand curve. At $40,000, consumers are unwilling to buy any SUVs. At $15,000, they purchase 6 million.

$$\text{Slope} = \frac{\Delta P}{\Delta Q} = \frac{\$(40,000 - 15,000)}{(0 - 6\,million)\,SUVs}.$$

Solving for b:

$$b = -\$0.0041750/SUV.$$

Choose any point on the demand curve to obtain the Y-intercept.
At $P = \$15,000$, $Q = 6$ million.
Solving for a:

$$\$15,000 = a - (-0.00417)\,(\$15,000)$$

and

$$a = \$15,000 + 0.00417 \times 6\,\text{million} = \$40,000$$

This value matches the Y-intercept in Figure 3.2.
We can represent demand as

$$P = 40,000 - 0.004175Q$$

Consumer surplus for SUVs is the area beneath the demand curve—maximum willingness to pay—minus what the consumers actually pay. Figure 3.2 shows consumer surplus at a price of $15,000. Consumer surplus (CS) is the triangle formed by the area beneath the demand curve minus total amount paid for the good.

Solving:

CS = 0.5 [(6 million − 0) SUVs × (40,000 − 15,000)]$/SUV

Simplifying:

CS = $75,000,000,000 ($75 billion)

To find CS at $20,000:

Substitute the new price into the linear demand equation and find Q equals (approximately) 4.8 million. Consumer surplus decreases to (approximately) $48 billion, a decrease of $27 billion.

Supply

Economists assume suppliers maximize profit. We judge this assumption to be good if it gives accurate predictions about the producer's price and quantity. Google is investing heavily in solar energy. They may claim their goal is to be carbon-free. We base our predictions on what companies do, not what they say they do. We will assume the company's goal is to maximize profit as long as the model predicts accurately.

The equation for linear supply is

$$Q = c_1 + d_1 P \tag{3.4}$$

where c_1 is the intercept term and d_1 is the slope.

We expect $d_1 > 0$ in the supply equation. The *law of supply* states that a higher price leads to an increase in quantity supplied, c.p. Marginal cost tells us why the law of supply holds. *Marginal cost* (MC) is the addition to total cost (TC) of producing one more unit. Marginal cost typically increases with production. In equation form:

$$MC = \frac{\Delta TC}{\Delta Q} \tag{3.5}$$

Typically, MC increases as output increases. Shale oil producers in Texas can make a profit at a price as low as $30 per barrel. Producers in North Dakota may need a price of at least $50 per barrel to cover their marginal cost. Producers in Alberta, Canada, extract oil from tar sands, and may need a price of $60 to cover their marginal cost. At $30, Texas supplies its oil. At $50, both Texas and North Dakota supply oil. At $60, Alberta adds its oil to oil supply. Therefore, as price increases, quantity supplied increases.

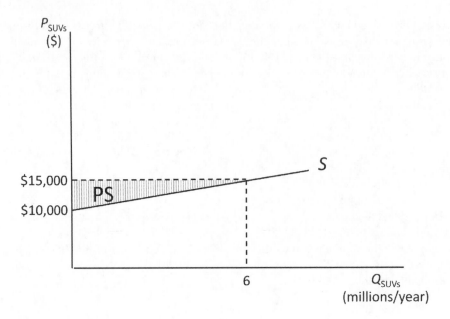

Figure 3.3 Producer surplus from SUVs.

Producer surplus (PS) is total revenue (TR)—price (*P*) × quantity (*Q*)—minus total cost, as measured by the area beneath the MC curve. Producer surplus is a similar measure to profit.[5] Figure 3.3 shows a supply curve for the SUV market, and shows PS at a price of $15,000.

Example 3.2

Using Figure 3.3, find the equation for the supply curve, assuming it is linear. Also find PS at *P* = $15,000.

Solution

We will use inverse supply, with price on the left-hand side of the equation. The graph shows that *a*, the price intercept, is $10,000. Solving for the slope (*b*):

$$b = \frac{\$(15,000 - \$10,000)}{(6 - 0) \text{ million SUVs}}$$

Simplifying and omitting units, *b* = 0.000833.
The equation for (inverse) supply is

$$P = 10,000 + 0.000833Q$$

Solving for producer surplus and omitting units:

PS = 0.5 × [(15,000 − 10,000) × (6,000,000 − 0)]

Simplifying,

PS = $15,000,000,000 ($15 billion)

Production

There are two steps to getting the cost of supply. The first step is to determine the relationship between inputs and outputs, a technical relationship. The second step is to determine the least-cost combination of inputs to produce a given output.

A production function relates inputs to output. The simplest characterization is to specify that output (Q) depends upon two inputs, capital (K) and labor (L):

$$Q = f(K, L)$$

We can easily add energy as a third input:

$$Q = f(K, L, E)$$

In some cases, we can add more inputs, such as materials (M):[6]

$$Q = f(K, L, E, M)$$

BMW produces cars at a factory in Spartanburg, South Carolina. The company makes extensive use of automation requiring a high amount of electricity, with relatively few workers on the shop floor. China has a growing car industry, and while they could emulate BMW, they choose more labor and less machinery and electricity. Whether a firm chooses a relatively capital-intensive process, such as the BMW operation, or a more labor-intensive one, such as the Chinese car companies, firms must achieve technical efficiency. *Technical efficiency* indicates that for a given combination of capital and labor, the firm will not waste inputs. If it is possible to produce a car using 6 units of capital ($6K$) and 4 workers ($4L$), BMW will not use $6K$ and $5L$. Similarly, if China can produce a car using $3K$ and $6L$, it is technically inefficient to use $6K$ and $6L$.[7] The reason? In order to maximize profits, it is necessary to achieve technical efficiency.

An *isoquant* depicts technically efficient input combinations to produce a given level of output. Figure 3.4 shows several isoquants for car production using capital and labor inputs.

As we move away from the origin, output increases, with Q_3 the highest level of output in the figure. Isoquants slope down, showing the substitutability of the inputs. The marginal rate of technical substitution (MRTS) is the slope of the isoquant:[8]

$$\text{MRTS} = \frac{\Delta K}{\Delta L} \tag{3.6}$$

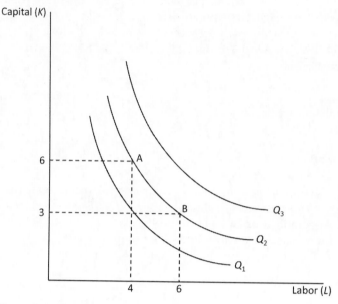

Figure 3.4 **Car production isoquants.**

Typically, MRTS decreases in absolute value as we move along the isoquant, giving the isoquant a convex shape. As we use more L relative to K, it requires increasingly large amounts of L to substitute for K, as each worker has less capital to work with. If the isoquant were linear, then it would be possible to substitute labor for capital at a constant rate and labor and capital would be perfect substitutes. We will not make this assumption, as it does not typically fit production conditions and so will not give accurate predictions.

Cost

To determine the least–cost input combination, we need to know the cost of the inputs (TC). If the inputs are labor and capital, the equation for total cost is

$$TC = wL + rK \tag{3.7}$$

where w is the wage rate and r is the cost of capital.

We rewrite the budget constraint as the equation for a straight line:

$$K = \frac{TC}{r} - \frac{w}{r}L \tag{3.8}$$

where the first term on the right–hand–side of the equation is the vertical-axis intercept and the second term (w/r) is the slope of the line. The negative sign on the slope indicates the budget constraint slopes down. We could add other inputs such as energy to the TC equation, but the expanded formulations do not allow graphical analysis where we prefer to use two-dimensional graphs with just an *x*- and *y*-axis.

The firm's objective is to maximize output subject to a budget constraint. The resulting choice of inputs will achieve productive efficiency. *Productive efficiency* denotes that the firm chooses the least-cost combination of inputs, capital-intensive in high-wage countries, labor-intensive in countries with relatively low wages, and energy-intensive where energy costs are relatively low. Productive efficiency includes technical efficiency as a necessary condition.

Figure 3.5 adds budget constraints (I_{SC}, I_{CH}) to the previous figure, where SC is South Carolina in the United States and CH is China.

The highest level of output the producers can achieve with their budgets is Q_2. We can easily understand why producers in China use a more labor-intensive and less capital-intensive production process to manufacture cars as compared to producers in the United States. Wages in China are lower relative to capital costs than in the United States; South Carolina achieves production efficiency with $4L$ and $6K$, while China chooses $6L$ and $3K$ to achieve the highest output level it can with the given budget constraint. At the points of tangency, the slope of the isoquant (MRTS) equals the slope of the budget constraint, so

$$\text{MRTS} = \frac{\Delta K}{\Delta L} = \frac{w}{r} \tag{3.9}$$

It should now be clear why South Carolina uses more energy relative to labor than does China.

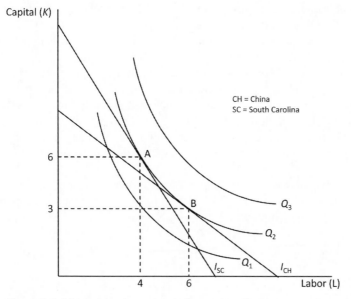

Figure 3.5 Maximizing car output for a given budget.

Additional cost concepts

A core concept in economics is opportunity cost. *Opportunity cost* measures cost in terms of the best forgone alternative. Marginal cost reflects opportunity cost. Total cost includes all costs. The *short run* (SR) is a period in which there is at least one fixed input. In the short run, there are *fixed costs* (FC)—costs such as capital costs that do not change with output—and *variable costs* (VC)—costs such as labor and energy that change with output. In the short run, fixed costs are *sunk costs*, costs that are irrelevant to short-run decision-making. As output increases, fixed costs do not change, so they are not part of marginal or opportunity cost. In the *long run* (LR), all costs are variable, including capital costs.

Average cost is an average of all costs. Short-run average cost is short-run total cost divided by output:

$$SRAC = \frac{SRTC}{Q} = \frac{TFC + TVC}{Q} = AFC + AVC \qquad (3.10)$$

Decision-making based upon average cost may lead to decisions that deviate from maximum profit because they include fixed cost. *Average fixed cost* (AFC) is overhead, which decreases as it is spread out over more units. Since fixed costs do not change with output, average fixed costs are also irrelevant to short-run decision-making. A firm must cover *average variable cost* (AVC) to justify short-run production.

Accounting cost counts *explicit costs* such as wages or interest payments to finance a nuclear plant. *Economic costs* include all costs relevant to opportunity costs including implicit as well as explicit costs. Implicit costs are costs for which there is no receipt, such as if the owner of a firm invests her own money or time in a project without receiving interest or wages. As accounting cost omits these costs, it can lead to incorrect decision-making. Accountants do include the implicit cost of depreciation to reflect the decrease in the value of an asset over time. However, they often base the depreciation formula on historical value, the original cost of the plant. Depreciation based on historical value does not reflect opportunity cost.

Coal plants are long-lived investments built to last for 40 years that can cost over $2 billion. Nevertheless, many of these plants are shutting down before their planned retirement or are being converted to run on natural gas due to the low cost of natural gas and in some places, the cost of carbon emissions. The fact that they cost $2 billion is a sunk cost. If the utility can produce electricity at a lower cost with nuclear energy, natural gas, or renewables, including the cost of meeting regulations on pollutants or carbon emissions, it should shut down the coal plant in the short run. In the long run, it should *decommission* the plant—dismantle the plant and clean up the site.

Alternatively, the utility may be able to sell the plant. However, its market value has nothing to do with its historical value of $2 billion. The value of the coal plant is whatever it is worth today, which may only be salvage value if the best use is to cease operations and sell the parts.

Supply and demand

We have seen the rise, fall, and rebound of SUV sales. When gas prices surged to $4 a gallon in 2008, demand for SUVs plummeted and owners offered to sell their cars at deep discounts. When gas prices fell below $2 a gallon in early 2016, SUV sales rebounded while sales of small cars lost market share. Supply and demand allow us to determine the price and quantity in the market, whether the market is for SUVs, small cars, or the gas that the SUV guzzles.

Equilibrium

Equilibrium is the point where supply and demand intersect. At the equilibrium price, the plans of buyers coincide with the plans of sellers. Figure 3.6 shows the equilibrium price and quantity for the SUV market for the demand and supply curves from Examples 3.1 and 3.2.

Example 3.3

Refer to Figure 3.6 and the equations we found for SUV demand and supply in Examples 3.1 and 3.2. Find equilibrium price and quantity, corresponding consumer and producer surplus, and social welfare.

Solution

We can solve for equilibrium using the algebraic expressions for supply and demand obtained earlier. The prices on the left-hand side of the two equations are equal at equilibrium, so we can set the right-hand sides equal to each other and solve for Q:

$$40,000 - 0.00417Q = 10,000 + 0.000833Q$$

Solving, $Q_e = 6$ million, and in turn $P_e = \$15,000$.
  Consumer surplus equals $75 billion (from Example 3.1) and producer surplus equals $15 billion (from Example 3.2), for a total of $90 billion.

Perfect competition

Under certain conditions, perfect competition generates an outcome that maximizes social welfare. When the invisible hand described in Chapter 2 applies, we will find that price equals marginal cost, the hallmark of efficiency. Furthermore, firms must find the lowest-cost method of production to survive in the long run. The market can generate efficient outcomes without any intervention by the government. This result requires certain conditions including an absence of externalities, no public good characteristics, and perfect information.

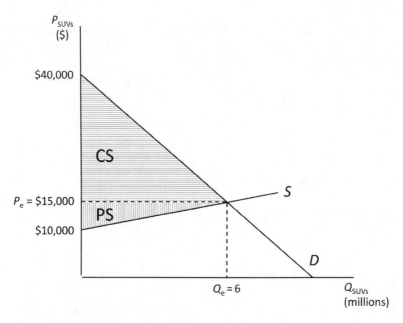

Figure 3.6 Equilibrium in the SUV market.

Assumptions of the perfectly competitive model

Industries vary according to the number of firms in the industry, whether they produce identical (homogeneous) or differentiated (heterogeneous) products, whether there is perfect information, and whether there are barriers to entry.

Perfect competition assumes:

1   A large number of buyers and sellers
2   Identical (homogeneous) products
3   No barriers to entry
4   Perfect information

We use the solar panel industry as an example of perfect competition. There are a large number of solar panel manufacturers. We assume consumers view solar panels as a commodity where one manufacturer is interchangeable with another. Finally, there must be complete information about price and quality. Finally, companies from the United States, China, and elsewhere must be free to enter (or leave) the industry.[9] According to Occam's razor, the model is appropriate if it is the simplest model that gives accurate predictions. If consumers do not see manufacturers as interchangeable, we would have to compare the predictions of the perfectly competitive model with those of monopolistic competition, which allows for differentiated (heterogeneous) products.

Short-run equilibrium

In the short run, the firm has at least one fixed input. It is typical to assume that the firm cannot adjust capital in the short run. *Capital* refers to equipment and machinery. Note that we are not referring to financial capital. The only way the firm can adjust production in the short run is to vary easily changeable inputs such as labor or energy.

For the simple case of labor and capital as the only inputs, and with capital fixed in the short run, the firm can only vary labor in order to change its output. Short-run total cost consists of fixed cost (capital costs) and variable costs (labor costs). When energy is included, energy costs are variable costs.

Figure 3.7a shows the solar panel firm. Figure 3.7b shows the individual solar panel industry; initially, there are 100 firms in the industry corresponding to S_1. Industry demand is initially D_1.

It is reasonable to assume that the solar panel firm has typical cost curves. Average total cost (ATC) and average variable cost (AVC) are U-shaped and MC is upward-sloping.[10] With 100 firms in the industry, the individual firm is a price taker, as it is too small a part of the industry to influence price. We use a lower-case q to denote the firm's quantity, and an upper-case Q to denote the larger industry quantity. The firm's demand curve (d_1) is horizontal; the firm can sell as much as it wishes at the industry price (P_1).

Total revenue for the firm is $P \times q$. Marginal revenue (MR) is the addition to total revenue (TR):

$$MR = \frac{\Delta TR}{\Delta q}$$

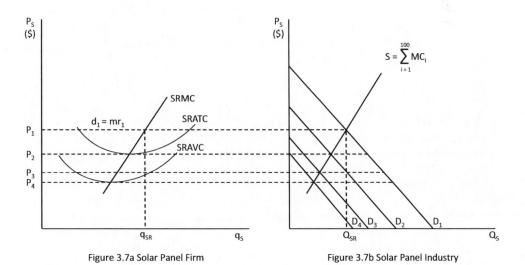

Figure 3.7a Solar Panel Firm   Figure 3.7b Solar Panel Industry

Figure 3.7 The competitive solar panel market in the short run.

For perfectly competitive firms, $MR = P = d$.

Profit (π) equals total revenue minus total cost:

$$\pi = TR - TC$$

At the profit-maximizing point, $MR = MC$, or for the competitive firm, $P = MC$. We can also write profit as

$$\pi = (P - ATC) \times q$$

The firm earns a profit as long as price exceeds ATC. At P_1, the firm earns a profit.

The last link between the firm and industry picture is the relationship between the firm's MC and industry S. Suppose the demand for solar panels decreases to D_2 due to a decline in home construction and price falls to P_2, just enough to cover minimum SRATC. At P_2, the firm breaks even as profit is zero. Below P_2, the firm has a loss. If demand falls further to D_3, the firm is losing money. However, in the short run the firm is better off operating than shutting down as long as price is above minimum SRAVC. The firm covers all of its variable costs, and contributes towards fixed costs. P_4 is the shut-down point. At any price below P_4, the firm is not even covering its variable costs, and minimizes its losses by shutting down.

Example 3.4

Consider an electric utility deciding whether to continue to operate a nuclear plant to produce electricity (in units of kilowatt hours (kWh)) or to shut it down temporarily. In the short run, the electric utility can decide how much labor to hire to operate the nuclear plant, but cannot increase the size of the plant nor sell it nor shut it down permanently. Average cost—the average of capital, labor, and fuel (uranium) costs—is \$0.15 per kWh. Labor cost is \$0.05 per kWh. Fuel cost is \$0.02 per kWh. Capital cost per kWh is \$0.08. The current price for electricity is \$0.12 per kWh. Should the utility continue to operate the plant in the short run?

Solution

Based on average cost, the utility is losing \$0.03 per kWh. However, if the utility shuts down in the short run, it will lose \$0.08 per kWh, a larger loss. By operating, it covers all of its labor and fuel costs and makes a contribution of \$0.05 per kWh to help defray its fixed capital costs.

Long-run equilibrium

In the long run, the solar panel manufacturer can vary its capital as well as its labor and fuel use. It can remain on the set of short-run cost curves shown in Figure 3.7a, or move onto different curves corresponding to either larger or smaller amounts of capital equipment. The long-run average cost curve is an envelope curve of SRAC curves, shown in Figure 3.8a.

We show a typical U-shaped long-run average cost curve. Each point on LRAC corresponds to a corresponding SRAC indicating the lowest-cost combination of K, L, and E to produce that level of output. Note that only at minimum LRAC is the corresponding SRAC also at a minimum. The LRMC intersects LRAC at minimum LRAC.

The typical situation is that the LRAC will initially display economies of scale—declining LRAC—as the scale of production increases. At some point, LRAC will begin to increase—diseconomies of scale—as the firm's large scale requires increasing layers of management. Between these two regions, LRAC will reach a minimum—constant returns to scale—as the factors that decrease and increase LRAC offset each other. That point corresponds to q_{LR}.

Figure 3.8b shows the industry. In the short run, there were 100 firms, each earning a profit. Since there are no entry barriers, new firms will enter until economic profit—total revenue minus total cost (including explicit and implicit costs)—equals 0.

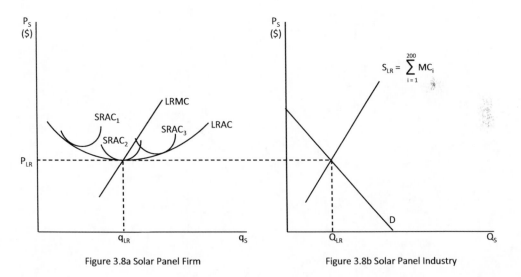

Figure 3.8a Solar Panel Firm   Figure 3.8b Solar Panel Industry

Figure 3.8 The competitive solar panel market in the long run.

Efficiency and social welfare

As stated earlier, the hallmark of efficiency is that price equals MC. All profit-maximizing firms operate where MR = MC. But in competition, price and MR are identical, so that P = MC. Recall that one of our interpretations of the demand curve is that it also reflects marginal benefit. When price equals MC, it also ensures that MB = MC.

In the long run, firms will enter until the last firm to enter—the marginal firm—earns zero economic profit. We still obtain the efficiency benchmark of P = MC (both SRMC and LRMC), but in addition P = minimum AC (both SRAC and LRAC). The result, one of the most remarkable in all of economics, is that firms in a competitive industry will arrive at the lowest-cost method of production to survive in the long run. This outcome coincides with Adam Smith's invisible hand that individuals acting in their own self-interest (consumers and firms) will end up accomplishing society's best interest.

We have developed a method of measuring society's best interest by aggregating the dollar gains of consumers and producers. In this case, we can demonstrate that perfect competition maximizes society's well-being by summing consumer and producer surplus and showing it is at a maximum at competitive equilibrium.

Figure 3.9 shows industry supply and demand for a competitive solar panel industry in the long run.

Consumer surplus is the upper left-hand-side triangle, while the lower left-hand-side triangle is producer surplus. It may seem odd that there is producer surplus, since

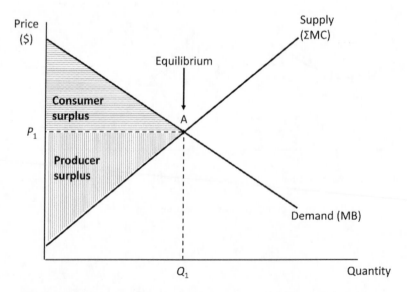

Figure 3.9 The competitive solar panel market maximizes social welfare.

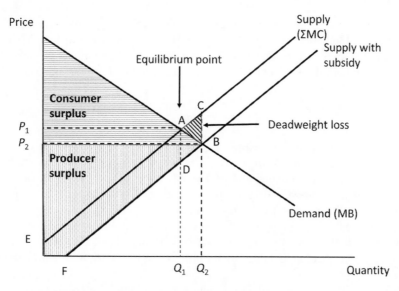

Figure 3.10 Social welfare loss due to subsidizing the competitive solar panel market.

the marginal firm is earning zero economic profits. To reconcile this puzzle, the infra-marginal firms have lower costs, perhaps due to lower costs of obtaining silicon. These infra-marginal firms will earn economic rent. *Economic rent* is a return in excess of what is needed to keep the resource in its current use. It is actually only the marginal firm that necessarily earns zero economic profit.

We now introduce a distortion to the market, such as a subsidy to solar panel producers.[11] A subsidy decreases the firm's costs and increases the firm's supply.

Figure 3.10 shows that the subsidy increases competitive industry supply. At the new equilibrium point, there is an increase in quantity to Q_2 and a decrease in price to P_2.[12] Consumers gain from the lower price and higher quantity. Producers also gain. They sell more, and with the subsidy, they receive a higher price than before, grossing P_2 and subsidy BC. Added surplus is EFBA. However, taxpayers pay area ECBF for the subsidy. On balance, there is a deadweight loss of triangle ABC. In essence, society is buying too many solar panels, as MC beyond Q_1 exceeds MB. The social welfare loss on unit Q_2 is distance BC, the difference between the MB and the MC of that unit.

Note that underlying our social evaluation is the assumption that a dollar is a dollar, whether it goes to consumers, producers, or taxpayers. This assumption underlies cost–benefit analysis (CBA). When economists claim they are focusing strictly on efficiency and leaving equity to be decided by other groups, that statement is not strictly correct. Most often, they are making the equity judgment implicit in CBA that a dollar is a dollar.

Market failure

We have just seen that when there are no market failures, perfect competition maximizes social welfare. An unjustified subsidy results in a deadweight loss. We now examine three other sources of market failure that arise in energy markets. In each case, the market outcome results in a deadweight loss as compared to the outcome that maximizes social welfare.

Monopoly

Gazprom is a Russian company that supplies oil and natural gas. The company monopolizes production in Russia. Gazprom Exports has a monopoly on exports from Russia. It exports to many countries in Europe, as well as to the Commonwealth of Independent Countries that were formerly part of the Soviet Union, such as Ukraine. Gazprom dominates the market for liquid natural gas (LNG) for countries that do not have their own natural gas supplies. Russia exercises its political power by threatening to interrupt supply for countries unwilling to abide by its political policies. Figure 3.11 shows the deadweight loss to monopoly—triangle ABC—compared to competition.

The profit-maximizing point for all firms is where $MR = MC$. For competitive firms, $P = MR$, so $P = MC$, the hallmark of efficiency. But for monopolists, $P \neq MR$. It can be proved that when a monopolist faces a straight-line demand curve, MR has the same vertical-axis intercept but twice the slope of demand.[13] Where competitive firms are price takers, too small to influence the industry price, monopolists are the industry and are price makers. In order to increase the quantity they sell, they must reduce price not only on the marginal unit, but on the infra-marginal units. As a result, MR is less than price.

To see this point, look at Figure 3.11.

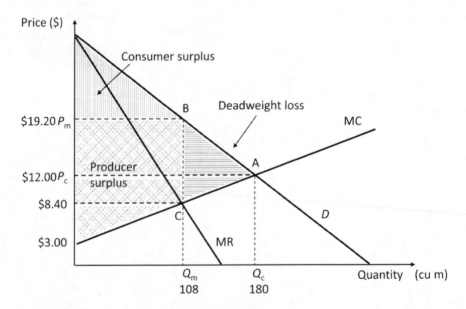

Figure 3.11 Social welfare loss due to Gazprom monopoly.

At a price of $19.20 per cubic meter (cu m or m³) of LNG, Gazprom sells 108 cu m. If they wanted to increase sales to 180 units, they would have to lower the price to $12. TR at $19.20 is $2,073.60. At $12, TR = $2,160.00. The incremental increase in revenue is $86.40 for the additional 72 units, or a little more than $1 in additional revenue for each of the additional units, way below the price.[14]

Triangle ABC is the deadweight loss (DWL) due to monopoly. Gazprom produces 108 cu m at a price of $19.20 per cu m, as compared to the competitive quantity of 180 cu m at a price of $12 per cu m. At $Q = 108$ cu m, MB = P = $19.20 (point B), while MC = $8.40 (point C). Society suffers a net loss of $10.80 by not producing this unit.

Example 3.5

Refer to Figure 3.11. Do you recommend Gazprom decreases price to $15?

Solution

To solve, we need the equation for demand. To obtain the slope of demand, compare prices and quantities at points B and A. When price decreases from $19.20 to $12, quantity increases from 108 to 180 cu m. So the slope is $7.20/72 cu m = $0.10/cu m.

If price decreases to $15, quantity will increase to 150 cu m. Total revenue will increase from $2,073.60 to $2,250. Incremental revenue is $176.40, or an average of $4.20 for each of the additional 42 units. As MC will be $8.40 or higher with the higher level of quantity, the profit-maximizing monopolist will not reduce price to $15.

You can also solve by obtaining algebraic equations for demand, MR, and MC.

Demand is

$$P = 30 - 0.1Q$$

For linear demand, MR has the same intercept but is twice as steep. So MR is

$$MR = 30 - 0.2Q$$

Since MC is linear,

$$MC = 3 + 0.05Q$$

At the profit-maximizing point, MR = MC, so

$$30 - 0.2Q = 3 + 0.05Q$$

Solving for Q, $Q = 108$. Substituting Q into the demand function, $P = 19.20.

Monopolists only retain their position if they can prevent entry in the long run. Typically, the monopolist's position weakens over time. Gazprom's high price and threats to interrupt delivery provide a powerful incentive for countries such as Ukraine to practice conservation, find alternative suppliers, and develop alternative fuels. It also creates the incentive for other producers, including Australia and the United States, to develop facilities to export their natural gas.

Externalities

Consider a competitive market for steel producers. In the absence of regulation, producers in a competitive market will minimize the cost of producing steel. They will disregard emissions from burning coal to provide heat for the steel furnace. The result is that a perfectly competitive market will charge too low a price, and produce too much steel, compared to the socially efficient price and quantity, as shown in Figure 3.12. The DWL to competition is triangle ABC. Society is better off with a lower quantity and a higher price.

Pigou (1932) proposed a tax to achieve the socially efficient solution. As shown in Figure 3.12, the tax should correspond to the external cost at the socially efficient quantity, distance CD, to ensure that the outcome will be efficient. If the external cost has a fixed relationship with the output, then we can tax the output. If the relationship between the output and pollution is variable and it is possible to meter pollution, we should set the tax equal to the external cost.

Firms can avoid the tax if they reduce emissions, or continue to emit and pay the tax. The outcome will typically result in some emissions, as is the case in Figure 3.12 at Q_2. However, these emissions are socially efficient in that a further reduction in steel production would result in a loss of benefits greater than the cost, including emissions.

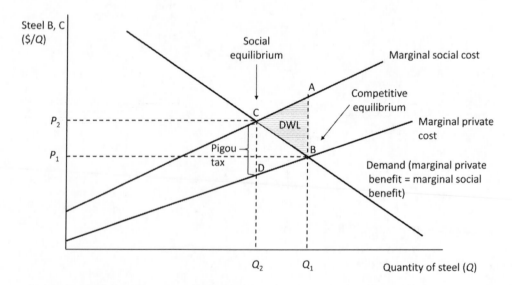

Figure 3.12 Pigou tax on steel plant emissions.

Ronald Coase (1960) challenged the Pigou solution. Consider the emissions from steel firms using coal to heat iron ore. The Pigou solution taxes steel output, or better yet, emissions from heating iron ore. It may be that a lower-cost solution is for people to not live near steel factories, so that factory emissions will not cause externalities. Coase's point is that there is joint causation; not only does the steel firm have an effect on nearby residents, but nearby residents have an effect on the steel firm. Sometimes it is lower cost for the steel firm to reduce its emissions, while at other times it is lower cost to not have residents near steel firms. There may be still other solutions that have an even lower cost to society, such as the steel factory paying residents to move, or the residents paying for the steel company to install a filter to reduce emissions.

The *Coase theorem* demonstrates that we will get the efficient outcome regardless of which party—the steel firm or nearby residents—is responsible for the cost of emissions from burning coal. Pigou implicitly assumes that society owns the right to zero emissions and that if a steel firm wishes to emit pollutants, it has to pay for that right. The alternative is that we do not own that right, and if we want steel producers to reduce their emissions, we will have to pay them to reduce emissions. We might pay for the emissions-reducing filter, or it may simply be cheaper to move away from their emissions.

There are implicit assumptions underlying the Coase theorem result. In order to get a socially efficient outcome regardless of the initial assignment of property rights, the two most prominent assumptions are that we can define property rights clearly and that transactions costs are zero.[15] Defining rights to the air is not easy. Surprisingly, the Coase theorem eventually paved the way towards doing just that, in the form of emissions trading, now referred to as cap-and-trade. In 1990, the United States introduced permit programs for sulfur and nitrous oxide emissions. While the programs did not include steel firms, they did cover most electric utilities. We discuss both Pigovian taxes and Coasean trading in detail in Chapter 14 on energy and the environment.

Public goods

Figure 3.13 shows the demand for a public good—abating steel plant emissions—for Arthur (A) and Ronald (R). The benefits are nonrival and nonexcludable, the characteristics of a public good. To get aggregate benefits, we vertically sum individual benefits, since both Arthur and Ronald benefit from each unit of abatement. The kink in the aggregate demand corresponds to where $MB_R = 0$.

The efficient point is where the sum of MBs to Arthur and Ronald equal the MC of abatement:

$$MB = \sum_{i=1}^{n} MB_i = MC$$

We can generalize the efficiency condition (and the graph) to contain more than two individuals.

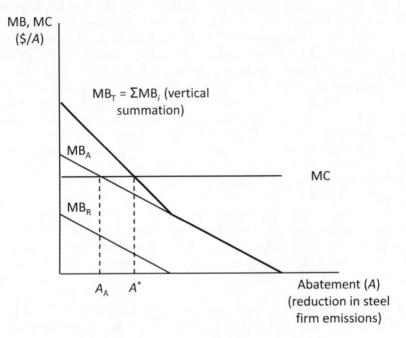

Figure 3.13 Steel plant emissions abatement as a public good.

Example 3.6

Arthur's marginal benefit from reducing steel plant carbon emissions is

$$\mathrm{MB_A} = 100 - 2A_\mathrm{A},$$

where A is units of abatement.

Ronald's marginal benefit from reducing steel plan carbon emissions is

$$\mathrm{MB_R} = 150 - 5A_\mathrm{R}$$

Marginal abatement cost (MAC) of reducing carbon is constant at $70.

What is the efficient reduction in carbon?

Solution

The sum of the vertical intercept points is $250, the starting point for aggregate demand. $\mathrm{MB_A}$ falls to 0 at $A_\mathrm{A} = 50$, while $\mathrm{MB_R}$ falls to 0 at $A_\mathrm{R} = 30$. So Ronald is unwilling to contribute to steel firm abatement beyond 30 units. At $A = 30$, Arthur is willing to pay $\mathrm{MB_A} = 40$. Beyond $A = 30$, the aggregate demand is identical to Arthur's demand. The aggregate demand has a kink at $A = 30$.

We can obtain the segment of demand where both Arthur and Ronald are willing to contribute by connecting two points. At $P = \$250$, $A = 0$. At $A = 30$, $MB_A = \$40$ ($MB_R = \$0$). Therefore, as price decreases from \$250 to \$40, quantity increases from 0 to 30, a slope of -7.

Aggregate demand between $A = 0$ and $A = 30$ is $MB_{A+R} = 250 - 7A$.

At $MC = \$70$, $P = \$70 = 250 - 7A$, and $A = 25.7$. In this case, Arthur pays his MB of \$48.60, while Ronald pays \$21.40. Note that the sum of the MBs = \$70. (What should Arthur and Ronald contribute if $MC = \$40$? In this case, we get $A = 30$, and Arthur pays \$40 while Ronald pays \$0.)

Example 3.6 provides a theoretical solution to paying for a public good, known as *Lindahl pricing*. However, if there is no way to exclude nonpayers, beneficiaries can understate their marginal benefits to avoid paying and free ride on contributions by others. In turn, since all participants have the same incentive, aggregate demand will understate the true marginal benefits.[16]

It may seem that when public goods are impure, so that it is possible to exclude nonpayers, we should exclude them, so that individuals cannot free ride. But efficiency still calls for taxing initial provision, not use. The MC_{use} remains 0, even if the good is excludable. Suppose the private sector offers weather forecasts to help electric utilities better forecast demand. As long as there is no MC for allowing an additional user to benefit from a produced forecast, the efficient use price remains 0.[17]

Coming full circle: social welfare

Social welfare measures net gain to society, where net gain is the difference between total benefits and total costs. In theory, social welfare considers both efficiency and equity. To this point, equity has been implicit. We have assumed that a dollar is a dollar regardless of who receives it.

This assumption may appear to be innocuous, but in fact, the underlying equity judgment could be viewed as highly controversial. A common view is that a dollar is more valuable to a poor person, who gets more from another dollar because she has fewer goods and services than a wealthy individual. By that reasoning, providing a dollar to a poor person adds more to social welfare than providing it to a wealthy person. This observation helps to justify *progressive* policies that redistribute income from the wealthy to the poor. It is common for electric utilities to add a surcharge on customer bills to assist low-income customers in paying their heating bills. Basic heat may mean the difference between life and death for a low-income customer, whereas raising the thermostat from 70 to 75 degrees may make a relatively small difference in well-being for other customers.

Despite the logic for weighting dollars to the poor more heavily, we stick with the conventional CBA assumption to weight all dollars equally. Weighting dollars unequally is difficult. How much more do we weight a dollar received by the poor as compared to the rich? If we do wish to consider a different equity criterion, we can do so (such as explicitly weighting a dollar to the poor twice as much as one to the rich). Other investigators can then accept or reject our equity assumption.

Summary

Static efficiency assumes that today's decisions are independent of future decisions. Supply and demand are key tools in static efficiency. We applied supply and demand to solar panels in a perfectly competitive setting, and worked through market failure scenarios such as Gazprom's monopoly, externalities from a steel company using coal to heat its furnace, and public goods characteristics of steel emissions abatement.

Social welfare measures net gain to society, the difference between total benefits and total costs. Social welfare takes equity into account. It is not unusual to favor low-income customers, such as when electric utilities provide heat even for customers who cannot afford it. However, CBA implicitly treats all participants equally by treating a dollar as a dollar, regardless of who receives it.

Perfect competition maximizes social welfare under certain conditions, such as the absence of externalities and public good characteristics. The hallmark of efficiency is that price equals marginal cost. In addition, firms in long-run competition must produce at minimum average cost in order to survive.

Market failure refers to situations where the market outcome is not socially efficient, although some use the term more broadly to include inequity. Externalities and public goods characteristics are often present in energy markets. While subsidies ordinarily reduce social welfare in perfectly competitive markets, they may be efficient in markets for carbon-free fuels such as solar energy if we do not price carbon emissions from fossil fuels.

Monopolies are a source of market failure. The Russian company Gazprom exercises market power in its sales of natural gas to countries that lack their own supplies. Gazprom charges too high a price and supplies too low a quantity, as compared to the socially efficient competitive outcome. However, if another firm enters the market, or a substitute product becomes available, a monopoly position will erode. Australia and the United States have plentiful supplies of natural gas, and can export natural gas and LNG to other countries.

In the energy market, the negative externality of pollution is one of the most common market failures. The Pigou tax assesses the producer for the cost of the pollution to third parties. The Coase theorem provides an alternative approach to the externalities problem by assuring efficient outcomes when there are clearly defined property rights and zero transactions costs. It has led the way to emissions trading.

Emissions are not only an externality, but a public goods dilemma, since the air belongs to everyone. Efficiency calls for a vertical summation of individual benefits, and setting the aggregate demand equal to the marginal cost of production. Use should be free, whether or not exclusion is possible. Lindahl prices provide a theoretical solution, but individuals have an incentive to free ride and understate their demands if the good is nonexcludable, such as the benefits from reduced steel plant emissions.

Market failures result in suboptimal outcomes with regard to economic efficiency and social welfare. Private efficiency focuses mainly on consumers and producers, while social efficiency takes into account all parties, including government and taxpayers. Social welfare also incorporates equity assumptions. We can accept the equity assumption underlying CBA that a dollar is a dollar, or choose to value dollars differently depending on the recipient.

Appendix 3A: Supply and demand basics

The *law of demand* states that price and quantity demanded are inversely related, other things constant. Consider the demand for gasoline. As its price rises, consumers reduce their purchases, holding other conditions constant. The Latin phrase *ceteris paribus* (c.p.) translates to "conditions equal" and is used to denote "other things held constant." "Other things" include income, prices of other goods, and any variables other than the price itself that could affect the demand for gasoline. It is also possible to interpret demand as showing marginal benefit or maximum willingness to pay.[18]

Figure 3A.1 shows a hypothetical demand for gasoline (G).
As the price of gasoline decreases from \$3 to \$2 per gallon, the quantity demanded increases from 600 gallons to 1,000 gallons per year for an average consumer. We can measure the response of quantity demanded to price by slope $\dfrac{\Delta P}{\Delta Q}$ but since quantity depends on price, it is more convenient in this case to use the inverse of slope: $\dfrac{\Delta Q}{\Delta P}$. Between points A and B, $\dfrac{\Delta Q}{\Delta P} = \dfrac{(600 - 1,000)\ gallons}{(\$3 - \$2)} = -400$ gallons/\$. As price decreases by \$1, quantity demanded increases by 400 gallons/year for the average consumer.

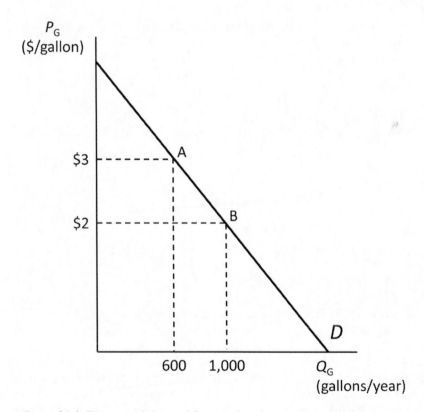

Figure 3A.1 The annual demand for gasoline for an average consumer.

Economists prefer a unit-free measure known as elasticity, which uses percentage rather than absolute changes. We can measure price responsiveness using *elasticity*, which measures the percentage change in a dependent variable with respect to a percentage change in an independent variable.

The *price elasticity of demand* is the percentage change in quantity divided by the percentage change in price:

$$E_p = \frac{\%\Delta Q}{\%\Delta P} = \frac{\Delta Q / Q}{\Delta P / P} = \frac{\Delta Q}{\Delta P} \times \frac{P}{Q} \tag{3A.1}$$

where E_p is the price elasticity of demand, and Δ is the Greek letter delta which stands for "change."

Equation 3A.1 shows the arc elasticity, where we calculate elasticity between two prices. We will use the midpoint formula for arc elasticity, which uses the average values $\overline{P}$ and $\overline{Q}$ for price and quantity, where

$$\overline{P} = (P_0 + P_1)/2 \text{ and } \overline{Q} = (Q_0 + Q_1)/2$$

Example 3A.1

Use the midpoint formula to calculate the price elasticity of demand for the prices and quantities in Figure 3A.1.

Solution

$$E_p = \frac{\%\Delta Q}{\%\Delta P} = \frac{\Delta Q / Q}{\Delta P / P} = \frac{\Delta Q}{\Delta P} \times \frac{P}{Q}$$

where $P = \overline{P} = (P_0 + P_1)/2$ and $Q = \overline{Q} = (Q_0 + Q_1)/2$.
The slope

$$\frac{\Delta Q}{\Delta P} = \frac{(1.000 - 600) \text{ gallons}}{\$2 - \$3} = -400 \text{ gallons/\$}.$$

Average price $\overline{P} = \$2.50$.
  Average quantity $\overline{Q} = 800$ gallons.

$$E_p = -1.25$$

As E_p is always negative, it is often written as an absolute value, in this case 1.25.

If $E_p > 1$ in absolute value, demand is elastic, indicating that the percentage change in quantity—$\%\Delta Q$—is larger than the percentage change in price: $\%\Delta P$. In example 3A.1, demand is elastic. If $E_p < 1$ in absolute value, demand is inelastic. If $E_p = 1$ in absolute value, demand is unit elastic, or unitary.

We can determine whether goods are substitutes or complements using a cross-price elasticity.

$$E_X = \frac{\%\Delta Q_A}{\%\Delta P_B} = \frac{\Delta Q_A}{\Delta P_B} \times \frac{P_B}{Q_A}$$ (3A.2)

To determine whether goods are substitutes or complements, we examine the sign of the cross-price elasticity. Suppose two goods are substitutes, such as SUVs and small cars. When producers reduce the price of small cars, their sales increase and sales of SUVs decrease. The cross-price elasticity is positive. For complements, such as gas and SUVs, a drop in the price of gas increases SUV sales, and the cross-price elasticity is negative.

The *law of supply* states that price and quantity supplied are directly related, *ceteris paribus*. On the supply side, the c.p. assumptions include the cost of resources and available technology, as well as additional assumptions such as the number of producers and expectations regarding future prices.

We can plot a supply curve and calculate price elasticity of supply in analogous ways to the demand side. Figure 3A.2 shows a supply curve for gasoline.

We can use equation (3A.1) to calculate the elasticity of supply. The inverse slope of supply, $\frac{\Delta Q}{\Delta P}$, is 400 gallons/$. The average values of P and Q are $2.50 and 800 gallons. The midpoint arc elasticity of supply is + 1.25. Elasticity of supply is always positive, as the law of supply states that an increase in price increases quantity supplied.

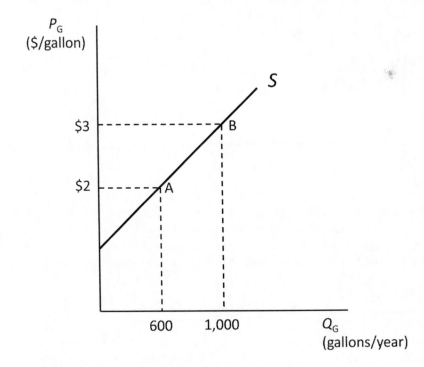

Figure 3A.2 The annual supply of gasoline.

Appendix 3B: The calculus behind supply and demand

We demonstrate the use of calculus using demand and supply. We begin with demand.

The slope at a point is

$$b = \frac{dQ}{dP}$$

where $\frac{dQ}{dP}$ is the derivative of Q with respect to P.

To calculate elasticity at a point:

$$E_p = \frac{dQ}{dP} \times \frac{P}{Q} \tag{3B.1}$$

If there are additional independent variables besides price:

$$E_p = \frac{\partial Q}{\partial P} \times \frac{P}{Q}$$

where $\frac{\partial Q}{\partial P}$ is the partial derivative of Q with respect to P. To obtain the partial derivative, differentiate the dependent variable, in this case Q, with respect to the independent variable of interest, in this case P, while treating all other independent variables such as income and the prices of other goods as constants.

The formula for cross-price elasticity is

$$E_X = \frac{\%\Delta Q_A}{\%\Delta P_B} = \frac{\partial Q_A}{\partial P_B} \times \frac{P_B}{Q_A} \tag{3B.2}$$

where Q_A is the quantity of the good, such as SUVs, and P_B is the price of another good, such as gasoline.

The formula for consumer surplus (CS) is

$$CS = \int_{Q_0}^{Q_1} (P - aQ)\, dQ \tag{3B.3}$$

If demand is linear, the formula will give the same answer as when we calculated the area of a triangle. If demand is nonlinear, the integral in equation (3B.3) gives an exact value, whereas a triangle provides only an approximation.

We can also show that for a monopolist, MR is twice as steep as demand:

$$TR = PQ = (a - bQ)Q$$

$$MR = \frac{dTR}{dQ} = a - 2bQ$$

MR has the same intercept as demand, but twice the slope.

Turning to the supply side, the differential calculus formula for marginal cost is

$$MC = \frac{d\,TC}{dQ} \tag{3B.4}$$

For two inputs I_1 and I_2, the marginal rate of technical substitution, which measures the slope of the isoquant, is

$$MRTS = \frac{dI_2}{dI_1} \tag{3B.5}$$

Notes

1 The U.S. EIA estimated technically recoverable reserves of 2,276 trillion cubic feet (tcf) as of 2013. Yearly consumption as of 2014 was about 27 tcf, so at that rate the supply would last about 84 years. Proved reserves are estimated recoverable reserves given present market conditions, while unproved reserves are technically recoverable with current technology, but not economically worth recovering. See EIA (2015).

2 There are alternatives such as multiplicative (or log-linear) demand. The log-linear form has a constant elasticity of demand, whereas elasticity changes along a linear demand curve. If we have reason to believe that elasticity is constant along the demand curve, we could choose the multiplicative form. There are other functions available, such as quadratic, cubic, and more elaborate functions. If we are using data to estimate demand, we can make our choice using statistical results.

3 Again, we choose the linear form for simplicity. We could use multiplicative (log-linear), quadratic, cubic, and other increasingly complex specifications if the gains from more accurate predictions exceed the cost of greater complexity.

4 If demand is not linear, the triangle is only an approximation. In Appendix B, we show how to get the exact value using integral calculus.

5 Producer surplus and profits are conceptually identical. However, producer surplus calculates total cost (TC) as the area beneath MC, which we will find provides total variable cost (TVC). In the short run, firms have both variable and fixed costs (TFC). Short-run profit is TR − TC, where TC = TVC + TFC.

6 Bendt and Wood (1975) introduced 'KLEM' in order to determine whether energy was a substitute for or complement to other inputs. In Chapter 11 on energy efficiency, we will discuss why it matters if energy is a substitute for or complement to other inputs.

7 In actuality, the Chinese government may have other objectives that do not lead to minimum cost. The government might command state-owned companies to hire more workers than otherwise identical privately owned firms would choose. The discussion assumes China uses profit maximization as a guide.

8 It is arbitrary which input goes on which axis. Had we chosen to put L on the vertical and K on the horizontal, then $MRTS = \Delta L/\Delta K$.

9 U.S. manufacturers including the now bankrupt Solyendra might argue otherwise. They have accused China of subsidizing domestic producers and then dumping solar panels, selling them in other countries for less than the price in their own country. Dumping could be a barrier to entry, as potential firms that are not being subsidized may not be able to compete with firms from China. Of course, Solyendra received subsidies as well, from the U.S. government.

10 Marginal cost is often J-shaped, first decreasing and then increasing. However, the firm only produces along the upward-sloping portion of MC, so for simplicity, we assume MC is linear and upward-sloping.

11 We are assuming there is no reason to subsidize solar panels. In a second-best world, where we are implicitly subsidizing fossil fuels by not charging for carbon emissions, there would be a justification for subsidizing solar.

12 This supply curve shows production even at a zero or negative price. With a large enough subsidy, producers will come out ahead even paying the customer to take the product. Electric utilities sometimes give away compact fluorescent bulbs (CFLs). The reason may be because they receive a large subsidy for programs promoting energy efficiency. Chapter 11 on energy efficiency will emphasize that energy efficiency is not the same thing as economic efficiency. Subsidies for economic efficiency may or may not improve economic welfare.

13 The proof requires calculus and is in Appendix B.

14 Incremental revenue measures the change in total revenue between two output levels. It differs from marginal revenue in that it allows for a larger quantity change. Marginal revenue usually denotes a one-unit change.

15 Coase (1960) may be the most cited article in economics. One branch of the literature concerns additional assumptions that may be required for the Coase theorem to hold. For example, if the wealthier party receives the rights, the poorer party may lack the income to achieve the same outcome as if the poorer party had gotten the rights; a wealth effect. The rebuttal is that the theorem concludes that the outcomes will be efficient, but they need not be identical. George Stigler is said to have referred to the results as the Coase theorem; Coase never used this term, and in fact thought the more important part of his paper was how to allocate rights when there are transactions costs.

16 While there are theoretical solutions as well as experimental proposals to overcome the free rider problem, there is as of yet no widely accepted real-world solution. If there were, we would be able to solve the climate change problem!

17 Increasingly, there are differentiated private sector forecasts, such as for individual utilities based on their service territory. In such cases, the $MC_{use} > 0$, as one utility's tailored forecast makes it less accurate for another utility with a different territory. Efficiency then calls for a positive use charge, and at the extreme, such forecasts are closer to private than to public goods.

18 Demand is derived from the theory of consumer maximization of utility. Consumers maximize utility subject to a budget constraint. At an initial price for an SUV, consumers maximize utility by purchasing their preferred amount of SUVs and all other goods. If the price of an SUV increases, they purchase fewer SUVs for two reasons. SUVs are now more expensive compared to other goods, a substitution effect. And consumers have less purchasing power.

References

Berndt, E., & Wood, D. (1975). Technology, prices and the derived demand for labor. *Review of Economics and Statistics*, 57, 376–384.

Coase, R. (1960). The problem of social cost. *Journal of Law and Economics*, 3, 1–44.

Pigou, A. (1932). *The economics of welfare*. London: Macmillan and Co.

Stigler, G. J., & Becker, G. S. (1977). De gustibus non est disputandum. *The American Economic Review*, 67(2), 76–99.

U.S. EIA. (2015). *Frequently asked questions: How much natural gas does the United States have, and how long will it last?* Retrieved September 5, 2016 from http://www.eia.gov/naturalgas/crudeoilreserves/

Chapter 4

Dynamic efficiency

Energy decisions over time

"Your money or your life?" "Take my life. I'm saving my money for my old age."

Jack Benny

"Extract oil now or later?"

The author of this text

Introduction

Chapter 1 introduced some of the major themes in this text, including whether we will run out of finite resources such as oil. It also introduced the related concern about whether our energy practices will be sustainable, allowing future generations to be as well off as we are today. In order to evaluate these questions, we need to apply a dynamic framework that is able to encompass how our use of resources today affects future resources and well-being. As concerns about sustainability go beyond efficiency into differing views about ethics, including equity, we touch upon the subject in this chapter but reserve a fuller treatment for Chapter 15 on energy sustainability.

There is enormous controversy over whether we will run out of fossil fuels. Geologists, for example, point to *Hubbert's peak*. M. King Hubbert, a Shell Oil geophysicist, predicted future production based on past discoveries, and the assumption of finite resources. In 1956, he predicted that U.S. oil production would peak in the early 1970s. Evidence supported this claim until the advent of hydraulic fracturing. Adherents of Hubbert view the upturn as temporary, and that production will resume its downward trend. As a result, they continue to call for energy conservation in order to extend the lifetime of oil supplies.

Most economists do not share this view. Economists generally favor a market approach to allocating resources, including finite resources such as oil. If indeed oil supplies are declining relative to demand, price will rise. Higher prices will bring about a decrease in quantity demanded, provide incentives for new technologies that can extract more oil out of existing reserves, and encourage the development of alternatives to oil.

There may be other reasons to conserve, such as to reduce emissions associated with oil use. We set aside externalities and public goods considerations in this chapter. We focus on the potential for a dynamic market failure, the possibility that markets leave too little oil and other finite energy resources for the future.

Dynamic efficiency, as developed by Harold Hotelling (1931), is the appropriate foundation for efficiency when it is necessary to consider allocation over time. Fossil fuels such as oil are nonrenewable resources, so that suppliers must balance extracting oil available today versus the future.

After discussing when to use dynamic efficiency, this chapter presents the dynamic efficiency framework, starting with the simplest setting of zero marginal cost and competition, and gradually introducing more realistic and complex assumptions, such as increasing marginal cost, monopoly, and the availability of backstop technologies such as renewable fuels if the current price rises sufficiently. We present a single numerical example to demonstrate dynamic efficiency, and use it throughout the chapter to demonstrate the effects of increasingly complex assumptions.

Hotelling's model assumes knowledge of energy prices now and in the future. In actuality, future prices are uncertain. We close the chapter with an introduction to energy market risk management tools. Energy producers may find it profitable to reduce or eliminate price uncertainty through the use of *derivatives*, financial instruments derived from the value of the underlying commodity. We will revisit risk management in later chapters, including specific tools for oil in Chapter 5.

Dynamic efficiency

Dynamic efficiency is the efficient use of resources over time. In deciding whether to extract another barrel of oil, the producer must compare its value today to its value in future periods of time. In making the comparison, it is necessary to recognize that the producer can invest today's profits, whereas sales that take place in the future forgo today's investment opportunities. To make present and future profits comparable, we must discount future profits to reflect forgone investment opportunities.

To make dollars comparable over time, we convert future values (FV) into *present value* (PV):

$$PV = \frac{FV}{(1+r)^t} \tag{4.1}$$

where r is the interest rate used to discount the future, and t is the number of years in the future when the earnings will be received.

For convenience, we use the real interest rate, r, adjusted to remove inflation. In the PV formula, the interest rate is the discount rate, and $1/(1 + r)^t$ is the discount factor. To demonstrate the application of PV, consider our willingness to spend money today to prevent the possibility of damage due to climate change 50 years from now.

Example 4.1

Suppose we could redesign car engines to emit less carbon at a cost of $10 million today to prevent $50 million in damage 50 years from now. Alternatively, we could invest $10 million today and get an average return of 4% per year over the 50-year period. Is the redesign of car engines dynamically efficient?

Solution

The present value of $50,000,000 to be received in 50 years, discounted at 4% is:

$$PV = \frac{\$50,000,000}{1.04^{50}}$$

$$PV = \$7,106,630.67$$

The PV is less than today's cost of $10 million. Redesigning the car engine is not a sound decision.

Another way to understand the solution is to find the future value of $10 million invested at 4% for 50 years. The future value (FV) is

$$FV = \$10,000,000 \, (1.04)^{50}$$

$$FV = \$71 \text{ million}$$

This amount exceeds the $50 million value 50 years from now for the engine redesign. If we invested the money, the future would be compensated for the $50 million in damage and have $21 million remaining to use in some other way. At 4% or any higher interest rate, we should save the funds rather than redesigning the car engine. (The interest rate would have to drop to approximately 3.25% before the engine redesign would be dynamically efficient.)

When to use dynamic efficiency

We use dynamic efficiency to include time considerations in evaluating efficient resource use. In deciding when to supply a nonrenewable resource such as oil, suppliers wish to maximize profits over the life of the resource, so they must balance selling the oil today versus selling the oil in the future. If a resource is renewable, but depletable, such as wood as a source of biomass energy, there are also dynamic aspects to using the resource today versus the future. For renewable resources that cannot be depleted, such as wind or solar energy, we do not need a dynamic framework, since the decision to use more wind or solar today does not impact future wind or solar supplies.[1] It may not be necessary to use a dynamic framework for coal, which, while finite, has a sufficient stock that using coal today has little effect on future supply. The same is likely true for uranium supplies. Natural gas is a less certain case. Estimated reserves are much larger with the advent of hydraulic fracturing. As supplies expand, the difference between the predictions of the static and dynamic models decreases. In deciding whether to use a static or dynamic framework, we must weigh the more accurate predictions of the dynamic framework against the greater analytic complexities.

For some products, particularly nonrenewable natural resources such as fossil fuels, there are good reasons to maximize value over time. Not only does this objective earn the maximum profit for the owner of that resource over the specified time period, it also creates the conditions and incentives necessary to encourage society to find alternatives. When we examine oil later in this chapter, we will compare the predictions for profit maximization and social welfare using a static model with a dynamic model that contains increasingly complex assumptions regarding supply and demand over time, as well as competition vs. monopoly.

Renewable vs. nonrenewable resources

Renewable resources can be divided into two categories: nondepletable and depletable. Solar and wind energy fit the renewable, nondepletable category so static analysis is sufficient to understand their usage. Biomass energy such as wood is an example of a renewable but depletable resource whose use sometimes benefits from a dynamic framework.

WOOD VS. OIL

A resource is nonrenewable if its replenishment rate is negligible in terms of a human lifetime. Oil was created millions of years ago as a product of sediments of fossilized plant and animal life under heat and pressure. This process continues to take place, but it will not produce meaningful additions to the world's supply of oil in one lifetime or even several lifetimes.

For renewable but depletable resources such as wood, it may still be necessary to include dynamic considerations. A decision to harvest the resource today must take into account the growth rate of the resource. It must also take into account the ability to exclude other firms from harvesting. A key difference in the analysis is that for the renewable but depletable resources, it is necessary to include a characterization of the growth rate of the resource. If the harvest rate is above the growth rate, then the resource will decline over time. If other firms cannot be excluded, there may be nothing left to harvest.

Box 4.1 All wood is not created equal

Developing countries use wood as a fuel for heating and cooking. The use of wood can lead to deforestation. An owner of a tree plantation will only be able to manage growth optimally if she can prevent poachers from cutting down the trees prematurely.

Wood is a major source of energy in developing countries, mostly by default. Indoor wood stoves have deleterious health effects on the occupants, while wood as a primary source of heating leads to indoor health effects, air pollution, and deforestation. Developing countries seek other sources of energy, such as renewables, to replace wood.

In developed countries seeking to increase the use of renewable energy, there can be controversy over whether wood should qualify as renewable. Some environmentalists fear that including wood as a renewable fuel will lead to premature harvesting of forests.

Duke Energy favored the inclusion of wood in meeting the North Carolina Renewable Portfolio Standard requirement. Duke asserted it could use wood without depleting it by managing a tree plantation sustainably, with equal rates of harvesting and replanting. However, environmentalists feared that Duke would also use forests containing old-growth trees which can better be characterized as nonrenewable resources. While it is possible to replace a 400-year-old oak tree, the new tree's rate of growth is slow enough that for all practical purposes, the tree will not be replaced for generations. Paper companies also protested that the use of wood for energy will drive up the cost of trees, making their product more expensive (Abt, Abt, Cubbage, & Henderson, 2010; Downey, 2010).

This chapter concentrates on the nonrenewable resources such as oil. Renewable, but depletable energy resources such as wood are not a focus of energy economics. They are a focus of courses in natural resource economics.

In the static framework of Chapter 3, a profit-maximizing producer was able to focus on the current time period without concern for future time periods. Models are simplifications of reality, and it is appropriate to use the static model when it provides sufficiently accurate predictions. Dynamic analysis involves additional complexity, as well as additional data in order to estimate total supply and forecast how demand and cost will change over time. Nevertheless, the study of some energy markets such as oil necessitates a dynamic model.

Competition in a dynamic framework

MC = 0

For simplicity, let us assume that the marginal cost of extracting oil is zero. We further assume that demand for oil is constant over time and the prices of substitutes and complements, income, and everything else affecting demand is constant. We also assume a competitive market.

With extraction costs of zero, the producer's profit maximization goal simplifies to maximizing total revenue over time. Also for simplicity, assume our producer has a fixed oil reserve that she must sell either today or one year from now. Revenue in each period is

$$TR_t = P_t Q_t \tag{4.2}$$

where TR is total revenue, P_t is price, and Q_t is quantity, and the subscript t denotes the time period.

In the simplified two-period framework, total revenue is

$$TR = TR_0 + TR_1 = P_0 Q_0 + P_1 Q_1 \tag{4.3}$$

We can generalize the formula for PV to consider funds received more than one year from now, as well as receiving funds in more than one future time period.[2] The general formula for maximizing total revenue is

$$PV = \sum_{t=0}^{T} (P_t \times Q_t) \frac{1}{(1+r)^t} \tag{4.4}$$

where Σ is the sum of the revenues received in each year, from the initial year 0 to the final year T, adjusted by the discount factor.[3]

The discount factor is raised to the year t because amounts received further in the future have a lower PV, as they forgo interest for a greater number of years. Also note that we do not discount sums received today ($t = 0$).[4] To keep the analysis as simple as possible, we restrict ourselves to the case where a producer chooses how much oil to sell today versus one year from now, along with our other starting simplifications of zero marginal cost and a competitive market. We will relax these assumptions later.

For the case of zero marginal cost in a two-period framework, the producer's goal is to maximize:

$$PV(TR) = P_0 Q_0 + \frac{P_1 Q_1}{(1+r)} \qquad (4.5)$$

When we are maximizing total revenue, it must also be true that the marginal revenue (MR_0), the addition to revenue from selling the last barrel today, should equal the discounted marginal revenue one year from now ($MR_1/(1 + r)$). Assuming competition, where P and MR are equal, price in period 0 (P_0) equals the discounted price in period 1 ($P_1/(1 + r)$).

To see that this statement must be true, suppose the last barrel sold today produces more revenue than the discounted value of the last barrel sold one year from now. Then, the producer should shift the last barrel sold one year from now to today. The producer should continue to shift barrels from next year to today until the marginal barrel produces the same PV in each period. This statement is an application of the *equimarginal principle*, which states that a rational decision-maker should allocate resources such that marginal profit is equal across periods.

Example 4.2

Market demand is

$$Q = 10 - 0.125P \qquad (4.6)$$

where Q is billions of barrels (BBL) of oil per year and P is price per barrel.

There is a total of 10 BBL of oil available to use in periods 0 and 1. Assume the interest rate is 10%. Marginal cost of extracting the oil is zero. What are the revenue-maximizing quantities of oil to extract in each period? What are the corresponding prices? Show that this solution maximizes social welfare.

Solution

We will lead up to a solution with a series of simpler problems.

Figure 4.1 depicts the demand for oil corresponding to equation (4.6). To begin, suppose the supply of oil is not limited. Then the problem is a standard static problem of the type found in Chapter 3. In competition, each producer will

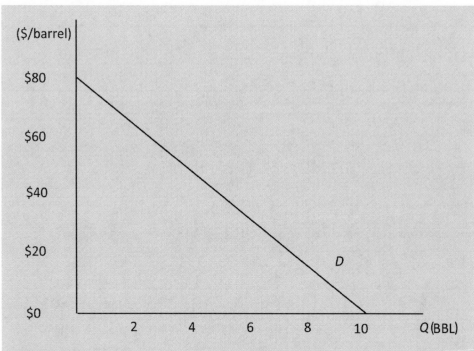

Figure 4.1 Demand for oil

supply output up to the point where price equals marginal cost. Since marginal cost is 0, price will be 0, and market supply will be $Q = 10$. This equilibrium outcome will maximize social welfare in the static setting. To verify, recall that

$$SW = CS + PS \tag{4.7}$$

$$CS = 0.5(\$80 - 0) \times (10 - 0) \text{ BBL} \tag{4.8}$$

$CS = \$400$ billion.

$PS = 0$ since $P = \$0$ and $MC = \$0$.

$SW = \$400$ billion.

To demonstrate that this solution maximizes social welfare, consider a marginal increase in price to $1:

$Q = 10 - (0.125 \times 1) = 9.875$ BBL

$CS = 0.5(\$80 - \$1)(9.875)$ BBL

$CS = \$390.0625$ billion

$$PS = (\$1 - \$0) \times 9.875 \text{ BBL}$$

$$PS = \$9.875 \text{ billion}$$

$$SW = \$390.0625 \text{ billion} + \$9.875 \text{ billion}$$

$$SW = \$399.9375 \text{ billion}$$

As price increases, CS decreases by slightly more than PS increases, so SW decreases. Raising price above $1 will reduce SW further. (For example, check that at P = $2, SW = $399.75 billion.) Therefore, to maximize social welfare, set price equal to marginal cost.[5]

Now suppose that society has only 10 BBL of oil in a two-period problem. If production today continues to be 10 BBL to maximize today's social welfare, there will be no oil one year from now and social welfare will remain at $400 billion.

In the two-period problem, selling all the oil today will no longer maximize the PV of SW. To demonstrate, suppose the producer sells 9 BBL today and 1 BBL a year from now.

Substituting Q = 9 BBL into the demand equation, consumers today will pay $8/barrel, while at Q = 1 BBL, next year's price will be $72/barrel.

$$CS_0 = 0.5(\$80 - \$8) \times (9)$$

$$CS_0 = \$324 \text{ billion}$$

$$PS_0 = (\$8 - \$0)(9)$$

$$PS_0 = \$72 \text{ billion}$$

$$CS_0 + PS_0 = \$396 \text{ billion}$$

$$CS_1 = 0.5(\$80 - \$72)(1)$$

$$PV(CS_1) = \frac{\$4 \text{ billion}}{(1.1)}$$

$$PV(CS_1) = \$3.364 \text{ billion}$$

$$PS_1 = (\$72 - \$0)(1)$$

$$PS_1 = \$72 \text{ billion}$$

$$PV(PS_1) = \frac{\$72 \text{ billion}}{(1.1)}$$

$$PV(PS_1) = \$65.454 \text{ billion}$$

$$SW_1 = CS_1 + PS_1$$

$$SW_1 = \$68.818 \text{ billion}$$

$$SW = SW_0 + SW_1$$

$$SW = \$464.818 \text{ billion}$$

Shifting one barrel of oil to the future increased SW by $64.82 billion. It is not surprising that SW increased, since the marginal barrel is worth $8 today and $72 in the future, or $65.45 in PV terms. According to the equimarginal principle, we should continue to shift oil to the future until its value today equals the PV one year from now.

Your intuition might be that we should sell 5 barrels today and 5 barrels one year from now. We find from equation (4.6) that

At $Q = 5$, $P = \$40$

SW_0 is

$$SW_0 = CS_0 + PS_0 = 0.5(\$80 - \$40) \times (5 - 0) + (\$40 - \$0) \times (5) = \$300.$$

$$CS_0 = \$0.5(\$80 - 40) \times (5 - 0) \text{ billion}$$

$$CS_0 = \$100 \text{ billion}$$

$$PS_0 = (\$40 - 0) \times (5 - 0) \text{ billion}$$

$$PS_0 = \$200 \text{ billion}$$

$$SW_0 = CS_0 + PS_0$$

$$SW_0 = \$100 \text{ billion} + \$200 \text{ billion}$$

$$SW_0 = \$300 \text{ billion}$$

Now consider period 1. Second period SW is $300 only if we do not discount revenues received in the future, that is, we implicitly assume an interest rate of 0%. Discounted social welfare one year from now is

$$SW_1 = \frac{\$300}{1.1}$$

$SW_1 = \$272.73$

$SW = SW_0 + SW_1$

$SW = \$572.73$

Recall that the interest rate is 10%. In PV terms, the fifth barrel sold today will add more to SW than the fifth barrel sold one year from now, so to maximize revenue, shift more production to the present. It makes sense to sell less than five barrels in the future, since the marginal barrel is more valuable in the present.

Using the equimarginal principle, we are now ready to find the revenue-maximizing solution. We want to find the quantities Q_0 and Q_1 that will satisfy:

$$P_0 = \frac{P_1}{1+r} \qquad (4.9)$$

Using the demand function from equation (4.5), inverse demand is

$$P = 80 - 8Q_0 \qquad (4.10)$$

Substituting inverse demand into equation (4.9),

$$80 - 8Q_0 = \frac{(80 - 8Q_1)}{1.1} \qquad (4.11)$$

Oil allocated over the periods must satisfy the constraint

$$Q_0 + Q_1 = 10 \qquad (4.12)$$

We now have two equations and two unknowns, so we can solve the system of equations for Q_0 and Q_1. We use the substitution approach,

$$Q_1 = 10 - Q_0 \qquad (4.13)$$

Substituting into equation (4.11):

$$80 - 8Q_0 = \frac{[(80 - 8(10 - Q_0)]}{1.1} \qquad (4.14)$$

Solving for Q_0, we obtain

$$Q_0 = 5.238$$

In turn:

$$Q_1 = 10 - 5.238$$

$$Q_1 = 4.762$$

Finally, we substitute our quantities into the inverse demand equation (4.10) to solve for P_0 and P_1:

$$P_0 = 80 - 8Q_0$$

$$P_0 = 80 - 8(5.238)$$

$$P_0 = \$38.10$$

$$P_1 = 80 - 8Q_1$$

$$P_1 = 80 - 8(4.762)$$

$$P_1 = \$41.90$$

As expected, the quantity sold in year 1 is slightly smaller than in year 0, and the price in year 1 is higher, to compensate for discounting revenue in year 1. Note that with no marginal costs, the price rises at exactly the rate of interest.[6] The intuition behind this result is that society should only save oil for the future if the return on oil is at least as great as the next best alternative. In this case, the marginal unsold barrel will reward producers with 10% more revenue than if that barrel were sold today.

This oil allocation will maximize PV (SW):

$$SW = SW_0 + SW_1$$

$$SW_0 = CS_0 + PS_0$$

$$CS_0 = 0.5(\$80 - \$38.10) \times (5.238)$$

$$CS_0 = \$109.74$$

$$PS_0 = (\$38.10 - 0)(5.238) = \$309.31.$$

$$PS_0 = \$199.57$$

$$SW_0 = \$309.31$$

$$SW_1 = CS_1 + PS_1$$

$$CS_1 = 0.5(\$80 - \$41.90) \times (4.762)$$

$$CS_1 = \$90.72$$

$$PS_1 = (\$41.90 - 0)(4.762)$$

$$PS_1 = \$199.53$$

$$SW_1 = \$290.24$$

$$PV(SW_1) = \frac{SW_1}{1+r}$$

$$PV(SW_1) = \frac{\$290.24}{1.1}$$

$$PV(SW_1) = \$263.86$$

$$PV(SW) = SW_0 + \frac{SW_1}{1+r}$$

$$PV(SW) = \$309.31 + \$263.86$$

$$PV(SW) = \$573.17$$

Total SW = $573.17 billion > $572.73 billion when output is allocated equally in each period. While the two numbers are close in this case, the result is just an artifact of the numbers in the example. The key takeaway is that allocating an equal amount of oil to each period will not maximize social efficiency.

Figure 4.2 shows the dynamic solution graphically.

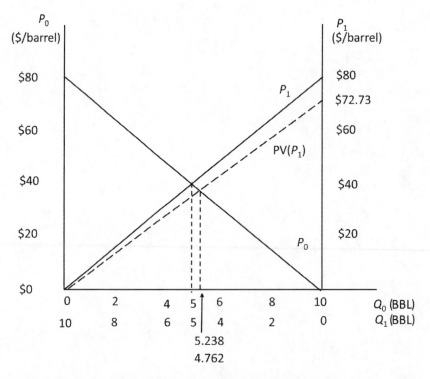

Figure 4.2 Allocating oil between two periods when MC = 0.

We graph demand for period 0 as in Figure 4.1, but we add a second demand curve for period 1, this time with quantity from right to left. At each price, $Q_0 + Q_1 = 10$, the total available supply. We have assumed demand is the same for both periods, so the curves are mirror images of each other. The demand in period 1 intersects the horizontal axis where $Q_0 = 0$ and $Q_1 = 10$. At this point, $P_0 = \$80$ and $P_1 = \$0$. Period 0 and period 1 demands intersect at $Q_0 = Q_1 = 5$.

We add a third demand curve that shows the discounted value of demand D_1. In this example the interest rate is 10%, so the vertical intercept of PV (D_1) is at PV $(P_1) =$ PV $(\$80) = \$72.73$. The horizontal intercept of PV (D_1) is at PV $(P_1) =$ PV $(\$0) = \$0$.

To find the revenue-maximizing point, look for the intersection of D_0 and PV (D_1) where $P_0 =$ PV (P_1). The prices are $P_0 = \$38.10$ and $P_1 = \$41.90$. The quantities at the intersection are $Q_0 = 5.238$ and $Q_1 = 4.762$. We showed earlier that this allocation also maximizes SW.

We have now completed Example 4.2. In this extended example, we have simplified the analysis by assuming that the marginal cost of production is zero and that the oil producer operates in a competitive market.[7] We proceed to incorporate alternative assumptions, beginning with marginal cost greater than 0.

MC > 0

We consider two cases, first where MC > 0 but is constant, and then when MC increases with increasing output.

Constant MC

The condition for profit maximization in a competitive market is to produce up to the point where price equals marginal cost. *Marginal net benefit* equals the difference between price (marginal benefit) and marginal cost, or in equation form:

$$MNB = P - MC \tag{4.15}$$

The equimarginal principle becomes

$$MNB_0 = MNB_1 \tag{4.16}$$

or for our two-period problem:

$$MNB_0 = \frac{MNB_1}{1+r} \tag{4.17}$$

Equivalently:

$$P_0 - MC_0 = \frac{(P_1 - MC_1)}{1+r} \tag{4.18}$$

To obtain social welfare, we sum up total net benefit (TNB), the area beneath the MNB curve. For our two-period problem:

$$PV(SW) = TNB_0 + \frac{TNB_1}{1+r}$$

Example 4.3

Marginal extraction costs are $20 per barrel. All other assumptions are unchanged from Example 4.2. Find the social welfare maximizing prices and quantities.

Solution

Using the same method as before, we solve for Q_0, Q_1, P_0 and P_1.

$$80 - 8Q_0 - 20 = \frac{(80 - 8Q_1 - 20)}{1.1}$$

$$60 - 8Q_0 = \frac{(60 - 8Q_1)}{1.1}$$

Substituting, $Q_1 = 10 - Q_0$,

$Q_0 = 5.12$ BBL, $Q_1 = 4.88$ BBL (BBL = billion barrels of oil)

$P_0 = \$39.04$, $P_1 = \$40.96$

$MNB_0 = 19.04$, $MNB_1 = 20.96$

$PV (SW) = TNB_0 + TNB_1$

$TNB_0 + TNB_1 = 0.5 \ \$(60 - 19.04) \times (5.12 \ BBL)$

$$+ \frac{0.5 \ \$(60 - 20.96) \times (4.88 \ BBL)}{1.1}$$

$$PV(SW) = \$104.86b + \frac{\$95.26b}{1.1}$$

$PV(SW) = \$104.86b + \$86.60b$

$PV(SW) = \$191.46b$, b = billion

Figure 4.3 shows the graphical solution.

We use MNB instead of D. We first plot MNB_0 which starts at $60 and falls to $0 at $Q_0 = 7.5$. We then graph MNB_1 from $Q_1 = 2.5$ BBL, corresponding to $Q_0 = 7.5$ BBL, and $Q_1 = 7.5$ BBL, corresponding to $Q_0 = 2.5$ BBL. By the equimarginal principle, the efficient point is now at the intersection of MNB_0 and PV (MNB_1).

Note that when MC > 0, $P - MC$ increases at the rate of interest. The producer will balance today's oil extraction with future extraction until the net present value of the profit contribution—$P - MC$—is the same in both periods. We will discuss this result in more detail shortly when we come to Hotelling's rule.

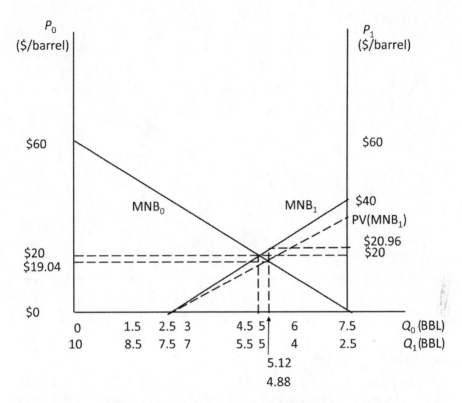

Figure 4.3 Allocating oil between two periods when MC > 0.

Increasing MC

A more realistic assumption is that the MC increases as the producer extracts additional oil. That is, the MC of extracting the marginal barrel is the highest.

Example 4.4

Let MC = 2Q, so that the first barrel costs $2 to extract, the second barrel costs $4, and so on. Other assumptions are the same as example 4.3. Find Q_0, Q_1, P_0 and P_1.

Solution

$$80 - 8Q_0 - 2Q_0 = \frac{(80 - 8Q_1 - 2Q_1)}{1.1}$$

Substituting $Q_1 = 10 - Q_0$,

$$80 - 10Q_0 - \frac{\{80 - [10 \times (10 - Q_0)]\}}{1.1}$$

Simplifying,

$$80 - 10Q_0 = \frac{(-20 + 10Q_0)}{1.1}$$

Multiplying both sides by 1.1,

$$88 - 11Q_0 = -20 + 10Q_0$$

Solving:

$$Q_0 = 5.14 \text{ BBL}, \ Q_1 = 4.86 \text{ BBL}, \ P_0 = \$38.88, \ P_1 = \$41.12$$

To check this solution, verify that $P_0 - MC_0 = \frac{(P_1 - MC_1)}{(1.1)}$. In both cases, the value is \$28.60.

Hotelling's rule

There is one sharp difference between the efficient outcome in the dynamic model as compared to the static model. Ordinarily, the hallmark of efficiency is that price equals MC, as is the outcome in a competitive industry. In the dynamic model, price exceeds MC, even in a competitive industry. Recall that even when MC was 0, price was greater than 0. How can this result be efficient? The resolution of this seeming paradox is that the difference between price and MC that arises with nonrenewable resources reflects the opportunity cost of selling the resource today instead of in the future. The difference between price and MC for nonrenewable resources is marginal net benefit, also known as *Hotelling rent*,[8] and its role in achieving dynamic efficiency is Hotelling's rule.

Hotelling's rule: The dynamically efficient allocation occurs when the PV of MNB for the last unit consumed is equal across time periods.

We summarize the cases of MC = 0 and MC > 0 in light of Hotelling's rule.

PRICE INCREASES AT RATE OF INTEREST WHEN MC = 0

In the simple case where the industry was competitive and MC was zero, price was greater than zero and rose at the rate of interest. In a static model, $P > MC$ indicates market power, but in a dynamic model, it need not. Even with competition, price exceeds MC because of the opportunity cost of selling now rather than later.

MNB INCREASES AT RATE OF INTEREST

With equal marginal costs in each period, the difference between production today and production one year from now is smaller than for MC = 0. In this case, MNB rises by the interest rate:

$$P_0 - MC_0 = PV(P_1 - MC_1).$$

Equivalently, Hotelling's rule implies that MNB, or Hotelling rent, grows at the rate of interest:

$$(P_0 - MC_0)(1 + r) = (P_1 - MC_1).$$

The opportunity cost of selling now rather than later—the PV of the difference between P and MC—is *marginal user cost*, or simply user cost.

Monopoly

It is sometimes said that a monopolist is the conservationist's best friend. While monopoly is ordinarily inefficient because it produces too little as compared to the competitive output, conservationists favor using less today and leaving more for the future. However, dynamic analysis and Hotelling's rule show that even competitive producers have a built-in incentive to conserve because they can earn a higher price as future supplies diminish. Naturally, they will have to discount the higher price to reflect that by receiving the price in a future period, they are forgoing the opportunity to invest current profits. Unless there is inefficiency due to a market failure associated with consumption, the competitive market results in the efficient amount of conservation.[9] From an economic efficiency perspective, monopolists over-conserve.

Example 4.5

Suppose a monopoly controls all 10 billion barrels of oil. Assume marginal extraction cost = 0. The firm faces (inverse) demand: $P = 80 - 8Q$. The discount rate is 10%, and the firm must choose how much oil to extract today and one year from now.

   Determine how much the monopolist will sell in each period. Compare the outcome to that of a competitive industry, and demonstrate that the monopoly allocation is inefficient.

Solution

To find quantities in each period, we apply the equimarginal principle. The monopolist chooses output where MR = MC. In this case, since MC = 0, the monopolist sets $MR_0 = PV(MR_1)$. As stated in Chapter 3, when (inverse) demand is linear, the equation for MR has the same intercept but twice the slope.[10]

The equation for MR is

$$MR = 80 - 16Q.$$

Applying the equimarginal principle that $MR_0 = PV\ (MR_1)$,

$$80 - 16Q_0 = \frac{80 - 16Q_1}{1.1}$$

Using $Q_0 + Q_1 = 10$,

$$88 - 17.6Q_0 = 80 - 16(10 - Q_0)$$

$$168 = 33.6Q_0$$

$$Q_0 = 5\ \text{BBL}$$

$$P_0 = 80 - 8(5)$$

$$P_0 = \$40$$

$$Q_1 = 10 - 5$$

$$Q_1 = 5\ \text{BBL}$$

$$P_1 = 80 - 8(5)$$

$$P_1 = \$40$$

The relevant calculations for CS, PS, and SW will follow in Table 4.1. Note that the equal quantities in the two periods are an artifact of the numbers in the example. In general, the quantities in the two periods need not be equal.

The monopolist produces less today than the corresponding competitive output of 5.24, thus over-conserving from an efficiency standpoint.[11] Also note that Hotelling's rule does not hold for the monopolist. Price rises by less than the rate of interest. In this particular case, price does not rise at all. The return on oil is less than the resources could be earning in another alternative. Dynamic efficiency calls for selling more today and saving less for the future.

Table 4.1 summarizes the results of the two-period model for monopoly and competition when $MC = 0$ and $r = 10\%$.

As we would expect, the PV of consumer surplus is higher for competition, while the PV of producer surplus is higher for monopoly. Competition maximizes the PV of social welfare.

Table 4.1 A comparison of results for monopoly and competition for the two-period dynamic model with MC = 0 and *r* = 10%

Case	Q_0 (BBL)	Q_1 (BBL)	P_0 ($)	P_1 ($)	PV(CS) ($b)	PV(PS) ($b)	PV (SW) ($b)
Monopoly	*5.000*	5.000	*40.00*	40.00	190.91	*381.82*	572.73
Competition	5.238	4.762	38.10	41.90	*192.21*	380.96	*573.17*

Notes: Figures in *italic* highlight expected findings: Monopoly has a higher price and a lower quantity in period 1, and higher producer surplus. Competition has higher consumer surplus and higher social welfare.

Other factors influencing dynamic efficiency

Change in demand

So far, demand has been constant over time. Global demand for oil may increase over time as countries increase their demand, which has been the case for developing countries in recent years.[12] We now allow demand to increase in period 1, as compared to period 0. We can increase demand by increasing the price intercept, decreasing the slope of the inverse demand curve, or both.

In Example 4.6, we begin with a case where the demand growth rate, *g*, is the same as the discount rate, *r*.

Example 4.6

Demand in period 1 increases by 10% as compared to period 0. Other assumptions are as in Example 4.2. Find prices and quantities that maximize social welfare.

Solution

Period 0: $P_0 = 80 - 8Q_0$

Period 1: $P_1 = 1.1\,(80 - 8Q_0)$

$P_1 = 88 - 8.8Q_0$

The competitive equilibrium occurs where

$P_0 = PV(P_1)$

$$80 - 8Q_0 = \frac{(88 - 8.8Q_1)}{1.1}$$

$$80 - 8Q_0 = 80 - 8Q_1$$

$$Q_0 = Q_1$$

$$Q_0 + Q_1 = 10$$

$$Q_0 = 5 \text{ BBL}$$

$$Q_1 = 5 \text{ BBL}$$

$$P_0 = \$40$$

$$P_1 = \$44$$

$$PV \text{ (SW)} = \$600^{13}$$

The general case is

$$a - bQ_0 = (a - bQ_1)\frac{(1 + g)}{(1 + r)}$$

When $g = r$, the ratio of $(1 + g)$ to $(1 + r)$ is 1, and the competitive outcome is to produce an equal amount in each period.[14] Contrast this outcome to the case where demand stayed constant. Efficiency called for producing more in the current period than one year from now.

When the growth rate in demand exceeds the discount rate ($g > r$), the efficient outcome in a competitive industry will result in a larger amount of oil available for the future period than the current period. If the growth rate in demand is lower than the corresponding rate of interest ($g < r$), we will produce more today than in the future period. However, today's amount will not be as large as if demand were constant ($g = 0$).

Change in total reserves

As reserves grow, the constraint on the firm's total production becomes less binding. The solution moves in the direction of the static case, where $P = MC$ in each period. The marginal user cost (MUC) decreases as there is a decrease in the opportunity cost of selling today, rather than in the future.

Example 4.7

Total reserves increase from 10 to 12 units. Other assumptions are the same as in Example 4.2. Find prices and quantities for the two periods that maximize SW.

$$Q_0 + Q_1 = 12 \tag{4.19}$$

$$80 - 8Q_0 = \frac{80 - 8Q_1}{1.1}$$

$$80 - 8Q_0 = \frac{80 - 8(12 - Q_0)}{1.1}$$

$$(80 - 8Q_0) \times (1.1) = 80 - 8(12 - Q_0)$$

$$88 - 8.8Q_0 = 80 - 96 + 8Q_0$$

$$104 = 16.8 \, Q_0$$

$$Q_0 = 6.19 \, \text{BBL}$$

$$P_0 = \$30.48$$

$$Q_1 = 5.81 \, \text{BBL}$$

$$P_1 = \$33.52$$

Outputs in each period are higher and prices lower with the increase in reserves compared to the earlier example when total reserves totaled 10 units. Note that price increased by 10% from period 0 to period 1, as we would expect when MC = 0.

Change in technology

A technological advance makes it possible to extract reserves at a lower cost.

Example 4.8

MC = Q. All other assumptions are the same as in Example 4.4. Find the welfare-maximizing prices and quantities for the two periods.

Solution

$$P_0 - MC_0 = PV(P_1 - MC_1)$$

$$80 - 8Q_0 - Q_0 = \frac{80 - 8Q_1 - Q_1}{1.1}$$

$$80 - 9Q_0 = \frac{80 - 9Q_1}{1.1}$$

Substituting $Q_0 = 10 - Q_1$,

$$88 - 9.9Q_0 = -10 + 9Q_0$$

$$98 = -10 + 18.9Q_0$$

$$Q_0 = 5.185 \text{ BBL}$$

$$P_0 = \$38.52$$

$$Q_1 = 4.815 \text{ BBL}$$

$$P_1 = \$41.48$$

A technological advance that reduces MC = 2Q to MC = Q results in an increase in today's production, leaving less for the future.

Change in backstop technology

A *backstop technology* is an alternative that is available at a price above the price of the current technology. Biofuels are a backstop technology for oil. As oil increases in price, cars can run on ethanol, switchgrass, and algae.

Figures 4.4a and b show the effect of a backstop technology on supply.

In period 1, equilibrium is at price P_1 and quantity Q_1. If demand increases to D_2 in period 2, equilibrium price increases to P_2 and equilibrium quantity increases to Q_2. If a backstop is available at price $P_B < P_2$, equilibrium is at P_B and equilibrium quantity is $Q_B > Q_2$. In Figure 4.4, the supply of the backstop is perfectly elastic, so there is no limit on the backstop energy source at that price. Solar cars could fit this assumption, although they might not be economical unless the oil price increases substantially. There may be a series of backstops available as the price of oil rises, starting with

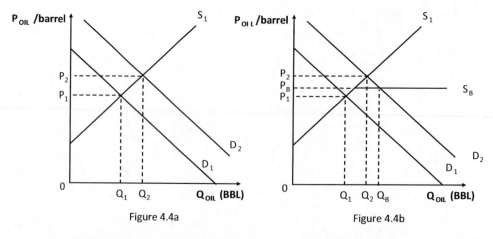

Figure 4.4a   Figure 4.4b

Figure 4.4 Effect of backstop technology on dynamic equilibrium.

ethanol, then a gas–electric hybrid, followed by an all-electric vehicle, and finally, a hydrogen vehicle.

Returning to the numbers in our extended example, suppose biofuels were available in infinite supply at a price of $40 per unit of oil-equivalent. Then, oil producers could not expect to receive more than $40 in the future period, or in PV terms, $\frac{\$40}{1.1} = \$36.36$. As compared to when there was no backstop and future price was $41.90, with a PV of $38.10, producers will now have a reason to shift more of their production to the present.

Using the equimarginal principle,

$$P_0 = \frac{P_1}{1+r}$$

$$\frac{P_1}{1.1} = \$36.36$$

$$P_0 = \$36.36$$

$$Q_0 = 5.455 \text{ BBL}$$

$$Q_1 = 4.545 \text{ BBL}$$

Since demand at next year's price of $40 is 5.455 and next year's oil production is only 4.545, biofuel production will equal 0.91 oil-equivalent units.

Change in interest rate

The higher the interest rate used to discount the future, the lower the PV of future dollars. Higher discount rates favor producing more of the nonrenewable resource today and leaving less for the future. The Hotelling rule maintains that the competitive market will allocate resources efficiently over time, setting aside the market failures (e.g., externalities and public goods) discussed in earlier chapters. However, as introduced earlier in this chapter, the outcome is only efficient if the interest rate that is used for discounting is the socially efficient interest rate.

Social vs. private discount rate

The discount rate firms use reflects their cost of capital. The private rate consumers use to decide whether to spend or save reflects their rate of time preference. The social rate of discount reflects society's willingness to consume today rather than in the future. The key point to note here is that if the private rate exceeds the social rate, as many suspect, we will discount the future too heavily, extracting and using more of our nonrenewable resources today, leaving less than the socially efficient amount for the future.

There is an argument that the social rate of discount should be no more than 3%, reflecting 3% growth in real GDP. The reasoning is that over a long period of time, an investment is not likely to exceed this rate.[15] If businesses can borrow at 5% at a time where prices are rising at a 2% annual rate, then the real interest rate is 3%, in line with the social rate of discount.[16] Historically, the real (inflation-adjusted) cost of borrowed funds may be close to 3%, in which case there is no difference between the real cost of borrowing and the social rate of discount.

To revisit the extended example, compare the amount of oil that will be extracted today if, using our original set of numbers, businesses make their decision using a 10% cost of borrowing vs. a 5% rate.

Using a 5% rate of interest and recalling that $Q_0 + Q_1 = 10$:

$$80 - 8Q_0 = \frac{80 - 8(10 - Q_0)}{1.05}$$

$$Q_0 = 5.122 \text{ BBL}$$

$$P_0 = \$39.02$$

$$Q_1 = 4.88 \text{ BBL}$$

$$P_1 = \$40.96$$

Table 4.2 summarizes the effect of a change in the interest rate for the competitive case.

At a lower interest rate, Q_0 is lower and Q_1 is higher. There is less reason to sell today, as the money you invest will only earn 5%.

Implications for sustainability

There is no guarantee that firms will leave at least as much for tomorrow as they produce today, and it is likely they will leave less. There are numerous conditions under which firms with a finite nonrenewable resource supply more now than in the future. There are cases where the firm may reserve more for the future, such as when they expect the rate of growth in demand to be greater than the discount rate.

If we define sustainability as leaving at least as much of a specific resource for future generations as is available to the present generation, unfettered markets are not likely to lead to strong sustainability. It is easier to achieve weak sustainability. Consider the case where a backstop technology such as biofuel is available. Using more oil today may leave less oil in the future. However, it may hasten the day when biofuel becomes cost-competitive with oil, so that the future will have at least as much oil-equivalent energy as we do today.

Strong sustainability is particularly relevant when there are no good substitutes for a resource, such as when contemplating clear-cutting the Amazon rainforest in order to extract oil. We may be able to replace oil with other energy resources or even by setting

Table 4.2 Effect of a change in the discount rate on dynamic efficiency price and quantity for MC = 0

r	P_0 ($)	P_1 ($)	Q_0 (BBL)	Q_1 (BBL)
0.05	39.02	40.96	5.122	4.88
0.10	38.10	41.90	5.238	4.762

Table 4.3 Discounting and the PV of $50 million to be received 20 years from now

Future value	Interest rate (%)	PV
$50,000,000	0	$50,000,000
$50,000,000	5	$18,844,474
$50,000,000	10	$7,432,181

aside monetary resources, but the rainforest provides resources for which there is no good substitute. Rainforests provide unique ecological services, as well as plants and animals that are not found elsewhere, in addition to storing carbon emissions.

While market efficiency may also achieve sustainability, the more common outcome is that we will leave less of a specific resource for the future than we consume today. This outcome is a consequence of discounting.

Consider the policy first presented in Example 4.1 where we considered spending $10 million today to redesign automobile internal combustion engines to prevent $50 million in climate-related losses 20 years from now. How much should we spend today to prevent the future loss? Using the PV approach and referring to Table 4.3, the maximum we would spend today to prevent the loss 20 years from now is

$$PV = \frac{\$50 \text{ million}}{(1+r)^{20}}.$$

At a 10% rate of interest, we would only be willing to spend $7.4 million today to prevent $50 million in damage 20 years from now. Similarly, a producer who borrows money at 10% would be indifferent between receiving $7.4 million today from the sale of oil and $50 million from selling oil 20 years from now. Therefore our producer favors selling oil today than 20 years from now, when $1 has a PV of less than $0.15. By the measure of strong sustainability, the future is likely to have less oil than we have today, and more carbon.[17] Our willingness to spend today to mitigate future damage is considerably larger with a lower discount rate. We are willing to spend almost $19 million to prevent the $50 million loss at a 5% interest rate. Only at an interest rate of 0% do we view today's dollar and a future dollar as equivalent. Advocates of strong sustainability argue that we should not discount the future, in essence requiring that we use a 0% rate of interest.

Economists argue that strong sustainability is too severe a constraint when resources have substitutes. Biofuels can substitute for oil in transportation, as can more fuel-efficient cars. Furthermore, the future may be just as well off with less fuel, but more financial resources to maximize social welfare. For a number of years, Norway has funded its pension system for seniors using oil revenues. The future may be just as well off with cash as with oil if the present generation sells oil today and invests the revenues in a pension system.[18] Future generations can use the savings to purchase oil, invest in biofuels, or for a retirement system. Twenty years from now, the money may be better spent on hyperloops, a proposal to use a pneumatic tube to transport people at 600 miles per hour, rather than oil.

More fundamentally, future generations have been better off than the previous generation at least since the Industrial Revolution. So there is an argument that the future will have more resources that we have today without our setting aside resources, as long as substitutes are available.

Furthermore, by slowing our current use of resources, we may reduce our rate of growth. Just as the choice of discount rate has an effect on PV, the rate of growth has an effect on future value. A small change in the growth rate has a large impact on future wealth. The Rule of 72 provides an approximation to calculate the time it will take for wealth to double. At a growth rate of 3%, income will double in 72/3 = 24 years. If the growth rate slows to 2%, that same doubling will take 36 years. So if we set aside $50 million today to prevent $50 million in climate-change related flooding costs 20 years from now, and in doing so, reduce the growth rate from 3 to 2%, the next generation will face repairing the flood damage with a substantially smaller economy than if our growth rate had been 3%.

Managing energy price volatility

So far, we have assumed that market participants know exactly what market conditions will be in the future. Most decision-makers are *risk-averse*, preferring less risk to more, c.p. One way to reduce the risk of energy price fluctuations is through *financial derivatives*, which are financial instruments that can reduce buyer or seller risk of changes in output prices (oil produced by drillers) or input price (oil purchased by refineries to produce gasoline). Using derivatives gives businesses more certainty for their business plans. Purchasers of derivatives pay a fee to lock in today's price, rather than taking a chance on an uncertain future price.

Southwest Airlines uses derivatives to reduce the risk of wide swings in the price of jet fuel. Jet fuel prices are a major component of airline costs, and an unanticipated increase in jet fuel prices can easily turn a profit into a loss. In early 2008, Southwest used derivatives to lock in supplies of jet fuel at the January 2008 price of approximately $100/barrel.[19] When fuel prices rose to a record of $147/barrel by July 2008, Southwest was protected from the record high prices.

Southwest uses derivatives primarily to *hedge*—reduce price uncertainty—not to earn a profit from the contracts. If the price of fuel collapses, as it did in the second half of 2008, Southwest could end up paying more for fuel than if it paid the market price.[20]

Economists generally endorse financial derivatives as facilitating efficient markets. The public view is often at odds. Many see *speculators*—individuals who buy and sell derivatives to earn a profit—as responsible for price spikes such as the soaring oil prices in July 2008. Speculators typically buy derivatives today with the hopes that they can profit from correctly predicting whether future price will be higher or lower. By jumping into the market today, the public sees them driving up today's demand, leading to higher prices. Economists actually see speculators as playing a valuable role in reducing price fluctuations. They profit if they buy when prices are low and sell when prices are high. So while they increase today's low price, they reduce the future high price.[21] While not their intention, they reduce price volatility and the associated risk of the commodity. We introduce this ongoing controversy here, providing more details in Chapter 5 on the oil market, including financial instruments.[22]

Summary

Dynamic efficiency is an appropriate framework for analyzing the optimal use of finite nonrenewable resources such as oil, where production today reduces the availability of the resource in the future. As dynamic efficiency is a more complex framework than static efficiency, its use depends upon how constrained the total supply is; while extracting oil at the current rate may exhaust supplies within 30 years, coal supplies would last two centuries at present rates of mining and so we would gain little from applying a dynamic framework.

Given the added complexity of a dynamic framework, it is worthwhile to simplify where possible. A useful starting point is to assume that marginal extraction cost is zero and that the industry is competitive. We can then consider more complex assumptions such as positive and increasing MC, noncompetitive markets, and backstop fuels that become viable if the current fuel price increases over time. There are some key findings in dynamic markets that differ from static analysis. In dynamic competitive markets, price exceeds marginal cost. The difference between price and MC is Hotelling rent, also known as marginal user cost, reflecting the opportunity cost of not owning the resource in the future if we extract and sell it today. Marginal user cost is the PV of NMB.

The biggest debate about finite, nonrenewable fuels such as oil is whether the market allocates them efficiently. Setting aside other potential sources of market failure, such as externalities or lack of competition, economists generally favor allowing the market to allocate such fuels. This perspective is in marked contrast to physical scientists, who want government to lessen our use today, and leave more of the resource for the future.

While a dynamic, competitive market leads to built-in conservation, the result may not satisfy a sustainability criterion. Sustainability requires that we leave as much of the resource for the future as we consume today, while dynamic efficiency generally leaves less of the resource for future generations than we consume today. The outcome is unlikely to satisfy strong sustainability. It can, however, satisfy weak sustainability if we invest today's receipts so future generations have at least as many resources as we consume today, although the form of the resources may differ. If there are no good substitutes for the resource, then there is a case for strong sustainability.

Over time, firms face price uncertainty. Market participants are typically risk-averse, and so are willing to pay to reduce price volatility. In energy markets, businesses can hedge against the possibility of higher prices in the future by purchasing financial derivatives. The purpose is to lock in a price today, rather than take a chance on the uncertain future price. The goal of hedging is to reduce price volatility, not to earn a profit.

Speculators, on the other hand, engage in such markets with the intent to earn a profit. The increased demand for financial instruments from speculators will drive up today's price of oil, leading to the concern that speculators contribute to high oil prices. However, the primary effect of speculators in the market is to smooth price fluctuations, a desirable outcome. If speculators are correct and prices rise, they will sell oil in the future for a profit. The increased supply will help to mitigate the price rise. On balance, speculators reduce price volatility.

Notes

1   We still need dynamic analysis to decide whether to invest in wind or solar in the first place, since the technology is a long-lived investment. We introduce levelized cost beginning in Chapter 6 on natural gas to show how to compare the cost of electricity generation using different fuels.

2   Courses in finance adapt the formula for other nuances, such as funds received on a quarterly basis. Such modifications do not change the fundamental concept of PV.

3   The proof of this extension of the basic PV formula is available in any finance textbook.

4   Confirming the intuition that we should not discount today's revenue or costs, the discount factor in year 0 is $(1 + r)^0$ which equals 1.

5   For simplicity, fixed cost also equals 0. Ordinarily, positive fixed cost will not affect the welfare-maximizing quantity. The exception is that if fixed cost exceeds the sum of CS + PS, then society is better off if the firm produces $Q = 0$. In this example, if fixed cost exceeds \$400, the product is not worth producing.

6   We have rounded our prices to the nearest cent. If we used the exact prices, price would rise at exactly the rate of interest.

7   Sustainability requires that we leave the future at least as much as we have today, showing that efficiency and sustainability are not typically the same. The dynamically efficient solution would not meet the sustainability criterion. Strictly speaking, we are using the definition of strong sustainability, where we must leave at least as much oil for the future as we have today.

8   Hotelling rent is a special case of Ricardian rent, which refers to the premium earned by a factor in inelastic supply.

9   We can get too little conservation if producers use "too high" a discount rate, which would favor present production over future production. We will touch upon the determination of interest rates later in the chapter.

10   The proof using calculus was in Chapter 3, Appendix 3B.

11   In fact, for this particular example, the static and dynamic solutions are the same, although that result will not hold in general. For an exercise, solve for the monopolist's static solution (no constraint on total quantity) and you will obtain $Q = 5$, whereas in competition, we got $Q = 10$. We see why monopoly is the conservationist's friend.

12   Some analysts predict global demand could decrease over time as we substitute different transportation fuels and different modes of transportation. For these analysts, peak oil is now more likely to mean peak demand than peak supply.

13   For practice, the reader should be able to calculate CS_0 and PS_0, PV (CS_1) and PV (PS_1) to obtain SW.

14   This solution meets the criterion for sustainability that we leave as much for future periods as we consume today. In this case, efficiency and sustainability coincide.

15   Historically, U.S. real GDP averaged 3% growth. In recent years, it has been 2% or less.

16   There remain additional issues, such as whether we should use the prime rate—the rate at which banks lend to their best corporate customers—or the rate consumers pay, which is likely to be higher to adjust for a higher risk of default. Then there is the issue of whether we should use the before- or after-tax rate of interest. Public finance courses cover these issues in detail.

17   The future will also be likely to have more carbon because carbon emissions accumulate in the atmosphere, and have a long half-life before they dissipate. So simply reducing emissions as compared to the current level will not necessarily reduce cumulative CO_2. It will take a very large emissions reduction to actually begin to reduce cumulative CO_2 emissions.

18   Norway is having difficulty maintaining its funds with the drop in oil prices. It may be that Texas has a more sustainable approach, investing oil revenues in their higher education system. In the debate over whether or not the United States should drill for oil in the Alaskan National Wildlife Refuge, Kotchen (2010) suggests that we give environmentalists a choice between no development (their initial position) and receiving tax revenues from oil sales that could be used for alternative environmental purposes, such as preserving other wilderness areas or developing alternative fuels.

19   They actually used oil price derivatives as a proxy for jet fuel prices. There are no financial instruments for jet fuel, but there is a high correlation between the two prices.

20   Some airlines followed Southwest's lead. They may have regretted locking in the June 2014 price when oil prices fell rapidly in the second half of 2008.

21   Speculators can also make money by betting on lower prices in the future. In this case, speculators sell today, reducing today's high price. They buy in the future, increasing tomorrow's low price, and in so doing, dampen price fluctuations.

22   Readers interested in the details of energy derivatives can refer to Dahl (2004), Chapter 15. Hull (2000) is a good source for readers interested in financial derivatives in general.

References

Abt, R., Abt, K., Cubbage, F. & Henderson, J. (2010). Effect of policy-based bioenergy demand on southern timber markets: A case study of North Carolina. *Biomass and Bioenergy, 34,* 1679–1686.

Dahl, C. (2004). *International energy markets: Understanding pricing, policies, and profits.* Tulsa, OK: PennWell Corporation.

Downey, J. (2010, October 18). N.C. will let Duke Energy count trees as a renewable biomass fuel. *Charlotte Business Journal.* Retrieved September 10, 2016 from http://www.bizjournals.com/charlotte/stories/2010/10/18/newscolumn4.html

Hotelling, H. (1931). The economics of exhaustible resources. *Journal of Political Economics, 39*(2), 137–175.

Hull, J. (2000). *Options, futures, and other derivative securities.* Upper Saddle River, N.J.: Prentice Hall International, Inc.

Kotchen, M. (2010). Oil and the Arctic National Wildlife Refuge (p. 56), in I. Parry and F. Day (Eds) *Issues of the day: 100 commentaries on climate, energy, the environment, transportation, and public health policy.* Washington, DC: Resources for the Future.

Part II

Conventional energy sources

Chapter 5

Oil

There at the creation of energy economics

"Formula for success—rise early, work hard, strike oil."

J. Paul Getty

"Formula for success—rise early, work hard, study energy economics."

The author of this text

Introduction

We study energy economics today largely because of the oil crises of the 1970s. The events demonstrated the central role of oil in the global economy and the unique characteristics of oil markets. In this introductory section, we identify these characteristics in order to set the stage for understanding the economics of oil.

First, oil is a global market. In the United States, oil is the largest source of energy, providing 36% of overall energy consumption according to recent U.S. Energy Information Administration statistics, of which 70% is for transportation. Oil is largely *fungible*, a commodity that is interchangeable. If the United States reduces its imports from OPEC, those countries will ship the oil to another country. If global demand for oil decreases, oil price will certainly decrease, but a decision to use less of one country's oil and replace it with another source, including a domestic supply, will have no effect on the global price. Exports and imports are necessary to align the two sides of the market. The United States imported 60% of its oil as recently as 2005. With the fracking revolution, that percentage is now closer to 25%. The United States is now allowing its producers to export oil for the first time since the 1970s.

Second, while oil is largely fungible, different grades of oil have different prices, depending on how easily they can be refined into premium products such as gasoline. The United States prefers to refine light sweet crude into gasoline. *Sweet crude* contains small amounts of impurities such as sulfur, in contrast to *sour crude* that contains more impurities. *Light crude* refers to a lighter-weight oil that contains a higher proportion of the light molecules used to make premium fuels such as gasoline. *Heavy crude* contains more heavy molecules, better for diesel or residual fuels that sell at a discount.

Third, it is necessary to deploy large amounts of resources to find and extract oil. In the wake of the oil price shocks, the United States built the Alaskan pipeline that allowed major oil companies to extract and transport the newly accessible oil. In the Gulf of Mexico, only large companies can afford deep-water oil exploration. Great Britain and Norway are among the countries that undertake drilling in the stormy conditions of the North Sea. Surprisingly, smaller companies led the way in the fracking revolution, more reminiscent of the industry's small-scale beginnings.

Fourth, given the pervasiveness of oil in production—transportation, oil used for heating and electricity, and the industrial use of petroleum feedstocks to make chemicals, plastics, and synthetic materials found in nearly all products—the oil market has a big impact on the macroeconomy. It has either caused or contributed to all U.S. recessions since 1973.

Fifth, a key aspect of the industry is infrastructure. Pipelines are the primary form of transportation for crude oil as well as gasoline, the major refined product. Pipelines frequently face environmental opposition due to fears that they will disrupt the land-scape, leak oil, or even pass through lands viewed as sacred by indigenous people. The alternatives are by ship, train, or truck, which present risks of their own. In 1989, the *Exxon Valdez* ran aground in Alaska's Prince William Sound, resulting in the largest oil spill in U.S. waters up to that time. In a later section, we will consider the *supply chain*, which describes each stage of production from initial exploration to delivery to the final customer.

The next section of this chapter provides a brief economic history of the oil industry. We then examine the uses of oil, with transportation the primary focus. We proceed next to oil production, including the supply chain. We then examine the market structure of oil, followed by its regulation. The penultimate section is on the use of financial instruments specific to oil and its price risks. We close with a summary.

A brief economic history

The modern history of oil began in 1859, in Titusville, Pennsylvania, motivated by a search for a cheaper alternative to whale oil, with whales being hunted towards extinction. A few years earlier, a Pennsylvania lawyer by the name of George Bissell hired "Colonel" Edwin Drake to drill for oil.[1] Drilling was a novel approach for finding oil. Drake struck oil, and a boom followed. He developed innovations to keep the hole from collapsing and to prevent groundwater from seeping into the well, innovations that led the way to the modern oil industry. While the original use was for kerosene lighting, there would be discovery of other by-products, particularly gasoline.

Box 5.1 Rule of capture

Property rights play a key role in the development of natural resources. In the 1800s, the legal regime for oil in the United States was the rule of capture. The owner of the resource is the first person to "capture" it. As oil flows, there is an incentive to capture not only the oil underneath your land, but also oil that flows to your land from land you do not own. Thus, all drillers have the incentive to drill as quickly as possible.

Is this property rights regime efficient? Recall Hotelling's rule. The equimarginal rule calls for balancing the value of extracting today with present value in the future. A driller who follows Hotelling's rule will likely find that no oil is left in the ground in the future. So the rule of capture leads to extracting the oil faster than the efficient rate.

In addition, drilling today has an external effect on extraction. As the oil is depleted, there is less pressure on the remaining oil, which makes it more expensive to extract. So excessive extraction today not only leaves too little for the future, but also reduces total extraction.

Unitization is potentially more efficient than the rule of capture. Owners may choose to pool interests. Then the majority decide when an individual owner can extract oil. Each owner gets a share of the rewards according to an initial contract. Majority rules are not necessarily efficient, but they may well be an improvement over first possession.

The next step in the evolution of the oil industry took place in Spindletop, Texas, in 1901. Drillers were originally seeking water when they hit oil, a "gusher" at a depth of over 1,100 feet. The amount of oil dwarfed anything that had come before, and ushered in the modern oil industry. The potential Texas sites lay far below the surface, and would require new techniques, such as injecting mud rather than water into the hole, to succeed.

Other parts of the world also discovered oil. Baku, Russia, on the shores of the Caspian Sea, now in modern-day Azerbaijan, could make a claim for the first oil well, with a hand-drilled well in 1848. By the 1870s, the Nobels introduced mechanical drilling and the Rothschilds financed a transcontinental railway. In 1909, a predecessor of today's BP found oil in Persia, today's Iran. The find was the start of the Middle East as a major source of oil which for many years would be controlled by companies from outside the region. Around the same time, Royal Dutch, which later merged with Shell and other producers, emerged as a leader in the discovery of oil in Indonesia. Similar consolidation of the oil refining industry took place in the United States, with the formation of Standard Oil.

Rockefeller and Standard Oil

The oil rush brought in many drillers and many companies. John D. Rockefeller was aware of the discoveries of oil in Titusville and surrounding areas. In the 1860s, Rockefeller began to build oil refineries. By 1868, Standard Works was the world's largest oil refinery. He founded Standard Oil in 1870, controlling 10% of the world's oil.

Rockefeller focused on efficient production, and so was able to underprice competitors and buy out less efficient firms. By 1871, he controlled as much as 90% of U.S. refined oil. His near-monopoly was in oil refining, not oil itself. In earlier chapters, we showed the deadweight loss that ordinarily results from monopoly as compared to competition. We demonstrate that loss in Example 5.1, but provide a counterargument in Box 5.2, suggesting that society actually benefitted from Rockefeller's amalgamation of less efficient firms.

Figure 5.1 depicts oil refining with representative figures for Rockefeller's production and price. If the industry is competitive, equilibrium price and quantity are at the intersection of supply and demand, at a price of $0.20 and a quantity of 800,000 gallons. If Rockefeller buys out the individual firms and establishes a monopoly, the profit-maximizing point is where marginal revenue (MR) intersects marginal cost (MC), at

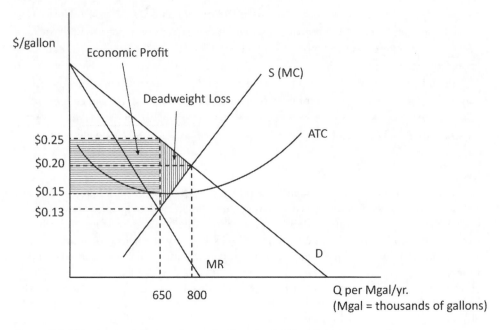

Figure 5.1 The deadweight loss from the Standard Oil refining monopoly.

a quantity of 650,000 gallons and a price of $0.25 per gallon. The objection to mono-
poly is that society suffers a deadweight loss. At the monopoly output, price, which
is also marginal benefit, exceeds marginal cost (MC). In Figure 5.1, MB = $0.25
and MC = $0.13 at the monopoly output, so that society would benefit from an
increase in output up to 800,000 gallons where MB = MC, the competitive
equilibrium.

Example 5.1

Referring to Figure 5.1, compare monopoly and competitive profit, assuming
ATC = $0.15 at both Q = 650 and Q = 800. Also find deadweight loss (DWL).

$$\pi = TR - TC$$

$$\pi = (P \times Q) - (ATC \times Q)$$

$$\pi = (P - ATC) \times Q$$

$$\pi_c = (\$0.20 - 0.15) \times 800 \text{ Mgal}$$

$$\pi_c = (\$0.05) \times 800 \text{ Mgal}$$

$$\pi_c = \$40,000$$

$$\pi_M = (\$0.25 - 0.15) \times 650 \text{ Mgal}$$

$$\pi_M = \$65,000$$

$$\text{DWL} = 0.5(\$0.25 - \$0.13) \times (800 - 650) \text{ Mgal}$$

$$\text{DWL} = 0.5(\$0.12) \times (150) \text{ Mgal}$$

$$\text{DWL} = \$9,000$$

By 1911, the antitrust laws caught up with Standard Oil. The Sherman Act of 1890 outlawed price fixing and the abuses of monopoly. Ida Tarbell, whose father had been driven out of the oil business, published *The History of the Standard Oil Company* (1904), which created a public uproar about Rockefeller's methods. The U.S. Supreme Court found Standard Oil violated the Sherman Act and broke up the company into smaller companies that came to be known as *the Majors*.

Box 5.2 Truth or myth: did Rockefeller use predatory pricing to gain a monopoly?

Predatory pricing, also known as cutthroat competition, takes place when a firm charges less than minimum average variable cost (AVC). We found earlier that firms will shut down in the short run if price is below minimum AVC. Conventional wisdom is that Rockefeller could more than offset those losses in the long run by convincing his rivals to sell their companies to him to avoid continued losses. Rockefeller could then raise price to monopoly levels.

John McGee (1958) rejected the argument that Rockefeller used predatory pricing to drive out the competition. McGee provides historical evidence to show that it was easy to enter oil refining, so Standard Oil would have had difficulty charging a high price to recoup its short-run losses. Hence, predatory pricing was not consistent with profit maximization.

McGee concludes that governments should protect competition, not competitors. Rockefeller's more efficient technology would explain why new firms would not enter the industry.

The Majors

In the twentieth century, oil transitioned from lighting and electricity generation to transportation. Henry Ford produced the Model T, the first mass–produced car. Ships began to use a low-grade gasoline known as bunker fuel, the name a legacy of when ships contained bunkers to store coal for fuel. Early aircraft used gasoline, and now use jet fuel, a form of kerosene.

After World War I, oil production throughout the world increased to the point that it was outstripping growth in demand. The Majors competed in the United States so as to not run afoul of antitrust laws. Outside the United States, they attempted to reach an agreement to not compete, known as the Achnacarry or "As-Is" Agreement that has served as a model for later attempts to restrict production, including OPEC.

In the 1930s, drillers continued to strike oil in Texas, adding to large supplies and falling prices. The Texas Railroad Commission, established in 1891 to regulate mono-polistic railroad practices, gained authority over buses and trucks, petroleum pipelines, gas utilities, and, in the early 1930s, Texas crude. They set quotas for each well. The Texas Railroad Commission was largely responsible for determining the price of oil until the early 1970s, when Texas oil production lost its dominance to OPEC.

The Middle East supplied much of the world's oil. Prior to the 1970s, major corporations won *concessions*—agreements spelling out how profits would be shared between the companies and the host country—and produced most of the Middle East oil. The typical concession split the net revenues 50/50 between the producer and the host country. The Texas Railroad Commission price was the basis for the price of crude throughout the world, adjusted for transportation costs from the United States, a practice known as *netback* pricing. However, the netback price was used even if production took place in the host country where there were no transportation costs.

In the 1950s, Getty, Occidental, and other new oil companies began producing oil from North Africa, paying taxes on the order of 50% to host countries, a precedent that had been set earlier by Venezuela. The increased supply and a European recession that reduced demand resulted in lower prices, which reduced tax revenues and began to stir dissatisfaction within the host countries.

Organization of Petroleum Exporting Countries (OPEC)

The decline in tax revenue caused Venezuela, Iran, Iraq, Kuwait, and Saudi Arabia to form OPEC in 1960. Qatar, Libya, Indonesia, the United Arab Emirates (UAE), and Algeria all joined in the 1960s, followed by Nigeria, Ecuador, and Gabon in the 1970s. Angola joined in 2007.

The seven largest oil firms, five of which were American (the others were Royal Dutch Shell and British Petroleum), had won the rights to produce oil in these countries from concession agreements. OPEC was unable to increase prices during the 1960s, but member countries were gradually able to win a greater share of revenues. In the after-math of the 1973 Arab–Israeli (Yom Kippur) war, the OPEC countries, displeased with the support for Israel, enacted an oil embargo. The governments of a number of OPEC members nationalized their oil industries. These countries felt they were being exploited, getting little in return for allowing the oil companies to operate in their countries. They also realized that if they coordinated their oil production decisions, they could get a higher price by restricting available supply. They could gain revenues and advance their economies, while at the same time punishing countries that aided their adversaries.

OPEC emerged as the dominant force in the determination of oil prices after 1973, reinforced by the 1979 Iranian revolution. The price of oil skyrocketed from $3 to $12 per barrel during the 1973 oil embargo. In 1979, the second price shock sent oil to almost $40 a barrel. The two shocks caused upheavals in the world's economies as well as redistributing wealth from the developed countries dependent on OPEC to the organization's member countries.

Oil demand dropped in the 1980s as a result of oil-induced recessions and conservation. The electric utility industry turned to other energy sources to generate electricity. On the supply side, OPEC countries exceeded their assigned quotas, making it difficult to maintain a high price. Also, the high prices of the 1970s encouraged non–OPEC production, including oil from Alaska, North Sea exploration by Great Britain and Norway, and production by the Soviet Union. By 1986, the price of oil had collapsed to just above $10 a barrel.

It was not until 2004 that the price of oil returned to 1980 levels. It reached $145 per barrel in June of 2008. Observers noted that the majority of trades were by speculators and not actual users of oil, leading to calls in some quarters to ban speculation. As the Great Recession took hold, oil followed an equally breathless collapse to under $40 by the end of that year. The price rebounded, hovering at $100 a barrel for 2011 and 2012. As pundits proclaimed ever-rising prices due to demands of emerging economies in China and India, they once again missed the importance of those high prices in stimulating supply and curtailing demand. The combination of hydraulic fracturing and horizontal drilling, initially expected to revolutionize the production of natural gas, had an equally dramatic effect on the oil supply, with the United States leading the way. By early 2016, oil prices briefly fell as low as $27 per barrel. In November of that year, OPEC met to rein in oil supplies, and prices increased to over $50 per barrel.

Oil consumption

Figure 5.2 shows that as of 2015, petroleum is the largest source of energy consumption, accounting for 36% of all energy consumed in the United States.

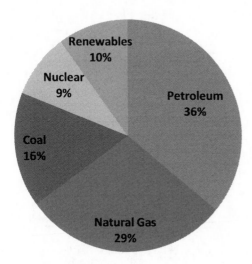

Figure 5.2 U.S. energy consumption by energy source, 2015. Adapted from U.S. EIA (2016a).

Oil as a transportation fuel

Oil dominates other energy sources as a transportation fuel. In the United States, petroleum—gasoline, diesel, and jet fuel—accounts for nearly 90% of energy used for transportation, of which cars and light trucks account for the largest portion.

Figure 5.3 shows that after a downturn that began in 2008 at the onset of the Great Recession, gasoline sales resumed their upward trend. The rebound is a combination of the economic recovery and lower gas prices due to increased fracking supplies. With the fall in gas prices beginning in July 2014, sales of full-size trucks and SUVs have increased their share of the market at the expense of cars. Sales have also slowed for gas–electric hybrids and electric vehicles.

Other uses of petroleum

After transportation, the largest use of petroleum is by the industrial sector. They use it for heating as well as powering equipment, and as a feedstock to make chemicals, plastics, and synthetic materials that are ubiquitous in almost all products. Petrochemicals made from petroleum include ethylene, propylene, benzene, toluene, and synthetic gas or syngas. Oil refineries use *cracking*—the process of breaking down larger carbon-based molecules into smaller and simpler ones—to produce these chemicals. Industry uses ethylene and propylene to make industrial chemicals as well as plastics and synthetic rubber. They use benzene in dyes and detergents, and benzene and toluene in poly-urethanes, a flexible material found in many products, including insulation and paints.

Residential and commercial uses make up all but a fraction of the remaining 5% of petroleum consumption. These sectors use petroleum-based products including paints, detergent, fertilizers, and pesticides. They also use synthetic fibers such as polyester, nylon, and acrylics in curtains, carpets, and clothing. They use plastic extensively. Make-up, perfume, dyes, and candles all make use of petroleum products.

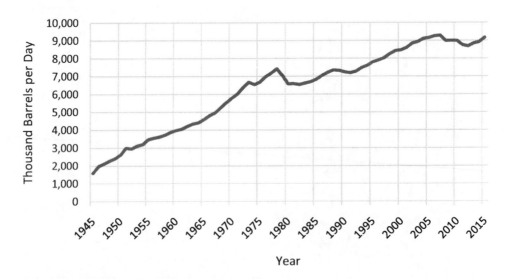

Figure 5.3 U.S. gasoline production. Adapted from U.S. EIA (2016b).

Petroleum accounts for only 0.1% of fuels used to generate electricity in the United States. It has declined in importance as other fuels have supplanted it as lower-cost burner fuels. The northeast United States still generates almost 10% of its electricity using oil, as well as fuel oil that is used directly for heating. While natural gas is growing in use throughout the United States including the Northeast, electric utilities in that region have found that they need fuel oil when natural gas prices rise or when they cannot obtain natural gas, as occurred during the 2014 Polar Vortex, a record cold snap.

Box 5.3 Fuel oil's last stand during the Polar Vortex

In January 2014, many parts of the United States experienced the Polar Vortex, with record cold temperatures sweeping down from the Arctic. Much of the country met record electricity demands with plentiful and low-cost natural gas, thanks to the hydraulic fracturing boom. The Marcellus shale in Pennsylvania is one of the major natural gas shale fields, but when the Polar Vortex hit, the Northeast was unable to get adequate supplies. There were numerous reasons, among them frozen gas wells in Pennsylvania, interruptible contracts that gave priority to natural gas companies whose customers depended directly on natural gas, and limited pipeline capacity.

Northeast U.S. utilities have dual-fuel boilers in their generating mix that can use either natural gas or fuel oil. When natural gas supplies ran low, the utilities switched over to fuel oil. In addition, natural gas prices in this region of the country spiked so high that fuel oil actually cost less. Natural gas prices, which had been in the range of $3–5 per million British thermal units (MMBtu), touched $100/MMBtu in the New York region. Comparing cost on a kilowatt-hour (kWh) basis, use of natural gas ordinarily translates to $0.05–0.08/kWh, while heating oil costs $0.20–0.30/kWh. With natural gas experiencing a 20-fold increase in price, the kWh cost soared to $1, making heating oil a relative bargain.

Oil production

Economists take a very different view of oil production than do physical scientists such as geologists and engineers. The divide is over the views of scarcity. Economists take a perspective of relative scarcity, whereas geologists and other physical scientists envision absolute scarcity.

Box 5.4 To peak or not to peak: that is the question

In 1956, M. King Hubbert predicted that U.S. oil production would follow a bell-shaped curve, peaking in the early 1970s. However, the model does include prices. OPEC has influenced world price. World prices also affect, and are affected by, conservation, substitution of other fuels, and new technologies.

The debate is analogous to the "Cassandra" and "Cornucopia" camps regarding running out of resources.[2] Physical scientists are pessimistic Cassandras who have warned repeatedly that we will run out of resources. Economists are the optimistic Cornucopians who foresee forces, including higher prices, that will lead to conservation, substitution, and technological advance. Earlier in the text, we discussed the famous bet between Paul Ehrlich, a well-known biologist, and Julian Simon, an economist whose 1981 book, *The Ultimate Resource*, saw human abilities and not physical limits as the determining factor in whether we will run out of resources.

Morris Adelman, one of the best known oil economists, cited the Kern River field in the San Joaquin Valley of California as evidence against peak oil theory. In 1942, the U.S. Geological Service (USGS) estimated reserves at 54 million barrels. By 1986, the agency set its estimate at 970 million barrels, based on existing technology. Between those years, the field produced 736 million barrels as technology improved.[3] Adelman (1993) stated, "Minerals are inexhaustible and will never be depleted ... How much was in the ground at the start and how much will be left at the end are unknown and irrelevant." Philip Verleger, an oft-quoted energy economist, states: "Technology moves so quickly today that any looming resource constraint will be nothing more than a blip. We adjust."[4]

Figure 5.4 shows U.S. production since 1920.

Beginning in 2009, with new fracking technology, oil production in the United States began to rise, in contrast to Hubbert's prediction. In 2015, production surged to 300 million barrels per month (10 million barrels per day), levels last seen in the

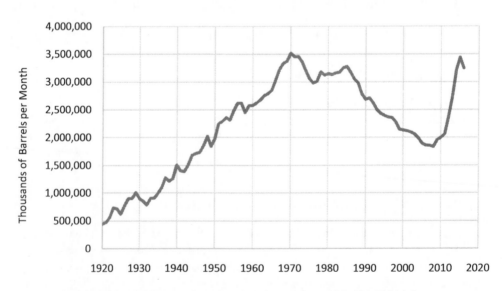

Figure 5.4 U.S. field production of crude oil. Adapted from U.S. EIA (2016c).

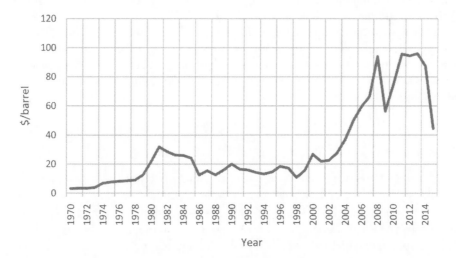

Figure 5.5 U.S. crude oil price. Adapted from U.S. EIA (2016d).

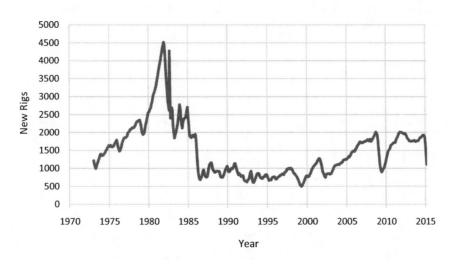

Figure 5.6 U.S. crude oil and natural gas rotary rigs in operation. Adapted from U.S. EIA (2016e).

early 1970s. After 2013, production started to turn down. Does this downturn indicate that the surge was only a blip on the way to peak-oil exhaustion? While geologists and other physical scientists would likely offer that explanation, economists would attribute the downturn to lower prices that accompanied record supplies, as shown in Figure 5.5.

When oil prices are low for an extended period, the quantity supplied will eventually decline. Hydraulic fracturing is a relatively quick process to start and stop. Lower prices mean lower profitability, or losses, for high-cost suppliers. Frackers can halt existing drilling, and postpone new drilling. Figure 5.6 shows U.S. drilling activity, reflecting the number of *rigs* (equipment used to drill oil wells). As prices dropped beginning in mid–2014, so did the number of new rigs.

Note that oil production need not drop even if new well completion decreases. Existing wells could achieve higher production levels, so that the net effect on oil production is a product of rig efficiency and the number of active rigs. Also, producers increase efficiency as they gain experience with fracking, allowing them to extract more oil from existing sites.

Box 5.5 Backstop technologies

One reason for skepticism about peak oil is backstop technology. Its availability creates a *choke price* at which producers will switch to the backstop. Consider the demand for fuel oil as an input into electricity production. While Hotelling's rule suggests that the price of fuel oil will rise at the rate of return on other assets, alternatives such as solar and wind may limit how high the price of fuel oil can get. If wind is available in essentially unlimited quantities, but is only economically attractive when the price of a kWh of electricity rises to $0.12/kWh, the demand for oil as a generating fuel has an upper bound. If the price of an alternative fuel falls below the cost of oil for electricity generation, then oil becomes the backstop technology for natural gas when its price soars or it cannot be delivered. Figure 5.7 shows oil as the backstop technology for electricity generation when natural gas reaches $0.20/kWh.

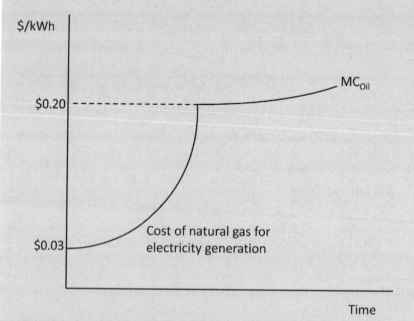

Figure 5.7 Oil as a backstop technology in electricity generation.

The Canadian province of Alberta contains oil sands with bitumen that can produce a liquid substitute for crude oil. Existing and new oil sands require a price from $45 to $80 per barrel or more to be economically competitive. Biofuels can also serve as carbon-free substitutes, even waste products such as used cooking oil. It may take an oil price of $150–200 per barrel to justify the switch to biofuels, lower if we put a price on carbon.

As long as there are backstop technologies, economists maintain that peak oil is irrelevant, as nonrenewable resources such as oil will never be fully depleted.

The supply chain for oil and gasoline

Porter (1985) introduced the value or supply chain. Its purpose is to identify value added at each step of the production process, and assist firms in determining which production stages offer opportunities for profit. Production begins at the *upstream* stage. The *midstream* stage takes the product from initial production to the final customer. The *downstream* stage is the final market.

Figure 5.8 depicts a supply chain for oil. Production of crude oil begins upstream with exploration and production. We associate this stage with oil well activities. Countries can use both domestic sources and imports of oil, depending on their relative costs.

The upstream stage of oil exploration has the highest risks and also the highest returns. In 2015, Shell Oil abandoned its exploration for oil in the Arctic after searching for nine years and spending over $7 billion. When they started exploration, oil sold for $100 per barrel, but was only half that value when they abandoned their efforts (Krauss & Reed, 2015).

The *Deepwater Horizon* disaster also shows the risks inherent in drilling for oil. BP was drilling for oil in the Gulf of Mexico when there was an explosion that resulted in deaths, damage, and an environmental disaster. BP as well as other companies connected

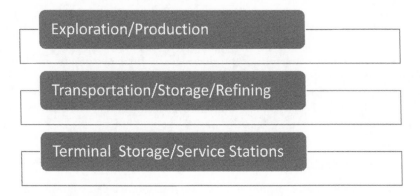

Figure 5.8 Oil supply chain.

with the disaster paid record fines and faced criminal and civil charges, including record fines.

The midstream processes include transportation, storage, and refining. Pipelines transport about 70% of gas in the United States, followed by ship and barge at 23%, trucking at 4%, and rail at 3% (Conca, 2014). With the rapid increase in production due to fracking, rail has increased its share, as building a new pipeline is a lengthy process (Gillies & Macpherson, 2015).

Some of the oil goes into storage tanks to assist in managing inventory. Production may outstrip consumption, in which case inventories increase. When inventories are particularly large, prices drop given the knowledge that there is additional supply available to meet demand. Oil demand has seasonal patterns, with the heaviest demand due to driving during summer. Companies may stockpile oil during off-peak seasons.

Oil refining distills crude oil into a variety of value-added products. The first stage is to heat the oil to distill it into lighter and heavier products. The next stage is cracking, breaking longer and heavier carbon chains into shorter and lighter ones. Gasoline is a lighter, more highly valued product that makes up the largest percentage of refined products. *Alkylation* combines lighter molecules into heavier ones, such as diesel fuel. The optimal distillation mix depends upon the market price of the refined products.

Box 5.6 Propane's pipeline blues

Liquefied petroleum gas (LPG) is a distillation product used as propane for heating fuel, mostly in rural areas. Production of propane increased with the surge in oil production from fracking. Yet in the winter of 2013–2014, there were propane gas shortages and its price soared from its normal range of $1–2/gallon to over $4/gallon. What happened?

The Polar Vortex played a role, as did a surge in the use of propane to dry crops quickly before the Arctic blast. Propane exports also increased. The supply chain came into play when a greater than normal number of pipelines shut down. There was also a drawdown in storage to meet record demands for heating.

History did not repeat itself the following winter. Despite another episode of Arctic air, inventories were sufficient to keep price at $2.50/gallon, and pipelines were serviced during off-peak times. Prices dropped to $2/gallon in the winter of 2015–2016.

At the downstream stage, the refined products go to final customers, including storage terminals, distributors, and gas stations. Upstream producers have gotten out of the downstream business of owning gas stations although many stations retain the large company names (BP, Shell, Exxon, etc.). Value-chain analysis shows gas station ownership to be a low-margin business.[5]

Market models of OPEC behavior

Now that we have reviewed oil consumption and production, we can examine the oil industry. We focus on OPEC, given its influence on the global market.

OPEC enjoyed lengthy periods where it could force up world price by limiting supply. Their strategy changed with the surge in U.S. oil production in 2009, when OPEC actually increased production and further depressed prices. One hypothesis for their change in strategy is that they hoped the low prices would bankrupt frackers. A second hypothesis is that they wanted to retain market share in order to be able to finance government expenditures. To better understand OPEC's decision-making, we examine market structure.

We present two oligopoly models—cartel and dominant firm price leadership—to explain OPEC behavior. *Oligopoly* models apply when there are a small number of firms in an industry that are interdependent. The models include a *reaction function* to capture how each firm responds to the decisions of other firms in the industry. There are many oligopoly models, as no single model has been developed that is general enough to predict accurately for all oligopolies.[6] How do we know which model is correct? Milton Friedman used the criterion that the best model is the one that predicts most accurately. At the same time, there is often a trade-off between accuracy and complexity. So we might modify the criterion to state that the best model is the simplest one that gives suffi-ciently accurate predictions for the purpose at hand, a restatement of Occam's razor.

Cartel model

Figure 5.9 depicts a cartel.

In a cartel, producers collaborate to set industry output and then allocate quotas to the cartel members. The intention is to mimic monopoly, producing industry quantity Q_m at corresponding price P_m. This is the price–quantity combination that corresponds to $MR = MC$ for a monopoly. In OPEC's case, industry supply is the sum of MCs for individual members.

Assuming all members are the same size and that there are n members, each country produces $q_m = Q_m/n$. OPEC holds periodic meetings to determine individual country quotas.

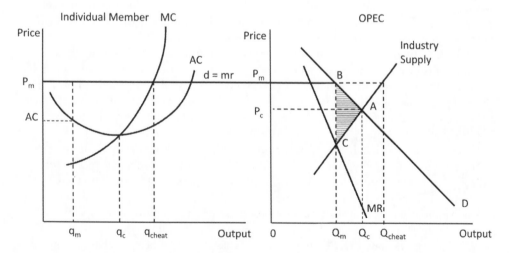

Figure 5.9 Cartel model applied to OPEC.

However, from an individual member perspective, the most profitable point is q_{cheat}. The individual member sees its demand (d) as infinitely elastic, since one member is too small to affect industry price. Individual marginal revenue (MR) is identical to demand and price, the horizontal line at P_m. Why q_{cheat}? Each firm has an incentive to produce more than its quota. However, if all firms cheat, industry quantity is Q_{cheat}. There is a surplus of oil ($Q_{cheat} - Q_m$), and price will fall. In the long run, if the cartel cannot enforce the quota, the industry will evolve into perfect competition.

While the cartel is desirable from the standpoint of OPEC members, it is inefficient in its use of global resources. Triangle ABC is the size of the deadweight loss. The reasoning is identical to why monopoly is inefficient.

Historically, cartels have had a short lifetime. In the United States, cartels are illegal under the Sherman Antitrust Act. While OPEC lies outside the reach of U.S. laws, the incentive for individual members to cheat makes market power difficult to maintain. Also, the cartel may not be able to prevent entry in the long run. It can invite new members, but they may find it more profitable to produce outside the group. As evidence of the difficulty of maintaining a cartel, when OPEC implemented the oil embargo in 1973, it produced just over 50% of world oil. In 2015, OPEC's share is just over 40%, and it has only retained that share by increasing production (U.S. EIA, 2016f).

Russia, Saudi Arabia, and the United States vie for the top spot in oil production, in the vicinity of 10 million barrels per day (mbls/day). Russia met with Saudi Arabia and other OPEC members in late 2016 and agreed to reduce its oil production, but it remains to be seen if they or OPEC will stick to the agreement.

The cartel model has the virtue of simplicity. It provides useful predictions on how OPEC sets quotas, and why they often exceed those quotas. The predictions are consistent with the cyclic history of high prices followed by collapsing prices. However, the model does not capture the disproportionate influence of Saudi Arabia.

Saudi Arabia as swing producer

Saudi Arabia has taken the role of *swing producer,* adjusting its output to maintain the organization price. Figure 5.10 shows how Saudi Arabian production influences the price of oil. The figure shows the price of West Texas Intermediate (WTI), a light sweet crude that is used as a benchmark for the U.S. price of oil.

Along the lines of a dynamic monopoly, Saudi Arabia (SA) balances today's net revenue of oil against the present value of net revenue in the future. Saudi Arabia has substantial spare capacity. When price falls below OPEC's target level, Saudi Arabia reduces production so that price will recover in the next period of time. If price is above the target, it is profitable to increase supply and accept a lower price in the next period. Prices since 2000 typically show this pattern.

Saudi Arabia has changed its strategy since the U.S. fracking dramatically increased U.S. supply. Traditionally, the Saudis would have cut production as the global price of oil fell. However, Figure 5.10 shows that they increased production, and asked the other members of OPEC to do the same.

The earlier discussion of the pitfalls of predatory pricing questions the wisdom of this strategy. If the strategy aims to drive frackers out of business, it only works if OPEC can prevent entry in the long run. Some frackers in Texas can cover their variable costs at prices as low as $30, while existing wells in North Dakota may need $70 to justify short-run

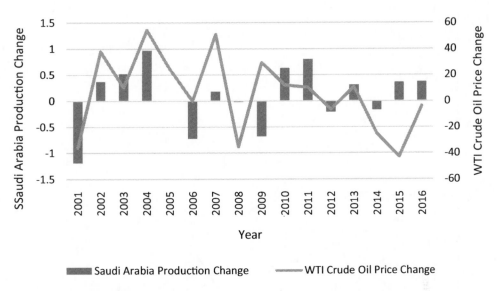

Figure 5.10 Saudi Arabia as the swing producer. Reprinted from U.S. EIA (2016f).

operation. OPEC may have difficulty achieving a price above the production cost of marginal frackers, perhaps in the range of $70–80 (Murtaugh, 2016). OPEC may have to settle for prices in this range or lower. Saudi Arabia can extract oil for $30 per barrel or lower and still make a profit, but Venezuela based its budget on $100 per barrel of oil.

Dominant firm price leadership model

We turn next to the dominant firm price leadership model to examine predictions. Figure 5.11 shows the dominant firm price leadership model for Saudi Arabia and the other OPEC members. The price leader, in our case Saudi Arabia (SA), determines price. The leader faces a residual demand (D_{SA}) that begins at P_A obtained by subtracting the supply of the competitive fringe (S_{CF}) from industry D (D_{OPEC}). The competitive fringe is composed of all the other OPEC countries, each of which is considered too small to influence industry price.

SA maximizes profits where $MR_{SA} = MC_{SA}$. Notice that MC_{SA} is to the right of the competitive fringe supply, which is the sum of the fringe MC curves; the dominant firm can produce more at a lower cost than the smaller firms combined. Dominant firm price is P_{SA} and quantity is Q_{SA}. The followers take P_{SA} as their price, and choose output Q_{CF} where $P_{SA} = MC$ (S_{CF}). Finally, OPEC supply is $Q_{CF} + Q_{SA}$. Note that price is lower and quantity is larger than the monopoly price and quantity predicted by the cartel model.

While the dominant firm price leadership model has the intuitively appealing aspect of emphasizing the role of Saudi Arabia, it does not necessarily capture the role of other members that do not simply accept the Saudi price. Instead, all the countries meet to negotiate price and output, so it is not obvious that this model does any better than the cartel model.[7]

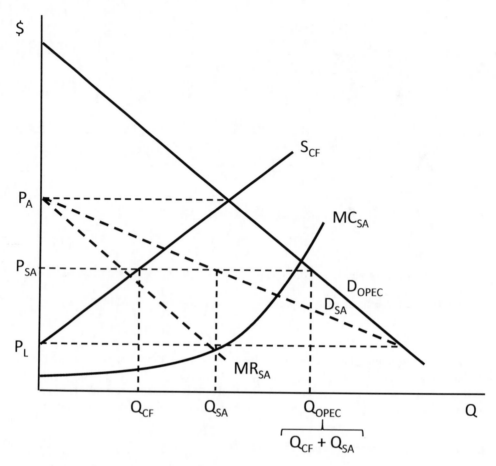

Figure 5.11 Dominant firm price leadership.

Environmental regulation

As the primary use of petroleum is for transportation, we focus on environmental regulations aimed at traditional gasoline vehicles. The process of oil combustion releases unwanted emissions, such as hydrocarbons (HCs), nitrogen oxides (NOx) and particulate matter (PM). NOx combines with HCs and sunlight to form ground-level ozone, a major component of smog. In addition to creating visible pollution, ozone irritates the eyes and lungs, especially for sensitive populations prone to respiratory problems such as asthma. Particulate matter enters the nose, mouth, and throat and eventually the lungs.

Vehicles emit carbon monoxide (CO), an odorless and colorless gas that can be fatal. However, carbon dioxide (CO_2) receives the most attention for its contribution to climate change. Figure 5.12 shows sources of CO_2 emissions in the United States. The largest emitters are transportation and electric power, with each responsible for just over a quarter of CO_2 emissions.

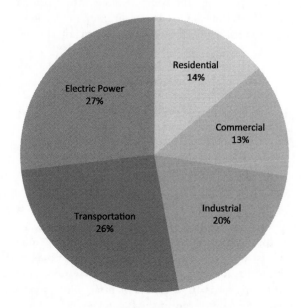

Figure 5.12 Percentage of carbon dioxide emissions by sector, 2015. Adapted from U.S. EIA (2016g).

Oil financial instruments[8]

In July 2008, the price of a barrel of oil according to the WTI benchmark hit a record of $147 per barrel. By the end of that year, the price plummeted as low as $32 per barrel. Oil prices returned to the $100 mark during the summer of 2014, only to collapse below $60 by the end of the year. Gas prices closed below $30 per barrel in early 2016, before rebounding to $50 within a few months. What is an oil market participant to do?

Chapter 4 introduced financial instruments as a way to manage energy price volatility. Here, we discuss three types of derivative contracts: oil forwards, futures, and options.

Forwards and futures

A forward contract gives the buyer the right to future delivery at an agreed-to price. The two parties decide on the volume of oil to be exchanged, as well as other customized terms. The forward market is an *over-the-counter (OTC) market*, which is not a physically based market, but simply exists wherever transactions take place. The parties in forward markets need not disclose the price to other parties. Trade journals such as *Platts Oilgram* provide some price information each day at the close of trading, which aids next-day traders. The journals do not report prices for a particular contract.

Futures contracts are similar, except they are standardized contracts that take place in organized markets. All participants in the market have complete price information.

Forward contracts arise as market participants see the need to reduce their price risk. Futures markets typically develop later if there are a large number of participants. There are a large number of oil market participants and so we will focus on the futures markets.

Futures contracts

There are two major futures exchanges for oil, the New York Mercantile Exchange (NYMEX) and the Intercontinental Exchange (ICE) in London.[9] The NYMEX bases its prices on WTI crude, while ICE uses Brent crude, extracted from the North Sea. Both are light, sweet crudes.

The first oil futures contract was the NYMEX contract for heating oil in 1978, with gasoline futures introduced in 1981 and crude oil following in 1983. European trading began in 1988 at the International Petroleum Exchange (IPE), the predecessor to ICE.

Contract size is 1,000 barrels (Mbbl. = 1,000 bbl).[10] If price per barrel is $70, a contract would cost $70,000. The contract is repriced at the end of each day, referred to as *marked-to-market*. The *spot price* is today's price. The *forward or futures price* is the price that buyers and sellers agree to today for future delivery. If the two sides expect prices to rise, the futures price will be higher than today's spot price. The buyer will have to pay more than $70/bbl today for oil delivered in the future.

Buyers can pay the full amount, or can open up a *margin account*. A margin account allows buyers to put down a percentage of the price, in effect borrowing money from the broker arranging the exchange. Buying on margin increases the potential rate of return as well as the risk.

Example 5.2

You decide to buy a NYMEX WTI crude oil futures contract at the price of $44.20 per barrel. The contract represents 1,000 barrels of crude oil to be delivered three months from now. However, instead of paying the full value of the contract, you only deposit an initial margin requirement of 10%. A week later, the price of crude oil jumps to $48.62. What will be your profit (or loss)?

Solution

Your contract has increased in value from $44,200 to $48,620. Your profit is $4,420. Had you invested the full amount, you would have a 10% return on your investment. However, by buying on margin, you earned $4,420 on an investment of $4,420, a return of 100%.

Before you get too excited about earning such a high return for one week's work, you will want to work out the consequences if the oil price drops to $40/bbl a week later. You would lose 10% if you had invested the full amount. If you used a margin account, you only invested $4,420 initially. As your investment has decreased in value by $4,000, you will receive a margin call from the broker who in effect loaned you

$40,000 to place an additional $4,000 in your account to return the margin to the initial amount. If you do not have an additional $4,000, you will have to sell your investment for a $4,000 loss. You will lose $4,000, about 90% of your initial investment.

Participants in futures markets can be hedgers or speculators. Hedgers reduce risk by buying or selling contracts to lock in a price. Speculators participate to earn a profit, and do not want to buy the underlying commodity. A speculator can make money by buying or selling a futures contract. Suppose an oil trader expects that future oil prices will be higher than today's spot price. The speculator should go *long*—buy a futures—in anticipation of higher future prices. The contract will be relatively cheap today, given today's spot price. If the speculator turns out to be correct and future price is higher, she will be able to sell the contract for more than she paid. Speculators can also potentially make money by going *short*, selling a futures contract when they expect price to be lower in the future. If they anticipate correctly, the buyer of the futures contract will pay them today's high price. When the contract becomes due, the seller can obtain the oil at the lower spot price, and profit by having obtained a higher price from the buyer in advance.

Speculators will not always guess right. Since *arbitrage*—the simultaneous buying and selling of an asset to take advantage of a price difference—should not exist in an efficient market, speculators will not routinely outguess the market. To the extent that they make money, it is because hedgers are willing to pay a premium over the current spot price to reduce their risk. By accepting the riskier side of the transaction, speculators earn compensation. The return to speculators is more attributable to their being less risk-averse than hedgers than to any ability to systematically outguess the market. There may be a speculator who outperforms the market for a short time, but unless there is a barrier that prevents other traders from learning the superior technique, the speculator will soon return to earning a market return and no more.

Another trading strategy is the *spread*, the difference between the price of the raw material such as crude oil, and the price of the finished products made from that raw material, such as gasoline or heating fuel. Recall that cracking refers to the process of refining oil. A *crack spread* is the difference between the price of the oil futures contract and the price of the product futures, such as gasoline. A refiner buying an oil futures contract for delivery of oil six months from now can simultaneously sell a gasoline futures contract. If oil prices fall, an adverse move for the refiner who bought at today's high price, the loss will be offset if gasoline prices also fall.

Options contracts

Options give the right, but not the obligation, to buy or sell the underlying commodity at a future time. A *call option* gives the right to buy the underlying commodity; a *put option* is the right to sell. The underlying commodity could be a product, a financial stock, or a futures contract. A three-month call option giving the right to buy oil at $60 has intrinsic value only if the oil spot price is more than $60. The predetermined price at which the buyer can purchase the commodity is the *strike* or *exercise price*. A buyer can trade an American option at any time, while a buyer of a European option can only trade it at expiration. The buyer pays an option price, or *premium*, for the contract. If the premium for a $60 call option on oil is $3, the buyer comes out ahead only if the price of oil rises above $63.

Example 5.3

A trader buys one European call option at a strike price of $50 per barrel that gives the right to buy 100 barrels of oil. The current price of oil is $48, the expiration is in two months, and the option premium per barrel of oil is $5. The trader can take this position for $500 using options rather than $5,000 using futures contracts. If oil is $65 at expiration, what is the buyer's dollar profit and percentage profit? What about if the price of oil is $46 at expiration? What about $53 at expiration?

Solution

The trader earns $1,500 for a net profit of $1,000 (ignoring the time value of money, which should be minimal for a two-month period). If the price in two months is below $50, the trader does not exercise the option and loses $500. There is no point paying $50 to buy $46 oil. Such a purchase would add an additional $400 loss.

Note that if oil settles between $50 and $55, the trader would exercise the option but still lose money. The profit from the sale would be less than $500, the initial option premium.

There are formulas for calculating option prices. Black, Scholes and Merton (1973) developed the capital asset pricing model (CAPM) to calculate the price of European put and call options.[11]

Summary

Oil has come a long way over the past two centuries, from being a nuisance to a valuable commodity with geopolitical consequences. By late in the nineteenth century, entrepreneurs found technologies to extract oil and use it for lighting, heating, and transportation. John D. Rockefeller gained control of the U.S. refining capacity shortly after. Either through superior efficiency or predatory pricing, he bought out other refiners and established a near-monopoly. The U.S. antitrust laws broke up the Standard Oil trust in 1911 to prevent the public from monopoly abuses. The "Majors," most of which were descendants of Standard Oil, still exerted substantial market power over oil, as exemplified by the Achnacarry Agreement of 1928. As Texas began to dominate production in the early 1930s, the Texas Railroad Commission set quotas on production that limited supply.

Private oil companies won concessions to produce in oil-rich but impoverished countries. Over time, these countries began to assert their dominance over the global market by nationalizing their oil industries and aligning their interests. This coordination led to the formation of the Organization of Petroleum Exporting Countries (OPEC), to limit supplies in order to increase profits. Their practices echoed those of Achnacarry and the Texas Railroad Commission to limit oil production and raise prices.

In the 1970s, OPEC imposed an embargo on countries opposed to their political policies. The resulting skyrocketing prices caused economic stagnation while creating incentives for consumers to seek out more fuel-efficient technologies. Since the 1980s, OPEC experienced periods of rising and falling power over price. Countries dependent on imports from OPEC increased domestic production to gain greater energy security.

The cartel and dominant firm oligopoly models offer predictions regarding OPEC strategy. The cartel model predicts agreement among members to mimic monopoly quantity and price, but difficulty in enforcing the agreement. The dominant firm model emphasizes the outsized influence of Saudi Arabia, with other organization members passively accepting Saudi Arabia's decisions. We base the choice of model on which appears to provide the more accurate predictions and which is simpler to use.

After two decades of low oil prices, OPEC has reasserted its market power since 2000. As prices soared, some analysts targeted speculators and the fast-growing economies of China and India as the culprits. By the end of that decade, the Great Recession followed by the advent of hydraulic fracturing led to a massive increase in supply and plummeting oil prices.

While many physical scientists predict the eventual exhaustion of oil supplies, economists do not share this pessimism. As supplies diminish, prices will rise, leading consumers to conserve, seek out alternative sources of energy, and reward new technologies that use less oil or that use different fuel sources. Economists are concerned about the externalities from the use of oil, particularly for transportation, which accounts for about 70% of oil use. Many of the negative externalities go unpriced, such as U.S. carbon emissions.

Participants in the oil market must cope with its high price volatility. Producers and consumers use a variety of financial instruments to reduce risk. Participants hedge by purchasing derivative contracts. Their strategy is to buy a contract that moves in the opposite direction from the underlying commodity. On the other side of the market are speculators, who accept greater risk in return for a premium. Forwards, futures, and options are the most widely used financial derivatives. Over the years, human ingenuity continues to find additional trading strategies such as crack spreads that offer new ways to hedge or speculate.

Notes

1 "Colonel" was appended to his name to give added respectability to an unproven technique, and Drake had no military connection.

2 Cassandra was a figure in Greek mythology doomed to have no one listen to her warnings, a punishment for having refused the advances of Apollo, son of Zeus. A cornucopia is a horn of plenty, used to provide nutrition to the infant Zeus while hidden from his father, Kronos, who believed he was to be overthrown by his children.

3 See Blackmon (2014) for this anecdote and more background on Adelman.

4 See Gold (2014), an energy columnist for the *Wall Street Journal*.

5 Gas stations earn about $0.03/gallon net of credit card fees and operating costs. Increasingly, gas purchases are primarily a way to get customers into associated convenience stores, where they purchase higher-margin secondary products such as snacks and beverages, and possibly car repairs.

6 Perhaps the most general oligopoly model is that of Stigler (1964). Game theory is an alternative to formal oligopoly models as a way to capture strategic behavior.

7 Griffin and Steele (1986) develop a hybrid model. Saudi Arabia and other large producers with excess capacity form a dominant group. The remaining countries compose two groups, one that maximizes price and the other that maximizes output. While this model is more realistic and is likely to provide more accurate predictions, it is also more complex. Whether or not it is a better model depends on the degree of accuracy needed for the purpose at hand.

8 Downey (2009) contains chapters on oil derivatives, Dahl (2004) has material on energy derivatives including oil, and Hull (1999) is a text on financial derivatives in general, with some specific information on oil and other energy derivatives.

9 The ICE trades in London, while its headquarters are in Atlanta.

10 There are varying stories over the origin of the abbreviation "bbl" for one barrel of oil. One claim is that barrels had varying sizes at first, but that over time there was greater acceptance of the 42-gallon barrel that is now standard (although oil now comes primarily through a pipeline, not in a barrel). Standard Oil used a blue 42-gallon barrel to identify the size, and bbl originally may have designated a blue barrel. This story is likely a myth, as documents from the 1700s already used the abbreviation. The most common abbreviation for 1,000 barrels is Mbbl, though some use Kbbl or Tbbl. One million barrels is MMbbl, where MM designates a thousand times a thousand.

11 A CAPM calculator is available online ("Black-Scholes Calculator," n.d.) The user must input strike price, the price of the underlying asset, time to maturity, the risk-free interest rate, and annualized volatility. Volatility is not directly observable and must be solved for in the Black–Scholes formula by inputting the other four variables. Historical volatility can be observed, but may not be an accurate measure of future volatility.

References

Adelman, M. (1993). *The economics of petroleum supply*. Cambridge, MA: The MIT Press.

Blackmon, D. (2014, June 10). Dr. Morris Adelman and peak oil theory. *Forbes*. Retrieved September 18, 2016 from http://www.forbes.com/sites/davidblackmon/2014/06/10/dr-morris-adelman-and-peak-oil-theory/

Black–Scholes calculator. (n.d.). Retrieved September 19, 2016 from https://www.mystockoptions.com/black-scholes.cfm

Conca, J. (2014, April 26). Pick your poison for crude—pipeline, rail, truck or boat. *Forbes*. Retrieved August 7, 2015 from http://www.forbes.com/sites/jamesconca/2014/04/26/pick-your-poison-for-crude-pipeline-rail-truck-or-boat/

Dahl, C. (2004). *International energy markets: Understanding pricing, policies and profits*. Tulsa, OK: Pennwell Publications.

Downey, M. (2009). *Oil 101*. New York: Wooden Table Press.

Gillies, R., & McPherson, J. (2015, November 7). After Keystone rejection, oil industry to rely on trains, other pipelines to move oil. *U.S. News and World Report*. Retrieved September 19, 2016 from http://www.usnews.com/news/business/articles/2015/11/07/without-keystone-industry-must-find-new-paths-for-oil

Gold, R. (2014, September 29). Why peak-oil predictions haven't come true: More experts now believe technology will continue to unlock new sources. *Wall Street Journal*. Retrieved September 18, 2016 from http://www.wsj.com/articles/why-peak-oil-predictions-haven-t-come-true-1411937788

Griffin, J., & Steele, H. (1986). *Energy economics and policy*. New York, NY: Academic Press.

Hull, J. (1999). *Options, futures, & other derivatives*. Englewood Cliffs: Prentice Hall.

Krauss, C., & Reed, S. (2015, September 28). Shell exits Arctic as slump in oil prices forces industry to retrench. *New York Times*. Retrieved December 2, 2016 from http://www.nytimes.com/2015/09/29/business/international/royal-dutch-shell-alaska-oil-exploration-halt.html

McGee, J.S. (1958). Predatory price cutting: The Standard Oil (New Jersey) case. *Journal of Law and Economics*, 1, 137–169.

Murtaugh, D. (2016, February 4). Texas isn't scared of $30 oil. *Bloomberg Business Week*. Retrieved December 2, 2016 from https://www.bloomberg.com/news/articles/2016-02-03/texas-toughness-in-oil-patch-shows-why-u-s-still-strong-at-30

Porter, M. (1985). *Competitive advantage: Creating and sustaining superior performance*. New York: Free Press.

Stigler, G. (1964). A theory of oligopoly. *Journal of Political Economy*, 72(1), 44–61.

Tarbell, I. (1904). *The history of the Standard Oil Company*. New York: McClure, Phillips & Co.

U.S. Energy Information Administration. (2016a). *U.S. energy facts*. Retrieved September 17, 2016 from http://www.eia.gov/energyexplained/index.cfm?page=us_energy_home

U.S. Energy Information Administration. (2016b). *U.S. product supplied of finished motor gasoline*. Retrieved September 17, 2016, from http://tonto.eia.gov/dnav/pet/hist/LeafHandler.ashx?n=PET&s=MGFUPUS2&f=A

U.S. Energy Information Administration. (2016c). *U.S. field production of crude oil*. Retrieved September 18, 2016, from http://www.eia.gov/dnav/pet/hist/LeafHandler.ashx?n=pet&s=mcrfpus1&f=m

U.S. Energy Information Administration. (2016d). *U.S. crude oil first purchase price*. Retrieved June 4, 2016, from https://www.eia.gov/dnav/pet/hist/LeafHandler.ashx?n=pet&s=f000000__3&f=m

U.S. Energy Information Administration. (2016e). *U.S. crude oil and natural gas rotary rigs in operation*. Retrieved September 18, 2016, from https://www.eia.gov/dnav/ng/hist/e_ertrr0_xr0_nus_cm.htm

U.S. Energy Information Administration. (2016f). *What drives crude oil prices?* Retrieved September 18, 2016 from https://www.eia.gov/finance/markets/supply-opec.cfm

U.S. Energy Information Administration. (2016g). *What are U.S. energy-related carbon dioxide emissions by source and sector?* Retrieved June 7, 2016, from https://www.eia.gov/tools/faqs/faq.cfm?id=75&t=11

Chapter 6

Natural gas

A new golden age?

"We knew the gas was there. We didn't know how to get it free."
George Mitchell (quote from National Public Radio Marketplace)[1]

"Natural gas could become the largest source of energy for generating electricity."
The author of this text

Introduction

In 2011, the International Energy Agency (IEA), an organization composed of oil-importing countries, proclaimed a Golden Age of Gas IEA (2011). There is great hope for natural gas to account for a larger portion of energy supplies. The technology of hydraulic fracturing coupled with horizontal drilling has led to a huge increase in extracting previously uneconomic natural gas from shale rock, particularly in the United States.

In 2013, the U.S. Energy Information Administration (EIA) estimated that the United States has 84 years of natural gas reserves at current rates of consumption. Although a finite resource, U.S. reserves are sufficiently large that we can use a static framework to understand production decisions. As compared to oil, domestic supplies better match demands in many countries. China and the EU have the potential for major increases in shale gas supply although they have not yet begun to extract significant amounts of the resource. In the EU, the government owns the property rights to minerals whereas in the United States, there is private ownership. EU governments have been hesitant to use the new technology given environmental concerns.

Natural gas is among the fuels that generate electricity. Historically, natural gas units were primarily used during peak hours. Coal and nuclear plants provided *baseload* plants that operate close to capacity at all hours. Natural gas is emerging as a baseload technology, due to its low cost in recent years and the expectation of continued availability and relatively low prices for the foreseeable future. It also competes with electricity for heating and cooking. Like oil, industry uses natural gas as a boiler fuel and a feedstock in chemicals and pharmaceuticals. It supplies fuel for a small fraction of vehicles, but will likely increase as it and other alternatives challenge the dominance of oil in transportation.

Natural gas is moving towards being a global market. Until recently, natural gas was a regional market because it was difficult and costly to export. It is necessary to convert natural gas to liquefied natural gas (LNG), build export terminals, and use specially designed tankers in order to transport it across oceans. Recipients must build import terminals. With the abundance of natural gas, these measures are increasingly worthwhile, and the cost of LNG has been dropping rapidly.

Transportation uses compressed natural gas (CNG) in modified internal combustion engine automobiles or in specially designed vehicles. Compression reduces the volume, although less so than LNG, a liquid. The cost of CNG is less than LNG, but still costly. CNG takes up more space than gasoline, a challenge for small vehicles.

There are three major regional markets for natural gas: North America, Europe, and Asia. North America is increasingly self-sufficient, with both the United States and Canada being major producers. Europe relies upon imports, especially from Russia. Their supply is susceptible to political pressures and they are looking to the United States as a supplier. China, Korea, and Japan are large consumers, and heavily dependent on LNG imports. Australia, Malaysia, and Indonesia are major exporters of LNG.

Until a world market develops, countries such as China that rely on imports will face challenges. For example, China has sought to import NG from Russia, but Russia will only sell to China at the high price it charges Europe. As well, China is among the countries with shale rock formations that likely hold huge reserves of natural gas. In fact, China likely has 50% larger reserves than the United States. However, China faces obstacles to extracting its reserves, including limited water and pipeline infrastructure, high population density, and immature fracking technology (Tian, Wang, Krupnick, & Liu, 2014).

Natural gas is not without its challenges. It is essentially methane, a potent greenhouse gas if it leaks into the atmosphere. The use of natural gas produces carbon emissions, although considerably less than coal or oil per unit of use. Natural gas price can be highly volatile. Fracking uses chemicals in the process of injecting water into cracks in the rock to prop them open and extract oil and natural gas. The method uses large quantities of water, as well as the potential for polluting water. Some regions have reported earthquakes in the vicinity of fracking activity. Nearby residents experience degradation of the environment, including the landscape, as well as construction traffic and noise. Fracking technology has been around since the late 1940s, but the breakthrough, and the controversy, have come only in the last decade when fracking combined with horizontal drilling took exploration for oil and natural gas from a gamble to a near certainty. If there is to be a Golden Age for natural gas, its advantages will have to outweigh society's environmental concerns. Just as nuclear energy has proved a lightning rod for fears both real (Fukushima) and fictional (*The China Syndrome*), fracking has ignited fears depicted in the documentary *Gasland* and *Gasland II*, as well as *The Promised Land*, a fictional account of drilling in Pennsylvania's Marcellus shale. New York state banned fracking, citizens of Denton, Texas, invoked home rule and voted to forbid further drilling, and in North Carolina, after the state gave the go-ahead for fracking, one county placed a three-year moratorium on it. LNG has its own environmental concerns. These concerns are about the construction and use of LNG ports and transportation, with risks of spills, fires, and explosions.

As with other sources of energy, we have to ask what the alternative will be if we reject using a potentially plentiful source of energy such as shale gas. Coal and nuclear energy as electricity-generating fuels have their own risks, which we explore in Chapters 7 and 8. Some advocate exclusive use of renewables and energy efficiency, which we evaluate in Chapters 9–11. They too have their downsides. The repeated theme of this book is that we must consider all available sources as part of our energy portfolio.

The next section of this chapter provides a brief economic history of the natural gas market from its beginnings as a regulated industry to the present, with competition playing an ever greater role. We then review production and the supply chain. We go on to cost, introducing the measure of levelized cost to compare natural gas to other energy sources. Next, we incorporate environmental considerations, including GHG emissions. We then examine the determination of price for a variety of market structures. We close with a summary.

Brief economic history of natural gas use

Throughout history, there have been reports of fires that were likely due to methane seepages associated with natural gas formations. Early on, natural gas was viewed as a nuisance. Natural gas found in conjunction with oil would often be *flared*—the controlled burning of natural gas produced in association with oil—or *vented*—the controlled release of unburned gases into the atmosphere—because its commercial value was not sufficient to pay for the infrastructure needed to get it to final users.

The first intentional drilling for natural gas was in the upstate New York town of Fredonia, by William A. Hart in 1827. The first use was predominantly for street lighting, until electricity began to replace it in the 1890s. In 1855, Robert Bunsen is widely credited with inventing the Bunsen burner, demonstrating the potential for natural gas to provide fuel for heating and cooking.

In 1891, the first pipeline was built, a necessary development in order to transport gas into individual houses. However, it took until after World War II for pipeline construction technology to advance to the point where numerous pipelines could be constructed. Most of the U.S. interstate pipeline system was constructed in the 1950s and 1960s.

Natural history

Natural gas gets its name because it is a naturally occurring gas. It is a mixture of hydrocarbon gases, with methane predominant (70–90%), ethane, propane, butane, and pentane, as well as carbon dioxide, nitrogen, and hydrogen sulfide.[2] The mix can vary, with "wet" natural gas containing hydrocarbon gases other than methane, "dry" natural gas almost all methane, "sour" natural gas containing sulfur, and "sweet" natural gas not containing sulfur. As with crude oil, "sweet" is better than "sour" in that it is necessary to remove impurities such as hydrogen sulfide in order to use the fuel. "Dry" natural gas has the advantage that it is closer to "pipeline-ready." With "wet" natural gas, it is necessary to separate methane from other *natural gas liquids* (NGLs)—compounds such as ethane, butane, and propane—some of which might corrode the pipeline, but which also have commercial value. On balance, wet natural gas can actually be more profitable, especially when natural gas prices are low and the price of NGLs high.

It is common to find natural gas together with oil, as both are fossil fuels formed over millions of years from the decomposition of plant and animal organic matter. Natural gas can also form where there are coal deposits, also a fossil fuel. While the value of NG as a fuel was first identified in the mid-1800s, it became a large-scale industry by the

1920s. NG prospered in the 1980s once it transitioned from a regulated industry to a deregulated one. Today, it is accelerating in its development with the massive increase in commercially feasible production.

Figure 6.1 contrasts the geology of conventional sources of natural gas with shale gas. Conventional gas forms in permeable rock formations that allow the gas to migrate until it reaches a cap rock, or seal, often made of shale, that prevents further migration. Gas that initially forms in shale cannot migrate very far, because shale is relatively impermeable. Prior to the advance in fracturing technology, shale gas was not economical to bring to the surface. Shale gas was originally categorized as an unconventional gas source, but that distinction is fading as U.S. production from shale now exceeds conventional sources.

Figure 6.2 shows conventional and unconventional sources of natural gas.

Shale gas is the largest unconventional source. Other unconventional sources include tight gas, coalbed methane, and gas hydrates. Tight gas is natural gas trapped in tight rock formations, while shale gas comes from the source rock itself. Source rock is the rock in which the natural gas actually formed. Unlike conventional natural gas, which is relatively easy to bring to the surface after vertical drilling, unconventional gas requires greater effort, such as hydraulic fracturing.

Coalbed methane is methane that formed alongside coal. When the coal was mined, the methane would be released. For many years, this methane was viewed as a nuisance, as it presented dangers to coal miners, such as gas explosions. Coalbed methane is "sweet" gas that is relatively free of hydrogen sulfides. Its commercial feasibility depends upon the price of natural gas. With the great increase in natural gas using hydraulic fracturing, there has been less extraction of coalbed methane in recent years.

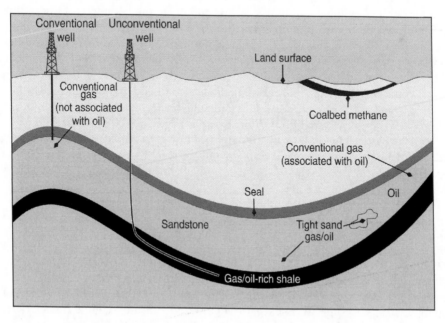

Figure 6.1 Schematic of the geology of natural gas resources. Reprinted from U.S. EIA (2016a).

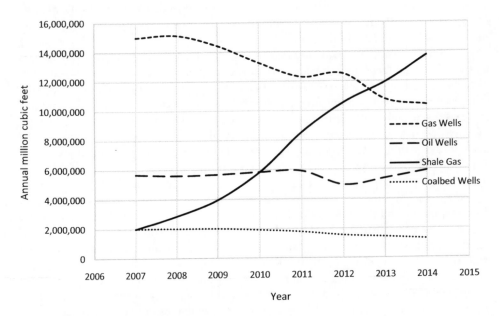

Figure 6.2 U.S. natural gas by well type (2007–2015). Adapted from U.S. EIA (2016b).

Gas hydrates represent still another potential unconventional source of natural gas. Methane hydrates are the most recently discovered source of natural gas. This source is found within icy crystals found in the Arctic and deep underwater. Commercial feasibility will depend upon how much natural gas can be recovered, as well as the cost premium for recovering this source, given its remote location. From an environmental perspective, there needs to be additional study of the role of gas hydrates in the carbon cycle. To the extent that the hydrates sequester carbon, extracting natural gas from hydrates could result in large releases of methane into the ocean floor, the ocean, or the atmosphere, and the threat of accelerated climate change.

Figure 6.2 shows the rapid growth of shale gas between 2007 and 2015. The large supplies have reduced price dramatically. In turn, low prices led to a sharp drop in new drilling. Drilling continued where shale oil and gas can be obtained at a low cost, such as the Barnett formation in Texas, but diminished in the high-cost Bakken Shield of North Dakota.

Regulation and deregulation

Natural gas had natural monopoly characteristics from its first commercial use in the 1850s until its deregulation in the 1980s. Because large amounts of capital were required for extraction, processing, and transport, one company could produce natural gas at a lower long-run average cost (LRAC) than if multiple companies competed in the same geographic area. Customers bought natural gas bundled with pipeline transportation. As pipeline distances increased, municipalities and eventually states recognized the need to regulate rates to prevent the exercise of monopoly power.

Box 6.1 Drilling down for the details behind pipeline economies of scale

A study by Leslie Cookenboo (1955) uses an engineering approach to examine fuel pipeline economies of scale. Pipeline throughput depends upon the diameter of the pipeline and the horsepower used to propel the fuel through the pipeline. For a given horsepower, throughput increases faster than pipeline diameter, hence there are economies of scale. Cookenboo (1955) examines oil pipelines, but the same reasoning applies to NG.

As pipelines extended across state borders, the U.S. Supreme Court ruled that interstate pipelines were subject to the Interstate Commerce Clause, so that natural gas was subject to federal regulation. In 1935, the Federal Trade Commission passed the Public Utility Holding Company Act (PUHCA) to limit the exercise of market power from mergers across state borders, and in 1938, with the passage of the Natural Gas Act, authority was given to the Federal Power Commission (FPC) to regulate rates for natural gas transported across state borders.

The 1938 Act regulated prices that pipelines could charge distribution utilities, but not the *wellhead price*, the price at the point of production. In the 1954 Phillips decision, the U.S. Supreme Court ruled that wellhead prices were subject to regulation. Regulation mimicked that of the electricity industry, with each natural gas producer receiving a rate of return based upon cost of service. However, unlike the electric industry, or for that matter interstate pipelines, there were a very large number of independent natural gas producers, rendering the determination of rates a large administrative burden. The regulatory approach created an unsettled industry.

In the 1970s, when oil prices soared, many customers turned to natural gas, including industrial customers needing boiler fuel and residential customers seeking to avoid increases in electricity prices linked to oil-fired generation. Natural gas was particularly good value for customers, as in 1959, the FPC, unable to keep up with the backlog of rate cases, had implemented "temporary" price ceilings. With natural gas prices capped, however, producers had no incentive to increase production, resulting in shortages. The FPC tried regional price caps to reduce the amount of regulation required, at the same time allowing the price of natural gas to double. The regional caps left intrastate, but not interstate, rates open to competition, causing severe shortages in states without their own natural gas producers. The end result was that customers abandoned natural gas as a viable energy source.

Relief for the natural gas industry slowly came with the passage of the 1978 Natural Gas Policy Act as part of the National Energy Act, the same Act that required utilities to purchase electricity from independent power producers and showed the feasibility of electricity deregulation. The Federal Energy Regulatory Commission (FERC) replaced the FPC, with the responsibility of phasing out NG price controls in favor of market-determined prices. During the phase-out period, there were challenges such as differentiating old gas, still subject to price regulation, and new gas that was not. Pipeline transporters challenged "take-or-pay" contracts forcing them to pay for gas even when prices rose and customers no longer demanded the gas.

A series of acts deregulated the NG industry, leading to its current structure. FERC Orders 436 and 636 gradually transformed the pipeline industry from a *merchant* role to a *transport-only* role. Prior to these acts, pipelines were in the merchant business of transporting and selling natural gas. In FERC Order 436, pipelines could voluntarily offer to transport natural gas for downstream customers. FERC Order 636 subsequently required *open access*, allowing pipeline customers to choose their transportation arrangements. Natural gas changed from a single bundled commodity delivered from wellhead to final customer to an unbundled product, with separate prices at the producer and pipeline stages. The Natural Gas Wellhead and Decontrol Act of 1989 decontrolled wellhead prices, with all "first sales" deregulated by 1993. Sales by pipelines and local distribution companies were excluded as they were not "first sales."

FERC Order 636 was the culmination of deregulation, requiring pipelines to offer nondiscriminatory pricing to customers. It ultimately established a market for these services, including electronic bulletin boards showing prices for unused capacity as well as available transport services where customers who experienced a change in demand no longer wished to purchase pipeline capacity.

Natural gas production

Supply chain

Figure 6.3 shows a natural gas supply chain.

We can envision the chain as "from wellhead to burner tip," beginning with drilling and well completion—the wellhead—to the final customer—the burner tip.

We begin with upstream production. Nonassociated natural gas is that found without oil. Associated natural gas is natural gas and oil found together, in which case it is necessary to separate the two, as well as to remove water. If the natural gas found with oil is not commercially valuable, producers might use venting or flaring although regulations increasingly prohibit such practices to reduce methane emissions, a potent GHG. Via small pipelines, producers transport natural gas from individual wells to a centralized processing station in the *gathering stage*. Assuming the natural gas is commercially valuable, *processing* separates pure natural gas—methane—from other natural gas

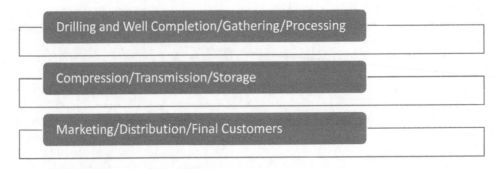

Figure 6.3 The natural gas supply chain.

liquids, such as propane or butane. Depending on the price of NGLs, they may be disposed of or sold. If the natural gas is sour, processing separates hydrocarbons and sulfides. Producers retain and sell NGLs, sulfur and other by-products when they have commercial value.

The midstream stage is primarily transport, with pipelines the primary means of transmission. It is first necessary to compress natural gas to facilitate transportation or to store it for later shipment. Most commonly, storage is underground in depleted oil and gas fields, aquifers, and salt caverns. Above-ground tanks also provide storage for liquefied or gas inventories. Mercaptan, a harmless chemical containing sulfur, adds a sulfur smell to the otherwise odorless gas to help detect leaks.

The distribution stage begins at the "city gate" where natural gas leaves the transmission pipeline for delivery to the local distribution company (LDC). The LDC can also store natural gas, in anticipation of peak demand during the winter heating season. Finally, the LDC distributes natural gas through small pipelines to end-use customers, including residential, commercial, and industrial sectors.

The motive for deregulation is to reduce cost, as compared to a regulated monopoly. Natural gas deregulation has done so, joining the deregulation success stories of trucking, the financial industry, and the airline industry. Under regulation, customers simply accepted the regulated price. Pipelines accepted the regulated wellhead price, distributors accepted the regulated pipeline price, and end-customers accepted the regulated distributed price. With deregulation, price at one or more of these stages may be determined by bilateral negotiations between a supplier and a customer, or a spot market that determines price based on multiple suppliers and customers.

Local distribution still has natural monopoly characteristics, as it would not be cost-effective to have competing distribution pipelines serving small retail customers. Most customers still buy natural gas from the LDC at a bundled price that includes not only the cost of the distribution, but the cost of the fuel. Nevertheless, some states allow marketers to offer end-customers a choice of suppliers.

As of 2014, about half of all U.S. states allowed retail competition. Figure 6.4 shows the top five U.S. states where customers who are eligible to choose their natural gas supplier choose to participate.

Georgia has the highest percentage of participating customers, followed by Ohio. California has the largest number of eligible customers, but the vast majority of customers stay with their incumbent LDC.

Processing

The natural gas transported through the transmission pipeline system and used in final product form for heating, cooking, and electricity generation, is pure methane. Raw natural gas, the natural gas that is initially extracted, is primarily methane, but needs to have impurities removed before it can be transported to or used by final customers.

Where natural gas is found with oil, it may have dissolved in the oil or may have separated from the oil. Where it is dissolved, it is necessary to separate the two and sell them if they are of sufficient commercial value. It is also necessary to separate other impurities including water, natural gas liquids (NGLs), and sulfur and carbon dioxide. NGLs such as propane and butane may have commercial value in themselves.

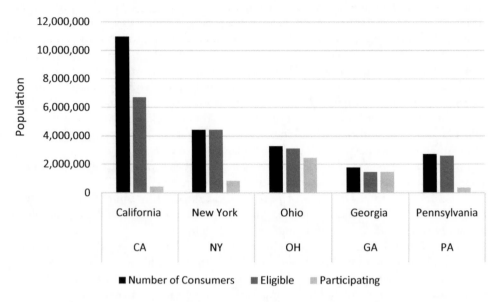

Figure 6.4 Top five states with participants in a residential choice program, 2015. Adapted from U.S. EIA (2016c).

If the natural gas is sour and contains hydrogen sulfides, the sulfides must be removed. Sour natural gas has a sulfur smell and is also corrosive. Again, it may be possible to collect the sulfur and market it separately.

With increasing concern about GHGs, flaring or venting is undesirable. At a substantial cost, *carbon capture and storage* (CCS) can capture CO_2 and then sequester it underground or in the ocean. Norway's Statoil uses CCS for oil and natural gas extracted from the North Sea. Note that these processes have their downsides, in addition to adding to cost. They may require large amounts of water, and there could be leaks from sequestered carbon over time (Neslen, 2015).

During transport of the natural gas through small gathering pipelines, it is necessary to prevent the natural gas from cooling to the point where it solidifies into gas hydrates, which can clog the pipeline. Pipelines use heaters to prevent the natural gas from cooling and scrubbers to separate out sand.

Delivery system

Natural gas is harder to transport than oil. It is much less dense and harder to handle. Compression condenses it before transportation. Pipelines transport the bulk of natural gas. Shipping by truck is an expensive alternative to pipelines, requiring compressing the gas and keeping it at a very low temperature. However, trucks may be necessary at times of peak demand or where pipeline construction lags new production.

Between continents, it may be more economical to transform natural gas from its gaseous state into liquefied natural gas (LNG) and use tankers for transport. LNG is a higher-cost alternative. In addition to the costs of liquefaction before exporting and regasifying after importing, and the cost of specially built tankers, LNG requires its own infrastructure including LNG ports and extensive safety measures.

The United States has developed a national network of transmission pipelines akin to an interstate highway system for gas. These pipelines typically have large capacities and stretch for hundreds or thousands of miles. During the many years of regulation when the transmission pipelines served a bundled merchant function, the system was subject to regulation as a natural monopoly. In some cases, the local utility controlled both gas and electric, a phenomenon that is resurfacing with consolidation in the electric utility industry and the increased use of natural gas to generate electric power.

Natural gas supplies and pipelines are complements. However, with the fracking boom, natural gas supplies have grown much faster than pipeline capacity. Fracking is a relatively quick process while capacity expansion takes a longer time. And as with oil pipelines, there is considerable opposition to pipeline siting. Consider the Atlantic Coast Pipeline that would transport shale gas from West Virginia to eastern North Carolina via Virginia. Residents near Shenandoah National Park in Virginia protested about the project, asking that the route be changed and trying to prevent participating companies from coming onto their properties.

Cost

In the United States, the share of natural gas used to generate electricity has increased dramatically in recent years, mostly at the expense of coal. Figure 6.5 shows the trends in the use of natural gas and other fuels with which it competes.

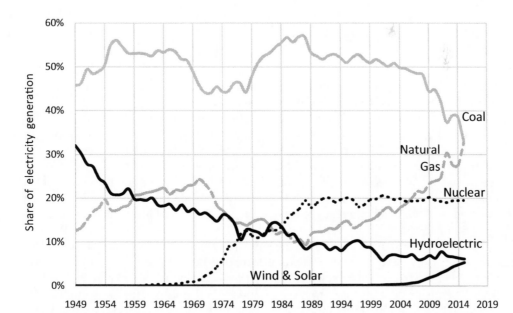

Figure 6.5 Annual share of total U.S. electricity generation by source (1949–2015). Adapted from U.S. EIA (2016d).

For many years, the share of coal in electricity generation hovered around 50%, with natural gas at most 25%. The most recent EIA statistics show that natural gas and coal each account for about one-third of electricity generation, with natural gas likely to overtake coal in the coming years. Two factors are primarily responsible for the rise of natural gas and the fall of coal during this period. Natural gas prices fell to historically low levels, as supply and reserves grew with the use of hydraulic fracturing. At the same time, concerns grew over the environmental consequences of coal use, resulting in accelerated plant retirements, conversions so that plants could run on natural gas rather than coal, and cancellations of new plants. Even though the United States did not impose a price for carbon emissions, utilities reduced their use of coal given the anticipation of future carbon controls.

Renewables, primarily wind and solar, have been rising dramatically in percentage terms, but from a low base, and make up a relatively small but growing proportion of electricity generation. Given that they are not available at all times and do not serve baseload, they compete with natural gas more than coal, an unintended consequence that would not please those who view coal as the fuel most in need of replacement.

Levelized cost

Levelized cost provides a simple technique for comparing the average cost of generating electricity using different fuels over the plant's lifetime. It shows the minimum price at which electricity must sell to break even. Equation (6.1) shows the formula for the levelized cost of electricity (LCOE), where costs include capital expenditures (I), operating and maintenance costs (M), and fuel expenditures (F):

$$\text{LCOE} = \frac{\sum_{t=1}^{n} \frac{I_t + M_t + F_t}{(1+r)^t}}{\sum_{t=1}^{n} \frac{E_t}{(1+r)^t}} \tag{6.1}$$

LCOE is total cost per unit of electricity generation (E), with numerator and denominator in present value (PV) terms.

Figure 6.6 shows levelized cost for plants entering service in 2022 (in \$2015/MWh) for natural gas, nuclear, and renewables plants.[3] Levelized cost was developed to compare the cost of conventional fuels that are available at all times and are under the control of the electricity dispatcher. This approach is less well suited for renewables for reasons we will discuss in Chapter 9, including intermittency. Nor do the comparisons reflect unpriced externality costs, although they do include priced externalities as well as subsidies. Also remember that Figure 6.6 is a 2016 forecast of plants that would begin operation in 2022.

The main point is that natural gas is the lowest-cost conventional fuel to produce electricity by a wide margin. The lowest-cost natural gas technology is a combined cycle plant. A combined cycle plant contains both a gas and steam turbine. Its efficiency comes from recapturing the waste heat from the gas turbine and reusing it for the steam turbine.

Should electric utilities needing additional capacity build natural gas plants exclusively? As we will see, natural gas prices can be highly volatile. Furthermore, if there is carbon pricing, the cost of natural gas would increase; nuclear energy and renewables would not.

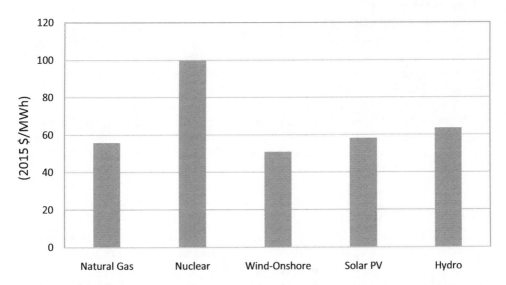

Figure 6.6 Estimated levelized cost of new electric generating technologies in 2020 (2011 $/MWH). Adapted from https://www.eia.gov/forecasts/aeo/pdf/electricity_ generation.pdf Table 1a p. 6.

Also, the production costs of renewables have been falling dramatically. Battery storage is likely to alleviate the intermittency problem eventually.

An additional justification for not relying exclusively on natural gas is diversification. During Hurricane Katrina in 2005, U.S. production shut down in anticipation of the hurricane and many processing facilities in the Gulf of Mexico were damaged, leading to temporary shortages of oil and natural gas. Similarly, the northeast United States was unable to obtain sufficient natural gas when facilities froze during the 2014 Polar Vortex. Where natural gas was available in the Northeast, price was as high as $100/MMBtu, as compared to $4/MMBtu before the event.

Capital costs

Natural gas plants traditionally had relatively low capital costs and relatively high fuel costs, making them better suited to run for a limited number of peak or shoulder hours than as baseload plants. Hydraulic fracturing has changed the equation by bringing down the cost of going deeper for natural gas. Fracking has a higher capital cost than conventional techniques that extracted supplies nearer to the surface. However, the lower fuel price due to the increase in actual supplies as well as estimated reserves has brought down the cost of natural gas sufficiently that it can now be considered for base-load electricity production.

As natural gas plants have not operated as extensively in the past, it remains to be seen how reliable they will be when they run continuously. We can anticipate new NG technologies specifically for baseloads.

Processing costs

NG processing is the cleaning stage between production and transmission. Until deregulation, the producer typically did the processing. With deregulation, producers often sell off the processing stage to concentrate on extraction. With the boom in shale exploration, Texas continues to be a major processor. Processors generally locate near production but there are exceptions such as the largest processor, located in northern Illinois in order to distribute its products to Chicago.

The Marcellus shale covers much of Pennsylvania and extends into New York and other surrounding states. They have limited processing capacity that will need to expand if it is to keep up with production. North Dakota also experienced a shale boom but had limited processing facilities.

Capacity and reliability

As the role of natural gas increases, electric utilities will increasingly have to consider its reliability as compared to other fuels. It has much more limited storage than coal, for example, and so utilities are dependent on secure pipeline deliveries. Weather events, such as extreme cold or hurricanes, can cause interruptions. Fortunately, shale gas has led to a more geographically dispersed supply, so there should still be natural gas available even in extreme weather.

There is also greater use of small-scale natural gas plants and *distributed generation*. Distributed generation is typically small-scale production that is built closer to where it is needed. Combined cycle natural gas plants can be built at small scale as well as utility scale.

Electric utilities will have to examine the availability of pipelines and need for increasing infrastructure such as additional processing or greater pipeline capacity. They will also need to consider holding excess reserves in the event of an interruption of their main supply. And electric utility system operators may need to have access to information on natural gas supplies elsewhere in case of emergency needs.

Natural gas will increasingly act as a reserve for solar during summer peak periods. It also has other uses, including heating and transportation. These uses are also expected to grow, which could, however, conflict with availability for electricity generation.

Greenhouse gas emissions and other environmental impacts

Natural gas is a cleaner fuel than coal or oil according to most observers. As an electricity-generating fuel, natural gas releases almost 50% less CO_2 than coal and 25% less than oil and gasoline. Table 6.1 shows a comparison of CO_2 emissions per kWh.

As regulations tighten on CO_2, sulfur, mercury, and nitrous oxides (NOx and NO_2), natural gas will become ever more advantageous as compared to coal, even if carbon emissions remain unpriced. Natural gas releases less NOx than coal, and almost no sulfur. Also, it is relatively free of the particulates that coal emits, associated with health issues such as asthma.

Howarth, Santoro, and Ingraffea (2011) questioned the environmental superiority of natural gas as compared to coal. They noted that a molecule of methane is estimated to be 21 times as potent at trapping heat as CO_2 over a 100–year period. They have a further concern about methane leaks in the drilling and distribution stages.

Table 6.1 Pounds of CO_2 emitted per million Btu of energy for various fuels

Coal (anthracite)	228.6
Coal (bituminous)	205.7
Coal (lignite)	215.4
Coal (sub-bituminous)	214.3
Diesel fuel and heating oil	161.3
Gasoline	157.2
Propane	139.0
Natural gas	117.0

U.S. EIA Frequently Asked Questions (2016) https://www.eia.gov/tools/faqs/faq.php?id=73&t=11.

Their position received vehement rebuttals. Methane dissipates from the atmosphere faster, and most of the methane in natural gas is consumed when natural gas is burned. Howarth and his colleagues used a 20-year analysis period rather than the more typical 100-year comparison, which makes methane look worse. The authors have also acknowledged the weakness of available data on methane leaks.

Both the U.S. Department of Energy and the U.S. Environmental Protection Agency have performed comprehensive studies of hydraulic fracturing. The DOE's National Energy Technology Laboratory released a 2014 technical report on a field study of a fracking operation in Pennsylvania's Marcellus shale over a one-year period, and found no detectable chemicals in groundwater or surface waters (U.S. DOE, 2014). In 2015, the U.S. EPA (2015) completed a five-year study examining the shale gas lifecycle at five stages: water acquisition, chemical mixing, well injection, flowback and produced water (wastewater), and wastewater treatment and waste disposal. It released preliminary findings in 2015 that found that the risk of contamination by hydraulic fracturing activities was very low. In 2016, they removed the conclusion that fracking did not contaminate water, finding insufficient evidence to make that claim (US EPA 2016).

Other findings are also mixed. Drollette et al. (2015) found no groundwater contamination attributable to fracking in the Marcellus shale region of Pennsylvania. However, DiGiulio and Jackson (2016) did find drinking water contamination due to fracking in Pavillion, Wyoming.

Fracking may trigger earthquakes. Ohio reported a possible link. In Oklahoma, there has been a dramatic increase in earthquakes that coincide with the use of hydraulic fracturing. While these earthquakes are generally mild, several earthquakes registered over 5 on the Richter scale, including one in September 2016. Clearly, fracking needs to avoid seismically active sites. The current debate is whether fracking is at fault (the author could not resist the pun) or whether the quakes are attributable to wastewater injection that can accompany fracking or conventional drilling.

There are also concerns about the large quantities of water used in the injection process. Water shortages are an issue in themselves. Water used for drilling is not available for agriculture. And water prices do not usually reflect its social cost. At a cost, companies can recycle more of the injected water, or make greater use of waste water. We can expect continued controversy over the effects of fracking, and continued studies of its benefits and costs (Jackson et al., 2014; Sovacool, 2014).

Determining price

Natural gas was regulated similarly to electricity until FERC gradually deregulated its sales beginning in 1978. Local distribution companies not subject to competition are still subject to rate-of-return regulation. We provide an intentionally brief introduction to regulation of natural gas, deferring a detailed look at rate-of-return regulation until we examine the traditional regulated electric utility in Chapter 12.

Determining price under regulation

Figure 6.7 shows a natural monopoly subject to rate-of-return regulation.

The natural monopoly has economies of scale, shown by declining long-run average total cost (LRATC) that justifies allowing a single firm to serve the market. In a competitive market, the hallmark of efficiency is that price equals marginal cost, corresponding to the socially efficient point where LRMC crosses D at point S, corresponding to quantity Q_s and price P_s. However, for the natural monopoly, LRATC is above LRMC at this point, resulting in a loss for the firm. While we will go into detail in Chapter 12 on how marginal cost pricing can overcome this dilemma, regulators often favor the simplicity of setting price equal to AC at point F, corresponding to Q_f and P_f, which results in a zero economic profit, comparable to the normal profit of competitive firms.

In addition to violating $P = MC$, another potential weakness of rate-of-return regulation is that if a firm can recover its capital costs, including a competitive rate of return, it has little reason to minimize those costs. Incentive-based programs, discussed in Chapter 12, attempt to correct this shortcoming by allowing firms to keep a portion of any decrease in cost or bear a portion of any increase in cost.

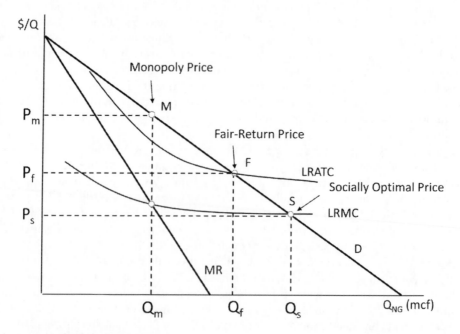

Figure 6.7 Regulated monopoly.

Box 6.2 Is the warm weather adjustment clause a cold concept?

Consider the weather-adjusted rate mechanism (WARM) employed by the Public Utility Commission of Oregon as well as other states and counties (although with less catchy acronyms). NG LDCs sell most of their NG during the winter heating season. In warm winters, they have below-average sales (increasingly likely if we are trending towards warmer winters due to climate change) and in cold winters, they have above-average sales. Under WARM, the Public Utilities Commission increases the per-unit price in warm winters and decreases the price in cold winters, to level out the revenues received by the company. LDCs argue that on balance, the effects cancel, so that the effects are a wash for customers.

This approach has some adverse effects. First, the price is only determined ex post, which is to say after the event. Customers set their thermostats based on the tariff price, only to get an unexpected surcharge in warm winters or rebate in cold winters. Second, the company has no incentive to take actions that might save customers money, such as taking advantage of lower prices at the wellhead from producers anticipating a warmer than normal winter or using derivatives contracts to reduce the risk of price volatility.

The policy is opposite to what would happen in a competitive market. Ski resorts are dealing with the effects of warmer winters and fewer customers. Imagine if the customers who did come received a note after the ski season with an extra assessment so the resort could stay in business. Instead, we would expect ski resorts to bear the risk, making more artificial snow, building indoor ski resorts as they do in Dubai, developing summer attractions, or going out of business.

Market determination of price

With deregulation, the basis of today's U.S. natural gas prices is the price at Henry Hub in Louisiana, the main U.S. distribution center. Figure 6.8 shows the decline in U.S. prices beginning in 2008, with the advent of fracking.

Other countries that do not have domestic supplies or do not make use of hydraulic fracturing have higher natural gas prices. Japan has limited and declining domestic supplies, and has been the world's largest importer of LNG. In the wake of the Fukushima disaster, they had to step up their LNG imports to record levels despite high prices, then in the range of $16–18/MMBtu as compared to the U.S. price of $2–4/MMBtu during that period. As of 2016, LNG supplies had increased substantially, and Japan was paying closer to $6/MMBtu (Meyer, Hume, & Sheppard, 2016).

Japan imports from a variety of countries, including Malaysia, Australia, the Middle East, and Russia. Russia had a practice of using long-term natural gas contracts tied to the price of oil rather than natural gas when they faced little competition from other countries. This practice increased the price they could charge when oil prices were high as compared to natural gas prices, and also reduced price volatility. As natural gas exports increase, Russia's price will have to compete with natural gas supplies of other countries.

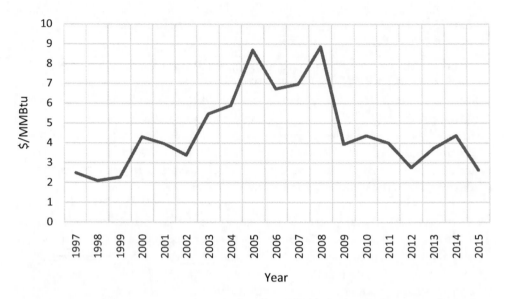

Figure 6.8 Trends in natural gas prices. Adapted from U.S. EIA (2016f).

Price depends upon demand and supply. Energy is an input, and so demand is a *derived demand* based upon the demand for output. There is utility from using an appliance, and the consumer is for the most part indifferent about the source of the energy to run the appliance. There may be some consumers willing to pay more for a less polluting source of energy, although most attempts by utilities to provide consumers with the option to pay a premium towards greater use of "green" energy have not made major inroads. There may also be differences in appliance performance, such as perceived or actual differences in comfort when using gas heat vs. electric heat. But for simplicity, the baseline assumption is that where the effects of the fuel input on appliance performance are indistinguishable, consumers seek the lowest-priced fuel.

In the short run, consumers have limited ability to switch fuels, but in the long run, they can make changes as they buy new energy appliances or replace existing ones. The most important energy choice that residential consumers face long term is the choice of fuel for heating.

Consumers have increasing choice on vehicle fuel. At a substantial cost, it is possible to convert existing vehicles to run on natural gas. Flex-fuel vehicles can run on more than one type of fuel. Natural gas buses run on CNG. One reason buses are more prevalent than cars is that it takes a large amount of space to store the natural gas. As with any alternative fuel vehicle, there is the chicken-and-egg problem of infrastructure. The limited number of refueling stations reduces the willingness of consumers to buy the vehicles. However, the small number of vehicles limits the willingness of filling stations to install separate natural gas fuel pumps (Corts, 2011).

In a competitive environment, price equals marginal cost. So at each stage of production, there would be no markup of price over cost. Gas field producers would make gas available at their marginal cost, processors would add the marginal cost of processing, transmission pipelines would add the marginal cost of transmission, and distributors such as electric utilities would add the marginal cost of their distribution pipeline services. In states that allow retail marketing, the marketers would shop around for the lowest-cost source of natural gas, and add in their own marginal costs to the price.

At any of these stages, a supplier with market power could mark up the price above marginal cost. If there is only one natural gas pipeline serving the local distribution company, it will charge a monopoly price unless regulation prevents it. If there are two or more pipeline companies, that may not be enough for competition. In Chapter 5, we examined the cartel and dominant firm price leadership models. Other oligopoly models may better fit natural gas pipeline decision-making. There are several *duopoly* models that predict behavior when there are two firms in the industry. The *Cournot model* assumes that one firm will react to the other firm's output, while the *Bertrand model* assumes that one firm will respond to the other's price. Increasingly, economists use game theory to model oligopoly strategies. If games have a *Nash equilibrium*, the individual firm decisions will lead to a stable outcome. We develop Cournot, Bertrand, and Nash equilibriums in Chapter 13 on electricity restructuring and deregulation.

Firms determine how much to buy by choosing the point where marginal revenue product (MRP) equals marginal factor cost (MFC). Monopsony models apply if there is only a single buyer. Japan is the primary buyer of LNG, and is able to choose from a number of suppliers.

In Figure 6.9, monopsony equilibrium is at point A, where MRP = MFC. Monopsony is the mirror image of monopoly, except that now there is a single buyer. Where MR was twice as steep as demand with monopoly, MFC is twice as steep as supply for the monopsonist. As the monopsonist increases its purchases, price increases and MFC increases twice as fast.[4] The company buys Q_{ms} at price P_{ms} corresponding to point B, whereas the competitive equilibrium at point C corresponds to a larger quantity of Q_c and a higher price P_c. Deadweight loss due to monopsony is the shaded triangle ABC.

Example 6.1

Referring to Figure 6.9, suppose that Japan paid $16/MMBtu in 2012. In that same year, Japan spent $75 billion on LNG, implying that it purchased approximately 4.7 billion MMBtu. Suppose that in 2013, Japan increased its purchases to 5 billion MMBtu, which pushed up the price to $16.5/MMBtu. Find the MFC.

Solution

$$MFC = \frac{[(\$16.5 \times 5 \text{ billion MMBtu} - (\$16 \times 4.7 \text{ billion MMBtu}]}{(5 \text{ billion MMBtu} - 4.7 \text{ billion MMBtu})}$$

$$= \$24.3 / \text{MMBtu}$$

Note that the incremental units actually cost Japan more than the price of $16.5/MMBtu, making it very expensive for a monopsonist to increase purchases.

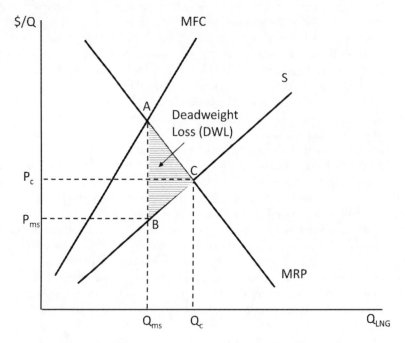

Figure 6.9 Determination of LNG monopsony price and quantity.

In fact, Japan has been reducing its LNG imports, not surprising given the high MFC it faced. In addition to slowly returning to nuclear energy, they have stepped up their use of renewables, increased energy conservation and efficiency, and are restructuring their electricity industry to be more competitive.

If there is one seller and one buyer, the situation is *bilateral monopoly*. An example is when a pipeline is a monopoly seller, and the LDC, the only buyer, is a monopsony. In this case, price can be anywhere between marginal cost and monopoly price, depending upon the relative negotiating skills. One convenient assumption is to assume both sides have equal negotiating abilities, in which case the price is midway between the monopoly and monopsony price.

The "holdup problem" from transaction cost economics is another example of market power. A customer buying from a distribution pipeline may be able to pay a low price if the pipeline has no alternative customers. *Asset specificity* refers to whether or not an asset has value in an alternative use. If it does not, the buyer may be able to gain the advantage, as the seller is better off with any price above variable cost than the alternative of receiving no revenue at all.

Where possible, it is desirable from an efficiency standpoint to have a competitive market, rather than monopoly, monopsony or bilateral negotiations. The competitive model fits U.S. wellhead production of natural gas. The EU does not have the same degree of competition. LNG accounts for about 20% of its supplies (Ratner, Belkin, Nichol, & Woehrel, 2013). Some of its supplies come from Russia with the threat of interruptions if countries do not support Russia's policies.

As the United States builds LNG export capacity, the global price gap will narrow. A small number of U.S. export terminals are operational, and many others have received approval. However, with low natural gas prices and the downturn in U.S. drilling activity, the approved plants may never be built. U.S. facilities are only part of the expansion of a global NG market. Other countries (importers) also have to build infrastructure, a chicken-and-egg world. So while regional price differences have been narrowing, natural gas is not yet a fully integrated global market.

Summary

Natural gas is at the forefront of energy discussions. The International Energy Agency (IEA) foresaw a Golden Age of Gas with enough natural gas reserves to meet demand for about 100 years. However, the key to the Golden Age is the controversial technology of hydraulic fracturing.

Conventional natural gas formed in permeable rock formations that allowed it to flow close to the surface, while gas from shale rock is far below the surface in tight rock formations. Drillers often find natural gas and oil together. They also find natural gas associated with coal beds. Unassociated natural gas refers to reserves that contain only natural gas.

Unconventional natural gas such as shale gas and coalbed methane refers to natural gas that requires unconventional technologies because it lies below the earth's surface in relatively impermeable rock formations. Given its prevalence, we can expect that shale gas extracted by fracking will lose its unconventional label.

Pipeline-ready natural gas, or methane, is dry natural gas, while wet natural gas contains NGLs. NGLs can compete with similar oil hydrocarbons, making wet natural gas sometimes more valuable than dry natural gas despite its higher processing costs.

Beginning in the 1930s, there was regulation of the natural gas industry as a natural monopoly along similar lines to the electricity industry. Natural gas transmission had the characteristics of a natural monopoly, with economies of scale justifying a small number of transmission pipelines.

The 1950s U.S. Supreme Court Phillips decision extended federal regulation to prices at the wellhead. During the 1970s, a tumultuous period in the oil markets, consumers turned to natural gas, but government-imposed price controls led to shortages and the abandonment of natural gas as a viable fuel for heating.

Price controls were gradually lifted, and by the 1980s, the FERC allowed for competition at the transmission level as well as at the wellhead. Where all stages of natural gas production had been bundled into a single commodity, FERC ordered the stages to unbundle. Instead of pipeline transmission companies having a merchant role in the delivery of natural gas, customers could now pay separately for transmission pipeline delivery. Energy marketers could help customers arrange for separate contracts with producers or processors, and then buy transmission services separately.

Modern-day hydraulic fracturing, which combines vertical and horizontal drilling into tight rock formations, has dramatically increased U.S. natural gas production and reserves and decreased price. The EU and China also have large shale reserves, although the geology is not as favorable for extraction. In addition, EU reserves are typically owned by governments, which have emphasized the environmental concerns.

Within some U.S. states, the push for natural gas has resembled a gold rush, with Texas, Oklahoma, Louisiana, Pennsylvania, and North Dakota adding shale oil and gas to their conventional production. North Dakota boomed, bringing energy wealth and jobs that resulted in the lowest unemployment rate in the country despite the Great Recession. However, the industry can turn off the spigot as quickly as it can turn it on, and some of the workers who flocked to the Dakotas moved on when prices plummeted.

Other states have hesitated to use fracking because of environmental concerns. New York banned fracking the Utica shale while Pennsylvania drills the adjacent Marcellus shale. Film-makers have made their opposition known in the documentary *Gasland* and its sequel, as well as the feature film *The Promised Land*. Hydraulic fracturing creates fractures in the shale by injecting a water–chemical mix under high pressure into the rock formation to create the fractures, with the chemicals acting to keep the fractures open long enough for the gas to escape towards the surface. This process raises concerns about the effects of the chemicals on water supplies. The process also raises the concern that it is contributing to earth tremors, which could be of particular concern if fracking takes place near an earthquake fault. Still another concern is that fracking requires large amounts of water, with little of it being recycled.

Despite these concerns, natural gas has advantages over coal, as it releases only half as much carbon and less NOx, sulfur and particulates. One way in which it might not be less benign is that pure natural gas is methane, a GHG estimated as 21 times as potent as CO_2 over a 100-year period. Howarth et al. (2011) have questioned the superiority of NG over coal given the heat-retaining potency of methane emissions from leaks during extraction, processing, and transport. Other researchers rebut this claim, but it raises the point that care must be taken to minimize methane emissions.

One major difference between natural gas and oil is that the former is more difficult to transport. Transportation via pipelines becomes uneconomical across oceans. As a result the market is not fully integrated, so that while natural gas prices are at historically low levels in the United States, prices are higher in importing countries. EU countries that obtain supplies from Russia pay a high price more closely aligned with oil prices than with natural gas, and risk supply interruptions if they go against Russia's policies. Japan imports most of its energy, including natural gas. LNG comes at a premium due to the cost of cooling the gas to a liquid, as well as the cost of import and export infrastructure and specially designed tankers to transport the liquid fuel. However, exports are increasing rapidly, and the market is moving in the direction of global integration.

While natural gas has numerous uses, including heating, cooking, and transportation, the fastest growth is in electricity generation. Due to its current low price and relatively low emissions, it is overtaking coal as the favored fuel for generating electricity in the United States. Natural gas is likely to grow unless the objections to fracking prove intractable. In addition to its use to generate electricity at peak and intermediate times, natural gas is increasingly viable as a baseload technology. Levelized cost shows combined cycle natural gas plants to have the lowest cost of the conventional fuels.

Despite its low cost, there is a case for keeping some diversification in the electricity mix. While natural gas has environmental advantages as compared to coal, it still emits carbon and NOx. It is subject to interruptions in production, processing, and transmission due to natural disasters such as hurricanes and Arctic cold waves. And while the price is low in early 2017, it has already risen considerably after dipping down to historically low levels.

Ultimately, the competitiveness of natural gas depends upon the structure of the market. At each stage of the supply chain, there is the potential for noncompetitive pricing. Natural gas markets also display situations with few sellers, such as only a single interstate pipeline serving a region, and few buyers, such as Japan being the dominant buyer of LNG. Such circumstances present opportunities for sellers to raise price above marginal cost, and for buyers to pay below the competitive price. Bilateral monopoly presents a battle between a monopolist and a monopsonist, where prices can fall anywhere between the monopoly and monopsony extremes, depending on relative bargaining power. Such markets may also be inefficient due to the transactions costs of strategic bargaining, such as with asset specificity and the holdup problem.

Formal oligopoly models such as cartels and dominant firm price leadership, as well as the duopoly models of Cournot and Bertrand, can predict strategies in non-competitive situations. Game theory can also suggest what strategies firms will employ in determining price and quantity.

Natural gas markets have evolved to more efficient markets with the move towards deregulation that began in the 1980s. With plentiful supplies and low prices, it is also becoming a more global market. Nevertheless, there will need to be continued vigilance to guard against the gaming of markets and environmentally short-sighted development if the industry is to deliver a Golden Age.

Notes

1 Tong (2012).
2 For more introduction about natural gas see NaturalGas.org.
3 The EIA no longer lists coal, as it anticipates no new construction due to climate change legislation. When it last included coal, the levelized cost with CCS was comparable to nuclear energy, and more expensive with CCS.
4 The relationship between S and MFC of an input in a monopsony market is analogous to that of D and MR of output in a monopoly market.
   MFC = ΔTFC/ΔX where TFC is total factor cost, X is input, and Δ stands for change.

References

Cookenboo, L. (1955). *Crude oil pipelines and competition in the oil industry.* Cambridge, MA: Harvard University Press.

Corts, K. S. (2011, Jan.) Flex fuel vehicles and alternative fuel infrastructure a chicken or egg question. *Resources for the Future.* Retrieved August 4, 2013 from http://www.rff.org/Publications/WPC/Pages/Flex-Fuel-Vehicles-and-Alternative-Fuel-Infrastructure-A-Chicken-or-Egg-Question.aspx

DiGiulio, D., & Jackson, R. (2016). Impact to underground sources of drinking water and domestic wells from production well stimulation and completion practices in the Pavillion, Wyoming, Field. *Environmental Science & Technology, 50*(8), 4524–4536.

Drollette, B. et al. (2015). Elevated levels of diesel range organic compounds in groundwater near Marcellus gas operations are derived from surface activities. *PNAS (Proceedings of the National Academy of Sciences), 112*(43), 13184–13189.

Howarth, R. W., Santoro, R., & Ingraffea, A. (2011). Methane and the greenhouse-gas footprint of natural gas from shale formations. *Climatic Change, 106*(4), 679–690.

International Energy Agency. (2011). *World energy outlook: Are we entering a golden age of gas?* Retrieved November 19, 2016 from http://www.worldenergyoutlook.org/media/weowebsite/2011/WEO2011_GoldenAgeofGasReport.pdf

Jackson, R. et al. (2014). The environmental costs and benefits of fracking. *Annual Review of Environment and Resources, 39,* 327–362.

Meyer, G., Hume, N., & Sheppard, D. (2016, March). Gas price tumble comes as markets are increasingly interlinked. *Financial Times.* Retrieved June 11, 2016 from http://www.ft.com/cms/s/2/3bc0116c-e681–11e5-a09b–1f8b0d268c39.html#axzz4BHRcxKiz

Neslen, A. (2015, March 23). Carbon capture battle stirs hopes, dreams and grim realities. *The Guardian, U.S. Edition.* Retrieved September 25, 2016 from https://www.theguardian.com/environment/2015/mar/23/carbon-capture-battle-stirs-hopes-dreams-and-grim-realities

Ratner, M., Belkin, P., Nichol, J., & Woehrel, S. (2013). *Europe's energy security: Options and challenges to natural gas supply diversification.* Retrieved September 30, 2016 from https://www.fas.org/sgp/crs/row/R42405.pdf

Sovacool, B. (2014). Cornucopia or curse? Reviewing the costs and benefits of shale gas hydraulic fracturing (fracking). *Renewable and Sustainable Energy Reviews, 37,* 249–264.

Tian, L., Wang, Z., Krupnick, A., & Liu, X. (2014). Stimulating shale gas development in China: A comparison with the U.S. experience. Resources for the Future Discussion Paper (July).

Tong, S. (2012). George Mitchell, 94, dies: Oil man unlocked fracking. *Marketplace, National Public Radio.* Retrieved October 1, 2016 from https://www.marketplace.org/2012/12/07/sustainability/new-petro-state/george-mitchell–94-dies-oil-man-unlocked-fracking

U.S. Department of Energy (DOE). (2014). *An evaluation of fracture growth and gas/fluid migration as horizontal Marcellus shale gas wells are hydraulically fractured in Greene County, Pennsylvania.* Retrieved September 19, 2016 from http://www.netl.doe.gov/File%20Library/Research/onsite%20research/publications/NETL-TRS-3–2014_Greene-County-Site_20140915_1_1.pdf

U.S. Energy Information Administration. (2016a). *Natural gas explained: Where our natural gas comes from.* Retrieved October 01, 2016 from http://www.eia.gov/energyexplained/index.cfm?page=natural_gas_where

U.S. Energy Information Administration. (2016b). *Natural gas gross withdrawals and production.* Retrieved October 16, 2016 from https://www.eia.gov/dnav/ng/ng_prod_sum_a_EPG0_FGG_mmcf_a.htm

U.S. Energy Information Administration. (2016c). *Natural gas annual, Table 26.* Retrieved October 16, 2016 from http://www.eia.gov/naturalgas/annual/pdf/table_026.pdf

U.S. Energy Information Administration. (2016d). *Monthly energy review.* Retrieved June 10, 2016 from http://www.eia.gov/totalenergy/data/monthly/#electricity

U.S. Energy Information Administration. (2016e). *Levelized cost and levelized avoided cost of new generation resources in the annual energy outlook 2016.* Retrieved October 16, 2016 from https://www.eia.gov/forecasts/aeo/pdf/electricity_generation.pdf

U.S. Energy Information Administration. (2016f). *Henry Hub natural gas spot price.* Retrieved October 01, 2016 from https://www.eia.gov/dnav/ng/hist/rngwhhdA.htm

U.S. Energy Information Administration. (2016g). *Levelized Cost and Levelized Avoided Cost of New Generation Resources in the Annual Energy Outlook.* Retrieved September 26, 2016 from https://www.eia.gov/forecasts/aeo/pdf/electricity_generation.pdf

U.S. Environmental Protection Agency (EPA). (2015). *Assessment of the potential impacts of hydraulic fracturing for oil and gas on drinking water resources.* Retrieved November 19, 2016 from https://cfpub.epa.gov/ncea/hfstudy/recordisplay.cfm?deid=244651

U.S. Environmental Protection Agency (2016). *EPA releases final report on impacts from hydraulic fracturing activities on drinking water.* Retrieved May 2, 2017 from https://www.epa.gov/newsreleases/epa-releases-final-report-impacts-hydraulic-fracturing-activities-drinking-water

Chapter 7

Coal

"Old King Cole was a merry old soul."

British nursery rhyme, originally dated 1708.

"Old King Coal may no longer be king."

The author of this text.

Introduction

Coal has two primary applications: metallurgical coal, also known as coking coal, for industrial applications and steam coal, also known as thermal coal, for electricity generation. In the United States, steam coal accounts for the vast majority of use, and in this chapter, we focus on the use of coal as an input in electricity generation.

For several decades, coal has been the largest source of fuel used to generate electricity in the United States, with a market share of 50% or more at its height despite a long list of negative externalities:

- Strip mining and mountaintop removal scar the landscape.
- The combustion of coal for electricity emits sulfur dioxide, a leading cause of acid rain, as well as health impacts, such as lung function impairment.
- It also produces nitrous oxide, which contributes to acid rain and is an ingredient in the formation of ground-level ozone, referred to as smog.
- Coal combustion emits mercury, which when ingested can damage development of the brain and nervous system.
- Combustion also releases heavy metals including arsenic and selenium, which can have toxic effects.
- Coal ash from combustion has impurities that can leach into soil and water.

Despite the lengthy list of negatives, coal was king of the generating fuels because of its availability, reliability, and low cost. However, the reign of King Coal is under attack.

In the late 1980s, climate change emerged as a dominant environmental policy problem. A series of meetings initiated by the United Nations, along with the formation of the Intergovernmental Panel on Climate Change (IPCC), culminated in the 1997 Kyoto Protocol, an international treaty originally signed by 192 countries to reduce GHGs below 1990 levels. The work focused attention on carbon emissions that increase the concentration of CO_2 in the atmosphere which are widely believed to be contributing to climate change. Electricity is the single largest source of carbon emissions, accounting for about one-third of anthropogenic (human–caused) emissions, and the combustion of coal to provide heat in the electricity generation process emits the most CO_2 on a per unit of electricity basis.[1]

Electric utilities have been shutting down a large number of coal plants before their planned retirement or converting them to natural gas, with lower carbon emissions per unit of electricity generated. U.S. utilities have no plans to build new coal plants in the near future.

The United States has not yet passed any legislation to restrict carbon emissions. However, coal plants typically have a 40-year lifetime, making new coal plants a high-risk investment. The U.S. Environmental Protection Agency has presented the Clean Power Plan, legislation that would restrict carbon emissions to the point that conventional coal plants could not meet the standard using current technology. The Clean Power Plan faces stiff court challenges, but utilities anticipate some form of carbon legislation that will render new coal plants untenable. Even if there is no federal legislation, states can take action to reduce carbon emissions.

Despite these dimming prospects in the United States, coal is still the dominant fuel in many developing countries. India is highly dependent on coal to further its economic development. China increased its coal use at a rapid rate to support economic growth, until it had to consider other alternatives due to high levels of air pollution as well as commitments to reduce its emissions of GHGs. Germany, a developed country, is returning to coal for a larger percent of its electricity generation after reducing its use of nuclear energy after Japan's Fukushima disaster and cutting back on wind and solar due to soaring subsidy costs. They have filled the gap with lignite, a highly polluting coal. Germany's carbon emissions are now rising, a stark reversal from when they first committed to renewable energy.

Consumption may no longer be on an inexorable rise, as U.S. consumption has declined sharply in recent years, and consumption in China has turned down. At least in the United States, carbon emissions have begun to decrease with the reduction in coal use (EIA, 2016a).

The next section of this chapter provides a brief economic history of coal use. We then consider production and the supply chain, from mining to processing to transport. Having laid out the links in the supply chain, we evaluate production cost. We consider market structure in the following section, with an emphasis on competition. We then return to environmental considerations. The final section is a summary.

A brief economic history of coal

Today's coal began forming 300 million years ago when swamps covered much of the earth. Layers of buried vegetation eventually formed peat, consisting of partially decomposed vegetation. Under heat and pressure, the peat was transformed into coal. While coal is a finite resource, the EIA estimates that at current rates of usage, the United States has enough coal to last approximately 250 years. Since today's use has a negligible effect on future coal supplies we use a static framework to evaluate optimal usage.

The Chinese used coal for heating 3,500 years ago (Chan, 2015). The region may have turned to coal as early as it did because of scarce woody vegetation. By AD 200, the Chinese burned coal in furnaces. At about the same time, there is evidence that the Romans used coal in Britain. Around AD 1000, China used coal in place of wood charcoal to produce iron and steel. Two centuries later, Britain shipped coal from Newcastle. They began underground mining soon after.

There was only limited use of coal until the early 1700s, when Britain discovered the process of making coke from coal. Coke burned hotter than coal and could melt iron ore so as to extract the pure metal (Speight, 2015, p. 45).

The Industrial Revolution in Great Britain in the 1700s needed a vast amount of fuel. With the invention of the steam engine and the factory system, it was now profitable to dig deeper for coal. There were expansive deposits throughout Britain, but their use brought dangers, including coal mine explosions and air pollution.

By 1885, coal had passed wood as the major energy source. It was a more compact source of energy and did not require large amounts of land for cultivation. Coal did require transportation from the mine to where it would be used, but this disadvantage declined as transportation costs decreased and the depletion of wood resources continued. Coal-fired trains or ships cost less than earlier technologies. Coal continued its ascendancy as the Industrial Revolution came to the United States.

The nineteenth century was the age of coal, but the twentieth was the age of oil. The internal combustion engine used fuel oil, without the need for labor to shovel coal into boilers required for trains, ships, and industrial equipment.

With electrification, coal found a new use as an electricity-generating fuel that was often cheaper than oil. Coal-fired plants dominated large urban areas, where the costs of transmission and distribution could be spread over many customers.

Since the middle of the twentieth century, global demand for coal has grown despite increasing environmental concerns. It has grown particularly quickly in the developing world since the widespread availability of coal offers energy security. Substantial coal reserves exist in many countries, and price has been more stable than for the other fossil fuels. Of the limited alternatives for electricity baseload power, coal has been the dominant technology, and given the objections to greater reliance on uranium, coal will be hard to replace in its entirety despite its shortcomings.

Coal's future depends upon clean-coal technologies that will enable power plants to burn coal with lower emissions. Clean-coal technologies include plants that operate at much higher temperatures and so use less coal to produce electricity, carbon capture and storage (CCS), and coal gasification that converts coal into a synthetic gas (syngas). Syngas is an alternative to natural gas. One use is in combined cycle plants. To date, these clean-coal technologies have required massive government subsidies, and the costs are multiples of initial projections. We discuss the costs, risks, and prospects for clean-coal technologies further in Chapter 10 on next-generation technologies.

Production and the supply chain

Figure 7.1 depicts the coal supply chain. The supply chain begins upstream with extraction from the coal mine. The next stage is processing, also known as cleaning, washing, preparation, or beneficiation, where it is necessary to remove noncombustible impurities from the run-of-mine (ROM) coal, the raw coal extracted from the mine. The midstream stage begins with transporting the coal from the mine to the end user, with

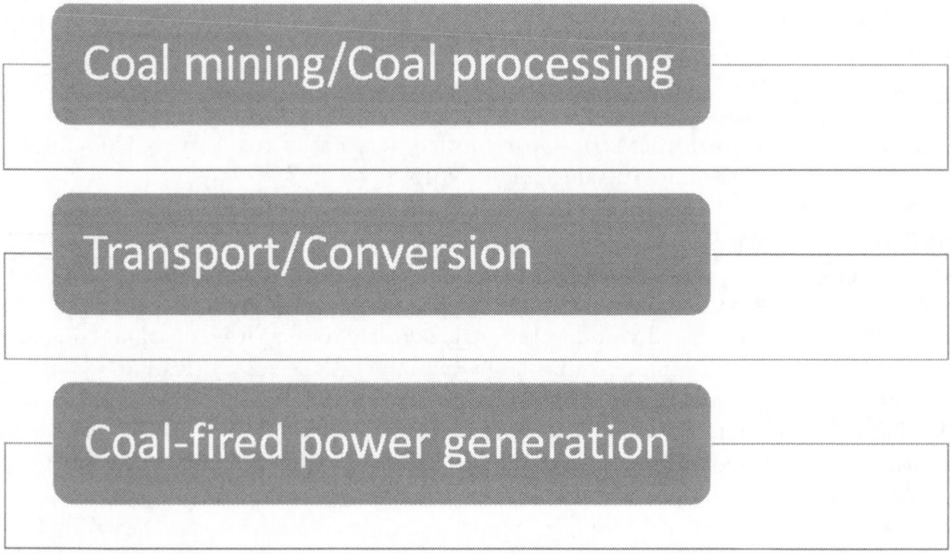

```
┌─────────────────────────────────────────────────────┐
│   Coal mining/Coal processing                         │
└─────────────────────────────────────────────────────┘

┌─────────────────────────────────────────────────────┐
│   Transport/Conversion                                │
└─────────────────────────────────────────────────────┘

┌─────────────────────────────────────────────────────┐
│   Coal-fired power generation                         │
└─────────────────────────────────────────────────────┘
```

Figure 7.1 Coal supply chain.

the option to convert the coal into synthetic or liquid form. Downstream, the end user receives the coal. We focus on electric utilities as end users of steam/thermal coal. The other end use is by industry, using metallurgical/coking coal, particularly to manufacture steel.

Extraction

Coal extraction uses underground and surface mining. The choice depends upon the amount of coal available underground and at the surface, as well as the associated costs of extraction and the effects on the environment. Surface mining predominates in the United States, whereas China needs underground mining to reach its deep deposits. Underground mining is both more dangerous and more expensive, but it provides many coal-mining jobs. There has been a rapid decrease in the number of underground mining accidents in developed countries, but less so in developing countries such as China. Developing countries typically have weaker mining regulations in order to reduce costs, a factor in the higher number of deaths.

Surface mining arouses opposition for degrading the environment. Surface mining calls for removal of layers of soil rock to expose the coal, in contrast to underground mining, where the rock remains in place during the extraction process. Mountaintop removal is a surface mining technique that removes the layers of the mountain to get at the coal seam, and faces particularly strong environmental opposition. There may be government requirements to restore the mountain landscape to the extent possible when mining is complete. We now consider surface and underground mining in more detail.

Mining operations—surface mining

Strip mining and mountaintop removal are types of surface mining. Producers use strip mining when the coal is close to the surface. Mountaintop removal uses explosives to remove the top levels of a mountain and access deposits that may be several hundred feet below. Even if there is a requirement to reclaim the landscape, it is not possible to completely restore the initial appearance. Nor is it likely that the company can fully restore ecosystems. Moreover, the debris contains chemicals that leach into surrounding soil and water.

The United States passed the Surface Mining Control and Reclamation Act (SMCRA) of 1977, aimed at unifying reclamation standards rather than the previous approach of leaving it to the individual states. Mining companies must post a performance bond as part of the original permit that allows extraction, with the bond returned partially or in full upon satisfactory restoration of the site. Reclamation increases the cost of mining, and a uniform policy has differential cost effects on regions that use different mining techniques. West Virginia has protested because since it has thinner coal seams, the legislation has increased their cost disproportionately; they spread the costs over fewer tons of coal per acre and have a narrower profit margin. The legislation may have contributed towards a shift in coal production to western states such as Montana and Wyoming (Misiolek & Noser, 1982).

Mining operations—underground mining

Underground mining is still the predominant form of mining in developing countries, as well as in developed countries where coal seams are deep. One technique is room-and-pillar that may be followed by a final stage of retreat mining. Room-and-pillar mining builds rooms into the coal mine, leaving pillars to support the roof. To maximize profit, the rooms and especially the pillars must be of optimum size. Pillars are left-behind resources, so larger pillars leave behind more resources. However, smaller pillars increase the chance of a mine collapse. Retreat mining removes the coal pillars to get the remaining coal, increasing the danger that the mine roof could collapse.

Location of supply

While almost all countries contain coal reserves, a few contain the largest coal deposits. The top ten countries account for close to 90% of world coal reserves; the United States, Russia, and China alone account for well over 50%. If we order countries by annual production, China is by far the largest, followed by the United States.

While the United States ranks second in production and consumption, China produces and consumes nearly as much coal as all other countries combined. China produced 3.68 billion tons of coal in 2015, but still needed to import 204 million tons, a little over 5% of production (EIA, 2014). The EU imports well over half of its coal. Japan is completely dependent on imports. The United States, South Africa, and Australia are self-sufficient, producing enough coal to meet their domestic needs. There is considerable debate in the United States about whether to allow coal exports, given the desire to reduce global carbon emissions.

Processing

Processing reduces the environmental damage caused by burning coal. Removing impurities and coal ash also increases the heat rate, reducing the amount of coal that must be burned to produce electricity, and, in turn, reduces carbon emissions. Processing coal also reduces transportation costs.

Steps in processing include crushing the coal and then cutting and sorting it into different sizes. Waste coal goes to an impoundment—an engineered settling basin—often as a coal slurry that is a mix of water and waste.

Pulverization often precedes combustion. Pulverization allows more of the coal to come into contact with the air and release its heat. A small percentage of the coal does not burn, leaving residuals such as coal ash.

Box 7.1 Is converting coal to syngas a better option?

Gasification is a "clean coal" technology. The gasifier replaces combustion, and operates at a higher temperature that converts coal into syngas, a synthetic gas that can potentially compete with natural gas. The clean aspect is the removal of harmful impurities prior to combusting the syngas. In addition, there is the capability of capturing carbon emissions during the combustion process. Companies either sell wastes such as minerals and sulfur or remove them to a waste site.

Syngas is still at a testing stage. Duke Energy built an operational syngas plant in Edwardsport, Indiana. The Duke Energy plant is a combined cycle plant in which they burn syngas as a combustion fuel, much like natural gas. When proposed, the estimated cost of the plant was under $2 billion, but rose to over $3 billion. In addition, natural gas was selling at $13/MMbtu when construction began, but with fracking, its price has been closer to $2–4/MMbtu. For now, syngas remains an expensive source of energy that results in higher electricity prices for Indiana ratepayers.

FutureGen was a project located in Illinois jointly funded by the U.S. Department of Energy and an international alliance of private coal companies and electric utilities, intended to explore combined cycle clean-coal technology including synfuels and carbon capture and storage (CCS). It experienced enormous cost overruns, and the project was suspended when the U.S. Department of Energy cancelled its funding.

Transportation

Rail transports most domestic coal. From a life-cycle standpoint, the large number of trains result in emissions from locomotives burning fuel, primarily diesel. In addition, there are coal dust emissions during transport. The dust can cover nearby vegetation and wash into nearby water. In turn, it can affect plants and the land and water life that depend on vegetation and water. While emissions due to rail transport are a smaller-scale environmental issue than those of coal extraction and combustion, they are a component of the supply-chain externalities.

Barges are an alternative when the supplier is near a waterway, and trucks are viable for short distances. These modes of transportation also emit coal dust during loading and unloading, as well as emissions from their combustion of fuel. Pipelines are a possible form of transportation for coal slurry. Water use can be an issue in dry regions. Exported coal uses ships, with larger-capacity ships for longer distances.

Box 7.2 Should an electric utility own its coal mines?

It is possible to vertically integrate production and end use. Ronald Coase (1937) first posited that firms will choose between doing production in-house or buying from other companies, depending on which costs less. Duke Energy Company bought four coal mines in Harlan County, Kentucky, in order to have dependable supplies. If the workers at an external supplier go on strike, the electric utility will need backup options, such as a large inventory of coal on site, to cope with the supply interruption. The utility may prefer to avoid such supply interruptions by owning its own mines.

Duke Energy was required to discontinue this practice, as the regulators were concerned that the utility was using an above-competitive price for coal in determining the price of electricity. With an external supplier, there is an explicit price, whereas when a company acts as its own supplier, it uses a "transfer price," the opportunity cost of using the resource to supply its own needs.

Harlan County USA, an Oscar-winning documentary, told a different story. It claimed that Duke Energy divested these mines after a tense conflict with the United Mine Workers Union.

Cost

The price of coal varies considerably, depending on its production costs, characteristics, and demand. Regional coal prices in the United States vary greatly. In 2015, Appalachian coal sold for about $45/ton, Illinois Basin coal closer to $30/ton, and Wyoming Powder River Basin coal as low as $10/ton (EIA, 2016b).

Extraction

Why do all users of coal not make exclusive use of Powder River coal? Extraction cost is not the only consideration. Additional factors that affect the choice of coal include heat and water content, sulfur content, ash, and transport costs.

Types of coal

Depending on geological conditions, coal has different characteristics that affect its usefulness as a source of heat and its environmental consequences. There are four major types—also referred to as ranks or grades—of coal: lignite, subbituminous, bituminous, and anthracite. As we move from the softest coal—lignite—to the hardest, the heat content increases and the moisture content decreases.

Lignite is the softest and anthracite the hardest, with hardness dependent on the amount of pressure on the vegetative materials during the formation process. Lignite, also known as "brown coal" because of its color, has a high water content, about 35%. From an environmental standpoint, lignite is the least desirable energy-producing coal. It has the lowest heat content and so requires the most coal to produce a unit of energy.

Bituminous coal is the most abundant and the most common coal used for electricity production. Subbituminous is the next most common. In contrast, anthracite makes up only about 1.5% of U.S. coal supplies. Anthracite was subject to heat and pressure applied over an extremely long time, making it the oldest, deepest, and hardest coal. As a result, it has the highest heat content, the lowest moisture, and the lowest ash.

Coal also has other characteristics that affect its desirability as a fuel to generate electricity. Electric utilities subject to restrictions on sulfur emissions are willing to pay more for low-sulfur coal.

The largest coal-producing region in the United States is the Powder River Basin in Wyoming and Montana. The grade is subbituminous, with properties between those of lignite and bituminous coal. It has a low heat content because of its relative softness. Utilities burning this coal must use a large amount to produce a unit of electricity, resulting in high carbon emissions. However, it is very low in sulfur and produces only a small amount of ash. Midwestern coal mined in Illinois is a bituminous coal with a high heat content, but also high sulfur. Appalachian coal from West Virginia coal is a bituminous coal with a high heat content, and a sulfur content midway between Wyoming and Illinois coal.

Box 7.3 High-sulfur coal makes a comeback

While electric utilities prefer low- to high-sulfur coal, there are other considerations. Transportation costs make up 40% of delivered coal costs, so utilities prefer coal from nearby locations. East Coast utilities buy relatively low-sulfur coal from West Virginia rather than lower-sulfur coal from the distant Powder River Basin. Customers in the Midwestern United States find it cheaper to buy high-sulfur coal from the Illinois Basin and scrub out the sulfur.

Increasingly, utilities have less concern about the sulfur content of coal as federal regulations require the installation of flue gas desulfurization (FGD) technology, known as scrubbers. Scrubbers remove 90% or more of sulfur emissions at a cost of about $360 million for a 1 GW plant.[2] Many utilities could achieve the same outcome at a lower cost using lower-sulfur coal, but no longer have that option.

Illinois lobbied for requirements that utilities install scrubbers.[3] It also pushed for federal subsidies to reduce their cost. In addition, the state pushed for financial incentives to utilities that buy in-state coal. In so doing, Illinois preserved demand for its high-sulfur coal.

While Powder River coal has the lowest sulfur content, it also has the lowest heat content compared to Illinois and West Virginia coal. It takes more Wyoming coal to produce a unit of electricity, as well as more expense to deliver a larger volume.

Buyers of coal also consider its ash content. Coal plants often have electrostatic precipitators (ESPs) to catch the particulates including fly ash before they go out into the atmosphere. The utilities store much of the ash in pits or ponds. Coal ash contains carcinogens and heavy metals so the ash must be kept out of soil and water.

The EPA does not regulate coal ash, but is under considerable pressure to do so since the catastrophic dam collapse in Kingston, Tennessee, in December 2008. That accident spilled 5 million cubic tons of coal residue into a nearby bay and eventually into the main channel of the Emery River. The courts found the Tennessee Valley Authority (TVA), the operator of the dam, negligent for not using recommended safety procedures. The TVA has spent over $1 billion on cleanup.[4]

Capital costs

Capital costs, the costs of constructing the coal-mining facility, depend upon the type of operation. Powder River Basin allows surface mining, while Appalachian coal is a mix of underground and surface mining. Underground mining typically has higher capital costs than surface mining. Within each category, there are a variety of types of mines. We referred previously to room-and-pillar and retreat mining, which are underground mining technologies, and surface mining techniques such as strip mining and mountaintop removal.

The cost of underground mining depends on factors including seam thickness, seam depth, and mining method. Key factors that influence the cost of surface mining include overburden ratio, mine size, and mining method. The overburden ratio refers to the ratio of rock removed per ton of coal.

The cost of extracting coal depends considerably upon the safety measures taken to prevent accidents. The United States has dramatically reduced the number of accidents and fatalities. While developing countries have also improved mine safety, accidents and deaths are still not uncommon. One major accident occurred in Turkey in 2014, with 301 miners killed. China has an improving safety record, but there are still close to 1,000 deaths per year, and the figure is likely underreported by the government. In contrast, there are fewer than 50 deaths from coal-mining accidents in the United States (Lelyveld, 2015).

Processing costs

Processing removes impurities such as sulfur or water content to reduce the amount of coal ash that will be created during combustion. There are capital costs as well as operating and maintenance (O&M) costs associated with coal-cleaning equipment as well as variable costs for coal-cleaning chemicals. In return, lower emissions and coal ash reduce end-user operating costs. Additionally, processed coal has higher thermal efficiency—a higher heat rate—so a steel manufacturer or an electric generator uses less coal to produce a given amount of heat, with lower GHG emissions.

Box 7.4 When is clean coal dirty?

Freedom Industries was a company located in Charleston, West Virginia, that stored an industrial chemical used to reduce coal ash. In January 2014, nearby residents reported an unusual licorice-like odor. Initially, the company denied that anything was wrong, but inspectors soon found a leak in a storage tank. The chemical had leaked into the nearby Elk River, so residents within the region were unable to drink the local water or use it for taking showers or washing dishes.

The West Virginia Department of Environmental Protection accused the state of lax regulation (including inspections of the storage tanks) prior to the accident (Field, Edwards, & Shoichet, 2014). Coal mining is the dominant industry in West Virginia. Politicians may be loath to regulate the industry vigilantly, for fear of losing campaign contributions. The industry is likely to claim that tougher regulation will drive up the cost of West Virginia coal, which will reduce sales and cost jobs.

Lax regulation can also drive up costs. There were costs to drinking bottled water that was trucked in, driving to a relative or a hotel to take a shower, potential health effects as well as the psychological toll of unknown health effects, court costs to ascertain the liability of Freedom Industries, and reputation costs to Charleston, West Virginia, for the notoriety of what locals call the Chemical Valley. Freedom Industries, which had undergone a management change shortly before the disaster, declared bankruptcy shortly after.

Transportation costs

Rail accounts for about 70% of coal transportation in the United States, with water and truck transit making up the remainder. Given its dominance, we focus on rail. Rail typically accounts for about 40% of the total delivered cost. Figure 7.2 shows rail costs as a component of the total cost of delivering steam coal to electric utilities.

Rail costs have trended higher since 2011 as coal competes with new supplies of oil and natural gas for rail transportation. The increase in transportation costs could hinder the ability of coal to reclaim market share from natural gas even if the price of natural gas increases.

Cost to generate electricity

The primary use of coal in electricity production is to fuel electricity baseload plants, although there are some smaller and typically older units that operate during intermediate, or shoulder, hours, when loads are above what baseload plants can serve, but below peak demand. The EIA lists baseload coal as having a capacity factor of 85%, indicating that on average the plant produces 85% of its *nameplate capacity*, the maximum electricity it can generate.

The capacity factor depends upon the percentage of available hours the plant runs. Plants may have both scheduled and unscheduled downtime. During off-peak seasons, when demand for electricity is relatively low, the utility performs routine

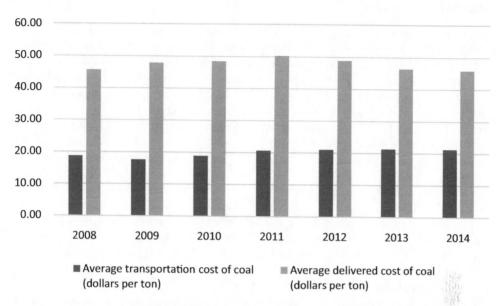

Figure 7.2 U.S. delivered cost of coal to electric utilities by rail, 2008–2014 ($/ton in real 2014 dollars). Adapted from *Rail continues to dominate coal shipments to the power sector*, by U.S. EIA (2016b).

plant maintenance. There are also unplanned outages, when a plant goes off-line unexpectedly.

Utilities also incur costs to meet environmental regulations, such as scrubbers to reduce sulfur emissions installed in baseload units. We earlier provided the initial cost of a scrubber for a 1 GW plant as $360 million, or $0.36 per watt. For a smaller 50 MW plant serving intermediate hours—hours where demand exceeds the baseload but is below the peak—the cost of a scrubber is approximately $1.14 a watt. And the technology may not even be feasible, given the size of the scrubber as compared to an intermediate-size plant.

In Chapter 6, we indicated that the EIA no longer lists coal in its comparison of levelized costs for producing electricity unless the technology includes carbon capture and storage (CCS). Conventional technologies no longer meet anticipated carbon restrictions. Before the EIA dropped conventional coal technologies from its listings, they had begun to add a 3% premium to the discount rate, reflecting the higher risk that electric utilities imputed to the likelihood of carbon restrictions. With the risk premium, the levelized cost of a new coal plant was comparable to new nuclear construction on a dollar per megawatt basis, and much higher than natural gas. There is little market experience with coal technologies with CCS, and their levelized cost is considerably higher than nuclear energy, or for that matter, natural gas combined cycle technology with CCS.

For plants already built, the relevant comparison is variable cost, such as O&M costs that vary with electricity production. Electric utilities have been shutting down existing coal plants or converting them to natural gas plants, reflecting that even without mandatory carbon restrictions, it is cheaper in many cases to use natural gas than coal, even taking into account the cost of conversion.

Market structure

Coal extraction at the *mine mouth*—the coal at the point of extraction—fits the characteristics for competition. The market supports a large number of mines operating at a small scale. For a given grade of coal, buyers view it as a commodity so that all that matters is price. As for barriers to entry, there are sizable capital costs, but we have earlier defined an entry barrier as a cost faced by new firms that was not faced by existing firms. If a new firm were unable to obtain mineral rights to mine for coal, that could be an entry barrier. Even so, existing mine owners face stiff competition from natural gas and other sources of energy that can also generate electricity. Coal's declining market share makes it difficult to charge above marginal cost.

Other aspects of the coal industry do not align with the competitive model. There is product differentiation among varieties of coal. Buyers consider sulfur and ash characteristics as well as heat content in determining which coal to buy. The largest four coal companies controlled 50% of sales until recently, so they may have had power over the price. However, the industry is under unprecedented pressure, with three of the top four going through bankruptcy, including Peabody Energy Corporation, the largest producer with almost 20% of industry production.

Competition may not fit the transportation stage, given the dominant position of the rail industry in transporting coal. It is often economical to have only one set of tracks between two points, and a small number of large railroads dominate the industry.

Competition

We begin by applying the model of perfect competition to the coal industry to see how well it fits the actual industry. The current picture suggests the model of perfect competition fits the industry reasonably well, with coal needing to compete with natural gas and even wind and solar as a source of fuel for electricity generation. If this market structure is competitive, we can use the model of perfect competition to predict price and quantity for the industry, as well as the behavior of individual firms.

Figure 7.3 depicts a perfectly competitive coal industry in long run equilibrium. Industry equilibrium is at the intersection of industry supply and demand. Industry price is $50/short ton and equilibrium quantity is 1 million short tons, approximately equal to total industry quantity in recent years. We depict a typical firm producing 50,000 short tons.[5] We assume there are a large number of small firms, so that each firm has a negligible effect on the industry price and output. Since price is unaffected by the firm's output, price, marginal revenue, and the firm's demand, are all identical.

Profit maximization for a competitive firm is where price equals marginal cost (MC). Competitive firms can make a profit or a loss in the short run, but in the long run, P = minimum LRAC and profit is zero. If firms earn a positive economic profit in the short run, new firms enter until profit for the marginal firm—the last firm to enter the industry—is zero; if firms are losing money in the short run, firms exit until the marginal firm earns a zero profit.

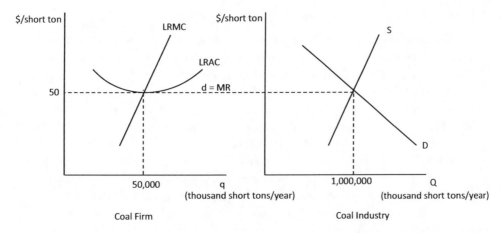

Figure 7.3 Competitive coal firm and industry.

Noncompetitive markets

Shortly before the Great Recession that began in December, 2007, coal prices rose to $190/ton, plunged to $65 by 2009, and then climbed to $140 by early 2011 (Els, 2014). Coal prices then declined rapidly through early 2016, briefly dropping below $50/ton, before a sharp rebound to over $80/ton later that year. As with oil, which followed a similar roller–coaster pattern, analysts cited drivers on both the demand and supply sides. On the demand side, the explanation for the 2009 price spike was that China and India needed more energy to fuel their economic expansions. On the supply side, the largest coal companies might have had the power to raise price by coordinating their production decisions, but there is no hard evidence.

We stated earlier that the four largest coal companies accounted for almost 50% of production in 2014, although concentration is declining with three of the largest having gone through bankruptcy. There is even more concentration within the Powder River area, where in 2011 four firms controlled 77% of sales (EIA, 2014).

Price fixing is illegal under U.S. antitrust law, but that does not mean it cannot occur. Coal producers would like to emulate OPEC. If successful, they would follow the cartel model described in Chapter 5 on oil. Another possibility is that coal industry behavior fits the dominant firm price leadership oligopoly model, except in place of a dominant firm setting price, the largest firms might coordinate their production decisions, with smaller firms on the competitive fringe accepting the dominant group's price.

Concentration on the buyer side can also lead to noncompetitive outcomes. If there is a single buyer, we have a monopsony. China is the largest buyer, and may be able to negotiate a lower price than smaller buyers.

The most common application of the monopsony model is that of a company town, where a firm is the only hirer of labor, and is able to pay a lower than competitive wage. At one time, coal company practices raised concerns of monopsony power.

Box 7.5 Did coal companies have a monopsony?

In 1956, "Tennessee" Ernie Ford recorded an old coal-mining song entitled "Sixteen Tons" that hit number 1 on both country and pop charts. The song refers to coal-mining conditions of the 1930s and 1940s, but resonates with listeners to the present day. Ford laments that he owes money to the company store.

Even in the 1950s, many coal companies issued scrip, a type of credit that could only be used in company stores. The payment was an advance against earnings, and had the effect of keeping the worker perennially in debt.

As long as the company was the only employer in town, a monopsony, it could pay below-competitive wages. Since the company store was also a monopoly, the company could sell products to workers at above-market prices. For graphs demonstrating how monopolists and monopsonists determine prices, refer to Figure 5.9 on OPEC and Figure 6.9 depicting Japan as the only buyer of LNG.

Fishback (1986) doubts the story of coal company exploitation. He notes that workers could relocate to hundreds of mines in coal-mining regions such as West Virginia. Also, workers at different companies would share information, reducing opportunities for companies to exploit employees. He also finds that after deductions for company-provided housing, doctors, fuel, and store purchases, workers received cash on payday amounting to between 30 and 80% of their wages. Based on his evidence, there was nothing monopsonistic about the company store after all.

Emissions and other environmental impacts

Coal's abundance of supply and wide geographic distribution of supplies would allow it to meet much of the world's demand for electricity generation. Instead, coal is under assault as a dirty fuel, at least in developed countries that factor in the external costs of coal production.

Externalities include sulfur emissions, particulates, mercury, coal ash, and carbon. In addition to affecting the air, coal production also pollutes water and soil, as well as degrading land. Chapter 14 on energy and the environment fully considers externalities. For now, we consider some key environmental consequences that pertain especially to coal.

Greenhouse gases and other emissions

In 1952, London experienced a toxic fog attributable in large part to the burning of coal. The fog led to 12,000 premature deaths as well as over 100,000 illnesses (Bates, 2002; Davis, Bell, & Fletcher, 2002). We referred at the beginning of this chapter to acid rain, a primary concern of the 1980s with its effects on water and forest ecosystems. The United States introduced emissions trading for sulfur as part of the 1990 Clean Air Act Amendments. While the initial purpose was to alleviate acid rain, the EPA found that health improvements—fewer cases of asthma, bronchitis, and emphysema—were by far the largest benefits. Increasingly, utilities are installing scrubbers to remove sulfur emissions. As a result, companies have less reason to engage in emissions trading, and that market has largely collapsed. Unfortunately, regulations favoring the installation of scrubbers may be a much higher-cost way of reducing emissions than the lower-cost measures such as using low-sulfur coal along with sulfur emissions trading.

Nitrogen oxide (NOx) also contributes to acid rain and smog. Smog forms when nitrogen combines with oxygen and heat. One major source of NOx emissions is from coal combustion in power plants. It is worst when summer heat adds to the mix. Power plant low-NOx burners reduce its formation by exposing nitrogen to more fuel and less air during the combustion process. Selective catalytic reduction (SCR) reduces NOx emissions much as scrubbers reduce sulfur emissions. Clean-coal technologies such as the liquefaction of coal into syngas before combustion produce energy with less NOx formation.

Particulates also damage health. There is legislation aimed at large and small particulate matter (PM). In the United States, the trend has been to regulate ever-smaller PM, as PM less than 2.5 microns (PM 2.5) may have more severe effects than larger particulates (PM 10).

More recently, the list of concerning and potentially regulated substances includes mercury, of which the primary source is emissions from coal-burning power plants.[6] A major source of current exposure to mercury is through eating fish. There are warnings to pregnant women to avoid species of fish with high absorption rates, as unborn babies are particularly susceptible to damage to the developing brain and nervous system. In 2011, the EPA proposed rules for lowering mercury, the Mercury and Air Toxics Standards (MATS). In 2015, the U.S. Supreme Court struck down MATS on the grounds that the EPA did not consider costs. In 2016, the EPA submitted a study that found benefits exceeded costs, and the U.S. Supreme Court allowed a lower court ruling in favor of the legislation to stand. Murray Energy, now the largest U.S. coal company, has filed a lawsuit challenging the EPA's decision that benefits of restricting mercury exceed costs (Walton, 2016). Nevertheless, many utilities have already reduced mercury emissions.

Developing countries have fewer environmental restrictions, and so experience all of these problems to a greater degree. Today, China is prominent among developing countries trying to combat dense smog due to coal-fired power plants, which currently account for 75% of electricity generation. South Korea blames its pollution on China, but makes its own contribution. Coal, much of it imported, currently accounts for 40% of Korea's electricity generation. South Korea continues to build new coal plants. While pollution in Seoul is not as bad as in Beijing, it still is much higher than in New York City.

There are heavy metals including arsenic that are by-products of coal production. In rural China, where cooking uses arsenic-rich coal briquettes, arsenic poisoning is a danger. Bangladesh also suffers from arsenic poisoning due to high levels of arsenic in the soil and groundwater near coal mines (Murcott, 2012). Arsenic also triggers a variety of cancers.

However, coal's fate most depends upon the future treatment of carbon emissions. CO_2 accounts for about 80% of GHG emissions. Figure 7.4 shows the relative contributions of various sectors in the United States to GHG emissions.

If we restrict GHGs to CO_2, electricity contributes close to 40%. Coal is responsible for about three-quarters of the electricity sector contribution, with natural gas responsible for most of the remaining one-fourth.

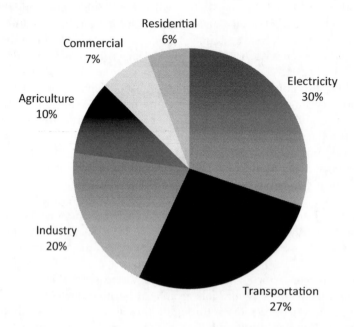

Figure 7.4 U.S. greenhouse gas emissions by sector, 2014. Adapted from *U.S. greenhouse gas emissions and sinks 1990–2014*, by U.S. EPA (2017).

EPA's contested Clean Power Plan (CPP) would restrict carbon emissions to a level that cannot be achieved by conventional coal plants but can by the current generation of natural gas plants. Many states, most of which are major coal producers, have sued to prevent the CPP from becoming law. The U.S. Supreme Court put a stay on the legislation in early 2016, delaying its enforcement.[7]

In the meantime, some states in the United States have initiatives to reduce their carbon emissions. The Regional Greenhouse Gas Initiative (RGGI) contains a number of northeastern states, while a California initiative now contains other states and even Canadian provinces.

The EU has a mandatory carbon trading program, which initially issued a large number of permits, resulting in a price for carbon considerably lower than what most economists estimate to be the value of carbon reduction. Allowance prices dropped below \$5/ton in mid-2016, while studies show the estimated value to society of reducing emissions is at least \$20/ton and some estimates are much higher. The EU is likely to reduce the number of permits available in future years.

Even if we reduce carbon emissions today, CO_2 will continue to accumulate for some time to come. CO_2 dissipates slowly, based on its half-life cycle. Of the carbon added to the atmosphere today, about half will remain 100 years from now.

Water contamination

Coal contributes to water contamination at a number of points in the supply chain. Coal mining (drainage from mines, mountaintop removal), processing (coal sludge, heavy metals), coal-fired electricity plants (mercury, thermal pollution, acid rain), and coal waste (coal ash, but also waste from scrubbers), all contribute to water pollution (SourceWatch, 2015).

Underground mining that takes place below the water table requires continuous pumping out of the water to prevent flooding. Abandoned mines are also subject to flooding. When water encounters sulfur-bearing minerals, it becomes acidic. As described earlier with reference to acid rain, acidic water can kill fish, and a study by Sams and Beer (2000) shows that rivers and streams near Appalachian coal mines cannot support fish populations. Tailings, the unwanted materials left over after the extraction of coal, and overburden, the rocks and soil removed to get to the coal, can exacerbate the problem depending on their method of disposal. If they mix with water, they increase acidity.

While the main objection to mountaintop removal is scarring of the landscape, it can also damage nearby forests and water. The rocks that contain sulfites acidify the water and reduce the species that can survive.

Coal processing produces sludge and heavy metal wastes that are another potential source of acidification. The U.S. federal government permits coal-mining firms to release a small amount of waste materials. Social efficiency compares marginal benefits and marginal costs, and so some discharge is optimal. However, firms pursuing maximum profit might exceed the legal standard. In May of 2014, the federal government fined Alpha Natural Resources, one of the largest U.S. coal firms, $27.5 million for releasing as much as 35 times the legal limit of toxic discharges from its mines, a record fine for violating water pollution standards. Why did they risk large fines and an additional $200 million in cleanup costs? They built in the probability of fines and cleanup costs as a cost of doing business.[8] We only read about the firms that get caught; firms that do not get caught presumably come out ahead—MC < MB—by exceeding the pollution limit.

Further down the supply chain, coal-burning power plants produce coal ash and heavy metals, mercury, thermal pollution, and acid rain. We have previously discussed all but thermal pollution, and will have more to say about coal ash shortly. Thermal pollution occurs when the water used in the combustion process increases in temperature before it is discharged to water outside the plant. The change in temperature can affect which species survive. Thermal pollution is not restricted to the use of coal for electricity generation. Nuclear energy heats up large amounts of water in the electricity-generating process.

Coal waste, including the heavy metals remaining after processing, can leach into the soil and water over time. A portion of toxic substances, such as mercury, will remain in the environment for some time to come, depending on the half-life cycle. Therefore, as we emit additional toxins, the effect is cumulative. While all types of coal mining can place metals in proximity to water or soil, mountaintop removal is a particular hazard, as it places a large amount of valley fill in direct proximity to water, plants, and soil. Initial low concentrations of heavy metals such as selenium can accumulate to levels 5,000 times as high as they make their way through the food chain (Lemly, 2009).

Finally, reducing one pollutant can have either a complementary or substitute relationship with other pollutants (Schwarz, 2005). A regulation reducing sulfur emissions can affect other emissions such as NOx, mercury, or coal ash. Also, regulating water can affect the substances released into the air. Firms complain that piecemeal regulation targeting one pollutant or one medium at a time increases regulatory uncertainty and cost. Where possible, regulators should consider the interrelationships among pollutants such as sulfur, mercury, and ash, as well as a multimedia approach that encompasses air and water. We go into more detail on the relationship among multiple pollutants in Chapter 14 on energy and environment.

Land degradation

Coal mining results in the deforestation and degradation of the landscape. These effects can remain long after the abandonment of coal-mining operations. In some cases, legislation requires the owner of the mine to restore the landscape, but the restoration is unlikely to restore the original ecosystem that existed prior to the mining operation. Nor will the restored landscape match the appearance of the original one, as the types of trees or plant species may differ from the vegetation that existed prior to mining. New growth is not the same as old growth.

Where reclamation takes place, as has been the case in the United States since the 1977 passage of the Surface Mining Control and Reclamation Act, there may be reuse of the land. However, if the cost of reclamation exceeds the value of the land, the land may be abandoned and reclamation will have to use designated tax revenues. The U.S. Department of the Interior (2016) has collected over $10 billion in fees from existing coal-mining operations, and redistributed about $7.5 billion to communities to reclaim land degraded prior to the passage of legislation. There remains $3 billion in abandoned sites still in need of reclamation.

Fires from underground mines can burn for decades or longer. A fire in Centralia, Pennsylvania, continues to burn more than 50 years after it started in 1962. Residents had to relocate and the Post Office has even removed the postal code. In addition to destroying coal, the fires release toxins and CO_2 emissions. They are difficult to extinguish, given their underground location and oxygen-rich atmosphere (Cray, 2010).

Human health effects

Studies of areas around coal-mining operations report higher rates of cancer, birth defects, and higher rates of death from chronic heart, respiratory, and kidney disease. China estimates premature deaths of 250,000 people, with a decrease in expected lifespan of 5.5 years due to air pollution, largely attributable to its reliance on coal (Ottery, 2013). There are corresponding figures for illness in China. Figures for 2011 are 320,000 children and 61,000 adults with asthma, 36,000 children with low birth weights, 340,000 hospital admissions, and 141 million sick days.

Box 7.6 Should coal miner deaths and illnesses count as externalities?

Economists usually assume that competitive wages include compensation for accepting higher risks. Gordon (2009) takes the argument one step further, arguing against government programs intended to protect the health of miners as unnecessarily driving up the cost of mining, reducing worker productivity, and costing jobs.

A coal miner engaging in retreat mining should receive a higher wage than one in a roof-and-pillar operation who does not do retreat mining. If each miner receives an extra $5,000 a year in salary for working in a retreat mine vs. roof-and-pillar, and faces a 1/1,000 greater chance of death, then a miner who takes the more hazardous position receives compensation reflective of valuing a statistical life at $5 million. Statistically speaking, of 1,000 miners, 999 will collect the extra annual compensation and survive, while one in 1,000 will not. In all, they receive total compensation of $5 million in exchange for the loss of one life.

Compensation for illness and injury is analogous. There is in fact a fund in the United States to compensate miners who develop black-lung disease, a potentially fatal bronchitis that is a common consequence of long exposure to coal dust.

Health effects do count as externalities when individuals are uninformed, or do not have a choice about accepting these consequences. This situation may have been more prevalent in the United States at the time "Sixteen Tons" was written. Today, it still may describe mining conditions in developing countries.

Summary

Coal provides a major share of electricity generation despite pervasive negative externalities for the environment and human health. Its favorable characteristics include large global reserves, low cost, and high reliability.

In this chapter, we have focused on the use of steam or thermal coal for electricity generation. Coal has been the largest source of generating fuel in the United States in the past, but natural gas will likely overtake it. Even though there is no federal program restricting carbon emissions, U.S. utilities are not building new coal facilities as they anticipate restrictions during the 40-year lifetime of a new plant. The U.S. EIA no longer calculates levelized cost for coal-burning power plants unless they have CCS. Given the unsuccessful and limited experience with these plants in the United States, new coal plants are not competitive at this time. Utilities are shutting down many existing plants before their planned retirement, or converting them into natural gas plants.

Coal extraction fits the characteristics of a competitive industry. There are a large number of firms, an absence of entry barriers, and for a given grade of coal, buyers care only about price.

In the United States, the top four firms controlled almost half of total sales, raising concerns that these firms might have power over the price. In 2008 and again in 2011, prices spiked to over $100 per ton. However, since 2011, the period when oil and gas production soared, coal's price has also fallen along with other energy prices. Of the top four coal-producing firms, three went into bankruptcy. With low natural gas prices and smaller coal firms, coal is likely to be a competitive industry.

While a particular grade of coal is a commodity where only price matters to the buyer, there is product differentiation because coal's characteristics differ according to its geological origins. Coal varies in heat content—the amount of Btus per ton of coal—with harder coals composed of more carbon molecules having higher heat content. Utilities in turn focus on heat rate—Btu/kWh, a measure of thermal efficiency. By using coals with higher heat content, utilities use less coal and also emit less CO_2.

Coals also vary in their ash content, which is subject to increasing regulation, and they differ in their sulfur content, an emission that has been regulated for decades. Coals also contain differing amounts of mercury, which can affect development of the brain and nervous system.

Transportation costs make up a large percentage of the price of delivered coal. Rail transportation is the most common delivery method. Even if coal extraction is a competitive industry, railroads are likely to have price power given limited competition. Railroads have been increasing their prices, as oil and natural gas producers with new supplies from hydraulic fracturing turn to rail when pipelines are not available.

Modern clean-coal technologies such as synfuels and CCS are not yet economical. Efforts so far have run far over budget. With low natural gas prices and the price of renewables falling, producers have less reason to invest in clean-coal R&D.

Outside of the developed nations, coal will likely continue to be a leading energy source. Developed countries with large reserves will seek to export coal when they cannot sell it in their domestic market, although doing so will make it more difficult to fight climate change. Developing nations will continue to use coal, making the argument that they need to achieve a higher stage of development before they can turn to cleaner but more expensive energy sources. There will be pressure for developed nations to develop lower-carbon technologies, as well as to subsidize cleaner alternatives in developing countries.

Notes

1   Coal had long led in total CO_2 emissions in the United States, but natural gas, which is used directly for heating as well as for electricity generation, is expected to surpass coal due to its rising use and coal's decline.
2   See Fahey (2010) for the cost estimate of a scrubber.
3   Rushton (2015) provides details on Illinois coal.
4   TVA was founded in the 1930s to bring electrification to an impoverished region. As there are no stockholders in this company, ratepayers will bear the majority of the costs. The utility had insurance that covered a portion of the costs.
5   In the United States, a short ton is simply a ton, or 2,000 lbs. The British long ton is 2,240 lbs., and the metric ton, or tonne, equals 1,000 kilograms or 2,204 lbs.
6   As early evidence of the potential harm from mercury (Hg), there is the "Mad Hatter" from Lewis Carroll's (1865) *Alice's Adventures in Wonderland*. In the 1800s, hatmakers used mercury to turn fur into felt and breathed its toxic fumes.
7   The plan was supported by the Obama Administration. Its prospects dimmed further with the 2016 election of Donald Trump, who has indicated that he does not plan to support it.
8   Ifill (2014). The second largest fine was $20 million, agreed to in a settlement between the EPA and Massey, another large coal company that was subsequently acquired by Alpha.

References

Bates, D. (2002). A half century later: Recollections of the London fog. *Environmental Health Perspectives, 110*(12), A735.

Carroll, L. (1865). *Alice's adventures in Wonderland*. London: Macmillan & Co.

Chan, E. (2015). Remarkable discovery shows humans were burning coal as fuel more than 3,500 years ago as world's earliest site of the activity is unearthed in China. *DailyMail*. Retrieved on October 2, 2016 from http://www.dailymail.co.uk/news/peoplesdaily/article-3202104/Remarkable-discovery-shows-humans-burning-coal-fuel-3-500-years-ago-world-s-earliest-site-activity-unearthed-China.html

Coase, R. (1937). The nature of the firm. *Economica*, 4(16), 386–405.

Cray, D. (2010, July 23). Deep underground, miles of hidden wildfires rage. *Time*. Retrieved October 12, 2016 from http://content.time.com/time/health/article/0,8599,2006195,00.html

Davis, D., Bell, M., & Fletcher, T. (2002). A look back at the London smog of 1952 and the half century since. *Environmental Health Perspectives*, 110(12), A734.

Els, F. (2014, June 4). *Halved since 2011, EPA rules to push coal price down another 20%*. Retrieved October 12, 2016 from http://www.mining.com/halved-since-2011-new-epa-rules-will-push-thermal-coal-price-down-another-20-40480/

Fahey, J. (2010, July 1). Why small coal-fired plants are going away. *Forbes*. Retrieved October 2, 2016 from http://www.forbes.com/forbes/2010/0719/outfront-obama-coal-energy-electricity-clearing-air.html

Field, A., Edwards, M., & Shoichet, C. (2014). West Virginia chemical spill shines spotlight on loose regulation. *CNN*. Retrieved December 26, 2016 from http://www.cnn.com/2014/01/13/us/west-viriginia-chemical-contamination/

Fishback, P. (1986). Did coal miners "owe their souls to the company store"? Theory and evidence from the early 1900s. *The Journal of Economic History*, 46(4), 1011–1029.

Gordon, R. (2009). The theory and practice of energy policy. In J. Evans & L. C. Hunt (Eds), *International handbook on the economics of energy*. Northampton, MA: Edward Elgar Publishing.

Ifill, G. (2014, March 5). Leading coal producer agrees to pay record fine to clean polluted waters across Appalachia. *PBS Newshour*. Retrieved October 12, 2016 from http://www.pbs.org/newshour/bb/coal-producer-pay-hundreds-of-millions-water-pollution/

Lelyveld, M. (2015). China cuts coal mine deaths, but count in doubt. *Radio Free Asia Commentaries*. Retrieved October 11, 2016 from http://www.rfa.org/english/commentaries/energy_watch/china-coal-deaths-03162015103452.html.

Lemly, A. D. (2009). *Aquatic hazard of selenium pollution from mountaintop removal coal mining*. Retrieved October 12, 2016 from http://www.filonverde.org/images/informe_selenio_en_minas_a_cielo_abierto.pdf

Misiolek, W., & Noser, T. (1982). Coal surface mine land reclamation costs. *Land Economics*, 58(1), 67–85.

Murcott, S. (2012). *Arsenic contamination in the world: An international sourcebook 2012*. London: IWA Publishing.

Ottery, C. (2013). *Map: Health impact of China's coal plants*. Retrieved October 12, 2016 from http://energydesk.greenpeace.org/2013/12/12/map-health-impact-chinas-coal-plants/

Rushton, B. (2015, May 14). A black outlook: Illinois coal in slump. *Illinois Times*. Retrieved October 2, 2016 from http://illinoistimes.com/article-15473-a-black-outlook.html

Sams, J., & Beer, K. (2000). *Effects of coal-mine drainage on stream water quality in the Allegheny and Monongahala river basins—Sulfate transport and trends* (Water Resources Investigations Report 99-4208). Retrieved October 12, 2016 from http://pa.water.usgs.gov/reports/wrir_99-4208.pdf

Schwarz, P. M. (2005). Multipollutant efficiency standards for electricity production. *Contemporary Economic Policy*, 23(3), 341–356.

SourceWatch. (2015, March 31). *Water pollution from coal*. Retrieved October 12, 2016 from Sourcewatch website: http://www.sourcewatch.org/index.php/Water_pollution_from_coal

Speight, J. (2015). *Handbook of coal analysis*. Hoboken, NJ: John Wiley & Sons, Inc.

U.S. Department of the Interior. (2016, December 15). *Reclaiming abandoned mine lands*. Retrieved December 27, 2016 from http://www.osmre.gov/programs/aml.shtm

U.S. Energy Information Administration. (2014). *Today in energy.* Release date: May 14. Retrieved October 7, 2016 from http://www.eia.gov/todayinenergy/detail.php?id=16271

U.S. Energy Information Administration. (2016a). *Quarterly coal report.* Release date: September 23. Retrieved October 2, 2016 from http://www.eia.gov/coal/production/quarterly

U.S. Energy Information Administration. (2016b). *Independent statistics and analysis: Coal.* Retrieved October 10, 2016 from https://www.eia.gov/coal/

U.S. Environmental Protection Agency. (2017). *Inventory of U.S. greenhouse gas emissions and sinks: 1990-2015.* Retrieved June 15, 2017 from https://www3.epa.gov/climatechange/ghgemissions/usinventoryreport.html

Walton, R. (2016, June 14). U.S. Supreme Court blocks latest challenge to MATS rule. *Utilities Dive.* Retrieved December 27, 2016 from http://www.utilitydive.com/news/us-supreme-court-blocks-latest-challenge-to-mats-rule/420855/

Chapter 8

Nuclear energy

"Our children will enjoy in their homes electrical energy too cheap to meter."

Lewis L. Strauss (1954)

"Nuclear energy has a history of costing far more than projected."

The author of this text.

Introduction

Nuclear energy provides about 20% of U.S. electricity generation, the third-largest source. The case for nuclear energy is that it is a highly reliable large source of carbon-free baseload power, with plants built to supply electricity throughout the day and night.[1] Uranium, the predominant fuel used in nuclear reactors, serves the same purpose as fossil fuels, to create heat and steam to power a turbine and generate electricity without the emissions associated with fossil fuels. It can also enhance energy security for countries such as the United States that have an abundant uranium supply. At current rates of use, the United States should have a 100-year supply, with a similar figure for global supplies. The price of uranium is at historically low levels.

The case against nuclear energy is its high cost as well as safety issues. Cost of a new plant can exceed $10 billion, and can take ten or more years to build. These factors combine to make the cost per unit of electricity higher than the cost of alternative fuels. To date, economies of scale dictate that nuclear plants are large. A reactor can deliver 1,000 MW (one gigawatt) or more. Nuclear power plants often contain two reactors at the same site to share common costs, enough to serve almost 1.5 million homes.[2] Since nuclear energy's inception as a source of electricity generation, its costs have escalated despite prophecies that as we gained experience with constructing and operating these plants, costs would decrease. Each nuclear plant has unique design characteristics, with each reactor built with custom parts on site. Further, safety requirements continue to increase, especially after each major accident.

Nuclear plants generate radioactive wastes as a by-product of electricity production. *High-level radioactive wastes*—the by-products of the nuclear reactions—remain active for up to 250,000 years. There is as yet no permanent solution to the storage of high-level wastes. The United States proposed Yucca Mountain in Nevada as a permanent site, but the plans are on hold. The temporary solution is to store wastes on site.

An alternative is to *reprocess* nuclear fuel, recycling spent fuel and using it to generate additional fuel. France, where nuclear energy accounts for the largest percentage of electricity at 70–80% of electricity production, is among a small number of countries that reprocesses its nuclear waste. In 1977, former U.S. President Jimmy Carter banned reprocessing due to fears of creating plutonium, which could be used to make nuclear weapons. While succeeding President Ronald Reagan lifted the ban in 1981, the cost of reprocessing exceeds using the cost of using new fuel as long as the price of uranium remains low.

The next section of this chapter briefly reviews the economic history of nuclear energy. We then highlight nuclear energy regulation. After that, there are sections on private and social costs. Private cost examines the capital costs of building nuclear plants, costs for plant operation and maintenance, and safety costs. Social cost includes negative externalities from spent fuel, including radioactive wastes and fears of nuclear proliferation. There are also subsidies to the industry, such as limited liability in the event of an accident and low-cost loan guarantees that reduce the cost of nuclear energy below its full cost to society. On the other side of the ledger, nuclear energy avoids the external costs of fossil fuel emissions, including carbon emissions. The final section is a summary.

A brief economic history of nuclear power

Ernest Rutherford, who won the Nobel Prize in Chemistry in 1908 for discovering the half-life of radioactive substances, went on in 1911 to propose a new model of the atom. His model resembled a solar system, with a dense nucleus that contained protons (positively charged particles) and neutrons (with no electrical charge) surrounded by orbits of (negatively charged) electrons. In 1917 Rutherford made another monumental discovery, that it was possible to split the nucleus of the atom by bombarding it with alpha particles. Alpha particles have an identical nucleus to a helium atom and contain two protons and two neutrons, and thus have a positive charge. The alpha particles would occasionally dislodge a proton in the nucleus of the original atom, changing it into a different element.

Fission is the splitting of atoms and the reaction releases energy (in the form of radiation). If the atom being split is of one of the heavier elements—such as uranium or plutonium—then the reaction releases at least two neutrons along with the energy. The extra neutrons then collide with and split additional heavy-element atoms which in turn release energy and at least two neutrons. Thus, a self-sustaining nuclear chain reaction occurs.

The fission process happens within fractions of a second. If left unchecked, the energy released through the fission reaction results in a violent explosion, releasing tremendous amounts of radiation, thermal energy, pressure waves (as the air around the explosion is compressed), radioactive particles, and electromagnetic pulses (EMPs) that could damage an electricity system. In 1942, Enrico Fermi, who had earlier discovered the fission potential of uranium, produced the first controlled, self-sustaining nuclear reaction.

Fermi's technology of using uranium and control rods was similar to today's nuclear reactor, but the immediate interest was in building a bomb to defeat Germany and the Axis powers and win World War II. Both the Axis and Allied countries raced to harness the energy released in a fission reaction to create an atomic bomb. Fermi was among the scientists who worked on the top-secret Manhattan Project, culminating in dropping fission-process atomic bombs on Hiroshima and Nagasaki, Japan.

With the end of World War II and the beginning of the Cold War—a competition between the United States and the USSR for control and influence over other countries and territory—the U.S. government sought peaceful uses for nuclear energy in order to maintain a ready supply of trained nuclear physicists and engineers and justify the continued experimentation with atomic weapons and nuclear power (Hewlett & Holl, 1989). The peaceful use of nuclear energy for electricity generation controls the reactor chain reaction to prevent an explosion. In 1946, the United States established the Atomic Energy Commission to oversee the development of peaceful civilian uses for nuclear energy as well as military uses. Commercial nuclear energy began in the 1950s.

In 1953, then President Eisenhower gave his "Atoms for Peace" address to the United Nations. The U.S. Navy studied the use of small, replaceable fission reactors to power its submarines and surface vessels. In 1957, the world's first large-scale nuclear plant began operations at Shippenport, Pennsylvania.

The United States built most of its nuclear plants in the 1960s and 1970s, reinforced by the goal of energy security in the wake of the Middle East oil embargo. However, there was growing discomfort about the safety of nuclear energy, with no permanent solution to storing nuclear waste. In 1979, an accident at Pennsylvania's Three Mile Island plant led to a virtual moratorium on new plant construction in the United States that continued for the next 25 years. In 1986, the most serious accident to date occurred at Chernobyl in the former Soviet Union. While plants in other parts of the world used different designs, the catastrophe reinforced the perception that nuclear plants were unsafe.

The new millennium saw the terrorist attacks of September 11, 2001 give rise to higher energy costs and renewed calls for energy independence. In addition, there was mounting concern about carbon emissions and climate change. There was talk of a *nuclear renaissance*, a return to building new nuclear plants, to reduce carbon emissions and increase energy security. In 2005, the U.S. Energy Policy Act aimed to propel that renaissance. The U.S. Department of Energy (DOE) proffered loan guarantees to electric utilities willing to build new plants with more advanced designs than existing plants. The goal was to gain experience and bring down the costs of the new technology. By 2007, the DOE had received 16 applications to build new reactors. However, when the Great Recession began shortly thereafter, many of the utilities withdrew their plans. And before the economy and the industry could fully recover, there was another nuclear accident.

In 2011, there was a massive earthquake and tidal wave that hit Japan and crippled the Fukushima-Daiichi nuclear energy facility. Japan, with almost no fossil fuel resources, turned to nuclear energy in the 1960s and 1970s to gain energy independence. By 2010, nuclear energy accounted for 30% of their electricity, second only to France. The Fukushima plant had met standards at the time it was built in the 1960s. However, subsequent studies showed that the region had been hit by earthquakes and tsunamis stronger than the ones for which the plant was designed. The Tokyo Electric Company had this information, but had not yet upgraded the plant. There is considerable evidence that Japan had a "*nuclear village*"—a culture of coziness between the company and the government—leading to lax regulation. Immediately after the disaster, Japan shut down all of its nuclear operations.

A number of other countries, Germany among them, accelerated their plans to phase out nuclear energy immediately after Fukushima. They made these decisions in the heat of the moment and not based upon economic reasoning. From an economic perspective, we need to evaluate nuclear energy compared to the alternatives. Germany sought to be a leader in renewable energy and provided large subsidies to wind and solar energy. The production of renewables skyrocketed, as did electricity prices and payments to producers. The government had to quickly reverse its course. As they cut back on their plans, the country turned to coal. Today, they find themselves with some of the highest electricity prices in the EU, and rising carbon emissions.

Japan, with few energy resources of its own, had high electricity prices even before Fukushima. After the disaster, they too provided incentives for renewable energy as well as turning to imports, including high-priced liquefied natural gas (LNG). They also built new coal-fired plants. They soon decided that they could not get by without nuclear energy. They have cautiously restarted several nuclear reactors, though not the ones at Fukushima.[3]

Fission vs. fusion

Nuclear energy has unique virtues, but also faces formidable problems that may threaten its future use. A nuclear power plant is much like one powered by fossil fuel. A heat source produces steam which drives a turbine and generates electricity. The difference is that the source of heat for a nuclear power plant is the heat released from the fission reaction. Unlike fossil fuel plants, there is no burning of fuel, and therefore there are no emissions at the electric-generating stage. It is the fission process that is a nuclear power plant's advantage over fossil-fueled plants—no carbon, NOx, or sulfur emissions—as well as its greatest weakness, the possibility of a release of radiation and radioactive particles.

Natural uranium contains different isotopes, configurations of the element with the same number of protons but different numbers of neutrons. Over 99% of natural uranium is composed of U^{238}, with the superscript representing the atomic weight of the nucleus. Only about 0.7% is U^{235}, the type that works best in conventional nuclear reactors.

U^{235} fissions relatively easily. Nuclear plants control the reaction by including a moderator to control the reaction and a cooling system to keep the reactor core that contains the uranium fuel rod assemblies from overheating. In conventional designs, ordinary (light) water is the moderator and the coolant; it slows the reaction and keeps the fuel from overheating. If the cooling system fails, there is a backup cooling system. In the Fukushima disaster, first the cooling system and then the backup cooling system failed, resulting in overheating and the partial or complete meltdown of the reactor core resulting in a release of radiation. As still another backup, most nuclear plants enclose the reactor core in a containment building. However, in the Fukushima accident, pressure built up to the point where radioactive gases breached the containment building. In the case of Chernobyl, the worst nuclear accident, the plant used a Soviet-designed reactor that had no containment building, and the disaster released large amounts of radiation into the atmosphere.

Box 8.1 There's more than one way to boil water

The most common reactor in the United States is a pressurized water reactor (PWR), followed by a boiling water reactor (BWR). The reactors use ordinary (light) water. The BWR boils water and creates steam inside the reactor vessel, and then pipes steam to the turbine. It recycles unused steam through a condenser to turn it back into water to reuse again. The PWR keeps the water under pressure to prevent it from boiling. The hot water is pumped from the reactor vessel where there is a second water supply away from the fuel source. The heat from the hot water creates steam to spin the turbine, drive the generator, and produce electricity. Unused steam is condensed back into water and used again to create heat.

As compared to the PWR, the BWR has a higher thermal efficiency—the amount of electricity produced per unit of fuel—since it has only a single circuit. The reaction is easier to control by monitoring the water around the core. The reactor is subject to less radiation, an advantage because some steels become brittle with exposure to high levels of radiation. It has fewer components and there is less pressure on the reactor vessel and components. However, the BWR requires a much larger reactor vessel because of the amount of steam that can be released during an accident. The design also allows a small amount of radiation to get into the turbine system, enough that workers near the turbine must wear protective clothing.

Nuclear fusion refers to the process of fusing atoms of lighter elements such as hydrogen and helium together. The result is an atom of a heavier element and a release of energy. A fusion reaction initially requires a large amount of energy from a fission reaction to begin and then uses some of the energy released to fuse additional atoms. The energy generated in a fusion reaction requires a magnetic or plasma field, as it is too hot for any material container.

In a 1954 speech to a group of science journalists, Lewis Strauss, the Chair of the U.S. Atomic Energy Commission, suggested a future in which nuclear power would generate "electrical energy too cheap to meter." In making his prediction, Strauss was apparently referring to his eventual hopes for nuclear fusion—replicating the process of the sun where atoms fuse together—but was not at liberty to talk about government-funded fusion research because of its overlap with weapons development (see Anderson, 2008).

The amount of energy from a nuclear fusion reaction is many times greater than from a fission reaction. Unfortunately, after decades of research, no one has successfully produced a controlled fusion reaction that produces more energy than it consumes. Research continues. In France, the International Thermonuclear Experimental Reactor (ITER, which in Latin means "the way") receives funding from an international consortium of countries. The consortium was organized in 2006 and estimated the cost of building the reactor at €5 billion. They projected construction would begin in 2012, but the project is a decade behind schedule, its projected cost has quadrupled, and the United States is questioning whether to continue providing funding (American Institute of Physics, 2016). MIT built a smaller-scale fusion reactor and announced a new record for the highest pressure achieved, one of the necessary conditions to create more energy than the reactor consumes. Ironically, the achievement took place in October of 2016, just as U.S. funding ended, with the money transferred to ITER (Thompson, 2016).

Regulation

These historical origins show that using nuclear power to generate electricity did not originate through the marketplace. The federal agency tasked with regulating and promoting civilian commercial uses—the U.S. Atomic Energy Commission (AEC)—served as more of an advocate than a watchdog. As an example, AEC promoted the 1957 Price–Anderson Nuclear Industries Indemnity Act, which limited the liability of nuclear firms in the event of an accident as necessary so that a fledgling industry would be able to find private financing.

The AEC's actions are consistent with Stigler's (1971) capture theory of regulation. Stigler expected that industry, which had concentrated interests, would have a greater incentive to influence regulators than the public, which had dispersed interests. The outcome is that instead of promoting overall social welfare, regulators favor the industries they regulate.

In 1975, the Nuclear Regulatory Commission (NRC) succeeded the AEC after there was strong dissatisfaction with the AEC's advocacy. Critics charged that the AEC standards were lax in several areas, including radiation protection, reactor safety, plant siting, and environmental protection.[4] There is evidence that the NRC continues to promote nuclear energy, consistent with capture. A 1988 Congressional investigation found that the NRC had a cozy relationship with the industry it regulated (U.S. Congress, 1988). In 2005, with the advocacy of the NRC, the Energy Policy Act extended Price–Anderson through 2025. The act also gave the industry production tax credits and the offer of loan guarantees for the construction of new more advanced reactors (Sovacool & Valentine, 2012). In a later section, we examine the size of these subsidies and how their removal would affect the cost of nuclear energy. We turn now to regulations on the treatment of spent fuel and its reprocessing.

Spent fuel

In countries that use nuclear power, the most prominent problem is the lack of a solution for long-term storage of nuclear wastes. In the United States, electric utilities pay a fee towards a permanent repository, yet to be established.

The temporary solution for U.S. nuclear power plants is to store used nuclear fuel at each reactor site. Spent fuel rods are contained in ponds with about 40 feet of water encased by reinforced concrete several feet thick with steel liners. As the pools near capacity, utilities move some of the older spent fuel to dry casks (U.S. NRC, 2015; Nuclear Energy Institute, n.d.). The NRC originally pronounced this method safe for 30 years, but recently extended it to 60 years.

Reprocessing

After nuclear fuel has been used to generate electricity, it is possible to reprocess (recycle) the unburned fuel and extract the remaining uranium and plutonium. The United States built three reprocessing plants, none of which are currently operating for civilian purposes due to fears that separated plutonium could fall into the wrong hands. Only one plant at Savannah River, Georgia, is active (although not for reprocessing) and, currently preparing mixed-oxide fuel (MOX), a mix of plutonium and uranium that is a possible alternative to enriched uranium but which presents the risk of stored plutonium.

When France committed to nuclear energy, it chose to reprocess its spent fuel. Other countries that reprocess include the UK, Japan, India, and Russia. While reprocessing has the disadvantage of creating plutonium, it has the advantage of reducing the amount of spent fuel and nuclear waste. At current prices of uranium, reprocessing increases the cost of generating electricity. Bunn, Fetter, Holdren, and van der Zwann (2003) concluded that uranium resources will very likely continue to be available at substantially below the breakeven price for reprocessing throughout the twenty-first century.

To fully evaluate the benefits and costs of reprocessing, we would also have to include benefits such as less mining of uranium, which presents problems similar to coal mining as well as additional concerns about radioactivity, and reduced amounts of spent nuclear fuel and nuclear wastes.[5] On the other side of the ledger, we would have to monetize the increased chance of nuclear proliferation with the greater availability of plutonium.

In the United States, the NRC and DOE continue to evaluate the possibility of resuming reprocessing (Croff et al., 2008; World Nuclear Association, 2016a). A study by Recktenwald and Deinert (2012) finds that reprocessing built in 2010 for a 100-year time frame would add about two mills (a mill is one-tenth of a cent) per kWh to the cost of nuclear energy produced, or about 2% of the average U.S. electricity price of $0.12 per kWh.

Private cost

Levelized cost

In Chapter 6, we introduced levelized cost as a way to compare the costs of fuels. Those figures showed the cost of nuclear energy is approximately $0.10 per kWh of generated electricity, considerably higher than natural gas, and according to Figure 6.6, higher than the cost of renewables.

While nuclear energy's capital costs are high and comprise about 75% of its total costs, fuel costs are low at about 10% (1¢/kWh) of total costs. Accordingly, it is expensive to build new plants because of high fixed costs, but relatively cheap to operate existing plants because of the low variable costs of fuel. The majority of plants in the United States have multiple reactors, which spreads out the fixed costs and brings down the cost per kW of capacity.

Operations and maintenance (O&M) costs account for most of the remainder. These fixed and variable costs include storing spent fuel and nuclear wastes. U.S. regulations require nuclear plant operators to contribute 0.1¢/kWh into a Nuclear Waste Fund towards a nuclear waste depository as well as another 0.1–0.2¢/kWh towards federal insurance to help pay for a possible nuclear accident.

Regulations also require that they set aside funds each year towards eventual plant *decommissioning*. Decommissioning includes reducing remaining radioactivity in the land and decontaminating and dismantling the structures. The wastes may continue to require on-site attention in the absence of a permanent depository. It is necessary to wait about 30 years after the plant has ceased operations for radiation levels to drop to a point when it is safe to begin decommissioning. Decommissioning costs account for 0.1¢/kWh (one mill/kWh).[6]

Capital costs

For the first time in decades, the NRC approved funding in March 2012 for the construction of four new nuclear plants—Vogtle 3 and 4, and Summer 2 and 3—as well as granting permission to the Tennessee Valley Authority (TVA) to complete the construction of Watts Bar Unit 2 so it can begin operations. Watts Bar 1 began operations in 1996, the last nuclear plant to do so. Watts Bar 2 is the first to enter into service since Watts Bar 1. The bankruptcy of Westinghouse threatens the completion of the four new plants.

A consortium of power companies led by the Southern Company of Georgia is building Vogtle units 3 and 4, which will be the first new nuclear plants built in the United States since the Three Mile Island accident. Together with units 1 and 2, the plant will be the largest in the United States. Vogtle 3 and 4 will each produce 1,100 MW, for a total of 2,200 MW. The initial estimated cost was $7 billion per plant, or $14 billion for the two plants. This results in an *overnight cost*—the cost as if the plant were built overnight so that there would be no financing costs—of $6,364/kW. Overnight cost represents the intrinsic cost of construction, setting aside the financing costs that depend on how long the project takes to complete. However, within three months of the funding being approved, the companies indicated cost overruns from a delayed federal licensing process of about $900 million, which pushed up the cost to $6,773/kW (Shapiro, 2012). The cost estimate now is closer to $9 billion per plant, and the plants, originally expected to operate beginning in 2016, now forecast 2019 or later.

A second consortium that includes South Carolina Electric & Gas Company and South Carolina Public Service Authority (Santee Cooper) is building the Virgil C. Summer units 2 and 3. The cost for the two units was originally $9.8 billion in 2008. They have reported delays of over one year and cost overruns attributable to fabrication and delivery of structural modules of over $1 billion (World Nuclear News, 2014).

The U.S. Energy Information Administration (EIA) shows an estimated 2015 overnight cost of a nuclear plant at $6,108/kW (in 2015 dollars), a 14% increase from the previous year when the cost had been estimated to be $5,366/kW. In comparison, a natural gas combined cycle plant has an overnight cost around $700/kW (U.S. EIA, 2015).

Other countries have not necessarily had the same history of rising capital costs. For one thing, the United States constructed its nuclear plants in the 1960s and 1970s, and they have resumed construction of new plants only recently. Lovering, Yip, and Nordhaus (2016) trace the history of construction costs for seven countries using overnight construction cost (OCC) as a metric.

For the United States, they find that OCC rose most sharply after Three Mile Island (TMI) as companies made expensive retrofits to meet new regulations. Construction times increased. While longer construction also leads to higher financing costs, OCC excludes those costs, so in their study rising costs were due to factors related to the new regulatory circumstances in the aftermath of TMI. There was mild cost escalation before TMI, while after this event, costs tripled and the plants took two years longer to build.

One of the justifications for offering subsidized loan guarantees to firms willing to undertake construction of commercially feasible advanced reactors is to allow for *learning-by-doing*, to bring down costs for future generators. If learning–by–doing occurs, we should observe it happening in France, with their extensive nuclear experience. France did experience falling costs with their initial reactors. However, during the 1971–1991 period of rapid expansion, costs escalated, although at a much lower rate than in the United States. Factors included rising labor costs, more complex reactors, and new regulations imposed after the Chernobyl accident in Russia. It was difficult to examine learning-by-doing, as France built reactors in pairs, but only had data on the aggregate facility and not the individual plants. However, the sobering finding is that even in the country with the most successful nuclear program, construction costs have risen over time.

Canada uses a different technology known as the Canada deuterium uranium (CANDU) reactor. It uses deuterium oxide (heavy water) as a moderator and coolant and natural, unenriched uranium as a fuel. With modification, it can also use enriched uranium, mixed fuels, or even thorium, a slightly radioactive element more abundant than uranium but more expensive from which to extract useful energy. CANDU's cost declined rapidly after the first plant that began operations in 1957. They began to build larger plants between 1971 and 1986 and experienced modest 4% annual cost escalation.

Germany experienced cost reductions after its first reactor in 1958, but 12% annual cost increases between 1973 and 1983. Japan, India, and South Korea offer more recent experience, as they continued building nuclear plants through the 1990s and 2000s. Japan shows the pattern of costs falling at first, followed by an 8% annual rate of escalation between 1970 and 1980, but then stable costs for the 27-year period between 1980 and 2007. India's early experience was a mix of falling and then rising costs, but their most recent experience between 2000 and 2003 showed falling costs. South Korea built its first reactor in 1971, and has experienced falling costs throughout the period, with a steady decline of 1% a year between 1989 and 2008, and an average decline of 2% over the entire history.

Lovering, Yip, and Nordhaus suggest isolating the drivers of lower costs rather than relying on learning-by-doing. They note that levelized costs rose by a smaller factor than construction costs, so there are opportunities to look for savings in O&M costs.

China announced a goal of building nuclear plants at home and for export at a rapid rate using a standardized design. They also planned to move construction crews from one site to another, so workers have experience in building nuclear plants. The objective was to bring down costs by using a standardized design and experienced workers. The initial evidence is that costs are higher than expected, due to a combination of construction setbacks and low demand (Thomas, 2016). India and Russia also have active building programs and may offer further data on recent experiences.

Operating and maintenance (O&M) costs

Of the $100/MWh levelized cost for plants entering service in 2022 (in $2015), capital cost was $75. Other than $1/MWh for transmission costs, fixed and variable O&M costs make up the remainder, with roughly equal shares. Fuel cost, included in variable O&M, is $6.91/MWh (less than 1¢/kWh). Uranium cost peaked in 2013, and has decreased each year since then, reducing fuel costs. Operating costs peaked in 2011, and have declined since then.

Variable O&M for nuclear energy at approximately $11/MWh is lower than for natural gas advanced combined cycle plants at close to $40. Plant operators who have nuclear plants available will use them before turning to natural gas, given the lower variable costs. Additionally, continuing to operate existing nuclear plants is a lower-cost decision than replacing them before their planned retirement.[7]

Additional costs due to Fukushima

The NRC mandated safety improvements in the aftermath of the Fukushima disaster. Measures include backup equipment in case a plant loses electrical power and cannot operate pumps to keep water high enough to cool the reactor. The equipment needs to be housed in a new building designed to withstand an earthquake. A second measure is instrumentation to show water levels inside the spent fuel facility. The NRC also issued a new vent requirement for boiling water reactors to prevent or lessen damage to the reactor core in the event of a serious accident. The industry also added two national response centers that have an extra set of backup equipment they can send to any plant within 24 hours. One cost estimate for the improvements is $4 billion (Kern, 2016).

Box 8.2 The cost of preventing the next Fukushima

Schwarz and Cochran (2013) ask what it would cost to prevent the next Fukushima. As most nuclear plants are not near oceans or on earthquake faults, they would spend less to make changes in response to the accident, so the estimates are an upper bound. The authors include four measures: relocating the plant 10 km (6 miles) inland, building a 15-m (50-foot) tsunami wall, using a lead acid battery backup system, and relocating the diesel generators to a higher site. The costs reflect a 4.7 GW plant the size of Fukushima, which contained six BWRs, operating at 80% capacity, for an average of 3.76 GW power production. For simplicity, the study uses overnight costs.

The additional cost of building the nuclear energy power plant 10 km inland would be approximately $30 million. A 15-m tsunami wall, more than twice the height of the one that protected the Fukushima nuclear power plant, would also add $30 million. The installation of a secondary emergency backup power system on the roofs of the reactor buildings, such as a series of lead acid batteries, would cost $1 million. Installing the primary emergency backup power system on the roofs of the reactor buildings of the Fukushima nuclear power plant would have protected the system from the 10-m high tsunami at a cost of at most $1 million.

The total costs associated with the four technological safeguards would have been an increase in capital costs of $62 million, $2.36/MWh, or only a little more than 0.2¢ (2 mills)/ kWh.

Using a damage estimate of $300 billion and an assumption that the event was a one-in-1,000-year event, annual expected damage is $300 million/year. Benefit per year exceeds cost by almost $240 million.

The additional safety measures should add no more to the cost of nuclear energy—about 0.2¢—than expenditures towards government insurance, a nuclear repository, or decommissioning.

Private cost revisited

As indicated earlier, U.S. EIA (2016a) estimates the levelized cost of nuclear energy for plants entering service in 2022 at $0.10/kWh. The cost includes NRC-required safety improvements from lessons learned at Fukushima.

We have introduced two of the major subsidies—limited liability and loan guarantees—that decrease the price of nuclear energy below its opportunity cost. We first consider the value of the subsidy that limits liability in the event of an accident. The method is from Schwarz and Cochran (2013).

Utilities pay into a fund that currently provides $12.6 billion in the event of an accident. In addition, they are required to have $300 million in private insurance. In all, the plants are responsible for just under $13 billion in damage.

Chernobyl and Fukushima had damage on the order of $300 billion. Sandia National Labs did a 1982 study for the NRC that property damage alone from a nuclear meltdown would be $300 billion, or $700 billion in current dollars. That amount does not include the estimated 50,000 fatalities. While the $700 billion figure can be debated, nuclear plants located near major population centers could well cause this amount of property damage (Hargreaves, 2011). To be conservative, we will use an estimate of $300 billion, the costs of Chernobyl and Fukushima. If there is an accident, the industry liability of just under $13 billion still leaves $287 billion paid for by society.

The world has experienced two serious nuclear accidents in the 60 years of nuclear plant operations, although neither has been in the United States; TMI was of a much smaller order of magnitude. We produce one-third of the world's nuclear energy, which would make the probability of a major accident in the United States 1/90. Given that the circumstances that occurred in the former Soviet Union and in Japan are less likely in the United States, the probability is probably lower. We will make a small adjustment to 1/100. The expected cost of a one-in-100-year accident of $300 billion is $3 billion. Assuming a 1,000 MW reactor with a 40-year life, an 8,766-hour year and a conservative figure of 80% utilization (nuclear plants typically achieve 90% or even higher), the present value of the subsidy is about $2/MWh, or 0.2¢/kWh, about 2% of the cost of a unit of nuclear-generated electricity.

Box 8.3 Battle of the Price–Anderson subsidy estimates

Dubin and Rothwell (1990) cite a 1973 study by Denenberg that estimated the value of the subsidy to be $23.5 million per reactor year. They find the estimate to be too low, as Denenberg bases the estimate on the probability of a worst case scenario of a single $40 billion accident whereas actual insurance covers all accidents between $40 and $60 billion. Their study finds the subsidy to be worth approximately $60 million per reactor year prior to 1982 and $22 million after 1988 changes that reduced the liability limitation. Heyes and Liston-Heyes (1998) find that Dubin and Rothwell underestimated the portion of damages that the nuclear operator would have to pay, resulting in too high a subsidy estimate. They find a lower subsidy value of $13.32 million before 1982 and $2.32 million after 1988, with all estimates in 1985 dollars. In a follow-up, Heyes (2002) converts the reduced subsidy to 2–3¢/kWh, with a wide range of uncertainty. Even the reduced estimate is an order of magnitude larger than the estimate in Schwarz and Cochran (2013).

We next calculate the value of the loan guarantee subsidy, again using the method in Schwarz and Cochran (2013). The cost of building a 1,000 MW plant is on the order of $5 million/MW (George & Cain, 2011). A 3% subsidy saves the utility $150,000/MW or $150 million for the 1,000 MW plant. Once again assuming an 8,766 hour year and 80% utilization, the subsidy is roughly $20/MWh, or about 20% of the cost of nuclear energy. Together, the removal of the two subsidies would increase the cost of nuclear energy by at least 20%, and possibly 40% or more given the estimates in Box 8.3. The revised cost is $0.12–0.14/kWh, making nuclear energy even less competitive as compared to other fuels.

Box 8.4 Financing construction work in progress: another subsidy?

It is a challenge to finance a risky $10 billion investment. Regulated utilities may undertake the expenditure if they expect to be able to recoup their investment through the rate base. Current law in most U.S. states requires a plant to be "used and useful" before it goes into the rate base. Utilities argue for construction-work-in-progress (CWIP), where they can receive payment as they incur the expense. They also try to recoup initial planning costs. If utilities recoup planning and construction costs before the plants are operational, utility customers pay higher rates for plants that are not producing electricity. And if the plants are never finished, ratepayers may get nothing in return. Utilities say that if they cannot collect these costs upfront, they will have to pay more to borrow money and it will cost consumers more in the end. Also, they need to spend money for planning, so that if the time comes when it is advantageous to build another nuclear plant, they are ready to go.

We further consider the two financing mechanisms in Chapter 12 when we look at traditionally regulated electric utilities. Investors also expect compensation for the risks of accidents as well as the risk that the plant never operates. Restructured utilities in a more competitive environment, which we consider in Chapter 13, have not undertaken any new nuclear plant construction.

Social cost

In order to evaluate nuclear energy as compared to fossil fuel alternatives, we need to compare social costs, including all relevant externalities. It is necessary to consider the costs of nuclear wastes that may remain radioactive for 250,000 years and for which there is no permanent storage solution. Nuclear energy also presents terrorism risks, both from enriching nuclear fuel into weapons–grade uranium or plutonium as well as the possibility of a physical or cyber attack on a nuclear plant. On the other side of the ledger, nuclear energy avoids external costs of fossil fuels, especially carbon emissions.

Nuclear waste

The United States has long pursued a permanent nuclear waste depository where all nuclear plants would ship their spent fuel and radioactive wastes. A single waste depository would make it easier to monitor the wastes than if they are at multiple locations.

Box 8.5 The saga of Yucca Mountain[8]

In 1982, the Nuclear Waste Policy Act established a timetable for the responsible disposal of nuclear wastes, with the DOE assigned the task of setting up a repository. U.S. utilities with nuclear plants and other nuclear facilities would pay the cost. Since 1983, U.S. utilities have contributed 0.1 ¢/kWh ($1/MW) to the fund. In 1987, President Reagan proposed Yucca Mountain in the remote deserts of Nevada far from any population centers as the site for a nuclear waste depository.

In 2008, after 20 years of discussion, the DOE applied to the NRC to license Yucca Mountain in Nevada for this purpose. That year was also an election year, and the Democrats won the presidency as well as obtaining a large majority in the Senate and the House of Representatives. Nevada Senator Harry Reid became Senate Majority Leader and campaigned against Yucca Mountain. In 2010, the Obama Administration decided to terminate the licensing proceedings and withdrew funds to continue their work from the NRC and DOE. The DOE and NRC suspended their efforts.

In 2010, the NRC ruled in the Waste Confidence Rules that the wastes, such as spent fuel rods, could stay on site for up to 60 years, an increase from the 30-year term established earlier. After a court challenge including a concern that the NRC had not sufficiently considered that a national waste depository might never be built, the NRC issued a new "continued storage" rule that the radioactive waste can be stored indefinitely—if no permanent storage facility is built.

In late 2013, a federal court ruled that the fee that utilities have been paying towards the depository since 1983 could no longer be collected until there were provisions to collect nuclear waste. By then, the fund had accumulated $30 billion, of which about $8 billion had been spent studying the Yucca Mountain site.

Shortly after the 2010 decision, several parties sued to restart licensing procedures. The NRC ordered the licensing proceedings restarted. In 2015, the NRC completed the report it had started before 2010, finding the site acceptable, but that the DOE did not have rights to the land or water needed to operate the repository. In 2016, Republicans won the presidency, and are likely to look more favorably on the Yucca Mountain site.

A blue ribbon panel was appointed when it appeared that Yucca Mountain would not be an option, and entertained a "consent-based" approach, where the government would compensate a location for storing wastes.[9] Private companies in Texas and New Mexico expressed an interest in providing interim storage facilities for used nuclear fuel.

The economic principle is based on a Pareto improvement approach where both sides gain. The concept was proposed in a different context when economist Larry

Summers, then at the World Bank, proposed in a leaked memo that countries submit bids for the amount they would be willing to accept in return for storing toxic wastes, with the lowest bid chosen. There was outrage from noneconomists over what some saw as abhorrent ethics, with poor countries likely ending up with the wastes. This ethical perspective objects to placing the poor in a dilemma where they accept a harmful product in exchange for money. From an economic standpoint, it is simply an example of a Pareto improvement. The poor likely get the waste, but since they volunteered, they must have received sufficient compensation to be better off.

Just as the United States may yet reconsider Yucca Mountain as a site for a permanent waste depository, it may also reconsider reprocessing of spent fuel. Reprocessing reduces waste considerably, as well as reducing externalities from mining. There is still waste, but the depository could be much smaller.

Terrorist threats

The possibility exists that the by-products of nuclear energy generation could be used for the development of nuclear weapons. Nuclear fuel cycles and nuclear weapon cycles are quite similar and, after utilization for nuclear energy, waste fuel rods contain elements required for the production of nuclear weapons. There remains considerable concern that Iran seeks to use uranium to build weapons, despite its claim that it is pursuing nuclear energy. However, the process of converting uranium or plutonium from peaceful to military purposes is difficult, expensive, and dangerous.

Natural uranium is over 99% U^{238} and less than 1% U^{235}. Nuclear plants require 3% U^{235}. Enrichment requires turning uranium into a gas, and then spinning it in a centrifuge at extremely high speeds, where the lighter gas with a slightly higher concentration of U^{235} separates from the heavier gas. It takes many rounds to enrich uranium to 3% U^{235}. To make highly enriched uranium—20% U^{235}—for crude and unreliable nuclear weapons—takes many more rounds of enrichment. Weapons-grade uranium—over 90% U^{235}—creates weapons as effective as the one used at Hiroshima, but is extremely difficult to make.

Plutonium (chemical symbol Pu) gives rise to the greatest concern among the nuclear fuels. When U^{238} absorbs a neutron, it becomes U^{239} which ultimately decays into Pu^{239}. This isotope generates enormous energy and destructive potential when it undergoes fission. Pu^{239} can be used for nuclear weapons, as it was in the bomb dropped on Nagasaki. Plutonium produced from spent fuel is typically 60–70% Pu^{239} compared with weapons-grade plutonium which is more than 93% Pu^{239}. Reprocessing increases the percentage, the argument underlying the U.S. ban on reprocessing. However, its use presents great challenges to the weapons builder from high rates of spontaneous fission and radiation (World Nuclear Association, 2016b).

Some reactors, known as fast breeder reactors, can create more plutonium and burn it along with uranium, disposing of the plutonium so it will not fall into the wrong hands. The reactor "breeds" more fuel by transforming abundant U^{238} into Pu^{239}. Some countries continue to use and research breeder reactors. The technology is not new, and its cost has been higher than the dominant technologies. Another option is to blend plutonium with uranium to create mixed-oxide fuel (MOX) that could burn in ordinary reactors and also render plutonium no longer usable for weapons. France, several other EU countries, and Japan use MOX. France and the UK produce MOX. Japan plans to do so by 2019. Although Duke Energy and the TVA have expressed interest in using MOX that would be produced at a plant under construction at the Savannah River Site in South Carolina, the United States has not given the go-ahead due to fears of nuclear proliferation from the plutonium on-site (World Nuclear Association, 2016c).

Finally, there is the concern that terrorists could attack nuclear facilities using ground or air attacks, with potentially devastating consequences especially in highly populated areas. The NRC has taken numerous measures to examine and strengthen the ability of nuclear plants to withstand attacks from jumbo jets, trucks, and from within. We further evaluate the threat of nuclear terrorism, cyber as well as physical, in Chapter 16 on energy security.

The costs of storing spent fuel and nuclear waste as well as the costs of protecting against terrorism are components of the social cost of using nuclear energy. They are difficult to measure, but it is important to do so. Otherwise, the public may treat the costs as if they are infinite, leading to the conclusion that we should not build any more nuclear plants. We need to monetize the risk and then evaluate the full social cost of nuclear energy compared to its alternatives.

Carbon emissions

In making societal decisions, we should count not only the external costs of nuclear energy, including catastrophic events such as the potential effects of radioactive fuel leaks, but also costs to society of emissions associated with the burning of fossil fuels. Referring to U.S. regulation, some of these emissions are subject to regulation and so the prices of fossil fuels internalize those costs. In previous chapters, we considered the effect of regulations on emissions such as SO_2 and NOx on fossil fuel producers and electric utilities.

As of 2016, the United States had not yet passed national legislation to reduce carbon emissions. If such a program is passed, it will increase the price of natural gas and especially coal while leaving the price of nuclear energy and renewables unaffected. Coal produces about 2.1 pounds of CO_2 emissions per kWh of energy produced, while natural gas emits about 1.2 pounds (U.S. EIA, 2016b). A carbon price will narrow the gap between the social cost of nuclear energy and fossil alternatives, and at a high enough price of carbon, nuclear energy would have a lower social cost than the fossil alternatives.

Given our levelized cost figure of $0.10 for nuclear energy, it is already competitive with coal. For utilities that are no longer building new coal plants and instead are turning to natural gas at a levelized cost of $0.06, nuclear energy does not become competitive with natural gas until we reach a carbon price of $80/ton. Where carbon trading does exist, price is generally $20/ton or less, although academic studies commonly choose a figure closer to $40/ton with the expectation that the figure will rise over time.

Box 8.6 Willingness to pay for carbon-free energy

Nuclear energy is a carbon-free source of energy, but also presents risks related to radioactivity in the event of an accident. Several economists have compared consumer willingness to pay (WTP) for nuclear energy or renewables, as compared to fossil fuels. When there are no markets to reveal this information, economists use *contingent valuation*, a survey method where economists ask questions to elicit consumer WTP.

One illustrative study is by Murakami, Ida, Tanaka, and Friedman (2015), who compare WTP in the U.S. and Japan for carbon reductions from nuclear energy and from renewable fuels. For a 1% decrease in GHGs, U.S. consumers are willing to pay $0.31 per month, while Japanese consumers are willing to pay $0.26 per month. U.S. consumers are willing to pay $0.71 per month and Japanese consumers $0.31 for a 1% increase in renewables and a 1% decrease in fossil fuels towards this goal. However, U.S. consumers are willing to pay −$0.11 and Japanese consumers −$0.72, *negative* amounts, for a 1% increase in nuclear energy and a 1% decrease in fossil fuels. This result indicates that consumers find the risks associated with nuclear energy exceed the benefits of lower carbon emissions. Japanese consumers showed greater negativity after the Fukushima crisis.

Summary

Nuclear energy as a source of fuel for electricity generation began in the 1950s, with the U.S. government wanting to find a peaceful use for nuclear energy beyond its military use. With a ready labor force of trained nuclear personnel, the government subsidized research and development into the use of nuclear power to generate electricity. The AEC both regulated and advocated its use.

The AEC predicted lower costs as the industry increased scale and gained experience, but instead it has had a history of cost overruns and lengthening construction times. Even with the continuation of subsidies such as limited liability and low-interest loans, electricity generated by nuclear energy continues to be more expensive than the alternatives of natural gas and renewables, although the latter also receive subsidies. However, there are few alternatives to nuclear energy as a baseload fuel.

Around 2000, there was talk of a nuclear renaissance as concerns about energy security and climate change intensified. Nuclear-generated electricity does not release carbon. The degree to which this factor favors nuclear energy will ultimately depend on the price society is willing to pay to restrict carbon emissions.

The Energy Policy Act of 2005 offered several inducements for nuclear plant construction. Electric utilities showed interest in the combination of tax credits and low-interest loans, as well as an extension of the Price–Anderson Act that limits liability in the event of a nuclear accident. A number of utilities cancelled their plans during the Great Recession that began late in 2007.

Just as economies were recovering from the depths of the recession, the 2011 nuclear accident at Fukushima reinforced concerns about the safety of nuclear reactors. Many countries, Germany among them, turned away from nuclear power even though the accident at Fukushima, and Chernobyl before it, had causes that were less likely for plants outside those countries. Chernobyl operated in an isolated environment with a flawed technology and less of a safety culture than plants outside the former Soviet Union. The Japanese government had a close relationship with their nuclear industry that likely contributed to lax regulation. There were reports that Tokyo Electric acted slowly on new information that the plant location was vulnerable to stronger hurricanes and tsunamis than it was designed for in the 1960s.

While many countries are hesitant about building new nuclear plants, and some are shutting down existing plants, the United States has recently completed Watts Bar 2, and Vogtle 3 and 4 and Summer 2 and 3 are under construction. China is trying to stand-ardize nuclear plant construction to bring down the costs, and wants to construct plants in China and in other countries. Korea, India, and Russia are building nuclear plants.

Nuclear energy has promised lower costs since its inception, but instead costs have generally risen, often by multiples of the initial cost estimates. While there is skepticism that nuclear energy will finally make good on its promises, it is the only available fuel that can currently deliver baseload fuel that is free of carbon emissions. Chapter 10 will consider a variety of next-generation alternatives, including nuclear energy technolo-gies such as small modular reactors, pebble bed, molten-salt, and thorium reactors as well as the elusive goal of commercially viable nuclear fusion.

Notes

1 Referring to nuclear energy as not contributing to climate change is somewhat of a simplification from a life-cycle perspective. Nuclear plants use water for cooling. Correspondingly, the production of electricity using nuclear energy warms the surrounding water, increasing evaporation. An increase in water vapor also allows the atmosphere to retain more heat and in that way has a similar effect as a higher concentration of CO_2 due to carbon emissions. See Mayumi and Polimeni (2012). There are also emissions at other stages of the supply chain, such as during mining and transportation.
2 Small modular plants are a next-generation technology. They exist, but are not yet cost-competitive, nor are they necessarily safer. We defer fuller evaluation of small modular nuclear plants until Chapter 10 on next-generation technologies.
3 The laws of supply and demand operate even when countries make decisions for noneconomic reasons. Japan has reduced its energy use as a result of its high energy prices. It plans to deregulate its electricity system in the hopes that competition will reduce the price of electricity and break the cozy relationship between the electricity industry and the government.
4 Surprisingly, this information comes from the U.S. NRC (n.d.), openly discussing the problems with its predecessor.
5 Uranium is a much more concentrated source of energy than coal, so the scale of uranium mining is much smaller.
6 Levelized cost also includes a contribution of 0.01¢/kWh for transmission lines needed in order for the electric producer to send electricity to customers.
7 According to Neuhauser (2016), operating costs increase as nuclear plants near retirement age or get an extension beyond their original planned retirement.
8 See YuccaMountain.org (2016) for information on the Yucca Mountain depository.
9 See the Nuclear Energy Institute (2016) for the interim proposal to store waste using the consent-based approach.

References

American Institute of Physics. (2016, June 10). *DOE recommends US stay in ITER, warns of potential delays to other projects*. Retrieved August 9, 2016 from https://www.aip.org/fyi/2016/doe-recommends-us-stay-iter-warns-potential-delays-other-projects

Anderson, C. (2008, Sept 12). The truth about "too cheap to meter" [Web log post]. Retrieved August 10, 2016 from http://www.longtail.com/the_long_tail/2008/09/the-truth-about.html

Bunn, M., Fetter, S., Holdren, J., & van der Zwaan, B. (2003). *The economics of reprocessing vs. direct disposal of spent nuclear fuel.* Belfer Center for Science and International Affairs, John F. Kennedy Harvard School of Government.

Croff, A. G., Wymer, R. G., Tavlarides, L. L., Flack, J. H., & Larson, H. G. (2008). *Background, status, and issues related to the regulation of advanced spent nuclear fuel recycle facilities.* ACNW&M White Paper, NUREG-1909. U.S. Nuclear Regulatory Commission. Retrieved October 19, 2016 from http://pbadupws.nrc.gov/docs/ML0815/ML081550505.pdf

Dubin, J., & Rothwell, G. (1990). Subsidy to nuclear power through Price–Anderson liability limit. *Contemporary Economic Policy, 8,* 73–79.

George, G., & Cain, C. (2011). *Beyond loan guarantees: Fostering U.S. nuclear investment in a post-Fukushima world.* Retrieved October 24, 2016 from http://www.bateswhite.com/assets/htmldocuments/media.739.pdf

Hargreaves, S. (2011, March 25). Nuclear industry shielded from big disaster costs. *CNN Money.* Retrieved October 20, 2016 from http://money.cnn.com/2011/03/25/news/economy/nuclear_accident_costs/

Hewlett, R., & Holl, J. (1989). *Atoms for peace and war, 1953–1961: Eisenhower and the Atomic Energy Commission.* Berkeley and Los Angeles, CA: University of California Press.

Heyes, A. (2002). Determining the price of Price–Anderson. *Regulation, 25*(4), 26–30.

Heyes, A., & Liston-Heyes, C. (1998). Subsidy to nuclear power through Price–Anderson liability limit: Comment. *Contemporary Economic Policy, 16,* 122–124.

Kern, R. (2016, March 11). U.S. nuclear industry largely safer after Fukushima accident. *Bloomberg BNA.* Retrieved August 22, 2016 from http://www.bna.com/us-nuclear-industry-n57982068435/

Lovering, J., Yip, A., & Nordhaus, T. (2016). Historical construction costs of global nuclear power reactors. *Energy Policy, 91,* 371–382.

Mayumi, K., & Polimeni, J. (2012). Uranium reserve, nuclear fuel cycle delusion, CO_2 emissions from the sea, and electricity supply: Reflections after the fuel meltdown of the Fukushima nuclear power units. *Ecological Economics, 73,* 1–6.

Murakami, K., Ida, T., Tanak, M., & Friedman, L. (2015). Consumers' willingness to pay for renewable and nuclear energy: A comparative analysis between the US and Japan. *Energy Economics, 50,* 178–189.

Neuhauser, A. (2016, March 30). Nuclear power, once cheap, squeezed by mounting costs. *U.S. News and World Report.* Retrieved October 19, 2016 from http://www.usnews.com/news/articles/2016–03–30/nuclear-power-once-cheap-squeezed-by-mounting-costs

Nuclear Energy Institute. (2016, January 21). *DOE considering consent-based interim fuel storage.* Retrieved October 21, 2016 from http://www.nei.org/News-Media/News/News-Archives/DOE-Considering-Consent-Based-Interim-Fuel-Storage

Nuclear Energy Institute. (n.d.). *Issues and policy: Used nuclear fuel storage.* Retrieved August 10, 2016 from http://www.nei.org/issues-policy/nuclear-waste-management/used-nuclear-fuel-storage

Recktenwald, G. D., & Deinert, M. R. (2012). Cost probability analysis of reprocessing spent nuclear fuel in the US. *Energy Economics, 34*(6), 1873–1881.

Schwarz, P., & Cochran, J. (2013). Renaissance or requiem: Is nuclear energy cost-effective in a post Fukushima world? *Contemporary Economic Policy, 31*(4), 691–707.

Shapiro, J. (2012, May 11). Vogtle nuclear project facing $900 million on cost overruns. *WABE90.1.* Retrieved October 19, 2016 from http://news.wabe.org/post/vogtle-nuclear-project-facing–900-million-cost-overruns

Sovacool, B., & Valentine, S. (2012). *The national politics of nuclear power: Economics, security, and governance.* London and New York: Routledge.

Stigler, G. (1971). The economic theory of regulation. *Bell Journal of Economics and Management Science, 2,* 3–21.

Strauss, L. L. (1954, September 16). *Speech to the National Association of Science Writers.* New York City.

Thomas, S. (2016, October 29). China's nuclear power plans melting down. *The Diplomat.* Retrieved December 28, 2016 from http://thediplomat.com/2016/10/chinas-nuclear-power-plans-melting-down/

Thompson, A. (2016, October 18). MIT breaks a world record for nuclear fusion: The record was broken on the day the reactor was scheduled to be shut down. *Popular Mechanics.* Retrieved October 23, 2016 from http://www.popularmechanics.com/science/energy/a23431/mit-world-record-nuclear-fusion/

U.S. Congress. (1988). *NRC coziness with industry: Nuclear Regulatory Commission fails to maintain arms length relationship with the nuclear industry: An investigative report.* Retrieved August 27, 2016 from https://babel.hathitrust.org/cgi/pt?id=pst.000013688240

U.S. Energy Information Administration. (2015). *Electricity market module.* Retrieved October 19, 2016 from https://www.eia.gov/forecasts/aeo/assumptions/pdf/electricity.pdf

U.S. Energy Information Administration. (2016a). *Levelized cost and levelized avoided cost of new generation resources in the annual energy outlook 2016.* Retrieved August 27, 2016 from https://www.eia.gov/forecasts/aeo/pdf/electricity_generation.pdf

U.S. Energy Information Administration. (2016b). *Frequently asked questions: How much carbon dioxide is produced per kilowatt hour when generating electricity with fossil fuels?* Retrieved October 23, 2016 from https://www.eia.gov/tools/faqs/faq.cfm?id=74&t=11

U.S. Nuclear Regulatory Commission. (2015). *Spent fuel storage in pools and dry casks key points and questions & answers.* Retrieved October 19, 2016 from http://www.nrc.gov/waste/spent-fuel-storage/faqs.html

U.S. Nuclear Regulatory Commission. (n.d.). *History.* Retrieved August 10, 2016 from http://www.nrc.gov/about-nrc/history.html

World Nuclear Association. (2016a, April). *Safeguards to prevent nuclear proliferation.* Retrieved October 21, 2016 from http://www.world-nuclear.org/information-library/safety-and-security/non-proliferation/safeguards-to-prevent-nuclear-proliferation.aspx

World Nuclear Association. (2016b, September). *Processing of used nuclear fuel.* Retrieved October 19, 2016 from http://www.world-nuclear.org/information-library/nuclear-fuel-cycle/fuel-recycling/processing-of-used-nuclear-fuel.aspx

World Nuclear Association. (2016c, October). *Mixed oxide (MOX) fuel.* Retrieved October 23, 2016 from http://www.world-nuclear.org/information-library/nuclear-fuel-cycle/fuel-recycling/mixed-oxide-fuel-mox.aspx

World Nuclear News. (2014, October 03). *Cost of Summer AP1000s increases.* Retrieved August 13, 2016 from http://www.world-nuclear-news.org/NN-Cost-of-Summer-AP1000s-increases-0310144.html

YuccaMountain.org. (2016, December). Retrieved December 28, 2016 from http://yuccamountain.org/

Part III

Alternative energy sources

Chapter 9

Renewable energy
Ready for prime time?

"We have one of the best solar potentials here in the United States in the world. . . . We're number one in the world in wind."

Robert F. Kennedy, Jr. (Collins, 2015)

"Cape Wind's proposal involves construction of 130 giant turbines whose windmill arms will reach 417 feet above the water and be visible for up to 26 miles. These turbines are less than six miles from shore and would be seen from Cape Cod, Martha's Vineyard and Nantucket."

Robert F. Kennedy, Jr. (2005)

Introduction

As the opening quotes show, there is great enthusiasm to increase our use of renewable energy. However, as its use has increased, there are also rising objections, in this case from the same person! Renewables offer the possibility of an inexhaustible, carbon-free fuel. Yet they impact views, affect ecology, and require large amounts of land.

In this chapter, we focus on commercially feasible renewable energy sources, such as wind, solar, biomass, and more briefly, geothermal. We also include hydropower, which while a conventional fuel, is renewable. We touch upon other water-based sources of energy, such as waves and tides. In Chapter 10, we will consider next-generation alternative energy sources including renewables such as hydrogen, Generation II biofuels, and small-scale hydro, as well as further developments in nonrenewable technologies, such as clean coal, modular nuclear plants, and battery storage.

Wind, solar, biomass, hydroelectric, and geothermal are renewable sources of energy. In contrast to nonrenewable fuels such as oil, coal, natural gas, and nuclear, renewable resources can replenish themselves. However, there are both exhaustible and nonexhaustible renewables. Wood is a renewable biomass resource, but is vulnerable to depletion if the rate of harvesting exceeds the growth rate of the trees. Geothermal is depletable if the rate of heat extraction exceeds the replenishment rate. Hydropower can be depletable if it uses slowly replenishing groundwater.

Solar energy is both renewable and nonexhaustible. The sun constantly replenishes itself through a process of nuclear fusion. Absorption of solar energy by one photovoltaic (PV) cell does not diminish the amount of solar energy accessible by other solar facilities. However, large-scale solar energy may compete with other land uses, such as farming.

Wind energy derives from the sun warming the Earth. Heating creates areas of varying air pressure, and as the air flows to equalize pressure, the result is wind.[1] As with solar energy, wind energy requires land and may impact views. It also interferes with the flight paths of birds and bats.

As nature provides these resources, their availability differs from place to place. These fuels are also intermittent, available only when the sun is shining or the wind is blowing. In the absence of electricity storage, these fuels cannot typically serve as base-load, as they are not available 24/7. While forecasts of availability are improving to the point where we can predict the next day's available sunlight or average wind speed with increasing accuracy, each passing cloud, tree shadow, or gust of wind can affect real-time availability. Battery storage is also an active area of investigation and we address its development in Chapter 10.[2]

Wind energy is often most available on mountain ridges and along coastlines. Despite the impetus for renewables from environmental advocates, the NIMBY (not in my backyard) phenomenon still arises. As one of the opening quotes shows, Robert F. Kennedy, Jr., a well-known environmentalist, has nevertheless been battling since 2005 to prevent the construction of Cape Wind, a project that would interfere with views from a Kennedy family compound in Massachusetts.[3]

Biofuels are renewable, but as with trees, they are exhaustible if the rate of harvest exceeds the rate of growth. It is common to think of biofuels made from crops, such as ethanol produced from sugarcane or from corn. One of the major concerns is that using a crop for biofuel reduces its availability for food. Former U.S. President George W. Bush promoted greater use of corn-based ethanol in his February, 2007 State of the Union address. By May, the price of tortillas had soared in Mexico, leading to street protests against the corn-based fuel.

The next generation of biofuels to be discussed in Chapter 10 seek to avoid the dilemma of food versus fuel.[4] Waste products may become biofuels, including a type of prairie grass called switchgrass, corn stover (nonedible parts of the corn plant), and even french fry grease.[5] These methods make food and fuel joint products rather than substitutes.

It would seem that the best source of energy is simply to burn waste. Doing so creates energy and saves on landfill space. To date, the plants have been costly, and require expensive technologies to control emissions. The EU uses the technology, while the U.S. recently built its first plant in twenty years.

The next section of this chapter provides reasons for using renewable fuels. After that, we examine government subsidies for producers and consumers of renewable fuels. We then look at their accelerating use, partly due to subsidies and partly to rapidly declining costs. We then examine resistance to their adoption, some of it due to the NIMBY phenomenon. The penultimate section considers hydropower and geothermal energy. The last section is a summary.

Why alternative fuels?

Solar and wind energy together account for only about 5% of electricity generation in the United States, but are experiencing high rates of growth. Onshore wind is approaching parity with natural gas on a levelized cost basis, with solar PV not far behind. However, levelized cost does not provide an apples-to-apples comparison, as it does not account for the intermittency of wind and solar energy. It includes current subsidies, but not unpriced externalities.

Germany, a country not known for its sunny climate, is a leader in solar energy. Why did the solar share in Germany grow so quickly? Germany makes use of *feed-in tariffs* (FITs). These set prices for solar and other alternatives above their costs, and may require utilities to purchase the alternative even if it exceeds the cost of traditional sources of energy. Typically, contracts are for a long period, such as 15 or 20 years.

Why would Germany and other countries want to accelerate the adoption of alternative fuels beyond what the marketplace would dictate? The primary impetus is to reduce GHGs, especially CO_2. Other reasons include improving energy security by using a domestic energy source, reducing pollution, and extending the life of fossil fuel supplies. Finally, there is the *learning-by-doing* argument presented in Chapter 8 for nuclear energy, where we subsidize the high-cost fuel now on the assumption that cost will decrease with greater experience.[6]

Advantages of renewable fuels

Solar and wind energy are typically viewed as carbon-free.[7] Biofuels do emit carbon when burned, but they also absorb carbon when the plant stock is growing. The net change in carbon depends upon the land use before the production of biofuels. If the biomass replaces a forest or a prairie, the replaced tree or crop releases stored carbon, which often exceeds any gains derived from the production of biofuels.

If indeed carbon emissions contribute to undesirable climate change, the first-best alternative is to incorporate these costs into the price of fuels. The evaluation of renewable fuels would then depend on whether they could meet energy needs at a lower cost than the full social cost of fossil fuels. However, where fossil fuel prices do not internalize carbon emissions, renewables are at a cost disadvantage. In such second-best situations where an externality goes unpriced, subsidies are justifiable on an economic efficiency basis by making the relative marginal costs of fossil fuels and renewables comparable.[8]

The EU does have carbon trading, which adds to the cost of fossil fuels, but not to the cost of nuclear, solar, or wind. Wind and solar also receive large subsidies in many EU countries, further promoting their use. Hence, carbon-free alternatives have a higher market share than in countries that do not price carbon or subsidize alternative fuels as heavily.

One surprising development, at least to traditional economists, is the growing number of companies in the private sector that are implementing green energy programs for reasons other than profit maximization. Facebook, Google, and Amazon have all made prominent announcements about their use of renewables for power-hungry data centers. Such voluntary efforts are a surprise insofar as we assume that competitive firms not subject to regulation will choose the lowest-cost method of production, based on private and not social costs.[9] Explanations for these voluntary efforts include: firms have ethical standards that override simple profit maximization, consumers are willing to pay more for greener products, and firms are willing to bear short-run costs in order to achieve long-term leadership in producing green products.[10]

Box 9.1 Do you get a "warm glow"?

If you are willing to give to charity, pay more for green energy, or contribute to carbon reduction, you may get a *warm glow*. Andreoni (1990) used this term to describe the good feeling you get from doing something charitable.[11]

Both green energy and carbon reductions have public goods attributes, which ordinarily result in a free rider problem that leads to underprovision by the market. Increases in green energy or decreases in carbon emissions are nonrival in consumption. Moreover, the two purchases are pure public goods, insofar as it is impossible to exclude non-purchasers from the benefits. However, Andreoni suggested that some people might get an additional benefit simply from the action, as you might get from donating to a worthy cause.

It is difficult to separate warm glow from getting utility directly from the desirable attributes of green energy and carbon reductions, in the form of lower emissions. Menges et al. (2005) attempted to distinguish the two. They looked at willingness to donate for green electricity. The study asked participants from two cities in Germany about their willingness to pay for different fuels. The researchers separately identified willingness to pay for warm glow and for direct benefits. Warm glow by itself was not enough to achieve a socially efficient level of green energy, so that government intervention could still be beneficial.

There is strong support for renewables, current costs notwithstanding. Environmental groups tout the cost savings that they believe are achievable with greater experience and greater scale. The prospects are tantalizing if we can harness the use of inexhaustible resources such as the sun and wind. If we can sufficiently bring down capital costs and better integrate intermittent fuels onto the electricity grid, fuel costs are zero.

Renewables avoid many of the problems of existing mainstream energy sources. There is no mining or drilling, no emissions, no wastes, and the source is inexhaustible. In addition, there are the related advantages of protecting ecosystems and extending the life of finite resources. The costs of these alternatives have been dropping at a rapid pace. For some purposes, wind, solar, and biofuels may already be the preferred fuel. Solar, wind, and biofuels are domestically available sources of energy that are not subject to supply interruptions from hostile foreign governments.[12] Electricity users in remote locations can use renewable energy off the electric grid for such uses as heating and cooking. Electricity users with access to the grid may still find it advantageous to have a separate source of energy to save money or as a backup to the grid. There is growth in distributed generation and in microgrids. *Distributed generation* offers power generation close to the user, while *microgrids* can operate separately from the centralized grid.

Political support

While the EU has historically led the way on promoting alternative energy, alternative fuels have enough political support that their market share has been growing worldwide. Their sources of support include (1) green jobs; (2) subsidies to green businesses; and (3) greater energy security.

While there is considerable resistance to taxes on existing fuels to discourage their use, it may be possible to counter this obstacle by a revenue-neutral approach that reduces unpopular or economically inefficient taxes such as the income tax with a tax on fuels that is actually economically efficient. There is considerable support for policies that provide green jobs, jobs in renewable energy industries and other sectors that improve the environment or focus on sustainability. There is also widespread support for subsidies that bring down the costs of alternatives, reduce dependence on fossil fuels, and increase energy independence.

Political support need not coincide with economic efficiency. The price per green job may exceed its value and subsidies may go disproportionately to political supporters. The well-known case of the U.S. solar energy firm Solyndra, which received millions in subsidies and then went bankrupt, is a high-profile example of what can go wrong. Critics maintain that the relevant government agencies knew of Solyndra's weaknesses when they made the loans, but that the owners of the company had provided campaign funding and were now receiving payback.[13]

China pursued a first-mover advantage in the production of solar panels and other inputs into solar production. They offered sizable subsidies. In fact, some observers blame those subsidies for driving down the price to the point where Solyndra was unable to be cost-competitive. Chinese firms were able to further reduce the selling price of solar technologies by disposing of silicon without addressing environmental considerations (Cha, 2008).

Recently, China has cut its subsidies. The ostensible reason was that input costs had fallen to the point where subsidies were no longer necessary. Another likely reason was falling world demand, making it unprofitable to continue to increase supply in the face of falling global prices.

In addition to providing direct financial incentives to alternative energies, many governments provide a guaranteed market via binding mandates. The EU has policies in place to achieve an average renewable share of 20% by 2020 (Yeo, 2016). The EU uses direct subsidies, as well as less obvious subsidies such as FITs.

In the United States, 29 of the 50 states and the District of Columbia have renewable portfolio standards (RPSs), with another eight states having voluntary goals. These programs require electric utilities to use an increasing share of alternative fuels to generate electricity, with the timetable and the qualifying fuels varying among the states. Some supporters call for a federal RPS, but for now, the decision to adopt RPSs is at the state level. We now examine subsidies, including RPSs and FITs, in more detail.

Government subsidies

In a second-best world in which fossil fuel prices do not fully incorporate externalities, the simplest way to level the playing field is to subsidize the price of alternatives. Environmentalists often lament the huge subsidies paid to fossil fuels, noting that the amount spent to subsidize renewables is much smaller. However, Badcock and Lenzen (2010) find that renewables often receive subsidies that are more generous on a per unit of electricity basis. Consumption efficiency requires the ratio of prices to equal the ratio of marginal utilities, where the ratio of marginal utilities is equal to the marginal rate of substitution (MRS). Production efficiency requires that the price ratio equals the ratio of marginal costs obtained from the production possibilities curve, known as the rate of product transformation (RPT). And it is well-known that the hallmark of *product-mix efficiency* where we achieve production and consumption efficiency, is that prices equal marginal costs, or equivalently, MRS = RPT.

Suppose there is an implicit subsidy for fuels by not including external costs in their prices, while alternative fuels do not receive a subsidy. Consumers equating their MRS to the price ratio will overuse fossil fuels and underuse alternatives, as compared to the efficient ratio.

As noted earlier, China provided subsidies to its solar industry. Germany subsidized its way to achieving its leading position in the use of solar energy. Japan offers generous FITs, with the downturn of its nuclear fortunes (Obe, 2011).

Beginning in 2003, with the introduction of gas–electric hybrid vehicles such as the Toyota Prius, the U.S. government subsidized alternative-fuel automobile purchases. The government phased out those subsidies, with the next round of subsidies targeting plug-in hybrids and electric vehicles. For a General Motors' Chevy Volt priced at $40,000, the price was closer to $30,000 after the tax incentives, still considerably more expensive than your typical Chevrolet. The Nissan Leaf listed at $37,000, and with discounts and tax advantages, you could get out the door for about $23,000, about the price of a conventional car. The Tesla model S, a luxury automobile that typically sells for $75,000, is still a luxury purchase at $65,000 even with the rebate.[14] Tesla is currently taking orders for a car it plans to introduce around 2018 that will list for not much more than the GM and Nissan offerings.

Renewable portfolio standard (RPS)

Analogous to the tax (price) and trading (quantity) approaches taken to reduce emissions, we can encourage the use of renewables by requiring their purchase at an above-market price using FITs or an above-market quantity using an RPS. The U.S. programs predominantly take the RPS quantity approach. Similar programs in the EU go by the name renewable obligations (RO), although in general, the EU favors FITs to an RPS.[15]

Box 9.2 Swine fuel

North Carolina established its Renewable Energy and Energy Efficiency Portfolio Standard program in August 2007. Its most singular feature is that the program requires a small amount of fuels made from swine and poultry wastes. Table 9.1 sets forth the following requirements for investor-owned utilities in North Carolina:[16]

The percentages are based on sales in the year in question, so that by 2015, utilities needed to use alternative fuels for at least 6% of electricity generation, including waste from pigs and poultry.[17] Perhaps not surprisingly, North Carolina is among the top states in poultry and hog production. Electric utilities have complained about the cost of

Table 9.1 North Carolina renewable portfolio standard requirements

- 2010: 0.02% from solar
- 2012: 3% (including 0.07% from solar)
- 2013: 3% (including 0.07% from solar)
- 2014: 3% (including 0.07% from solar + 170,000 MWh from poultry waste)
- 2015: 6% (including 0.14% from solar + 0.07% from swine waste + 700,000 MWh from poultry waste)
- 2016: 6% (including 0.14% from solar + 0.07% from swine waste + 900,000 MWh from poultry waste)
- 2017: 6% (including 0.14% from solar + 0.14% from swine waste + 900,000 MWh from poultry waste)
- 2018: 10% (including 0.20% from solar + 0.14% from swine waste + 900,000 MWh from poultry waste)
- 2019: 10% (including 0.20% from solar + 0.14% from swine waste + 900,000 MWh from poultry waste)
- 2020: 10% (including 0.20% from solar + 0.20% from swine waste + 900,000 MWh from poultry waste)
- 2021: 12.5% (including 0.20% from solar + 0.20% from swine waste + 900,000 MWh from poultry waste)

Adapted from DSIRE (2016)

meeting quotas for these nascent technologies, especially in light of lower-cost subsidized solar energy. The state also counts energy efficiency towards meeting the overall renewables requirement.

As of 2015, North Carolina claimed fourth place among the 50 states in the total amount of installed solar energy. While attributable in part to having lots of sunshine, the RPS requirement and a substantial state tax subsidy over and above federal subsidies provided momentum. In that same year, the state froze the RPS requirement at 6% and allowed the solar tax to expire, a reminder that states can choose whether to adopt RPSs and how much to subsidize alternative fuels.

As with tradable emissions, an RPS in theory has the advantage that it provides an incentive to producers of alternative energies to bring down their costs. Assuming that utilities want to meet the mandate at the lowest possible cost, producers will be able to gain a larger share if their fuel decreases in price, as has been the case for solar (due at least as much to subsidies as to innovations) (Downey, 2016). North Carolina partially defeated this efficiency advantage by mandating the type of alternative. The irony is that swine and chicken producers were politically successful in getting special set-asides, but then could not provide the product commercially in time to meet the deadline. This situation is a reminder of the inefficiency of command-and-control regulations, as compared to incentive-based approaches. To achieve maximum efficiency, the type of alternative fuel should be flexible.

Another issue is defining what fuels qualify. The Duke Energy Company refers to energy efficiency as "the fifth fuel," and gets credit for energy efficiency towards meeting the renewables share. Duke's position may help explain why North Carolina is one of only four RPS programs that count energy efficiency towards meeting the renewables standard. It has also successfully sought permission to include wood as a renewable, to use wood chips alongside coal chips as fuel to produce electricity. Environmentalists opposed the inclusion of wood as a renewable, fearing Duke will cut mature trees in North Carolina forests.

By its very nature, an RPS is a command-and-control program, in that it drives up the cost of producing electricity by requiring the use of high-cost alternatives. Restricting the alternatives that meet the conditions of the mandate only adds to the inefficiency. We must be cautious about assuming that just because some by-product is a negative externality, we are better off converting it into electric power.

In a first-best world, prices internalize the costs of all externalities and there would be no need for a program such as an RPS. If alternative fuels were cost-competitive, we would use them; otherwise, we would use fossil fuels, and since their prices would include all their costs to society, we would be allocating our resources efficiently. In a second-best world, some subsidy for alternatives is defensible, but the relevant question is whether an RPS is the best way to achieve the goal.

One way to increase program efficiency is to allow trading of renewables. For example, North Carolina does allow its utilities to meet the standard by buying renewable energy produced out of state, such as wind energy from Texas. Similar to emissions trading programs, utilities buy and sell renewable energy credits (RECs). The overall cost is less than if every utility had to adhere to the exact same standards.

By this reasoning, the larger the region over which trading can take place, the greater the potential cost savings, which seemingly suggests the desirability of a national RPS in the United States. However, given the diversity of energy types, both conventional and renewable, it would be a significant challenge to harmonize all of the regional interests. Would the national program include set-asides for chicken and hog wastes? Would an EU system give two credits for offshore wind, and only one credit for onshore wind, as in the British RO? Moreover, given that an RPS is only justifiable in the second-best world of implicit subsidies for conventional fuels, it is questionable whether imposing a standard on all regions, both those regions that have adopted an RPS and those that have not, will be welfare-enhancing. Finally, there is the question of enforcing an RPS. North Carolina has delayed the set-asides for hog and chicken waste several times. It is one thing to set standards, another to achieve them.

Allowing energy efficiency and trading improves RPS efficiency. The equimarginal principle reminds us to compare the marginal costs of alternative ways of achieving a unit of carbon reduction. States that exclude energy efficiency or trading from their RPS are likely to spend more to achieve carbon reductions.

Feed-in tariffs (FITs)

Feed-in tariffs (FITs) provide a long-term contract that sets price based on the cost of a renewable, which is usually above the utility's cost of generating electricity. These rates have been a popular way to accelerate adoption of alternative energy, especially in Europe. Producers favor this approach over an RPS because it offers them a guaranteed price. Typically, the mandated price decreases over time, in anticipation of costs that decrease with larger-scale production and longer experience.

Just as the RPS has the disadvantage that producers are uncertain about the future price, the FIT has the problem that utilities are uncertain about the long-term quantity. Germany and Spain have achieved their large shares of solar energy with FITs. However, both countries have cut back on the generosity of their offerings, finding the programs to be very costly.

In addition to solar energy provision by companies, individual customers have found it profitable to supply excess energy. Of course, it could also happen that input costs rise for renewables producers, such as when China reduced the subsidies to its solar panel manufacturers, in which case there may be less alternative energy available than anticipated.

In a regulated regime, the higher cost of providing electricity passes on to customers. Should the industry undergo restructuring, utilities may find themselves with stranded costs. They agreed to purchase the high-priced fuels while regulated, expecting that they could recoup this money. With deregulation, consumers have a choice of where to purchase their electricity. Consumers are likely to find a better price from suppliers who obtain their electricity from lower-cost supplies.

Box 9.3 Net metering

Another way to incentivize the use of alternative fuels is through net metering. Most commonly, customers receive compensation for generating electricity with solar PV. The program may be similar to a FIT, or customers may only pay (or gain payment) for the net amount of electricity use. Residential customers are likely to use more electricity than they generate during peak times, but may generate more than they use during the off-peak.

It is common to compensate households for net generation using the retail rate but this rate need not result in efficient electricity generation. If the utility could generate a marginal unit of electricity at a lower cost, then households produce too much solar generation if they are paid retail prices. Alternatively, if solar for electricity generation offsets the use of coal and associated carbon emissions, it may be socially efficient to require the utility to pay above the retail rate. As we would expect, constraining the utility to pay the retail rate at all times is not likely to be efficient. However, determining what rate to pay requires knowledge of what fuel solar is displacing, corresponding carbon emissions, and the value we place on lower carbon emissions.

In order to pay a different rate than the retail electricity price, the electric meter has to be capable of separating consumption from production. Increasingly, electric utilities are installing smart meters capable of two-way transmission—so the utility can receive as well as generate electricity—and two-way communications—so the utility can measure consumption and production at different times of use. These meters allow the utility to charge and pay different rates depending on whether the household is a consumer or a prosumer (producing rather than consuming energy).

The rising tide of alternative energy

Wind and solar make up a rapidly rising percentage of the electricity mix, and biofuel use in transportation is likely to increase as well. Table 9.2 shows the composition of energy sources used to generate electricity as of 2015.

In the United States, renewables make up about 13% of electricity generation, with hydro responsible for almost half. Wind accounts for nearly 5%, the largest share of nonhydro renewables, while solar has a share of only 0.6% despite having the fastest growth rate.

In the EU, renewables account for more than one-fourth of electricity generation, but much of the total is due to preexisting hydro energy. However, growth is due to wind, solar, and biofuels. The renewables share of hydro in electricity production is around 44%, with wind over 25% and biomass and waste, mostly wood, approaching 20%. Solar has a 10% share, but the most dramatic growth rate.

Countries with relatively large amounts of nonhydro renewables are Portugal, Spain, Germany, Denmark, Finland, Sweden, and Austria. The EU as a whole generates 24% of its electricity from renewables, with 11% from hydro and 13% from other renewables (Eurostat, 2016).

We cited Germany earlier for its growth in solar and wind. As of 2015, renewables account for 31% of electricity generation, with rapid growth in absolute and percentage terms. Renewables primarily replaced nuclear energy and not coal, so carbon emissions have not really declined appreciably (Hoff, 2016).

The EU had the subgoal of renewables accounting for 10% of transport fuels by 2020. Renewables for transport include liquid biofuels, hydrogen, and electric vehicles where the electricity has been generated from renewables. By 2014, 6% of transport fuels were from renewables. In 2016, it was announced that the EU was scrapping the goal after 2020. Biofuels were found to be having a larger than expected effect on land use changes, causing deforestation and food scarcity. They also added to the cost of transportation fuel (Simon, 2016). The discontinuation of the renewables transportation goal shows why there can be resistance to renewables, to which we turn next.

Table 9.2 Major energy sources and percent share of total U.S. electricity generation in 2015

- Coal = 33%
- Natural gas = 33%
- Nuclear = 20%
- Hydropower = 6%
- Other renewables = 7%
  - Biomass = 1.6%
  - Geothermal = 0.4%
  - Solar = 0.6%
  - Wind = 4.7%
- Petroleum = 1%
- Other gases = <1%

Adapted from U.S. EIA (2016a)

Barriers to acceptance of alternative fuels

Private cost of alternative fuels

In comparing costs of conventional and alternative fuels, we begin by comparing their levelized cost. Table 9.3 shows projections for 2022 from the 2016 EIA Annual Outlook (U.S. EIA, 2016b).

Geothermal is the lowest-cost source, but has limited geographic availability. We discuss its status later in the chapter. Onshore wind has an LCOE projected to be lower than natural gas advanced combined cycle plants by 2022 if we include projected subsidies. Solar PV is almost at parity with natural gas given the 30% federal subsidy on solar installations. Hydroelectric is cheaper than solar if solar does not receive subsidies; with current subsidies solar has a lower cost per MWh.

The EIA divides technologies into dispatchable and nondispatchable, a reminder that wind and solar are not under the control of the electricity dispatcher. We discuss pumped storage for hydro later in the chapter, which allows some storage capability— allowing dispatch when it is needed.

The low-capacity factors for nondispatchable technologies are a reminder that wind and solar are intermittent. For a given megawatt of capacity, solar may only be able to deliver megawatt hours one-fourth of the time, and wind around 40% of the time. While levelized cost does take into account capacity factor, it does not take into account that wind and solar may not be available when they are needed. Nor does it reflect the hours of availability. Wind energy may be most available during low-value nighttime hours when electricity demand is low. In the summer, solar energy drops off in early evening, just when residential customers are getting home. California has found that it is necessary to quickly ramp up its natural gas plants, with an additional cost for having

Table 9.3 Estimated LCOE (2015 $/MWh) for plants entering service in 2022

Plant type	Capacity factor (%)	Levelized capital cost	Fixed O&M	Variable O&M (including fuel)	Total system LCOE	Total LCOE including tax credit
Dispatchable technologies						
Natural gas advanced combined cycle	87	15.4	1.3	38.1	55.8	55.8
Advanced nuclear	90	75	12.4	11.3	99.7	99.7
Geothermal	91	27.8	13.1	0	42.3	39.5
Nondispatchable technologies						
Wind	42	43.3	12.5	0	58.5	50.9
Solar PV	26	61.2	9.5	0	74.2	58.2
Hydroelectric	60	54.1	3.1	5	63.7	63.7

Adapted from *Levelized cost and levelized avoided cost of new generation resources in the annual energy outlook 2016*. Retrieved November 5, 2016 from https://www.eia.gov/forecasts/aeo/pdf/electricity_ generation.pdf to start them in advance of when they are needed to avoid a power shortage. The duck curve refers to the shape of load, a flat tail at night supplied by fossil fuel, solar filling in the duck's belly during the day, and then natural gas ramping up to meet the neck and head of the duck.

Social cost comparison

How do alternative fuels compare if we include the cost of carbon emissions? The literature contains numerous estimates of our willingness to pay for reductions in CO_2, and actual markets such as the EU Environmental Trading Scheme (EU-ETS) give some indication. One of the best-known estimates from the literature is from Nordhaus (2011), who since the early 1990s has estimated the potential damage from rising CO_2. He estimates the damage of carbon emissions at \$44/metric ton (and CO_2 emissions at \$12/metric ton, on the order of €9 at the time of the study).[18] In 2016, EU emissions traded for as little as €5.50/metric ton CO_2. Many believe that the EU issued an excessive number of permits to get industry support for the program, resulting in a permit price lower than society's WTP for carbon reductions.

Schwarz and Cochran (2013) show the levelized cost of conventional fuels adjusted for a price for CO_2 emissions starting at \$20/ton (about €16 at the time of the study). Natural gas emits about 1.2 pounds of CO_2/kWh, or 0.6 ton/MWh (U.S. EIA, 2016a). A carbon price of \$20/ton would add \$12/MWh to the price of natural gas, for a total of \$68/MWh. Given the levelized costs shown in Table 9.3, wind would have the lowest levelized cost at a carbon price of \$20/ton even without subsidies. Solar energy would also be cheaper with existing subsidies, but more expensive than natural gas without subsidies.

Intermittent and nondispatchable characteristics

While the ability to predict wind and solar availability for short periods such as a day in advance is improving, some forecasting challenges are unavoidable. It may be possible to predict with a high degree of accuracy that the sun will be available for 80% of available minutes on a next-day basis. However, there is no obvious method for predicting the exact time when clouds will block the sun. On average, there will be the need to generate energy using a different source for one of every five minutes. In order to meet demand, utilities will have to add backup power, such as natural gas units that can ramp up quickly when the sun goes behind a cloud.

Intermittency of wind and solar presents a challenge to the operation of the electric grid. It is necessary to balance electricity demand and supply at each instant.[19] Nature, not the grid operator, dictates when renewables will be available. Sudden increases in supply, such as when solar energy quickly increases after a passing cloud, can threaten the stability of grid operation. As with other technical problems, there is ongoing progress in lessening the magnitude of these issues, such as better cloud forecasts or diversified sources of wind and solar energy to provide a more stable supply. Also, combining wind and solar can make their aggregate output more predictable. For example, solar is not available at night, while wind is available both day and night. By combining resources, solar output will be available during the day, and to the extent that the utility also has access to wind, there will be energy during the night as well (Traube et al., 2008).

Paul Joskow (2011) makes the case that while solar energy appears to have a higher levelized cost than wind, it tends to be more available during summer peaks, when the value of electricity is highest. Even then, we have encountered the sudden drop-off around 6 PM, requiring the rapid ramp-up of standby natural gas. Wind availability is not as highly correlated with the peak. In fact, Texas, the state that generates the largest percentage of its electricity using wind, gives away electricity off-peak hoping that consumers will transfer demand from peak hours (Krauss & Cardwell, 2015).

Environmental shortcomings

The effectiveness of wind is highly dependent on its location. In the United States, wind has high potential in coastal and mountain areas, but faces considerable opposition from those who find the towers detract from the landscape. Positioning wind towers offshore substantially increases the cost of construction, as the towers must withstand the constant assault of ocean waves. Offshore towers can also affect ocean ecosystems.

Both wind and solar require land. Entergy (n.d.) provides a comparison of how much land would be required for nuclear, solar, and wind to supply 1,800 MW, based on the plants running at 90% of capacity. In actuality, while nuclear plants have a capacity factor of 90% or over, solar has a capacity factor of 25% and wind close to 40%. Therefore, the actual solar requirement would be about 3.5 times the given figure, and about 2.5 times for wind. Consider the amount of land needed for a two-reactor 1,800 MW nuclear plant. Such a plant would serve approximately 1.8 million homes. It would encompass about 1,100 acres (a football field is about 1 acre) or 1.7 square miles. If solar energy produces the same amount of power, it would require 7.4 acres of photovoltaic solar panels, and 13,320 acres in all (21 square miles). For wind, it would take 720 2.5 MW turbines, requiring 108,000 acres, or 169 square miles. While the comparison does not include biofuels, they require far more land than wind, and corn-based ethanol in the United States uses far more land than Brazilian ethanol produced from sugarcane.

There are other environmental concerns. Solar panel construction uses silicon, which can pollute if there is improper disposal. Wind towers present a danger to birds (and bats) with their sharp blades. There have been numerous complaints about low-frequency noise emitted by turbines. Biofuels take the place of other land uses, raising concerns about their effect on ecology and food supply.

There is no completely benign source of energy, and society must evaluate the full social costs in ranking different fuel alternatives. Some might point to hydroelectric as a benign fuel, envious of Norway's ability to meet almost 100% of its electricity generation needs with hydro. We turn next to hydro and then geothermal sources.

Other currently available renewables

Hydropower

Hydroelectric plants have produced electricity for more than a century. Hydroelectric plants still make up almost half of today's renewable energy, although their share is declining.

Relative to wind and solar, electric system operators of hydroelectric plants have more control over electrical output. Hydro has the unique characteristic among renewable sources that it can serve as a type of electricity storage. The pumped-storage process pumps water from a lower to a higher level during times of excess capacity and releases it when demand warrants. The released power drives the turbines that in turn generate electricity.

Hydro does have drawbacks, such as during drought conditions. Norway has experienced droughts in recent years, and has sometimes had to import energy. When California introduced competition to its electricity industry in 2000, it had hoped to import electricity from its lower-cost hydro-rich neighboring states. When a drought struck, Oregon and Washington needed all of their hydropower.

For many years, hydro had a benign reputation, as it does not require mining or drilling, and does not result in emissions. That view has faded with the recognition of the impact of dams, to the point where many countries do not anticipate new hydro facilities. The building of dams has undesirable impacts on the environment (disruption of fish migration), agriculture (floods that periodically replenished soil nutrients no longer occur), and communities. In addition, silting can eventually clog the turbine intakes, depending on the geology and amount of silt in the water.

There is relatively little potential for additional hydroelectric plants in developed countries because they have dammed most of the suitable sites, and environmental concerns pose obstacles to new projects. The developing world has much more potential for new projects.

Polimeni et al. (2014) provide a case study of the Yali Falls Dam in Cambodia. The authors surveyed the local population on the changes they had experienced after the opening of the dam, including water availability, disease, and effects on the ecology. For example, while the dam reduced flooding, the villagers now experience less severe but less predictable and more frequent floods, depending on when the dam operators choose to release water.

China built the Three Gorges Dam to generate large amounts of electricity, as well as to reduce reliance on coal and to alleviate an area of severe flooding. However, it forced the relocation of over 1 million people, as many villages along the route are now under water.[20]

Hydropower may have growth opportunities if it can be done economically on a small scale of 30 MW or less. Compare that capacity to the Three Gorges Dam, with 22,500 MW, generated using 32 turbines, each 700 MW. As small-scale hydropower is not yet cost-competitive, we delay further consideration of its potential to Chapter 10 on next-generation alternatives.

There are a number of other technologies that use water to generate electricity. They may also play a growing role, such as wave, tidal, and ocean power. As with other forms of hydro, the viability of these sources depends on geographic location. Moreover, as with other renewable fuels, they are intermittent, providing variable levels of electricity depending on the time of day, height of the tide, and height of the waves.[21] The first utility-scale wave motion generators were tested off the coasts of Portugal and Scotland. The UK estimates it is possible to provide about 14% of its electricity demand using wave power alone. The U.S. Electric Power Research Institute (EPRI) estimates that wave power could meet 6% of domestic demand (Jacobson, Hagerman, & Scott, 2011).[22]

If these innovative forms of water-based energy become cost-competitive, would they offer renewable energy with no environmental disadvantages? One technology to harness wave power bears a resemblance to dams, with similar implications for the environment. Other techniques involve long chains of pontoons that float up and down as waves move past and generate electricity using submerged turbines. There will certainly be opposition to locating such equipment in scenic coastal areas. Perhaps the greatest disadvantages are the unknown factors about how harnessing the power of waves and tides will affect ecological systems.

Geothermal

If you have ever observed geysers or bathed in hot springs, you were enjoying the effects of the earth's heat. Geothermal energy directly provides heat for hot water and possibly home heating. It can provide heat with the use of a heat pump. Finally, it can create heat and steam to drive a specially designed turbine and generate electricity.

The geology of Iceland, with its volcanic activity, favors the use of geothermal energy for both electricity production and heating. More than 25% of Iceland's electricity comes from power plants that use geothermal energy (hydro makes up almost all of the remaining electricity production, with fossil fuels accounting for only 0.1%). Geothermal accounts for about 90% of heating and hot water in buildings (Islandsbanki Geothermal Research, 2010). Heat pumps are able to make use of geothermal heat near the earth's surface.

In absolute terms, the United States is the top producer of geothermal energy for electricity, with most of that production at The Geysers, a geothermal field north of San Francisco. On a relative basis, geothermal supplies only 0.4% of U.S. energy production, just behind solar at 0.6% (U.S. EIA, 2016c).

The potential for greater use of geothermal is likely, using binary cycle power plants that can run with less heat, and with improvements in drilling and extraction technology. We consider these new advances along with other alternative fuel technologies that are under development in Chapter 10 to follow.

Summary

This chapter focuses on renewable energy sources that are commercially feasible today. Among the currently available alternatives are wind, solar, biofuels, hydro and geothermal. Wind and solar are the two most rapidly growing alternatives. While alternative fuels account for close to 15% of all fuels in the United States, nearly half is hydro. Wind accounts for almost 5%. Solar provides less than 1%, but has the fastest growth rate. Geothermal is behind solar as a percentage.

Onshore wind and solar photovoltaic energy are approaching parity with natural gas in generating electricity as measured by levelized cost. Wind is closer to being competitive than is solar. However, even as these alternatives reach parity with fossil fuels, they have challenging aspects. Both wind and solar are intermittent sources of energy. Until batteries can store energy cost-effectively, the electric utility dispatcher does not have control over when these sources will be available. Solar does have the advantage that it tends to be available on hot summer days, when needed for air conditioning, but it is less available in winter when needed for heating. It also drops off sharply at sundown, requiring rapid ramp-up of high-cost natural gas peaker units. Wind is often available at night when demand is low.

Renewables stretch supplies of fossil fuels, reduce emissions of GHGs and other pollutants such as SOx, NOx, and particulates, and increase energy security by replacing imported fossil fuels with domestic sources. In the absence of first-best policies such as carbon taxes or cap-and-trade, countries have increasingly turned to renewable portfolio standards (RPSs) and feed-in tariffs (FITs) to promote renewables.

These second-best methods focus respectively on quantity and price. An RPS demonstrates a long-term commitment to increasing use of renewables and possibly other alternatives fuels such as energy efficiency, to produce electricity, but does not assure a profitable price. It does have the virtue of providing an incentive for producers to seek efficiencies so that they can increase their share of the mandated percentage of alternative fuels. Feed-in tariffs offer a long-term contract with a guaranteed price that decreases over time with the anticipation of cost efficiencies. However, countries such as Germany that have relied on FITs have found it to be a very expensive program, as utilities are expected to buy alternative fuels at above-market prices, and to pay a higher price for more expensive alternatives such as solar than for less expensive resources such as wind.

While renewables avoid many of the external costs of fossil fuels such as pollution and waste emissions, they have the disadvantage of requiring larger amounts of land to generate equivalent amounts of energy. Biofuels in particular use large amounts of land, and they can result in carbon emissions if their development is at the expense of a previous land use such as a forest. Further, biofuels such as corn-based ethanol drive up the cost of food by siphoning off a portion of the crop that would otherwise have gone to food.

While traditional hydro energy accounts for the largest share of renewable energy, it also has the least potential for growth. Most nations have already dammed their suitable sites, and there is increasing resistance to its visual impact and its effect on ecosystems. We include the possibility of small-scale hydro in the next chapter. Tidal and wave energy also may emerge as alternatives.

Finally, geothermal energy can be a low-cost renewable energy source when the earth's heat is close to the surface. While geothermal is a renewable resource, it is possible to deplete the heat if the rate of use exceeds the rate of replenishment. As with other fuels, there is ongoing research to make greater use of geothermal energy, such as binary cycle power plants that can run on less heat.

Notes

1 Personal conversation with Manda Adams, formerly of the Department of Geography and Earth Sciences, UNC Charlotte and now at the National Science Foundation, and Adams and Keith (2013).

2 According to Archer and Jacobson (2007), wind could potentially provide baseload energy if we interconnect wind farms. Wind sources are more diversified than solar energy, which is only available during the day unless we connect solar facilities over very far distances. We can also connect wind and solar energy facilities to diversify their availability.

3 As will be discussed, offshore wind is less unsightly as well as able to take advantage of winds that are stronger and steadier. However, offshore wind is more expensive to construct, and it would affect the aquatic ecosystem. And the towers may still be visible from the beach.

4 On almost a daily basis, there is excitement about a new biofuel that will not require as much land and water as existing ones. One such biofuel is the jatropha tree, which has seeds that can be used for oil. It turns out that while the jatropha tree does not need much water and can grow on poor quality land, it will only bear a good harvest of seeds with plentiful water and good nutrients. Farmers in particular have been burned numerous times by the next great hope for alternative fuels. See Charles (2012).

5 Even human wastes are an option. See Sevcenko (2016).

6 Despite these arguments, solar growth has slowed in Germany. Electricity prices have risen as a result of the high cost of solar, and in turn, FITs have fallen, resulting in lower production. It is also important to distinguish between solar capacity and solar production. See Wirth (2016). Also, Wilson (2015) notes that Germany produces very little solar energy in its cloudiest months.

7 Practitioners of life-cycle analysis make the point that no energy source is carbon-free when viewed from cradle to grave. The production of solar panels and wind turbines requires energy that emits carbon. Transportation of materials also emits carbon.

8 Ramsey (1927) introduced the rule that where products cannot be priced at marginal cost, the markup should depend on the inverse of the price elasticity of demand. To minimize deadweight loss, the markup should be small for goods with elastic demands and large for goods with inelastic demands.

9 Behavioral economists offer explanations outside of the traditional assumptions of rational behavior. Akerlof and Kranton (2000) allow for identity in decision-making. If the trait of caring about the environment is more closely associated with females, women might be more supportive of the environment insofar as it reinforces their identity as female.

10 The last reason has the flavor of the Porter hypothesis, one aspect of which says that firms are trying to achieve a first-mover advantage. See Porter and Van der Linde (1995). We will discuss the hypothesis in more detail in Chapter 16 on energy sustainability. For now, suffice it to say that neoclassical economists are skeptical of the hypothesis, comparing it to finding $20 bills on the sidewalk. Economists reason that such savings are rare, or someone else would have already found them. There is the additional possibility of greenwashing, where a firm markets itself as green, but closer examination shows the firm has exaggerated its claim. For example, Amazon may be selling renewable energy to the electricity grid rather than using renewable energy for its data centers. See Carrington (2015).

11 Akerlof and Kranton (2010) further distinguish warm glow from identity. You may give to charity because you receive a warm glow, but how do you decide which charity? You may give to your alma mater because of identity.

12 However, the materials such as rare earth metals that are used to construct alternative energy technologies may be limited. For example, rare earth metals are needed for wind energy turbines as well as for hybrid vehicles. To add to the challenge, the needed materials may also raise security issues, as is the case for wind turbines where the needed rare metal is found primarily in China. See Chandler (2012).

13 Of course, pointing out losers does not provide information on the overall program. Factcheck. Org, an independent report done at the behest of the Obama Administration after relentless criticism of the DOE program with repeated mention of Solyndra, found that while oversight could be improved, the failure rate of subsidized renewable energy programs was less than had been anticipated by the U.S. Congress. See Farley (2012).

14 Lippert (2015) writes that carmakers apparently lose money on each electric car sold in the United States, but are required to produce a specified percentage of zero-emission cars in the state of California. They do so because on balance, they are better off losing money on a small number of electric vehicles and making money on a large number of other vehicles than not meeting the California requirement. Again, it is worth pointing out that from the perspective of life-cycle cost, electric vehicles are not truly zero-emissions, as the electricity used to charge the car results in emissions during the electricity-generating process.

15 As with taxes and trading, the two approaches are theoretically identical under simplifying assumptions. In practice, differences arise as they do for taxes and trading. Just as Weitzman shows the nonequivalence of taxes and trading under supply uncertainty, Marschinski and Quirion (2014) show differences between RPSs and FITs under uncertainty.

16 A summary is available at the website of U.S. Department of Energy (n.d.).

17 Buckley and Schwarz (2003) describe the technologies to convert these wastes into fuel.

18 A metric ton (also referred to as a tonne) equals 1,000 kilograms, or 2,204 pounds. It is more common to express the price in terms of CO_2 than carbon, but the two taxes are equivalent based on carbon making up about 37% of the weight of CO_2.

19 We are setting aside the existence of excess capacity. That issue is considered in the chapters on electricity.

20 The U.S. built the Hoover Dam during the Great Depression to supply electricity to the desert southwest. The dam is as high as a 60-story building. Even then, it was controversial because of its anticipated cost. It is still controversial for dramatically altering the flow of the Colorado River. Today, democratic countries would be unlikely to be able to carry out such a massive public works project requiring massive relocations.

21 Waves and especially tides are more predictable than wind. However, as with other renewables, nature, and not a grid operator, dictates when they are available. And it is still necessary to transmit their power to an electric grid.

22 In another endeavor, Norwood (2016) describes a consortium of North Carolina universities including UNC Charlotte and industry professionals studying the feasibility of using wave and tidal power in the waters near the North Carolina Outer Banks. Currently, the investigators are finding that power from using the Gulf Stream appears to be the most promising source of ocean power.

References

Adams, A., & Keith, D. (2013). Are global wind power resource estimates overstated? *Environmental Research Letters, 8*(1), 1–9.

Akerlof, G., & Kranton, R. (2000). Economics and identity. *Quarterly Journal of Economics, 115*(3), 715–753.

Andreoni, J. (1990). Impure altruism and donations to public goods: A theory of warm-glow giving. *The Economic Journal, 100*(401), 464–477.

Archer, C., & Jacobson, M. (2007). Supplying baseload power and reducing transmission requirements by interconnecting wind farms. *Journal of Applied Meteorology and Climatology, 46*, 1701–1717.

Badcock, J., & Lenzen, M. (2010). Subsidies for electricity-generating technologies: A review. *Energy Policy, 38*, 5038–5047.

Buckley, J. C., & Schwarz, P. M. (2003). Renewable energy from gasification of manure: An innovative technology in search of fertile policy. *Environmental Monitoring and Assessment, 84*(1–2), 111–127.

Carrington, D. (2015, November). Amazon's wind farm links nonexistent. *Carolina Journal, 24*(11). Retrieved November 2, 2016 from http://www.johnlocke.org/acrobat/cjPrintEdition/cj-nov2015-web.pdf

Cha, A.E. (2008, March 9). Solar energy firms leave waste behind in China. *Washington Post*. Retrieved October 31, 2016 from http://www.washingtonpost.com/wp-dyn/content/article/2008/03/08/AR2008030802595_pf.html

Chandler, D. (2012, April 9). Clean energy could lead to scarce materials. *MIT News*. Retrieved October 31, 2016 from http://news.mit.edu/2012/rare-earth-alternative-energy–0409

Charles, D. (2012, August 21). *How a biofuel dream called Jatropha came crashing down*. Retrieved October 30, 2016 from http://www.npr.org/sections/thesalt/2012/08/22/159391553/how-a-biofuel-dream-called-jatropha-came-crashing-down

Collins, S. (2015, April 24). Robert F. Kennedy Jr. says alternative energy is key for a true free market economy. *Annenberg Media Center neon tommy Annenberg Digital News*. Retrieved December 29, 2016 from http://www.neontommy.com/news/2015/04/robert-f-kennedy-jr-talks-america-environment-and-true-free-market-economy

DSIRE (Database of State Incentives for Renewables & Efficiency). (2016, September). *Renewable energy and energy efficiency portfolio standard*. Retrieved November 4, 2016 from http://programs.dsireusa.org/system/program/detail/2660

Downey, J. (2016, March 21). How N.C. biogas plant, swine waste would help Duke Energy meet state regs. *Charlotte Business Journal*. Retrieved November 4, 2016 from http://www.bizjournals. com/charlotte/blog/power_city/2016/03/duke-energy-should-meet–2017-n-c-swine-waste-power.html

Entergy. (n.d.). *Backgrounder—a comparison: Land use by energy source—nuclear, wind, and solar*. Retrieved November 6, 2016 from http://www.entergy-arkansas.com/content/news/docs/AR_Nuclear_One_Land_Use.pdf

Eurostat. (2016, July). *Renewable energy statistics*. Retrieved November 5, 2016 from http://ec.europa. eu/eurostat/statistics-explained/index.php/Renewable_energy_statistics

Farley, R. (2012, June 1). *Romney's solar flareout: He misrepresents Obama's green-energy program using false and twisted facts*. Retrieved October 31, 2016 from http://www.factcheck.org/2012/06/ romneys-solar-flareout/

Hoff, S. (2016, May 24). *Germany's renewables electricity generation grows in 2015, but coal still dominant*. Retrieved November 5, 2016 from http://www.eia.gov/todayinenergy/detail.php?id=26372

Islandsbanki Geothermal Research. (2010). *Iceland geothermal market report*. Retrieved November 6, 2016 from http://skjol.islandsbanki.is/servlet/file/store156/item61173/version3/2010%200419% 20Iceland%20Geothermal%20Energy%20Market%20Report.pdf

Jacobson, P., Hagerman, G., & Scott, G. (2011). *Mapping and assessment of the United States ocean wave energy resource*. Electric Power Research Institute. Retrieved November 7, from http://www1.eere. energy.gov/water/pdfs/mappingandassessment.pdf

Joskow, P. L. (2011). Comparing the costs of intermittent and dispatchable electricity generating technologies. *American Economic Review, 101*(3), 238–241.

Kennedy, R. Jr. (2005, December 16). An ill wind off Cape Cod. *New York Times: The Opinion Pages*. Retrieved December 29, 2016 from http://www.nytimes.com/2005/12/16/opinion/an-ill-wind-off-cape-cod.html

Krauss, C., & Cardwell, D. (2015, November 8). A Texas utility offers a nighttime special: Free electricity. *New York Times*. Retrieved November 6, 2016 from http://www.nytimes.com/2015/11/09/ business/energy-environment/a-texas-utility-offers-a-nighttime-special-free-electricity.html

Lippert, J. (2015, August 3). California has a plan to end the auto industry as we know it. *Bloomberg Markets*. Retrieved November 4, 2016 from http://www.bloomberg.com/news/articles/ 2015–08–03/california-regulator-mary-nichols-may-transform-the-auto-industry

Marschinski, R., & Quirion, P. (2014). Tradable renewable quota vs. feed-in tariff vs. feed-in premium under uncertainty. *Fondazione Eni Enrico Mattei Nota di Lavoro, 99*.

Menges, R., Schroeder, C., & Traub, S. (2005). Altruism, warm glow and the willingness-to-donate for green electricity: An artefactual field experiment. *Environmental & Resource Economics, 31*, 431–458.

Nordhaus, W. (2011). *Estimates of the social cost of carbon: background and results from the RICE–2011 model* (Cowles Foundation discussion paper No. 1826). New Haven, CT: Yale University.

Norwood, J. (2016, March 11). Energized: Coastal Studies Institute rides cutting edge of energy research. *ECU (East Carolina University) News Services*. Retrieved November 6, 2016 from http:// www.ecu.edu/cs-admin/news/UNC-CSI-Energy.cfm

Obe, M. (2011, August 13). Tokyo seeks big growth in solar, wind power. *Wall Street Journal*. Retrieved November 4, 2016 from http://www.wsj.com/articles/SB1000142405311190391810457 6504362770587244

Polimeni, J., Iorgulescu, R., & Chandrasekara, R. (2014). Trans-border public health vulnerability and hydroelectric projects: The case of Yali Falls Dam. *Ecological Economics, 98*, 81–89.

Porter, M., & Van der Linde, C. (1995). Toward a new conception of the environment–competitiveness relationship. *Journal of Economic Perspectives, 9*(4), 97–118.

Ramsey, F. (1927). A contribution to the theory of taxation. *The Economic Journal, 37*(145), 47–61.

Sevcenko, M. (2016, January 16). Power to the poop: One Colorado city is using human waste to run its vehicles. *The Guardian*. Retrieved October 30, 2016 from https://www.theguardian.com/

environment/2016/jan/16/colorado-grand-junction-persigo-wastewater-treatment-plant-human-waste-renewable-energy

Simon, F. (2016, updated May 9). Green transport target will be scrapped post–2020, EU confirms. *EurActiv.com*. Retrieved December 29, 2016 from https://www.euractiv.com/section/transport/news/green-transport-target-will-be-scrapped-post–2020-eu-confirms/

Traube, J., Hansen, L., Palmintier, B., & Levine, J. (2008). *Spatial and temporal interactions of wind and solar in the next generation utility*. Presented at WINDPOWER 2008 Conference & Exhibition. Retrieved from http://www.rmi.org/Knowledge-Center/Library/2008–20_WindSolarNGU

U.S. Department of Energy. (n.d.). *Renewable energy and energy efficiency portfolio standard*. Retrieved November 9, 2016 from http://energy.gov/savings/renewable-energy-and-energy-efficiency-portfolio-standard

U.S. Energy Information Administration (2016a). *Frequently asked questions: What is U.S. electricity generation by energy source?* Retrieved November 5, 2016 from http://www.eia.gov/tools/faqs/faq.cfm?id=427&t=3

U.S. Energy Information Administration. (2016b). *Levelized cost and levelized avoided cost of new generation resources in the annual energy outlook 2016*. Retrieved November 5, 2016 from https://www.eia.gov/forecasts/aeo/pdf/electricity_generation.pdf

U.S. Energy Information Administration (2016c). *Table 7.2a Electricity net generation: total (all sectors)*. Retrieved November 6, 2016 from http://www.eia.gov/totalenergy/data/monthly/pdf/sec7_5.pdf

Wilson, R. (2015, August 11). *Germany will never run on solar power. Here is why*. Retrieved October 31, 2016 from https://carboncounter.wordpress.com/2015/08/11/germany-will-never-run-on-solar-power-here-is-why/

Wirth, H. (2016). *Recent Facts about Photovoltaics in Germany*. Freiburg, Germany: Fraunhofer ISE. Retrieved October 31, 2016 from https://www.ise.fraunhofer.de/en/publications/veroeffentlichungen-pdf-dateien-en/studien-und-konzeptpapiere/recent-facts-about-photovoltaics-in-germany.pdf

Yeo, S. (2016, October 2). Who's hitting the EU's 2020 renewables target—and holding it back? *CarbonBrief*. Retrieved October 31, 2016 from https://www.carbonbrief.org/whos-hitting-the-eus–2020-renewables-target-and-whos-holding-it-back

Chapter 10

Next-generation alternatives
The future or flavor of the month?

"A simple chemical reaction between hydrogen and oxygen generates energy, which can be used to power a car, producing only water, not exhaust fumes. With a new national commitment, our scientists and engineers will overcome obstacles to taking these cars from laboratory to showroom, so that the first car driven by a child born today could be powered by hydrogen, and pollution-free."

George W. Bush[1]

"The most common question I hear in regards to energy economics is 'Have you heard about the new energy source___?'"

The author of this book

Introduction

Fill in the blank in the above author's quote with algae, hydrogen, nuclear fusion, ocean currents, and even antimatter. Will these alternatives take their place in a transition from fossil fuels and the accompanying carbon emissions, or will they fade into obscurity? Are they tomorrow's energy future, the next hydraulic fracturing that might provide electricity and transportation at a lower cost and with fewer externalities than current alternatives? Alternatively, will they be the next "flavor of the month," the next "cold fusion" that would revolutionize the production of energy if they were truly feasible and economical, but instead prove to be a mirage or a money pit?

The job of the economist is not to be omniscient, but to make use of the economic system to provide proper incentives for entrepreneurs to develop alternatives, based on considerations of risk and return. Economists can also highlight market failures, the limitations of markets in providing proper incentives. A third role of economists is to help design government programs that will be the most likely to improve society's welfare. In developing these programs, we should be aware that the government will not be omniscient either. We are more likely to gravitate to next-generation alternatives cost-effectively if we augment markets when there is reason to believe that government can improve upon the outcome. Where possible, economists favor incentive-based programs over command-and-control.

The next section of this chapter will distinguish a next-generation alternative from today's alternatives. In the following three sections, we examine next-generation renewables, nonrenewables, and prospects that fall outside those categories such as fuel cells and batteries. We then consider the role of markets and government in providing proper incentives for development of alternatives. The final section is a summary.

What is a next-generation energy alternative?

Next- (or second-) generation technologies are in the research phase and have not yet achieved commercial feasibility. Therefore, the factors differentiating current and next-generation technologies are: The technology that will emerge for the future power source is still unsettled; the current cost of the next-generation technology is prohibitively high; and the infrastructure needed to make the alternative viable is not yet in place. It might be more accurate to separate technically feasible technologies from those that are not yet feasible, referring to the latter as "beyond the next (or third) generation," but the distinction is not always clear-cut. To demonstrate the distinction between current and next-generation alternatives, we consider automobile technology.

Alternatives to the automobile combustion engine

There are alternatives to the gas combustion engine, some of them in the early phase of commercial feasibility. Electric vehicles (EVs) are available, ranging from the $30,000 (before subsidies) Nissan Leaf to luxury Tesla models. Porsche plans to bring out its own model in the luxury category. Faraday, copying Tesla by naming its company after a famous energy scientist, is also developing an EV. Google and Apple have also announced plans to participate in the EV market.

Box 10.1 Is the hydrogen vehicle the car of the future or a lot of hot air?

Consider hydrogen as an energy source, such as for hydrogen vehicles. In his 2003 State of the Union address (see the quote that opens this chapter), then U.S. President George W. Bush pledged $1.2 billion towards the development of hydrogen vehicles. Bush envisioned combining hydrogen and oxygen to generate energy, with a by-product of water but no carbon or other unwanted emissions. He projected the child born in 2003 to be the first driver of a hydrogen vehicle, just one generation away in 2023.

The technological road that these vehicles take is at a juncture. The new vehicles will either contain a combustion engine like today's gasoline vehicles, with hydrogen replacing the traditional fuel, or they will run on hydrogen fuel cells in combination with a battery. As hydrogen is a gas and is difficult to compress or liquefy, the combustion engine version will require a large and expensive tank. Fuel cells and the accompanying battery are expensive as well. There are numerous potential electrolysis technologies for separating hydrogen from water or other molecules, necessary since hydrogen does not exist alone. Each technology requires energy to achieve the separation, and for the technology to be viable it must produce more energy than it consumes. There is also the question of whether the fuel used to bring about the reaction is a fossil fuel or a renewable. The cost at the current time is astronomical where the separation method is feasible. Much of the research is still at the experimental stage to see if it is possible to separate the hydrogen from another element by using other elements to initiate the chemical reaction at an affordable cost. Moreover, there is little infrastructure available to transport hydrogen or to fuel a hydrogen vehicle.

Former President Bush's program to promote additional research to speed the development of hydrogen vehicles is an example of government efforts to "pick winners." EVs offer an alternative to conventional cars as well as to hydrogen vehicles. Car companies are doing enormous research on EVs, with the hope that they can one day be profitable without government subsidies. It is uncertain whether hydrogen vehicles will offer enough of an advance over EVs to gain acceptance.

What is the alternative to the government attempting to pick winners? The market offers incentives in the form of high rewards for high-risk investments. Toyota, developer of the Prius, a successful gas–electric hybrid vehicle, is introducing the Mirai, a hydrogen fuel-cell automobile. Honda is also developing a hydrogen fuel-cell vehicle. For now, the cars cost about $60,000 and refueling is expensive, if you can find fuel. The United States has only about a dozen refueling stations, with ten of them in California (Davies, 2015). Talk about range anxiety![2] Nor is there much in the way of infrastructure to ship hydrogen from production facilities to distribution centers. In addition, steam-reformulating natural gas—a process that combines natural gas and steam that releases GHGs—is the primary method of production for the hydrogen in the fuel cells.

The decision to produce hydrogen-cell vehicles is not purely market-based. As with the Prius, Toyota or Honda looks for programs like those introduced by the Bush Administration to assist in subsidizing hydrogen research and development.

With the abundance of natural gas, we can expect continuing efforts to increase the market share of natural gas vehicles. For now, the niche is primarily large vehicles such as buses that can accommodate the large tanks needed to hold natural gas. There are also compressed natural gas (CNG) vehicles, with smaller tanks, longer range between fill-ups, but more expensive fuel.

There are next-generation biofuels that move beyond corn- or sugar-based ethanol to feedstocks that will not compete with human food supplies, although they may affect animal food supplies. Former President George W. Bush singled out switchgrass in his 2006 State of the Union Address, but there is also wheat straw, corn stover from the inedible parts of the plant, and woody stalks from plants. Food wastes, such as recycled grease from cooking French fries, or cooking grease that consumers dispose of improperly that ends up in municipal water systems, can provide energy.

Which technologies will emerge as winners? None of us is likely to have a crystal ball. We need to make use of markets to motivate next-generation alternatives, and where markets are subject to failures we need to consider if government can improve the outcome.

Incentives to develop next-generation energy alternatives

What is driving the pursuit of next-generation alternatives? The first driver is concern about GHG emissions. In the absence of a price on carbon, next-generation measures that reduce carbon emissions are candidates for second-best approaches. There is also more attention to *net energy* considerations—energy input vs. energy output—and life-cycle emissions. From a life-cycle perspective, we need to account for carbon emissions at each step of the supply chain, including extraction and transportation.

A second driver is fuel cost. As recently as June of 2014, oil sold for over $100 per barrel. However, oil prices quickly fell. Low energy prices weaken the incentive to invest in long-term, highly speculative alternatives.

Global population is a third driver. World population will increase, putting a greater strain on existing resources including nonrenewable fuels. Growing population is a concern for those who believe that oil supplies will inevitably decline and we will need to develop new energy resources to meet greater global demand.

While markets play a major role in allocating today's fuels, they play only an indirect role in promoting long-term alternatives. If entrepreneurs who perform research and development (R&D) cannot patent it, markets will underprovide this activity. R&D has public goods characteristics. Once a producer makes a discovery, there is no cost to allowing others to use that discovery. Moreover, in the absence of patents, there may be no way to prevent others from free-riding on your innovation. Patents are not a perfect remedy, as they grant long-term monopoly rights and therefore also underprovide R&D.

Where markets fail, there is the potential for government to improve resource allocation. If the market underprovides R&D, the government may be able to provide an incentive to promote it. Patents are one way. Subsidies are another. Private or not-for-profit organizations can also provide incentives.

We need innovations in promoting R&D if next-generation energy technologies are to make it to commercial development. *Awards* are an alternative to the patent system, with successful developers receiving a large cash prize. For example, the X Prize Foundation is a nonprofit organization that awarded $10 million to the first nongovernmental entity to successfully launch a reusable manned spacecraft twice within two weeks. There are a range of X Prizes in energy and environment, including $20 million for breakthrough technologies to convert CO_2 emissions into useful products including alternative fuels (see X Prize, 2015). However, the approach suffers from identifying the area to award the prize, making the prize large enough to be a sufficient reward, and providing a continuous incentive for R&D.

Next-generation renewable energy

Wind, solar, and biomass will take new directions as the next generation of alternatives aims to overcome some of the drawbacks of today's commercially available alternatives. Hydro will also see potential changes, especially if we include wave and tidal energy as forms of hydro.

Wind

In order to make further inroads as a cost-competitive alternative to fossil fuels, wind can reduce costs directly, or indirectly by increasing its reliability and capacity factor. These changes can be incremental, such as redesigning the turbine blades to capture the wind more effectively, or novel, such as suspending the wind apparatus above the earth where winds are strong and consistent.

Onshore development

Current capacity factors are around 40%, so in the absence of battery storage, the next generation of technologies will look for innovations that increase wind's capacity factor. A recent Wind Program publication by the Office of Energy Efficiency & Renewable Energy, a division of the U.S. Department of Energy (n.d.-a), reports on selected research projects aimed at next-generation wind technologies. Towers are scaling up to increase capacity. To achieve these gains, rotor blades are longer and lighter. Innovative turbine blade design captures more wind and can make use of slower wind speeds.

Drivetrains—composed of a gearbox and generator—are more reliable, and control systems can better measure available wind and optimal use. The drivetrain is contained within a gearbox that converts the blade rotation of 12–20 rotations per minute (for a 1 MW turbine) into the faster 1,800 rotations per minute that the generator needs to generate electricity. The majority of wind tower failures occur within the gearbox, which is heavy and expensive. Next-generation gearboxes will be simpler, will run at a lower speed, and will use advanced components and improved circuit design. The goal is longer gearbox longevity, along with lower cost and greater reliability. There are explorations of direct-drive generators that operate at lower rotational speeds and do not require gearboxes.

Wind towers also require a yaw mechanism to face the wind turbine rotor perpendicular to the wind. If the two are not perpendicular, the amount of wind power will be lower and the blades will be subject to greater fatigue, cracks, and shorter life. Improvements can better control the wear that results from torque due to changing wind conditions. Yaws contain a brake to control the angle of the tower as the wind direction changes, as well as an inverter to convert DC power produced by the turbine into AC power used on the electric grid. Simplified design integrates the brake and inverter.

The National Wind Technology Center, located at the National Renewable Energy Laboratory (NREL) in Boulder, Colorado, in collaboration with private company Siemens Energy, is measuring the characteristics of airflow for a 2.3 MW wind turbine. Among the objectives is to study blade fatigue. Turbine blades undergo stress from their use, and longer blade life would increase cost-effectiveness. A facility at Clemson University SCE & G Energy Innovation Center (n.d.) designs and tests innovative drivetrain concepts. They also have a grid simulator that mimics real-world conditions and the interaction between wind energy and the grid.

Offshore wind

Offshore wind is currently much more expensive than onshore, given the challenges of building offshore and the punishment of ocean conditions. The reward is stronger and steadier wind, as well as fewer objections to impairment of the *viewshed*—the geographical area that is visible from a location—since the towers are located far from shore. Offshore wind has the potential to provide more capacity than onshore installations. The aforementioned DOE Wind Program is supporting research in three areas: technology development, market acceleration, and advanced technology demonstration.

Conventional tower foundations are not practical in deep water. Companies are examining a variety of floating platforms. Offshore turbines must be able to withstand greater corrosion due to seawater exposure and operate with less maintenance, given the cost of transporting repair crews and equipment from shore.

Integrating offshore wind energy into existing grid infrastructure remains a problem. Moreover, just as there is concern about land-based wind impacts on birds and bats, offshore wind can in addition impact aquatic life. Lastly, construction of offshore wind power requires use of available ports, vessels, and supply chain infrastructure. The DOE funded a number of offshore wind projects to study how to reduce the costs of planning, construction, and operating offshore wind plants.

Box 10.2 Up in the air

Rather than going offshore, why not go up, where winds are even stronger and steadier? Some of the objections are the same as for existing wind energy, including airflow uncertainty, land requirements, and the effect on views. Consider that one site with promising wind conditions is above New York City. Additional concerns are how to safely suspend airborne turbines thousands of feet above the ground, keep them up in high winds, and not interfere with aviation.

Airborne turbines could ultimately cost less to construct. They would avoid giant steel and concrete towers, or the yaw mechanism that keeps standard turbines facing into the wind as the wind direction changes. Current prototypes include a wind turbine that combines elements of a windmill and a blimp and others that resemble kites (Calderone, 2013).

Solar

Solar photovoltaic (PV) vs. thermal

Solar PV and solar thermal are both available in today's market, with solar PV pulling ahead because its levelized cost is only about half that of solar thermal. The costs of solar PV have fallen quickly enough that they should soon be able to compete without subsidies.

Solar PV is available when an individual customer installs solar panels on the roof of a house, or when an electric utility operates large-scale wind farms. Solar PV converts sunlight into electricity. Individual customer solar electricity is a form of *distributed generation* (DG), electrical generation produced on-site, rather than by an electric utility at a central location.

Sunlight causes a chemical reaction that converts photons—particles of light—into electrons of direct current (DC), and an inverter converts the power to alternating current (AC), the current used on power grids.[3] This source of electricity is only available during daylight hours at times when clouds or even trees do not obscure the sun. Typically, customers make use of energy from the grid, with the option of substituting solar energy when it is available or even selling electricity back to the grid when they use less than the available solar energy.

Solar panels are semiconductors containing silicon or other conductive materials. Silicon is a widely available and inexpensive material, the same material that largely composes sand and is transformable into glass. However, silicon is relatively inefficient at converting sunlight to electricity.

Thin-film technology is the primary alternative to silicon. The materials are cheaper, but less efficient. Thin-film technologies operate on the same principles as silicon solar cells, but use different layering and photovoltaic materials. Silicon dominates today, but advances in thin-film efficiency could allow it to make inroads. A cadmium compound is one of the alternative materials, but its ingestion could have adverse effects on kidney function. As of now, the cadmium is not recycled.

Solar thermal uses the sun's heat rather than its light, and generates heat rather than electricity. At the DG level, individual customers can place solar collector panels that absorb heat on their roofs. Most panels contain a liquid, such as water, that heats up and flows through pipes to a storage area in either liquid or gas form. The most common use is for hot water heaters, but it is also possible to use the technology to heat a house. Commercial and industrial customers can also install solar thermal DG systems. The collectors are most efficient where the sun's intensity, as measured by insolation (not to be confused with insulation), is high, such as in a desert area. They do not require full sun, although solar intensity is likely to be lower on cloudy or cold days. Since the heat is stored, it is available on cloudy days or at night.

When used on a large scale, solar thermal is referred to as concentrated solar power (CSP). At large scale, it is primarily an alternative way for the electric utility to generate the heat needed to create steam to drive a turbine that generates electricity. It can produce a large amount of energy that can power a large number of households, as well as commercial and industrial operations.

We now consider new forms of technically feasible solar technology that could provide alternatives to the leading solar technologies of today.

Next-generation solar

INNOVATIONS IN SOLAR PANELS

In place of silicon, other materials would produce more electricity or could make better use of partial sunlight. Current silicon technologies have a physical limit on how much electricity they can produce.

Perovskite—a mineral composed of calcium, titanium, and oxygen—could double the maximum conversion rate of photons to electrons from about 33% to 66%. Perovskite occurs naturally in the Ural Mountains of Russia, but synthetic perovskite is relatively cheap and easy to produce (Casey, 2016). It can also yield a variety of translucent colors, which will allow new architectural designs. Solar cell efficiency improvements occur by layering the mineral into the solar cells. One problem is that perovskite is unstable in air. The solution is to sandwich it under a stable material such as lead, but that material raises health concerns. There is ongoing research to find alternatives to lead in the layered solar cell.

The U.S. DOE's SunShot program (n.d.-b) funds efforts to make solar energy cost-competitive with other forms of electricity by 2020. To accomplish this goal, they are funding research on next-generation PVs. The program provides competitive grants for projects that increase efficiency, lower costs, improve reliability, and design more secure and sustainable supply chains. The project began in 2011, with $24.5 million in funding for 23 projects. In 2014, the DOE awarded 10 grants and $14 million, including a grant for $1.3 million to Duke University aimed at commercialization of perovskite and the replacement of lead as a layer in the perovskite solar panel.

INNOVATIONS IN CONCENTRATED SOLAR POWER

Advances will be in uses and technology. One advance would be the use of solar thermal for air conditioning. Air conditioning accounts for a large percent of household electricity use during the summer.

Using heat to generate cold sounds like an oxymoron, but is in fact in the development stage. A chemical refrigerant changes phases from liquid to gas, and the phase change requires heating the liquid. Solar thermal heats the refrigerant to a higher temperature than the conventional air conditioning technology, which reduces the work of the compressor—a device that pressurizes fluids—in converting the refrigerant liquid into a gaseous state and therefore reduces the required energy to provide cool air.

Given that solar thermal is currently not cost-competitive with solar PV, what are other anticipated developments that could give solar thermal the edge beyond air conditioning? The DOE SunShot program has funded a number of projects aimed at advancing CSP at the utility scale, with the goal of reducing levelized cost to $0.06/kWh or less by 2020. Projects include advances in the components of thermal technology, including the collector, receiver, storage, heat transfer fluids, and power cycle subsystems, as well as technologies that reduce O&M costs. The program looks for transformative technologies that can break through existing efficiency and temperature barriers.

In addition to stand-alone facilities, work is taking place on using solar thermal as part of hybrid technology, such as augmenting coal plant production to achieve lower emissions. Duke Energy has attempted one application to date, which evaluated the cost of integrating solar thermal energy with existing coal and natural gas plants for a plant in North Carolina. The rationale was to leverage the lower cost and higher reliability of fossil-fueled plants with the environmental advantages of renewables. On balance, there was too low a level of solar intensity to achieve economic viability. The outcome suggests that utility-level CSP is more promising in the southwestern United States, with its deserts and year-round hot sun.

In 2015, SunShot provided $32 million in funding through CSP: APOLLO (Advance Projects Offering Low Levelized Cost of Energy Opportunities). They funded 14 industry and academic projects. The largest grant for over $5 million went to Southwest Research Institute in San Antonio, Texas, for a novel compressor design to be developed with Samsung Techwin America. General Electric's GE Global Research division received almost $4 million to team with the Southwest Research Institute on a better compressor design in a CSP tower. Los Alamos National Laboratory has funding to develop a better heat-pipe-based technology.

Next-generation biofuels

Today's first-generation biofuels generally use biomass—organic plant and animal materials—and compete directly with food for crops and land. The objective of next-generation biofuels is to use inorganic materials that will not drive up food prices. Furthermore, next-generation biofuels can improve upon the ratio of energy output to energy input. Since next-generation biofuels are much more expensive, the only way to make an economic case for them is that costs will come down, or that the cost of conventional fuels will go up.

Alternatives to food-based ethanol

The conversion of switchgrass to cellulosic ethanol would reduce GHG emissions as compared to corn ethanol. In his 2006 State of the Union address, former President George W. Bush announced funding for research, with the goal that switchgrass would be competitive within six years. That goal remains elusive; while switchgrass grows much more densely than corn and is plentiful, the cost of converting it into gasoline remains high. Current U.S. DOE figures report a cost equivalent of $5.26 per gallon (Moulton, 2015).

An alternative to switchgrass or other woody crops and forest residues is to use corn stover, the nonfood part of corn plants. Again, there would be large reductions in GHGs. Corn stover is less expensive than switchgrass, but more expensive than corn ethanol. Miscanthus is a grass that is not native to the United States, but is introducible and has a comparable cost per gallon to corn stover (Larson, 2015). Miscanthus would become competitive at a lower price of carbon than the other alternatives, given its lower carbon emissions.

These technologies are at a very early stage of development. While costs will no doubt come down over time, there is limited incentive for private companies to plow dollars into the technologies when gas prices are low and carbon prices are low or zero. If carbon prices were $100/ton, these alternatives would attract considerable commercial interest.

Some species of algae and seaweed are also convertible into ethanol. These sources are actually third-generation biofuels, as they come from aquatic organisms and not land-grown crops. Algae break down via fermentation that transforms the sugars into ethanol. However, there are other profitable uses of algae, leaving a limited amount to convert to ethanol. Nor is its use economical on a commercial scale. It is currently more expensive than plant-based ethanol.

Next-generation biodiesel

Diesel fuel is a heavier, denser by-product of the refining process than gasoline. Diesel vehicles get more miles per gallon because there is more energy in the denser fuel. The EU pursued diesel vehicles as a way to reduce GHG emissions. U.S. consumers were less willing to embrace the technology after negative experiences with U.S.-produced diesel vehicles. The engines are also more expensive to build. Diesel cars had a large share of the European market until the Volkswagen scandal showed that diesel emissions were higher than claimed.

To the extent that the market for diesel fuel for automobiles recovers and that other uses for diesel such as for trucks, trains, ships, and military vehicles are still viable, there is an incentive to search for alternatives that emit fewer pollutants, including GHGs. Not only can algae produce ethanol, but it also produces a type of oil that is transformable into biodiesel fuel for automobiles or jet fuel. However, the U.S. General

Accounting Office found that the military was spending $150 per gallon on algae-based jet fuel when conventional oil-based jet fuel was selling for $3 per gallon (Clemente, 2015). Rapeseed oil is another source of biodiesel, although it and other oils for biofuels are also food sources, presenting the same issue as conventional biofuels where food and fuel compete.

Jatropha is among the nonfood plants that yield oil. It attracted attention a decade ago, until researchers discovered that it yielded too few seeds to produce enough petroleum to be profitable. The latest round, titled Jatropha 2.0 by SGB, its producer, is a hybrid plant that yields enough seeds to be competitive with $100 per barrel oil. It is also usable as jet fuel. Whether the company can commercialize the technology remains an open question (Woody, 2013).

Oil left over from cooking food is also a source of biodiesel. Converting these wastes to oil turns a negative externality into a useful product. These wastes otherwise clog drains and end up in landfills. Diesel vehicles can run using these fuels, and any of the next-generation biofuels can blend with conventional biofuels.

Even plant and animal matter that ends up in landfills can produce fuel. As it decomposes, it emits methane, which is natural gas. Capturing it to use as fuel also diverts it from the atmosphere, where methane would otherwise be a potent GHG. The use of an *anaerobic digester* can accelerate the decomposition process. Bacteria, in the absence of oxygen, break down the wastes to produce methane, which is usable as an automobile fuel and for cooking.

Nonrenewables

Carbon capture and storage (CCS)

Coal and natural gas are the leading fuels for generating electricity. However, both fuels, as well as oil, emit carbon. With coal emitting the most carbon per unit of electricity generated, there is a wide perception it will need to incorporate CCS to remain viable. The technology could also reduce emissions from natural gas-burning power plants. To date, CCS attempts such as Duke Energy's Edwardsport plant and the DOE FutureGen project have cost much more than projected, as detailed in Chapter 7 on coal. However, given the large amounts of available coal, there is a strong incentive to pursue this technology.

Conceptually, the method is similar to sulfur removal, with a simple three-step supply chain. The first step is to separate CO_2 from other gases that are by-products of electricity production or industrial processes. The second is to transport the CO_2 gas much as we would transport natural gas, using pipelines, tanker trucks, or ships. The third step is to store the gas deep underground, or to transport it to companies that have a use for it.

Box 10.3 Bubbling over with creative reuses of CO_2

Do you enjoy carbonated beverages? The thirst quencher is CO_2. One option is to transport the gas where it has a positive, rather than a negative value. The U.S. DOE (n.d.-c) is funding a variety of creative uses, such as the following three representative projects.

Alcoa and partner companies will capture and convert CO_2 in flue gases from exhaust into mineral carbonates to convert alkaline clay to carbonate-enhanced clay for soil remediation. Calera, a company that focuses on beneficial reuses of CO_2, and partner companies also have an innovative process for converting CO_2 in flue gas to carbonates for use in the construction industry. Research Triangle Institute (RTI), a nonprofit consulting firm affiliated with the University of North Carolina at Chapel Hill, North Carolina State University, and Duke University, will work with partners to produce pipeline-ready synthetic natural gas from CO_2 and waste fuel.

The Global CCS Institute (n.d.), established in 2009 with start-up funding from the Australian government and international membership of businesses, governments, and nongovernmental organizations, has a lengthy list of existing reuses including beverage carbonation, wine making, coffee decaffeination, water treatment, and perhaps of greatest interest to the subject of energy, enhanced oil recovery. CO_2 injection makes it possible to recover oil that would otherwise be unrecoverable. The CO_2 reduces the viscosity of the remaining oil so that it can flow to the surface for easier extraction. The CO_2 can remain permanently in the well. A similar use is to inject CO_2 along with other propping agents to prevent cracks from closing during hydraulic fracturing to enhance oil and gas extraction.

The Institute also notes emerging uses. It can enhance coal bed methane recovery, geothermal power generation, and nuclear energy production. The Institute also lists mineralization along the lines funded by the DOE. It can also produce methanol, a racecar fuel, which has fuel properties similar to ethanol. The Methanol Institute (n.d.) is a global trade association that lobbies for greater use of this alternative energy.

Nuclear energy

The unique attributes of nuclear energy—no carbon emissions and a highly reliable source of baseload generation for the production of electricity—ensure that nuclear energy will continue to receive consideration as a way to provide electricity despite its high cost and radioactive wastes. The future viability of nuclear energy will require consideration of smaller-scale reactors, alternative designs and fuels, and a breakthrough in nuclear fusion. We now consider these prospects.

Small nuclear reactors

The primary driver for small reactors is the lower financing cost. A second impetus is to supply power in remote locations that do not have access to the electric grid. Smaller size also allows construction on brownfields, potentially contaminated sites such as former coal plant sites (World Nuclear Association, 2016). Small modular reactors (SMRs) typically have a capacity of 300 MW or less (as low as 10 MW) compared to 1,000 MW conventional large-scale reactors. However, the production of nuclear energy appears to enjoy economies of scale, so the cost of producing energy is higher for SMRs. While capital costs may be less daunting than for large plants, investors will still not be interested if they are not cost–competitive with large nuclear plants, much less natural gas and renewable sources of energy. There also may be less expensive ways of serving off–the–grid customers, such as solar, wind, and natural gas.

Small is not necessarily safer. To replace large reactors, we would have to build multiple small reactors. While radioactive wastes would be smaller per reactor, total wastes could be larger given the much larger number of plants. There is also the fear that terrorists could attack nuclear plants, and having to protect many small sites is likely to be more expensive than protecting one large site.

The future of SMRs rests on bringing down their cost per MW of power as well as improving their safety. Westinghouse, faced with bankruptcy from the cost of its latest-technology, also has designs for small-scale. The DOE has invested in small-scale nuclear. In particular, it provided support to NuScale Power LLC, affiliated with Fluor Corporation, for a new technology SMR. The plan is for a 50 MW reactor, with the opportunity to build multiple reactors at a site.

NuScale is expected to be first to the market because it uses a light-water cooling system similar to conventional reactors. Alternative cooling systems such as molten salt reactors are likely to operate at a higher temperature and higher efficiency. The plants are designed to be underground, a safety advantage as they are less accessible to terrorists. The company estimates the cost at $5,000/kW, compared to U.S. Energy Information Administration estimates of $4,700/kW for a conventional nuclear plant, $4,600 for a carbon sequestration coal plant, and $1,800 for a gas-fired plant with CCS (World Nuclear Association, 2016). The company sees a market in remote areas that need small power plants and do not have access to natural gas. Flatbed truck or rail can transport the small-size components, also facilitating additional units to meet growth in demand.

Alternative designs and fuels

One motivation for encouraging new nuclear plants is to evaluate changes in technology since the 1970s. New construction includes the plants at Vogtle and Summer in the southeast United States as well as the Olkiluoto 3 plant in Finland. Vogtle and Summer both use the Westinghouse (now majority owned by Toshiba) AP1000. The AP1000 is a Gen III+ design (there was also a Gen III AP600, but very few Gen IIIs were built). Gen II technology refers to plants built in the 1970s. The new plants require less land and promote cheaper, safer, and simpler design with fewer components such as pumps, valves, and cables. One prominent feature is passive safety, where the plant proceeds to shut down automatically if it detects a malfunction rather than requiring human intervention.

As referred to in Chapter 8 on nuclear energy, costs for the Vogtle and Summer plants are way above estimates and the projects are years behind schedule.[4] Olkiluoto 3 in Finland also has an unfavorable performance to date. As of 2015, it was nine years behind schedule and three times over budget. It would use a new European pressurized reactor (EPR) technology. It was originally estimated to cost €3 billion and to begin operating in 2009. Areva, a multinational public–private company and major builder of nuclear plants, saw this project as an opportunity to launch a revival in its business. Instead, the company has fought with TVO, the Finnish electric utility, over who is at fault for construction mistakes along the way, some due to inexperienced builders.

They have cancelled a proposed second plant, Olkiluoto 4, although Finland still plans to build a new nuclear reactor at a different location.

Generation IV may become available around 2030. The plan is for revolutionary, rather than evolutionary changes. Generations II and III primarily used light-water reactors. Gen IV includes other designs, such as *molten salt reactors* (MSRs). MSRs convert uranium into a liquid rather than a solid fuel. They are a simpler design which should result in lower costs. They have the potential to be safer, as they operate at a lower temperature that does not present the threat of meltdown. The spent fuel stays in the plant, so there is no nuclear waste needing disposal. However, once the plant is no longer operational, the entire site will be nuclear waste. Furthermore, it may be decades before these reactors are ready for use, at which time renewables and next-generation technologies may be still lower cost. All of these alternatives depend upon funds for R&D. There is no reason to expect a change from a history of cost overruns and schedule delays, so investments in these new technologies should include multiple cost estimates in deciding the best use of R&D dollars (Locatelli et al., 2013).

While there are ample supplies of uranium, it is still a finite resource. Other fuels can replace uranium. The most widely discussed alternative is *thorium*, a source of fuel that was actually considered in the early days of nuclear plants. It is a slightly radioactive metal found in rocks and soils. It can be used in combination with uranium as well as by itself. It can be burned in pressurized-water reactors and MSRs. The cost of extraction is lower than for uranium. It produces less radioactive waste and is less likely to lead to a plant meltdown. Moreover, it cannot be used for nuclear weapons. The obstacle is extracting the energy value at a competitive cost. That achievement will require additional R&D.

Box 10.4 A fuel with MOXie

Plutonium, typically recovered from reprocessing reactor fuel, can be used in nuclear plants. In the form of a mixed oxide fuel known as MOX, 95% uranium oxide and 5% plutonium oxide, Duke Energy and the Tennessee Valley Authority (TVA) were among U.S. utilities that received DOE funding to perform tests using MOX fuel. In its 2003 proposal to the U.S. Nuclear Regulatory Commission, Duke Energy (2012) cited MOX fuel as a mature technology widely used in Europe, and as a way to reduce weapons-grade plutonium supplies.

Duke Energy cited the availability of supplies from the Savannah River site in South Carolina as an advantage of the fuel. That site, owned by the DOE, has the proclaimed purpose of safely handling nuclear materials and preventing nuclear proliferation. At the time of the Duke Energy proposal, Savannah River anticipated building the only manufacturing plant for MOX in the Unites States. Opponents raised concerns about nuclear proliferation in processing, transporting, and using such fuels (Friends of the Earth, 2009). Duke Energy abandoned its plan to use MOX in 2009 and the TVA has not moved forward.

By 2014, Savannah River had not completed the MOX manufacturing plant and requested a 10-year extension. Areva, a leader in construction of the facility, reported it 70% complete as of 2016 despite "meager funding" (Areva, 2016). After more than a decade of cost overruns and delays, the Obama Administration announced its intent to discontinue funding for the facility. While it faces extinction, South Carolina raised the specter of lawsuits to fund the completion and eventual operation of the facility (Bergengruen & Fretwell, 2016).

Nuclear fusion

Nuclear fusion is the holy grail of nuclear energy. Fission releases energy by splitting atoms, while fusion releases much more energy by fusing atoms of relatively abundant deuterium and rarer tritium, hydrogen isotopes of differing weights. Fusion reactions take place on the sun, but to make fusion useful on earth, the reaction needs much higher temperatures than those found in the core of the sun and on a much smaller scale. It will also need to generate sufficient tritium for an ongoing reaction (Arnoux, 2016). Fusion is much harder to control than fission, and much more expensive. However, if it were to succeed, it would produce less radioactive material and have a nearly unlimited fuel supply.

The first step will be to produce net energy, more energy output than the energy input into the reaction. The most prominent test facility is the international thermonuclear experimental reactor (ITER), described in Chapter 8 on nuclear energy. Recent announcements from ITER suggest that the technology will not be ready for commercialization until 2050 (Cockerill, 2016).

The fusion device is a donut-shaped torus referred to as a tokomak. ITER is the largest tokamak ever built. The process heats the fuel (consisting of hydrogen isotopes deuterium and tritium) to over 100 million degrees Celsius, at which temperature the fuel becomes a plasma. The plasma is difficult to work with and must be confined, protected from contamination, and kept from cooling. The technique is magnetic confinement. It takes a great deal of energy to create the magnetic fields, the challenge of creating positive net energy to be used in power plants. In a commercial fusion power plant, the heat from the reaction would produce steam to drive turbines and generate electricity (Culham Centre for Fusion Energy, n.d.).

Box 10.5 The superconducting supercollider

There have been alternative attempts to achieve nuclear fusion on a large scale. In 1989, Texas won a contract to build the superconducting supercollider, a particle accelerator that accelerates particles (electrons) using electromagnetic waves. The collisions release energy and subatomic particles (Freudenrich, n.d.). The primary objective was to produce the Higgs boson or "God particle," a subatomic article that gives atoms their mass.

The superconducting supercollider ultimately fell victim to excessive cost and construction delays, and the U.S. Congress cancelled the project in 1993. CERN (Conseil Européen pour la Recherche Nucléaire, or the European Organization for Nuclear Research), a European consortium of 21 member states and Israel located in Geneva, Switzerland, now carries on fusion research and receives U.S. funding. Using their large Hadron collider, CERN confirmed the existence of the Higgs boson "God particle" and investigates the use of high-speed particles for fission and fusion (Weinberg Foundation, 2013).

Ongoing work couples particle accelerators with thorium fuel nuclear reactors to produce fission required to start the fusion reaction. The elemental particles collide and form muons, subatomic particles that are much heavier than an electron. When a muon replaces an electron, the nuclei in atoms draw much closer together making fusion easier. Muon-catalyzed fusion can take place at much lower temperatures.[5]

Other next-generation alternatives

Water power

Hydroelectric power is one of the earliest sources of energy to generate electricity. Most of the suitable sites for dam-building have been taken. The future will require new ways of using water to create energy, including small-scale hydro and wave and tidal power.

Small-scale hydro

Hydropower typically uses large dams that create energy as water falls a large distance and drives a turbine, which in turn generates electricity. Hydropower depends upon the distance and the volume of water. Hoover Dam, built during the Great Depression, is as tall as a 60-story building and has a 2,000 MW capacity. It changed the Colorado River from a mighty fast-flowing river to a sluggish water flow that changed the river's ecology. Next-generation hydro will avoid large dams and their ecological consequences. Small-scale hydro from 5 to 100 kW is designated micro hydro, and the smallest scale below 5 kW is pico hydro.

Small hydro can connect to the electric grid or work in an isolated area off the grid. As with large hydro, small hydro makes use of lakes, streams, and rivers. The run-of-river classification requires a weir—a low dam built across a river to raise the level of water upstream—to divert water, and accounts for the majority of small hydro. The other method is to use existing water infrastructure, such as infrastructure for drinking water or wastewater.

To be economical, the hydropower source must be near consumers. There must be sufficient stream flow. Other energy sources need to be available if the area experiences seasonal variation such as droughts.

Wave and tidal power

These sources of power depend upon the size of waves and changes in tides. Technologies exist to harness these sources, but further commercialization depends upon bringing costs down to competitive levels. While waves and tides provide an inexhaustible source of energy, building and maintaining the plants is expensive. Moreover, the energy must be transported to shore. These sources do have the advantage of being more predictable than wind or solar, although they are not as predictable as traditional baseload sources such as fossil fuels and nuclear energy (Silverstein, 2013).

There are several types of wave energy technologies. They typically drive hydraulic pumps using buoys or floats to harness the power from the rise and fall of waves. Tidal power often uses a structure similar to a dam to take advantage of locations with large differences between high and low tides. The method can affect water quality and marine life, although to a lesser extent than large dams as tidal power does not require a permanent impediment to water flow. As with any offshore power source, there can be objections to their effect on views or on recreational or ecological uses.

The U.S. DOE (2015) has awarded funds for next-generation marine energy systems. The emphasis is on extending the lifetime of the technologies to reduce their cost. The technologies need to survive potentially harsh conditions, which present uncertainties in the cost of installation, operation, and maintenance. One project is by M3Wave LLC of Salem, Oregon. The company will develop a wave-energy converter that sits on the ocean floor and utilizes pressure waves that sit below ocean waves. The project seeks to minimize effects of sediment transport and reduce required maintenance. Verdant Power, Inc. has a tidal project in New York's East River and aims to reduce uncertainty by operating three turbines as a single system, with optimal spacing of the turbines and support structures and reduced installation, operation, and maintenance costs.

Fuel cells and batteries

Fuel cells

Earlier in the chapter, we discussed fuel cells as a next-generation source of energy for transportation. Their other major use will assist with the production of electricity. They can be incorporated in the electric grid or be off the grid as distributed generation. Hydrogen fuel cells can provide heat and electricity, and provide energy at the generation source or elsewhere using transmission much like electricity (Renewable Energy World, n.d.).

Fuel cells will likely see use sooner in commercial transportation than in passenger vehicles because of their size. Large trucks, buses, rail, ships, and manned and unmanned aircraft are candidates for hydrogen cells.

Box 10.6 Hydrail on track?

Stan Thompson of Mooresville, North Carolina has promoted hydrail—trains powered by hydrogen fuel cells—since 2003, with the original goal to have a hydrail train connect Mooresville and Charlotte, a 30-mile distance. Mr. Thompson champions the need for funding R&D today to make it an eventual reality. He led the way for an annual global conference on hydrail that launched in Charlotte in 2005 with the cooperation of North Carolina's Appalachian State University. After holding the conference in other North

Carolina locations as well as Canada, Germany, Spain, and Turkey, the tenth annual conference in June of 2015 was held in Mooresville (Steimer, 2015). As compared to diesel engines, the trains would have the environmental advantage of emitting water rather than pollutants. However, as with any hydrogen vehicle, the net advantage depends on whether fossil fuels or renewables supply the power for hydrogen cells.

North Carolina is not the only place seeking to make hydrail work. Germany plans to launch a passenger rail service using a hydrogen-powered train manufactured by the French Company Alstom. On a smaller scale, the Caribbean island of Aruba runs a streetcar powered by batteries along with hydrogen fuel cells. Dubai has an initial route of a hydrogen-powered trolley system in operation (O'Sullivan, 2016).

For hydrogen to achieve its carbon-free objective, hydrogen electrolysis must use fuels that are emissions-free. Hydrogen and renewables can form a virtuous circle, as not only can emissions-free renewables produce hydrogen, but hydrogen can be stored, overcoming the intermittency issue that reduces the value of wind and solar. The less virtuous part is whether hydrogen electrolysis uses renewable fuels, and the cost. To the extent that we use renewables to produce hydrogen, the cost of hydrogen is dependent on the cost of renewables.

In addition, as with all next-generation technologies, capital costs need to come down for hydrogen to be cost-competitive. There is also the cost of storing hydrogen. Stored hydrogen can serve more than one use, thus increasing its value. It can supply electricity to the grid or off-grid for fuel-cell electric vehicles. It can also provide a feedstock for industries using hydrogen, such as ammonia production. Hydrogen suppliers can balance hydrogen uses depending upon its value for electricity as compared to transportation or industry uses (Melaina & Eichman, 2015).

Batteries

Batteries differ from fuel cells in that they store electricity but do not produce it. Electric utilities are beginning to incorporate grid-scale battery storage that can smooth out fluctuations in the availability of intermittent energy sources or outages in conventional generation. Batteries also allow distributed generation, either connected to the grid or independent of it. As with other distributed generation, batteries can serve remote locations. Electric vehicles can store electricity, and supply it to the grid when the vehicle is not in use.

The lithium-ion battery is the most common. It presents several challenges. In some uses, it has caught fire.[6] Bolivia, which controls over half of the world's lithium, may exercise political muscle much as Saudi Arabia has done with oil. Bolivia and other producers also face environmental challenges. Bolivia's supplies are in formerly pristine salt lakes. Tourists used to come to these landscapes that have since been altered by construction equipment and transformation of large lakes into small bodies of water.

Batteries are currently an expensive source of electricity. However, they provide *ancillary services*—value to the electricity supply chain by increasing reliability—such as backing up renewables or stabilizing voltage. In order to properly compensate the use of batteries, payment will need to reflect the value of greater electric system reliability.

As with other next-generation technologies, the market will underprovide R&D. The DOE supports projects in this space as in other areas of innovative energy technologies.

The role of markets and governments in next-generation technology

We have previously discussed efforts by car manufacturers to pursue hydrogen vehicles, but it is likely to be underprovided given the public goods characteristics of R&D. Florida Power and Light (FPL) engages in solar energy activity using current as well as next-generation technologies. Electric utilities are not completely independent of the public sector, as conventional utilities are subject to regulation. FPL can propose research that they will only do if they can win approval to include the costs in their rate base. Their DeSoto Next-Generation Solar Energy Center uses current solar PV technology despite the next-generation in its name. It produces enough solar energy to power about 3,000 homes. The FPL Martin Next-Generation Clean Energy Center teams solar with natural gas. The sun produces heat to drive the turbines, assisted by natural gas at night or when the weather is overcast. FPL Space Coast Next-Generation Solar Center is a third installation. It is a public–private partnership with the National Aeronautics and Space Administration (NASA). The solar PV technology is again more conventional than it is next-generation, with a scale of providing electricity for over 1,100 homes from grid-based power (FPL, n.d.).

Other next-generation examples involving private firms are generally in cooperation with public funding. CERES Technologies is a privately held company with a solar PV line of business. They have a $20 million partnership with a campus of the State University of New York to accelerate the development of next-generation solar PV systems using new computer-chip technologies. CERES will supply tools needed to work on copper indium gallium (CIG) selenide, or CIG-based PV technology (New York State, 2012). The DOE SunShot Initiative also provides funds.

The major impetus for next-generation fuel alternatives is to mitigate climate change. To date, most of the focus has been on CO_2. In the absence of a price for carbon emissions, both current and future alternatives to fossil fuels are a hard sell. However, firms and consumers may still invest in these technologies based on subjective calculations of the likelihood that carbon constraints are coming or for reasons of warm glow, identity, or sustainability.

Summary

Next-generation technologies are not yet commercially feasible. The factors differentiating current and next-generation technologies include: the technology for the future power source is still unsettled; the cost is prohibitively high; and the infrastructure needed to make the alternative viable is not yet in place. Three factors drive the pursuit of next-generation alternatives: the concern about the effects of GHG emissions, high fuel costs, and growing global population. The role of the economist is to clarify the roles of markets and governments to provide socially efficient levels of next-generation alternatives.

Next-generation renewables include wind, solar, and biofuels. For wind energy, a major task is to increase its capacity factor. Solar PV can utilize solar panels that more efficiently convert sunlight into electricity with innovative materials such as perovskite. Solar thermal currently lags behind solar PV, but the DOE has targeted projects to reduce its levelized cost, as well as new uses such as air conditioning and working in combination with coal and natural gas to reduce emissions. The objective of next-generation biofuels is to use inorganic materials that will not drive up world food prices. Next-generation hydropower will be small scale in order to avoid the use of dams and their ecological consequences. For wave and tidal energy, technologies exist to harness these sources, but their costs are high and they have environmental consequences.

Next-generation nonrenewables include CCS, nuclear energy, fuel cells and batteries. There is strong impetus to develop CCS technology given the large amounts of available coal and natural gas. The future viability of nuclear energy will require consideration of smaller-scale plants, alternative designs and fuels, and a breakthrough in nuclear fusion. Small nuclear reactors are easier to finance and allow construction and operation in remote locations off the grid. However, nuclear fusion technology is the holy grail of nuclear energy. Fusion produces less radioactive material and has a nearly unlimited fuel supply, but it is much harder to control than fission and much more expensive.

Fuel cells or batteries can be at grid-scale or off the grid as distributed generation. They supply electricity and ancillary service. They also offer an alternative to gasoline-powered vehicles. We will likely see their use sooner in commercial transportation than in passenger vehicles, given their space requirements.

Technology advancement is the instrument to commercialize these next-generation alternatives. However, R&D has public goods characteristics, making it difficult for private companies to prevent others from using unpatented technologies. The incentive is also weaker when gas prices are low and carbon prices are either low or zero. The market alone is not able to provide a socially efficient level of technology advancement. Government funding, such as by the DOE, is prominent in developing these next-generation technologies. Nongovernment organizations such as X-Prize are another channel for rewarding next-generation energy entrepreneurs.

Notes

1 Electrifying Times (n.d.) reprints the section of the speech on hydrogen vehicles.
2 Electric vehicles offer a range of between 100 and 300 miles. Consumers experience range anxiety about their ability to find a recharging station before the car runs out of its charge.
3 Go Solar California (n.d.) contains a simple explanation of how we get electricity from solar panels.
4 Smith and Narioka (2016) report that Toshiba is suffering large losses and steep drops in stock market shares from its acquisition of Westinghouse. They are now discovering unexpected labor force inefficiencies with a new subcontractor at the Georgia and South Carolina sites.
5 "Cold fusion" got a bad name when two professors from the University of Utah announced they had achieved nuclear fusion at room temperature. Other scientists were unable to replicate the reaction. However, the technique did not involve particle accelerators or muons.
6 You may recall Samsung cancelled sales of its Galaxy 7 phones after a number of them burst into flames. They used lithium-ion batteries surrounded by a flammable liquid.

References

Areva. (2016, February 9). *Significant progress on MOX project achieves 70% completion*. Retrieved November 11, 2016 from http://us.arevablog.com/2016/02/09/significant-progress-on-mox-project-achieves–70-completion/

Arnoux, R. (2016, February). *Tritium: Changing lead into gold*. Retrieved November 11, 2016 from https://www.iter.org/mag/8/56

Bergengruen, V., & Fretwell, S. (2016, February 9). Obama plans to scrap MOX plant; SC leaders livid. *The State*. Retrieved November 11, 2016 from http://www.thestate.com/news/local/article59334313.html

Calderone, L. (2013, October 15). High altitude wind energy. *Altenergymag*. Retrieved November 9, 2016 from http://www.altenergymag.com/content.php?post_type=2156

Casey, T. (2016, February 5). Yes, solar can go lower (perovskite solar cells, that is). *CleanTechnica*. Retrieved November 11, 2016 from https://cleantechnica.com/2016/02/05/yes-solar-can-go-lower-perovskite-solar-cells-that-is/

Clemente, J. (2015, June 17). Why biofuels can't replace oil. *Forbes*. Retrieved November 11, 2016 from http://www.forbes.com/sites/judeclemente/2015/06/17/why-biofuels-cant-replace-oil/#71f11a9a362b

Clemson University SCE & G Energy Innovation Center. (n.d.). Retrieved November 9, 2016 from http://clemsonenergy.com/

Cockerill, R. (2016, May 4). At the forefront of scientific endeavor—Air Liquide and ITER: The largest cryogenics plant. *Gasworld*. Retrieved November 11, 2016 from https://www.gasworld.com/free-feature/air-liquide-and-iter-the-largest-cryogenics-plant/2010380.article

Culham Centre for Fusion Energy. (n.d.). *The tokamak*. Retrieved November 12, 2016 from http://www.ccfe.ac.uk/tokamak.aspx

Davies, A. (2015, October 28). Boy, Honda's not giving up this whole hydrogen car thing. *Wired*. Retrieved November 9, 2016 from https://www.wired.com/2015/10/honda-clarity-hydrogen-fuel-cell-sales/

Duke Energy. (2012, February 27). *The MOX project*. Retrieved March 19, 2016 from http://nuclear.duke-energy.com/2012/02/27/the-mox-project/

Electrifying Times. (n.d.). *President Bush 2003 State of the Union Address promotes hydrogen cars*. Retrieved December 30, 2016 from http://electrifyingtimes.com/state_of_the_union_2003.html

Florida Power & Light. (n.d.). *Solar energy centers*. Retrieved November 12, 2016 from https://www.fpl.com/clean-energy/solar/energy-centers.html

Freudenrich, C. (n.d.). *How atom smashers work*. Retrieved November 12, 2016 from http://science.howstuffworks.com/atom-smasher2.htm

Friends of the Earth. (2009, March 16). *DOE's plans to use plutonium fuel (MOX) jolted by Duke Energy's withdrawal from program*. Retrieved November 11, 2016 from http://www.commondreams.org/newswire/2009/03/16/does-plans-use-plutonium-fuel-MOX-jolted-duke-energys-withdrawal-program

Global CCS Institute. (n.d.). *CO_2 reuse technologies*. Retrieved November 11, 2016 from http://hub.globalccsinstitute.com/publications/accelerating-uptake-ccs-industrial-use-captured-carbon-dioxide/1-co2-reuse-technologies

Go Solar California. (n.d.). *How solar works*. Retrieved November 11, 2016 from http://www.gosolarcalifornia.ca.gov/solar_basics/how.php

Larson, D. (2015, March 4). *Miscanthus-based ethanol boasts bigger benefits, higher profits*. Retrieved November 11, 2016 from http://aces.illinois.edu/news/miscanthus-based-ethanol-boasts-bigger-environmental-benefits-higher-profits

Locatelli, G., Mancini, M., & Todeschini, N. (2013). Generation IV nuclear reactors: Current status and future prospects. *Energy Policy, 61*, 1503–1520.

Melaina, M., & Eichman, J. (2015). *Hydrogen energy storage: Grid and transportation services.* Golden, CO: National Renewable Energy Laboratory.

Methanol Institute. (n.d.). Retrieved November 11, 2016 from http://www.methanol.org/

Moulton, A. (2015, January 29). *Energy Department helping lower biofuel costs for the nation.* Retrieved November 11, 2016 from http://energy.gov/eere/articles/energy-department-helping-lower-biofuel-costs-nation

New York State. (2012, August 29). *Governor Cuomo announces $20 million partnership between SUNY College of Nanoscale Science and Engineering and Ceres Technologies in Ulster County.* Retrieved November 12, 2016 from https://www.governor.ny.gov/news/governor-cuomo-announces–20-million-partnership-between-suny-college-nanoscale-science-and

O'Sullivan, F. (2016, September 26). Germany has the world's first hydrogen-powered passenger train. *Atlantic Citylab.* Retrieved November 12, 2016 from http://www.citylab.com/commute/2016/09/germany-hydrogen-passenger-train/501575/

Renewable Energy World. (n.d.). *Hydrogen energy.* Retrieved November 12, 2016 from http://www.renewableenergyworld.com/hydrogen/tech.html

Silverstein, K. (2013, June 6). Tidal energy could be next big wave. *Forbes.* Retrieved November 12, 2016 from http://www.forbes.com/sites/kensilverstein/2013/06/06/tidal-energy-could-be-next-big-wave/#667cb25341cf

Smith, R., and Narioka, K. (2016, December 29). Toshiba shares plunge further over problems at nuclear-power subsidiary. *Wall Street Journal.* Retrieved December 30, 2016 from http://www.wsj.com/articles/toshiba-shares-crash-after-write-down-warning–1482905903

Steimer, J. (2015). Mooresville hosts international hydrail conference. *Charlotte Observer.* Retrieved November 12, 2016 from http://www.charlotteobserver.com/news/business/article25180096.html

U.S. Department of Energy. (2015, December 28). *Energy Department awards $10.5 million for next-generation marine energy systems.* Retrieved November 12, 2016 from http://energy.gov/eere/articles/energy-department-awards–105-million-next-generation-marine-energy-systems

U.S. Department of Energy. (n.d.-a). *Next-generation wind technology.* Retrieved November 9, 2016 from http://energy.gov/eere/next-generation-wind-technology

U.S. Department of Energy. (n.d.-b). *About the sunshot initiative.* Retrieved November 11, 2016 from http://energy.gov/eere/sunshot/about-sunshot-initiative

U.S. Department of Energy. (n.d.-c). *Innovative concepts for beneficial reuse of carbon dioxide.* Retrieved November 11, 2016 from http://energy.gov/fe/innovative-concepts-beneficial-reuse-carbon-dioxide–0

Weinberg Foundation. (2013). Renowned physics lab CERN turns its big thinking to energy's future, as Thorium Energy Conference kicks off. *Weinberg Next Nuclear.* Retrieved November 12, 2016 from http://www.the-weinberg-foundation.org/2013/10/25/renowned-physics-lab-cern-turns-its-big-thinking-to-energys-future-as-thorium-energy-conference-kicks-off/

Woody, T. (2013, December 24). Start-up uses plant seeds for a biofuel. *New York Times.* Retrieved November 11, 2016 from http://www.nytimes.com/2013/12/25/business/energy-environment/start-up-makes-gains-turning-jatropha-bush-into-biofuel.html

World Nuclear Association. (2016, October 17). *Small nuclear power reactors.* Retrieved November 11, 2016 from http://www.world-nuclear.org/information-library/nuclear-fuel-cycle/nuclear-power-reactors/small-nuclear-power-reactors.aspx

XPrize. (2015, September 29). *New $20 million XPrize aims to tackle CO2 emissions from fossil fuels.* Retrieved November 9, 2016 from http://carbon.xprize.org/press-release/new–20-million-xprize-aims-tackle-co2-emissions-fossil-fuels

Chapter 11

Energy efficiency

The cheapest fuel?

"Many analysts now regard modest, zero or negative growth in our rate of energy use as a realistic long-term goal."

Amory Lovins (1976)

"Many economists now regard proposed fuel requirements of 54.5 miles per gallon as an economically inefficient goal."

The author of this text

Introduction

Energy efficiency is sometimes referred to by those in the electricity industry as the "fifth fuel," after coal, natural gas, nuclear, and renewables.[1] Oil authority Daniel Yergin (2012) has even suggested that energy efficiency should be the new "first fuel." He tells of Boeing's latest airplane, the 787 Dreamliner, whose developers chose a 20% reduction in fuel use over a 20% increase in speed. From an economic perspective, the first fuel is the one with the lowest social cost. Yergin suggests that energy efficiency comes first, implying that it is the cheapest fuel. However, increasing a plane's fuel economy requires resources just as if we use renewables or burn more fuel. It is possible that energy efficiency uses fewer resources, but in order to draw the conclusion that it is the cheapest fuel, we must include all the resources that make up opportunity cost.

Yergin uses the terms "energy efficiency" and "conservation" interchangeably, but others distinguish between the two terms. *Conservation* is saving fuel by using fewer energy-using goods and services, while *energy efficiency* is using less energy to achieve a fixed level of goods and services, or the same amount of energy to achieve more goods and services. The equation for energy efficiency is

$$\text{Energy efficiency} = \frac{\text{Energy output}}{\text{Energy input}}$$

An example of energy conservation is turning down the thermostat from 72° to 68° in the winter and wearing a sweater. An example of energy efficiency is insulating the attic so it takes less energy to heat your home to 72° in winter. In this case, energy output is comfort, which requires less energy input when you increase insulation. Neither conservation nor energy efficiency necessarily increases economic efficiency, which calls for getting the most value from scarce resources and deciding how much insulation you should install. More insulation is not privately efficient if the additional insulation cost exceeds the savings from lower energy use, although it may be socially efficient if we include the value of lower emissions.

Both conservation and energy efficiency are physical measures, not economic measures. The higher efficiency of the Dreamliner did not come free. It required extensive R&D as well as the use of lighter-weight materials that are typically more expensive. For the energy efficiency measures to be economically efficient, the benefits must outweigh the costs.

At the same time, energy efficiency has external effects that could justify its adoption even if private costs are higher. Lower energy use means lower emissions. If we are to slow climate change, energy efficiency may achieve carbon reductions at a lower cost than replacing fossil fuels with renewable energy.

In this chapter, we examine energy efficiency from an economic perspective. We first examine physical measures such as energy conservation and energy efficiency from an economic perspective of benefits and costs. We then consider energy efficiency in production and consumption. We follow with a section that examines the possibility of an energy efficiency gap, a potential market failure whereby consumers purchase less than the economically efficient amount of energy efficiency. We then consider the rebound effect, where an increase in energy efficiency leads to greater use of energy-using technology, partially offsetting energy savings. The penultimate section revisits government options for correcting market failures if there is an energy efficiency gap or other failures specific to energy efficiency decisions. The final section provides a summary.

Energy efficiency and economic efficiency

Energy efficiency vs. economic efficiency

Many observers view energy efficiency as low-hanging fruit. McKinsey & Company (2010) identified 38 different approaches to reducing GHGs, evaluating each approach based on tons of CO_2 equivalent avoided and the societal cost (taxes and subsidies excluded) per ton avoided. The GHG marginal abatement cost is in Figure 11.1. For example, the cost of substituting carbon-free solar PV for carbon-emitting fossil fuels is just under €20/ton of CO_2 equivalent avoided, about $28/ton avoided based on 2010 exchange rates.[2]

Of the 38 energy-saving options, 20 had a negative cost, meaning the monetary savings from using less energy would outweigh the additional capital costs of the more efficient technology. The negative cost substitutions included switching from incandescent lightbulbs to LED lights in homes, driving hybrid cars, and landfill gas electricity generation. A few alternatives (geothermal energy and some land management practices) had approximately zero costs of switching. Finally, 13 approaches reduced GHGs at a positive cost, including nuclear, wind, solar, and some technologies incorporating CCS.

From an economic perspective, we should adopt all measures up to where marginal cost (MC) equals marginal benefit (MB). McKinsey's point is that implementing negative cost measures would reduce carbon emissions and save money. The same

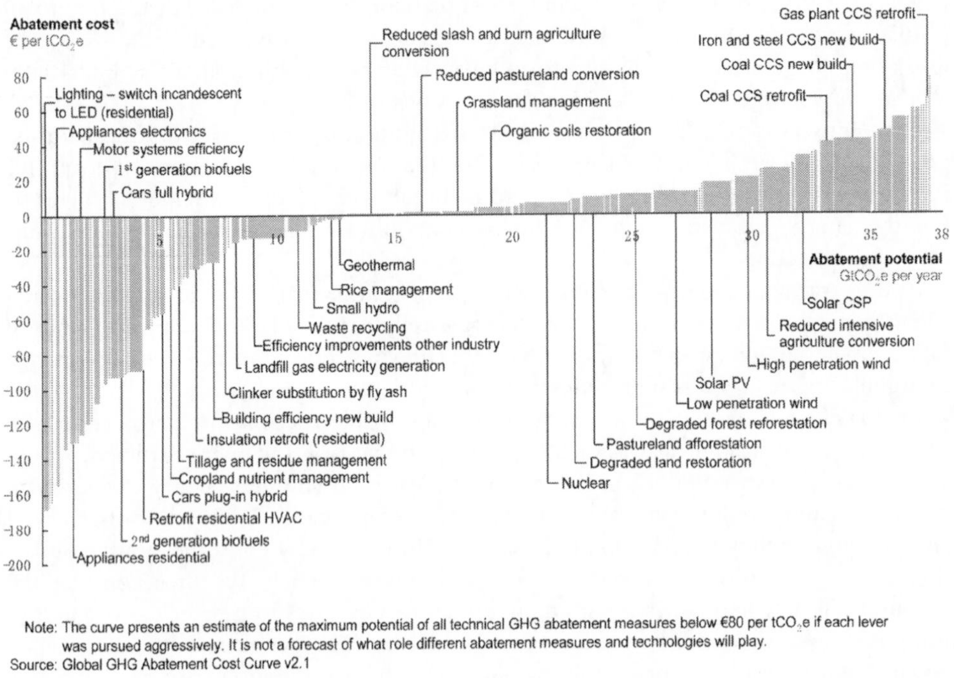

Note: The curve presents an estimate of the maximum potential of all technical GHG abatement measures below €80 per tCO₂e if each lever was pursued aggressively. It is not a forecast of what role different abatement measures and technologies will play.
Source: Global GHG Abatement Cost Curve v2.1

Figure 11.1 Energy efficiency opportunities for carbon abatement. Reprinted from *Impact of the Financial Crisis on Carbon Economics*: Version 2.1 of the Global Greenhouse Gas Abatement Cost Curve, by McKinsey & Company (2010). Reprinted with permission.

applies to measures with a marginal cost near zero. Society also benefits from implementing other approaches as long as MB ≥ MC. Estimates of MB range from $20/ton to $200, with a few estimates even higher. If we use a conservative figure of €20/ton ($28 based on the 2010 exchange rate) as a benchmark, then all measures except solar CSP and CCS technologies would produce a net social benefit. In fact, over 10 million gigatons of CO_2 equivalent reductions can be achieved for a negative cost, what economists would call a Pareto superior opportunity!

Consider a switch from incandescent to LED lighting in the residential sector, which according to Figure 11.1 would reduce carbon emissions while saving over €160/ton of abatement! The claim is that the high upfront cost of LED lighting would be more than offset by the long life of the bulb and low energy usage. The result would be a much lower levelized cost than Thomas Edison's incandescent bulb that dominated lighting since 1879. Efficiency experts professed equal zeal for compact fluorescent lights (CFLs), but the LED is still more energy-efficient. In fact, countries including the United States passed legislation to phase out incandescent bulbs in favor of CFLs and LEDs (Lee, 2013).

Why have we not made all these changes? Is it market failure? Do we need more stringent regulations to force the adoption of the technologies where MB is at least as great as MC? Economists suggest another possibility, that McKinsey & Company are not capturing opportunity cost. There may be transactions costs to switching technologies, and consumers might find differences in the services they provide.

Box 11.1 Are CFLs a bright idea?

Economists would ask why legislation to phase out the incandescent bulb would be necessary if there are energy-efficient alternatives with a negative opportunity cost. One reason may be that McKinsey is not measuring the opportunity cost of switching. Consider the CFL. Assuming consumers can correctly evaluate the costs and are willing to pay the higher upfront costs, there is no guarantee the bulbs will last the advertised five or ten years. The manufacturers note in small print that if users turn the lights on and off frequently, their lifetime will be much shorter.

Some users find CFL lighting quality inferior. The incandescent gives off a yellowish light that is reminiscent of a candle, whereas the CFL is a whiter light. And CFLs contain mercury, which means that when the bulbs do burn out, the consumer must dispose of them carefully, often requiring a special trip to a facility that is willing to accept them. Should the CFL break, the advice is to evacuate the room. If a consumer vacuums up the waste, it may be necessary to throw away the vacuum (U.S. EPA, 2016).

While environmentalists might maintain that CFLs and incandescent light bulbs provide identical characteristics other than the greater longevity of the CFL, residential users may see it differently. They not only weigh upfront costs compared to electricity bill savings, but also such characteristics as lighting quality, ease of use, and waste disposal. Government legislation to impose more energy-efficient lighting could result in a loss of economic efficiency, forcing consumers to buy CFLs when they prefer incandescents.

Energy expert Amory Lovins (1989) makes the case for energy-efficient lighting:

> Imagine being able to save half the electricity for free and still get better services! . . . You get the same amount of light as before, with 8 percent as much energy overall—but it looks better and you can see better. . . . It is doing more with less.

While noneconomists may view energy efficiency as the closest thing to a free lunch, economists give no special credence to energy efficiency for its own sake. We are interested in economically efficient energy use. Minimum energy use need not coincide with minimum total cost. We need to consider opportunity cost, which can differ from the calculations done by McKinsey, to arrive at the options that produce the largest net benefits. To the extent that energy use has externalities such as undesired emissions of sulfur, NOx, and carbon, social welfare requires that we set marginal social benefit

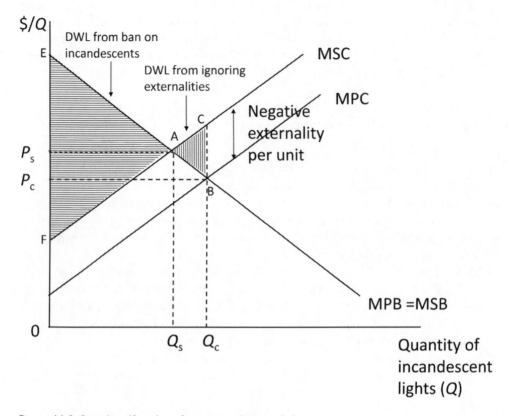

Figure 11.2 Social welfare loss from incandescent lights.

equal to marginal social cost, resulting in a lower level of energy use than the market outcome, as shown in Figure 11.2.

Examining Figure 11.2, the competitive market for incandescent lights results in price P_c and corresponding energy use Q_c, where the subscript c corresponds to the competitive market outcome. To the extent that their use results in more electricity use and accompanying undesirable spillovers to society such as sulfur, NOx, particulates, and carbon, the marginal social cost (MSC) exceeds the marginal private cost (MPC). Triangle ABC shows the deadweight loss (DWL) from unpriced negative externalities from using incandescent bulbs.

Economists would suggest a tax on incandescents sufficient to reduce use from Q_c to Q_s as one way to reduce the use of the last-generation technology. However, banning the bulb goes too far. A ban at $Q = 0$ compared to Q_s results in underproduction— DWL triangle AEF—which is much larger than the DWL from overproduction. Of course, if the marginal external cost (MEC) of incandescents is larger, a ban could be preferable. If MEC is so large that the social supply curve is everywhere above the demand curve, then a ban would be socially efficient.

Energy intensity

Energy intensity **measures** energy use per unit of output:

$$\text{Energy intensity} = \frac{\text{Energy input}}{\text{Energy output}}$$

It is common to calculate energy intensity at a macroeconomic scale, with energy input an economy-wide measure and gross domestic product (GDP) the output measure. It would appear that energy intensity is nothing more than the inverse of energy efficiency, but a change in energy intensity can occur for reasons other than a change in energy efficiency.

Energy intensity depends not only on energy efficiency at the firm level, but on the industry mix. For example, as the United States became more service-oriented, U.S. energy intensity decreased because services are less energy-intensive than manufacturing. Furthermore, a shift within manufacturing to less energy-intensive industries would also decrease EI. Another factor affecting energy intensity is energy price. For example, as energy prices rise, we expect energy intensity will decrease, and these effects are likely to be transitory. However, if energy prices are high for an extended period, they will spur technological change that will bring about further reductions in energy intensity that will be long-term (Wing, 2008).

Figure 11.3 shows energy intensity and energy use per capita, measured as an index with 2005 as a base year where the index equals 1.0. Thus, both energy intensity and energy use per capita cross at an index of 1.0 in 2005. Energy intensity (energy use per dollar of GDP) has trended down since 1980 and the prediction is that it will continue to decline. For many of these years, energy intensity declined even though per capita energy use was relatively constant, because GDP (the denominator of energy intensity)

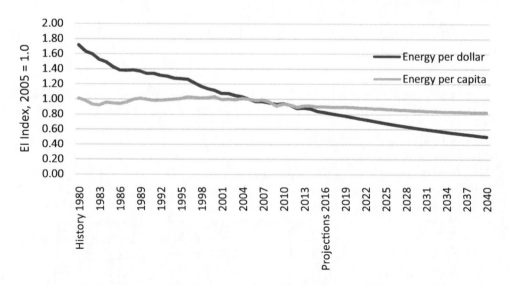

Figure 11.3 U.S. energy intensity history and projections. Adapted from *Annual Energy Outlook* 2015 (p. 17), by U.S. EIA (2015).

was growing. During the Great Recession that began in December 2007, energy intensity was relatively flat. Per capita energy use declined, but GDP also declined, leaving energy intensity little changed. Note that the overall trend of decreasing energy intensity was not necessarily due to an increase in energy efficiency, although that was likely an additional factor. The third contributing factor was the shift towards services and less energy-intensive manufacturing sectors.

Energy efficiency in production

Energy input–product output relationship

The demand for energy is derived from the demand for output. In order to maximize profit, firms use inputs efficiently to minimize the cost of producing output. Production is a first step in analyzing cost. In order to consider energy efficiency, we need to include energy as an input in the production function.

With the inclusion of energy, the production function is

$$Q = f(K, L, E)$$

where K is quantity of capital, L is quantity of labor, and E is quantity of energy.[3]

Energy efficiency is Q/E, the average product of energy (AP_E). Economic efficiency makes use of the marginal product of energy (MP_E), and the use of average product could lead to inefficient decisions.

The firm's objective is to maximize output for a given level of budget, or equivalently, to minimize the cost of a particular level of output. In order to use resources efficiently, firms minimize the total cost of producing a given level of output:

$$B = P_K K + P_L L + P_E E$$

where B is the budget constraint and P_i is the price per unit of input i.

Short run

In the short run, when capital (K) is fixed, optimization requires marginal revenue product (MRP) to equal marginal factor cost (MFC):

$$MRP_i = MFC_i$$

where $MRP_i = MP_i \times P_Q$ and P_Q is the price of output.

That is, optimization occurs when the MRP, the addition to revenue from an additional unit of each input, equals the price of the input. As shown above, MRP is the marginal product multiplied by the price of the product. Implicitly, we are assuming that product output price is constant, which is the case when output is sold in a competitive market. We are also assuming constant input prices, the case when input markets are competitive.

For variable inputs such as E and L:

$$MRP_L = P_L \text{ and } MRP_E = P_E$$

Example 11.1

A car manufacturer can produce one more car from its automated plant using 120 MWh (120,000 kWh) of electricity with labor and capital fixed. Each MWh sells for $100/MWh (10¢/kWh), and a car sells for $20,000. Do you recommend producing more cars?

Solution

Compare MRP to MFC. $MRP_E = MP_E \times P_Q$.

$$MP_E = \frac{1 \text{ car}}{120 \text{ MWh}}$$

$$MP_E = \frac{0.0083 \text{ cars}}{\text{MWh}}$$

$$MRP_E = \frac{0.0083 \text{ cars}}{\text{MWh}} \times \$20,000$$

$$MRP_E = \$166.67$$

$MFC_E = \$100/MWh$. Since $MRP_E > MFC_E$, produce the additional car. Intuitively, the cost of producing an additional car is $12,000 (120,000 MWh × $0.10/MWh), which is less than the $20,000 selling price of the car.

Typically, MRP will eventually decline as production increases, limited by more intensive use of fixed capital. When we get to the point where $MRP_E = MFC_E$, we have reached the optimal level of production.

Long run

In the long run, optimization occurs when the ratio of the marginal products of the inputs equals the ratio of the input prices:

$$\frac{MP_K}{r} = \frac{MP_L}{w} = \frac{MP_E}{P_E}$$

where r is the interest rate (the cost per unit of K), w is the wage rate (the cost per unit of labor), and P_E is the cost per unit of energy.

Figure 11.4 shows cost minimization for a decrease in the price of energy. In our graph, we depict energy on the horizontal axis and capital on the vertical axis. The production function is shown by the curved line known as an isoquant. The *isoquant* depicts the K, E combinations to achieve a particular level of output, for given levels of other inputs such as labor and materials (M). The isoquant depicts a physical relationship based on the production function. To address the relevant economic

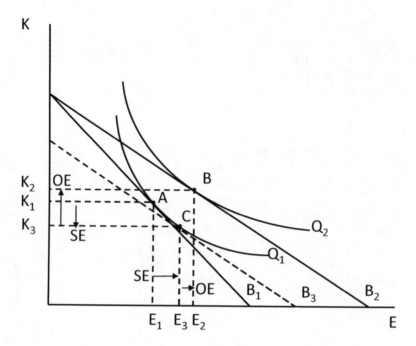

Figure 11.4 The effect of a decrease in energy price on the use of capital and energy.

question of what combination of K and E to choose, we add the budget constraint—the straight line—to the figure. We use a straight line budget constraint because we assume that the price of each input stays constant regardless of the amount of input used, which holds in a competitive input market. The optimal mix occurs at the tangency of an isoquant and a budget constraint.

Initially, assume the firm has budget B_1. It can achieve a maximum output of Q_1 by operating at point A with capital K_1 and energy E_1. Budget constraint B_2 shows a decrease in energy price. The firm can now achieve a higher level of production Q_2 corresponding to point B. The optimal amount of energy increases from E_1 to E_2. In the figure, capital increases from K_1 to K_2. However, energy increases by more than capital.

The move from A to B contains two effects, an output and a substitution effect. The energy *substitution effect* will always bring about an increase in the use of energy if the energy price decreases. As energy price decreases, the firm can produce more output, the *output effect*. As output increases, the firm will typically increase the use of all inputs.

To decompose the price effect into the substitution effect and output effect, we construct a third budget curve B_3 that is parallel to B_2 but tangent to the original isoquant Q_1. On B_3, the firm is paying the lower energy price, but we have taken away the extra purchasing power that allowed the firm to increase output. The firm minimizes the cost of producing Q_1 at point C. The substitution effect (SE) is the move along the original isoquant from A to C. Energy use increases from E_1 to E_3, while capital decreases from K_1 to K_3.

The move from C to B is the output effect (OE). The firm can produce additional output as its purchasing power increases with the lower price of energy. The output effect generally leads to greater use of both inputs.

The move from A to B is the *gross effect* that includes the substitution and income effects. The *net effect* is the substitution effect alone. In Figure 11.4, energy and capital are gross complements, but net substitutes. In the two–input case, the inputs can be gross substitutes or complements, but they are always net substitutes.

Recall that labor that has been assumed constant in Figure 11.4. With three inputs, a pair of inputs can be net substitutes or complements. To determine gross substitutability or complementarity, we can use the elasticity of (technical) substitution (EOS or σ), which measures how the percentage change in the ratio of inputs, such as K/E, changes with respect to a percent change in the price ratio:

$$\text{EOS}(\sigma) = \frac{\text{Proportionate change in input ratio}}{\text{Proportionate change in the ratio of input prices}}$$

An elasticity of substitution greater than 1 indicates gross substitution, while an EOS < 1 indicates gross complementarity.

Many studies have examined the relationship among energy, labor, and capital to discern whether they are substitutes or complements, motivated initially by concerns about the effect of the oil price shocks of the 1970s on the economy. If energy and capital are complements, higher oil prices reduce the use of energy and capital, with both effects slowing down the economy. If there is energy–capital substitution, then higher energy prices lead to greater use of capital in place of energy, which helps to offset the negative impact of higher energy prices. Berndt and Wood (1975) found energy and capital to be substantial gross complements, which implied that higher energy prices reduced the use of both energy and capital, which both led to a negative effect on the economy. Energy and labor were weakly substitutable. There have been many studies since then examining the relationships between energy, capital, and labor based on the elasticity of substitution, but there is unfortunately no consensus on the relationships among the three inputs, making it difficult to determine the effect of a change in oil price on the macroeconomy. There are many explanations given for the inconsistent results, including different datasets, different econometric estimations, and whether there are three inputs—K, L, and E—or four—K, L, E, and M—as in the Berndt and Wood model. However, energy costs are now a much smaller percent of total production costs than in the 1970s, so there is consensus that a rise in energy prices has a smaller effect on the economy now than in the 1970s.

A simpler measure of input substitutability is the cross–price elasticity. If an increase in the price of energy reduces energy use, as we would expect, and the firm increases capital equipment in order to maintain output, the cross–price elasticity is positive and the two inputs are substitutes. If the firm reduces both capital and energy as the price of energy increases, energy and capital are complements.

Energy input–energy output relationship

Another perspective on energy efficiency is to consider how to produce a unit of energy output (kWh) with less energy input. For example, combined-cycle gas turbine (CCGT) plants recapture waste heat from the initial conversion of natural gas to drive a gas turbine, and the waste heat provides additional heat to drive a steam turbine. Thus, combined-cycle plants produce a given amount of energy output with less energy input than a simple cycle turbine that does not recapture waste heat. The common measure of this sort of energy efficiency is plant efficiency, with the CCGT converting close to 60% of the natural gas into electricity production, while a simple cycle natural gas plant is closer to 30%. The combined-cycle natural gas plant, combined with the lower price of natural gas, contributed to the growth in the use of natural gas to generate electricity.

While the combined-cycle plant has higher *thermal efficiency*—the ratio of energy output to energy input—the simple cycle plant can ramp up more quickly and so can serve during peak hours when there is a quick need for additional power. The simple cycle plant is also smaller and therefore has lower initial capital costs. On balance, the simple cycle generator has a higher cost per kWh of electricity produced, which is why electricity costs more to produce during peak hours.

Box 11.2 Is coal in critical condition?

As discussed in Chapter 7, the future of coal is in question, with limitations on CO_2 emissions the greatest threat. If coal is to improve its position, it will need to reduce the carbon emissions associated with its use. While the most obvious way is through the implementation of CCS, energy efficiency could have a role as well. Conventional coal technology has a thermal efficiency of about 35%, which means 35% of the energy from coal is converted to electricity and 65% is lost as waste heat. This technology is referred to as subcritical, which means that at the operating temperature and pressure of the plant, water is a liquid that has not yet reached the critical temperature where it turns into steam, and so the water must be boiled to create steam. Increasingly, the technology of choice is to use supercritical coal plants to generate energy. These plants use higher operating temperatures and pressures, and at these higher levels, water is steam, increasing efficiency to 40%. Ultra-supercritical plants that operate at still higher temperatures and pressures are primarily in the demonstration phase, and if they reach commercialization, will further increase efficiency to 45%. The Chinese government is encouraging the adoption of ultra-supercritical plants.

Supercritical and ultra-supercritical plants use less coal energy to generate a unit of electricity, and so also release less CO_2. The electricity-generating equipment requires materials that can withstand higher temperature and pressure, for example nickel alloy, an expensive material. At this point, supercritical technology is cost-competitive with subcritical, so firms are willing to adopt this technology on economics alone. Even if there are no restrictions on carbon emissions, firms incorporate some probability that there will be restrictions, making this technology lower in expected cost than subcritical technology.

It is possible to integrate CCS with any of these technologies, although the cost of CCS depends upon which technology is used. Currently, CCS is not yet commercially viable. There are potential competing technologies, most notably the integrated gasification combined cycle (IGCC), which is still primarily at the demonstration phase. Most coal plants use pulverized coal. By pulverizing coal into small pieces, it burns more easily. IGCC converts coal into a gas (syngas), which burns even more efficiently than a pulverized solid. The combined-cycle process captures some of the waste heat to power a turbine and create additional electricity. Again, installing CCS adds to the cost of the IGCC which is not yet competitive even without CCS. The energy efficiency of IGCC is comparable to that of supercritical technology.

Environmentalists have not rallied around so-called "clean coal" technologies. The technologies would reduce carbon emissions, but not as much as carbon-free renewable fuels.

Energy efficiency in consumption

Energy efficiency in consumption is probably the form with which you are most familiar. When you consider the purchase of a car, a house, or a new appliance such as an air conditioner, you are likely to evaluate energy efficiency. Buyers of cars, appliances, and homes are willing to pay more for cars that get more miles per gallon, air conditioners that use less energy in the summer, and homes with more insulation to keep energy bills lower year-round.

From an economic standpoint, the goal of the consumer is to maximize utility subject to a budget constraint. Consider a household that wishes to maximize its wintertime comfort, as represented by the thermostat setting, for an existing heating unit.[4] Its objective is to maximize $U(t, Z)$, where t is indoor temperature, a proxy for comfort, and Z represents all other goods. Utility is constrained by the household's available budget $B = P_t t + P_z Z$, where P_t is the price of comfort and P_z is the price of a composite of all other goods.

The price of a unit of comfort depends upon energy efficiency. An increase in energy efficiency effectively reduces the price of a degree of comfort. Figure 11.5 shows consumer utility maximization with respect to outputs using the same graphical technique that we used to show firm output maximization with respect to inputs.

In Figure 11.5, an increase in energy efficiency from increased insulation results in a shift of the budget constraint from B_1 to B_2. Maximum utility is at the tangency of the budget constraint with utility, and maximum utility increases from U_1 to U_2. The household with more home insulation chooses a relatively large increase in comfort at tangency point B as compared to point A, such as by turning up the wintertime thermostat setting from t_1 to t_2. The household with more insulation also has an increase in all other goods (moving from Z_1 to Z_2). To isolate the substitution effect of increased insulation, we constrain household income to B_3 so that the consumer returns to the original utility curve. The consumer now maximizes utility at point C and corresponding thermostat setting t_3. The move from t_1 to t_3 is a substitution effect, while the move from C to B and the increase in thermostat setting from t_3 to t_2 is an income

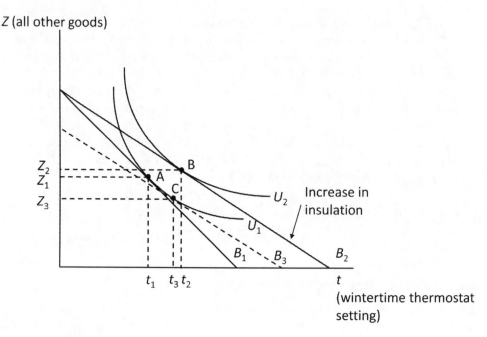

Figure 11.5 The effect of an increase in energy efficiency on thermostat setting.

effect, analogous to the output effect for firms. Households that choose more insulation have the primary motive of reducing their energy bills, but our analysis shows that they may have a secondary motive of increasing their comfort level. This secondary effect, often overlooked by energy efficiency advocates, is known as a *rebound effect*, and is important enough to have its own section later in this chapter.

Energy efficiency and electric utility capacity

Energy efficiency in consumption reduces the demand for energy that must be supplied by an electric utility. However, the reduction only indirectly affects the amount of capacity that the utility has to have on hand. If a household buys a programmable thermostat to set back temperature during winter nights, utilities will not have to supply as much energy during hours when households are asleep. While the thermostat saves energy, it may not reduce the amount of capacity that the utility will need to maintain, as capacity is based on maximum demand for energy, which for a winter-peaking system typically occurs around daybreak and sunset. The distinction between energy use and capacity demand is the distinction between kilowatt hours (kWh) and kilowatts (kW).

The most general definition of energy is the ability to do work. Energy = power × time, where power can be measured in kilowatts (kW) and time in hours. A 60 W bulb that burns for one hour uses 60 Wh. Energy efficiency refers to using less energy to accomplish a given task. Energy efficiency need not reduce the kilowatt capacity required to provide that energy. A 60 W bulb that burns for 30 minutes out of every 60 will use 30 Wh, but will still place a demand of 60 W on the electricity system.[5]

Consider a small appliance such as an air conditioner (A/C). The amount of energy use depends upon the technology as well as the size. Typically, you choose a larger capacity to cool a larger area. In turn, the electric utility provides you with the energy (kWh) to run your A/C, but also must be able to meet the demand for power (kW) when the A/C is running. An energy-efficient low-capacity room unit may use 2,000 kWh annually, 10–15% less than a conventional unit. However, when the A/C kicks in, the utility must have the capacity to supply the power to meet the initial demand surge.

In short, energy efficiency saves energy (kWh) that may not be in direct relation to savings in capacity (kW). Energy efficiency programs such as LEED and ENERGY STAR focus on energy use. However, much of the cost of providing electricity depends upon the available supply of capacity. The focus on energy efficiency should also address the extent to which it reduces peak demand.

Energy efficiency gap

The primary economic justification for government to play a role in energy decisions is a market failure leading to a socially inefficient outcome. The *energy efficiency gap* refers to the difference between observed levels of energy efficiency and cost-effective optimal energy efficiency. If such a gap exists, consumers undervalue a dollar of energy savings, and the market fails to produce the economically efficient outcome. Parry, Evans, and Oates (2014) refer to this market failure as "the misperception problem." For example, Allcott and Wozny (2014) find that drivers value a dollar in saved fuel as equivalent to $0.76 saved in the purchase price of a new car, a gap in present value terms over the lifetime of the vehicle of 32%.

Example 11.2

Consider the decision to purchase a 60W LED bulb. The typical household uses a 60W bulb two hours per day. Assume an incandescent bulb costs $1 and lasts one year (2 hours per day for 365 days). The LED has an initial cost of $20, will last 20 years (equivalent to 14,600 hours of use), and will use 90% less energy than an equivalent incandescent bulb. The price of electricity is $0.10/kWh. Compare the annual energy cost of the two bulbs, and indicate which one the consumer should buy based upon cost.

Solution

The incandescent uses 60 W for two hours per day for each of 365 days, or 43,800 Wh/year (60 W × 2hrs/day × 365 days) = 43.8 kWh, for an annual energy cost of $4.38. Including the initial cost of buying the bulb, the annual cost is $5.38. The LED provides 20 years of lighting, using about 6W/hour or 4.38 kWh for two hours over 365 days, about $0.44 in annual energy costs. The upfront cost is $20, or about $1 a year over the life of the bulb, for an annual cost of $1.44. The LED has a much lower cost.

We have not incorporated present value into the calculation, which makes the comparison closer. Both bulbs cost $20 over 20 years for the bulbs, but the incandescent has a lower cost in PV terms since the purchases are spread over 20 years, whereas the full purchase price of the LED is upfront. If discounted at 5%, the present value of the cost of buying and using incandescent bulbs purchased for $1 for each of the next 20 years is $67.05 (PV=$\sum_{t=1}^{20} \frac{\$(1+4.38)}{1.05^t}$), vs. $28.80 (PV = $20 + $\sum_{t=1}^{20} \frac{\$0.44}{1.05^t}$) for the LED (assuming that we pay for the LED upfront). So based on the numbers, consumers should purchase LEDs.[6]

Despite the cost savings, consumers may still choose the incandescent light. Consumers may perceive differences in quality and convenience as they did with CFLs. However, we wish to focus on the energy efficiency gap, so for now we assume the two bulbs have identical characteristics. Consumers may be unwilling to pay one dollar today to save $1 in present value in future energy costs.

Although identified by some as a paradox, we will use the term "energy efficiency gap" to describe consumer undervaluation of energy savings to distinguish it from the Jevons paradox. In 1865, the British economist William Stanley Jevons noted that as energy-efficient technology advances, we are likely to use existing appliances more intensively (the intensive margin) as well as use more appliances (the extensive margin). The *Jevons paradox* is that energy-efficient appliances may not end up reducing energy use. In the next section, we discuss the rebound effect, whereby we make more intensive use of energy-efficient appliances and therefore save less energy than if we did not increase intensity of use. However, this action is not a market failure. If the price of energy is low, it is efficient to use more of it.

Reasons for an energy efficiency gap

High discount rate

The origin of the energy efficiency gap traces back to studies by Hausman (1979) and Dubin and McFadden (1984) who found that consumers used an implicit discount rate higher than the market discount rate when making energy efficiency decisions. Hausman examined the purchase and utilization of room air conditioners, while Dubin and McFadden examined the purchase and utilization of water and space heaters. Both studies found an implicit discount rate of around 20%, higher than the market discount rate.

Example 11.3

Jerry is comparing two refrigerators, a standard model and an energy efficient one. The refrigerator life is expected to be 10 years. The energy-efficient model costs $100 more, but saves $20 a year in energy costs. The market discount rate is

10%, but he implicitly applies a 15% rate to energy efficiency decisions. Should Jerry buy the energy-efficient model? Will he?

Solution

Evaluate an annuity of $20 for 10 years, discounted at 10% minus the upfront premium of $100 to determine if he should buy the energy-efficient refrigerator. Do the same calculation using an above-market discount rate of 15% to decide if he will buy it. The benefit is $\sum_{t=1}^{10} \dfrac{20}{(1+r)^t} = \$122.89$ if discounted at 10% > $100. So he should buy it. At a 15% discount rate, the present value of the annuity is $100.38, only $0.38 more than the cost. So he will buy it, despite using an above-market discount rate in this particular case, although it is a close call. If he applies a discount rate above 15%, he will not buy the energy-efficient model and we will have an energy efficiency gap.

Bounded rationality

Bounded rationality is a cognitive explanation of why consumers do not make energy-efficient choices. Where consumers face difficult decisions, they use *heuristics*—simplified decision rules—rather than attempting to evaluate benefits and costs. Consumers may have in mind a payback period of three years or less for an energy investment. In the above example, the payback period for the energy efficient refrigerator at a 15% discount rate was 10 years, the amount of time it took to recoup the initial $100 premium for the energy-efficient appliance. Consumers may require energy efficiency investments to pay off more quickly.

Behavioral economics offers alternatives including bounded rationality to understand consumer decisions. Behavioral explanations refer to psychological motivations that lead to outcomes that diverge from rational utility maximization. For example, *framing* may influence consumer choice. Reducing energy bills from $200 to $190 or $20 to $10 both save $10, but the consumer may view the second reduction as more valuable if she views it as a 50% rather than a 5% saving. Bounded rationality is not, strictly speaking, irrational behavior nor a market failure, but rather a recognition of the high costs of obtaining more accurate information. In any case, to the extent that consumers view energy efficiency decisions as difficult, they may use a rubric other than the market interest rate in making energy efficiency decisions.

Principal/agent problems

Energy inefficiencies including the energy efficiency gap can arise from the divergent interests of principals and agents. The *principal/agent problem* refers to situations where the principal has an objective and relies upon the agent to achieve it, but the agent has a different objective and so may fail to do what the principal seeks.

Box 11.3 Who pays the energy bill in multiunit housing?

A classic principal/agent problem relevant to energy is that of owners and tenants. Owners have longer-term objectives than tenants, and so are more likely to invest in energy efficiency. Tenant agents may behave in inefficient ways, such as opening the windows on a cold winter day when the building owner sends more heat than the tenants prefer.[7]

There are a number of potential market failures when it comes to energy use in multiunit residential housing. In a single family home, the owner captures energy savings while she lives in the home, as well as capitalizing energy efficiency improvements at the time of sale. The potential buyer is likely to examine energy bills and pay more for a better insulated home with energy-efficient doors and windows. In rental housing, a renter could potentially reduce energy bills by investing in energy efficiency, but there are numerous reasons why the renter would underinvest. The renter cannot capitalize the value of the improvements, as the renter will not sell the unit. The renter also may not plan to stay in the apartment for a long enough period to recoup the investment.

In New York, where multiunit buildings make up a large percentage of the housing stock, many buildings are master-metered, with a single energy bill for the entire building, rather than submetering, where the tenant pays. With master-metering, rents reflect owner energy costs, but individual renters have little reason to engage in energy-efficient actions. Suppose a renter needs to replace a window, and a more energy-efficient window would reduce energy use by 10%. If other renters do not replace their windows, the master-metered bill might decrease by 1% or less, a negligible effect.

If it is the owner's responsibility to replace the window and there is master-metering, it would seem the owner would have the proper incentive, since the owner gets the energy savings. However, the energy efficiency gap suggests that renters are unwilling to pay the full cost of energy efficiency savings, so that the owner will not be able to fully recoup the savings by raising the rent. Also, since the renter does not pay the bill, New Yorkers and other master-metered tenants will use energy almost as if it were free, since they get the full benefits of their action and do not perceive much connection between their personal energy use and their rent. So New Yorkers may leave the windows open even on a cold winter day.

Might the Coase theorem resolve these inefficiencies? Could landlords compensate renters for efficient actions? If there is submetering, would owners be able to fully capitalize any investments in energy-saving actions? There are substantial transactions costs that might prevent these agreements, starting with the adversarial relationship between landlords and tenants. Even if the two sides are willing to negotiate, the energy efficiency gap, imperfect information, and high turnover of tenants who cannot recoup long-term investments, leave considerable uncertainty that the two sides will reach an efficient outcome.[8]

Appliance manufacturers have an incentive to advertise high energy savings, but consumers cannot observe the savings upfront and may choose to discount the manufacturers' claims. Electric utilities also advertise energy-saving programs. Kaufman and

Palmer (2010) find that electric utility projections of energy savings exceed actual savings. Furthermore, utility reports of projected savings are larger than reports by independent third parties. These results are consistent with incentives that utilities have to overreport savings to the extent that regulators compensate utilities based on savings.

Reasons why there may not be a gap

There are rebuttals attesting that there are unobserved variables that explain why energy efficiency decisions are rational, and that there is no gap. Consider a residential consumer who declines to get an energy efficiency audit, even one offered at no charge. There is a time cost to the resident of being at home when the audit is done. Then there is the aforementioned question of the motive of the company performing the audit; the company may try to promote the purchase of energy-saving measures that may not be worth the cost. Additionally, there is a time cost associated with evaluating energy efficiency. If an energy-efficient refrigerator saves $125 over an expected 10-year lifetime, less in terms of PV, and costs $50 more after available rebates for a net savings of less than $75 in PV, it may not be worth the time to carefully evaluate a decision for what is likely to be a small net benefit.

There may also be quality differences among the appliances. Consumers hesitated to buy compact fluorescents given their experience with standard ones. Consumers claimed to prefer the yellow-tinged incandescent to white fluorescent. There are also the mercury-related issues of breakage and disposal. If studies fail to account for these variables when they infer a discount rate, they will overstate the discount rate consumers use in making these decisions.

Allcott and Greenstone (2012) find the energy efficiency gap is either small or zero, suggesting that government should not provide incentives for consumers to adopt greater energy efficiency than the market would dictate. They review numerous energy efficiency studies, including weatherization, automobile and appliance markets, and landlord–tenant agency problems and maintain that studies have not used the best available econometric techniques, throwing the findings of a gap into doubt. We need additional state-of-the-art studies before we assert there is a role for government in energy efficiency decisions.

Rebound effect

The Jevons paradox showed the possibility of a rebound effect so that greater energy efficiency can lead to less than proportional energy savings. The effect is now referred to most often as the rebound effect, although there are other names such as takeback, the Khazzoom (1980) effect, or simply the marginal—or substitution—effect (David Friedman (1987)).[9]

In his book, *The Coal Question*, Jevons referred to the increasing use of coal after the invention of the steam engine. Jevons actually proposed that coal use would increase, not decrease, with the more efficient steam engine, hence the Jevons paradox. Jevons was describing an extreme rebound effect, where the effect is so large that increased technical efficiency actually leads to an increase in energy use. This extreme form of rebound is now known as the *backfire effect*.

Consider an energy efficiency policy implemented with the goal of reducing carbon emissions. A policy aimed at more energy-efficient buildings, to reduce the 40% of energy use attributable to the building sector, could make it attractive for building users to install more energy appliances to take advantage of low energy use per appliance. Additional appliances could partially offset the energy savings promised for the more efficient building, and could swamp the energy savings completely if the building attracts a population that welcomes the opportunity to use more appliances at a lower cost per appliance. So carbon emissions could decrease by less than anticipated, or in an extreme case increase. The effectiveness of energy efficiency as a way to reduce carbon emissions depends on whether the rebound effect exists, and if it does exist, its magnitude.

The rebound effect lessens the energy savings from an energy efficiency improvement, and is a negative from the perspective of energy efficiency advocates. However, it can be a positive from the vantage point of economic efficiency. For some consumers, one of the reasons to buy a vehicle that gets 50 miles per gallon is to be able to drive more, the rebound effect. While intensive driving may reduce fuel savings, the consumer is better off than if she were not permitted to drive more miles. The rebound effect increases consumer utility and is an example of a market at work, not a market failure.

Box 11.4 Coming in from the cold

David Friedman (1987) asked whether people in a cold city such as Chicago would set their thermostats lower in the winter than people in warmer climates such as Santa Clara, California. Friedman concluded that people in cold climates keep their houses warmer despite the higher cost of heating. The reason is that denizens of colder climates find it worthwhile to better insulate their houses, resulting in a lower marginal price of comfort. Those who expect colder houses in cold climates due to the higher cost of heating are confusing average prices based on total energy use with marginal prices that determine use for a rational consumer.[10]

Dewees and Wilson (1990) challenged Friedman's conclusion, noting that the cost of heating depends not only on insulation, but also on humidity and the temperature of walls and other surfaces. Older homes in particular, built before the 1973 energy crisis, are likely to have little insulation and be difficult to heat. Insulation can reduce energy use by retaining moisture and reducing heat loss radiated through walls. Dewees and Wilson provide preliminary evidence that wintertime thermostat settings need not be higher in Chicago than Santa Clara. Schwarz and Taylor (1995) suggest that investigators have been measuring net rebound (they use the term net take-back), the difference between ordinary rebound due to the price effect noted by Friedman, and the opposing humidity and heat radiation effects introduced by Dewees and Wilson. Schwarz and Taylor find a small, but statistically significant, net rebound effect, so that on balance, they affirm Friedman's hypothesis of warm houses in cold climates.

Taxonomy of rebound effects[11]

There are both direct and indirect rebound effects, and they occur at both micro-economic and macroeconomic levels. Direct rebound is the price effect of an energy efficiency improvement, including both the substitution and income effects. This effect can be obtained using the price elasticity of demand for energy. Indirect rebound is the inframarginal effect of spending the extra income on other goods.

Gillingham et al. (2014) further distinguish between a pure rebound effect, due to a decrease in the implicit price of energy from an energy efficiency gain, and a total rebound effect that includes other changes brought about by the change in energy efficiency. A pure price effect occurs if there is an improvement in energy efficiency that causes no change in product characteristics nor the cost of producing the product. A policy change, such as a requirement that U.S. automobiles achieve higher miles per gallon, is likely to affect the characteristics of the vehicle—smaller, lighter materials, slower acceleration, less safe, less comfortable—as well as the vehicle cost (lighter materials cost more). If consumers perceive the changes in product characteristics as negative, total rebound will be less than pure rebound.

Magnitude of rebound effects

If rebound effects are small, then the offset to energy savings will be small. If rebound effects are large, or at the extreme, there is backfire, energy savings from energy efficiency gains will be small or even negative. The most likely case is that there is a modest rebound effect.

Davis (2008) and Davis et al. (2013) examine appliance programs. In the first study, consumers received new energy-efficient clothes dryers at no cost to replace their less efficient dryer. The price elasticity with respect to energy use was −0.06, a modest rebound effect. The second study focused on a program in Mexico where consumers could trade in their air conditioners and refrigerators for more energy-efficient models, a program with a similar flavor to the U.S. Cash for Clunkers program. Gillingham et al. (2009) remind the reader that the measured response reflects direct effects and changes in energy services, and in this case the new dryers had a larger capacity and were gentler on clothes. The second study found a large rebound effect, with energy use decreasing only 7% for refrigerators, and increasing (backfire) with the air conditioner replacement.

Less is known about the magnitude of macroeconomic rebound effects, although despite the Jevons paradox, backfire is unlikely. Macroeconomic rebound includes leakage and growth. *Leakage* is the counterpart to the micro direct effect, as an energy efficiency improvement in one country will reduce the price of energy in others. If the United States requires cars to meet higher mileage requirements and the net effect is that gasoline use decreases, the price of gas will decrease globally and global gas will increase. There is an indirect effect at the macro level due to respending the additional income. The most widely cited macro effect is the Jevons effect of economic growth. Higher energy efficiency increases productivity and consequently, investment. Investment increases directly in the affected sector, but can spill over into other sectors. Much as the invention of the Internet initially increased the productivity of the military sector but spilled over into other sectors, the latest generation of fuel-saving aircraft from Boeing and Airbus will likely spawn energy efficiency improvements in other transportation modes such as rail and car. Gillingham et al. (2014) suggest a macro rebound effect of 10–20% as a starting point, awaiting further studies that overcome concerns about existing studies.

Government intervention to encourage energy efficiency

Standards vs. incentive-based approaches

Economists generally advocate incentive-based (IB) approaches over standards. IB approaches such as taxes and trading provide incentives for participants to achieve the objective at least cost. Standards can achieve the objective, but do not guarantee the least-cost solution.

Voluntary vs. mandatory standards

CAFÉ, ENERGY STAR, and LEED are energy efficiency programs that use standards. The first program is a mandatory program, while the other two are voluntary. Mandatory programs impose a standard regardless of the cost of achieving it. Voluntary programs allow self-selection, so the parties that choose to participate are those who can do so at relatively low cost. From this perspective, voluntary standards are more efficient than mandatory ones.

One obvious improvement to the mandatory CAFÉ program is to allow manufacturers to trade the right to produce high-mileage cars. The U.S. government introduced this feature in its proposed standard for 2025 of 54 miles per gallon. If gas prices remain low and consumers favor SUVs and full-sized trucks, it will be increasingly difficult to achieve the standard. Economists would add that there is increasing question as to why we should try. If the reason is to reduce carbon emissions, economists would prefer IB programs such as carbon taxes or cap-and-trade.

ENERGY STAR and LEED are voluntary programs. Firms only participate if they see net benefits to doing so, which could be in the form of subsidies received, green marketing, or heading off mandatory regulations. Firms can pursue the LEED standard if benefits, including energy savings and any marketing cachet, exceed any additional costs of meeting the requirements.

LEED standards are not likely to be economically efficient. The standards focus on benefits, not benefits minus costs. In addition, owners of energy-inefficient buildings can opt out of the program. It may be exactly those firms whose energy use and consequent emissions are imposing the largest costs on society.

Government failures

Government failures such as inefficient regulation or responding to political incentives affect many areas of the economy. We now address two government failures particularly relevant to energy efficiency.

Free riders

Participants in energy efficiency programs may have taken the action even in the absence of the program. This effect is sometimes referred to as a *free-rider problem*, although it is a different effect from the one that arises with reference to public goods. This second type of free-rider effect is when someone gets a benefit from a program without doing anything. Hence, the government and taxpayer pay a cost to reward participants, but are not getting any benefits.

Howarth et al. (2000) examine two programs sponsored by the U.S. EPA—Green Lights and ENERGY STAR Office Products—and find both programs have net benefits. In the case of Green Lights, firms invested in cost-saving lighting systems that they did not purchase prior to the program. Firms participating in the ENERGY STAR program purchased more energy-efficient products. The authors find limited rebound effects, so that there are net energy savings. They argue that the programs overcome market failures such as bounded rationality. However, they do not mention free riding. In other words, what would these firms have done in the absence of the programs?

It is difficult to identify free riders in designing energy efficiency programs. Surveys intended to detect potential free riders are not likely to elicit truthful responses. If asked "Would you buy compact fluorescent lights in the absence of a subsidy?" you would likely answer in the negative if you believe you may be eligible for free or subsidized CFLs from the organization asking the question.

Identifying free riders in an energy efficiency program requires a counterfactual to determine what actions the individuals would have taken if the program had not been implemented. There have been some attempts to estimate the size of the free rider problem so as to ascertain the net benefit of an energy efficiency program, but there does not appear to be much progress in preventing the problem in the first place.

Picking winners

In energy efficiency and other arenas of government intervention, critics express the concern that unlike markets, the government is not playing with its own money. In the market, a firm making a mistake will bear the consequences, whereas a government entity may be able to transfer the cost onto taxpayers. Critics conclude that as a result, the government is not likely to be nearly as good as the market at "picking winners." Examples include government investments in solar energy such as Solyndra, and clean coal such as the plant in Edwardsville, Indiana. Solyndra went bankrupt shortly after receiving government funds, and the Edwardsville plant had a series of sizable cost overruns before its completion. The government CAFÉ program requires carmakers to increase fleet mileage, but consumers have not always embraced small American-produced cars, preferring the safety and comfort of larger vehicles despite guzzling more gasoline.

Summary

Energy efficiency—energy required per unit of output—is a popular goal of public policy, but does not necessarily coincide with economic efficiency or maximum social welfare. The *rebound effect* demonstrates this potential conflict. An increase in energy efficiency could increase *energy intensity*—units of energy input per unit of output—by reducing the implicit price of using energy to produce a unit of output. Energy efficiency advocates would view rebound as negative as it reduces net energy savings. From an economic standpoint, it would be viewed as positive by allowing consumers to increase their utility from purchasing a more energy-efficient product, setting aside emissions such as carbon. If there is no price for carbon emissions, the rebound effect would work against carbon reductions.

Negative externalities attributable to energy use are a common justification for government intervention such as subsidies to encourage the purchase of energy-efficient appliances. Another justification is that there may be an *energy efficiency gap*, with consumers unwilling to spend a dollar today to save the present value of a dollar in energy costs tomorrow. However, subsidies may go to *free riders*, which in this context refers to decision-makers who would have made the purchase even in the absence of the subsidy.

If there are to be rewards or penalties to encourage energy efficiency, we can use standards or incentive-based programs. Economists prefer incentive-based programs such as taxes and cap-and-trade to standards such as CAFÉ, deferring to standards only if there is a special situation that prevents incentive-based programs from working or from being implemented.

Notes

1 Why is oil omitted? At least in the United States, it accounts for less than 1% of the fuel used for electricity generation.
2 The values in the figure are in euros. At the time of the study, the euro was worth about $1.40, so €20 = $28. Using 2016 exchange rates, the value of a euro would be closer to $1.10, so €20 = $22.
3 Sometimes it is useful to add a fourth input, M, for materials, in which case output depends upon "KLEM." Berndt and Wood (1975) introduced this specification.
4 In actuality, comfort may also depend upon humidity, wind speed, the tightness of the building envelope, and so on. We consider those complications later in the chapter.
5 Electric utilities typically refer to capacity as demand. Industrial customers pay separate demand (kW) and energy (kWh) charges. The demand charge assesses the customer's highest use over a short interval, such as 30 minutes. The purpose of the demand charge is to provide an incentive to the customer to reduce their maximum demand for capacity, which should help reduce maximum utility system load. Utilities are considering the use of residential demand charges, especially for customers who use solar energy. These customers consume less energy from the utility, but still require capacity, as they still need the utility grid when the sun is unavailable.
6 If you assume you purchase your first incandescent bulb today, then you would sum from $t = 0$ to $t = 19$ in calculating PV. You will then find a slightly higher levelized cost for the incandescent, strengthening the case for the LED as the lower-cost alternative.
7 True story. The author grew up in New York City, where owners paid the energy bill and supplied heat to all tenants over which tenants had no control. If the apartment got too hot, the lowest-cost remedy from the renter's perspective was to open the window.
8 Schwarz (1991) did not find evidence consistent with the Coase theorem. Landlord and tenant decisions did not move towards efficiency even where transactions costs were relatively low, such as in a building with a small number of units, or where the owner lived on site.
9 Harry Saunders, in a 1992 paper looking at the macroeconomic energy effects on energy use of microeconomic energy efficiency policies calls it the Khazzoom–Brookes postulate, with British economist Len Brookes sharing the credit for similar findings in the 1980s.
10 We are setting aside the issues of whether consumers actually know the marginal price. Some literature suggests consumers only know the average price.
11 Much of the remaining material on the rebound effect is based upon the excellent survey by Gillingham, Rapson, and Wagner (2014).

References

Allcott, H., & Greenstone, M. (2012). Is there an energy efficiency gap? *Journal of Economic Perspectives* 26, 3–28.

Allcott, H., & Wozny, N. (2014). Gasoline prices, fuel economy, and the energy paradox. *Review of Economics and Statistics 96*, 779–795.

Berndt, E., & Wood, D. (1975). Technology, prices, and the derived demand for energy. *Review of Economics and Statistics, 57*(3), 259–268.

Davis, L. (2008). Durable goods and residential demand for energy and water: Evidence from a field trial. *RAND Journal of Economics, 39*, 530–546.

Davis, L., Fuchs, A., & Gertler, P. (2013). Cash for coolers: Evaluating a large-scale appliance replacement program in Mexico. *American Economic Journal: Economic Policy, 6*, 207–238.

Dewees, D., & Wilson, T. (1990). Cold houses and warm climates revisited: On keeping warm in Chicago, or paradox lost. *Journal of Political Economics, 98*, 656–663.

Dubin, J. A., & McFadden, D. L. (1984). An econometric analysis of residential electric appliance holdings and consumption. *Econometrica, 52*(2), 345–362.

Friedman, D. (1987). Cold houses in warm climates and vice versa: A paradox of rational heating. *Journal of Political Economy, 95*, 1089–1097.

Gillingham, K., Newell, R. G., & Palmer, K. (2009). Energy efficiency economics and policy. *Annual Review of Resource Economics, 1*, 597–620.

Gillingham, K., Rapson, D., & Wagner, G. (2014). *The rebound effect and energy efficiency policy* (Discussion Paper 14–39). Washington, D.C.: Resources for the Future.

Hausman, J. (1979). Individual discount rates and the purchase and utilization of energy-using durables. *The Bell Journal of Economics, 10*, 33–54.

Howarth, R., Haddad, B., & Paton, B. (2000). The economics of energy efficiency: Insights from voluntary participation programs. *Energy Policy, 28*, 477–486.

Kaufman, N., & Palmer, K. (2010). *Energy-efficiency program evaluations: Opportunities for learning and inputs to incentive mechanisms.* (Discussion Paper 10–16). Washington, D.C.: Resources for the Future.

Khazzoom, J. D. (1980). Economic implications of mandated efficiency in standards for household appliances. *The Energy Journal, 1*, 21–40.

Lee, J. (2013, December 27). Why people still use inefficient incandescent light bulbs. *USA Today.* Retrieved October 26, 2016 from http://www.usatoday.com/story/news/nation-now/2013/12/27/incandescent-light-bulbs-phaseout-leds/4217009/

Lovins, A. (1976). The road not taken? *Foreign Affairs, 55*(1), 65–95.

Lovins, A. (1989). *The negawatt revolution—solving the CO2 problem—keynote address.* Retrieved October 27, 2016 from http://www.ccnr.org/amory.html

McKinsey & Company. (2010). *Impact of the financial crisis on carbon economics: Version 2.1 of the global greenhouse gas abatement cost curve.* Retrieved October 29, 2016 from http://www.mckinsey.com/business-functions/sustainability-and-resource-productivity/our-insights/impact-of-the-financial-crisis-on-carbon-economics-version–21

Parry, I., Evans, D., & Oates, W. (2014). Are energy efficiency standards justified? *Journal of Environmental Economics and Management, 67*, 104–125.

Saunders, H. (1992). The Khazzoom–Brookes postulate and neoclassical growth. *The Energy Journal, 13*, 131–148.

Schwarz, P. M. (1991). Does apartment energy efficiency improve when tenants pay the bill?" *International Journal of Energy Systems, 11*, 91–95.

Schwarz, P. M., & Taylor, T. N. (1995). Cold hands, warm hearth? Climate, net takeback, and household comfort. *The Energy Journal, 16*, 41–54.

U.S. Energy Information Administration. (2015). *Annual Energy Outlook 2015.* Retrieved December 8, 2016 from http://www.eia.gov/outlooks/aeo/pdf/0383(2015).pdf

U.S. Environmental Protection Agency. (2016). *Cleaning up a broken CFL: Recommendations for when a CFL or other mercury-containing bulb breaks*. Retrieved October 27, 2016 from http://www2.epa.gov/cfl/cleaning-broken-cfl#instructions

Wing, I. S. (2008). Explaining the declining energy intensity of the U.S. economy. *Resource and Energy Economics*, *30*, 21–49.

Yergin, D. (2012, Nov 11). Energy efficiency: The new "first fuel." *The Huffington Post: The Blog*. Retrieved August 30, 2016. http://www.huffingtonpost.com/daniel-yergin/energy-efficiency-_b_1084604.html.

Part IV

Electricity

Chapter 12

Traditional electricity regulation
The calm before the storm

"Democracy is the worst form of government except all those other forms that have been tried from time to time."

Winston Churchill[1]

"Regulation may be the worst way to run the electricity industry except compared to the alternatives."

The author of this text

Introduction

Electricity regulation began in the 1930s, largely on the basis that its production exemplified a natural monopoly. A *natural monopoly* is a firm with *economies of scale* (EOS)—declining long-run average cost in the relevant range of demand—and so in the long run there will be only one firm in the industry, as any firm that operates at a smaller scale will have higher average costs than the largest firm. For many years, electricity production displayed economies of scale in all three stages of production—generation, transmission, and distribution—so that a single firm in the market could achieve lower average costs than if that firm were broken up into more than one firm to create competition. The purpose of regulation was to pass on the benefits of EOS to consumers. In the absence of regulation, the monopolist would maximize profit by restricting output in order to raise price.

Key court decisions such as the 1877 U.S. Supreme Court case Munn vs. Illinois established that the government can regulate industries "affected with the public interest."[2] Public utility regulation sets price in a quasi-judicial process. The electric utility periodically comes before the commission to determine allowed profit, and which costs can be included in the rate base.

Under regulation, public utility commissions (PUCs) allow utilities a "normal" rate of return. Typically, the rate of return on capital allows a markup over average costs, which leads to several distortions. First, efficiency calls for prices to equal marginal cost, not average cost. Second, the Averch–Johnson (AJ (1962)) effect indicates that firms earning a rate of return on capital use too much capital compared to other inputs such as labor. Third, recall that Stigler (1971) raised the concern of regulatory capture, where regulators gain from acting on behalf of the firms they regulate rather than in the interest of consumers.

Economists have long proposed marginal-cost-based rates, with Electricité de France implementing marginal cost pricing as early as the late 1940s (Boiteux, 1960; Boiteux,

Clemens & Clemens, 1964). There are also alternatives to rate-of-return regulation, such as incentive regulation, that encourage utilities to decrease the costs of production. Incentive regulation induces utilities to reveal their actual costs, by allowing them a share of the added profit that comes from more efficient practices.

The AJ effect and regulatory capture are among the reasons why the prices of regulated firms may be higher than rate-of-return regulation suggests. Regulated firms inflate cost by building too much generating capacity, or by managers choosing more generous employee *perquisites* (*perks*)—thicker carpeting or longer vacations—than a comparable competitive firm would offer (Williamson, 1964). Skeptics of regulation such as Stigler questioned whether we might not be better off with unregulated monopoly. They planted the seeds that led to deregulation and restructuring, the subject of Chapter 13.

The next section of this chapter presents a brief economic history of electricity and its regulation, followed by a section that provides an overview of the electric utility. We then develop the traditional approach to regulating electricity, followed by a section on alternatives that stop short of restructuring or deregulation. The final section is a summary.

A brief economic history of electricity and its regulation

The origins of electricity

While people had known about electricity for eons as a result of phenomena such as electric eels, magnetic attraction, and lightning, Thomas Edison successfully demonstrated the first application of commercial significance, the incandescent bulb, in 1879. In 1882, he built the first electric utility, Pearl Street Station in New York City, making it possible to use electric lighting on a large scale.

Edison initially had to compete with preexisting means of lighting, from whale oil to gas to kerosene. His biggest fight was between his distribution network, which used direct current (DC), and a rival method by George Westinghouse, which used alternating current (AC).

Box 12.1 "The war of the currents"

Edison received a patent for the first incandescent bulb in 1880, and in the same year, another patent for his direct current (DC) electrical system.[3] Direct current, current that runs continually in the same direction, like in a battery or a fuel cell, was the standard in the United States at that time. However, DC had some challenges. It lost significant energy when it was transmitted long distances, and it was difficult to increase or decrease the voltage. Edison hired Nikola Tesla to find solutions. Tesla proposed an AC system, where a rotating magnet results in the electric current switching direction. The voltage could be stepped up or down, and using a higher voltage and a lower current resulted in less heating of the wires and in turn lower electricity losses.

Edison found Tesla's solution "splendid," but claimed it was impractical (King, 2011). Tesla left Edison to work for George Westinghouse. Tesla had a number of patents that

Westinghouse bought. At first, Westinghouse only served markets not yet served by Edison. Edison, determined to maintain dominance, attacked the safety of AC power, going so far as to electrocute dogs and horses and hooking up the first electric chair with a Westinghouse AC generator, resulting in the gruesome death of convicted ax–murderer and electric chair guinea pig William Kemmler.

However, Westinghouse triumphed, winning the bid for the 1893 Columbian Exposition in Chicago, the first all-electric world's fair. His bid was half that of the Edison Company. The next triumph was in 1896, when Westinghouse harnessed the power of Niagara Falls, first sending power to Buffalo in upstate New York, and after building a series of generators, to New York City.

A modern irony is that DC is beginning to make inroads against AC. With as much as 20% of total electricity demand due to DC appliances, there would be cost savings by avoiding using an inverter to convert AC power. Microgrids using DC could meet these needs. Electric vehicles run on DC, and in addition to using power they can also supply power to the grid. Solar panels and data centers run on DC, and their users may prefer to stay off the AC grid. LED lighting is another rapidly growing use of DC electricity. While generating plants still use AC, and devices such as electric motors do as well, transmission lines increasingly use DC. It is easier to handle DC power, which maintains a constant voltage, and has lower line losses. Edison may yet prevail.

Predecessors to electric lighting

Long before the appearance of modern concerns about peak oil, there were concerns about peak whale oil. Whale oil was in use from the mid–1700s through the mid–1800s. It had a number of uses, chief among them lamp oil. Whale oil was far superior to its predecessors. Whaling was one of the world's largest industries. Citizens of that time feared that the extensive hunting for whales would lead to their extinction. Looking back, some economists question whether we would have hunted the whales to extinction. Just as economists are skeptical of the peak oil theory that predicts we will exhaust our oil supplies, there are those who refer to the "whale oil myth." Greater scarcity increases prices, which stimulate the incentive to substitute other resources and find new technologies.[4]

Kerosene was distilled from petroleum in 1849, and provided a longer-lasting and better-smelling fuel. In the 1860s, John D. Rockefeller improved the efficiency of petroleum processing, increased kerosene production and eventually established Standard Oil. Gas lighting had already emerged by the early 1800s. Initially, the source was gas from coal, followed by natural gas by the late 1800s. Gas provided brighter lighting, allowing longer working hours and accelerating the Industrial Revolution, and was the first fuel provided by a central utility.

Electric lighting was initially more expensive than gas. It required large centralized generating facilities and infrastructure, as well as expensive rights of way. As the main use was for nighttime lighting, the cost remained high until a daytime demand could be found. It was not until about 1930 that electric systems had sizable daytime demands, with increasing use of industrial motors and railways. By the late 1920s and early 1930s, electric lighting supplanted gas as the leading source of illumination.

The evolution of U.S. electric utility regulation

In the early days of the U.S. electricity industry, there was no regulation, resulting in high prices in some areas and redundant services in others. Initially, municipalities granted franchises to gas and electric companies, with long-term contracts that generally led to high prices. Some cities, such as Chicago in the 1880s, allowed multiple electric companies. Competition was only viable in larger cities, and even there, it was short-lived.

By 1900, municipal governments were establishing public utilities regulation. New York was among the earliest states to establish a public utilities regulatory commission, gradually moving away from municipal regulation. In 1907, Wisconsin introduced regulation based on the company's assets, the foundation for rate-of-return regulation.

Electric utilities formed *holding companies*. These companies owned stock in other firms that allowed them to control decision-making and gain market power. General Electric controlled over 200 electric companies by 1924 through the use of 9 holding companies. In turn, the company required all their subsidiaries to purchase equipment from General Electric.

The Federal Power Commission (FPC) was established in 1920 to oversee federal hydroelectric projects. In 1935, the FPC gained power over interstate electricity transmission and wholesale electricity prices. In the 1944 U.S. Supreme Court case of Federal Power Commission vs. Hope Natural Gas, the court refined the definition of "fair return" introduced in the 1898 case of Smyth vs. Ames. Rate-makers now had to balance the competing interests of stockholders and consumers.

In 1935, the passage of the Public Utilities Holding Company Act (PUHCA) aimed to prevent abuse of market power. It abolished electric utility holding companies except for those benefiting geographically neighboring utilities. PUHCA viewed electric utilities as natural monopolies with economies of scale in generation, transmission, and distribution.

In 1965, there was a massive blackout that hit all of New York, parts of seven surrounding states, and portions of eastern Canada. That event led to the establishment of the North American Electric Reliability Council (NERC) in 1968 to oversee the wholesale supply of electric power. The 1970s saw the most fundamental changes to the industry since the 1930s, in the wake of rising electricity prices due to dramatically higher prices for fuels needed for generation.

The Federal Energy Regulatory Commission (FERC) replaced the FPC in 1977 to facilitate industry changes. In 1978, the passage of the Public Utilities Regulatory Policy Act (PURPA) required electric utilities to buy electricity at avoided cost from *qualifying facilities* (QFs), typically small solar producers or cogeneration facilities—also referred to as combined heat and power (CHP)—that produced reusable waste heat along with generation. PURPA showed that nonutility operators could produce energy. However, PURPA contributed to much higher electric rates than would have existed had the electric utilities generated the power themselves. *Avoided cost*—the cost of building new capacity to meet demand—often exceeded the cost at which utilities with available capacity could meet demand. These high prices were an impetus for states to consider deregulation and restructuring in the electricity market, the subject of the next chapter.

Overview of the electric industry

There are three stages—generation, transmission, and distribution—necessary to get electricity from the electric utility to the final customer. Electricity is a *secondary source* of energy, generated from *primary sources* such as fossil fuels. When burned, these fuels produce heat and steam to rotate the turbine that moves the generator, producing an electric current. Transformers step up the voltage before the electricity passes through high-voltage transmission lines, and then step down the voltage before the electricity travels through distribution lines to end-use customers.

A unique aspect of electricity is that demand must equal supply at each instant. While batteries can store electricity, their integration into the electricity system is in the development stage.[5] Regulated utilities maintain excess generating capacity to ensure that customers receive electricity whenever they flip the switch. Although it is impossible to guarantee perfect reliability, electric utilities in developed countries set a very high standard, such as a loss of load probability (LOLP) of one day in ten years. To achieve such a high standard, regulated electric utilities have a margin of excess capacity on the order of 15%.[6]

Developing countries may experience interruptions of power even on a daily basis. Over half a billion people in India lost power in the summer of 2012 during a two-day blackout. Electric capacity in India is insufficient to meet demand. Government-regulated prices for distribution are low, which results in little growth in the distribution system even as the government tries to expand generating capacity (Zhong & Chaturvedi, 2014).

In both developed and developing countries, retail prices do not typically reflect real-time conditions, and so when demand threatens to exceed supply, customers do not get a price signal that would encourage them to cut back on their use. Excess capacity is a costly alternative to using prices to signal when capacity is tight.

Customer sectors

Industrial sector

The availability of electricity led to the electrification of industry as firms found new applications and substituted electricity for other fuels in production. Electric lighting improved factory safety and lengthened the hours when production could take place. While electric lighting was one stimulus for the advance of industry, electric motors, also used in street railways, were the biggest driver.

The industrial sector—manufacturing, mining, agriculture, and construction—accounts for just over a quarter of total U.S. electricity use, with residential and commercial use each exceeding one-third, as shown in Figure 12.1. Transportation is a small fraction despite the growth of the electric vehicle sector.

Both primary fossil fuels and secondary electricity power industrial processes. Motors account for about half of energy use in manufacturing, followed by process heating and cooling at about 20%. Electrochemical processes, heating, vacuuming, and air conditioning (HVAC) and lighting, each approach 10%.

Figure 12.2 shows that electricity use declined during the Great Recession before recovering, but has barely grown since 2010 (U.S. Energy Information Administration, 2016a). Industrial use has been flat or has even declined since 2010.

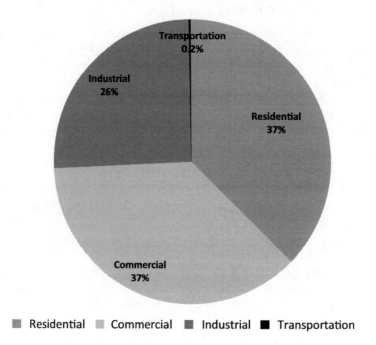

■ Residential   ■ Commercial   ■ Industrial   ■ Transportation

Figure 12.1 Electricity consumption by sector, 2015. Adapted from *Retail Sales of Electricity, Monthly*, by EIA, 2016.

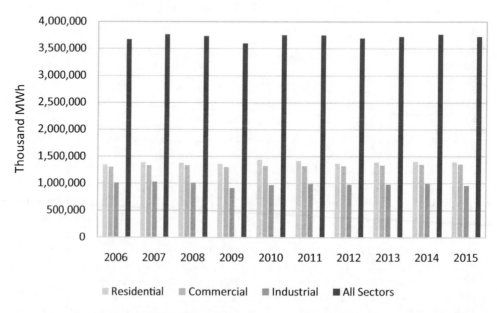

Figure 12.2 Annual retail electricity sales by sector, 2006–2015. Adapted from *Electric Power Monthly: With data for September 2016* (U.S. EIA, 2016b). Retrieved November 13, 2016 from https://www.eia.gov/electricity/monthly/pdf/epm.pdf.

Commercial sector

Commercial buildings account for nearly 20% of energy consumption, with office space, retail, and educational facilities about half of that amount. As of 2015, lighting, heating, and cooling and ventilation account for almost half of commercial energy consumption.[7] The commercial energy sector also includes outdoor street lighting and water and sewage treatment, but these uses are a small percentage of overall commercial demand. The major emphasis is on reducing energy use in buildings.

Residential sector

Residential energy consumption made up 22% of primary energy consumption as of 2009, equal to 54% of building energy consumption, both figures slightly larger than for the commercial sector. While space heating, water heating, and air conditioning are the largest energy uses, air conditioning is the largest electric use. Lighting is second, but electronics is the fastest growing. Natural gas has a growing share of space heating, leaving electricity with a declining share.

As was shown in Figure 12.2, despite rebounding immediately after the recession, residential use then dropped and now appears to be flat. The American Council for an Energy-Efficient Economy (ACEEE) suggests the leveling is due to energy efficiency, while the EIA notes slower home sales during the period (Nadel, 2014; U.S. EIA, 2016c).

Global trends in electricity use

For many years, the assumption in the United States and elsewhere was that electricity use would always increase. Year-after-year U.S. demand grew 2–3%. Growth slowed after the year 2000 as the industrial sector cut its electricity use. Electricity use by all three sectors dipped during the Great Recession. Even as the economy has recovered, Figure 12.2 suggests that electricity use will grow at a slower rate than before the recession, if it grows at all. Slowing electricity demand has contributed to a surprising drop in GHG emissions.

There is increasing discussion of the reasons that electricity demand is slowing or even shrinking, including greater energy efficiency and disruptive technologies. *Disruptive technologies* are technologies that could change the electric utility business model, such as individuals installing solar panels on their roof, demanding less power from the centralized grid and selling power back. Electric vehicles could supply electricity as well as demand it; the vehicles store electricity to power the car, and can then provide excess electricity back to the grid.

While U.S. electricity use has been slowing, China has increased its use by more than enough to offset any U.S. decline. China is the second-largest electricity consumer, after the United States, although it does not rank among the leaders in per capita consumption. China's electricity use was climbing at double-digit percentages, but the growth rate has slowed dramatically to less than 1%. Slower economic growth may be a contributor, as well as reducing reliance on heavy industry (Bloomberg, 2016).

Since 2000 China has been generating nearly 80% of its electricity using coal, making it the world's largest producer of GHGs (International Energy Agency, 2005). In recent years, China has been increasing its investment in renewables at a rapid pace and decreasing its use of coal, a necessary step if the world is to have any hope of slowing or stopping the accumulation of GHGs.

India is the third largest energy consumer and is experiencing rapid economic growth and modernization. The country currently has little air conditioning, but it is rapidly becoming more widespread, which will contribute substantially to growing electricity demand.

The European Union shows flat or declining electricity use. If there is any growth, it will be smaller than in the United States or the developing world (Eurostat, 2016).

The electric system supply chain

Figure 12.3 shows a supply chain for the traditional regulated electric utility. The initial stage is the generation of electricity by the electric utility; then the electricity is sent through transmission lines, and finally through distribution lines to the final customers. Some large industrial customers receive power directly from the transmission system.

Generation

Figure 12.4 reviews the primary energy sources that generate electricity in the United States. Other countries use a different mix of fuels. France depends heavily on nuclear energy for about three-quarters of its total electricity generation. Until the Fukushima disaster, Japan had also emphasized nuclear energy, with that source accounting for about 30% of its generation. Norway relies almost exclusively on hydropower, which allows them to have low electricity prices and low emissions. Iceland also uses hydropower extensively, along with rising use of geothermal energy. They use only a small amount of fossil fuels.

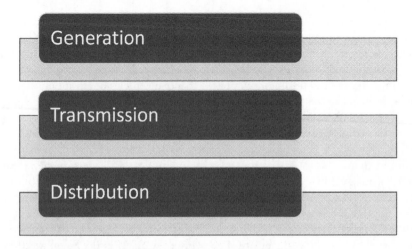

Figure 12.3 A simple electric system supply chain.

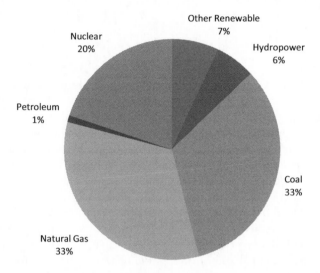

Figure 12.4

Figure 12.4 U.S. net electricity generation by energy source, 2015. Adapted from *What is U.S. electricity generation by energy source?* (U.S. EIA, 2016d).

Transmission

Transmission lines transport electricity long distances so that electricity generation can take place far away from the final customer. The transmission system also allows utilities to send electricity to other utilities. The FERC has jurisdiction over interstate transmission. Intrastate transmission falls under state regulation.

Transmission systems are critical in making sure that electricity gets to final customers. Just as generators can have outages, transmission lines can malfunction due to overloading or overheating. The North American Reliability Corporation (NERC) sets out reliability standards that FERC enforces. For example, the standards require redundancy in transmission lines in case one line fails.

Generation and transmission is a joint decision for regulated utilities. Regulated utilities only consider their own service area in building transmission. As it may make sense for transmission lines to serve more than one utility, FERC supports, but does not require, regional transmission organizations (RTOs) and independent system operators (ISOs) that supervise transmission capacity that serves multiple utilities.

Distribution

Distribution lines carry electricity for relatively short distances. In the United States, they are mostly within a state, so FERC is not involved. After a storm when people have lost their power, they press for transmission and distribution lines to be buried. In addition, there is an advantage to not having power lines crisscrossing the landscape. As usual in economics, there is no such thing as a free lunch. The cost of burying lines is much higher than for overhead lines, particularly in highly populated urban areas, and the cost of repairs is also higher.

Regulating the electric industry

State regulations

Who regulates?

In the United States, a state Public Utilities Commission (PUC) determines in-state rates, typically using rate-of-return (RoR) regulation. The commission determines retail rates, with separate tariffs for residential, commercial, and industrial customers.

The case for regulation depends upon comparing two imperfect alternatives, a market likely to have limited competition vs. regulation subject to government failures. In order to set prices, regulators must estimate cost from utility information. Utilities may inflate costs due to the AJ effect and regulatory capture. If utilities can recoup costs, they have less incentive to minimize costs than private, profit-maximizing firms. Managers of regulated firms have more latitude to pursue their own interests.

Regulators may also favor the industry they are regulating due to capture. The industry has more incentive to influence the regulatory body than consumers, since benefits to individual ratepayers are small and diffuse, while benefits to the utility are large and concentrated.

Box 12.2 The political economy of electricity regulation

In North Carolina, commissioners are political appointees, with one commissioner serving as chair. The party in power will typically appoint commissioners who reflect their view. With a Republican Administration in office, appointed commissioners will tend towards a more laissez-faire approach to regulation, whereas Democratic appointees will see a greater need for regulatory vigilance.

In North Carolina, Duke Energy, headquartered in Charlotte, and Progress Energy, headquartered in Raleigh, proposed a merger. The Progress Energy CEO was to be in charge of the combined company, while the headquarters would be in Charlotte. Within hours of the merger, there was a decision to install the head of Duke Energy as the CEO of the combined company. The PUC took the utility to task, asking for details of correspondence that had led to the decision. It is not obvious why the PUC should have any say in who should head up the combined company. One possible reason for the commission's concern is that the Progress Energy CEO would better protect the interests of Raleigh, where the commissioners live.

The political composition of the PUC is also likely to influence the allowed rate of return. The North Carolina Attorney General, a Democrat who has since been elected Governor, wanted to hold a proposed electric utility rate increase at 2.2%. The Attorney General cited difficult economic times for consumers. Republicans supported the recommendation of the PUC for an increase of about 7.5%, and a return to stockholders in the range of 10%.

Stigler and Friedland (1962) examined the 50 U.S. states, comparing prices and quantities for the years 1912–1937, a time span covering periods before and after regulation. They found little evidence that regulation had reduced rates. Their findings led them to ask whether deregulation, the subject of the next chapter, would work better.

Economists skeptical of deregulation look for ways to improve regulation rather than eliminate it. Later in this chapter, we focus on *incentive-based regulation*, a system whereby it is in the firm's self-interest to reduce costs.

Rate-of-return regulation

The most common form of regulation of electric utilities is RoR regulation. Figure 12.5 shows a natural monopoly, with economies of scale shown by declining long-run average cost. Economic efficiency calls for setting price (marginal benefit (MB)) equal to marginal cost (MC). However, it is possible for MC to lie below average cost at the corresponding quantity. The regulatory compromise is average cost pricing, where average cost crosses the demand curve. The corresponding quantity results in a deadweight loss, because price (marginal benefit) exceeds MC. Other government failures including the AJ effect and regulatory capture can add to welfare losses.

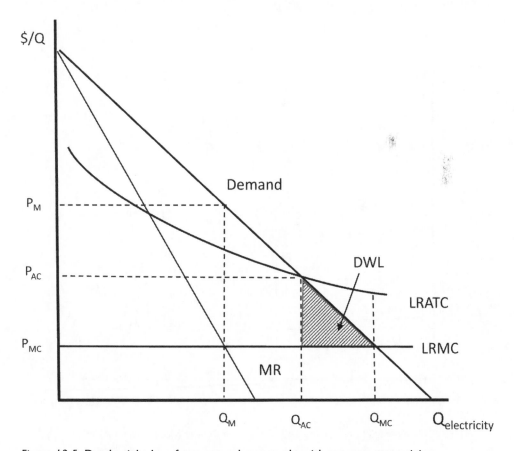

Figure 12.5 Deadweight loss from natural monopoly with average cost pricing.

Figure 12.6 shows that the AJ effect adds to social welfare loss in two ways. By over-using capital relative to labor, average cost (LRATC') is higher than if the firm chose the minimum-cost combination of inputs (LRATC). The intersection of LRATC' and D is at a lower quantity and higher price, increasing the deadweight loss triangle from ABA to AEF. There is an additional inefficiency from the higher cost of producing each of these units, shown by the rectangle $EHGP_{AC'}$.

Regulatory capture has an analogous effect. If there is both an AJ effect and regulatory capture, ATC would be higher due to both effects, with a corresponding larger deadweight loss triangle at the further reduced quantity, and an additional efficiency loss rectangle due to higher ATC.

DETERMINING AVERAGE COST

Economics offers little guidance for allocating fixed costs, so the utility commission uses rules of thumb. If a utility serves more than one state, the PUC uses accounting formulas to allocate costs among states. The allocation of the costs of the distribution system is straightforward, as distribution is typically within one state. Other expenses, such as the expenses of the administrative headquarters, production, and the transmission system, can fall within more than one state.

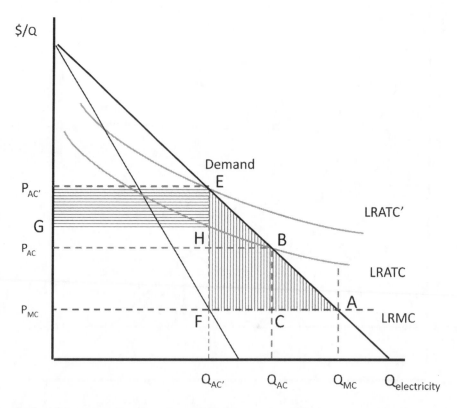

Figure 12.6 Average cost pricing and added dea dweight loss due to AJ effect.

Commissions allocate production and transmission costs based on measures of usage. Measures could be in proportion to each area's share of peak demand, or according to energy usage. Commissions allocate administrative facilities in proportion to the number of customers, or share of peak demand and energy use, or share of total revenue. Commissions allocate taxes (federal, state, and local) using similar measures. The commission attempts to separate costs between regulated and nonregulated services. Nonregulated operations are typically riskier, and their costs should not be borne by regulated customers.

DETERMINING THE REVENUE REQUIREMENT

The equation for determining the revenue requirement is:

$$\text{Rev. Req.} = \text{Rate Base} \times \text{Rate of Return (RoR)} + \text{Operating Expenses}$$

The rate base equals net investment = investment − (accumulated) depreciation.

Investment equals generation, transmission, and distribution capital equipment as well as other investment from buildings to vehicles. In most case, the items must be *used and useful*—providing value to current ratepayers in order to be paid for by current ratepayers—as established in the 1898 Smyth vs. Ames case. Accumulated depreciation uses accounting formulas to determine the total decrease in value of investments since their original purchase.

Box 12.3 Pay me now or pay me later? Construction work in progress

Utilities prefer to recoup construction-work-in-progress (CWIP), while ratepayers may prefer that assets not be included in the rate base until they are used and useful and actually producing energy. Utilities protest that investment is a multi-year process, and if these costs can only enter into the rate base upon completion, the needed funds will be lumpy, increasing substantially in years when new equipment is placed in service and resulting in rate shocks. The utilities argue for CWIP to smooth out changes in the rate base and to reduce the costs of borrowing, since lenders will see the investments as less risky.

The issue arises when utilities consider building a nuclear plant, which can take ten years or more to construct and which has high up-front capital costs up to 80% of overall costs. The opposition to CWIP stems from allowing higher costs before the plant is complete, including the possibility that the plant might never be completed. Utilities may be less careful about cost overruns if they know they can include those costs in the rate base. Given the history of nuclear reactor cost overruns and unfinished plants, it is easy to understand why there is vigorous opposition to applying CWIP for electric utility assets, particularly new nuclear plant construction.

The rate of return must be sufficient to allow the utility to attract additional capital under prudent management, commensurate with risk, as established in the FPC vs. Hope and Munn vs. Illinois cases cited earlier. The benchmark is zero economic profit, which is the normal return earned by competitive firms. This return includes a return on equity (a return to shareholders) as well as a return on debt (a return to bondholders). Equity includes common as well as preferred stock. Debt includes long- and short-term bonds. Common stock and long-term bonds make up the majority of the financing.

Holders of common stock face the highest risk and expect the highest return to compensate for that risk. In the event of bankruptcy, common stock may be worthless. Holders of preferred stock are a higher priority of repayment if the company faces bankruptcy. Bondholders are a higher priority than preferred stockholders. Note that all investors in the utility may receive less than one dollar for each dollar invested in the event of bankruptcy.

Example 12.1

Consider the firm with the hypothetical capital structure given in Table 12.1. The table lists the composition of investors and their expected RoR, given commensurate risk. Determine the allowed RoR on capital for this utility.

Table 12.1 Determining electric utility allowed rate of return

	Percent of capital structure	Cost of capital (k)
Common equity	40	10%
Preferred equity	5	8%
Long-term debt	45	5%
Short-term debt	10	3%

Solution

The weighted cost of capital determines the allowed rate based on the percentage of investment financed from different categories of debt and equity. Holders of common stock expect a 10% return. Short-term bond holders expect a 3% return. The weighted average of the four categories of investment is

$$RoR = (0.4 \times 0.1) + (0.05 \times 0.08) + (0.45 \times 0.05) + 0.1 \times 0.03)$$

$$RoR = 0.0695$$

If the PUC grants a 6.95% return on the utility's rate base, the utility will have enough net revenue—revenue less cost of items in the rate base—to compensate holders of capital investment at the returns shown in Table 12.1. The utility can issue short-term bonds with a 3% return, long-term bonds at 5%, and have enough remaining revenue that it can provide a return to preferred stockholders of 8% and 10% to common stockholders.

The determination of the cost of common equity is highly contentious. Where the cost of debt and preferred equity is set in advance, the cost of common equity is based on market conditions. Expert witnesses provide evidence on a fair RoR on capital, such as 10%. The utility needs to receive a discounted cash flow sufficient for it to make the target. The discounted cash flow (DCF) is

$$DCF = \sum_{t=1}^{n} \frac{Earnings}{(1+r)^t}$$

where earnings t years from now must be discounted using the discount rate (r).

As compared to a low-risk investment such as a treasury bill, the discount rate incorporates a risk premium to reflect higher-risk investments such as common equity with greater earnings volatility. There are formulas such as the capital asset pricing model (CAPM) to determine the equity risk premium. The CAPM formula is

$$R_c = R_f + \beta \times (R_m - R_f)$$

where R_c is the risk-adjusted discount rate (also known as the cost of capital), R_f the rate of a risk-free investment such as a short-term treasury bill, R_m the rate of return on a market benchmark such as the S&P 500, and β (beta) is a measure of riskiness, the return of the asset as compared to return of the market.

The cost of debt is the average cost of the utility's borrowed funds at any time, a lower rate than the cost of equity. It is typically an exact calculation based on a past (historical) year, unless the PUC uses a procedure based on a future test year, in which case they estimate the cost of debt. As long as the historical year is a good predictor of the future, the use of a historical year should insure that the utility will recoup its costs in a future year. However, commissions may instead construct a future test year if, for example, they expect inflation in the coming year.

In addition to recovering capital costs plus a fair RoR, the utility also needs to be able to recover its operating and maintenance (O&M) costs. In contrast to capital costs, which only vary in the long run, some O&M costs are variable in the short run. Short-run O&M costs include labor and fuel costs and any other costs that recur repeatedly, such as maintenance services that depend upon production. The PUC holds periodic hearings where the utility defends costs under its control as reasonable to include in the rate base. Some O&M costs can be passed on automatically, such as a fuel cost adjustment aimed at allowing the utility to adjust its costs for unexpected changes— up or down—without a rate hearing.

Adjustment clauses have the advantage of not penalizing the firm for factors outside the firm's control, but the disadvantage that the firm has little incentive to hold down these costs. An electric utility that can pass on the fluctuating costs of fuel directly to its customers has no reason to consider hedges such as futures or options contracts on fuel costs.

Commissions typically allow utilities to pass on costs due to extreme events such as hurricanes. The utility may also be able to pass on costs of nuclear plant decommissioning, infrastructure replacement, and energy efficiency program expense. Automatic adjustments save time and money, as well as reducing utility company risk. The disadvantage is that the utility has little incentive to minimize these costs, and thus it passes the risk onto ratepayers.[8]

RATE CLASSES

Utilities set different rates for residential, commercial, and industrial classes. Industrial customers are typically the largest users, and usually pay the lowest rates. The lower average cost of distribution per unit of electricity provides an argument for a lower price per unit for these customers. Industrial customers who buy electricity directly from the transmission system get an even lower price. By the same argument, residential customers buy a relatively small amount of energy, and so the average cost of providing distribution lines is relatively high. Commercial customers fall in between.

As noted earlier, economic theory does not provide much guidance in allocating fixed costs. Recall that profit-maximizing firms set MR = MC, and fixed costs do not enter into the MC calculation. Similarly, social welfare maximization calls for MSB = MSC. Again, fixed costs do not affect MSC. Their only relevance to social welfare is that a large fixed charge could prevent a low-income customer from consuming electricity in the first place. Such exclusion is inefficient insofar as the consumer's MB will exceed MC for a certain number of units of electricity, yet consumption will be zero if the fixed cost exceeds the customer's ability to pay. To the extent that social welfare includes income distribution considerations, the high fixed charge is also regressive, taking a higher percentage of the low-income consumer's income and driving up the average cost per unit consumed.

Arbitrary rules for allocating capacity costs can be based on percent of customers, percent of peak energy demand, or percent of energy sold. Residential customers may account for 90% of customers, but only 50% of peak demand, and 40% of energy sold. What is their responsibility for fixed costs? Residential customers prefer their share be determined by energy sold. Industrial customers prefer their share to be determined based on number of customers.

In turn, the utility can recover costs using fixed charges or charges that depend on use. Residential customers pay an energy charge—a cents/kWh charge—that recovers usage-based costs, along with a fixed customer charge to recover nonusage-based costs. The energy charge can be flat, or it can increase or decrease with energy consumption.

Example 12.2

Calculate monthly bills for residential customers using 500, 1,000, and 1,500 kWh who face a fixed customer charge of $10 and a per-unit rate of $0.10/kWh. How would the monthly bills be affected if the first 500 kWh are priced at $0.07 and additional kWh are priced at $0.13? What if the first 500 kWh are priced at $0.13 and additional kWh are $0.07?

Solution

Table 12.2 summarizes the rates and shows the calculations.

Table 12.2 Monthly bill calculation for three residential rates ($)

	Flat	Inverted block rate	Declining block rate
Customer charge	10.00	10.00	10.00
First 500 kWh	0.10	0.07	0.13
Over 500 kWh	0.10	0.13	0.07
Customer bill			
0 kWh	10	10	10
500 kWh	60	45	75
1,000 kWh	110	110	110
1,500 kWh	160	175	145

The example is *revenue-neutral* for a customer using 1,000 kWh; that is, all three rates produce the same amount of revenue. The simplest rate, or *tariff*, contains a flat energy charge along with a customer charge. A customer with low demand prefers an increasing block rate—also known as an inverted block rate—with a low charge for initial kWh and an increasing per-unit charge beyond certain thresholds. For the customer using 500 kWh, a customer charge of $10 plus an energy charge that begins at $0.07/kWh, increasing to $0.13 beyond 500 kWh, results in a $45 monthly bill, with each kWh priced at $0.07/kWh since customer use does not exceed the 500 kWh threshold. A customer using 1,500 kWh would prefer a declining block rate, with a price of $0.13 applied to the first 500 kWh, and $0.07 for all use beyond the threshold. The large user now pays $145, while the small user pays $75.

Declining block rates provide an incentive to use large amounts of electricity. Utility companies may target these rates to attract large industrial customers. Increasing block rates encourage users to conserve electricity. They also help to reduce the bills of small customers, who may have limited income.

Alternative forms of regulation

Marginal cost pricing

While regulators have largely dismissed marginal cost pricing on the premise that the firm will lose money, there are a number of ways to overcome this concern, including a fixed customer charge, a declining block rate, or using *dynamic prices* that correspond to time-varying marginal cost.[9] We have already addressed fixed charges and declining block rates. We now consider prices that depend on time of use.

Peak load pricing

In the absence of economical storage, efficient pricing calls for higher prices during peak periods, and lower prices at other times. In addition to seasonal patterns, utilities experience daily patterns, such as higher demand when industry places the greatest demand on the system. Residential demand may peak in the evening. The system peak depends upon the aggregated loads of residential, commercial, and industrial customers. A typical summer-peaking system peaks on a hot July or August afternoon.

The typical electric utility has a portfolio of generating technologies. Production efficiency calls for running the generators in *merit order*, from least expensive to most expensive depending on the level of demand.

During off-peak hours, the utility employs baseload units that typically run continuously. Coal and nuclear units provide baseload power. As natural gas has become cheaper, these units are increasingly part of the baseload mix. Baseload units have high capital costs and low operating costs. Peak units have lower capital costs, but higher operating costs.[10] It is economical to run the baseload units at all hours and spread out the high capital costs, and only use the peak units for a limited number of hours.

There are transactions costs to using time-varying electricity rates. Meters must read and record customer usage by time of use. Also, the utility needs to inform customers of changing prices. Utilities have offered time-varying rates to large industrial and commercial customers, where the large load justifies the additional costs. *Smart grids* are capable of two-way communication, and so will allow greater use of time-differentiated rates.

Boiteux (1960) first championed the benefits of marginal cost pricing and introduced the Green Tariff (Tarif Vert) shortly after France nationalized its electricity industry in 1946, creating Electricité de France. Day rates exceeded night rates, with higher rates during the peak winter season.

Boiteux provides a simple explanation of the principles of marginal cost pricing (Boiteux et al., 1964). Suppose a utility has seven generating plants. In his example, all plants use coal, but have differing operating efficiencies, so that the cost of the most efficient plant is \$0.01/kWh, the cost of the second plant is \$0.02/kWh, up to \$0.07/kWh for the seventh plant. As electricity demand increases, the utility starts with the most efficient plant, fully using the capacity of each plant except the marginal plant, the last plant that is needed to meet demand. At night, if demand can be met by fully using the most efficient plant and partially using the second plant, the price would be \$0.02/kWh. During the peak period, if the utility fully utilizes six plants, and partially utilizes the seventh plant, the price is \$0.07/kWh. Note that the price for each unit of electricity during a given period equals the cost of the marginal plant, \$0.02 during the night and \$0.07 during the peak in Boiteux's example.

The marginal plant covers its short-run marginal cost, while the infra-marginal plants earn rent, since price exceeds their marginal costs. The firm needs these revenues in order to cover long-run marginal cost. If short-run marginal cost exceeds long-run marginal cost, capacity is below the efficient level and the utility should build an additional plant. If short-run MC is less than long-run MC, the firm should reduce its capacity. The firm is at optimal long-run capacity when short-run and long-run MCs are equal.[11]

Figure 12.7 shows a utility with higher demand during peak hours.

The figure shows the social welfare gain to charging a higher price during the peak hours when demand is high (D_p) and a lower price during the off-peak hours when demand is low (D_0). At the flat rate P_f, peak consumption is Q_1', and MC exceeds MB. The efficient point corresponds to price P_1 and quantity Q_1. The right-hand shaded triangle shows the social welfare gain to charging the efficient peak price, as compared to the flat rate. The left-hand shaded triangle is the gain from charging an off-peak price lower than the uniform rate.

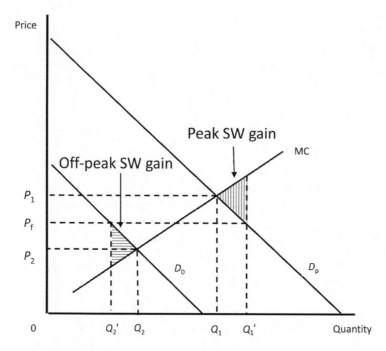

Figure 12.7 Social welfare gain to peak load pricing.

The utility can also use an intermediate or shoulder price between the peak and off-peak price when demand is high but not as high as during the peak. A shoulder price can help avoid the problem of shifting peaks. If there is only a peak and off-peak price, the peak price may shift the highest demand to the off-peak.

The likelihood of a shifting peak depends upon price elasticity and cross–elasticity. If the peak ends at 6 p.m. and consumers can easily delay running the dishwasher to 7 p.m., then implementing an intermediate price at 7 p.m. could prevent a shifting peak. Of course, there are always transactions costs associated with a more complex tariff, such as the need for the utility to inform consumers and for consumers to keep track of the rates.

Example 12.3

Under a flat rate of $0.10/kWh, a customer uses 100 kWh during each of 12 peak hours beginning at 8 a.m. and ending at 7:59 p.m. The customer uses 50 kWh during each of the 12 off-peak hours of 8 p.m. through 7:59 a.m. An electric utility introduces an economic experiment with the goal of estimating peak, off-peak, and cross-price elasticities. Table 12.3 shows consumer use under the base case of flat rates, a premium for peak hours, and a discount for off-peak hours. Based on the numbers in Table 12.3, determine the peak and off-peak price elasticities and the cross-price elasticities.

Table 12.3 Peak load pricing example

Period	Price during peak hours ($/kWh)	Price during off-peak hours ($/kWh)	Average hourly consumption during peak hours (kWh)	Average hourly consumption during off-peak hours (kWh)
Base case	0.10	0.10	100	50
Experiment 1	0.12	0.10	90	54
Experiment 2	0.10	0.06	95	62

Solution

To determine peak price elasticity, compare experiment 1, where peak price changes, to the base case. The (starting point) formula for peak period price elasticity is

$$\varepsilon_{P_P} = \frac{\% \Delta q_P}{\% \Delta p_P}$$

$$\varepsilon_{P_P} = \left(\frac{q_1 - q_B}{p_1 - p_B} \right) \times \frac{p_B}{q_B}$$

Substituting the numbers for the base case and experiment 1:

$$\varepsilon_{P_P} = \left(\frac{90 - 100}{0.12 - 0.10} \right) \times \frac{0.10}{100}$$

$$\varepsilon_{P_P} = -0.5$$

The cross-price effect of peak price on off-peak energy is

$$\varepsilon_{x_{O,P}} = \left(\frac{54 - 50}{0.12 - 0.10} \right) \times \frac{0.10}{50} \varepsilon_{x_{O,P}} = 0.4.$$

Off-peak elasticity is

$$\varepsilon_{P_O} = \frac{\% \Delta q}{\% \Delta P}$$

$$\varepsilon_{P_O} = \left(\frac{q_2 - q_B}{p_2 - p_B} \right) \times \frac{p_B}{q_B}$$

$$\varepsilon_{P_O} = \left(\frac{62 - 50}{0.06 - 0.10} \right) \times \frac{0.10}{50}$$

$$\varepsilon_{P_O} = -0.6$$

Finally, the effect of off-peak price on peak energy use is

$$\varepsilon_{x_{O,P}} = \left(\frac{95 - 100}{0.06 - 0.10} \right) \times \frac{0.10}{100}$$

$$\varepsilon_{x_{O,P}} = 0.125$$

Own-price elasticities, such as the peak and off-peak price elasticities, always have a negative sign. The cross-price elasticities can be positive or negative. In this case, the cross-price elasticities have a positive sign, indicating the two goods are substitutes. As the price of energy increases in one period and its quantity decreases, the quantity of energy increases in the other period.

Critical peak pricing (CPP)

Utilities set peak and off-peak prices many months in advance. The utility may have the capability of adding a surcharge to the peak price when the next-day forecast is very high. The surcharge can achieve a large efficiency gain as the price better reflects real-time conditions. Table 12.4 shows an illustrative CPP tariff.

The mild CPP rate could be a transition rate as customers adapt to the new rate. The steep CPP rate is the permanent rate.

Demand reduction (DR)

If a utility has determined how responsive customers are to peak prices, it can also pay customers to reduce demand, referred to as *demand reduction* (DR). In theory, subsidizing a customer to reduce demand during peak hours can achieve the same outcome as charging a higher peak period price. One advantage of a subsidy is that customers are more likely to support the program, since they receive payments rather than risking higher bills.

THE USE OF A BASELINE

One downside to a subsidy is determining a *baseline*, what use would have been in the absence of a subsidy. The difficulty is determining a *counterfactual*, the consumer's behavior in the absence of the subsidy. Suppose customers get a payment for reducing their use during peak hours. Customers have an incentive to boost the baseline, as they receive a subsidy for the baseline minus current usage. The higher the baseline, the larger the total payment the customer receives.

Utilities also use the baseline concept for a variant of dynamic prices. Customers may resist dynamic prices, concerned that they may see major bill increases. To reduce this risk, utilities offer their large industrial and commercial customers a hybrid rate. Customers pay a flat rate for all units included in the baseline, and then a dynamic price

Table 12.4 Illustrative critical peak pricing rate ($)

	Flat rate	Mild CPP rate	Steep CPP rate
Customer charge	10.00	10.00	10.00
Energy charge (kWh)			
Nights/weekends	0.08	0.06	0.04
Mornings/evenings	0.08	0.08	0.10
Afternoon peak	0.08	0.12	0.18
Critical peak hours		0.20	0.30

for deviations above and below the baseline. Customers pay the hourly price for increments above the baseline, and receive the hourly rate for reductions below baseline. The customer and the utility jointly determine the baseline, such as usage for the same month from the previous year. The hybrid rate appears to be efficient, as the customer still faces the correct marginal price. However, Chao (2011) has shown that the customer has an incentive to inflate the baseline, as demonstrated in Example 12.4.

Example 12.4

Two customers normally have identical usage of 100 kWh during the peak hours beginning at 8 a.m. and ending at 7:59 p.m. (12 hours) and 50 kWh during the remaining off-peak hours. Both customers initially pay a flat rate of $0.10 per kWh. The peak load rate is $0.12 during the peak hours and $0.06 during the off-peak. Customer A's baseline is 100 kWh during the peak and 50 kWh during the off-peak. Customer B strategically shifts use prior to the new rate and establishes an inflated baseline of 110 kWh during the peak and a deflated baseline of 40 kWh during the off-peak.

Once the customers are on the new rate, suppose they show no change in usage as compared to their normal use. Which customer will receive the lower bill?

Solution

As customer A does not deviate from the baseline, she will pay the flat rate for all units and receive the same bill as before. She will purchase 100 kWh during the 12 peak hours and 50 kWh during the off-peak hours, all priced at $0.10, for a daily bill of $15 (and a monthly bill of $450 if she has the same pattern for 30 days).

If customer B's normal usage is the same as customer A's, usage during peak hours will be 10 units below the baseline, while off-peak usage will be 10 units above baseline. Customer B pays $0.10 for the baseline peak of 110 units, but then receives $0.12 for the deviation below the baseline of 10 units. During the off-peak, customer B pays $0.10 for the 40 baseline units, and then $0.06 for the 10 units above baseline. The daily bill is ($11 − $1.20) for the peak hours, and ($4 + $0.60) for the off-peak hours. The daily bill for baseline usage remains at $15, but the customer receives $1.20 for reducing peak usage by 10 kWh below baseline and pays $0.60 for increasing usage 10 kWh above baseline during the off-peak, for a daily bill of $14.40 (and a monthly bill of $432). The $0.60 saving represents 4% of the $15 bill. For a large industrial customer with a utility bill of $10,000 per month, a 4% reduction is a $400 monthly saving, and almost $5,000 per year.

Utilities using a baseline in a dynamic rate risk getting less revenue than they anticipate.[12]

Other alternatives

Energy efficiency

Regulatory commissions may want to reward customers for saving energy, but they will have a difficult time devising incentives for the utility to offer energy conservation programs. Utilities get a return on capital, so they have an incentive to increase load, not reduce it. Ideally, we would like to develop a tariff that offers the proper incentive, based on marginal costs. Instead, the easiest path for the regulator is to pay the utility to offer energy-efficient devices to consumers. One common program is for the utility to offer compact fluorescent lamps (CFLs) at a discount, or even give them away. Utilities will only offer such technologies if they receive compensation, as they would otherwise lose revenues from selling less electricity.

Suppose a customer saves 1 MWh, allowing the utility to postpone building a new plant.[13] If the utility is allowed a 10% return on capital, the utility is forgoing the return on an additional unit of capital. To make the utility whole, it must receive $0.10 for each $1 no longer going into capital expansion. The customer gets $0.90 of each $1 saved by reducing electricity use, with $0.10 going to the utility. Environmentalists may prefer that the customer receives the entire amount. However, the utility will then have no motivation to encourage customers to save energy.

Decoupling

One method of encouraging utilities to offer energy-saving incentives is *decoupling*, where the utility's revenues no longer depend upon sales. If sales decrease because of energy efficiency, regulators will adjust rates upward so that revenue remains constant.

As with baselines, there is the potential for gaming. If utility sales decrease, it may be hard to distinguish whether the downturn is due to energy efficiency, a slowing economy, or customers generating their own electricity off the grid.

Instead of customers reducing energy use, the utility can contract with customers to shut off selected appliances using *load control*. For example, the utility can offer customers a $10 per month reduction in their summer bills for allowing the utility to shut off their air conditioner during hours when electric loads approach system capacity.

Box 12.4 Does load control really reduce electricity use?

As an alternative to a fixed monthly payment, there have been programs that reduce the hourly price during the summer months for customers who allow the utility to shut off their air conditioner. Instead of paying $0.10/kWh, customers signing up for the load-control program might pay only $0.08/kWh.

Such a program encourages the customer to use more electricity in general, and to use the air conditioner more intensively in particular, a rebound effect. At the lower electricity price, the customer may now choose 70 °F instead of 75 °F as the summer-time thermostat setting. Load will actually increase, due to an overall increase in appliance use and, in addition, more intensive use of appliances.

Incentive regulation

Under traditional RoR regulation, the utility has an incentive to inflate capital costs. *Incentive regulation* provides an incentive to reveal costs accurately.

Price depends upon average cost according to the following formula:

$$P_t = C_t + s\,(C_t - C_e)$$

where P_t is price in period t, C_t is actual cost in period t, C_e is average cost estimated in advance, and s is a sharing parameter between 0 and 1.

Suppose s equals 0.5. If actual costs are below estimated cost, price will decrease, but by only half the decrease in cost. Customers benefit from lower cost, but so does the utility, as it gets to keep half of the cost reduction. If actual costs are above the cost estimate, the utility only gets to recoup half of the cost increase. The best strategy for the utility is to reveal cost truthfully.

A common version of incentive regulation is price–cap regulation:

$$P_t = P_{t-1}\,(1 + \Delta CPI - X)$$

where P_t depends on P_{t-1}, the price in the previous period, and the difference between the percent change in the consumer price index (ΔCPI) and the expected percent change in annual productivity X.

If the utility can increase productivity faster than the estimated rate, it will increase its profit as P_t reflects the lower expected productivity increase. The following year, price decreases because the X factor—the expected productivity increase—is now set higher.

Incentive regulation is not without its challenges. Utilities will suffer if exogenous factors—factors not under their control—reduce profit. Fuel costs could increase during the year, leaving utilities with a smaller residual profit. In turn, utilities will put pressure on the regulator to consider Y factors, such as fuel costs, in the interim period. However, if regulators adjust rates frequently, then utilities have little reason to minimize fuel costs and other factors that may not be completely exogenous.

Summary

This chapter reviews traditional electric industry regulation. The first application of electricity of major significance was electric lighting, developed by Thomas Edison, who also built the first large-scale power station in the United States.

The electric industry includes three production stages: generation, transmission, and distribution. Electricity transmission takes place over long distances at high voltage. The next stage is distribution to residential, commercial, and industrial end users at a lower voltage. In the United States, industrial electricity use accounts for roughly one-fourth of overall use, with residential and commercial use each exceeding one-third.

Utilities set different rates for each of these customer classes. Fixed costs use accounting formulas to apportion shares. Customer charges do not vary with the volume of use. Energy charges are per-unit prices for energy consumption. They may be flat, declining, or increasing with usage. Declining block rates serve a promotional purpose, attracting large users to the utility system. Increasing block rates encourage conservation and energy efficiency. They also favor smaller users, who typically have lower incomes.

In the United States, the natural monopoly character of electric utilities led to the establishment of state public utilities commissions. The PUC uses rate-of-return (RoR) regulation. The RoR price equals the average cost of producing electricity, including a fair return on capital costs. However, the RoR may be higher because of the Averch–Johnson (AJ) effect and regulatory capture. The AJ effect maintains that utilities subject to RoR regulation overinvest in capital relative to labor. Regulatory capture states that the regulators favor the utility over ratepayers. The AJ effect and regulatory capture are examples of government failure. To justify regulation, one must compare imperfect alternatives, such as unregulated monopoly, imperfect regulation of natural monopoly, and restructuring to allow competition, the subject of the next chapter.

Economic efficiency entails marginal cost rather than average cost pricing. A common argument for average cost pricing is that utilities will lose money if price equals marginal cost, since MC < AC. A fixed charge or a higher price for initial units of electricity can eliminate the objection.

Time-varying marginal cost pricing is a third way to overcome this problem. Peak load pricing charges higher prices when demand approaches capacity. Critical peak pricing can be more efficient than peak load pricing by sending out a price surcharge closer to real time. Dynamic pricing is possible with the smart grid, which can provide real-time information on individual customer use of electricity.

There are additional proposals to improve economic efficiency, including payments for demand reduction and energy efficiency, decoupling revenues from sales, and incentive regulation. Each of these alternatives presents difficulties in implementation. As well, utilities need to determine customer baselines accurately or risk compensating customers for illusory load reductions and falling short on revenue projections.

Notes

1   Churchill (1947, November 11), speech, House of Commons. Please see Churchill (1974, p. 7566).
2   The Regulatory Assistance Project (2011) provides an excellent overview.
3   In 1878, Sir Joseph Swan invented and patented a competing light bulb. Initially, each sued the other for patent infringements before joining forces to start the Ediswan Company.
4   North and Miller (1980, pp. 4–6) are skeptical of the view that whales would have been hunted into extinction for their oil had petroleum not been discovered.
5   We discussed this technology in Chapter 10 on next-generation technologies. Battery storage at customer-level and utility scale will fundamentally alter the production of electricity whether in regulated or restructured markets.
6   The standard may be determined by convention, such as LOLP of one day in ten years, or by economic efficiency. Economic efficiency compares the marginal benefit of avoided power outages to the marginal cost of additional capacity.
7   Statistics are from the U.S. DOE (2011), and Center for Climate and Energy Solutions (n.d.).
8   Lien and Liu (1996), Golec (1990), and Kaserman and Tepel (1982) investigated the effects of the fuel adjustment clause on the utility's cost of energy, as well as proposing reforms such as allowing utilities to hedge fuel costs without commission approval, while at the same time eliminating the automatic fuel cost adjustments.
9   Another approach is the Ramsey rule. Ramsey (1927) maximizes social welfare subject to a breakeven constraint, and shows that price should be marked up over marginal cost according to the inverse of elasticity.

10 Note that if one generating plant had lower capacity and lower operating costs than a second unit, it would never be economical to run the second plant.

11 When there is demand or supply uncertainty and little or no storage, it is no longer optimal to have zero excess capacity. Insufficient capacity could result in shortages and the need to ration electricity.

12 Chao (2012) has a proposal for a baseline that gives the incentive to reveal demand accurately. Mohajeryami, Doostan, Asadinejad, and Schwarz (2016) examine the potential revenue losses to a utility that employs the most common baseline calculation methods.

13 But 1 MWh compared to what? If the utility has to establish a baseline, we are back to the problem of the customer having an incentive to inflate the baseline.

References

Averch, H., & Johnson, L. (1962). Behavior of the firm under regulatory constraint. *The American Economic Review, 52,* 1052–1069.

Bloomberg. (2016, January 19). China's slowing power consumption highlights clean energy gains. *Bloomberg News.* Retrieved November 14, 2016 from http://www.bloomberg.com/news/articles/2016–01–19/china-s-slowing-power-consumption-highlights-clean-energy-gains

Boiteux, M. (1960). Peak load pricing. *The Journal of Business, 33,* 157–179.

Boiteux, M., Clemens, E., & Clemens, L. (1964). The green tariff of the Electricité de France. *Land Economics, 40,* 185–197.

Center for Climate and Energy Solutions. (n.d.). *Electricity Overview.* Retrieved November 14, 2016 from http://www.c2es.org/technology/overview/electricity

Chao, H. (2011). Demand response in wholesale electricity markets: The choice of consumer baseline. *Journal of Regulatory Economics, 39,* 68–88.

Chao, H. (2012). Competitive electricity markets with consumer subscription service in a smart grid. *Journal of Regulatory Economics, 41,* 155–180.

Churchill, W. S. (1974). *Winston S. Churchill, his complete speeches, 1897–1963,* vol. 7: *1943–1949,* R. R. James (ed.). New York/London: Chelsea House Publishers.

Eurostat. (2016). *Statistics explained.* Retrieved November 15, 2016 from http://ec.europa.eu/eurostat/statistics-explained/index.php/File:EU–28_Evolution_of_electricity_supplied_(in_GWh),_2000–2015_annual_data;_2008–2015_monthly_cumulated_data_update.png

Golec, J. (1990). The financial effects of fuel adjustment clauses on electric utilities. *Journal of Business, 63,* 165–186.

International Energy Agency. (2005). China, People's Republic of: Electricity and heat for 2005. Retrieved November 28, 2016 from https://www.iea.org/statistics/statisticssearch/report/?country=China&product=electricityandheat&year=2005

Kaserman, D. L., & Tepel, R. C. (1982). The impact of the automatic adjustment clause on fuel purchase and utilization practices in the U.S. electric utility industry. *Southern Economic Journal, 48,* 687–700.

King, G. (2011, October 11). *Edison vs. Westinghouse: A shocking rivalry.* Retrieved November 29, 2016 from http://www.smithsonianmag.com/history/edison-vs-westinghouse-a-shocking-rivalry–102146036/?no-ist

Lien, D., & Liu, L. (1996). Futures trading and fuel adjustment clauses. *Journal of Regulatory Economics, 9,* 157–178.

Mohajeryami, S., Doostan, M., Asadinejad, A., & Schwarz, P. M. (2016). Error analysis of customer baseline load (CBL) calculation methods for residential customers. *IEEE Transactions on Industry Applications, 53* (99), 5–14.

Nadel, S. (2014, February 25). U.S. electricity use is declining and energy efficiency may be a significant factor. [Web log comment]. Retrieved November 14, 2016 from http://aceee.org/blog/2014/02/us-electricity-use-declining-and-ener

North, D., & Miller, R. (1980). *The economics of public issues.* New York: Harper and Row.

Ramsey, F. P. (1927). A contribution to the theory of taxation. *The Economic Journal, 37,* 47–61.

Regulatory Assistance Project. (2011). *Electricity regulation in the U.S.: A guide.* Montpelier, Vermont: The Regulatory Assistance Project.

Stigler, G. J. (1971). The theory of economic regulation. *The Bell Journal of Economics and Management Science, 2,* 3–21.

Stigler, G. J., & Friedland, C. (1962). What can regulators regulate? The case of electricity. *Journal of Law and Economics, 5,* 1–16.

U.S. Department of Energy. (2011). *Buildings energy data book.* Retrieved November 14, 2016 from http://buildingsdatabook.eren.doe.gov/

U.S. Energy Information Administration. (2016a). *Manufacturing energy consumption survey.* Retrieved November 13, 2016 from http://www.eia.gov/consumption/manufacturing/

U.S. Energy Information Administration. (2016b). *Electric power monthly: With data for September 2016.* Retrieved November 13, 2016 from https://www.eia.gov/electricity/monthly/pdf/epm. pdf

U.S. Energy Information Administration. (2016c). *Electric power monthly.* Retrieved November 14, 2016 from https://www.eia.gov/electricity/monthly/epm_table_grapher.cfm?t=epmt_5_1

U.S. Energy Information Administration. (2016d). What is U.S. electricity generation by energy source? Retrieved November 16, 2016 from https://www.eia.gov/tools/faqs/faq.cfm?id=427&t=3

Williamson, O. (1964). *The economics of discretionary behavior: Managerial objectives in a theory of the firm.* Englewood Cliffs, NJ: Prentice Hall.

Zhong, R., & Chaturvedi, S. (2014, June 11). Scorching heat exposes India's power woes. *The Wall Street Journal.* Retrieved November 13, 2016 from http://online.wsj.com/articles/scorching-heat-exposes-indias-power-woes 1402491922

Chapter 13

Electricity restructuring and deregulation

The path forward?

"The verdict is in: California's experiment with electricity deregulation is not just a mess; it's a certifiable failure, according to everyone from the state governor to the very utilities that initially backed the scheme."

Charles Feldman (2001)

"As Thomas Edison said in an earlier quote in this text, there is no such thing as a failure, as California showed us what did not work. We have learned from their mistakes."

The author of this text

Introduction

Chapter 12 examined traditional regulation and attempts to make it more efficient. In this chapter, we consider the possibility that the best remedy is *deregulation*, or at least *restructuring* to introduce competition in the electricity industry. Electricity presents unique challenges, such as the need to balance supply and demand at each instant, the inability of the electricity dispatcher to control electricity's path through the transmission lines, and the complexity of integrating the grid to handle intermittent fuels such as wind and solar. We will find that it is more correct to speak of restructuring than deregulation, as the industry has introduced new forms of regulation such as independent system operators and regional transmission organizations to make sure that electricity is available when you flip the switch.

We will examine representative experiences in deregulation and restructuring, beginning with the transformation of the UK electricity industry from a government-owned to a privatized system, and efforts in the United States by California to force incumbent utilities to *divest*—sell off—generating assets and buy their generation through a power exchange supplied by independent power producers and possibly other states. California in particular shows what can go wrong with the transformation, so we look at ongoing efforts by PJM in the northeastern United States and the Electric Reliability Council of Texas (ERCOT) in Texas that have proved viable. (PJM—the letters stand for Pennsylvania, New Jersey, and Maryland, the original states that formed the organization.) It is still an open question as to whether deregulation and restructuring have delivered their promise of lower costs, lower prices, and greater economic efficiency.

The next section provides a brief economic history of the move to deregulate and restructure the electricity industry. After that, we introduce reasons for restructuring.

We then examine the UK and California approaches. In the penultimate section, we examine the ongoing PJM wholesale market in the northeastern United States and restructuring in Texas under the auspices of ERCOT. The final section is a summary.

A brief economic history of electricity deregulation and restructuring

The modern movement towards introducing competition to the electricity industry had roots in the early 1980s with the election of conservative governments in the United States and the UK. Ronald Reagan and Margaret Thatcher championed markets and sought a less interventionist role for government. A number of other industries underwent deregulation in the United States, beginning even before the election of former President Reagan, including banking, airlines, and trucking. Industries formerly regarded as natural monopolies underwent deregulation in the 1980s, including telecommunications and natural gas. Market advocates cited successful deregulation in those industries, particularly natural gas, to push for changes in electricity.

The electricity industry had in fact started its history as largely unregulated and competitive. As described in Chapter 12, Edison and Westinghouse battled with each other with their rival direct current (DC) and alternating current (AC) transmission systems. Individual generating plants initially produced small amounts of power, compared to the overall market, so there was room for more than one producer. The New York City area had more than 30 electric companies as of the year 1900 and Chicago more than 45 (Isser, 2015).

Consolidation began to take place as generators became larger and companies recognized the potential for higher profits through monopolization. By the 1930s, after consumer outcry over high prices, the Federal Power Commission (FPC), originally established to coordinate federal hydroelectric projects, expanded its mission to regulate interstate commerce in electricity and natural gas. States established public utilities commissions (PUCs) to supervise in-state practices. State and federal laws initiated the longstanding model of treating electric utilities as natural monopolies subject to regulation, allowing a single vertically integrated firm providing generation, transmission, and distribution, to serve the local electricity market.

As has been discussed throughout this text, the 1970s gave birth to the modern study of energy economics with the doubling of oil prices in 1973, and a second oil price shock in 1979. At that time, oil was widely used to generate electricity and so the price of electricity rose steeply during that decade. The Public Utilities Regulatory Policy Act (PURPA) of 1978 introduced changes to alleviate the crisis in the electricity industry. It required electric utilities to purchase alternatives such as wind and solar energy at *avoided cost*, what it would have cost utilities to add generating capacity. The goal was to conserve existing fossil fuels. If a secondary goal was to reduce electricity prices, it had the opposite effect, as even at the high cost of oil and natural gas in the late 1970s, alternative fuels were still more expensive. However, the law had a historic tertiary effect, which was to show the feasibility of non–utility generation. The Act also created the *Federal Energy Regulatory Commission* (FERC) to supplant the FPC and to oversee new and more competitive institutions arising in both natural gas and electricity.

Electricity in 1980 was much as it had been 50 years earlier. A single utility controlled a given region with vertically integrated generation, transmission, and distribution.

Regulators based price on the average cost of supplying the integrated service. The service worked, but the utility had little incentive to innovate. Instead, its main incentive was to expand capacity to keep up with demand. Advocates for deregulation envisioned challengers to the entrenched monopoly and incentives for innovation to reduce cost and address consumer wants.

PURPA had shown the feasibility of competitive generation in renewable energy, primarily solar. The 1980s brought innovations in smaller-scale natural gas generation. Natural gas industry deregulation had demonstrated the potential to separate ownership of generation from that of transmission, a model which regulators could potentially apply to electricity. Another way to introduce electricity competition was to force utilities to divest generation assets to independent power producers. A third alteration of the electricity supply chain was to allow independent marketers to sell electricity to final customers.

Marketers could offer choices beyond shopping around for the lowest price. Consumers might be willing to pay more for green power produced from nonpolluting renewables. They might opt for *interruptible rates*—giving the utility the right to interrupt service—or *load control*—allowing the utility to centrally control appliances to reduce demand at times of tight capacity—in return for a lower electricity bill. Utilities might reimagine their mission as sellers of customer services rather than simply an electric commodity. They could compete in the sale of energy-using or energy-saving technology. Consumers might become *prosumers*, selling power to the electric utility when we have more than we need from our solar panels, wind turbines, and electric vehicles. Batteries could allow customers and utilities to store excess electricity until there is demand for it. Unless . . . say the advocates, we keep our 1930s-style regulation.

Opponents caution that regulation has served us well, providing low-cost, highly reliable, and equitable service. There is nearly universal access to the electric grid, with subsidies as needed to make sure almost everyone can access this necessity of life. Electricity may be more essential and more complicated than other industries that have deregulated successfully.

Restructuring

Originally, advocates of a transformed electric system proposed deregulation. They pointed to successes in deregulated airlines, banking, trucking, telecommunications, and natural gas. These industries demonstrated both static and dynamic efficiency gains, with lower costs and prices in the short run, and even larger dynamic gains from new entrants, technological advances, and innovative products.

The United States and the UK helped lead the way in electricity reform. The United States passed the Energy Policy Act (EPAct) in 1992 to build upon PURPA. While the EPAct was not limited to electricity, it played a major role in encouraging competition in the electricity industry, allowing *independent power producers* (IPPs)—nonutility generators (NUGs) who could sell to utilities—beyond the first wave of renewables producers whose existence depended upon PURPA requirements that utilities buy their product. In addition, existing electricity utilities could sell to other utilities as well as to emerging wholesale power markets. The wholesale markets bought and sold power, introducing auction mechanisms to identify the lowest-cost suppliers and customers with the greatest willingness to pay.

Prior to the passage of the 1992 EPAct, vertically integrated investor-owned utilities (IOUs) dominated U.S. electricity production. Individual states could choose to pursue electricity reform subject to the supervision of FERC. In the UK, the government owned utility assets. The UK broke up its *Central Electricity Generating Board* (CEGB)—created in the late 1950s to plan the electricity system centrally—into three regional generating companies, two of them privatized fossil fuel generators and one public company that operated nuclear plants, and a public national transmission company.

Deregulation movements in both countries sought to transform the industry to a privatized, competitive market by the year 2000. Other countries pursuing deregulation and restructuring have chosen paths based on the British and American models, transforming a public system into a privatized one or restructuring investor-owned regulated monopolies into competitive firms in those facets of the industry where competition is viable.

The original intent was to deregulate electricity markets, much as had taken place in the natural gas industry. Just as natural gas production was now fully competitive, with no price controls at the wellhead, electricity generation would follow suit as long as there was room for multiple generators to meet market demand. Transmission and distribution lines, or "wires," still had economies of scale sufficient to maintain natural monopolies at those stages. However, as with natural gas, transmission would now offer open access, with a requirement to allow nondiscriminatory transport to both utility and nonutility generators. In addition, there could be competition at the retail stage of the supply chain, with marketers shopping around for the lowest-cost suppliers. Marketers could also offer consumers differentiated products, such as green power using renewable sources, time-differentiated prices, or load control.

Over time, the term "electricity restructuring" has replaced deregulation, as it has not been possible to eliminate government intervention. Instead, the government has formed new entities, such as *independent system operators* (ISOs) and *regional transmission organizations* (RTOs) to help facilitate competitive bidding among generators and high reliability in transmitting power. With the growing prominence of distributed generation, *distribution system operators* (DSOs) coordinate independent generation from wind, solar, and other localized generation, such as electric vehicles, with the centralized grid.

Electricity has three stages of production—generation, transmission, and distribution—and a fourth, if we separate the merchant stage. Transmission and distribution remain natural monopolies; we only want one set of transmission and distribution connections. Most of the attention is on generation, where independent power producers share the market with large electric utilities.

After PURPA led to the first generation of independent producers of renewable energy, new natural gas technologies provided the breakthrough for further small-scale generation. Small-scale natural gas units resemble jet engines. Rather than needing to be located at a centralized location, the smaller units allow *distributed generation* (DG)—where the units can locate closer to customers—reducing transmission distances and line losses, the fraction of electricity lost during transmission. The combined-cycle gas turbine (CCGT) is the most common type of natural gas unit, with smaller-scale units that can operate away from the central utility, or larger units for utility-scale operations. Increasingly, customers use wind and solar units for distributed generation.

The retailing function can also be economical at a relatively small scale. Texas, which is at the forefront of electricity restructuring among U.S. states, has the largest role for electricity sold through marketers, requiring its residential customers to shop around for the best electricity price.

Challenges for electricity deregulation

Electricity markets present challenges beyond those of other deregulated markets. One challenge is that electricity transmission depends on the laws of physics. The dispatcher generating electricity at one point, or *node*, cannot control its path if there is more than one transmission circuit, or branch. There is no simple way to identify the supplier of a given electron to a given buyer. Kirchhoff's laws dictate how current and power flow. The voltage law states that electricity will travel along the different branches depending on impedance (resistance), with more of the electricity taking the path of least resistance. Furthermore, a branch may have limited capacity, so electricity will need to take a different path if one branch is at capacity. Example 13.1 demonstrates these physical realities.

Example 13.1

Consider the following simple transmission network, with three nodes A, B, and C, two generators, one at A and the other at B, and one customer at C. Customer C has a demand of 5 MW. Both generators are capable of supplying 5 MW. Generator (Gen) A has a constant MC = $30/MW, Gen B has a constant MC = $40/MW. Initially, assume capacity on each line is unconstrained. Find the equilibrium price. Then suppose line AC is limited to 3 MW. Find the equilibrium price.[1]

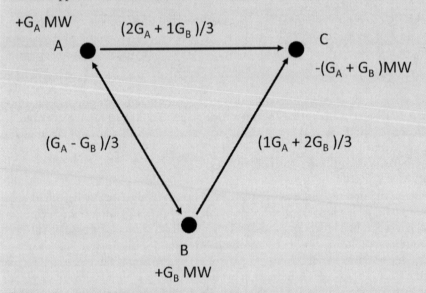

Figure 13.1 Electricity price allowing for Kirchhoff's voltage law.

Solution

Some of the electricity from Gen A will follow the direct path (AC) and some the indirect path (AB, BC). Assuming all paths have the same impedance (resistance) and are of equal length, there is twice as much resistance on the indirect path.[2] Therefore, if Gen A produces 1 MW, 2/3 goes directly (A to C) and 1/3 indirectly (A to B to C). Similarly, when Gen B produces 1 MW, 2/3 goes directly (B to C) and 1/3 indirectly (B to A to C). On line AB, the two currents from the generators are equal but flow in opposite directions, so on balance there is no net power on this line. In a competitive market and with unconstrained line capacity, Gen A will bid \$30 to supply power while Gen B will bid \$40. Gen A will be the lowest bidder and will supply all 5 MW at a price of \$30.

In the constrained case:

$$G_A + G_B = 5 \text{ but } (2 G_A + G_B)/3 \leq 3.$$

Solving for G_A and G_B using the two equations and assuming the constraint is binding,

$$\frac{[(2G_A + (5 - G_A)]}{3} = 3$$

$$G_A + 5 = 9$$

G_A cannot exceed 4 and G_B cannot be less than 1 is the least-cost solution. Once line AC is at capacity at MW = 3, Gen B will need to contribute to meet C's demand for 5 MW. For each additional MW at point C, Gen B will need to produce 2 MW more, and Gen A will need to produce 1 MW less because: $(2/3)*2 + 1/3 (-1) = 1$ is the lowest-cost solution since any increase in Gen A would overload line AC. Price at C will be $2*\$40 - 1*\$30 = \$50$, even though price is \$30 at node A and \$40 at node B. This type of *nodal pricing* is also known as *locational marginal pricing* (LMP).

In addition, producers may recognize market power opportunities. Gen B may recognize that it is the marginal unit and may bid higher than \$40/MW. Gen A may recognize that it now receives more than \$30/MW, and so may not expand transmission capacity on line AC even if it is efficient to do so.

Other complicating factors for deregulating electricity include the need to meet electricity demand at each instant, unless economical storage is possible. If supply is insufficient to meet demand, the system can suffer catastrophic failures such as the massive blackout that occurred in 2003 throughout the northeastern and Midwestern U.S. states and into Ontario, Canada.

Demand also varies continuously. As Example 13.1 suggests, deregulated prices will be volatile. Furthermore, it is challenging to price electricity to recoup the cost of peak generating units, since demand may only require their use for a few hours every year.

The FERC expanded its regulatory responsibilities to guard against the exercise of market power by firms in the electricity market, as well as to create new entities to make sure the industry operates efficiently. The 1992 Energy Policies Act gave FERC *wheeling* authority, allowing one utility to transfer electricity through transmission and distribution lines to another utility. FERC recommended the creation of ISOs and RTOs to supervise the transformed markets. ISOs and RTOs have the responsibility of matching demand and supply, necessitating day-ahead, hour-ahead, and real-time prices. Originally, ISOs supervised individual states while RTOs spanned more than one state, but as ISOs could grow over time to encompass more than one state, it is common to refer to an ISO/RTO. Some regions, such as the southeastern United States, chose to remain without ISOs or RTOs on the premise that they would be better off—for example, having lower electricity prices—without forming a competitive wholesale market to provide electricity to individual utilities.

Figure 13.2 shows the locations that have established these entities.

There are seven ISO/RTO organizations in the United States. California, New York, and Texas have within-state organizations, while New England, northeast states, Midwest states, and southwest states have regional organizations. Later in this chapter, we will focus on PJM, the regional transmission organization that operates

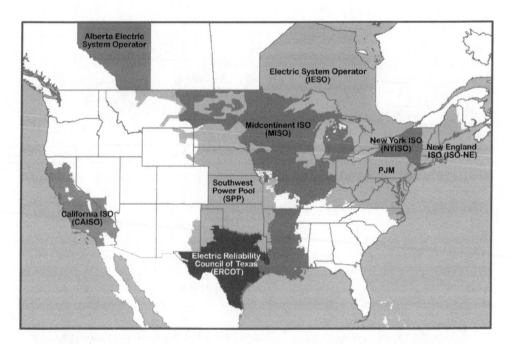

Figure 13.2 Locations of U.S. ISOs and RTOs. Reprinted from *Regional Transmission Organization (RTO)/Independent System Operators (ISO)*, by FERC (2016a).

an electricity wholesale market for a group of northeastern states and ERCOT, the organization that oversees most of Texas.

These organizations have to reconcile the complexities of electricity production. In addition to accounting for the electricity dispatcher's inability to control the transmission path that generated electricity will take, they must provide *ancillary services*, operations beyond generation and transmission that maintain grid stability. For example, electric utilities need to maintain reserves to assure they will meet demand. *Spinning reserves* are generators that run even when they are not generating power, in case they need to *ramp up*—bring up generating resources—on short notice. These reserves are even more important as utilities increase their use of renewable resources such as wind and solar, which do not provide continuous power and are not under the control of the grid operator.

Transactions costs

Restructured markets typically separate ownership of generation (G) and transmission (T). The role of transmission has changed from marketing electricity to providing transportation. If G and T coordinated their operations, as is the case with vertical integration, generators might not have the correct incentives regarding transmission capacity. They could choose to limit capacity to increase the price of electricity, as was shown in Example 13.1.

While a simple textbook perspective suggests gains to separating transmission from generation, Oliver Williamson (2002) delineated *transactions cost economics*—cost considerations when comparing transactions that take place within the firm to the costs of contracting outside the firm—and suggests caution before concluding that the two functions should be separate. The two stages are subject to a *holdup problem*. Holdup can occur with firm-specific assets. Generation has little value without transmission and transmission has little value without generation. A generator that cannot transmit its electricity will be at a disadvantage, and a transmission line can take advantage of this situation and charge an above-competitive price to the generator. Similarly, there is little value to owning transmission if there are no generators willing to use it. In that case, the holdup problem is that generators can offer less than the competitive price to owners of transmission if generators can choose among alternative transmission lines.

Both sides are aware of these potential problems, and will have a reason to sign a long-term contract to prevent holdup. Both sides have an incentive to make sure the other party will use their services over a long period to justify the initial investment in G or T. However, contracting is not free. So the relevant comparison between integrating and separating G and T is the possibility that under integration, too little transmission will be built while under separation, firms may be hesitant to build G or T in the first place unless they can arrange a long-term contract and are willing to bear the associated transactions costs from contracting.

Some empirical studies show vertical integration can be more efficient. Mansur (2007) finds that vertical integration both mitigates market power—wholesale prices are lower—and limits its distributional impacts—retail consumers pay lower prices—in the PJM market. The integrated firm sells to the wholesale electricity market, but also buys from it. In turn, it sells to the retail market where it is subject to price regulation.

Thus, it has less of an incentive to use market power to raise price in the wholesale market than a firm that does not sell in the retail market. In essence, if it raises price in the wholesale market, it ends up having to buy wholesale electricity at a higher price and cannot recoup the difference from retail customers. Mansur suggests that requiring utilities to divest their generating assets, as was done in California, may lead to greater market power in the wholesale market. Bushnell et al. (2008) also find that vertical integration reduces wholesale prices.

Two paths to restructuring

The UK

The UK electricity industry was publicly owned beginning with its nationalization in 1947. In England and Wales, the CEGB generated and transmitted electricity to 12 area boards that in turn distributed electricity and supplied it to customers. The price was set according to a bulk supply tariff based on the CEGB's marginal cost.[3]

The British Electricity Act of 1989 set in motion plans to deregulate the electricity industry to take effect on March 31, 1990, with the focus on England and Wales. The CEGB was split up into four entities. National Power plc and Powergen plc were private fossil-fuel-generating companies created to compete with each other and eventual new entrants.[4] The UK transferred nuclear facilities to Nuclear Electric, which remained a public company. The fourth company, the National Grid Company (NGC or "The Grid"), owned and operated the high-voltage transmission system, separating generation from transmission. They also created a wholesale market—the Electricity Pool—in which generators offered to supply electricity, and customers larger than 1 MW offered to buy. The NGC was responsible for balancing generation and demand, akin to an ISO. The UK transformed the area boards into 12 regional electric companies (RECs) with a monopoly over distribution in their region. The UK sought a more dynamic industry, with RECs replacing less innovative public bureaucracies, resulting in lower generating costs and lower prices as well as more service options. RECs could invest in generation in the hope of creating more competition, as it would take some time before independent power producers would enter the market. The Office of Electricity Regulation (OFFER or Ofgem, after the merger of gas (Ofgas) and electricity markets (OFFER) in 1999) monitored prices. Economist Stephen Littlechild headed the regulatory office.

ISOs supervise two types of wholesale markets, pools and bilateral trades. The UK model created a pool, where generators bid how much they are willing to supply at a particular price. The NGC arranges the bids from lowest to highest to create a supply curve. To determine demand, the NGC also receives willingness to pay from the RECs. Demand and supply determine price on a day-ahead basis in 30-minute blocks, with additional markets to handle differences between day-ahead and real time. End-use customers, typically relatively large industrial customers, can also buy directly from the wholesale market. Smaller customers can choose among entities selling electricity, with customers who do not wish to choose staying with a default supplier.

Figure 13.3 shows the determination of price in a day-ahead power pool. Market price is at the intersection of demand and supply, with all producers receiving the

$/MWh

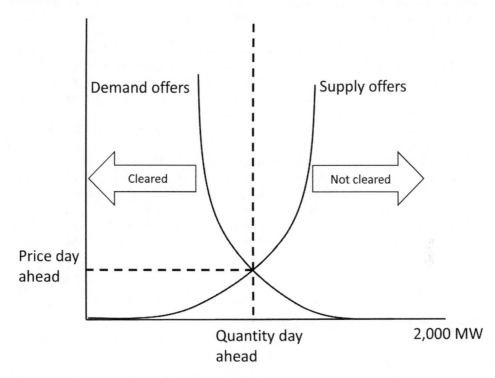

Figure 13.3 Determination of price in a power pool.

marginal price. Infra-marginal producers earn rents, which cover capacity costs. Solar and wind producers, for example, have zero marginal fuel costs, but substantial capacity costs. The marginal producer only covers short-run marginal cost.

To a lesser extent, the UK also makes use of bilateral trade. In these markets, a single buyer coordinates with a single seller. They agree on a price that applies only to that particular trade. Other buyers and sellers negotiate their own price. The ISO has a more limited role in that case, since there is no need to determine price. The ISO still has to make sure that the electricity system can meet demand. There must be sufficient transmission and distribution lines to transport generated power to the final customer.

Buyers and sellers can also arrange long-term contracts to reduce the risk of spot prices. We will shortly discuss a financial instrument that emerged in the UK known as *contracts for differences* (CFDs), which effectively allowed parties to agree on price in advance even though they exchanged electricity at the spot market price.

In order to make sure there is not excessive demand on transmission or distribution systems, markets can develop for transmission and distribution pricing. One approach is a market for transmission rights, to determine who receives transmission when demand exceeds available capacity. The UK also introduced retail competition, so that customers could choose their supplier. The UK continues to regulate distribution, but with incentive regulation as discussed in Chapter 12. Prices increase at the rate of inflation minus an expected productivity gain.

Green and Newbery (1992) analyzed the initial years of the UK restructuring, and questioned the gains from creating what was effectively only two firms, a *duopoly*. National Power plc and Powergen plc were the only private generating firms that could compete. Nuclear Electric plc remained in the public sector, and nuclear energy is baseload energy that typically operates at a constant level at all times regardless of wholesale price. It would take several years before IPPs entered the market and increased the number of competitors.

Several models predict duopoly behavior, which is the simplest type of oligopoly. In *oligopoly*, there are only a few firms in the industry. Oligopoly has few enough firms that they are interdependent, with each firm taking into account the decisions of other firms in the industry in making its own decisions.

One way to characterize the interdependence is to specify a reaction function, as in the Cournot duopoly model.[5] Firm 1 bases its output decision on its price, as well as what it expects firm 2 to supply:

$$Q_1 = f(P_1, Q_2)$$

Similarly, the reaction function of firm 2 is

$$Q_2 = f(P_2, Q_1)$$

In equilibrium, each firm will charge the same price. In the simplest case, where the firms have identical marginal costs, they will also produce equal quantities. Figures 13.4a and b show the Cournot duopoly model.

Figure 13.4a shows market demand D_0 and firm 1's initial derived demand D_1, based on the assumption that firm 2 will produce the monopoly output Q_0 and charge the monopoly price P_0. Based on this assumption, firm 1 maximizes profit at Q_1 and P_1. In turn, firm 2 would adjust its demand, based on firm 1 producing quantity Q_1. And in turn, firm 1 will adjust its output and price until in equilibrium, both firms will produce an equal output and charge the same price, given that we have assumed they have identical marginal cost.[6]

Figure 13.4b shows reaction functions for two firms, and the determination of equilibrium in the Cournot model. The horizontal intercept on firm 1's reaction function is firm 1's output corresponding to the assumption that firm 2 is producing monopoly output. Moving up along firm 1's reaction function, each point corresponds to a smaller output for firm 2; the vertical intercept corresponds to firm 2 producing no output and firm 1 producing monopoly output.

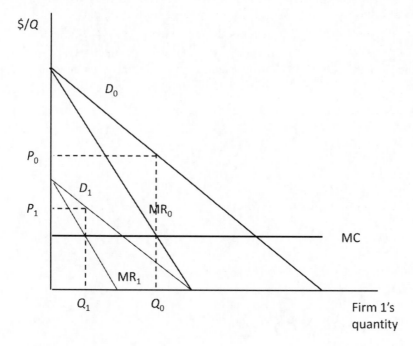

Figure 13.4a Firm 1's derived demand in the Cournot model.

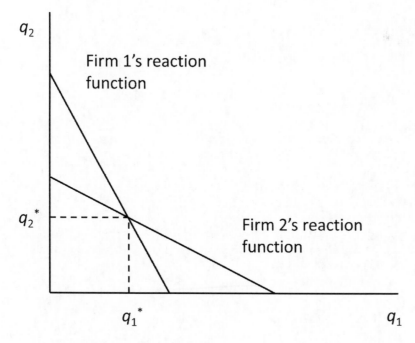

Figure 13.4b Cournot reaction functions.

Example 13.2

Market demand is $P = 120 - Q$, where P is price per MWh and Q is quantity of MWh. National Power and Powergen are the only firms supplying electricity to the RECs, and behave according to Cournot assumptions. They each have constant marginal costs of \$20/MWh. Find each firm's equilibrium price and quantity.

Solution

To find firm 1's reaction function:

$$P_1 = 120 - Q_1 - Q_2$$

$$MR_1 = 120 - 2Q_1 - Q_2$$

Setting $MR_1 = MC$:

$$120 - 2Q_1 - Q_2 = 20$$

Firm 1's reaction function is

$$Q_1 = 50 - \frac{Q_2}{2}$$

For firm 2:

$$120 - 2Q_2 - Q_1 = 20$$

Firm 2's reaction function is

$$Q_2 = 50 - \frac{Q_1}{2}$$

Since $Q_1 = Q_2$,

$$Q_1 = 50 - \frac{Q_1}{2}$$

Solving,

$$1.5 \times Q_1 = 50.$$

$$Q_1 = 33.3$$

Since $Q_1 = Q_2$,

$$Q_2 = 33.3$$

Substituting into demand:

$$P_1 = 120 - Q_1 - 33.3$$

$$P_1 = 120 - 33.33 - 33.33$$

$$P_1 = \$53.33$$

Analogously,

$$P_2 = \$53.33$$

At equilibrium:

$$Q_1 = Q_2 = 33.33 \, MWh$$

$$P_1 = P_2 = \$53.33/MWh^7$$

Bertrand formulated an alternative duopoly model, where each firm sets a price, reacting to the price set by the other firm. This assumption leads to each firm selling at a price equal to its MC, an outcome closer to the competitive outcome than the Cournot equilibrium prices. A reader who has lived through price setting by gas stations on opposite corners has probably witnessed Bertrand behavior, where prices are competitive, but has also witnessed cases where prices at that intersection are higher than at other gas stations, where Cournot might give more accurate predictions. There is no obvious way to know when duopolists will behave according to Cournot predictions or Bertrand predictions. Firms are better off in the Cournot equilibrium, as price is above the competitive level. If there are only two firms, the Cournot outcome appears more likely, as we would expect that it takes more than two firms to get a competitive outcome, as demonstrated by the outcomes in the UK when there were only two generating firms.

The problem with many oligopoly models including the Cournot and Bertrand duopoly models is that the underlying assumptions about firm behavior do not stem from profit maximization. For example, the Cournot assumption that firms choose their profit-maximizing quantity based on the residual demand once the rival firm has chosen its quantity is arbitrary.

In Chapter 5 on oil, we examined the cartel and dominant firm price leadership models. In the cartel model, firms try to mimic monopoly. In the dominant firm model, the largest firm derives its demand by subtracting supply of the competitive fringe firms from market demand and then maximizing profit. We could also apply these models to the electricity market. However, there is no underlying rationale derived from profit-maximizing behavior to indicate when firms will collude, when small firms will follow the largest firm, or when the Cournot or Bertrand model will best predict the outcome. In the absence of theoretical underpinnings, we will need to see which model predicts most accurately by using data to compare the model predictions.[8]

Game theory is an alternative approach to modeling strategic behavior. Games may be cooperative or noncooperative, static one-period games or dynamic multiperiod games, simple strategies, where a player always chooses the same strategy, or mixed strategies, where a player may use different strategies in different periods. Here we consider only one-period games with simple strategies.

The underlying rule is that each player attempts to choose a best strategy, based upon the other player's strategy. In most simple games, a player chooses the outcome that is best without regard to the other firm's profit. For example, if strategy A gives firm 1 a profit of $100 and firm 2 a profit of $50, and strategy B gives firm 1 a profit of $90 and firm 2 a loss of $20, firm 1 would choose strategy A; firm 1 does not consider the greater harm to firm 2.

Example 13.3

National Power and Powergen are each deciding independently whether to charge a high price or a low price to the RECs. The table shows the respective (National Power\Powergen) profit payoffs (in $) depending on the price strategies.

National Power\Powergen	High price	Low price
High price	100\80	60\100
Low price	150\50	70\70

What price will each company charge? Moreover, what will be the corresponding profits?

Solution

Consider National Power's (NP) decision. If NP think Powergen (PG) will charge a high price, what is NP's best strategy? NP will submit a low price in order to earn $150 rather than $100. If NP thinks PG will charge a low price, NP will also charge a low price, as $70 in profit is better than $60. In this example, NP has a *dominant strategy*—the same strategy regardless of what the other player does—which is to charge a low price.

As for PG, if it thinks NP will charge a high price, it is better off with a low price. If it expects NP to price low, it will do the same. PG also has a dominant strategy of a low price. The game's outcome will be that both generators will charge a low price and each will earn a profit of $70.

This outcome turns out to be a Nash equilibrium. A *Nash equilibrium* is a stable outcome, such that neither player would choose to change strategies once each player knows the other player's strategy. The Cournot equilibrium shown earlier is also a Nash equilibrium.

Notice that had they stuck to a high-priced agreement, they would have each done better. Such a game is a *prisoner's dilemma*, a game in which the Nash equilibrium does not lead to the best outcome for the players. To avoid the prisoner's dilemma, the two players could find a way to convert a noncooperative game into a cooperative game. If they know they will play this game repeatedly, the payoff for preventing the prisoner's dilemma is greater. They may be able to build up trust that if they agree to a high price, they will stick to the agreement.[9] If they cannot cooperate, they may have to resort to threats of retaliation if a firm violates the agreement. In order for a threat to work, it must be credible; that is, the potential violator believes that the other player will be better off if it carries out the threat than if it does not.

Returning to the analysis of Green and Newbery for the restructuring of the UK electricity market, they find that Cournot quantity setting best fits the data, with the two generating firms setting equilibrium price above MC. The authors concluded that two generating companies were not enough to lead to vigorous competition.

Further restructuring of the UK market took place in the late 1990s. The two generating companies could buy retail providers, but in return had to divest additional generation. In addition, the government sold off shares in the companies it had retained. U.S. as well as EU companies bought generating assets. Distribution companies had to separate distribution from retail sales, although they could continue to own both. This change was to prevent the RECs from using profits from their distribution monopolies to subsidize their retail activities, which could allow them to undercut other retailers and discourage retail competition. The other major change was a merger of gas and electricity markets.

New Electricity Trading Arrangements (NETA), a reform of the UK wholesale electricity market, passed in 1997, and began in 2001. OFFER took steps to prevent generators from forcing up the price by withholding electric power. Also, there were now eight generating companies, rather than two. Even so, relatively few trades actually took place at the pool price. Most trades used bilateral contracts.

Box 13.1 Staying out of the pool

Generators and RECs required to use the electricity pool may want to avoid its price volatility. In the UK market, they often got around the pool spot price by using *contracts for differences* (CFDs). The buyer and seller agree in advance on a price at which they will exchange electricity. If the future spot price differs from the agreed-to price, they exchange electricity at the spot price, but then one company makes an offsetting payment to the other firm so that the net effect is that the buyer and seller exchange electricity at the price they agreed to in advance.

Consider the following hypothetical example. On January 1, 1994, National Power agrees to deliver 100 MWh of electricity to London Electricity on April 1, 1994 at 14:00 hours (2 p.m.) at a price of $80/MWh, or $8,000 for 100 MWh. On April 1 at 14:00 hours, the actual spot price is $100/MWh. London Electricity pays $10,000 to National Power for 100 MWh. National Power makes a side-payment to London Electricity of

$20/MWh, or $2,000 in all, so that the effective price is $8/MWh. London Electricity wins from the CFD, while National Power loses.

So why would National Power agree to such a contract? Neither side knew what the future spot price would be. Had it been $6/MWh on April 1 at 14:00 hours, London Electricity would have written a $2,000 check to National Power. Both sides found it advantageous to agree in advance on the future hourly electricity price, and not risk a big loss. At the same time, each side sacrificed the possible savings from a favorable move in the electricity price.

The UK showed that electricity restructuring was possible. However, the experience did not paint a clear picture of the net benefits of doing so. A cost–benefit study performed by Domah and Pollitt (2001) found net benefits, such as higher labor productivity in nuclear plants, but that most of the benefits went to the producers. Government gained from sales proceeds and net taxes. Towards the end of their study, they found consumers beginning to gain from lower prices.

California

Under traditional rate-of-return regulation, California had some of the highest electric prices in the United States. In addition, rates in the neighboring states of Oregon and Washington—states with access to large amounts of hydroelectric power—were below the U.S. average. In the late 1990s, California restructured its electricity industry, seeking to bring in lower-priced generation from IPPs and to import electricity from lower-cost neighboring states.

The restructuring required the three major investor-owned utilities—Pacific Gas and Electric, Southern California Edison, and San Diego Gas and Electric—to sell most of their natural-gas-generating assets, retaining only nuclear and hydro plants. They sold the units to *merchant* generators who could buy divested assets or build their own on a speculative basis. Each company owned between 6 and 8% of the state's capacity. Ordinarily, market shares below 20% are not high enough to trigger concerns about market power.

In addition, California did not allow the three utilities to sign new long-term contracts for electricity. The objective was to force the utilities to buy electricity on the spot market, thus introducing competition at the generating stage. In particular, California anticipated buying lower-cost electricity from neighboring states that could generate electricity more cheaply.

Furthermore, the utilities had to allow wheeling by providing open access to their transmission and distribution lines to competing generators, electricity service providers (ESPs), and wholesale marketers. Retail customers could choose an ESP, or, if they did not exercise the right to choose, receive service from their default supplier (the local distribution company (LDC)).

California Assembly Bill AB1890, passed in September 1996, created a wholesale market along with two new institutions to supervise wholesale transactions. The California approach used a novel hybrid of two separate organizations to supervise a power pool and bilateral trading. The California Power Exchange (PX) was a nonprofit organization that oversaw the pool and was in charge of the wholesale spot market, while the California Independent System Operator (CAISO) would coordinate all trades, whether from the PX or from a bilateral transaction. It would also administer transmission congestion contracts, ancillary services such as spinning reserve, and real-time balancing of supply and demand.

In order to make the transition politically palatable, the state ordered an immediate 10% reduction in rates, as well as capping retail rates to protect customers. Advocates thought that rates after deregulation would go down, so the price caps would not be binding. Restructuring also created a mechanism to allow utilities to recover stranded costs by allowing the utilities to keep the difference between the fixed retail rate and the variable wholesale rate, with the expectation that the retail rate would exceed the competitive wholesale rate.

As it turned out, the northwest United States experienced a severe drought, so that the neighboring states had no excess hydropower to export. Instead, the California utilities had to buy from independent power producers, some of which had bought generation from the three utilities. The price was high, easily 10–20 times the usual price. While some of these high prices were on peak summer days, there were also price spikes on fall and spring days when we would expect prices to be low.

Retail customers, protected from the soaring wholesale prices by price caps, increased their demand as the temperature soared on unusually hot summer days. The three utilities tried to find supplies, typically at a cost much higher than the retail rate. They introduced rolling blackouts and brownouts when they could not guarantee sufficient supplies. At the same time, they lost money on the electricity they were selling. The utilities experienced financial strain and even bankruptcy. Smaller IPPs that did not receive payment shut down, exacerbating the electricity shortages.

Borenstein (2002) and other studies found that even firms with relatively modest market shares were able to exercise market power due to unique characteristics of the electricity industry. Enron, which briefly had the highest market capitalization of any company in the United States, participated in the California wholesale market and was later found to have engaged in illegal schemes to drive up prices. For example, they encouraged suppliers to perform unnecessary maintenance to reduce available supply. El Paso Corporation, a Texas energy company, withdrew large amounts of its natural gas pipeline capacity, another factor in high California prices. Both companies engaged in phantom trades, reporting energy trades that never actually occurred, but drove up prices. In the wake of the charges of market manipulation in California, Enron eventually declared bankruptcy, taking down the venerable accounting firm of Arthur Anderson in the scandal. Some El Paso traders also received convictions and jail sentences.

Figure 13.5 shows a typical supply and demand graph for electricity. The electricity market presents special challenges. Retail demand is almost completely inelastic, since customers typically pay fixed rates that do not reflect wholesale rates. Supply is relatively flat during most production periods, but increases steeply when demand approaches capacity. During these hours, the utility operates its peak units that need to be able to ramp up quickly. Historically, these units have been natural gas generators with high fuel costs and low capital costs. However, the utility needs to recover the capital cost of these units over a relatively small number of hours.

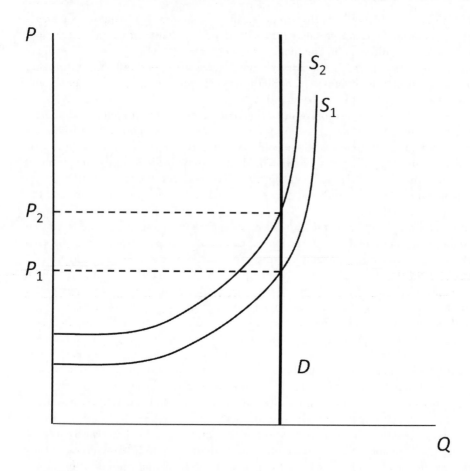

Figure 13.5 Supply and demand in the electricity market.

Since both demand and supply are inelastic during peak hours, any shift in the curves causes a large price change. A decrease in demand could cause a large decrease in price. While good news for consumers, producers could find themselves unable to cover average cost, particularly for the peaking units. All units receive the market-clearing price (P_1), which may be enough to cover infra-marginal units such as coal and nuclear baseload units, but not the marginal peak period units that set the LMP. Ordinarily an increase in demand would lead to higher prices for customers, but with prices frozen, utilities must increase production, again turning to high marginal-cost peaking units without receiving a higher price.

Who profits? Wholesale producers can profit. Infra-marginal producers can profit. They may recognize that they can profit even more if they withhold supply, as shown by S_2 in Figure 13.5. Even a small decrease in supply can lead to a large price increase, given inelastic demand. Wholesale suppliers can recognize this effect even without collusion, and even if their market share is only 5% of overall capacity. If there is collusion, then all producers can withhold supply, and we have an explanation for the extreme price spikes that occurred in California even during off-peak times.

Which oligopoly model best predicts the prices generators charged during California's attempt to deregulate its electricity industry? Puller (2007) compares competition, collusion, and Cournot, and finds Cournot provides the best fit. Using individual firm data, he concludes that the high prices were due to high cost and inelastic demand rather than collusion. Nevertheless, we have already referred to Borenstein (2002) and other studies that showed that even firms with small market shares can exercise market power even if they do not collude.

Other examples of electricity deregulation and restructuring

While the failure in California slowed the momentum of electricity deregulation and restructuring, particularly at the retail level, a number of states and regions in the United States have forged ahead, especially at the wholesale level.

Figure 13.6 shows states with active or suspended electricity restructuring as of 2010, the most recent map posted by the U.S. Energy Information Administration (EIA). As of 2014, the EIA reported that 16 states plus the District of Columbia have active programs, while 7 states started deregulation but have suspended it. We consider two restructuring efforts that receive wide attention: PJM, covering many northeastern states, and ERCOT, covering most of Texas.

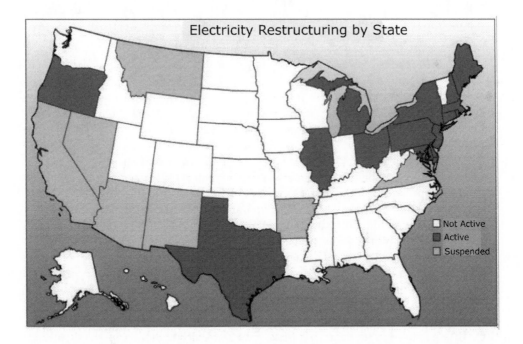

Figure 13.6 Electricity restructuring by state. Reprinted from *Status of electricity restructuring by state*, by EIA (n.d.).

PJM

PJM is an ISO/RTO that coordinates the movement of electricity among 13 states and the District of Columbia. The three letters represent the initial utilities of Pennsylvania and (New) Jersey that formed the first power pool in 1927, followed by Maryland utilities in 1956. It became an ISO in 1996 and introduced wholesale pricing in 1997. In 2001, PJM became the first fully functioning RTO and is now the largest in the United States.

In addition to an energy market that balances supply bids by participating utilities with wholesale customer demand, PJM operates a reliability pricing model to optimize transmission availability, and demand response to encourage demand reductions at times of highest use or for other reasons such as air quality concerns.

PJM uses locational marginal prices (LMPs). One notable feature of PJM pricing in the initial stages of the wholesale market was the difference between price in the western and eastern portions of its territory. Low-cost production using coal took place largely in the west, in states such as West Virginia, Pennsylvania, and Kentucky, while the east contained the population centers but not the low-cost energy sources. There was chronic congestion of transmission capacity in transporting electricity from west to east, resulting in much higher LMPs in the east. PJM introduced new pricing structures to help allocate constrained transmission capacity, including financial transmission rights (FTRs) and auction reserve rights (ARRs), which allow holders to hedge the cost of moving power from different points on the transmission grid based upon LMPs. Based on these markets, PJM does a 15-year forecast of transmission needs. In addition, the hydraulic fracturing boom from the Marcellus shale along with the decline in coal is pushing the production of low-cost electricity closer to the east (Sitaram, 2016).

ERCOT

The electricity system of much of the state of Texas has no interconnections with other states and so there is no interstate transmission of electricity. As FERC only regulates interstate electricity, most of Texas is not subject to FERC regulation. ERCOT is the ISO/RTO, but it is subject to state and not federal law.

Legislation introduced in 2002 called for deregulation and restructuring. Texas leads the United States in allowing consumers to choose their retail energy provider (REP). Legislators expected that competition among REPs would bring energy prices down. The prominence of REPs is a major distinction from California. In California, IPPs could gain from withholding supplies, whereas in Texas, REPs will seek out low-priced generation. With Texas restructuring more than ten years old, the debate continues as to whether it has led to higher or lower prices. Industry has likely benefited, as their high use justifies shopping around for the best deal. Residential users have also shopped around, with a large percentage of users switching suppliers. However, the nonprofit organization Texas Coalition for Affordable Power (2016) found that at least through 2014, Texans in deregulated parts of the state would have paid less for electricity if they had lived in the regulated parts of the state, although the gap was shrinking.

One surprise is that Texas has become a leader in renewable fuels. Clemente (2016) connects the wind boom to the ease of building transmission in Texas as compared to other states. Without the need for FERC approval, Texas can take advantage of wind in the western part of the state and transfer it to the population centers in the eastern part. Spindle and Smith (2016) note that at the same time Texas restructured, it also incorporated a renewable portfolio standard. Some customers have been willing to pay extra for green power.

ERCOT takes a more passive role of supervising bilateral trades as opposed to a power pool with its associated day-ahead, hour-ahead, and real-time exchanges. ERCOT still has to balance loads, again on a day-ahead, hour-ahead, and real-time basis. It still has to contract for balancing energy.

Kiesling and Kleit (2009) focus on why restructuring in Texas has worked where other efforts such as those in California have failed. Just as California faced a perfect storm of problems that led to failure, Texas has unique circumstances including being the only state that is not subject to FERC regulation. Each restructuring experience offers lessons for the future, but no two experiences are likely to be the same.

Summary

This chapter reviews electricity industry restructuring experiences in the U.S. and UK. In the traditional regulated electricity industry, investor–owned, vertically integrated monopoly utilities (IOUs) dominate the market due to economies of scale. In the United States, PURPA (1978) showed the feasibility of nonutility generators (NUGs), also called independent power producers (IPPs). In addition, the successful deregulation of other industries, especially the natural gas industry, stimulated the demand for further reform in the electric industry. The Energy Power Act (EPAct) of 1992 was the first effort to deregulate the U.S. electricity industry. It allowed IPPs to sell into wholesale power markets. It also allowed existing electricity utilities to sell outside their service region, a practice known as wheeling.

A textbook view of deregulation is to increase competition through separating generation and possibly retailing from transmission and distribution. Independent power producers compete in generation and, where consumers choose their power company, retail energy providers (REPs) offer consumers more than one electricity supplier. Electricity transmission and distribution remain a natural monopoly subject to rate-of-return regulation.

This standard textbook approach to deregulation ignores transactions costs. For example, a generator with more than one choice of transmission pipeline may be able to cut the price it offers to pay for transmission, the holdup problem. In order to reduce transactions costs, ISOs and RTOs are the government entities established by FERC for supervising the transformed regional markets and facilitating competitive bidding.

Electricity deregulation is also more complex than deregulation of other industries due to the distinctive characteristics of electricity. These complexities have changed the discussion on electricity reform from deregulation to restructuring. First, Kirchhoff's laws indicate that electricity transmission from one node to another need not follow the shortest path. This physical property combined with different generating costs at different sites requires nodal pricing—also called locational marginal pricing (LMP)—for efficiency. However, electricity generators may be able to exercise market power by withholding supplies and therefore cause efficiency loss. In addition, supply must meet demand at each instant in the absence of economical storage capability and the consequence is the need for additional capacity that may serve only a small number of hours, which drives up the marginal cost and price for meeting peak demand. Excess demand can cause brownouts or even blackouts.

It is also challenging to price electricity due to the continuously changing costs. Utilities may not be able to recoup their investment, the problem of stranded cost. Still another factor is that retail rates do not vary while wholesale rates do. As a result, retail demand in the electricity market does not respond to changes in the wholesale price.

The United States and the UK demonstrate differing approaches to electricity restructuring. In the 1990s, the UK privatized government-owned utilities into a number of retail generating companies that produced electricity, and regional electricity companies that purchased electricity. By the year 2000, California had had a less successful restructuring experience, deregulating the wholesale price but not the retail market. They also required the electric companies to sell natural gas generation to nonutility generators and prohibited them from signing long-term contracts for electricity. When wholesale prices soared, the electricity system suffered brownouts, blackouts, and even bankruptcy of some of the legacy electric utilities.

Although California's failure slowed down electricity restructuring in the 2000s, there have been advances such as PJM and ERCOT. Technology advancement, in addition to institutional arrangements, is important for the success of electricity restructuring. Small-scale generation, particularly for natural gas, increased competition. The improving efficiency of renewable energy increases its practical application. Smart grids enable real-time pricing, which is fundamental for establishing market prices.

There is not yet conclusive evidence that restructuring increases social welfare. In particular, restructuring has not necessarily delivered lower consumer prices nor lower costs. California's initial attempt at deregulation led to higher costs and prices. The UK's initial efforts that split the government-owned generating company into three firms, only two of which were private generators, was not sufficient to bring down cost and prices. As more generators entered production, social welfare increased, with benefits to large industrial customers that purchased directly from generators. The benefits may now be reaching residential customers.

The PJM wholesale market introduced competition in electricity generation throughout the northeastern United States. However, costs and prices were initially lower in the western portion of their territory, where generators used low-cost coal. It was expensive to distribute this electricity to the densely populated eastern section because of transmission constraints. With falling natural gas prices, resistance to the use of coal, and added transmission lines, the price gap has shrunk so that more retail customers are benefiting from the PJM wholesale market.

Texas has always provided low-cost state electricity, which has continued to be the case with restructuring. However, while prices have decreased over time in ERCOT's territory, these customers might have experienced larger price drops under regulation, based on prices paid by the customers in Texas who are still subject to regulation.

We can anticipate a dynamic future for the electricity industry, as states within the United States as well as countries throughout the world compare the merits of regulation and restructuring. With growing use of distributed generation, such as wind and solar energy but also electric vehicles and batteries, as well as the greater implementation of a smart grid capable of real-time metering and two-way communication, the utility of the future will look very different from the utility of the past. It will no longer be enough for a utility to keep the lights on. The utility of the future will confront challenges from third-party generators, calls for green power and energy efficiency, and the implementation of new technology.

Notes

1 This example follows the presentation of Griffin and Puller (2005, pp. 6–8).
2 Impedance refers to obstacles to AC electric current, including resistance (the opposition of the current that causes heat) and reactance (opposition due to a change in current or voltage due to capacity and electromagnetic force (EMF)). Resistance is the DC counterpart, where there is resistance but not reactance.
3 Bulk supply refers to the aggregate of electric generating plants, transmission lines, and related equipment, either within one utility or within a group of utilities interconnected with transmission. The term is interchangeable with wholesale power supply. For a glossary of energy terms, see the Independent Energy Producers Association (2016).
4 The UK uses the plc designation for public limited company, equivalent to the U.S. term inc. for publicly traded companies.
5 Tremblay and Tremblay (2012) summarize duopoly models including Cournot.
6 If the two firms have different marginal costs, the firm with the lower MC will have a larger equilibrium output than the firm with the higher MC.
7 In Example 13.2, the coefficient for Q in the demand equation equals 1, so it is easy to get the derived demand equation. For more complex problems, it is necessary to use calculus, such as when this coefficient is not equal to 1, or when the two firms have different marginal costs or marginal cost increases with output, or when there are more than two firms.
8 Also in Chapter 5, we discussed the Stigler (1964) oligopoly model, which does derive firm behavior from an assumption of profit maximization.
9 This strategy works better if the players do not know how many times they will play. If they do know, then a player has an incentive to violate the agreement in the last round. But if the other player knows the agreement will unravel in the last round, that player has an incentive to violate the agreement in the previous round. In turn, the first player, knowing the second player will not stick to the agreement, violates it a round earlier. By recursive reasoning, neither player will stick to the agreement and we are back to the prisoner's dilemma.

References

Borenstein, S. (2002). The trouble with electricity markets: Understanding California's restructuring disaster. *Journal of Economic Perspectives, 16*(1), 191–211.

Bushnell, J. B., Mansur, E. T., & Saravia, C. (2008). Vertical arrangements, market structure, and competition: An analysis of restructured US electricity markets. *American Economic Review, 98*(1), 237–266.

Clemente, J. (2016, October 11). The great Texas wind power boom. *Forbes.* Retrieved November 26, 2016 from http://www.forbes.com/sites/judeclemente/2016/10/11/the-great-texas-wind-power-boom/#7f0a7798192b

Domah, P., & Pollitt, M. (2001). The restructuring and privatisation of electricity distribution and supply businesses in England and Wales: A social cost–benefit analysis. *Fiscal Studies, 22*(1), 107–146.

Feldman, C. (2001). The California power quagmire. *CNN.com.* Retrieved November 29, 2016 from http://www.cnn.com/SPECIALS/views/y/2001/01/feldman.power.jan3/

Green, R. J., & Newbery, D. M. (1992). Competition in the British electricity spot market. *Journal of Political Economy, 100*(5), 929–953.

Griffin, J., & Puller, S. (2005). *Electricity deregulation: Choices and challenges.* Chicago, IL: University of Chicago Press.

Independent Energy Producers Association. (2016). *Glossary of energy terms.* Retrieved November 23, 2016 from http://www.iepa.com/Glossary.asp

Isser, S. (2015). *Electricity restructuring in the United States: Markets and policy from the 1978 Energy Act to the present*. New York, NY: Cambridge University Press.

Kiesling, L., & Kleit, A. (2009). *Electricity restructuring: The Texas story*. Washington, DC: The AEI Press.

Mansur, E. T., (2007). Upstream competition and vertical integration in electricity markets. *Journal of Law & Economics*, *50*(1), 125–156.

Puller, S. (2007). Pricing and firm conduct in California's deregulated electricity market. *Review of Economics and Statistics*, *89*(1), 75–87.

Sitaram, S. (2016). How power generation changes are impacting energy prices in the Mid-Atlantic [Web log post]. Retrieved December 3, 2016 from http://blogs.constellation.com/energy4business/energy-prices-in-the-mid-atlantic

Spindle, B., & Smith, R. (2016, August 29). Which state is a big renewable energy pioneer? Texas. *Wall Street Journal*. Retrieved November 26, 2016 from http://www.wsj.com/articles/which-state-is-a-big-renewable-energy-pioneer-texas–1472414098

Stigler, G. (1964). A theory of oligopoly. *Journal of Political Economy*, *72*(1), 44–61.

Texas Coalition for Affordable Power. (2016). *Electricity prices in Texas*. Retrieved November 26, 2016 from http://tcaptx.com/wp-content/uploads/2016/06/TCAP-ElectricityPricesinTX-Snapshot-A-Final.pdf

Tremblay, V., & Tremblay, C. (2012). Quantity and price competition in static oligopoly models. In *New Perspectives in Industrial Organization* (pp. 241–277). New York: Springer-Verlag.

U.S. Energy Information Administration. (n.d.). *Status of electricity restructuring by state*. Retrieved November 26, 2016 from http://www.eia.gov/electricity/policies/restructuring/restructure_elect.html

Williamson, O. (2002). The theory of the firm as governance structure: From choice to contract. *Journal of Economic Perspectives*, *16*(3), 171–195.

Part V

Energy policy

Chapter 14

Energy and the environment

"Never doubt that a small group of thoughtful, committed citizens can change the world; indeed, it is the only thing that ever has."

Margaret Mead, quoted in Richardson (1982)

"Never doubt that citizens and countries will free ride on the provision of public goods such as climate change contributions."

The author of this text

Introduction

Throughout this text, you have read about energy and no doubt noticed its inextricable relationship to the environment. It is now time to give that connection its own chapter. Consider how the following stories make headlines: oil spills, hydraulic fracturing, coal ash leaks, nuclear plant accidents. When we choose which of these conventional energy sources to use, we immediately contemplate their environmental consequences.

We seek remedies for our environmental challenges with less conventional sources of energy, such as: energy efficiency, renewable fuels, and next–generation alternatives. Energy efficiency—negawatts instead of megawatts—meets our energy demands with less energy. Renewables promise inexhaustible sources of energy without depleting our remaining nonrenewable fuels and their environmentally damaging consequences. However, these alternatives pose their own environmental challenges. By reducing the energy cost of using our technology, energy efficiency promotes more use of technology, the rebound effect. Wind towers impede views, and the flight paths of birds and bats. Solar requires land and resources such as silicon. In addition, they require backups for when they are not available, which brings us back to conventional fuels and their consequences.

We continue to search for next-generation alternatives: hydrogen vehicles, capturing solar by suspending solar collectors above the earth or water power deep in the ocean to make use of the energy from waves and currents, and biofuels made from fast-growing plants. We look for lower-cost ways to accomplish carbon capture and storage (CCS) so that we do not need to keep hundreds of years of coal locked up in disuse. We explore new nuclear technologies and new fuels that might not have the nightmare consequences of uranium or plutonium, while pursuing nuclear fusion as an energy source.

In order to facilitate these goals we need to get the prices right and the institutions in place that will reward entrepreneurs who reduce the social cost—the private cost as well as the external cost—of energy. As long ago as 1920, A. C. Pigou proposed a tax equal to marginal external cost to maximize social welfare and correct market failure due to externalities. If we want frackers to reduce their use of underground aquifers and fresh water, we need to examine whether they are paying the full costs of their water use. If we increase that price, they will have more reason to recycle water or turn to grey water, the wastewater we produce every time we take a shower or brush our teeth. If we do not want piles of coal ash, we want market prices that encourage producing less ash in the first place, safer means of storing the ash, or potentially beneficial reuses such as in concrete. Getting the prices and institutions to align with our societal preferences will provide the incentive for the next Edison, Tesla, Faraday, or Musk.

Elon Musk can pursue his vision beyond the electric car named in honor of Nikola Tesla. Musk has presented the Hyperloop, the equivalent of a pneumatic tube that would whisk passengers on a high-speed sled from Los Angeles to San Francisco in 30 minutes at speeds on the order of 700 miles per hour (Farrington, 2016). Meanwhile, Faraday Future tries to out-Tesla Musk on the automotive front. Faraday Future aims to produce an electric vehicle built more quickly than Tesla and able to anticipate your needs.[1] While its Silicon Valley headquarters is within miles of Tesla's headquarters in Palo Alto, California, it is one of several ventures into electric vehicles with the backing of Chinese investors both in this country and in their own. In addition, Google and Apple are looking to play a role.

The big breakthrough may be hydrogen vehicles. Toyota hopes to take the lead in hydrogen automobiles, and already has a hydrogen fuel-cell car called the Mirai (the Japanese word for future) available in showrooms.[2] Stan Thompson of Mooresville, North Carolina, just outside of Charlotte, promotes Hydrail, a train run on hydrogen. Hydrogen gas takes up more volume than a liquid fuel, so it is easier to use as a transportation fuel in large vehicles such as train engines.

To integrate energy and environmental concerns, we first need to see if markets reflect the value of those objectives. If they do not, we need to assess our demands for the environment: what we are willing to pay for fewer oil spills, less coal ash and carbon emissions, and safer nuclear energy. We then may need government's involvement to modify prices, laws, and other institutions to maximize social welfare.

In this chapter, we begin by tracing the increasing attention to the environment since 1970. That year marked the first Earth Day as well as the passage of the Clean Air Act, effectively the start of the modern environmental movement in the United States. We then examine the relationship between energy and environment, especially conventional oil, natural gas, and coal and their impacts on emissions of sulfur, NOx, mercury, particulate matter, and carbon. Next we consider environmental regulation and the distinction between command-and-control (CAC) approaches such as technology and performance standards and market-based approaches such as taxes and cap-and-trade. The focus is on U.S. regulation, but we also visit international frameworks aimed at mitigating global environmental problems. The final section is a summary.

Growth of the environmental movement

What triggered the modern environmental movement? In the United States, artists of the mid–1800s Hudson River School painted landscapes of the natural environment that piqued interest in protecting wilderness areas. In the late 1800s, John Muir described a pristine wilderness that would become Yosemite National Park. In the early

1900s, President Theodore Roosevelt helped establish national parks in the United States to conserve unique wilderness sites. In 1949, Aldo Leopold wrote of the land ethic in *A Sand County Almanac*.

Some observers point to Rachel Carson's *Silent Spring* as the tipping point for the environmental movement. Her 1962 book on DDT, a pesticide that had been used extensively to increase agricultural production, exposed devastating effects on wildlife. The public's heightened awareness of business practices that could harm humans as well as wildlife paved the way for President Richard Nixon to establish the U.S. Environmental Protection Agency (EPA) in 1970.

The EPA is a far-reaching and controversial government agency. Its responsibilities include protecting air, water, and land to protect the environment and public health. The Clean Air Act (CAA) was passed in 1970, followed by the Clean Water Act (CWA) in 1972. There is little doubt that U.S. air and water quality are far better today than they were in 1970, but the controversy is over whether benefits have exceeded costs, particularly since the agency can promulgate new regulations as long as there are benefits and is not required to consider costs. As a result, the agency continues to tighten standards that are likely to yield ever smaller marginal benefits and larger marginal costs, since the easier changes have already been made.

In 1978, the town of Love Canal in upstate New York detected carcinogens in its water that turned out to be a legacy of the Hooker Chemical Company that had its prime in the 1950s. The town had to be completely evacuated. Although the EPA had just passed the Resource Conservation and Recovery Act (RCRA) in 1976 aimed at solid waste, the agency vowed to prevent future Love Canals and in 1980 passed the Comprehensive Response, Compensation, and Liability Act (CERCLA) that required industry to contribute funds (known popularly as the Superfund) towards cleanup of future abandoned and contaminated sites. By 1995, the EPA aimed at cleaning up brownfields which are potentially contaminated sites, but below the level required for Superfund cleanup.

The CAA has been amended several times, most notably in 1990 when the program introduced incentive-based (IB) regulation in the form of emissions trading. The approach can be traced back to Coase (1960) where he proposed that clearly establishing property rights and allowing parties to negotiate will lead to a socially efficient outcome. Prior to the 1990 amendments, the dominant approach was CAC using technical or performance standards to reduce emissions.

Economists cheered the use of the "cap-and-trade approach" as more efficient than CAC. Under technology standards, all firms must use a required technology to reduce emissions, such as a scrubber to reduce sulfur. Under performance standards, all firms must reduce emissions by the same percentage, although they have flexibility on the technology to achieve the standard. Emissions trading allows further efficiency gains by allowing producers capable of reducing emissions at low cost to sell permits to firms with higher marginal abatement costs (MACs). The result is that firms with lower MACs reduce their emissions by more than firms with higher MACs, which is a further efficiency gain. The 1990 amendments first introduced emissions trading for sulfur followed by nitrous oxide (NOx). NOx emissions are an ingredient in ground-level ozone often referred to as smog.

Electricity generation using fossil fuels emits sulfur and NOx, with coal the worst offender. Utilities subject to emissions trading had to evaluate their use of coal. They could switch to low-sulfur coal. They could install a scrubber to catch sulfur emissions.

They could substitute other fuels that emit less sulfur and NOx. They could reduce electricity production. Alternatively, they could buy permits as an alternative to higher-cost mitigation.

In 2014, the EPA proposed the Clean Power Plan (CPP) to reduce carbon emissions. The plan sets state-specific standards in conjunction with emissions trading to reduce costs. However, many states, among them major coal-producing ones, sued to stop implementation of the plan. In early 2016, the U.S. Supreme Court delayed its implementation pending settlement of the legal challenge. The 2016 elections brought an administration less supportive of regulation including the CPP, further reducing its chances of implementation.

Relationship between energy and the environment

Primary and secondary energy production impact the environment.

Box 14.1 When is a zero emission vehicle not zero emissions?

California has long been an impetus for the production of electric cars because of its Zero Emission Vehicle (ZEV) program. The California Air Resources Board (CARB) began its ZEV program in 1990, with a target that 2% of vehicles sold in the state be emissions free in 1998 and 10% in 2003. They list plug-in electric vehicles (PEVs) and hydrogen electric vehicles that qualify. In 1996, as a result of pressure from carmakers, they dropped the 1998 requirement. Car companies have continued to fight the restrictions on the grounds that the technologies were immature, leading to high-priced cars that consumers were unwilling to buy. CARB had to settle for hybrid gas–electric vehicles labeled partial zero emissions vehicles (PZEVs).

Despite the resistance to the program, CARB revised the program in 2015 with sweeping reforms. As of 2015, the requirement was still only 2.7%, barely more than the target originally set in 1998 and then repeatedly delayed. The latest revision calls for 4.5% by 2018, increasing by 2.5% per year to achieve 22% by 2025 (California EPA, 2016). There is talk of a 100% emissions-free fleet by 2030 (Howe, 2015).

Automakers have little choice but to meet the ZEV requirement, given the large number of cars they sell in California. They take a loss on ZEVs to meet the mandate in order to sell conventional vehicles at a positive profit margin. The program is technology-forcing, which from an economic perspective represents a highly inefficient form of regulation.

But the most egregious objection is that PZEVs are not really ZEVs, in that they use electricity, a secondary source of energy. While there are zero gasoline emissions, there are emissions at the electric plant. If electric plants use coal, there will be substantial carbon emissions along with sulfur, NOx, particulates, and mercury. Other fuel sources emit less carbon, but as we have said, there is no externalities-free source of energy to generate electricity. ZEVs may reduce carbon emissions, but the vehicles should be renamed. A more accurate name would be REVs (Remote Emission Vehicles) to signify that there are emissions, just at a remote location.

We next consider the environmental effects of fossil fuels and then secondary energy production of electricity using these primary fuels.

Energy production and the environment

Development of oil and gas fields

OIL SPILLS

In addition to externalities from the use of oil for transportation—sulfur, NOx, particulates, and carbon—we now count oil spills, an externality from transporting oil. If oil spills were unregulated, oil companies would still take precautions because lost oil means lost revenue to the company. However, they would not have an incentive to internalize all externalities, such as damage to fish. As a result, we need regulations to reduce the number of spills to the socially efficient point.

We are unlikely to eliminate oil spills. In fact, from an economic perspective, we do not want to eliminate all oil spills; it would be too expensive. The United States, Russia, and Saudi Arabia are the top three oil-producing countries, each yielding approximately 10 million barrels, or 420 million gallons, per day. Figure 14.1 demonstrates the determination of the number of oil spills that would occur with and without regulation.

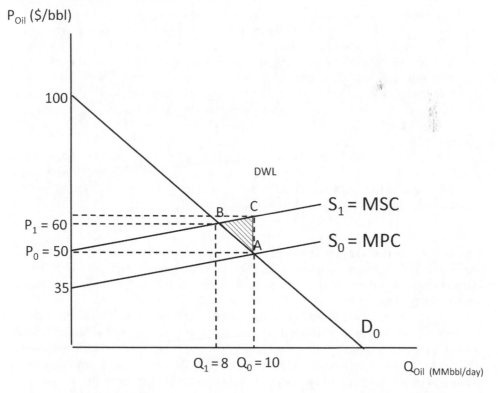

Figure 14.1 Optimal number of oil spills.

Oil producers consider their marginal private costs of oil production, as shown by supply curve S_0. Given demand for oil D_0, the market quantity is 10 million barrels per day at a price of $50 per barrel.

Oil producers include the cost of their resources, as well as the expected cost to them of a potential oil spill. But if there are no regulations concerning oil spills, they will not account for costs to the environment that they do not bear, such as lost fish or lost income to fishers.[3]

Supply S_1 includes all marginal social costs, both private and external. As shown for simplicity, marginal external cost is constant per unit of oil, so the two supply curves are parallel. Also for simplicity, we are initially assuming that the only way to reduce oil spills is to produce less oil.

Example 14.1

Referring to Figure 14.1, what is the price and quantity of oil if there is no regulation of oil spills? Calculate the associated social welfare loss.

Solution

In the absence of laws requiring oil producers to pay for damage to others from oil spills, the companies will only consider private costs. They do have some incentive to prevent oil spills, since they bear the costs of lost revenue from oil that ends up in the ocean. Supply S_0 includes those costs. The unfettered market outcome results in price $P_0 = \$50$ per barrel of oil and quantity $Q_0 = 10$ million barrels per day. According to the figure, there is a marginal external cost (MEC) of $15—the difference between the y-axis intercepts for the two supply curves— per barrel. If this cost were internalized, supply would decrease to S_1 and price increases to $P_1 = \$60$ per barrel of oil while quantity decreases to $Q_1 = 8$ million barrels per day, with producers able to pass on $10 of the $15 cost increase to consumers.

There is a deadweight loss (DWL) triangle (triangle ABC) to the unfettered market. We know that at $Q_1 = 8$ million barrels per day, MSC = $60 = MPC + MEC. Since MEC = $15, MPC = $65 at point C. DWL = $0.5 \times (10 - 8)$ MMbbl $\times \$(65 - 50)$ per barrel = $15 million.

The most straightforward remedy to correct the problem is a tax of $15 per barrel on oil output, the Pigou prescription using the "polluter pays" principle. The remedy assumes the government can accurately measure the MEC and that the government acts in society's best interest.

Coase would add that it assumes that the lowest-cost solution to achieve the welfare-maximizing outcome is to reduce oil production. The Coase approach calls for clearly defining property rights and then allowing negotiations. The *Coase theorem* states that we will obtain the socially efficient outcome regardless of the initial assignment of property rights. Therefore, whether we initially assign the rights to fishers or to the oil company, the outcome will be the same and it will maximize social welfare. If fishers have the right to oil-free water, then oil producers would compensate fishers for allowing oil production. Alternatively, we could assign the property rights to oil producers. While they would have some built-in incentive to protect against oil spills, they would still produce more oil than is socially optimal. However, fishers would have an incentive to compensate oil producers for fewer spills corresponding to the welfare maximum.

Another insight from the Coase approach is that the parties involved know more about the costs of alternative solutions than does the government. Moreover, if the government asks them about their costs, the parties have reasons to misrepresent those costs. Oil companies will claim that a tax on oil aimed at reducing spills will damage their prospects, particularly if they have to compete in a global market where other countries do not impose a similar tax.

However, the primary insight from the Coase perspective is that negotiations may lead to lower-cost solutions than the Pigou tax approach. It may be that fisheries should not be located near oil refineries, rather than expecting oil refineries to reduce spills. If the only externality of an oil spill is damage to fish, removing fish removes the damage.[4] This remedy may cost society less than requiring refineries to modify their plants to reduce oil spills.

The Coase theorem assumes zero transactions costs, so that fishers and oil companies can negotiate without cost. There are likely to be transactions costs involved in negotiations particularly if there are more than two parties. If there is one oil company and 100 fishers, it may matter who has the property rights. If the oil company has the right to spill oil, the fishers may try to negotiate a deal where they compensate the company for using a double-hulled ship for transportation rather than a single-hulled one. If negotiations are successful, all fishers win. However, the benefit of the new technology has public goods characteristics of nonrivalry and nonexclusion. All fishers benefit from the new technology and none can be excluded from the benefits. We are back to the free-rider problem, where everyone has the incentive to enjoy the benefits without paying the costs. Therefore, even if the double-hulled ship increases social welfare, we may not get it. Hence, in the wake of the massive 1989 *Exxon Valdez* oil spill in Prince William Sound, Alaska, the government imposed a new requirement that oil shippers must use double-hulled ships.[5]

Does that mean that the better solution is to assign the rights to the fishers? In this case, the oil company would need to reach an agreement with 100 fishers. One or more of the fishers might recognize the financial stakes for the oil company, and try to extract a large portion of the producer surplus. However, if enough fishers pursue this strategy, we end up with a holdout problem. Fishers who hold out for a large percentage of the stakes could push the settlement above the cost of installing the new technology, even if settling with the fishers would be a lower-cost solution. Therefore, in the presence of transactions costs, it does matter who has the property rights. Furthermore, negotiations may not lead to the social-welfare-maximizing outcome.

Transactions costs are pervasive in dealings over environmental externalities, which would seem to reduce the relevance of the Coase theorem to multiparty externalities such as oil spills. Nevertheless, the thought experiment of assignment property rights and negotiating solutions led the way to J. H. Dales (1968) proposing the emissions trading approach.

Example 14.2

The table below shows oil company profits and fishing industry losses from oil spills. Assume oil companies have the property right to spill oil and there are ten fishers in all. What is the social–welfare–maximizing amount of oil? Explain negotiations that will lead to the socially desired outcome. Ignore transactions costs. Now, still ignoring transactions costs, what will be the negotiated outcome if fishers have the right to pristine water? Finally, revisit the two cases when the fishers face transactions costs of reaching an agreement, explaining whether public goods characteristics or holdout problems could prevent the socially desired outcome.

Barrels of oil	Oil company total profit ($)	Number of fish	Fish industry (10 firms) total profits ($)
0	0	10	100
1	40	9	90
2	70	7	70
3	90	4	40
4	100	0	0

Solution

If the oil company has the property rights and there are no negotiations, it will maximize profits at 4 barrels of oil (or more, but the table stops at $Q_{oil} = 4$. Fishers lose $40 from the last barrel of oil, while the oil producer gains only $10 in additional profit. So the fish industry and the oil producer can strike a deal anywhere between those two values (say $25 if they are equally good negotiators, but anywhere between $10 and $40 will prevent the oil company from producing the fourth barrel. Negotiations will also prevent the third barrel of oil, with a deal between $20 and $30 (again, $25 is a possibility if the two sides agree to the middle value). Fisheries can offer up to $20 to prevent the second barrel, but the oil company will not accept less than $30. So the oil company will produce $Q_{oil} = 2$.

If fishers have the property rights, they will produce 10 fish and earn $100 in an unfettered market. It is worth up to $40 to the oil company to produce the first barrel and only costs the fishers $10. Therefore, there is room for a deal. The same is true for the second barrel, with the deal between $20 and $30. The oil company is willing to pay up to $20 to increase output to $Q = 3$. However, the fishers will refuse any offer less than $30. So we again arrive at $Q = 2$. This quantity also maximizes social welfare, as we can see if we calculate total profit for the two industries. Total profit at $Q = 2$ is $140, the largest total for any oil output level.

This outcome may also strike you as fair, as each party gets $70. However, there are 10 fishers, so each of them gets $7. More importantly, the Coase theorem is strictly about maximizing social welfare and not about fairness. After all, each side would like to have the property rights, but the Coase theorem simply states that from a social welfare standpoint, it does not matter who has the initial property rights.

Returning to the case where the oil company owned the right to pollute, 10 fishers must now unite to make an offer. It is worth $40 to them to reduce oil production from $Q = 4$ to $Q = 3$, and only costs the oil producer $10. Therefore, society is better off if the oil company does not produce the last barrel. But it may not happen. If each fisher pays a fair share, she will contribute at least $1 and no more than $4. However, fishers free ride if they recognize that they will get the benefit of less oil production even if they do not contribute. That is, fewer oil spills have public goods characteristics; everyone benefits simultaneously and no one can be excluded. So why contribute?

If instead the rights go to the fishers, the oil company can afford to offer up to $40 for the right to produce the first barrel. Anything over $10 makes the fishers better off. In the absence of negotiations, fishers might agree to a total payment of $25, or $2.50 each. However, suppose five fishers recognize that the oil company gains $40 by producing the first barrel, and each one asks for $7. Since the other fishers will want at least $1 to accept the deal, and more likely $2.50, the total ask exceeds $40 and the deal collapses. This time, the holdout problem prevents a welfare-maximizing outcome.

Before a spill, a demand curve shows maximum willingness to pay, such as $40 to reduce oil output from 4 to 3 barrels. In the 1989 *Exxon Valdez* and BP (British Petroleum) *Deepwater Horizon* oil spills, society was faced with damage already done. Then the role of the courts is to put a dollar value on damage. If all that matters is fish revenue and the oil company is liable, the courts could simply require the company to pay damages to fishers for lost revenue.

The calculation is more difficult for forgone tourism, as in the aftermath of the Gulf Coast oil spill. Finding that number requires estimation of a counterfactual. We can only estimate how many tourists came in earlier years when there was no oil spill and use that approximation for how many would have come this year had the oil spill not occurred, doing our best to hold constant other factors such as weather, shark attacks, and other factors that also affect tourism. The courts estimate forgone revenues by comparing what tourists would have spent in the absence of an oil spill to spending by the actual tourists who did come.

We can measure use values by *revealed preference*, what we actually do. Two common approaches are the hedonic approach and the travel cost approach. The travel cost approach estimates willingness to pay based on distance traveled to the site. As distance increases, fewer tourists come to a site. The travel cost method estimates the associated cost of the trip, of which the largest amount is typically the value of time to get to the site. We then construct a demand curve, with the cost of travel on the vertical axis and the number of visitors on the horizontal.

The hedonic approach estimates the value of an environmental amenity from a complementary private good such as housing. Other things constant, housing values are higher further away from the likely spill path of an oil refinery. With house prices on the left-hand side of a regression equation and distance from contamination due to an oil spill and any other variables that influence home prices on the right, the estimated coefficient for the distance variable indicates willingness to pay to live further from the contamination.

Environmental economists distinguish between use and nonuse values, distinguishing between active and passive uses. Use values such as eating fish or visiting the Gulf Coast are relatively easy to measure because we routinely place values on these uses when we eat at seafood restaurants or stay at coastal hotels. Nonuse values are existence values, willingness to pay for the resource even if we never intend to use it. You may simply value clean water for its own sake, not for any utilitarian uses. Nonuse values can be much larger than use values. You may have never been to the Gulf of Mexico, nor do you expect to go. However, you might still be willing to pay to prevent oil spills that coat shorebirds in oil even if you will not ever see them.

It is more difficult to estimate nonuse values, because we do not reveal our preferences by actions. Here, the best we can do is ask questions about value, the *stated preference* approach. Contingent valuation (CV) asks people their willingness to pay to prevent damage or willingness to accept compensation for damage. Stated preferences are not nearly as trustworthy as revealed preferences, as people are not using their own money.

While you may be skeptical of the answers produced by CV surveys, it is the standard technique when it is necessary to estimate nonuse values. A blue-ribbon panel was formed immediately after the *Exxon Valdez* oil spill and the results of the subsequent CV study were used in court (Arrow et al., 1993). Still, the *Exxon Valdez* case dragged on for years, with numerous increases and decreases in damages owed as the case worked through the appeals process. In the end, total damage payments were approximately $1 billion. In addition, Exxon spent over $2 billion on restoration and cleanup. Carson et al. (2003) put the damages at $2.8 billion in an initial study, revised upward to a little over $7 billion when the authors revisited the statistical analysis.

The BP *Deepwater Horizon* case took six years. The settlement calls for BP to pay $8.8 billion for restoration to address natural resource damage assessment, by far the largest environmental damages ever assessed. Economic studies are relatively recent, one examining the effect of the spill on condominium values and another on oyster consumption (Winkler & Gordon, 2013; Morgan et al., 2016). Both are use value studies. A federal CV study estimates BP *Deepwater Horizon* damages at $17 billion.[6] More CV studies should soon follow now that the court phase is over.

HYDRAULIC FRACTURING

Will natural gas have a Golden Age? Will it be the bridge to a clean energy future? Or is the Golden Age already over? The answers to these questions rest with fracking, unlocking previously inaccessible natural gas using fracturing technology of drilling down a mile or more in concert with horizontal drilling up to several miles. This combination has altered the search for oil and natural gas from a 1 in 100 gamble to a near certainty. With it, the United States has joined the Saudis and the Russians as one of the three largest oil producers and has positioned natural gas to surpass coal as the leading fuel for electricity generation.

We also know the perils of the technology including water pollution and depletion, earthquakes, and methane leaks. Nearby residents may deplore or embrace the technology depending on whether it threatens their well water or promises a buyout of their property. So how do we weigh the benefits and costs? The hedonic method that we presented for oil spills is also suitable to evaluate fracking. Studies are only now starting to appear, as the phenomenon is recent and so there are only a few years of data.

One study by Mason, Meuhlenbachs and Olmstead (2015) reviewed existing studies of the benefits and costs of accessing natural gas (as well as oil). Benefits include lower energy prices to consumers, profits to producers, and less dependence on imports from unfriendly regimes. Costs include negative externalities to air, water, and quality of life in surrounding regions. They find the benefits so large that their recommendation is to use the technology while studying how to reduce the costs.

Another study by Meuhlenbachs, Spiller and Timmins (2015) uses the hedonic method to examine property values of houses with and without well water atop the Marcellus shale in Pennsylvania. Houses with well water depend on the local ground-water where the threat from fracking is greater. Note that while we do not know if fracking will contaminate the water, expectations affect property values. Their results find substantial negative effects on the value of houses with well water as well as houses where drilling operations are visible. They find small positive effects for houses with piped-in water that are near drilling operations, suggesting price increases when there is potential for royalty payments. They conclude that the next step is to better determine the actual effects of fracking on groundwater, as the current negative impact is based on expectations, not evidence.

There is concern that fracking can increase earthquakes. Oklahoma has long been an oil-and-gas producing state. In 2013, the state experienced 109 magnitude 3 or greater earthquakes. In 2014, the number was 585 and in 2015, there were 907 tremors. The quakes were concentrated in areas of drilling activity. The culprit may be wastewater disposal rather than fracking itself (Oklahoma Secretary of Energy & Environment, n.d.).

DEVELOPMENT OF ENVIRONMENTALLY SENSITIVE AREAS

There is often a conflict between energy development and environmental uses. In Chapter 6 on oil, we reviewed a study by Cicchetti and Freeman (1973) that compared two potential routes for the Alaskan pipeline and showed that the one chosen was inferior on cost and environmental criteria.

Oil companies have long wanted to drill for oil in the Alaskan National Wildlife Refuge (ANWR). Environmentalists have fought development, mostly on the argument that caribou migrate through this region. As few of us will travel to ANWR, much less see any caribou migrating, cost–benefit analysis (CBA) would weigh the estimated value of the oil to the willingness-to-pay to protect the reserve and its caribou. Kotchen and Burger (2007) estimated the social benefits of the oil net of extraction costs at $250 billion, using a price per barrel of around $50. The only way to estimate the environmental cost would be a CV study, given that the loss is a passive use. Kotchen and Burger do not undertake such an analysis. However, they use the oil benefits to determine that the breakeven amount to compensate individuals would be between $600 and $1,800 per person.

Dwight Lee (2001) suggested a thought experiment offering environmentalists a choice of preserving ANWR or being able to spend the revenues on other environmental objectives. If they received 10% of the revenues from drilling that they could spend as they wished, would they accept the deal? Lee suggests that framing the decision as an opportunity cost might bring about a breakthrough in the long stalemate between environmentalists and oil companies. Lee points to the Audubon Society, which owns the Rainey Wildlife Sanctuary in Louisiana and has allowed supervised drilling.

Coal mining

There was widespread opposition to coal even before concerns about carbon emissions and climate change. There were widely publicized deaths to coal miners trapped in mines and breathing poisonous methane gas. Massey Energy owned a coal mine in West Virginia where, in 2010, an explosion killed 29 miners. The company CEO received one year in jail given evidence of numerous safety violations. China, the largest producer and consumer of coal, still mines extensively underground and suffers mine explosions and deaths.

Coal mining is a risky occupation, but in a competitive market where workers are compensated for risk, there is no externality and no need for government intervention. In the case of the Massey Energy explosion, the market failure was that the company covered up safety violations, so workers were not fully compensated for their risks.[7]

Electricity production and the environment

As was discussed in Box 14.1, energy affects the environment whether in primary or secondary form. Coal mining has environmental consequences at the upstream end of the coal supply chain when it is mined and at the downstream end when it is a generator fuel. We now turn to the environmental effects of coal- and natural-gas-fired electricity generation.

Emissions

We have encountered carbon emissions and climate change throughout the text and do not repeat that discussion here. There are additional consequences such as particulates and coal ash. In this section, we focus on sulfur and NOx emissions as well as mercury.

SULFUR DIOXIDE (SO_2)

In the 1980s, the United States connected SO_2 with acid rain. SO_2 was already included in the 1970 CAA. The regulations led to more use of low-sulfur coal. In 1978, the United States passed New Source Performance Standards (NSPSs) that effectively required new plants to install flue gas desulfurization equipment (scrubbers). Scrubbers remove approximately 90% of sulfur emissions. As this technology cost about $100 million dollars (Lazar & Farnsworth, 2011), some utilities could meet the standard at a lower cost simply by substituting low-sulfur coal. States that produce high-sulfur coal had reason to favor the new rule requiring scrubbers to protect their market.

Box 14.2 When is a new source new?

New legislation often exempts electric utility facilities built prior to its passage due to the high cost of retrofitting existing plants. This legislation creates an incentive to extend the life of existing plants rather than build a new one, since existing plants face less stringent regulation. It also creates an incentive to modify existing plants as long as the modifications do not trigger the new laws.

The U.S. EPA defines when an existing plant has been modified to the point that it is closer to a new plant. It applies NSPSs to new plants as well as sufficiently modified existing plants.

The 1990 CAA amendments introduced emissions trading, which greatly reduced the cost of meeting SO_2 regulations. Utilities with a high MAC bought permits while utilities with low MACs sold permits. Ironically, the largest benefit by far turned out to be health improvements, with those benefits alone justifying the program. In another irony, the program collapsed in 2012 because of new rules that had in effect required scrubbers, after which the demand for sulfur emissions contracts dropped precipitously (Schmalensee & Stavins, 2013).

NOx

The 1990 CAA amendments also proposed a 1995 start for a nitrous oxide (NOx) trading market. NOx reacts with volatile organic compounds (VOCs)—a group of chemical compounds that easily enter the air—and sunlight to form low-level ozone popularly known as smog. In addition to reducing visibility, smog can cause respiratory problems and other illnesses.

Box 14.3 China makes Olympian efforts to clean the air

As China is the world's largest consumer of coal in conjunction with rapidly growing automobile use, it is also experiencing dangerous levels of smog. Beijing suffers levels of pollution many times that of U.S. cities.

As China prepared to host the 2008 Summer Olympics, athletes and spectators were concerned about Beijing's air pollution. The Chinese government took a variety of CAC measures to clear the air during the Olympic events. They restricted automobile travel during the period and required many plants to stop production.

Econometric studies often seek natural experiments in which people are subject to a change in environmental conditions over which they have no control. There have been numerous studies of Beijing during the 2008 China Olympics as compared to usual levels of air pollution.

China's data may be suspect, making studies more difficult. For one thing, the government may underestimate pollution to lessen international condemnation. A study by

Chen et al. (2013) combined Chinese data with upper-atmosphere U.S. National Aeronautics and Space Administration (NASA) data used for verification. They found a 25% reduction in air pollution, but the improvement was temporary. They did not examine the health effects of the temporary improvement. Also, they left as an open question whether resources could have been used more efficiently by reducing pollution over a broader area or for a longer time.

MERCURY

The 2008 U.S. EPA Mercury and Air Toxics Standards (MATS) called for reduction of mercury emissions from coal-fired power plants. Mercury can affect the development of the brain and nervous system, especially for infants in the womb. The government has warned pregnant women to limit their intake of fish species that have high mercury concentrations.

U.S. coal-burning power plants are the largest source of mercury emissions. The MATS rules were challenged by 20 states emboldened by the Supreme Court ruling that put a stay on the CPP. However, the Supreme Court denied the request of the states, leaving the rules in place.

HOLISTIC CONSIDERATIONS

A holistic approach would consider relationships among pollutants, where those pollutants end up, and sources of pollution. Policies to reduce sulfur may also affect emissions of NOx. Emissions may affect both air and water. In addition, electricity production affects water use, and vice versa.

U.S. utilities have asked for greater certainty about regulatory standards. In addition to frequent changes in the standards, the EPA typically focuses on one pollutant at a time. They may tighten the standard on sulfur, followed later by a more stringent standard for NOx. Moreover, just when the utilities have adjusted to those regulations, the EPA announces restrictions on mercury, carbon, or even coal ash.

When utilities take measures to meet a standard on one pollutant, it can affect other emissions. Using more low-sulfur coal reduces sulfur emissions, but increases coal ash. Putting in a scrubber reduces sulfur and mercury emissions. So the cost-minimizing solution in response to a regulation targeting one emission may not be the lowest-cost choice if there is a subsequent change in the standard for other emissions (Schwarz, 2005). Utilities make the case that the EPA should consider multiple pollutants when it sets standards, rather than a piecemeal approach.

In addition, it is common to focus on one medium at a time, such as air, land, or water. There may be separate regulations for release of mercury into the air and water, where a multimedia approach would integrate those two mediums. In 1998, the EPA promulgated its first multimedia regulation, known as the Cluster Rule, aimed at pulp and paper mill emissions into air and water (Gray & Shadbegian, 2015). This industry generates air pollutants as it creates power-generated steam for its dryers and water pollution from residuals in the water as the paper is dried. By proposing both sets of regulations at the same time, pulp and paper mills could choose the best strategy to minimize the cost of meeting the joint regulations.

A third joint consideration is the energy–water nexus (Malinowski et al., 2015). The nexus is that energy production requires water and water production requires energy. Nuclear energy requires large amounts of water for cooling. Transporting water over long distances requires energy-using pumps. Regulations to reduce carbon emissions that favor nuclear energy may increase the use of water. Regulations that restrict water extraction in drought-stricken areas could lead to importing water from distant locations and greater use of energy. From the perspectives of user and societal cost, we should consider a more holistic approach.

Regulations

In the introduction to this chapter, we noted the importance of prices, law, and other institutions in providing a framework for using energy in a socially optimal manner. Markets alone may not provide the proper incentives. Negative externalities such as pollution are pervasive in the use of conventional sources of energy. The market underproduces public goods such as R&D into future energy alternatives. We explore key U.S. state and federal regulations as well as international attempts to address global environmental problems.

Environmental regulation of energy production

The United States has both federal and state environmental regulations. In some cases, states adopt regulations even when there is a federal regulation, as long as the state regulation is at least as stringent. In other cases, the federal government may not have a regulation, but the states adopt their own rules.

The theory of fiscal federalism sets out when it is more efficient to regulate at the federal level vs. the state level. The benefit of federal legislation is economies of scale where constituents throughout the country jointly consume the output. That benefit must be weighed against heterogeneous preferences, such as states that prefer less stringent laws. The battle between these two principles is evident in states suing to prevent the passage of the CPP. Coal-producing states in particular have opposed the plan, no doubt recognizing the economic damage it will do to the coal industry, its workers, and its multiplier effect on other industries and workers as coal industry workers and management have less income to spend on other goods and services. However, some of the states joining the suit do not mine coal. Those states may prefer state to federal regulation.

Oil production

On- and offshore drilling rights can be owned by the federal government or by the states. From a fiscal federalism perspective, the rights should go to the level that can maximize social welfare. One distinctive characteristic of the United States is that private parties can own mineral rights and the associated right to drill for what is under the surface. We came across this distinction earlier as a reason why the shale boom started in the United States, but is less likely in continental Europe where the government owns the mineral rights.

One complication described in Chapter 6 is that oil flows to whoever drills first. Under the rule of capture, the oil belongs to whoever brings it to the surface, leading to pumping out the oil as quickly as possible. This incentive conflicts with dynamically efficient oil use as well as with sustainability. Some states deter this occurrence by rules that share the revenues from oil production depending on relative shares of mineral rights near the drilling.

U.S. regulation of oil and gas resides primarily with the states except for offshore drilling. In some states, localities can establish laws that supersede state laws, depending on state constitutions.

There are other environmental regulatory agencies besides the EPA. The Bureau of Land Management (BLM) oversees federally owned land including sites believed to contain oil and gas deposits. The BLM may lease those properties or hold auctions to sell the rights. The BLM is responsible for making sure companies that lease land for oil and gas exploration meet all environmental laws. Some properties are more valuable in other uses such as for recreation or wilderness, or cannot be used safely for oil and gas drilling, in which case the BLM controls the land for recreation or passive uses.

The BLM and other federal agencies are subject to the National Environmental Policy Act (NEPA) of 1969 that established a framework for evaluating benefits and costs. Agencies must prepare an environmental assessment and an environmental impact statement. Despite NEPA and environmental impact statements, we have seen that the route chosen for the Alaskan pipeline was inferior from a cost and environmental standpoint. However, NEPA did not require an independent review of impact statements. The EPA was established the following year at least in part to overcome the weaknesses of NEPA.

Most oil production is onshore. It is less costly to access conventional oil and gas on land than under the sea. The lead in onshore production is likely to increase with hydraulic fracturing, although at a higher cost than conventional onshore supplies and higher than some offshore supplies.

In the United States, most offshore drilling rights reside with the federal government, with the states having the right to pass more stringent legislation. In the United States, the states own the rights three miles out to sea, with federal rights extending to 200 miles from shore.[8] Most of the activity is in the Gulf of Mexico, and until recently, the U.S. government had not leased rights on the east and west coasts for several decades. The BP *Deepwater Horizon* oil spill reinforced opposition to offshore drilling, despite tougher regulations aimed at the building and operation of offshore drills as well as real-time monitoring to detect leaks.

In deciding whether to lease offshore drilling rights, the United States evaluates energy potential against environmental considerations. The federal government collects revenue on onshore and offshore leases. Just before the BP *Deepwater Horizon* disaster, the federal government had been planning to allow leasing of some nearby coastal waters. States have rights out to 3 miles from shore, so if the federal government reinstitutes offshore drilling, states can pass legislation forbidding it. There were vigorous debates in North Carolina and Florida about whether the environmental risks to the coasts were worth the potential revenues. The decision would also depend upon the value of the resources, which was over $100 per barrel in June of 2014 but much lower since then.

Natural gas production

We have seen that in the United States, private parties own the subsurface mineral rights while in the EU the government owns those rights. U.S. federal legislation permits fracking, explicitly exempting it from the CWA and the Safe Water Drinking Act, as well as the RCRA passed in 1976 and then reinforced by CERCLA and Superfund.

States can choose to regulate fracking or even forbid its use. If states do permit fracking, local areas can challenge the state's supremacy. Ordinarily, state law supersedes local law, but there are exceptions such as Home Rule where local law can be supreme. A few localities in Colorado and Texas argue that frackers cannot drill within a specified distance of "Home-Rule" localities.

The EPA is working on regulations to reduce methane emissions associated primarily with natural gas drilling. As discussed earlier in the text, Howarth (2015) claims natural gas is worse than coal given the potency of methane emissions. While his finding has been attacked for ignoring the longer duration of CO_2 effects, there is no disputing that methane emissions contribute to the climate change problem.

Environmental regulation of electricity production

Federal

CLEAN AIR ACT

The CAA regulates a number of electric utility emissions. In addition to sulfur and NOx, there are proposed regulations for mercury. NOx as well as VOCs and particulate matter (PM) can all contribute to ground-level ozone, which is also regulated by the EPA. States that violate the ozone standard risk losing federal highway funds.

Wind can transport emissions far from where they are emitted. North Carolina attributed high concentrations of emissions to electricity production in Tennessee. The EPA has promulgated several pieces of legislation to address interstate transport by requiring states to reduce emissions that harm a neighboring state, but there have been court challenges.

CLEAN WATER ACT

U.S. power plants are the largest water users of any industry. Many electric plants withdraw large amounts of water from a lake, river, or ocean. Most plants have a cooling tower to condense the steam back into water and then release the water. Concerns include aquatic life that may be trapped by the cooling system, water lost to evaporation, and the temperature of the released water.

The EPA currently requires utilities to use the "best available technology" to cool the water (Natural Resources Defense Council, 2011). The lowest-cost technology at one time was once-through technology that uses the water once and then releases it back into a body of water. A closed-loop system that recirculates the water is more expensive but uses less water. As it became more difficult to find sites with access to large amounts of water, almost all plants incorporated closed-loop systems. Dry cooling uses air rather than water to cool the steam (Dorjets, 2014).

NUCLEAR WASTE POLICY ACT

This Act addresses disposal of spent nuclear fuel. The interim solution was that utilities would store it on-site. Utilities also had to pay into a fund intended to finance a permanent site.

In 1987, Yucca Mountain in Nevada was identified as a suitable site for spent fuel. Radioactive waste must remain isolated for thousands of years. Not surprisingly, Nevada disagreed with the site choice. In 2010, with a Democratic President in office and a Democratic Congress majority led by a senator from Nevada, the site was rejected. Utilities continue to store the spent fuel locally.

Another alternative is to reprocess the fuel. The United States banned reprocessing in the late 1970s out of fears that stored plutonium could be used for weapons. The ban was lifted in the early 1980s, but the method has not been used. The United States has transported spent fuel to a facility in Savannah River, Georgia, that currently has the mission to reprocess weapons-grade plutonium into plutonium–uranium mixed oxide (MOX) fuel for nuclear reactors (Nuclear Watch of New Mexico, 2017). The fuel has not been used, given concerns about utilities having inventories of plutonium that could be used in weapons.

Some countries do reprocess their nuclear fuel. Reprocessing does not reduce radioactivity, but by reducing the amount of fuel used, it reduces nuclear waste. France relies heavily on nuclear energy and uses reprocessing. Even though Japan reprocesses spent fuel, one of the major concerns in the Fukushima disaster was damage to the storage area that could have released dangerous amounts of radioactivity.

The U.S. Congressional Budget Office produced a 2007 report comparing reprocessing with direct disposal. They cited previous analyses showing that the cost of reprocessing was at least 25% more (Orszag, 2007). The cost of nuclear reprocessing plants have cost far more than projected. A Japanese plant had a capital cost of over $20 billion and the Savannah, Georgia, MOX plant cost over $7 billion, way over estimates. China is evaluating reprocessing, with cost estimates between $3 billion to over $9 billion depending on capacity, but the eventual cost could be much higher (Bunn, Zhang, & Kang, 2016).

State

The United States has no national standard on carbon emissions or on the use of renewable fuels, but states have implemented renewable portfolio standards (RPSs) that set quotas for using renewable fuels to generate electricity. Some states choose to restrict carbon emissions. California has a cap-and-trade program that covers almost all industries including utilities. The Regional Greenhouse Gas Initiative (RGGI) uses carbon cap-and-trade to reduce utility carbon emissions in nine northeastern states.

We would expect requirements to use more alternative fuels or emit less carbon to increase electricity prices. Borenstein et al. (2015) report that the effects of the California program on electricity prices have been small, and an analysis of RGGI actually finds that after an initial period of higher electricity prices, energy efficiency measures funded by revenues from auctioning permits have actually reduced electricity prices (Hibbard, Okie, Tierney, & Darling, 2015).

International

The United Nations has led international efforts to head off climate change. In 1988, the UN helped establish the Intergovernmental Panel on Climate Change (IPCC). In turn, the IPCC has influenced subsequent UN programs such as the 1992 UN

Framework to Combat Climate Change (UNFCCC) and the 1992 Kyoto Protocol. Representatives of nearly 200 countries met in Paris at the end of 2015 to set goals to restrict warming to less than 2°C.

Again, we would expect that agreeing to restrict emissions will increase electricity prices. To date, carbon prices have been low, due to the program initially issuing large numbers of permits as well as the global recession that began in 2008.

Policy options

We have made a case for incentive-based programs rather than command-and-control. CAC should be reserved for situations such as toxic wastes. Spent fuel from nuclear plants is not suitable for an IB approach such as cap-and-trade. We want tight control over inventories of uranium and plutonium.

Although the United States has not yet instituted a carbon trading market, governments elsewhere are increasing their use of IB programs. China has seven cap-and-trade pilot programs. British Columbia implemented a carbon tax, implementing offsetting tax cuts elsewhere in the economy.

There are also CAC policies that add flexibility. Some RPSs allow trading among states to meet standards. The proposed U.S. CPP sets state-specific carbon reductions but gives states flexibility in how to meet the standard and would allow trading among states.

Summary

The U.S. government established formal environmental protection in the 1970s, including the EPA, NEPA, the CAA, and the CWA. The goal of regulations on energy production is to achieve socially optimal outputs. CAC using technical or performance standards can reduce emissions, but at a high cost. Economists prefer incentive-based regulations when possible. The U.S. government adopted market-based approaches with the 1990 CAA amendments. The cap-and-trade system reduced the emissions of SO_2 at a lower cost than the CAC alternative.

Two economic theories contribute to the design of market-based governmental regulations of primary and secondary energy production. The Pigou tax internalizes the external costs of energy production. The remedy assumes the government can accurately measure the marginal external cost and that the government acts in society's best interest. The Coase theorem offers another approach to internalizing externalities and can be more efficient than the Pigou tax approach. As long as the property right is assigned to one party, the other party negotiates to a point where marginal benefit from the negotiation equals its costs. The negotiations approach has the potential to be more efficient because the economic actors in the market often have better information than the government. One issue with the Coase approach is transaction costs, especially a negotiation involving many parties. Also, the Coase theorem pertains strictly to efficiency and not fairness.

Cost–benefit analysis is a fundamental instrument for the government to evaluate its regulations on energy production and environmental impacts. Its implementation, however, is difficult because many environmental impacts have no market. The hedonic and the travel cost approaches provide an estimate of use values. Contingent valuation can measure use and nonuse values.

From the economics perspective, the level of regulation should be set based on the criteria of maximizing social welfare by maximizing net benefits. There are both federal- and state-level regulations. In essence, the benefit of federal legislation is economies of scale where constituents throughout the country jointly consume the output. That benefit, however, must be weighed against heterogeneous local preferences.

Notes

1 Faraday is named in honor of Michael Faraday's 1831 discovery of electromagnetic induction and Faraday's law involving the use of magnetic current to create an electric field.
2 The current price of the Mirai for UK customers willing to deal with range anxiety given the absence of hydrogen refueling stations is £66,000 (equivalent to about $100,000) (Sharman, 2015).
3 If it is hard for you to imagine a world without penalties for oil spills, substitute ships disposing of trash. When the ocean was seen as an inexhaustible resource, cruise ships simply dumped out trash, including excess oil, into the ocean. It was the lowest-cost solution to them and as long as society believed the ocean could absorb the trash without any consequences, the lowest-cost solution to society. When society altered its view and saw consequences to dumping oil and other trash in the ocean, the rules changed and there are now penalties for polluting the ocean.
4 Recall that economics takes an anthropocentric view. Fish only count to the extent that we count them. If we care about their well-being over and beyond the loss to the fishing industry, we as a society can incorporate that concern by establishing laws and other institutions to bring about the socially preferred outcome. However, the fish do not get to vote.
5 The Oil Pollution Act of 1990 required that new tankers be built with double hulls. However, single-hulled tankers already in operation were not required to add a second hull because of the prohibitive retrofitting cost.
6 John Whitehead and Tim Haab have an environmental economics blog. The number comes from their entry of March 5, 2016. Please see Whitehead (2016).
7 A hedonic approach uses wages to infer the value of a statistical life. Workers are compensated for riskier jobs. But if they do not know the risks, then the inference is not valid.
8 All countries now have rights to waters up to 200 miles from shore.

References

Arrow, K., Solow, R., Leamer, E., Portney, P., Randner, R., & Schuman, H. (1993). Report of the NOAA panel on contingent valuation. *Federal Register, 58*, 4602–4614.

Borenstein, S., Bushnell, J., Wolak, F. A., & Zaragoza-Watkins, M. (2015). *Expecting the unexpected: Emissions uncertainty and environmental market design.* NBER Working Paper 20999.

Bunn, M., Zhang, H., & Kang, L. (2016). *The cost of reprocessing in China.* Retrieved June 21, 2016 from http://belfercenter.ksg.harvard.edu/files/The%20Cost%20of%20Reprocessing-Digital-PDF.pdf

California Environmental Protection Agency. (2016). *Zero emission vehicle (ZEV) program.* Retrieved January 9, 2017 from https://www.arb.ca.gov/msprog/zevprog/zevprog.htm

Carson, R., Mitchell, R. C., Hanemann, W. M., Kopp, R. J., Presser, S., & Ruud, P. A. (2003). Contingent valuation and lost passive use: Damages from the Exxon Valdez oil spill. *Environmental and Resource Economics, 25*, 257–286.

Chen, Y., Jin, G. Z., Kumar, N., & Shi, G. (2013). The promise of Beijing: Evaluating the impact of the 2008 Olympic Games on air quality. *Journal of Environmental Economics and Management, 66*(3), 424–443.

Cicchetti, C., & Freeman, A.M. (1973). The Trans-Alaska Pipeline: An economic analysis of alternatives. In A. C. Enthoven & A. M. Freeman III (Eds), *Pollution, resources, and the environment* (pp. 271–284). New York: W.W. Norton & Company.

Coase, R. (1960). The problem of social cost. *Journal of Law and Economics*, *3*, 1–44.

Dales, J. H. (1968). *Pollution, property and prices: An essay in policy-making and economics*. Toronto: University of Toronto Press.

Dorjets, V. (2014). Many newer power plants have cooling systems that reuse water. Retrieved June 21, 2016 from http://www.eia.gov/todayinenergy/detail.cfm?id=14971

Farrington, D. (2016, May 11). Elon Musk's hyperloop dream has its 1st public demo. *NPR.ORG*. Retrieved January 9, 2017 from http://www.npr.org/sections/thetwo-way/2016/05/11/477645103/elon-musks-hyperloop-dream-is-about-to-have-its–1st-public-demo

Gray, W., & Shadbegian, R. (2015). *Multimedia pollution regulation and environmental performance: EPA's cluster rule*. Resources for the Future Discussion Paper, RFF DP 15–26.

Hibbard, P. J., Okie, A. M., Tierney, S. F., & Darling, P. G. (2015). *The economic impacts of the regional greenhouse gas initiative on nine Northeast and Mid-Atlantic states*. Retrieved January 9, 2017 from http://www.analysisgroup.com/uploadedfiles/content/insights/publishing/analysis_group_rggi_report_july_2015.pdf

Howarth, R. (2015). A bridge to nowhere: Methane emissions and the greenhouse gas footprint of natural gas. *Energy Science and Engineering*, *2*(2), 47–60.

Howe, M. (2015, August 7). California aims for all new cars to be emissions free by 2030. Retrieved January 9, 2017 from http://gas2.org/2015/08/07/california-aims-new-cars-emissions-free–2030/

Kotchen, M., & Burger, N. (2007). Should we drill in the Arctic National Wildlife Refuge? An economic perspective. *Energy Policy*, *35*, 4720–4729.

Lazar, J., & Farnsworth, D. (2011). *Incorporating environmental costs in electric rates*. Retrieved June 22, 2016 from file:///C:/Users/CoB_User/Downloads/RAP_LazarFarnsworth_Incorporating EnvironmentalCostsinElectricRates_2011_10%20(1).pdf

Lee, D. (2001). To drill or not to drill: Let the environmentalists decide. *Independent Review*, *6*(2), 217–226. Retrieved June 18, 2016 from https://www.independent.org/pdf/tir/tir_06_2_lee.pdf

Malinowksi, P. A., Stillwell, A. S., Wu, J. S., & Schwarz, P. M. (2015). Energy–water nexus: Potential energy savings and implications for sustainable integrated water management in urban areas from rain-water harvesting and gray-water reuse. *Journal of Water Resources Planning and Management*, *141*, 1–10.

Mason, C., Muehlenbachs, L., & Olmstead, S. (2015). The economics of shale gas development. *Annual Review of Resource Economics*, *7*(1), 269–289.

Morgan, O. A., Whitehead, J. C., Huth, W. L., Martin, G. S., & Sjolander, R. (2016). Measuring the impact of the BP Deepwater Horizon oil spill on consumer behavior. *Land Economics*, *92*(1), 82–95.

Muehlenbachs, L., Spiller, E., & Timmins, C. (2015). The housing market impacts of shale gas development. *American Economic Review*, *105*(12), 3633–3659.

Natural Resources Defense Council. (2011). *Power plant cooling water and Clean Water Act section 316(b): The need to modernize U.S. power plants and protect our water resources*. Retrieved June 21, 2016 from https://www.nrdc.org/sites/default/files/powerplantcooling.pdf

Nuclear Watch of New Mexico. (2017). *SRS—Savannah River site*. Retrieved January 9, 2017 from http://nukewatch.org/activemap/NWC-SRS.html

Oklahoma Secretary of Energy & Environment. (n.d.) *Earthquakes in Oklahoma: FAQS*. Retrieved January 9, 2017 from http://earthquakes.ok.gov/faqs/

Orszag, P. R. (2007). *Costs of reprocessing versus directly disposing of spent nuclear fuel*. Washington, D.C.: Congressional Budget Office. Retrieved January 9, 2017 from https://www.cbo.gov/sites/default/files/cbofiles/ftpdocs/88xx/doc8808/11–14-nuclearfuel.pdf

Pigou, A. (1920). *The economics of welfare*. London: Macmillan and Co.

Richardson, J. (1982). *Making it happen: A positive guide to the future*. U.S. Association for the Club of Rome. ISBN–13: 978–0942718003.

Schmalensee, R., & Stavins, R. (2013). The SO_2 allowance trading system: The ironic history of a grand policy experiment. *Journal of Economic Perspectives*, *27*(1), 103–122.

Schwarz, P. (2005). Multipollutant efficiency standards for electricity production. *Contemporary Economic Policy, 23*(3), 341–356.

Sharman, A. (2015, October 25). Toyota bets the future car will be fueled by hydrogen. *Financial Times*. Retrieved June 16, 2016 from http://www.ft.com/intl/cms/s/2/a2d9151e–7427–11e5–a129–3fcc4f641d98.html#axzz4BjglFp6y

Whitehead, J. (2016, March 05). The BP/Deepwater Horizon federal CVM study estimated damages of $17 billion [Web log post]. Retrieved January 9, 2017 from http://www.env-econ.net/2016/03/the-bpdeepwater-horizon-federal-cvm-study-estimated-damages-of–17-billion.html

Winkler, D., & Gordon, B. (2013). The effect of the BP oil spill on volume and selling prices of oceanfront condominiums. *Land Economics, 89*(4), 614–631.

Chapter 15

Energy and sustainability

"There is something fundamentally wrong in treating the earth as if it were a business in liquidation."

Herman Daly (1977)

"What makes achieving sustainability so hard is that there are always more immediate problems that require our attention."

The author of this text

Introduction

Sustainability in its most widely recognized definition requires that we use today's resources in a way that does not leave the future worse off. The term is becoming ubiquitous in every aspect of the economy, from statements of business objectives to university curricula, due to an understanding that the economically viable resources of the earth are limited. Energy sustainability is a prominent focus, being the combination of investment in energy efficiency and renewable energy resources. We contrast the economic approach to sustainability with the perspective of physical scientists. Physical scientists see physical limits to resources, or *absolute scarcity*. Economists think in terms of *relative scarcity*, or opportunity cost. Opportunity cost will slow the use of scarce resources before depletion due to lowered economic viability. As supply diminishes, prices will rise, and there will be an incentive to find substitutes and new technologies.

Robert Solow, winner of the Nobel Prize in Economic Sciences in 1991, stated:

> It is very hard to be against sustainability. In fact, the less you know about it, the better it sounds. The questions that come to be connected with sustainable development or sustainable growth are genuine and deeply felt and very complex. The combination of deep feeling and complexity breeds buzzwords.
>
> (Solow, 1993, p. 179)

Sustainability has indeed become a buzzword. There are so many interpretations and it is so widely used, that it threatens to lose any meaning (Schwarz et al., 2009). Nevertheless, Solow (1993) provided a definition that has proven useful in economics, "[The best thing I could think of is to say that] it is an obligation to conduct ourselves so that we leave to the future the option or the capacity to be as well off as we are." The key distinction between Solow's definition and earlier interpretations of sustainability is the term "capacity," which opens the idea that technological progress may improve sustainability.

As sustainability has aspects of a global public good and there are no global governments, countries have attempted to come together on the topics of climate change mitigation and sustainability. The United Nations has been at the center of these efforts. However, we do face the challenge that the UN is not a world government, and cannot impose laws unless countries agree to them. Global public goods face the free-rider problem. Countries may maximize their individual well-being while other countries make sacrifices, but they are not required to contribute to the public good. Economics suggests that achieving global agreements will be very difficult. Nevertheless, it can also provide insights into how to make progress, such as rewarding richer countries not only for progress within their country, but also for contributing financially to achieve progress in poorer countries.

The next part of this chapter takes up definitions of sustainability as they pertain to energy economics. We then focus on energy sources as components of a sustainability strategy. The next part addresses energy conservation and efficiency. We then examine consumption strategies aimed at electricity use. The final section is a summary.

Meaning of sustainability

The most widely known definition is that put forward in 1987 by the Bruntland Commission as "development which meets the needs of current generations without compromising the ability of future generations to meet their own needs" (Bruntland, 1987). Economists shy away from the term "needs," perhaps because of its Marxist connections in the phrase "From each according to his abilities, to each according to his needs." Economists find it difficult to distinguish needs and wants, preferring to base their analysis on what people want and are willing to pay for, or in short, *revealed preference*. Moreover, when it comes to future generations, we do not know their preferences. The safest assumption is that they will have the same preferences we do. However, the value of ecosystems is likely to rise over time, with rising incomes and increasing population. As income increases, people want more of *normal goods*— where demand increases with income—and want more of public goods as population increases. As countries develop, they are better able leave a resource endowment for the future, rather than depleting resources for today simply to survive. In addition, since ecology and other environmental resources have benefits that are nonrival and nonexcludable, the sum of benefits increases with rising population. Therefore, we can make a case that investing in the future will have increasing benefits as income and population increase.

A key question is whether we need to provide specific resources, the debate between weak and strong sustainability. Where resource substitution is possible, economists favor weak substitutability, such as selling more today and investing the proceeds, be it in alternative sources of energy, better universities, or simply cash in the bank that the next generation can spend as it wishes. Sustainability advocates outside economists are more likely to call for strong sustainability, the need to endow the future with specific resources. The case is strongest for ecological systems on which life depends and for which there are no human-made substitutes. Examples of ecological systems include the water cycle, coral reefs, tropical rainforests, and even the entire planet.

In fact, some view the term "sustainable development" as an oxymoron, and that we need to abandon economic growth in favor of other objectives. The implication is an economic growth rate of zero or even less. Advocates of a *simple life* call for smaller houses, eating locally, and other ways that conserve existing resources. They argue that correlation of happiness with materialistic possessions or economic growth is not a universal concept, citing indexes that include countries with simpler lives and fewer material possessions outranking countries with higher well-being as measured by the standard of per capita *gross domestic product.*

Sustainability can also have multiple dimensions, with frequent reference to the "triple-bottom line" that refers to economic, environmental, and social sustainability. Economic sustainability calls for using resources today in ways that will allow future generations to achieve at least as productive an economy. Environmental sustainability focuses on leaving future generations in an equal or better position with respect to environmental resources and ecosystems, including air and water. Social sustainability, the least well-defined, most nebulous, and farthest from typical economic considerations, refers to developing institutions that empower citizens today and in the future. The goals might include human rights, greater equality, and even happiness. Advocates would argue that not everything that is worth doing is measurable, and that social sustainability should be included along with economics and environment as the three pillars of the achievement of sustainability.

Economists caution that there are always trade-offs. Pursuit of sustainability could be at the expense of efficiency. Given a choice between a present and future of $10,000 in each time period and another growth path that generates $20,000 to today's citizens and $15,000 to the next generation, only the first path is sustainable. Yet the second would seem clearly preferable to all but an extreme devotee to outcome equality.[1] We also know that redistributing income can dull incentives to produce. If today's generation invests more of the proceeds from using resources today for the benefit of the future, they may have less motivation to use those resources as efficiently as possible. This trade-off is little different from increasing the tax rate on the last dollar earned; there is less reason to earn that last dollar.

Limits to Growth *revisited*

Herman Daly proposes *steady-state growth*, a slightly less stringent recipe than was put forward by *Limits to Growth*. The premise is that all growth is not equal. He would only allow growth that leaves intact ecosystem systems necessary for our survival. Daly's proposal will slow the rate of depletion of nonrenewable resources such as oil, but will not stop it. Therefore, his concept will not fully satisfy calls for strong sustainability. *Limits* adherents see the need for a fundamental change in our economic system, a move away from materialism and a move towards equality.

Economists would level similar criticisms at Daly's paradigm as they do at *Limits*. It ignores the role of relative scarcity in leading to higher prices, which in turn motivates substitution and advances in technology. Economists have been labeled optimists, or Cornucopians, for claiming that technology will always come to the rescue. A further point for optimism is dematerializing, as we shift from manufacturing to a services economy. That shift has also been a factor in lower energy intensity, so that each unit of output uses less energy. *Limits* adherents are among the pessimists, or Cassandras, fearing the collapse of our ecological systems, and in turn our economic system, which requires nature's resources to survive.

The debate about "IPAT" helps to crystallize the opposing perspectives (Ehrlich & Holdren, 1971). According to this equation:

$$I = P \times A \times T$$

where I is impact on the environment, P is population, A is affluence, and T is technology.[2]

Increases in population, affluence, or technology have a negative impact on the environment. As there is recognition that advances in technology can reduce environmental impact, IPAT adherents assume that even in cases where the use of additional technologies does not have a negative environmental impact, growth in population and affluence will outstrip the effects of resource-conserving technology.

Either way, economists note the absence of price in the relationship. We also question the claim that population and affluence effects will outweigh technology effects. Nordhaus (1992) and Weitzman (1999) find the resource-conserving aspect of new technology to greatly outweigh concerns about absolute resource scarcity. Furthermore, once a country reaches a critical point of development, affluence increases the demand for environmental quality. In addition, affluence also curtails population growth, as families and countries with higher incomes choose to have fewer children. Economists reject the IPAT framework on multiple grounds.

Paul Ehrlich, an ecologist whom we encountered earlier in the text, is one of the originators of IPAT along with scientists Barry Commoner and John Holdren.[3] Recall that Ehrlich made a wager with economist Julian Simon about the direction of resource prices. Ten years later, five minerals, all chosen by Ehrlich, had fallen in price, consistent with Simon's optimistic view of technology and going against Ehrlich's pessimistic view of absolute scarcity of nonrenewable resources.

Ehrlich and other *Limits* adherents have repeatedly warned about running out of resources, environmental catastrophe, and population devastation, but have had to extend the deadlines for when these events will happen when the disasters have not occurred as predicted. Ehrlich, Donella Meadows, and other well-known pessimists say their vindication will come when the catastrophe occurs. Economists are willing to run the risk.

Ethics

Philosophers view sustainability as an *ethic*. Ethics attempt to distinguish right from wrong and virtuous from nonvirtuous. The sustainability ethic extends these considerations to future generations. *Deep ecology* maintains that humans have no special place in the universe, with plants and animals having an intrinsic right to their place in the ecosystem. Taken to an extreme, environmental terrorists bury projectiles in trees to cause injury to anyone who attempts to cut the tree down. Economics claims to avoid ethics because of the difficulty of reaching widespread agreement on what is ethical.

Sometimes unknowingly, we do use ethics. The economic assumption that consumers maximize utility is a form of *utilitarianism*, an ethic developed by philosopher Jeremy Bentham in the late 1700s. Utilitarianism counts the ends, but not the means. Lying may be permissible if it results in greater total utility.

We also maintain an *anthropocentric* perspective, measuring utility by what makes us better off. Consider our choice of which endangered species to protect. Studies have found that we place greater emphasis on *charismatic megafauna*. A lesser extreme is animal rights, as espoused by the philosopher Peter Singer (1975). Singer is a utilitarian philosopher who builds upon Bentham's original reasoning that those who can suffer should count in finding maximum well-being. Not only would Singer's perspective make a stronger case for saving endangered species, going beyond the anthropocentric perspective of economics that we should save them if it makes us better off, but it would question the concept of animals as pets.

The sustainability ethic to include future generations asserts that representing generations as yet unborn is simply the right thing to do. Immanuel Kant developed deontological ethics whereby certain things are intrinsically good—the means are worthwhile for their own sake—as opposed to teleological or consequentialist ethics, where what matters is the ends or instrumental value, such as providing pleasure to individuals.

Economists are hesitant to assert a claim that there are intrinsically good behaviors, as there is no widespread agreement on what these might be. Yet we may be unaware of our assumptions, as we place efficiency and possibly social welfare as our top priorities, viewing equity and sustainability as open to debate.

While economics is hesitant to impose a sustainability ethic, we would advocate that should we pursue that goal, we do so in an efficient way. After all, it would be unethical to use more than the efficient amount of resources to mitigate climate change, given other pressing objectives such as helping the impoverished citizens of today achieve a higher standard of living. In fact, Thomas Schelling noted the paradox of spending large sums to protect the future instead of protecting the poorest of today's citizens (Schelling, 1997). Adding to the paradox is that if the last 200 years are a guide, future generations will be better off than the citizens of today. Therefore, those of us with lower incomes are spending money to help what is likely to be a wealthier future generation.

Dynamic energy market conditions

Economics addressed topics related to sustainability long before the term became ubiquitous. The Hotelling rule addresses the extraction of oil over time, with the implication that competitive markets will efficiently balance oil extraction between now and in the future. However, given the current interest in sustainability, the relabeling of some work that predates the sustainability movement has occurred in order to expand the sustainability umbrella.

Consider whether we use oil sustainably. Physical scientists typically believe we do not. M. King Hubbert, the Shell Oil geologist who in 1956 put forward the Peak Oil hypothesis, predicted that U.S. oil production would peak around 1970. Given that oil is a nonrenewable resource, production would inevitably decline after "Hubbert's Peak." The implication is that given finite reserves, we need to slow the rate of extraction if we are to leave future generations with at least as much productive capacity as we have today.

Hotelling's rule provides dynamically efficient extraction over time, but does not guarantee the use today will not compromise the ability of future generations to achieve at least as much productive capacity as the present generation. It does explain why producers will choose to leave some oil in the ground for the future, but does not explicitly consider sustainability. It is, in fact, possible that dynamically efficient production will extract the entire supply within a finite number of years, leaving no oil for some future generation.[4]

Impacts of growing global demand for energy

As global population grows and developing countries advance, global energy demand is likely to increase. The oil price spike in 2009 when oil rose to $147 per barrel was widely attributed to what was expected to be an inexorable thirst for more energy in China, with India and other developing countries not far behind. Even after oil plummeted to near $50 by the end of that year, analysts still cited the inevitability of higher demand when prices topped $100 per barrel midway through 2014. However, prices since then have retreated closer to half that amount.

If demand is growing, why have prices not risen? For one thing, demand did not rise with the onset of the Great Recession, nor has it resumed its prerecession growth. Consider U.S. energy consumption as shown in Figure 15.1.

During the recession, consumers used less petroleum as they cut their automobile traveling while spending less due to concerns about income and jobs. Energy efficiency also kicked in, as higher gasoline prices led to the purchase of more energy-efficient vehicles. Overall, we can expect demand to resume its upward movement with a strengthening economy, but the trend is likely to be a smaller increase as energy efficiency advances with new technology.

Assume that demand does increase. Can the outcome be sustainable? Physical scientists would say it is not. There is only a limited amount of oil, and at some point,

Quadrillion Btu

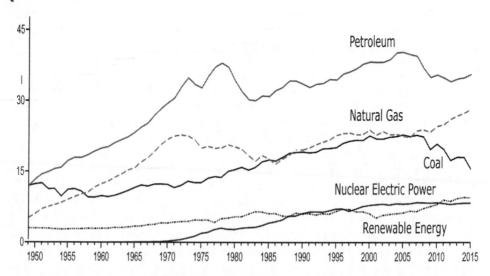

Figure 15.1 U.S. energy primary consumption, 1949–2015. Adapted from Monthly Energy Review, by EIA, 2016. Retrieved January 13, 2017 from https://www.eia.gov/totalenergy/data/monthly/pdf/mer.pdf.

we will have used it to the point where future generations will have less, and eventually none. Furthermore, they cite the laws of thermodynamics, noting that matter is neither created nor destroyed. However, as we use energy, its *entropy*—the amount of disorder in the molecules—increases, resulting in a less useful form of energy. Nevertheless, by Solow's definition, the outcome is sustainable as long as we do not compromise future *capacity*. As demand increases and other factors remain constant, price will rise. Higher prices will stimulate the use of substitutes, such as hybrid and electric vehicles, and at a high enough price, hydrogen vehicles, as well as other forms of transportation—public transportation, bicycling, even walking.

Solow also advocates a policy that echoes *Hartwick's rule* (Hartwick, 1977). To assure sustainability, invest the rents derived from the consumption of nonrenewable resources today into productive resources for tomorrow, assuming the two are substitutable as far as maintaining productive capacity is concerned. The willingness to substitute physical for natural capital is weak sustainability, and scientists outside of traditional economics advocate strong sustainability, where we leave future generations at least the level of natural resources that we enjoy today.[5] Some observers have noted that strictly speaking, strong sustainability would not allow us to use any of our nonrenewable resources, as the future would then have a smaller supply than today's generation, and have labeled such a requirement *absurdly strong sustainability*. To make strong sustainability a viable concept, we can view strong sustainability as requiring the preservation of certain natural capital such as ecosystems necessary to sustain life. The two perspectives differ on the degree to which we can substitute one type of capital for another.

In its weakest form, we can simply invest the rents from today's consumption of natural resources so that the future has sufficient money to compensate for any damage. Alternatively, the future can use the proceeds to mitigate damage in the future.

Natural scientists contest the notion that we can damage our ecosystems and somehow compensate the future. They are among scientists, some of them economists, who established a new discipline they entitled "ecological economics" with a focus on natural resources, particularly ecosystems, that they see as essential to the world's well-being and for which there are no good substitutes.[6] They would contend that the buildup of carbon in the atmosphere threatens not only economic prosperity, but also the earth's ecosystem and the survival of the planet. On local levels, developing countries may depend upon forests to help purify water, but with limited income and a lack of alternatives, will cut trees for firewood at a rate that will leave future generations impoverished. Water has many uses including hydropower, but the building of hydroelectric facilities can change ecosystems and could damage plant and aquatic life.

Supply considerations

Strong sustainability argues against depleting our nonrenewable resources, particularly oil. The original 1972 *Limits to Growth* volume focused on running out of oil and other nonrenewable resources, then shifted its focus to pollution in the 1992 update, and in the most recent 2002 update focuses on population. Regardless of the primary focus, they call for limits to growth before we overshoot the earth's ability to withstand the challenges of fossil fuel use, pollution, and population.

Economists do not find the *Limits* framework to be credible. Underlying assumptions arbitrarily assume exponential growth for factors such as population and pollution, while other factors grow little if at all, such as technology. Most fundamentally, prices do not adjust despite the depletion of a resource.

In 1798, Thomas Malthus famously predicted that population would outstrip food supplies, leading to cycles of exponential population growth followed by starvation. His predictions have not happened for developed countries, and economists reject predictions by *Limits to Growth* advocates that population will bring about ruin in the future, or the notion that the earth has a fixed *carrying capacity*, so that there is some upper limit on the number of humans the planet can hold. Those who today embody the perspective that increases in population threaten human well-being are *neo-Malthusians*. Advocates of the need to limit population growth may wear the name with honor, while economists invoking the term may be using it in a disparaging way.

Nevertheless, as on the demand side, let us extrapolate the consequences of depletion of traditional fuels over time. If we use our supplies of fossil fuels without regard to future generations, we will also leave them a buildup of environmental problems including pollution and climate change, a secondary reason why an upward trend in their use is seen as unsustainable. In order to change the status quo, we need environmental regulations restricting their use.

In 1976, Amory Lovins coined the "soft path" as using renewables rather than the "hard path" of fossil fuels. He also advocated energy efficiency, or negawatts instead of megawatts, in a keynote address at the 1989 Montreal Green Energy Conference. Sustainability advocates invoke business considerations. They cite the hypothesis of Richard Porter that businesses benefit from sustainability. Economists are dubious that businesses "leave $20 bills lying on the sidewalk," and focus on the costs should society incorporate sustainability as a goal.

Sustainable energy

An energy source is sustainable if its use does not reduce future energy resources. Typically, we are referring to strong sustainability and the use of renewable resources. Their use today does not reduce the supply available to the next generation.

Clearly, wind and solar energy meet the definition. Hydroelectricity is also sustainable as long as the use of water does not exceed its depletion. So-called "fossil water," such as groundwater in an underground aquifer, may take a long time to regenerate and so while renewable, is depletable. If the rate of use exceeds the rate of regeneration, then it is not a sustainable source. The same distinction holds for geothermal power. Tapping into the earth's heat as a source of energy is sustainable unless its use can deplete the source of heat. Biomass can be sustainable if it does not degrade soil quality.

We focus here on commercially feasible alternatives. Sources such as wind, solar, and biomass are also domestic sources, providing energy security. Sources such as wave and tidal power, and experimental technologies such as nuclear fusion, are in Chapter 10 on next-generation alternatives.

Wind and solar energy

Advocates of sustainability call for a transition to the soft path advocated by Amory Lovins as quickly as is feasible. They call for the immediate retirement of coal plants due to environmental concerns, with climate change at the top of the list. They may tolerate natural gas as preferable to coal because of lower carbon emissions, but still not acceptable other than during the transition to carbon-free energy generation. There is little agreement on nuclear energy, some willing to allow it in the mix as a carbon-free source of fuel, and others rejecting it due to the unsolved problem of storing radioactive waste, the risk of catastrophe, and concerns about uranium or other radioactive elements falling into the wrong hands. What is clear is that sustainability advocates prefer renewable energy.[7]

Box 15.1 Solar loses its flare

Both wind and solar are declining in cost rapidly. Yet governments typically subsidize their use. Setting aside sustainability, the advent of hydraulic fracturing combined with horizontal drilling allowed natural gas to substitute for coal and accelerated coal plant retirement. However, its low cost has also slowed the adoption of renewable fuels.

A number of countries have taken leadership positions in speeding the transition. Germany provided large inducements to use solar energy. The country set ambitious targets for renewables as a percentage of electricity generation of 35% by 2020, 50% by 2030 and 80% by 2050 (Wirth, 2016). Yet Germany has cut back on subsidies given the budget impact, and installations have slowed in the last few years. To meet the gap, they have stepped up use of lignite, also known as brown coal, a particularly dirty coal.

Spain has had a similar trajectory, second to Germany in PV installations until it drastically cut its subsidies. Unlike Germany, Spain has a sunny climate, so solar energy has a better chance to succeed on its own than is the case in Germany. Spain has a target that 20% of its electricity generation will come from renewables by 2020, with both wind and solar prominent (Klessmann et al., 2013).

Biomass energy

Biomass energy is energy from plants, and it is the most ancient of fuels, used ever since the first humans burned wood for heat and cooking fuel. Wood is still widely used, but it is rarely sustainable. The use of wood can result in deforestation if the rate of harvesting exceeds the growth rate. Forests store carbon, but then release it when trees are cut down. The indoor use of wood for cooking and heating can hurt the health of residents. Wood smoke emitted through chimneys contributes to air pollution.

Other sources of bioenergy range from crops grown for their energy content, such as fast-growing trees, grasses, and algae. Ideally, biomass sources used for energy should not compete with food uses, which is not the case for corn used to make ethanol. Corn stover—corn stalks, leaves, and husks—contains energy, but we must also consider the larger amount of energy needed to extract the energy from biomass and convert it into usable energy.

Waste to energy is another source of biomass. There have been attempts at trash-burning power plants. Such plants hold out a vision of a Pareto improvement, as we not only produce energy from a plentiful source, but also eliminate unwanted trash. Charlotte, North Carolina, constructed such a plant, but soon found that air pollution in the surrounding area exceeded the allowed standard. We also have to consider the type of trash. In one case, a plant was burning medical refuse, which emitted unpleasant odors as well as causing concerns about health effects. In addition, we have to consider the cost of building and operating the plant, as well as the energy content of the trash.

If we do not recycle the trash, we will have to dispose of it. One common result is to store the trash at a landfill. The public dislikes landfills, as much of the trash does not decompose, and landfills often occupy economically viable land. Where there is decomposition, methane gas forms. If methane escapes, it is a potent GHG. If captured, it is a fuel, equivalent to natural gas. We can accelerate the process with anaerobic digestion. There are commercially available technologies that contain the waste and maintain a temperature that favors decomposition and the production of methane. As always, there is no such thing as a free lunch, or even free trash. There is a cost to the digester, and we have to consider how much usable methane energy we are able to capture.

Trash comes in all different shapes and sizes, from French fry grease to hog manure. At a cost, many of these wastes can be biomass for bioenergy.

Hydroelectric

Large-scale hydro facilities were the earliest forms of electricity generation. While once regarded as benign, we have since recognized the effects of hydroelectric plants on ecological systems, particularly aquatic plants and fish. In any case, there are few remaining sites for building dams to generate electricity.

Wave and tidal power still require underwater structures that can interfere with aquatic life. Nor will they be available widely. Tidal power in particular is only suited to where there is a large and rapid change in water level, such as in the Bay of Fundy in Nova Scotia, Canada.

Algae

Algae are an alternative source of biomass to woods or grasses. It can be done, but at what cost? After ten years of investigating algae as a source of fuel, Exxon abandoned its efforts as too costly (Carroll, 2013). Upfront investment costs per unit of energy are high, and it is not known whether the technology is scalable and the per-unit cost reducible to where it will ever be commercially competitive.[8]

Nuclear

Nuclear energy represents the elephant in the room. While uranium is a nonrenewable resource, the discussions around the use of nuclear energy do not focus on concerns about limited supplies. If the United States were to continue to run its existing nuclear fission plants, supplies should last approximately 200 years. If we could affordably extract uranium from the ocean floor, we could have 65,000 years of supply (*Scientific American*, 2009). Another means of extending uranium supplies is to reprocess the nuclear fuel as is done in France. Then there are alternative nuclear plant technologies, as well as plants that run on different fuels, such as thorium, or a mix of fuels, such as mixed oxide fuel (MOX), typically a blend of plutonium and uranium. These alternatives, as well as nuclear fusion, were detailed in Chapter 10 on next-generation technologies. For now, we have existing nuclear technology, the only large-scale carbon-free energy source.

As the topic of this chapter is sustainability, we can envision two scenarios, one in which we include, however reluctantly, a role for nuclear energy, and one in which we do not. If we include nuclear energy, we have a highly reliable technology that can limit the use of coal, and to a lesser extent, natural gas, as a source of baseload electricity generation. We can expect that the cost of generating a unit of power from new construction will exceed the cost of fossil fuel alternatives by a wide margin, as promises of cheap, affordable nuclear energy have proven false since its beginnings in the 1950s as an electricity-generating fuel.

In the absence of nuclear energy, we will still need baseload power, the power that runs 24/7. The current choices are coal, nuclear, and increasingly natural gas. Some locations can tap into hydro or geothermal. Baseload energy sources are *dispatchable*— under the control of the system operator when needed. Of the renewable fuels, only biofuels qualify. Wind and solar are not dispatchable, as the dispatcher cannot vary their production to match demand, and as they are available only intermittently. Increasingly, battery storage will give the system operator greater control over their use. However, battery storage is not yet mainstream because of the cost of storing electricity, as detailed in Chapter 10 on next-generation alternatives. Given present alternatives, a diminishing role for nuclear energy means that natural gas will expand its role as a bridge to the future of renewables. There will also be great pressure to keep coal in the mix. Are there ways to use coal in a way that is consistent with sustainability? We turn to that energy source next.

Coal

Sustainable coal may appear to be an oxymoron, and sustainability advocates will likely push for no new coal plants and accelerated retirement of plants in operation. In order to meet electricity baseload demand, coal and nuclear are the longtime options, with natural gas increasingly a third option. Again, hydro is only an option for locations with access to water, and there is little opportunity for new hydro construction. Geothermal also depends upon the availability of geology favoring heat and pressure near the earth's surface. Therefore, there is much attention on ways to use coal without the potentially dire consequences for the environment, including climate change.

Given the large supplies of coal, we must carefully consider options to use this resource in a more sustainable fashion. Coal also has the advantage of wide distribution throughout the world, an important consideration for energy security, the subject of the next chapter. We consider advanced combustion and carbon capture and storage (CCS) as the principal means to improve coal's sustainability profile.

Advanced combustion

Coal gasification transforms solid coal into a synthetic gas, or syngas, much like burning natural gas. In combined-cycle plants, the first cycle involves burning the fuel to drive a combustion turbine while the second cycle uses the exhaust heat to boil water and produce steam to drive a steam turbine. During the process, sulfur is removed. While NOx does not form, ammonia and particulate matter (PM) do and they can also be removed. CO_2 is also easier to separate and capture than from conventional coal plants. While a combined-cycle plant increases efficiencies by both burning the original fuel and reusing waste heat, the plants will require further efficiency gains to become cost-competitive (U.S. Department of Energy, n.d.).

Coal plant technology is advancing by producing energy more efficiently from coal. Heat rate measures the energy input required to produce a unit of electricity output. Gross output is the amount produced at the generating stage, while net output is the amount of electricity delivered to the transmission grid and available to customers after deducting electricity needed to operate the generating unit. A unit with a higher heat rate burns less coal to produce electricity, and so emits less carbon (and less of other unwanted emissions).

Supercritical and ultra-supercritical power plants operate at higher temperatures and pressures than conventional coal-fired power plants. They achieve higher heat rates, and therefore higher efficiencies, because at high temperature and pressure, gas and water coexist, reducing the energy needed to boil water and generate steam. It will not come as a surprise to any student of economics that the higher efficiency comes at a cost, in this case higher up-front capital costs. Nevertheless, supercritical plants are becoming the new "conventional" technology, and in China, new plants increasingly use ultra-supercritical technology. As China uses more coal than any other country, it has a particularly strong motivation to develop technologies for its continued use, while mitigating its own environmental problems and reducing carbon emissions to lessen climate change.

Carbon capture and storage (CCS)

It is unlikely that coal will have a place in a low-carbon future unless coal plants can incorporate CCS. CCS equipment captures carbon emissions before they leave the plant and injects them into storage such as old salt mines and oil and gas wells. In fact, one possible use is to inject CO_2 into existing oil and gas wells to increase pressure and recover additional deposits. If the CO_2 is stored but not reused, there is the possibility of eventual leakage. The technology is usable with natural gas plants, but since they are lower emitting, the carbon reduction is smaller.

CCS borders on next-generation technology in that much of today's efforts are at the demonstration stage, and that projects to date have huge cost overruns. Coal will not be a viable technology in a carbon-constrained future if CCS cannot become cost-effective. This statement is not an endorsement of governments funding projects without regard to cost. It is saying that there is a lot at stake for countries with abundant coal. Producers and workers have already experienced severe declines. Unless coal can overcome this hurdle, it may well be that existing plants will go into early retirement and there will not be new plants built.

If coal plants are to meet sustainability criteria, we will have to consider retrofitting existing plants as well as incorporating the technology in new plants. Retrofitting appears to be prohibitive in cost, given the redesigning required for existing plants to accommodate the technology. Installing the technology on new plants might add $0.09–0.15/kWh to the cost of coal-generated electricity, considerably more than the cost to generate power using natural gas plants and comparable to the cost estimates of new nuclear power plants. With the cost of natural gas low, and the cost of renewables declining, it is hard to see a path for CCS. Coal devotees will no doubt call for continued subsidies for CCS, but the record of accomplishment has not been good. It is not obvious what would allow CCS to become cost-competitive, unless we rule out the use of carbon-emitting fuels and nuclear energy. There is always the possibility of new technology, but the same is possible for nuclear fission and fusion, battery storage, and hydrogen vehicles.

Energy efficiency and conservation

Before sustainability became a ubiquitous concept, there was "reduce, reuse, and recycle." That simple phrase also expresses a ranking. In terms of sustainability, the best option is to reduce our use of resources. To do so, we could dematerialize—consume less—or find technologies that are less energy-intensive. Alternatively, we could shift our consumption to products that use less energy. In addition, the shift to a more service-oriented economy and away from manufacturing has also lessened our energy consumption. However, increasing populations throughout the developing world make it likely that global energy consumption will increase.

Reuse is not as highly ranked from a sustainability perspective, as it means we have produced something in the first place, vs. forgoing production. Still, it is an alternative to the throwaway society where everything gets a single use. Reuse is likely to call for less energy than new production. When grocery shopping, you could use a cloth bag repeatedly rather than plastic or paper. Alternatively, you could reuse your paper bags or return the plastic ones. Reuse is quite prevalent within the developing world due to a lack of wealth, and many products have multiple uses throughout their existence.

Recycling ranks third of the three R's. Here, we find new uses for existing products. We are producing new goods, but using previously harvested resources rather than newly harvested virgin materials. Recycling aluminum cans to make additional cans, or using the aluminum to make car parts, saves aluminum. It may or may not save energy, as compared to producing cans using new aluminum. Recycling plastic bottles to make new bottles, clothing, or even car seats, keeps the bottles out of landfills and reduces trash. However, there are many instances where recycling costs more than new production, including higher energy usage. Some of the products you dutifully recycle may not be worth recycling from a cost standpoint, and may still end up in a landfill eventually. Recycling is quite common within international trade, as the largest exports from developed nations to developing nations are the recycled materials that fuel the economies of the developing nations.

Negawatts vs. megawatts

Using less energy—negawatts in Amory Lovins's catchphrase—calls for less consumption or less energy-intensive consumption. While Chapter 11 on energy efficiency makes clear that using less energy need not be consistent with economic efficiency—driving a Smart Car may not be "smart" if there is not enough space for the family or their luggage—companies and consumers may find opportunities where using less energy is economically efficient. Claims that pursuing sustainability is simply a component of cost saving are too strong; using resources sustainably may or may not save money. Nevertheless, if reducing energy use is coincident with profit maximization, it is the preferred path if sustainability is also a goal.

Consumers may save less energy than might seem justified to an outside observer. While it might be due to market failures such as applying too high a discount rate, lack of financing for the initial investment, or asymmetric information where the consumer underestimates the cost savings, it could also be that the monetary savings do not justify the explicit and implicit costs. In addition to the costs of installing a more energy-efficient model—say triple-glazed vs. double- or single-glazed windows—there are transactions costs to obtaining the information needed to make a decision. In addition, the manufacturer's word is not likely to be an impartial source of information.

Even if consumers do buy the more efficient version, energy savings are likely to be smaller than forecast. The consumer with triple-glazed windows should benefit from lower electricity bills. However, the cost per unit of comfort also decreases, as less heat escapes to the outside. As a result, the consumer might choose to turn up the thermostat. In addition, the extra energy bill savings can go to buying more energy appliances. Taking the reasoning one step further, if electricity demand decreases, its price decreases, so that other consumers will increase their electricity demands. All three phenomena are types of rebound effects.[9]

Joskow and Marron (1992) examined electric utility conservation programs and found the cost per kWh saved was substantially higher than conservation advocates proclaim, about double the cost. An energy audit may seem like low-hanging fruit as a way to reduce costs and energy use. However, the consumer has to be at home during the audit, has to consider scrapping existing appliances, and has to evaluate the impartiality of the auditor. Electric utilities or efficiency advocacy groups may gain from adoptions of efficiency measures.[10]

Energy efficiency

Energy efficiency entails using less energy to achieve a given outcome, or the same amount of energy to achieve a greater outcome. Triple-glazed windows allow you to maintain a given level of comfort while reducing your electricity bills.[11] Moreover, a poorly insulated small house may use as much energy as a well-insulated larger one. Better insulation, either in the form of triple-glazed windows or wall and ceiling insulation, is likely to increase energy efficiency. It is likely to save energy as well, although the rebound effect of choosing a more comfortable thermostat setting will partially offset the energy savings.

The rebound effect is economically efficient, as you are making more use of energy now that it costs less per unit of comfort. Refrigerators have gotten more energy-efficient over time, but they have also gotten larger. There is likely to be a net energy saving, but again, it may be smaller than would be predicted based on an engineering estimate that predicts 25% lower energy use. That would be true if other things were held constant, including the size of the refrigerator, the inside temperature setting, how long the consumer leaves the door open, and the like.

On a macro scale, studies have examined economic development, measures of well-being such as average life span, and energy intensity of production. Some studies show that it was possible to reduce energy intensity while increasing well-being. Other studies showed the reverse.[12]

Consumption strategies

While sustainability advocates prefer energy conservation or negawatts, Herman Daly was willing to accept *steady-state growth*, which includes a stable level of energy use while leaving ecosystems intact. We consider several energy practices sympathetic to this objective, although Daly would not necessarily approve of these methods.

Renewable portfolio standards

Renewable portfolio standards (RPSs) set targets for the minimum amount of renewable energy as a percentage of total energy used to generate electricity. Over half of the U.S. states have voluntarily adopted RPSs. The state can decide the timetable, stringency of the targets, and the resources that qualify as renewable.

In the United States, California is often a leader in environmental measures. It established an aggressive RPS in 2002, with a goal of 33% renewables by 2020, and interim targets of 20% by the end of 2013 and 25% by the end of 2016. A recent extension sets a target of 50% by 2030. California's renewable mix includes solar, wind, geothermal, small hydro, and biomass (California Energy Commission, 2016).

California has by far the most geothermal energy of any state in the country, and this source of energy was by far the largest source when the RPS was established. California did not need to do much at first to achieve its renewables goals because geothermal was quite extensive before the RPS adoption. However, as California cannot easily expand the use of geothermal, other renewables need to account for growing percentages. Biomass was the second largest amount when the RPS began, again having attained this level prior to RPS. It is growing modestly. Small hydro was the third largest source prior to and at the establishment of RPS. However, several years of extreme droughts experienced by California have caused hydro to shrink. These trends point to wind and solar as the required growth areas. Wind capacity has been growing rapidly, although we must remember that the wind may only blow enough to produce usable energy one third of the time. In addition, recall that the production of wind does not always occur when needed. There is the example of Texas that has actually been giving away wind energy produced during the nighttime hours. Solar is now growing at the fastest rate. While wind is still the largest source, solar has passed biomass and will likely overtake geothermal by 2020.

Compare the California experience with North Carolina. North Carolina is the only state in the southeastern United States to establish an RPS. The program started in 2007, with a target of 12.5% renewables by 2020 and an interim target of 10% by 2018. These targets are for investor-owned utilities, with lower targets for electric cooperatives and municipal utilities. The current target is 6%, and there have been several attempts to freeze the requirement at that level or even abandon the RPS. So far, the legislation is intact.

The North Carolina RPS includes the renewables allowed by California, although the state has negligible geothermal power. However, the North Carolina version has some distinct features. It allows energy efficiency to count towards the renewables target. It also has minimum requirements for some specific technologies. There is a surprisingly modest minimum for solar of 0.2% by 2018. Most surprising to those unfamiliar with North Carolina, there are minimums for swine and poultry waste. Recently, the main investor-owned utility, Duke Energy, has been stepping up its use of hog waste despite the high cost of transforming it into usable energy. North Carolina is a leading producer of hogs and chickens, and these industries successfully lobbied to include these sources of energy. It has been a battle to meet the minimums, with technology in its infancy and cost high. There have also been disputes about whether the utility can count out-of-state conversion of waste to energy. Duke Energy has also fought to count wood as biomass, while environmentalists have been concerned that Duke will cut mature trees.

Feed-in tariffs

Feed-in tariffs (FITs) have a similar objective to RPSs. They take a price approach, whereas RPS is a quantity approach. The distinction is similar to the use of Pigou taxes—a price approach—and cap-and-trade—a quantity approach—to achieve environmental goals. Just as taxes and trading are equivalent under simplifying assumptions, FITs and RPSs can achieve equivalent goals. FITs promote long-term contracts between producers of renewable fuels and utilities. The long-term feature encourages long-term investments, since suppliers have certainty about price for a long period of 15–20 years. Prices typically decline over the course of the contract to reflect expected cost declines. Lower-cost renewables such as wind receive a lower price per unit.

In the United States, there have been legal questions that have discouraged the use of FITs, so states have chosen RPSs as the path of less resistance. A common legal position is that FITs are illegal at the federal level. The Public Utilities Regulatory Policies Act (PURPA) of 1978 that required utilities to buy from independent power producers at the utility's avoided cost does not allow a payment above avoided cost. This amount may not be enough to make it profitable to provide renewable energy, such as for solar PV. If states were to implement FITs, in the absence of a federal policy, they would face the legal issue of whether their standard would have to meet the federal requirement limiting the payment for renewables to avoided cost.

In the EU, there is wide use of FITs. Germany and Spain used this policy to drive the adoption of wind and solar. The tariffs were a success if measured by the increase in the use of renewables, but a failure if measured by the cost to the German and Spanish governments and their taxpayers. Solar PV growth increased faster than expected, resulting in unsustainable payments to the producers. The German government committed itself to payments of about $0.90/kWh for 20 years, whereas current contracts pay about $0.20. The contracts do have a built-in reduction, such as $0.05 per year, but the beginning payments caused a very large increase in solar PV, and even with the annual price reductions, producers are making a sizable profit (Paulos, 2014).

Demand response mechanisms

Chapter 12 describes marginal cost prices for electricity. The objective is to properly price fuel and capacity to lessen the amount of excess capacity that utilities have built historically. Initial attempts set a higher price for peak hours and seasons. As metering technology allows, utilities can consider rates that more nearly reflect real-time costs, such as day-ahead or hour-ahead prices. Between these extremes, rates such as *critical peak pricing* (CPP) provide day-ahead notice that the next day's rates will contain a surcharge. CPP attempts to capture much of the benefits of real-time pricing, but with a simpler rate structure and less sophisticated metering requirements.

While economists generally endorse *dynamic prices*, consumers have resisted. Consider residential customers, most of whom pay flat rates that do not vary with real-time conditions. Customers with high use during peak hours will experience higher bills with cost-based rates, and so have no reason to switch to variable rates. In addition, there are transactions costs to monitoring rates. They also face higher risk. In contrast, when they pay flat rates, it is the utility that absorbs the risk if flat rates do not recover real-time costs.

One way to lessen resistance is to pay consumers to reduce their use. Customers who reduce their use during peak hours receive payment for supplying negawatts. In return for overcoming consumer resistance to dynamic prices, we introduce additional complexity. What is the correct price to pay consumers? Is it the avoided cost of new capacity or simply the avoided cost of short-run fuel? In addition, how do we know the amount by which consumers have reduced their use? As discussed in Chapter 12, we need a customer baseline load (CBL), the amount customers would have used under their previous rate. Determining a *counterfactual* is not easy, although there are numerous methods for approximating baselines. In addition, consumers have strategic motivations for inflating the baseline, so that they receive payments for large reductions, some of which are illusory. A resident can cool her house to 68 degrees during the CBL determination period, knowing that ordinarily, she keeps the temperature at 72 degrees. On an event day, if she simply leaves the thermostat at 72 degrees, she will receive payments as if she ordinarily set the thermostat at 68 degrees.

There is also the issue of whether consumers receive the retail rate, the wholesale rate, or some combination, for load reductions. A similar issue exists for customers who install solar panels and are able to sell electricity to the utility when the household produces more electricity than it needs. The household commonly receives the retail rate, but the value depends on when the production of electricity occurs. Electricity supplied during peak hours has a higher value than electricity supplied off-peak. As described earlier, Texas wind power produced at night has close to a zero value.

Summary

Sustainability is a widely used concept, but it has many interpretations. The economic approach sticks to its traditions in interpreting sustainability and in contributing solutions to achieve it. Efficiency is the fundamental standard for economists to judge a sustainable action. There is always a trade-off between generational consumption of natural resources. In conserving natural resources for the future, the current generation is making a sacrifice. Policies and behaviors that maximize intergenerational social welfare are the economic approach, but need not produce a sustainable outcome. The Hotelling rule is the standard economic approach to dynamic efficiency.

Economists emphasize relative scarcity as compared to the absolute scarcity perspective common outside economics. Market prices represent the relative scarcity of a resource. Economists tend towards the view of weak sustainability which is that different resources are substitutable. Relative scarcity incentivizes people to pursue other substitutes. Technology advancement can decrease the depletion rate of a scarce resource, as can searching for good substitutes. Instead of stopping the use of certain resources, economists recommend investing the rents from today's consumption of natural resources to compensate future citizens.

Economists advocate government regulations to restrict the uses of resources when there are negative externalities. An increase in the use of natural resources causes pollution issues and possible climate change. Discontinuing their use is a solution to the issues, but the cost is too high when weighed by efficiency criteria. Governments should implement regulations to internalize externalities with the goal of maximizing social welfare.

Maximizing social welfare is the ethic of economics, which is based on utilitarianism. In addition, economists hold an anthropocentric perspective. The perspective does not include intrinsic values of other plants and animals, nor intrinsic good behaviors. This emphasis on efficiency differentiates the economic approach from the sustainability approach.

Energy use is sustainable if it regenerates at least as fast as the rate of its use. Traditional fossil energies are not sustainable. Wind, solar, and biomass are widely used sustainable energies. They also are relatively clean as compared to fossil fuels. The major issue, however, is that they cannot yet replace current technology for various reasons: they are nondispatchable, intermittent, and in some cases, high-cost. Nuclear energy is an alternative that presents problems of radioactive waste and use of fuels for weapons. Clean-coal technologies, especially advanced combustion, increase the energy-generating efficiency of coal and reduce its environmental impact.

Energy efficiency is not the same as economic efficiency. If energy is low-cost, conserving energy may be consistent with sustainability but not efficiency. Another issue is that energy efficiency effectively reduces the cost of using energy. The lower implicit price results in higher use, partially offsetting the energy efficiency savings, known as the rebound effect. This effect is consistent with economic efficiency, as the consumer is using more energy now that it implicitly costs less.

Both command and market approaches can stimulate the growth of sustainable energy. Some states have adopted RPSs that require minimum percentages of sustainable energies; FITs use an above-market price to encourage renewables use. Dynamic pricing charges consumers the marginal cost of production. It increases efficiency because it incentivizes consumers to respond to prices. Another market instrument is demand response: pay consumers to reduce their electricity use. Two difficulties, however, reduce its accuracy: determining a customer baseline load, and the price to pay customers for demand reduction.

Notes

1 See Perman et al. (2003, p. 41) for the original example.
2 It may be more accurate to express the relationship as $I = f(P, A, T)$, as the relationship need not be strictly multiplicative.
3 See Ehrlich and Holdren (1971) and Commoner (1972). John Holdren served as President Obama's senior advisor on science and technology beginning in 2009 through a series of appointments. He and Paul Ehrlich originally targeted population growth as the major concern. Ehrlich, with his wife Anne, first gained fame with the bestseller, *The Population Bomb* (1968).
4 Hotelling (1931) specifies that supply will run out if demand is fixed over time and linear ($Q = a - bP$). It will decrease asymptotically but will not run out if demand is exponential ($Q = aP^b$).
5 It is also possible to include *intermediate sustainability*. It would distinguish categories of capital, such as natural and human-made, and while it would permit some substitution between the types

of capital, it would not permit a reduction in natural capital below the threshold level needed to maintain life services.

6 Ecological economics established its own association and journal in 1989.

7 They like energy conservation and efficiency even better, as it involves no resources at all. We discuss this option in a later section of this chapter. From a life cycle perspective, even nuclear energy and renewable energy sources emit carbon. Uranium must be mined and transported for nuclear energy, solar panels require the use of silicon, wind towers require materials in their construction.

8 We leave most of this discussion to Chapter 11 on next-generation fuels, but add one reference for convenience. See Carriquiry, Du, and Timilsina (2011).

9 See Schwarz and Taylor (1995) for a study of the effects of home insulation on thermostat setting.

10 Of course, a major problem is that utilities may gain more from selling megawatts than negawatts. The task of economics is to get the prices right, so that utility conservation programs will offer the correct incentive for pursuing lower energy consumption.

11 In fact, you may be more comfortable even at the same thermostat setting because you have reduced drafts.

12 Jorgenson et al. (2014) finds that well-being increases while energy intensity decreases, but also reports two earlier studies that found the opposite.

References

Bruntland, G. (1987). *Our common future*. Oxford: Oxford University Press.

California Energy Commission. (2016). *Renewables portfolio standard*. Retrieved January 11, 2017 from http://www.energy.ca.gov/portfolio/

Carriquiry, M., Du, X., & Timilsina, G. (2011). Second generation biofuels: Economics and policies. *Energy Policy, 39*(7), 4222–4234.

Carroll, J. (2013, March 8). Exxon at least 25 years away from making fuel from algae. *Bloomberg.com*. Retrieved June 5, 2016 from http://www.bloomberg.com/news/articles/2013–03–08/exxon-at-least–25-years-away-from-making-fuel-from-algae

Commoner, B. (1972). A bulletin dialogue: on "The Closing Circle"—response. *Bulletin of the Atomic Scientists*, 17–56.

Daly, H. (1977). *Steady-state economics*. Washington, D.C.: Island Press.

Ehrlich, P. R., & Holdren, J. P. (1971). Impact of population growth. *Science, 171*(3977), 1212–1217.

Hartwick, J. (1977). Intergenerational equity and the investment of rents from exhaustible resources. *American Economic Review, 67*, 972–974.

Hubbert, M. K. (1956). *Nuclear energy and the fossil fuels*. Retrieved April 16, 2016 from http://www.hubbertpeak.com/hubbert/1956/1956.pdf

Jorgenson, A., Alekseyko, A., & Giedraitis, V. (2014). Energy consumption, human well-being and economic development in central and eastern European nations: A cautionary tale of sustainability. *Energy Policy, 66*, 419–427.

Joskow, P., & Marron, D. (1992). What does a negawatt really cost? Evidence from utility conservation programs. *Energy Journal, 13*(4), 41–74.

Klessmann, C., Rathmann, M., de Jager, D., Gazzo, A., Resch, G., Busch, S., & Ragwitz, M. (2013). Policy options for reducing the costs of reaching the European renewables target. *Renewable Energy, 57*, 390–403.

Lovins, A. (1976). Energy strategy: The road not taken? *Foreign Affairs, 55*(1), 65–96.

Nordhaus, W. (1992). Lethal model 2: The limits to growth revisited. *Brookings Papers on Economic Activity*, 1–59.

Paulos, B. (2014, June 04). *Are the legacy costs of Germany's solar feed-in tariff fixable?* Retrieved January 11, 2017 from https://www.greentechmedia.com/articles/read/germany-moves-to-reform-its-renewable-energy-law

Perman, R., Ma, Y., McGilvray, J., & Common, M. (2003). *Natural resource and environmental economics*. Harlow, UK: Pearson Addison Wesley.

Schelling, T. (1997). The cost of combating global warming. *Foreign Affairs, 76*(6), 8–14.

Schwarz, P., & Taylor, T. (1995). Cold hands, warm hearth? Climate, net takeback, and household comfort. *Energy Journal, 16*(1), 41–54.

Schwarz, P., Inyang, H., & Mbamalu, G. (2009). Sustaining sustainability: Approaches and contexts. *Journal of Environmental Management, 90*(12), 3687–3689.

Scientific American. (2009). How long will the world's uranium supplies last? Retrieved June 6, 2016 from http://www.scientificamerican.com/article/how-long-will-global-uranium-deposits-last/

Singer, P. (1975). *Animal liberation: A new ethics for our treatment of animals.* New York: HarperCollins.

Solow, R. (1993). Sustainability: An economist's perspective. In: R. N. Stavins (Ed.), *Economics of the environment: Selected readings* (pp. 179–187). New York: W. W. Norton and Company.

U.S. Department of Energy. (n.d.). *How coal gasification power plants work.* Retrieved January 11, 2017 from http://energy.gov/fe/how-coal-gasification-power-plants-work

Weitzman, M. (1999). Pricing the limits to growth from materials depletion. *Quarterly Journal of Economics, 114*(2), 691–706.

Wirth, H. (2016). *Recent facts about photovoltaics in Germany.* Retrieved June 5, 2016 from https://www.ise.fraunhofer.de/en/publications/veroeffentlichungen-pdf-dateien-en/studien-und-konzeptpapiere/recent-facts-about-photovoltaics-in-germany.pdf

Chapter 16

Energy security

"An ounce of prevention is worth a pound of cure."

Benjamin Franklin (1735)

"The Strategic Petroleum Reserve may not be worth its cost."

The author of this text

Introduction

The modern study of energy economics, as well as concerns about energy security, began with the 1973 Middle East oil embargo. That event showed the vulnerability of economies to interruptions in the supply of oil and consequent rising prices. Since that time, importing countries have sought to reduce their exposure to supplies from hostile regimes. Most of the efforts focus on the supply side, such as increasing domestic production of oil or shifting to other fuels. Another supply-side effort is a *strategic petroleum reserve* (SPR), which stores oil to meet future contingencies such as interruptions or rapid price increases. Countries may also expend a portion of their military budget to protect oil supplies.

It is also possible to increase security by decreasing demand. Countries have reduced energy intensity steadily since 1973, redoubling their efforts after the second oil shock of 1979. Businesses faced with higher energy prices modified their production processes to reduce energy intensity and the consequent demand for energy as an input. Commercial and residential sectors modified lighting and installed insulation to reduce their use of vulnerable and expensive energy. Consultants advise all three sectors on how to reduce energy use, including audits to highlight opportunities to increase energy efficiency.

Energy security can apply to other potential threats to supply, such as terrorist attacks on the electricity grid. The attacks may be on the physical system or cyber attacks that inflict damage on the computer system or the electric grid, the supply chain of generation, transmission, and distribution that carries electricity from suppliers to customers. Responses include greater safeguards of the facilities or quick-start backups should a part of the generating system be disabled.

Economics requires that we consider both costs and benefits of increasing our energy security. Neither is easy to measure, but in the absence of monetary considerations, we cannot compare the wisdom of shoring up security vs. resources allocated to other energy issues such as reducing air pollution or spending the money on issues outside energy, such as education, health care, or national defense.

In this chapter, we focus primarily on energy security as it applies to oil, but also consider electricity security. After this introduction, we define energy security. As with sustainability, the term is more useful if we can agree on what it means. We then visit measures taken since the 1973 embargo, followed by current issues in energy security. We consider threats to the electricity system in a separate section. Before closing the chapter, we evaluate key areas of energy security from a cost–benefit standpoint. Oil issues include the effects of import instability and the military costs of protecting that source of supply. There are potential costs from oil price volatility as well as interruptions in supply. Electricity issues include outages and grid modernization to make the network more secure. The final section is a summary.

Definition of energy security

The International Energy Agency (IEA) defines *energy security* as "the uninterrupted flow of energy at an affordable price." In fact, the IEA, an organization of OECD and other countries working together to achieve safe and reliable energy, was formed in 1974 as a countervailing response to OPEC's actions. Much as we built our discussion of sustainability beginning with the Bruntland definition, we can also use the IEA definition as a starting point for energy security. Just as sustainability often incorporates economic, environmental, and social dimensions, the European Commission—the executive body in charge of legislation promoting the interest of the EU—broadened energy security considerations of uninterrupted supplies and affordability to include environmental concerns and sustainable development. In this chapter, we focus on the economic aspects, having considered environment and sustainability in the previous two chapters.

Much as the original Bruntland sustainability definition required elaboration on the term "need," Labandeira and Manzano (2012) ask that we ascertain the meaning of "affordability." They recommend that we compare benefits to costs, much as we would do for any other objective. They also note that the definition should address the heterogeneity of energy sources. Oil is needed for transportation, but less so for electricity. The EU needs natural gas for electricity generation, and Japan needs LNG. Moreover, what supply is sufficient to ensure continuous availability? It is evident we cannot afford to stockpile enough oil to eliminate price instability or to prevent any chance of a shortage.

Metcalf (2014, p. 156) finds existing definitions more political than economic, and proposes an economic definition of energy security as "the ability of households, businesses, and governments to accommodate disruptions of supply in energy markets." He seeks to clear up three areas of confusion common to policy discussions. The first is that ever since the 1973 pronouncement of Richard Nixon to achieve energy independence, the focus has been to reduce imports from politically unfriendly regimes to protect us from price shocks. As oil is a global commodity, domestic oil prices will adjust to world oil price, so we cannot protect ourselves against a global shock even if we reduce imports to zero. While there is not free trade of oil in all countries—the United States only recently allowed oil exports for the first time in four decades—the general principle holds that oil will flow to the country willing to pay the highest price. Metcalf calls for demand-side reductions as the way to energy, or more specifically oil, independence.

A second potential source of confusion according to Metcalf stems from Bohi and Toman (1996), who envision energy security as an externalities issue. They cite costs such as the oil stockpile premium and military preparedness. Metcalf sees the emphasis on externalities as misplaced, in that the larger energy security costs may be bottlenecks in specific locations, such as in Japan in the wake of Fukushima and natural gas supplies in the northeastern states during the Polar Vortex. There are also macro effects on the business cycle from energy price instability, and micro effects from interruptions to energy. Farrell, Zerriffi, and Dowlatabadi (2004) argue that it is better to view energy security as a public good, rather than an externality, as it is both nonrival and non-excludable. However, we will make use of the externalities construct as it proves useful in clarifying the economics of energy security.

A third area of confusion is that low prices need not enhance energy security. Low prices weaken the incentive for energy efficiency, which works against energy security. In addition, lower revenues weaken investor incentives to pursue improvements or additions to energy infrastructure.

Metcalf suggests that the most important issue may be the differing perspectives of policy-makers and economists. Policy-makers recognize that the need for energy security may influence foreign policy, such as working with Saudi Arabia despite human rights differences or concerns about terrorism. He suggests that economists should consider incorporating these political realities in their future energy security research.

History of oil security since 1973

OPEC and the 1973 embargo

In the aftermath of the 1973 Arab–Israeli War, the Middle East members of OPEC instituted an oil embargo against the United States and other countries that had provided support to Israel. The price of oil shot up from $3 to $12 a barrel. The second shock followed during the Iranian Revolution in 1979 when the United States allowed the deposed Shah of Iran to seek medical treatment in the U.S., resulting in the Iran hostage crisis with Iran holding American hostages for 400 days. The second shock took the price of a barrel of oil from $14 a barrel to almost $36 by 1981. These shocks triggered severe stagflation, a combination of high inflation and unemployment.

In 1973, President Nixon declared a goal of energy independence by 1980. However, there was pressure to take immediate action. The President had already imposed wage and price controls for a three-month period in 1971 to stem rising inflation, and the first response to the oil crisis was to put a ceiling on the price of gasoline. Figure 16.1 shows the gasoline market subject to a price ceiling.

Curves S_0 and S_1 represent pre- and post-embargo gasoline supplies. Equilibrium shifts from A to B. Price soars from $0.35 to $0.70, while quantity demanded decreases from 230 to 160. However, there is pressure for the government to protect consumers, especially the poor, from such a large price increase, so the government caps the price at $0.50. Consumers now wish to purchase 190 gallons, but suppliers are only willing to make available 100 gallons, leaving a shortfall of 90 gallons.

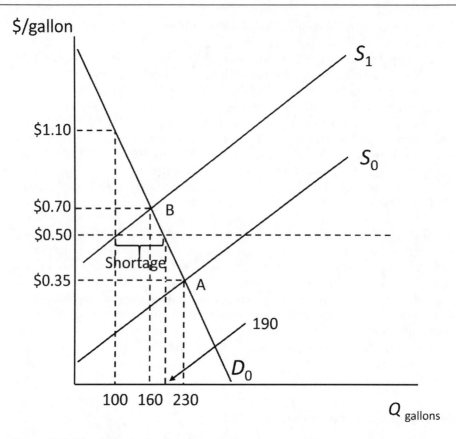

Figure 16.1 The 1973 Arab oil embargo and price controls.

Example 16.1

Refer to Figure 16.1 and calculate the deadweight loss of capping the price at
$0.50, given the post–embargo equilibrium price of $0.70.

Solution

In the absence of the price ceiling, equilibrium would be at point B, corresponding
to a price of $0.70 and a quantity of 160 gallons. At a price ceiling of $0.50,
suppliers' vertical distance between $1.10 and $0.50, and the horizontal distance
between a quantity of 160 and 100 gallons, form the deadweight loss triangle:

$$DWL = 0.5 \times (\$1.10 - \$0.50) \times (160 - 100) = \$18$$

Consumers waited for gas as long lines of cars formed. Angry motorists waited for
hours to fill their tanks, with quantity demanded at 190 and quantity supplied at 100 in
our stylized example. Wealthy motorists paid low-income individuals to sit in line and

fill the tanks. To get around the price controls, gas station owners required drivers to get a car wash with a fill-up. Where a car wash was $5 before the embargo, it now cost $10, with the gas station owner attempting to extract rents from consumers in Figure 16.1 willing to pay as much as $1.10 for the limited supply.

The government now saw that its plan to protect consumers, especially low-income consumers, had backfired. When prices soared in 1979 after the second oil price shock, the United States instituted a rationing system. The government assigned days when drivers could buy gas depending on whether the last number on their license plate was odd or even.[1] The rationing scheme did make it harder for gas station owners to extract rents, but did nothing to alleviate the shortage.[2] One hypothesis is that it caused even longer lines, as drivers topped off the tank more frequently since they could not fill up the following day.

In addition to price controls, President Nixon signed a law in 1974 mandating a national speed limit of no more than 55 miles per hour. The motivation was that cars run more efficiently at lower speeds, thereby reducing the demand for gas.

Box 16.1 Why drive 55?

Oil prices collapsed in the early 1980s as consumers adapted to high energy prices and reduced their energy use. With gas demand falling, OPEC found it more difficult to maintain a high price of oil. Yet the speed limit remained in place until 1995 when President Clinton lifted the national limit.

There had been no lack of calls for its repeal. While it is evident that the limit had outlived its original purpose, the new justification was that the slower limit saved lives.

Economists were active in seeking its end. Forester, McNown, and Singell (1984) performed a cost–benefit analysis of the limit and found that costs far outweighed the benefits. While driving slower saves lives, it costs time. The authors value a statistical life using hedonic wage studies, and value time according to a fraction of forgone earnings. Fuel savings, reduced injuries, and lives saved come to between 0.35 and 0.42 of the costs of forgone time.

In 1975, the United States banned crude oil exports as another supply strategy to achieve energy independence. We have already indicated that supply-side strategies do not reduce the global price of oil, although they would cushion the impact of oil supply interruptions by foreign suppliers.[3]

The 1970s also saw soaring electricity prices as well as natural gas shortages. Oil was a major generating fuel for electricity, and as its price soared, electricity producers turned to natural gas as an alternative source of generation. At the same time, consumers looked to natural gas as an alternative to electricity to heat their homes, and industry sought to use more natural gas for its industrial processes. However, the 1954 U.S. Supreme Court Phillips decision capped natural gas wellhead prices. The consequences for natural gas were predictable. Substitute millions of Btus of natural gas for gallons of oil in Figure 16.1 to tell the story. The winters of 1977 and 1978 were severe in many parts of the country, and when customers could not obtain natural gas, they abandoned it in large numbers as an unreliable source of fuel.

The United States passed the Public Utilities Regulatory Policy Act (PURPA), part of the National Energy Act, in 1978. The Act promoted energy conservation and alternative fuels. The most noteworthy provision was that electric utilities were required to purchase power from qualifying facilities (QFs), mostly small independent power producers using renewable energy. The short-term consequence was to drive up the price of electricity, as in some cases utilities had to buy the alternative fuel even if they could have produced at a lower cost using their own generating facilities. Nevertheless, the Act opened the door to independent power production and the possibility of competition at the electricity generation stage.

The Natural Gas Policy Act was also passed in 1978, and phased in decontrol of natural gas prices. The phase-in period was messy, with "old gas" still subject to controls, while gas under new contracts was decontrolled. Naturally, there were attempts to get out of the old contracts. Despite inauspicious beginnings, the Act eventually led the way to full decontrol of natural gas prices at the wellhead. The 1980s and the 1990s saw the separation of natural gas production and transmission, with transmission lines transformed from a merchant function to solely a transport function.

Prices and price volatility

U.S. price controls aimed at curtailing the price shocks likely exacerbated the effects. Domestic suppliers had little reason to increase their supplies or invest in R&D to uncover new supplies or better technologies. Consumers had less reason to conserve and identify energy efficiencies.

The combination of high prices and price volatility not only were instrumental in the malaise of the 1970s but culminated in a deep economic downturn in 1980. In fact, there has been a rise in oil prices just preceding each recession since 1973, including the ones in 1991, 2001, and 2008.

In 1990, Iraqi dictator Saddam Hussein invaded Kuwait. One of his motivations for the invasion was Kuwaiti oil. Iraqi troops had quick success in overrunning Kuwait, but the United States drove them out several months later. As the Iraqis fled, they set fire to Kuwaiti oil fields. The intention of this "scorched earth policy" was to destroy any resources that might be of value to the enemy.

During the initial invasion, price per barrel of oil rose from $18 pre-invasion to slightly over $40 by late fall of that year, largely due to interrupted Kuwaiti and Iraqi production. Once the United States drove Iraq out, prices fell quickly and dramatically. The United States experienced a short eight-month recession that closely coincided with the duration of the conflict.

The 2001 terrorist attack on U.S. targets including New York's World Trade Center towers also contributed to a spike in the price of oil. The price spike was brief, as concerns about the world economy and weakening demand ultimately reduced the price of oil. By 2003, the United States had invaded Iraq on the premise that Iraq had weapons of mass destruction that would unleash acts against its own people and possible terrorism. Since the United States never found any weapons, one alternative hypothesis is that it wanted to protect its oil interests.

The Great Recession that began in 2008 was primarily due to the global meltdown of financial institutions. However, oil prices were also a factor, with a barrel of oil spiking to $147 that same year. Once the recession took hold, oil prices plummeted.

The primary explanation for the run-up in oil prices was rapidly increasing demand in developing countries, especially China. The Great Recession took the wind out of those expectations of increasing demand in developed and developing countries.

Explanations for the 2008 oil price spike

In the 2000s, developing countries and China in particular had a virtually insatiable demand for energy. While the U.S. government could not do much about rising demand outside the United States, policy-makers turned to oil speculators inside the country as culprits in the 2008 price spike. *Speculators* take a higher-than-average risk in return for higher-than-average profits.

As we have reviewed in earlier chapters, economists generally believe that speculators serve a useful role, and actually reduce price volatility. If speculators anticipate rising prices in the future, they buy today in the hopes of selling at a higher price. Buying today does increase today's price, but putting more oil on the market later actually reduces the future price. Speculators also provide useful information regarding future price expectations (Smith, 2009). While there were investigations into alleged market manipulation by speculators, there was no convincing evidence. When oil prices collapsed as quickly as they had risen, pundits who were happy to have low prices did not ask if speculators were responsible. Moreover, while many speculators made money during the ride up, just as many lost money on the way down. By the end of the year, oil was selling for $40 a barrel.

By 2014, oil edged its way back over $100 a barrel and once again, prognosticators pointed to higher oil prices henceforth. They again saw developing countries inevitably demanding more energy, possibly reinforced by the actions of oil speculators. Believers in peak oil offered a third explanation; there were too many global dollars chasing too few barrels of oil.

After the summer of 2014, oil markets again confounded these projections of forever rising prices. By the end of 2014, prices were half of their summer highs. Prognosticators had not factored in the deluge of oil from fracking. Furthermore, Saudi Arabia broke from its past role of swing producer for OPEC, and kept up its oil production to maintain its market share. By early 2016, oil had dipped below $27 per barrel. Saudi Arabia reevaluated its strategy and by the end of 2016, OPEC countries had agreed to restrict oil supplies and price rebounded to over $50 per barrel. Time will tell if they are successful in sticking to their agreement and preventing cheating within OPEC, as well as there being the temptation of producers outside OPEC to increase production.[4]

Current issues in primary energy security

Falling energy prices and imports reduce security concerns

When energy prices decline and imports from unfriendly regimes shrink, energy security becomes a less pressing issue. More abundant fossil fuels all lessen the urgency of traditional energy security concerns. The issue has less urgency in the United States with the advance of hydraulic fracturing, inroads of renewables such as solar and wind energy, and slower growth in energy demand. There is discussion of the possibility that peak oil demand is closer to reality than peak oil supply.[5]

With the lessened concerns, the United States is beginning to export oil and liquefied natural gas (LNG). There are diminishing subsidies for renewables given their declining costs as well as the new reserves of fossil fuel. Speculators are no longer the center of attention. In short, there is less reason to interfere with market outcomes based on energy security considerations.

Natural gas

While the United States has pursued fracking and reduced its dependence on foreign suppliers, the EU has resisted the technology. EU governments own mineral rights, and have taken a cautious approach until they can better resolve environmental issues. A consequence is that much of the EU is dependent for its natural gas on Russia, which has threatened to cut off supplies to countries that support Ukraine where Russia seeks to increase its influence.

The EU has begun to look towards the United States as an alternative supplier, in the form of LNG. However, it takes years to build new export facilities in the United States, and EU countries must have LNG import terminals. While natural gas companies in the United States have been getting the right to build terminals, low natural gas prices of recent years reduce the profitability of exercising those rights. Moreover, the United States can expect that Russia, as well as other exporters, will reduce price to hold on to their market share and impose losses on U.S. exporters, much as some observers think OPEC has done in the oil market.

We can anticipate additional safety measures for domestic natural gas and LNG for export. Natural gas pipes can leak methane and be subject to explosions. The Aliso Canyon California fire was the worst natural gas leak in U.S. history. It began in October 2015 and it took until February 2016 to stop the leak. Nearby families complained of headaches, nausea, and nosebleeds, along with above-average incidences of nose and throat infections, causing the relocation of over 2,000 households of the affluent Porter Ranch neighborhood of Los Angeles. Pipeline infrastructure is aging, and with it the chance of increased leaks and fires as well as lost energy. LNG has a good safety record under ordinary conditions. However, terrorists and saboteurs could find LNG facilities and tankers inviting targets (Kaplan, 2006).

Climate change

Climate change is likely to cause more extreme weather events that could affect energy supply and in turn energy security. Stronger and more frequent storms can affect energy infrastructure on a temporary or permanent basis. In advance of hurricanes, it may be necessary to shut down stages of the energy supply chain, such as off-shore drilling rigs. Long term, weather changes could destroy facilities or call for redesign, much as the earthquake and tsunami at Fukushima called into question the design of nuclear plants. Extreme temperatures will increase the demand for energy and the cost of its interruption, as in European heat waves in recent summers that resulted in illnesses and deaths. In the northeastern United States, the Polar Vortex rendered natural gas production and transport inoperable during a time of record demand for electricity.

Climate change may be responsible for droughts, which is a threat to hydroelectric power, as well as causing competition for the water that supplies the energy for hydro-electric power. California has experienced repeated droughts, although it is now experiencing increased flooding. In the years surrounding its initial restructuring of electricity, it had hoped to obtain low-cost hydro energy from neighboring states. When those states entered into a drought, they no longer had excess energy, leaving California highly dependent on external natural gas supplies and market manipulation by Enron and other independent power producers. Drought now plagues a number of African countries. Zambia had been able to obtain almost all of its electricity from low-cost hydropower and was able to prosper and attract industry. That progress is under threat, as repeated drought has reduced the availability of hydropower and industries now experience frequent interruptions in the electricity supply (Onishi, 2016).

Heat and drought increase fire risk. In 2016, the Fort McMurray wildfires in the Canadian oil sands region of Alberta, Canada, shut down oil production and required a mass evacuation.

Restrictions on carbon may mean the end of coal production. Natural gas emits only about half as much carbon as coal per unit of energy. But it also emits methane, which is more potent than CO_2 as regards its effect on retaining heat, although with a shorter atmospheric life. We can expect further restrictions on methane, including the practice of flaring unwanted natural gas, and leaks during production and transportation.

Nuclear energy

Nuclear energy offers a carbon-free alternative, but it comes with its own issues, some of which involve energy security. Nuclear proliferation is a concern because fissile materials, such as uranium and plutonium, are the active materials within nuclear and radiological weapons, including weapons of mass destruction. In fact, there was much consternation over Iran's plans to construct nuclear plants, arising from the fear that they were actually enriching uranium for weapons.

There are also fears concerning the creation of weapons from stolen spent nuclear fuel. There have been cases where nuclear reactor spent fuel could not be fully accounted for. In the 1970s, the United States banned reprocessing of nuclear fuel out of fear of nuclear proliferation. Reprocessing separates out unused uranium and plutonium. Nuclear and radiological weapons made from plutonium are a primary worry because of their relative ease of construction.

Nuclear catastrophes can be due to accidents or to terrorist events. We have to decide the level of protection, from the system used to monitor plant operation to the thickness of the plant's walls. It costs more to defend against airplane attacks of the type employed on 9/11 than against truck attacks. Small modular nuclear reactors are on the horizon, though not yet cost-effective. While small-scale reactors might reduce the repercussions of a terrorist attack, they also require monitoring of many more facilities, and constitute a larger number of targets.

Regardless of the size of the facility, and whether or not we allow reprocessing, there is still nuclear waste. Recycling reduces waste but does not eliminate it. The United States has still not agreed on a centralized waste storage site, withdrawing permits for the use of Yucca Mountain in Nevada after a long period of evaluation. Therefore, the waste continues to be stored on-site in pools, a temporary solution in the hope that a permanent solution will emerge. While it will be very difficult for terrorists to make use of this highly radioactive material, the pools could make tempting targets for an attack. As shown by the accident at Fukushima, it is necessary to evacuate a large population near a damaged nuclear facility, and there is the immediate threat of illness and death to persons near the plant. Workers brought in to contain the event are at great risk of illness or death from radiation.

Energy infrastructure

Energy delivery requires infrastructure, the equipment and structures to provide the commodity to the final customer. We set aside electricity infrastructure, including the grid, for the next section on electricity security.

Earlier, we noted that aging natural gas pipelines are subject to leaks and fires. Aging oil pipelines are also increasingly prone to breaks that can result in oil spills. Oil transport by truck or rail is also subject to spills. The events may be accidental or the result of terrorism. The 1989 *Exxon Valdez* oil spill may have had several contributing factors including poor weather, inadequate crew training, and possibly alcohol consumption by the captain (History, n.d.). The 2010 BP *Deepwater Horizon* oil spill had numerous contributing factors, including the concrete cementing operations, the malfunctioning of the blowout preventer, and inability to recognize an unexpected change in the well's pressure. In the next section of this chapter, we encounter the 2003 northeastern U.S. blackout of the electricity system, which had such mundane origins as a tree bringing down a transmission line, causing a series of cascading failures.

Terrorist events present a different set of challenges. Farrell et al. (2004) refer to critical infrastructure protection (CIP), which is protection of infrastructures, including energy, critical to national security. We briefly discuss aspects of oil, natural gas, and nuclear infrastructure here, deferring electricity infrastructure to the next section of this chapter.

Oil and natural gas

We have discussed the Iraqi "scorched-earth policy" when they set Kuwaiti oil facilities on fire. There have also been attacks on oil production facilities in Nigeria. While these events have not involved terrorism, they demonstrate the vulnerability of oil infrastructure to terrorist attacks. We have reviewed the vulnerability of pipelines to accidents, and they are potential terrorist targets as well. Oil refineries are another vulnerable part of the supply chain. Then, there have been terrorist attacks on oil storage facilities in Libya. Oil tankers are another potential target.

Another threat to oil supplies is to block key shipping channels, such as Iran's warning that it would close the Straits of Hormuz to Persian Gulf oil shipments if countries did not support its policies. The Bosporus Strait separates the European and Asian sides of Istanbul in Turkey, and during a recent coup attempt, oil prices gyrated as countries contemplated the possibility that shippers would have to take an alternate route. The Strait of Malacca that separates Malaysia and Indonesia is a key channel for shipping oil to South and East Asia. It is potentially subject to piracy and terrorism.

Natural gas has similar vulnerabilities along its supply chain. According to Farrell et al. (2004), it is more vulnerable than oil because of its pressurized contents. Pipelines and LNG tankers transport highly pressurized supplies, so their targeting would lead to more violent explosions. However, the authors see natural gas as less vulnerable than electricity since pipelines run underground, whereas much of the electricity transmission and distribution system is above ground. In addition, natural gas can be stored, whereas electricity supply must be available to meet demand at each instant until large-scale storage becomes economical.

Nuclear energy[6]

Nuclear energy differs from other fuels in that it involves inherently dangerous materials, fuels and wastes. As a result, nuclear facilities have greater security requirements than other energy sources. In the United States, the Nuclear Regulatory Commission (NRC) inspects nuclear facilities. While nuclear plant operators pay into a fund intended for a permanent waste facility, the funds do not cover security risks.

There are risks at several steps of the supply chain, beginning with fuel transportation, which is vulnerable to interruption. The major threat is to nuclear reactors. Given the 9/11 attack, the containment buildings are tested to withstand airplane attacks. There are also measures in place against an armed attack. However, simulation may not reveal the repercussions were there to be an actual attack.

Spent fuel is highly radioactive, and as no country has established a permanent disposal site, the rods are placed in cooling ponds and then into dry storage or directly in dry casks awaiting a permanent disposal site. The United States stores the casks outside the containment building, which leaves them more vulnerable than when stored inside the building, such as in Germany. A loss of coolant caused by sabotage or terrorism could result in fires and release of radioactivity.

Electricity and energy security

Given the critical role electricity plays, there are many safeguards to prevent electricity interruptions. Outages are rare in the United States and other developed countries, but more frequent in developing countries such as India.

We focus on the safeguards in the United States to prevent accidents. We also consider additional measures needed to protect the system against deliberate acts to damage it, such as acts of terrorism. The attacks may be physical attacks on the plant or cyber attacks on computer systems.

Outages

Consumers place a high value on being able to flip a switch and having the lights come on. Despite the fact that the last major blackout in the United States was in August of 2003, the consequences were dire enough that it led to a careful examination of the causes, followed by reforms establishing mandatory rather than voluntary reliability standards. Fifty million people lost power throughout the northeastern and Midwest United States and on into Ontario and Quebec, Canada. At least 11 people died and the estimated damage was $6 billion.[7] Congress gave the Federal Energy Regulatory

Commission (FERC) expanded powers over regional transmission operators to strengthen the transmission system and impose fines for safety violations.[8]

FirstEnergy, an Ohio-based utility, had not performed its routine tree-trimming program. An overgrown tree touched a high-voltage power line, which shut down that line. An alarm system failed to go off that would have warned FirstEnergy to redistribute power to other lines. As system operators tried to figure out the reason for the loss of power, overheated lines touched more overgrown trees, cut off those lines, and there was a cascading effect as power went to other lines. There was high summertime demand, adding to the strain. The Midwest Independent System Operator (MISO) also had computer system problems, and when they eventually recognized the gravity of the situation and contacted FirstEnergy, they realized that FirstEnergy had not identified the problem.

The northeast blackout involved human error. In addition to mandating and enforcing reliability standards, a second measure was to create the North American Electric Reliability Corporation (NERC) to oversee the process. There are also ongoing efforts to upgrade the century-old electric grid. New sensors that monitor in real time give better information on grid operations. There is more cooperation among different transmission regions, so that multiple operators can spot a problem in one region of the country.

Natural disasters can also test the resilience of the electrical grid. Even small deposits of ice on overhead transmission lines can lead to multi-day outages. Customers typically question why utilities do not bury lines underground, which would have a second advantage that they are more difficult to attack. They are also preferable aesthetically. However, they would be more expensive to access in the event that there is a repair problem. As with any reform to improve electricity reliability, we need to compare benefits to costs. The next section of this chapter will provide some instances of the evaluation of the benefits used to determine what energy security measures pass the test.

Burying lines for new developments is more cost-effective than making the change for existing developments. Retrofit requires participation of all affected parties, including other affected utilities such as cable and phone, and residents who may pay higher bills as well as the disruption of a construction project. These measures may not be worthwhile for a once in ten years ice storm or a once in a lifetime hurricane. In addition, underground lines could be more vulnerable to flooding. Hurricane Sandy knocked out power to approximately 8.5 million customers in the northeastern United States, and with climate change, there may be more storms like Hurricane Sandy. Therefore, a one-size-fits-all solution for whether to bury power lines is unlikely.

Grid modernization

Most discussion of grid modernization involves the *smart grid*, which will use digital technology and be able to provide real-time data on electric system usage. The most common deployment will allow two-way transfer of electricity. In 2009, as a response to the Great Recession, the United States provided the Department of Energy (n.d.-a) with $4.5 billion to support smart grid endeavors as part of the American Reinvestment and Recovery Act.

The use of upgraded technology should provide information that will reduce the like-lihood of physical or cyber attacks on electricity infrastructure. The grid is "self-healing," meaning that the troubled part of the system is isolated, and power rerouted to the working parts of the system. The process will use more automation and rely less on human operators. By speeding identification of outages, it will allow a quicker recovery.

However, the smart grid also introduces new security concerns (Clemente, 2009). It will need new and extensive transmission lines to reach remote wind and solar power. These lines will require monitoring. Hackers can get into the system. Saboteurs could manipulate services to households and businesses, possibly shutting them down or disrupting the system.

Microgrids

Damage to the grid can be immense because transmission is highly interconnected. The traditional grid makes use of highly centralized generation, typically large-scale coal, natural gas, and nuclear plants. It uses hydroelectric power for pump storage where available, and uses a small but growing share of renewables such as wind and solar for intermittent electrical production.

The microgrid is a local grid separate from the main grid and close to energy users. It is powered by *distributed generation* (DG), typically small-scale power such as rooftop solar, batteries, or local generators. While the DG and the microgrid connect to the transmission system, they have the capability to operate independently. They can also provide electricity where demand is far from transmission lines, advantageous if it is cheaper to have an autonomous grid. In the event of an outage, the microgrid can still provide power.

Customers served by microgrids have an independent source of power should disasters damage the regional transmission system. Control is local, facilitating quick action in the event of an impending disaster. As microgrids often rely on intermittent sources such as wind and solar, they require battery storage to allow operation inde-pendent of the main grid. Battery storage can be more affordable at the microgrid scale than at utility scale. The systems are easiest to justify for hospitals, the military, and universities with critical needs or favorable economics.

Electric utilities have not always welcomed microgrids. There have been disagree-ments over payments towards transmission, similar to the disputes with customers generating their own solar energy. Customers on a microgrid may argue that they make limited use of the utility's grid. The utility counters that it still needs to build the system to supply energy when the microgrid cannot meet the customer's demand. The utility also has to keep backup generation that can ramp up quickly whenever the microgrid is not available (Lott, 2012).[9]

Costs and benefits of energy security

In this section, we consider several of the major themes we have touched upon in considering energy security and the costs and benefits of increased security. We consider oil price shocks and their effect on the macroeconomy. We also visit attempts to value the SPR and to separate out military costs of protecting oil supplies. Lastly, we consider costs and benefits of reducing energy outages and implementing the smart grid.

Oil prices and oil price shocks

The oil price shocks of the 1970s led to a search for energy independence to protect against the consequences of supply interruptions, higher oil prices, and price volatility. The impetus was on building domestic supplies, which protects against supply interruptions but offers less protection against price spikes.[10]

We reviewed the costs and benefits of energy efficiency in Chapter 9, so we will not repeat that discussion here, other than to note that Metcalf (2014) has added a macroeconomic benefit to the microeconomic ones noted in most discussions of reducing energy use. Here we consider the effects of oil price shocks on the macroeconomy and evaluate measures to cushion those shocks. As Metcalf notes, we should not conflate energy security and low prices. We saw that price controls were not an effective way to increase energy security.

We first laid out the case against monopoly from a social welfare perspective in the foundation chapters, with a more detailed examination of OPEC's strategy and its consequences for oil in Chapter 5. Greene (2010) puts the total impact on the U.S. economy from OPEC for the year 2008 at $500 billion. Of this amount $330 billion is a transfer from U.S. consumers to U.S. oil producers, who receive the global price. Therefore, a large portion of the $500 billion is a transfer, not a loss. Only $75 billion is lost production due to higher prices. Price shocks make up $150 billion of the losses due to the dislocations of responding to sudden changes in energy input costs. With U.S. GDP approaching $15 trillion, the efficiency cost due to noncompetitive oil pricing is approximately 5% of GDP, but only 1.5% if we net out transfer costs. Greene suggests measures costing less than 1% of GDP, including further reductions in oil intensity, greater substitution of other energy resources for oil, and increasing domestic oil production. For example, Greene finds increased fuel requirements for automobiles to be worthwhile.

Oil price shocks have a diminishing effect on the economy as oil costs become a smaller share of production costs. The first oil shock had such a large effect because many countries had been accustomed to low oil prices, and so had not given much attention to energy efficiency. In the decades since the initial shock, countries have reduced their energy usage per unit of output, as measured by energy intensity. In so doing, we have reduced our vulnerability to further shocks. Where the 1970s was a period of high unemployment and inflation in the United States, oil prices now have a much smaller effect on inflation because they account for a much smaller percentage of production costs. While oil price spikes can still contribute to the likelihood of a recession, they have a muted impact on the overall economy as compared to the 1970s malaise and the deep recession of the early 1980s.

Brown and Huntington (2013) estimate a premium taking into account projected world market conditions, probable oil supply disruptions, and world market responses to those disruptions.[11] The estimates incorporate expert opinions regarding the probability of oil disruptions of a given severity and duration. For example, the probability of oil market interruptions is high, but not on the scale of the 1970s events. They come up with estimates for domestically produced oil of $3 per barrel and $5 for a barrel of imported oil, with the difference being that domestic oil boosts the share of stable supplies while imported oil increases the share of unfriendly supplies. Based on their expectation of oil prices of $80 or above, they suggest that the size of these premiums call for only moderate policy responses.

We can compare the energy security premium to other oil externalities. Parry and Small (2005) found the optimal Pigou tax for externalities to be $0.83, counting the external costs of carbon emissions ($0.06), air pollution ($0.18), congestion ($0.32), and accidents ($0.27), but not energy security. Converting the per-barrel cost of the energy security premium to a per-gallon cost, energy security adds $0.10 to the optimal tax. It would account for just over 10% of the optimal tax of $0.93.

Security petroleum reserve (SPR)

One early response to energy security was to stockpile oil. The United States started the SPR in 1975, with the reserves buried in underground salt domes along the Texas and Louisiana Gulf coasts. The DOE maintains the SPR, which has a capacity of 714 million barrels. Recent figures show it contains just under 700 million barrels.

In theory, the purpose of the SPR is to reduce the market and political power of foreign suppliers. In response to withholding oil by a foreign supplier, we would tap into our reserves, thus increasing our price elasticity (Yücel, 1994). In reality, we have only used the reserve three times, the most recent in 2011 when the United States released 30 million barrels in response to Middle East unrest. The other countries of the IEA also reduced their stockpiles. In total, the IEA members released 60 million barrels (U.S. DOE, n.d.-b). Considine (2006) finds that buildups or drawdowns of the U.S. SPR have negligible effects on the world price of oil, and that for it to have an effect, the amounts would have had to be much larger.

At least in the United States, there seems to be a de-emphasis on the SPR. There had been a proposal to increase its capacity, but it was dropped in 2011.

Military costs

The 1990 Iraqi invasion of Kuwait and the 2001 terrorist events triggered military responses by the United States. The Kuwait response was at least partially motivated by protecting oil supplies. Iraqi oil is a possible factor in the U.S. invasion of Iraq in 2003. It is difficult to disentangle the portion of military spending that goes towards oil protection, but there have been attempts.

Investigators affiliated with Resources for the Future (RfF) have addressed the question. They view military spending as an externality, in that neither oil producers nor consumers take into account the cost of energy security in their production and consumption decisions. Delucchi and Murphy (2007) estimate the hidden cost of military expenditures. The authors cite past estimates ranging from zero, by Parry and Darmstadter (2003) of RfF, to upwards of $1 a gallon (about $0.25 a liter) by Ogden, Williams, and Larson (2004). To narrow the range of answers, Delucchi and Murphy focus on how much the United States would reduce military spending if U.S. highway transportation did not use oil. They arrive at $0.03–0.15 per gallon. Delucchi (2012) provides an update to the earlier study, looking at reduced military spending if the United States curtailed its use of oil for freight shipping. He arrives at a cost of up to $10 billion a year, counting monetary costs but not nonmonetary costs of injuries and lost lives. Using a range of $3–30 billion, the cost translates to a modest $0.02–0.20 premium, based on the price of diesel fuel in 2004.

Brown and Huntington (2013) estimate the oil security premium externality from price instability by estimating the loss in GDP due to the cost of imported oil as compared to the use of domestic oil. The midpoint estimate for domestic oil is $2.28 per barrel and $4.45 for imported oil, a difference of $2.17. At a 2009 price of $40 a barrel, the security premium is about 5.5%. If gas sells for $2 a gallon when oil is $40 a barrel, the premium for imported oil adds about $0.23, a modestly higher figure than the one obtained by Delucchi and Murphy based on military expenditures.

Electricity outage costs

Value of lost load (VoLL) is an estimate of the cost of unsupplied electricity. Figure 16.2 shows the consumer surplus loss if actual supply falls short of the amount needed to satisfy demand at the market price:

$$VoLL = \Delta CS/\Delta EC$$

where CS is consumer surplus and EC is electricity consumption.

Outage cost for residential consumers is forgone utility from the loss of electricity to operate household goods and services such as heating, cooling, and lighting. Industrial

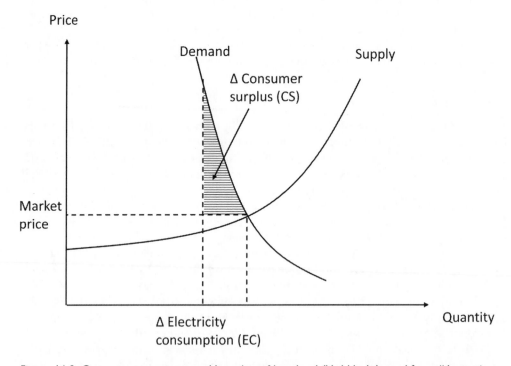

Figure 16.2 Outage cost as measured by value of lost load (VoLL). Adapted from "Assessing energy supply security: Outage costs in private households" by A. J. Praktiknjo, A. Hahnel, and G. Erdmann, 2011, *Energy Policy*, 39(12), p. 7826. Copyright 2011 by Elsevier Ltd.

customers lose profit due to production downtime. Commercial customers such as stores forgo business.

The literature has obtained estimates using macroeconomic models, market-based methods, and contingent valuation surveys. Figure 16.2 shows the market-based approach, where VoLL on a per kWh basis would be the average value per kWh based on forgone consumer surplus if an outage were to occur. Contingent valuation would ask consumer willingness to pay to avoid a hypothetical outage. It may be possible to get real-world information, such as compensation for accepting a load-control device. Note that we expect the VoLL to greatly exceed the price given large forgone consumer surplus when demand is inelastic.

Praktiknjo, Hähnel, and Erdmann (2011) use a macroeconomic approach and provide estimates for residential, commercial, and industrial customers in Germany, as well as an overall figure using a weighted average of the sectors. For the residential sector, they use a Monte Carlo approach that factors in the probability of different household activities, such as cooking, using the computer, or watching TV. They also take into account the value of time as a function of the wage rate. The third factor in their model is electricity consumption. For commercial and industrial customers, the loss is the monetary value of forgone production.

The overall value is approximately €8.5/kWh, with €15.7/kWh for residential customers, €2.5/kWh for industry, and €6.06/kWh for the commercial enterprises.[12] They note that their residential estimate is close to that of similar macroeconomic studies of neighboring countries.

These numbers give some guidance on the value of energy security. The values show that some customers may lose more value during a shortage. In addition, there is heterogeneity within a sector. Hospitals may have a high VoLL if they have no alternative source of electricity, as patient lives depend on electricity. However, for exactly that reason, many hospitals do have backup generation, in which case the loss may be small, simply the additional cost of using their own auxiliary power rather than that of the electric utility.

The damage also depends on the duration of the outage, which could be seconds or days. Electricity systems take into account how quickly different sources of power can be restored, with a very short time for renewables, followed by natural gas and then coal. Nuclear energy takes several days to get back to full power after a shutdown. Utilities also build redundancies into their electric system, such as excess generating capacity or additional transmission lines in case one line goes out of service.

Smart grid

The current electric grid does not meet the needs of a restructured electricity industry where there are opportunities for competition, nor can it provide for two-way transfers of renewable energy. The smart grid can meet these needs, along with the capability to detect malfunctions in the transmission and distribution systems. In addition to these functions, a third benefit of implementing the smart grid is energy security. The smart grid would reduce the number and duration of outages.

The DOE requested the Electric Power Research Institute (EPRI) (2011) to estimate the costs and benefits of the smart grid, breaking down the itemization for several of the key advances offered by a smart grid, although there are no monetary values for cybersecurity. EPRI obtains a benefit estimate of $600 billion vs. $120–170 billion in cost (both in net present value), but according to Joskow (2012), EPRI used too high a VoLL of $5,000–10,000/MWh. On a kWh basis, $5–10/kWh does not seem to be out of line with the outage cost estimates in the previous section. So given the dearth of estimates, EPRI's figure provides a start and suggests that benefits exceed costs even before monetizing the benefits of cybersecurity.

Summary

This chapter reviews the economic perspective on the energy security issue. Energy security does not equate to low energy prices from the economic perspective. Cost–benefit analysis (CBA) can evaluate a policy or an action to enhance energy security. Energy security is a complex issue composed of a number of facets. This complexity often causes disparities between different perspectives. A good CBA analysis needs to quantify the concerns including political and social perspectives. Doing so will decrease the gap between the various perspectives on the energy security issue.

Most approaches to the energy security issue in the United States focus on the supply side, based upon the historic origins of replacing the oil that was lost in the Middle East oil embargo. The oil market has been secure since then, but there are costs to maintaining security.

The initial responses to the oil crises of the 1970s of price controls and rationing likely exacerbated the crises. Producers decrease energy output because of the low price. Consumers increase purchases compared to what they would buy at the new equilibrium price. The quantity gap in the market as a consequence of the price control causes a social efficiency loss. The ban on oil exports was another policy aimed at preserving domestic supply in the United States. Its negative consequence is that the oil companies have less incentive to exploit domestic oil since they cannot sell it to the world. The decreased supply in the world increases the global oil price and thus hurts American consumers due to the higher cost of imports.

One economic approach is to treat energy security as a type of externality. The externality is the higher social energy cost of imports compared to domestic production. One reason is that energy imports can be more volatile. The military cost of protecting foreign energy sources is another type of externality; buyers and sellers of energy do not take this cost into account. Domestic supplies avoid these costs. Electricity outages also cause externalities. The smart grid can reduce externalities by making it easier to detect and repair interruptions in transmission or distribution.

Decreasing energy demand is another efficient way to increase energy security. The demand from the United States affects the energy price in the world due to its large quantity. The decreased demand would lower the energy price and therefore enhance American consumers' benefits. The decreased demand also lessens the impacts from energy supply disruptions.

The United States has reduced its reliance on crude oil imports due to the domestic production boom and decreased energy intensity. These actions have reduced the energy security concerns that are a legacy of the 1970s, but new threats are emerging. Climate change causes extreme weather which threatens the availability of hydropower. Terrorist attacks can cause electricity outages by physical damage to electricity transmission, and by attacking nuclear power plants or obtaining nuclear fuels to manufacture weapons. Cyber attacks can undermine electricity systems. These new threats need new answers that require comparing the costs and the benefits to prioritize our responses.

Notes

1 The arrangement led to a black market in license plates, so that some drivers purchased an additional plate so that they would have one ending in odd numbers and one in even numbers. So-called vanity plates costing a small surcharge that the buyer can customize with a particular phrase were assigned specific days as well.

2 New York and New Jersey brought back this system in 2012, when Hurricane Sandy led to panic buying because of fears that gas would not be available.

3 There were exceptions to the ban, such as allowing some Alaskan crude to go to Japan. The major oil companies were large campaign contributors, and also recognized the opportunity for increased profits if they could elude price controls. By 2015, with the United States now rivaling Saudi Arabia and Russia in oil production as a result of fracking technology, U.S. oil companies made a compelling case that the embargo no longer made sense, if it ever did.

4 For a book-length treatment on the determinants of oil prices, see Aguilera and Radetzki (2015). They reject a number of the usual suspects, including OPEC, demand by developing countries, and speculators, as the primary causes.

5 The McKinsey consulting firm has raised the possibility that we may soon see an era of declining global demand for oil (Roelofsen, Sharma, Sutorius, & Tryggestad, 2016).

6 This discussion follows the analysis of Farrell, Zerriffi, and Dowlatabadi (2004).

7 See Minkel (2008). EPRI (2011) put the damage at $10 billion.

8 New Yorkers in particular remembered the blackout of 1977, where there was widespread looting. Before that, some remember the blackout of November 1965. I was doing algebra homework at the time, and finished my assignment by candlelight.

9 For a fuller treatment of microgrids and the consequences of electric utilities, see Sioshani (2014).

10 As Metcalf (2014) stated, even if the United States were to eliminate oil imports, a supply shock elsewhere would still increase U.S. prices. Metcalf recommended demand reductions as a more effective strategy.

11 Kilian (2014) shows the econometric challenges to sorting out the cause and effect of oil price shocks, including accounting for demand changes due to higher prices.

12 Given exchange rates in 2011, multiply by 1.4 to obtain the dollar equivalent.

References

Aguilera, R., & Radetski, M. (2015). *The price of oil*. Cambridge, UK: Cambridge University Press.

Bohi, D., & Toman, M. (1996). *The economics of energy security*. Dordrecht, the Netherlands: Springer.

Brown, S., & Huntington, H. (2013). Assessing the U.S. oil security premium. *Energy Economics, 38*, 118–127.

Clemente, J. (2009). The security vulnerabilities of the smart grid. *IAGS Journal of Energy Security*. June. http://ensec.org/index.php? option=com_content&view=article&id=198:the-securityvulnerabilities-of-smart-grid&catid=96:content&Itemid=345

Considine, T. (2006). Is the strategic petroleum reserve our ace in the hole? *Energy Journal, 27*(3), 91–112.

Delucchi, M. (2012). The cost of protecting oil in the Persian Gulf. *Resources for the Future: Policy commentary*. http://www.rff.org/blog/2012/cost-protecting-oil-persian-gulf

Delucchi, M., & Murphy, J. (2007). U.S. military expenditures to protect the use of Persian Gulf oil for motor vehicles. *Energy Policy, 36*, 2253–2264.

Electric Power Research Institute. (2011). *Estimating the costs and benefits of the smart grid: A preliminary estimate of the investment requirements and the resultant benefits of a fully functioning smart grid*. Retrieved

January 12, 2017 from https://www.smartgrid.gov/files/Estimating_Costs_Benefits_Smart_Grid_Preliminary_Estimate_In_201103.pdf

Farrell, A., Zerriffi, H., & Dowlatabadi, H. (2004). Energy infrastructure and security. *Annual Review of Environmental Resources, 29*, 421–469.

Forester, T., McNown, R., & Singell, L. (1984). A cost–benefit analysis of the 55 MPH speed limit. *Southern Economic Journal, 50*(3), 631–641.

Franklin, B. (1735, February 4). An ounce of prevention is worth a pound of cure. *Philadelphia Gazette.*

Greene, D. (2010). Measuring energy security: Can the United States achieve energy independence? *Energy Policy, 38*, 1614–1621.

History. (n.d.). *The Exxon Valdez captain's conviction is overturned.* http://www.history.com/this-day-in-history/the-exxon-valdez-captains-conviction-is-overturned

Joskow, P. (2012). Creating a smarter U.S. electricity grid. *Journal of Economic Perspectives, 26,* 29–48.

Kalicki, J., & Goldwyn, D. (2013). *Energy and security,* 2nd edn. Washington, D.C.: Woodrow Wilson Center Press and Baltimore, MD: Johns Hopkins University Press.

Kaplan, E. (2006, February 27). Liquefied natural gas: A potential terrorist target? Retrieved January 11, 2017 from http://www.cfr.org/natural-gas/liquefied-natural-gas-potential-terrorist-target/p9810

Kilian, L. (2014). Oil price shocks: Causes and consequences. *Annual Review of Resource Economics, 6*, 133–154.

Labandeira, X., & Manzano, B. (2012). Some economic aspects of energy security. *European Research Studies, 15*(4), 47–63.

Lott, M. C. (2012, December 18). Guest post: Are microgrids the key to energy security? [Web log post]. Retrieved January 12, 2017 from https://blogs.scientificamerican.com/plugged-in/guest-post-are-microgrids-the-key-to-energy-security/

Metcalf, G. (2014). The economics of energy security. *Annual Review of Resource Economics, 6*, 155–174.

Minkel, J. R. (2008, August 13). The 2003 northeast blackout—five years later. Retrieved from January 11, 2017 from http://www.scientificamerican.com/article/2003-blackout-five-years-later/

Ogden, J., Williams, R. H., & Larson, E. D. (2004). Societal lifecycle costs of cars with alternative fuels/engines. *Energy Policy, 32*, 7–27.

Onishi, N. (2016, April 12). Climate change hits hard in Zambia, an African success story. *New York Times.* Retrieved January 11, 2017 from http://www.nytimes.com/2016/04/13/world/africa/zambia-drought-climate-change-economy.html

Parry, I., & Darmstadter, J. (2003). The costs of U.S. oil dependency. *Resources for the Future Discussion Paper,* 03–59. Retrieved July 17, 2016 from http://www.rff.org/files/sharepoint/WorkImages/Download/RFF-DP-03-59.pdf

Parry, I., & Small, K. (2005). Does Britain or the United States have the right gasoline tax? *American Economic Review, 95*, 1276–1289.

Praktiknjo, A., Hähnel, A., & Erdmann, G. (2011). Assessing energy supply security: Outage costs in private households. *Energy Policy, 39*(12), 7825–7833.

Roelofsen, O., Sharma, N., Sutorius, R., & Tryggestad, C. (2016). *Is peak oil demand in sight?* Retrieved January 11, 2017 from http://www.mckinsey.com/industries/oil-and-gas/our-insights/is-peak-oil-demand-in-sight

Sioshani, F. (2014). *Distributed generation and its implications for the electric utility.* Oxford, UK, Waltham, USA and San Diego, USA: Academic Press, an imprint of Elsevier.

Smith, J. (2009). The 2008 oil price shock: Markets or mayhem? *Journal of Economic Perspectives, 23*(3), 145–164.

U.S. Department of Energy. (n.d.-a). *Recovery act: Smart grid investment grant program.* Retrieved January 12, 2017 from http://energy.gov/oe/recovery-act-smart-grid-investment-grant-sgig-program

U.S. Department of Energy. (n.d.-b). Strategic petroleum reserve. Retrieved January 12, 2017 from http://energy.gov/fe/services/petroleum-reserves/strategic-petroleum-reserve

Yücel, M. (1994). Reducing U.S. vulnerability to oil supply shocks. *Southern Economic Journal, 61*(2), 302–310.

Chapter 17

A comprehensive energy policy
The big picture

"You can't see the forest for the trees."

John Heywood (1546)[1]

"Energy economics helps to see the forest and not just the trees."

The author of this text

Introduction

A *holistic* policy recognizes interrelationships. A *piecemeal* energy policy considers each energy source in isolation. Currently, there is a policy for oil, another one for natural gas, a separate focus on coal, one more for wind, another for solar, and maybe one more for energy efficiency. In fact, there may be multiple policies for each energy source, sometimes working in opposite directions. Piecemeal policy runs the risk of producing an outcome that does not minimize the social cost of meeting our energy needs. In recent years, U.S. natural gas production and use have grown rapidly while coal has declined. Coal is at a disadvantage because it emits more carbon than does natural gas. However, coal has lost its cost advantage to natural gas as a source of electricity-generating fuel even without an explicit price for carbon.

If a new policy wishes to make greater use of abundant reserves of coal, the challenge to accomplish this goal will be larger if we consider coal and natural gas together than if we isolate coal. It will take sizable subsidies for coal to regain market share as an electricity-generating fuel as long as natural gas prices remain at historically low levels. In a carbon-constrained world, where firms pay for carbon emissions or cannot exceed prescribed levels, the cost of coal will be at an even greater disadvantage. We may find that when we evaluate policy for these two fuels jointly rather than in isolation, we should not subsidize coal unless economical methods emerge to decrease carbon emissions from coal, such as lower-cost methods of carbon capture and storage (CCS), the use of synthetic coal, coal gasification, or ultra-supercritical technology.

We can use similar reasoning when evaluating the prospects for nuclear energy. A piecemeal approach considers the prospects for nuclear energy based on its being free of carbon emissions. A holistic approach would encompass renewable fuels such as wind and solar, which are also carbon-free. With nuclear energy's history of cost overruns while renewable costs continue to drop quickly, the case for the former is harder to make. Nuclear energy does have the virtue of providing a dependable source of baseline energy, whereas renewables will not be able to do so until battery storage becomes economical. In evaluating whether to promote a greater role for nuclear energy, we need to consider the strides in providing renewable energy economically as well as its prospects for a higher capacity factor through the availability of battery storage or next-generation technologies that can produce energy more efficiently using alternative technologies and materials.

The holistic view suggests anticipating how the energy landscape and the provision of electricity will change with battery storage. It also suggests that society may gain from government support for R&D without picking winners. The U.S. Department of Energy could make funds available for research in battery storage, nuclear fusion, or other alternatives, rather than picking one or the other. It is closer to the X-Prize approach of offering a substantial reward for the next breakthrough that changes the energy landscape.

Energy efficiency provides another source of carbon-free fuel, even if the fuel itself is invisible. Policies to promote the use of carbon-free fuels should allow for energy efficiency as well as renewable energy or nuclear fuel. The societal goal is to use our least expensive resources first, where that cost includes the price society places on carbon and other emissions. We cannot assume that energy efficiency is necessarily the cheapest fuel. We have to compare the costs of greater energy efficiency, such as weatherizing a home or building more fuel-efficient transportation, to the value of the fuel savings and the value society places on lower emissions. When fuel prices are low and society places a low value on carbon emissions, the case for energy efficiency is weaker.

Amory Lovins (1976) presents energy policy as the soft path vs. the hard path. When he first wrote these words, he proposed the *soft path* as the road that had not yet been taken—energy efficiency and a shift to renewable fuels—with less reliance on the *hard path*—oil, natural gas, and coal—business as usual. A comprehensive policy needs to encompass both paths, with the goal of satisfying our energy requirements at the lowest social cost, including private costs of production and external costs to society of the negative by-products.

First- and second-best policies

A *first-best* policy is one where we get the prices right. In order to maximize social welfare, it is necessary that price equals marginal social cost. Marginal social cost is the sum of marginal private cost and marginal external cost. Marginal private cost is the cost of private resources—including labor, capital, and energy—while marginal social cost includes external costs, with carbon emissions prominent in discussions of the external costs of energy.

If we are to pursue first-best policies, we would need to have a price for carbon emissions, in addition to prices for sulfur, NOx, particulates, and mercury, assuming the benefits of monitoring and enforcing emissions requirements exceeds the cost. In the United States, at the time of writing of this book, there is no federal policy regarding carbon emissions, although some regions have adopted their own programs. In the absence of a market for carbon emissions or other external costs, we are in a second-best world where the usual efficiency rules may not apply. If companies can emit carbon freely, there is an implicit subsidy for fossil fuels. We are violating the rule for social efficiency, since fossil fuel price is below marginal social cost. In that case, setting price equal to marginal social cost in other related markets, such as renewable fuels or economic efficiency, may no longer maximize social welfare. Maximizing social welfare in a second-best world calls for subsidizing substitutes for fossil fuels. The first-best rule would fully price all fuels, but if we do not, the best we can do is to get the relative prices right.

Inevitably, we make energy policy in a second-best world. The modern study of energy economics emanates from the early 1970s when OPEC gained market power over the price of oil. We have been in a second-best world in oil and related energy markets as we try to offset the distortion of oil prices exceeding competitive levels. As oil prices collapsed from the lofty heights of $100 per barrel in June of 2014 to under $30 per barrel by early 2016, some commentators expressed concern that energy prices were too low. When OPEC met in late 2016 and committed at least verbally to reducing output, some commentators expressed relief that oil prices were back above $50 per barrel. Setting aside external cost considerations, this economist disagrees with these commentators. In a first-best world, competition is necessary to achieve the socially efficient outcome. A cohesive energy policy should start with market outcomes. As we introduce energy market failures, market outcomes including competition need no longer be efficient.

When markets fail, government has the potential to improve resource allocation. However, government failure is also possible, where its intervention leads to still greater inefficiency. In the 1970s, the U.S. government imposed price controls on gasoline, and then rationed its supply by limiting the size of purchases and by the day of the week depending on the last digit of your license plate. Instead of paying higher prices, consumers paid with their time, stuck in hour-long lines at gas stations to top off their gas tanks. Wealthier drivers paid someone else to wait in line, or paid the station owner for an overpriced car wash tied to the purchase of price-controlled gas. Electric utilities turned from oil to natural gas as a source of generating fuel. However, natural gas was subject to its own set of price controls that also resulted in shortages and a loss of confidence in natural gas as a heating fuel.

Government regulation in the late 1970s required electric utilities to buy alternatives such as solar energy at above-market prices. This rule added to market inefficiencies, insofar as the utilities could have met demand at a lower cost using their available generating units. Proponents of renewable fuels, including then President Jimmy Carter, may have cheered the use of solar, including the installation of panels on the White House roof. Economists did not cheer, as our criterion is the best use of scarce resources. While the 1978 legislation did have the advantage of showing the feasibility of independent power production, it did so in an inefficient way, expanding the use of solar when there were alternatives with lower social costs.

Incentive-based policies vs. command-and-control

If markets produce an inefficient outcome and we look to government to improve it, economists usually advocate incentive-based (IB) policies over command-and-control (CAC). IB solutions make use of markets, whereas CAC replaces them. The two major IB approaches are taxes and trading. Pigou made the case for corrective taxes when markets did not internalize externalities, such as a tax on a coal company that pollutes nearby water. Coase identified the fundamental problem as transactions costs, not externalities, and saw the solution as clearly establishing property rights and then allowing negotiations of those rights. He preferred his approach to that of Pigou, as he felt the parties involved had a better knowledge of the costs of the externalities and of preventing them than did the government. More importantly, the parties could choose from a variety of solutions to minimize costs, which could lead to lower-cost solutions than Pigou's tax. Under Pigou, the coal company pays a tax on its emissions and reduces output of the offending product if it is cheaper to do so than to pay the tax. With Coase, other outcomes are possible. If the coal company has the property right, homeowners can pay the coal company to reduce emissions, buy bottled water, or move away. The lowest-cost method depends on the transactions costs of establishing property rights, negotiating those rights, and monitoring and enforcing the agreement. In some cases, the most efficient outcome is to do nothing and live with the externality, as might be the case for electromagnetic field (EMF) radiation from high-voltage electricity trans-mission lines passing through remote areas.[2]

The leading IB approaches are Pigou-style taxes and Coase-style trading. Electric utilities subject to a carbon tax can reduce electricity output, install technology to capture the emissions, or substitute alternative fuels. If trading is the method, electric utilities can pursue these options and more such as offering consumers the option to pay a premium for carbon-free fuels. In addition, electric utilities that can only abate at a high cost can buy additional permits to emit from utilities with low abatement costs. In an offset system, they could get credit for reducing carbon emissions by paying to eliminate gas-guzzling cars or fuel-intensive manufacturers. They could pay for carbon-reducing technology in developing countries to earn credits towards pollution reduction. Cap-and-trade might lead to the same outcome as the Pigou tax. However, it enlarges the possibilities and it could lead to a lower-cost solution.

We have just compared static efficiency. Over time, different approaches lead to different dynamic savings. Firms that successfully innovate in ways that reduce carbon emissions will reduce their tax obligation, or will need fewer permits. However, as the demand for permits decreases with innovations, permit values decline, giving a weaker incentive to innovate over time than the fixed tax price.

While economists recommend that we "need to get the prices right," there is a danger of doing so in a piecemeal fashion. Considering the parts without the whole will result in inefficient substitution from one source to another, and in inefficiency as busi-ness makes decisions only to find that they would have done things differently if all the policy pieces were determined together.[3] In this final chapter, we will lay out a holistic energy picture. By incorporating the full social costs of energy, we will be able to make maximum use of the power of the market mechanism for determining our energy future. At the same time, we will illuminate areas where the public needs the govern-ment to make the best use of energy resources. Such roles may include subsidies for R&D, or for leveling a playing field that has favored fossil fuels via subsidies, or path-dependent historical accidents that have favored, in Amory Lovins's terms, the hard path over the soft path.

Energy-using sectors

Transportation

Oil comprises the largest source of energy use in the United States, and almost all of it goes to transportation. For the first time since 1979, transportation is now the largest source of carbon emissions, as electric utilities have reduced emissions by replacing coal with natural gas, and to a lesser extent, renewables (Vine, 2016). Low gasoline prices have spurred consumers towards SUVs and full-size trucks and away from fuel-efficient gasoline cars as well as alternative-fuel vehicles.

If we are to reduce carbon emissions from oil, we will need to reduce the share of conventional gas-combustion vehicles, especially SUVs and full-size trucks that get fewer miles per gallon. The first-best policy is to price externalities, with the primary unpriced externality being carbon emissions. Implementation of a carbon price would lead to vehicle drivers paying the full social cost of their vehicle choice, with drivers weighing the higher cost of gasoline for SUVs and full-size trucks when evaluating a vehicle purchase. However, as we found in an earlier chapter, talk of the demise of SUVs was premature then, and it is premature now. If fewer drivers purchase SUVs, their price will fall. We can also expect manufacturers to improve their gas mileage, or to make a version with a hybrid engine. Our job is not to target the SUV for extinction, but to get the prices right. We can then let the market determine the future of SUVs.

Economists prefer IB policies that achieve the goal of reducing carbon at the lowest cost. The policies have the secondary effect of stretching out oil supplies. In addition, lower use of oil has energy security benefits, as it reduces the need for imports.

The IB policies are carbon taxes and carbon trading markets. Economists are divided on which is the better alternative. Pigou taxes reduce unwanted emissions, and the government can spend the revenues on other desirable programs, or use the revenues to offset less desirable taxes, referred to as a double dividend. Emissions taxes also encourage dynamic efficiency, since firms that can find technologies that cut carbon emissions can reduce their carbon-tax liability. A downside is that industry knows more about the cost of reducing carbon emissions than does the government, and has little reason to reveal these costs accurately. Instead, businesses have an incentive to exaggerate the costs to try to discourage the government from setting a high tax.

A carbon emissions market has the advantage that the government does not need to determine where to set the tax. It simply sets the quantity of emissions permits, and leaves it to firms to buy and sell permits, depending on their marginal abatement costs. Of course, true efficiency requires setting quantity at the optimal level.[4] The government can auction permits to raise revenue, but it is common to give away the permits. Giveaways have the advantage over taxes that they can garner industry support, whereas businesses will oppose taxes. Trading is likely to have smaller dynamic benefits than taxes, as cost-saving technology will reduce firm willingness-to-pay for permits. The lower permit price reduces the gains to carbon-reducing technologies, so there is a smaller incentive to pursue these technologies than is the case with taxes, where innovations do not affect the tax level.

If we do not implement taxes or trading, we will have to consider second-best remedies. One widely used approach is to subsidize the purchase of alternative-fuel vehicles. Initially, the U.S. government subsidized gas–electric hybrids, most notably the Toyota Prius. We can give a second-best rationale for the subsidy with the argument that there is an implicit subsidy for fossil fuels as long as there is no carbon price. Subsidies are popular because the winners get a sizable benefit while the losers, taxpayers who finance the subsidy but do not receive one, may not be aware of the cost. In addition, the costs are small and spread out, reducing the likelihood that taxpayers will object.

As gas–electric hybrid vehicles gained market share, the government phased out the subsidy and turned to electric vehicles. Producers claim that were it not for the subsidy, they would lose money on these vehicles. The subsidies to buyers are typically credits or deductions on income taxes, and their effect depends upon how much they reduce an individual's taxes, with the wealthy benefiting most.

California requires that carmakers produce a percentage of vehicles that qualify as zero-emissions vehicles (ZEVs). From a life–cycle standpoint, we must recognize that ZEVs including qualifying electric vehicles require electricity, so unless the electric generator uses carbon-free power, there are still emissions.

The Cash-for-Clunkers program offered several thousand dollars to buyers who traded a low-mileage vehicle for a high-mileage one. We have cautioned that some buyers could be free riders who were planning to trade their old clunker for a newer higher-mileage car even without a subsidy. Again, the gains are large and concentrated, while the cost to taxpayers is small and diffuse, making this program politically feasible.

All of these programs have the weakness that the government is picking winners, first hybrids, then electrics, perhaps hydrogen vehicles next. The approach is also vulnerable to regulatory capture. The U.S. government has imposed a gas–guzzler tax since the late 1970s. There is room for lobbying by car manufacturers, with the tax based on undisclosed laboratory tests that can differ from the mileage figures posted publicly in vehicle windows. In addition, manufacturers have lobbied for a more lenient standard for trucks and SUVs, which U.S. regulations have defined as trucks.

The government CAFÉ standard is a long-standing regulatory program that has required the average car in a manufacturer's fleet to achieve an increasingly stringent number of miles per gallon, with the latest proposal set at 54.5 mpg by 2025. It has the advantage that it does not attempt to pick winners, as compared to programs that specifically target a segment of the auto industry. As was discussed earlier in the text, manufacturers are lobbying against this standard, with the credible argument that if gas prices are low and so consumers favor large, low mpg vehicles, it will be very difficult to achieve such a high average figure.

If the CAFÉ program continues, albeit at a less ambitious mpg requirement, there is hope that it will allow car manufacturers to trade permits, so that manufacturers who have a comparative advantage in building high-mileage cars could sell permits to companies that find it more difficult to produce high-mileage vehicles profitably. By incorporating an IB approach, there is an improvement in the efficiency of the CAFÉ program. The least efficient program is to ban SUVs and high-mileage trucks. Consumers get considerable utility from these larger vehicles, and as long as they pay the full social costs including carbon emissions, consumers should have the option to purchase size and possibly safety over fuel economy and lower emissions.

Carpooling and congestion pricing are less direct ways of reducing gasoline use. Highways can provide a lane for carpoolers. There is the dilemma of whether there need to be only two passengers or more than two to qualify.[5] Americans are sufficiently reluctant to carpool that the designated lane may not attract many cars, thereby adding to the congestion in the other lanes.

Congestion pricing can relieve congestion and increase social efficiency, as well as produce revenue. Congestion wastes time as well as fuel. The government or a private company can build and operate the toll road. However, we need to take into account own- and cross-price elasticities. A higher toll reduces the number of cars. It may shift the cars to a different time of use, which is beneficial if it moves cars from peak hours to less travelled times but not if it simply shifts the time of the peak. It also moves vehicles to different lanes or different roads, which could increase congestion on those roads.

To recap, economists prefer IB approaches such as taxes and trading if possible. If we cannot implement first-best approaches, we have the difficult task of identifying the second-best approach that can accomplish the goal at a minimum cost to society. We should avoid CAC performance standards that impose the same requirement on all participants, because it is more efficient to allow a party that can achieve the goal at a lower marginal cost to do more abatement than another party with a higher marginal abatement cost. If we do implement CAC, we should particularly avoid technology standards that not only require all participants to reduce an objectionable behavior by the same proportion, but to use the same method to accomplish the reduction. GM may build a high-mileage diesel car, while Ford may achieve the goal by using lighter-weight materials to build a car.[6] There is no way a government (or an economist) is smart enough to be able to imagine all the ways to minimize the cost of achieving a goal.

Electric utilities

Our starting point is again to price external costs as long as the benefit to society of reduced emissions exceeds costs of monitoring and enforcement. In the United States, we regulate a number of electric utility emissions, including SO_2, NOx, and particulates. Again, economists prefer IB policies. The Clean Air Act amendments of 1990 introduced the IB approach of cap-and-trade for SO_2 and NOx emissions, but recent legislation led to utilities installing scrubbers to reduce sulfur emissions, leaving permits almost worthless and the trading market near collapse. The CAC scrubber requirement increased the cost of achieving the goal of reduced emissions, as utilities might have been able to achieve the goal at lower cost using low-sulfur coal or switching to natural gas or other fuels that are lower in sulfur. However, now that utilities have installed scrubbers, there is much less value to continuing an IB approach on top of a technology standard.

In the absence of a federal program to limit carbon emissions, some states have chosen to start cap-and-trade programs, notably California in the west and the Regional Greenhouse Gas Initiative (RGGI) that includes a number of Northeast states. The California Exchange has a low permit price. Contributing factors include a weak recovery from the Great Recession, a renewable portfolio standard (RPS), and uncertainty about whether the program will continue beyond 2020. There is also the disadvantage that trades can only take place within the California Exchange, so we lose the efficiencies that come from trading among different states. Quebec and Ontario have linked with California's cap-and-trade exchange, increasing efficiency for both California and the two Canadian provinces.

As states are free to enter or leave RGGI, its gains may be modest. The coalition appears to have set initial goals that were easy to achieve. Even then, if a state finds it costly to reduce emissions, and fears those costs will reduce its competitiveness with neighboring states, it may exit the coalition, as New Jersey has done (Jones, 2016).

The EU has a carbon cap-and-trade program, but for much of its existence it has had at best a modest effect. The EU issued a large number of permits to gain industry support for the program, and so permit prices have been low. Studies put the value of carbon reductions at \$40/ton (almost €40/ton using exchange rates as of early 2017), while the EU Environmental Trading System (EU-ETS) permits trade for about €5.

The Canadian province of British Columbia has had a carbon tax since 2008, and it is currently C\$30/ton (about US\$22.50 at 2017 rates of exchange). Alberta initiated a C\$20 tax in 2017, due to rise to C\$30 in 2018. Both provinces use the tax revenues to reduce other taxes or they go towards environmental programs.

Twenty-nine U.S. states and the District of Columbia have chosen an RPS. These programs have an element of CAC by requiring electric utilities within a state to meet a renewables requirement even if electric utilities have lower-cost generators. As with the voluntary emissions-trading programs, voluntarily adopted RPS programs may not set ambitious targets for renewables if they fear that the state will decide to terminate the program (Cochran, 2015). They may be a high-cost way to achieve carbon reductions. These programs can also cause the inefficiencies discussed earlier when two programs target the same goal, as we saw with SO_2 when recent regulations led to the installation of scrubbers, bringing about the collapse of the sulfur emissions trading program. If states had a tax or trading system, there would be no need for an RPS. If states have an RPS system, it reduces the value of a trading system, as RPS reduces the use of sulfur-emitting fossil fuels.

Piecemeal approaches come in many shapes and sizes, in this case multiple programs aimed at the same objective. A cohesive approach would recognize that if there is an IB program with a price that truly reflects the marginal social cost of carbon emissions, there is no longer a need for an RPS, as industries should not use a second-best approach if a first-best one is in place. Of course, if governments introduce an excess of permits or too low a tax, we do not have a first-best situation. The effect on social welfare of multiple programs becomes a difficult empirical question, and the theme of this final chapter is a cohesive approach with one first-best program, rather than a piecemeal approach with two second-best programs.

Feed-in-tariffs in the EU serve a similar purpose to RPS in the United States. Both programs have a CAC flavor, as they target renewable fuels as the best way to reduce carbon emissions. The programs define acceptable energy sources. Some programs may recognize wood as a renewable fuel, others may include energy from swine and chicken waste, and still others count energy efficiency as equivalent to renewables. Even though nuclear energy also is carbon-free, it is not a renewable fuel and is at a relative disadvantage in the presence of an RPS or a FIT. The programs rarely count existing hydro energy, nor even additional sources of hydro.

Some observers urge a federal RPS to unify the U.S. programs. We can shed light on the use of RPSs and whether or not a federal RPS would increase welfare by using our holistic framework. We now know that RPS is a second-best approach, and that a properly designed tax or trading program would be preferable. However, in the absence of a proper tax or trading program, RPS is a candidate for the next best alternative.

Would a federal RPS be better? We can enhance RPS efficiency by allowing trade among states. Trading allows states with a comparative advantage in renewables to provide a greater percentage of those renewables. If Nevada can transport electricity to Oregon, it is likely to have a lower-cost source of solar energy, given its sunny desert climate as compared to Oregon's rainy reputation. Even within Oregon, the dry eastern half of the state can ship power to the cloudy western half. The larger the trading sphere, the more RPS can reduce the inefficiency of mandating renewables as an alternative to a tax or trading system. Just as with CAFÉ standards for vehicles, trading reduces CAC program inefficiencies. However, some states already allow trading, so that Oregon may be able to get credit towards meeting its requirement by importing energy from Nevada without the need for a federal RPS. The federal RPS does have the advantage that in the absence of a federal tax or trade program, it would offset the implicit subsidy to fossil fuels by requiring all states to increase their use of renewables as a second-best approach to reducing carbon emissions. The downside is if it imposes a one-size-fits-all approach, requiring sunny states such as Nevada, cloudy states such as Oregon, and windy states such as Wyoming, to all meet a common standard.

The U.S. Environmental Protection Agency (EPA) proposed a Clean Power Plan (CPP) under the administration of President Obama that has the potential to improve social welfare. It would set a separate standard for each state based upon the cost of reducing emissions for that state, and would allow trading among states to reach the standard. The plan faces formidable obstacles to adoption, with the U.S. Supreme Court suspending its enforcement pending many states, chief among them coal-producing states, raising legal challenges. The legal challenge to the plan is the accusation that the EPA has overreached its authority. It faces a further challenge because the new administration of President Trump has not expressed willingness to advocate for the CPP.

Aside from the legal and political questions, a state-specific plan imposed at the federal level assumes that the central government has good information on the cost of achieving the goal at the state level. It is more likely that the states have better information. This same criticism applies to a federal RPS. The states are in a better position to evaluate whether wind, solar, wood, waste, energy efficiency, or even nuclear energy, is the least-cost method of reducing emissions in the absence of a first-best policy. Despite the absence of carbon taxes or trading at the federal level, U.S. utilities have dramatically reduced their use of coal and carbon emissions. Utilities may be anticipating the eventual pricing of carbon, or the main impetus might be low natural gas prices. They are also adopting more wind and solar, attributable to falling renewables prices, subsidies, RPS, and regional cap-and-trade programs.

Electric utilities have programs that reward customers for using energy more efficiently, such as offering LED lights at a below-market price or demand reduction (DR) programs that pay customers to use less energy during peak hours. Such programs put utilities in the odd position of encouraging consumers to use less of their product. We should be cautious about assuming that the utility has the right incentive to encourage energy efficiency. Such programs are a more natural fit for producers of appliances and builders of homes, and we turn to the industrial and buildings sectors next.

Instead, economists advocate marginal cost pricing for electricity, preferably with all external costs included. As utilities implement a smart grid capable of providing real-time information on prices, as well as the ability to buy as well as sell electricity, society stands to gain as long as the benefits exceed the cost of implementing the new grid. Consumers facing the full social cost of electricity can evaluate the annual savings from LEDs vs. their upfront costs. High peak period prices will reduce the need for the utility to build new plants. Government need not intervene unless there is a market failure in how consumers make their energy use decisions, such as an energy efficiency gap whereby consumers discount future energy savings at an above-market interest rate and so underinvest in energy efficiency.

Industry

Industry has reduced its energy use, mostly attributable to reducing its energy intensity, although energy use also dropped during the Great Recession. It is notable that industry has been reducing energy intensity since 1980 as firms adjusted to high energy prices. In addition to individual firms choosing less energy-intensive production processes, the U.S. economy has also shifted towards less energy-intensive manufacturers and away from manufacturing in general towards services, which use less energy per unit of output.

Firms have reduced energy intensity in response to market forces such as higher energy costs. The trend is not a consequence of a government regulatory program. Profit-maximizing firms need to move away from high-priced inputs if they are to compete successfully in a competitive market. Businesses have also expressed the desire to use sustainable practices, which would also reduce energy use.

The motive for sustainable practices is less clear, as it does not always coincide with profit maximization or private efficiency. Sustainability can differ from social efficiency as well. Other possible motives are warm glow and green marketing. Businesses proclaim the desire to do good for society, although economists are skeptical that firms will deviate from profit maximization. Firms may be able to attract more customers by advertising their sustainable practices. Google, Amazon, and Facebook use energy-intensive data centers, where they claim they use 100% renewable fuels. The claim may lead consumers to believe the data centers themselves run on renewables, but a more accurate claim would make clear that these companies buy renewable energy credits to offset their energy use. Data centers run 24/7, while wind and solar energy are intermittent, so until battery storage is available at a competitive cost, data centers will require electricity powered from continuously available conventional sources such as fossil fuels and nuclear energy.

As with other sectors, carbon pricing would reinforce energy intensity and sustainability trends. A carbon price increases the cost of fossil fuels, with commensurate rewards to firms that can reduce their energy use. We once again survey second-best possibilities since we cannot count on the U.S. government to introduce tax or trading systems to reduce GHGs.

While there are some regulatory programs aimed at reducing energy use and increasing energy efficiency, much of the change in industry energy use is due to market forces. Programs that reward energy efficiency include informational programs such as EPA's ENERGY STAR that provides buyers with information on energy savings with more energy-efficient appliances or building materials. In turn, manufacturers shift towards selling appliances that are more efficient. ENERGY STAR is a voluntary program, and, in that sense, is a Pareto improvement. Setting aside market failures such as the energy efficiency gap and behavioral failures such as the inability to calculate benefits and costs, businesses can decide whether they save money by buying appliances that are more efficient. ENERGY STAR may improve buyer information, but as with any program, we have to compare benefits of providing the information to costs, including the costs to the government and in turn to taxpayers.

Buildings and commercial users[7]

Buildings account for 40% of primary energy consumption, with industry the second largest user at around one-third, and transportation the third largest use at almost 30%.

Residential and commercial buildings each account for about one-half of building energy consumption. Almost 60% of commercial use is for heating, cooling, and lighting, directly through primary energy use as well as secondary use to generate electricity. As buildings are long-lived, many of the improvements will require retrofitting existing stocks, although there is also room for improvements in new construction.

We proceed to second-best possibilities for reducing energy use and its associated emissions. Leadership in Energy and Environmental Design (LEED) certification encourages businesses to construct energy-efficient buildings; the certification may serve as green marketing as well as reducing operating costs. To the extent that the energy-efficiency improvements save money, they would be accomplished by the market and do not require government programs or even encouragement from LEED. If building owners have imperfect information, LEED as well as ENERGY STAR can provide information on savings from energy-efficient practices. The American Council for an Energy Efficient Economy (ACEEE) also provides information, as does the American Society for Heating, Cooling, and Air Conditioning Engineers (ASHRAE). Energy audits are another source of information.

Market incentives as well as subsidies encourage measures such as triple-glazed windows and adding insulation. Government subsidies should first identify what market failure they are trying to overcome. If there is no market failure, the government should stay out, unless the motive is equity rather than efficiency. The rationale for voluntary government programs such as ENERGY STAR or nongovernment programs such as LEED is that building owners and users have imperfect information.

The McKinsey study showed programs that would reduce energy use, some of them at a negative cost, and a number of others with a cost below €20. Implicitly, McKinsey is saying that consumers have less than perfect information. Economists question whether McKinsey has measured opportunity cost as opposed to accounting cost. While CFL and LED bulbs will save energy over the course of their lifetime, consumers may not like the illumination as much as an incandescent bulb. In addition, consumers must make a special trip to a city-owned facility to dispose of the mercury contained in CFL bulbs.

Ideally, carbon pricing would provide the proper incentive of what light to use. In the absence of an IB program, it is best that the government not pick winners. There is no reason to ban the incandescent bulb to force the buyer to use CFLs or LEDs if carbon is unpriced. In that eventuality, we should find the program that reduces carbon emissions at the lowest cost per ton. It could be a switch to an LED, as McKinsey suggests, or it could be motion sensors to turn off lights when no one is using a room. We must also compare the cost of transportation, industry, and electric utility measures to reduce carbon emissions, and then arrange the options in merit order. We can include all sectors, as opposed to focusing on each sector in isolation. We start with the lowest-cost method, and proceed to higher-cost ones if we desire more carbon reductions than the lowest-cost method can achieve.

The other major area for energy savings in commercial buildings is heating, ventilation, and air conditioning (HVAC). Insulation may be cost-effective at reducing heat loss or retaining the benefits of air conditioning. Energy-efficient windows might achieve the benefits at a lower cost. As usual, we should be wary of programs that target a particular action, such as subsidies for more efficient windows. The government is unlikely to have the information to subsidize the most efficient measures, and the subsidies may go to buyers who would have bought the more efficient technology even without the subsidy. Moreover, insofar as the building owner fully internalizes lower energy bills or can capitalize the expenditures by selling the building at a higher price, the market alone can achieve the socially efficient solution. However, in the case of rented or leased buildings, neither the occupants nor the owner can capture the resale value of energy-efficient improvements, and the government may have the potential to improve efficiency.

Government buildings may also suffer from split incentives, since the government workers do not get back the savings from energy efficiency. One way to provide an incentive is to allow departments to keep a percentage of energy savings to use towards a desired program. At the same time, taxpayers save money. The concept is analogous to electric utility incentive regulation, where a utility that reduces its cost below the expected level keeps a portion of the savings, with ratepayers getting a portion as well.

There is a justification for government R&D programs to correct for market under-provision of goods with public goods characteristics. Society gains from making tech-nological advances widely available. Furthermore, it may not be possible to exclude others from using the technology other than by a patent-granting monopoly, which motivates R&D but also results in underprovision of the eventual innovation. The DOE sponsors research to develop energy efficiency and create zero-emissions build-ings (ZEBs) that produce enough renewable energy to offset their energy use. There are also government facilities, such as Oak Ridge and Argonne National Labs, that perform energy research including energy efficiency measures such as HVAC research and weatherization.

Remember that such programs need not be socially efficient. In the energy efficiency chapter, we discussed the recent study that showed that a program to weatherize the homes of low-income owners had little effect, and had a very high cost per ton as a way to reduce carbon emissions (Fowlie, Greenstone, & Wolfram, 2015).

Buildings and residential users

As with commercial building uses, the largest residential use is HVAC. Lighting and water heating are the next largest uses. Electronics, refrigeration, and cooking follow. The same programs and cautions that apply to commercial users and buildings apply here. In the absence of a first-best tax or trading program, we need to choose the second-best program that achieves the objective at lowest cost.

Typically, the ultimate objective is to reduce carbon emissions by reducing energy use. Household technologies, including heating, cooling, lighting, and electronics are available in energy-efficient varieties at a price premium over less efficient versions. The EPA offers estimated savings through the ENERGY STAR program, and there may be state or federal incentives to help defray the price premium. From an economic perspective, energy-efficient appliances vary in their effectiveness.[8] Energy-efficient air conditioners may have the greatest potential to save energy, but they also have the largest rebound effect. Consumers who buy the energy-efficient model may respond to energy bill savings by adjusting their thermostat to achieve greater comfort. Energy-efficient refrigerators save energy, but the payback period may be close to ten years. In the absence of rebates, only consumers who use a low discount rate will purchase the more efficient model. While consumers typically do not adjust the interior temperature of the refrigerator, rebound can occur if the consumer purchases a refrigerator with a larger capacity or more features. The savings are smaller for energy-efficient washing machines, and smallest for dishwashers. As a result, the per-unit cost of carbon reductions is high.

While energy-using devices including TVs and computers are increasingly energy-efficient, the bigger story is that consumers continue to buy more appliances. Appliances and electronics now use more electricity than HVAC (U.S. EPA, n.d.). On balance, energy consumption is relatively flat or decreasing in recent years for all sectors—industrial, transportation, commercial, and residential (U.S. EIA, n.d.)—attributable to lower energy intensity.

Markets and government

A comprehensive and cohesive energy policy has to start with markets. Where they work, they provide an economically efficient outcome. They bring together consumers and producers in a way that achieves the best interests of society. There is no need for government intervention to achieve the best outcome. For energy, markets are the starting point but not the ending point. In energy, negative externalities are ubiquitous. Where there are negative externalities, markets such as gasoline or electricity over-produce and underprice output. Where the market fails to produce an economically or socially efficient outcome, the government has the potential to improve the outcome.

Government has intervened in most energy markets. It has regulated a number of unwanted emissions, from lead in gasoline to sulfur, NOx and particulates from burning fossil fuels to generate electricity. The EPA has promulgated regulations for mercury. However, there is not yet a federal regulation for carbon emissions. The lack of a price for carbon has led to less efficient policies, and not enough attention to which of the policies achieves the goal of reducing carbon emissions at the lowest cost per ton. In many cases, the government has imposed more than one regulation at a time, risking further losses in efficiency when the multiple policies are at cross-purposes. As an example we discussed in this chapter, California's cap-and-trade regime would be a first-best policy if the state were not simultaneously imposing an RPS. The RPS greatly reduces the demand for permits, since firms are constrained in their use of fossil fuels and therefore only need a small number of emissions permits.

A comprehensive energy policy would be much easier to achieve if we had a carbon price. However, as long as we do not, we will have to evaluate policies for their effects on carbon and the cost of achieving the reduction.

Summary

Energy policy typically takes a piecemeal approach, examining one energy source or one policy at a time, but such an approach risks missing connections among sources or conflicts among policies. A major purpose of economics is to provide a framework for holistic thinking, in this case to formulate a cohesive energy policy that does not miss the forest for the trees. A policy to save coal cannot ignore the reasons for the emergence of natural gas as the largest fuel source for electricity generation nor the fast growth of renewables. An objective to encourage the use of renewables in electricity cannot overlook the emergence of transportation as the largest emitter of CO_2.

Economics provides clarity on first- vs. second-best approaches. First-best approaches are typically IB approaches—taxes and trading—that make use of existing markets. Second-best approaches have elements of CAC regulation—replacing rather than augmenting existing markets with uniform requirements for all firms or prescribed methods to achieve the goal. By chance, regulators might pick the lowest-cost solution, but IB approaches allow for a wider range of solutions with the likelihood that there will be a lower-cost solution than the CAC approach. Throughout this final chapter, we have contrasted the efficiency and simplicity of the first-best tax or trade solution as compared to the alternatives that have arisen given the unwillingness to implement a tax or trading system. Programs such as CAFÉ standards, subsidies for alternative-fuel vehicles, and RPSs have higher social costs than taxes or trades. If the goal is to reduce carbon emissions, the CAC programs may achieve the goal, but at a higher cost per unit of reduction.

Given that we live in a second-best world where there are preexisting distortions such as an absence of a carbon market, we then have to compare second-best solutions to minimize the loss of social welfare. If we use a CAFÉ program, we can improve it by incorporating trading of mileage requirements among manufacturers. This program has the advantage that it does not attempt to pick winners, whereas singling out hybrids, electric vehicles, or hydrogen vehicles does.

Transportation has overtaken electricity as the largest emitter of fossil fuels. It is also the primary use of oil, still the largest component of energy use in the United States. If we are to reduce carbon emissions, we will need to reduce the dominance of the gasoline combustion engine. A CAFÉ program may be the best we can do in the absence of carbon taxes or trading. It is more evenhanded than subsidies for specific alternatives, which also have the characteristic that they mostly benefit taxpayers in high tax brackets.

Electricity use has been flat or declining as all sectors—industrial, commercial, and residential—reduce energy intensity enough to offset higher use of electric appliances. Carbon emissions have decreased even faster, with coal losing market share to natural gas, which emits only about half as much carbon. Renewables are a small but growing share, but will replace natural gas more than coal until battery storage allows them to be available at all times as a baseload fuel.

Again, tax or trade systems are the most efficient way to reduce emissions. In their absence, RPS or FIT programs may be the best we can do. They have the weakness that they still pick winners, defining what fuel sources qualify—wind, solar, biofuels—and which do not—nuclear energy and existing hydro—even though they all are carbon-free sources of energy. CAC technology standards are still less efficient, requiring the adoption of scrubber technologies to reduce sulfur or CCS to reduce emissions from coal when there are likely to be lower-cost alternatives.

Industrial energy use has been declining at the fastest pace, with the long-term trend to reduce energy intensity. In addition, there has been a shift toward fewer energy-intensive manufacturers and an even more significant trend from manufacturing in general towards less energy-intensive service industries. Industry has responded to higher energy prices, with the market rather than government being the impetus for higher energy efficiency and lower energy intensity. Industry has also adopted green programs and sustainability objectives that may have motives other than profit maximization. These actions have also reduced energy use, and have been a surprise insofar as we assume that firms single-mindedly pursue profit maximization.

There have been some modest government programs, such as the EPA's ENERGY STAR, that provide information on energy savings from more energy-efficient appliances. As businesses have a choice of appliance, the programs are worthwhile if the value of the information exceeds the cost of running the program. In some cases, the government removes the less efficient alternative, as in the case of Edison's light, and in some cases, less energy-efficient technologies. Such bans may actually reduce welfare if the new technologies have higher manufacturing costs or less desirable characteristics, such as inferior lighting or higher disposal costs. We also have to bear in mind that energy efficiency programs may save less energy than anticipated if there are rebound effects, whereby adopters of more energy-efficient technologies use the technology more intensively, or use the monetary savings to buy more energy-using technologies.

Buildings are the third major energy-using sector and actually the largest user at 40% of total energy use. The largest use is HVAC for both commercial and residential occupants. Other major uses are lighting and appliance usage. The building stock turns over slowly, so in order to reduce energy use and emissions, programs have to target improvements within existing buildings as well as new construction.

LEED has targeted new construction. Architects and not government initiated the program. It has increased the energy efficiency of buildings, but has an arbitrary points and grading system that does not seek to identify the lowest-cost way to reduce carbon emissions. Like other green efforts by industry, one motive may be marketing to buyers willing to pay more for environmentally friendly outputs. In turn, buyers may value warm glow or identity benefits from the purchase of green goods. The EPA's ENERGY STAR focuses more on improving the energy efficiency of building operations by providing information on energy performance of building components. Both programs are voluntary, and in that sense, worth doing if information benefits exceed program costs.

Economists advocate starting with markets, and augmenting them if needed to maximize societal welfare. Where they do not, we consider the possibility that government may improve welfare. As we have seen throughout this book, energy markets frequently fail to produce the outcome that maximizes social welfare. We have also seen that government can fail, due to incomplete information, capture by industry, or motives other than efficiency such as pursuing votes or money. The goal of a holistic energy policy is to do the best we can in an imperfect world to choose policies that move us in the direction of achieving societal objectives that balance energy use with other objectives such as emissions reductions.

Notes

1 John Heywood included it in a book of proverbs as "You can't see the wood for the trees," the British version of the saying. And no, it's not, "You can't see the forest through the trees," which totally changes the meaning.
2 Salzberg (2014) concludes that there is no credible evidence showing that EMFs cause cancer. Even so, if people think they do, and do not like the look of high-voltage transmission lines running near their property, the best societal outcome is to build them away from property or bury them underground.

3   Schwarz (2005) compares environmental policies that target one emission at a time vs. a single policy that considers multiple emissions. It is lower cost to society if firms know the requirements for both sulfur and NOx than if they meet a sulfur requirement and then later must meet a NOx requirement. To meet the sulfur requirement, they might switch to low-sulfur coal, which could actually increase NOx.
4   Holland and Yates (2013) provide a model to determine the more general objective of an efficient level of permits rather than the narrower goal of minimizing abatement costs.
5   There have been instances of drivers using inflatable dummies so it looks as if there are more passengers in the car!
6   The EU adopted high-mileage diesel cars as a way to reduce emissions. However, Volkswagen, a leading producer of diesel automobiles, was using technology to only limit emissions when the car went through testing, and to release higher emissions at other times. It was convicted and had to pay record fines. As I write these words, Fiat Chrysler is under investigation for a similar offense. U.S. consumers have not warmed to diesels, and these scandals make it less likely that the United States will look to diesels as an emissions-reducing strategy.
7   Center for Climate and Energy Solutions (n.d.) is a good source of information on buildings and energy use.
8   Schwarz, Depken, Herron, and Correll (2017) have a working paper comparing appliances, where they find small, but significant, increases in the purchase of ENERGY STAR appliances in states that have higher energy prices. Energy-efficient appliances have a relatively small effect on reducing carbon emissions. Jacobsen (2015) finds no price response in the purchase of ENERGY STAR appliances.

References

Center for Climate and Energy Solutions. (n.d.). *Buildings overview.* Retrieved January 7, 2017 from https://www.c2es.org/technology/overview/buildings

Cochran, J. (2015). *Do state-level RPS policies in the U.S. deliver anticipated benefits? Examining the impact of federalized energy and environmental policy on electricity price and quantity, use of renewables, and carbon emissions* (Doctoral dissertation). Retrieved from ProQuest Dissertations and Theses database. (ProQuest No. 3744306).

Fowlie, M., Greenstone, M., & Wolfram, C. (2015). Do energy efficiency investments deliver? Evidence from the Weatherization Assistance Program. NBER Working Paper No. 21331.

Heywood, J. (1546). *The proverbs of John Heywood: Being the "Proverbes" of that author printed 1546.* Retrieved January 8, 2017 from https://www.archive.org/stream/proverbsofjohnhe00heywrich/proverbsofjohnhe00heywrich_djvu.txt

Holland, S., & Yates, A. (2013). Optimal trading ratios for pollution permit markets, completed manuscript presented at UNC Charlotte workshop. Retrieved January 8, 2017 from http://bryan.uncg.edu/econ/files/2013/10/Holland-Yates-Michigan.pdf

Jacobsen, G. (2015). Do energy prices influence investment in energy efficiency? Evidence from Energy Star appliances. *Journal of Environmental Economics and Management, 74*, 94–106.

Jones, B. (2016). *The regional greenhouse gas initiative: A three-article study on the decision to join and the impacts of a cap and trade market* (Doctoral dissertation). Retrieved from ProQuest Dissertations and Theses database. (ProQuest No. 10161974).

Lovins, A. (1976). Energy strategy: The road not taken? *Foreign Affairs, 55*, 65–96.

Salzberg, S. (2014, September 1). Do high voltage power lines cause cancer? *Forbes.* Retrieved January 8, 2017 from http://www.forbes.com/sites/stevensalzberg/2014/09/01/do-high-voltage-power-lines-cause-cancer/#69b605e17f1c

Schwarz, P. M. (2005). Multipollutant efficiency standards for electricity production. *Contemporary Economic Policy, 23*(3), 341–356.

Schwarz, P., Depken, C., Herron, M. & Correll, B. (2017). The effect of U.S. electricity prices on the purchase of energy-efficient appliances and implications for the effects of carbon pricing. Working paper.

U.S. EIA. (n.d.). *Consumption & efficiency*. Retrieved January 7, 2017 from http://www.eia.gov/consumption/

U.S. EPA. (n.d.). *Energy and the environment: Electricity customers*. Retrieved January 7, 2017 from https://www.epa.gov/energy/electricity-customers

Vine, D. (2016, June 20). Transportation emissions roll over power sector emissions [Web log post]. Retrieved January 8, 2017 from https://www.c2es.org/blog/vined/transportation-emissions-roll-over-power-sector-emissions

Index

All references to figures are shown in *italics* and tables are in **bold**.